The Catalog of Kits

The Catalog of Kits

by

Jeffrey Feinman

William Morrow and Company, Inc.

New York   1975

Copyright © 1975 by Jeffrey Feinman

Printed in the United States of America.
1 2 3 4 5 79 78 77 76 75

Book Design by Morris Berman Studio

Library of Congress Cataloging in Publication Data

Feinman, Jeffrey.
    The catalog of kits.
    Includes index.
    1. Handicraft—United States—Directories.
2. Handicraft—United States—Catalogs. I. Title.
TT12.F44   745.5'025'73   75-12590
ISBN 0-688-05283-5

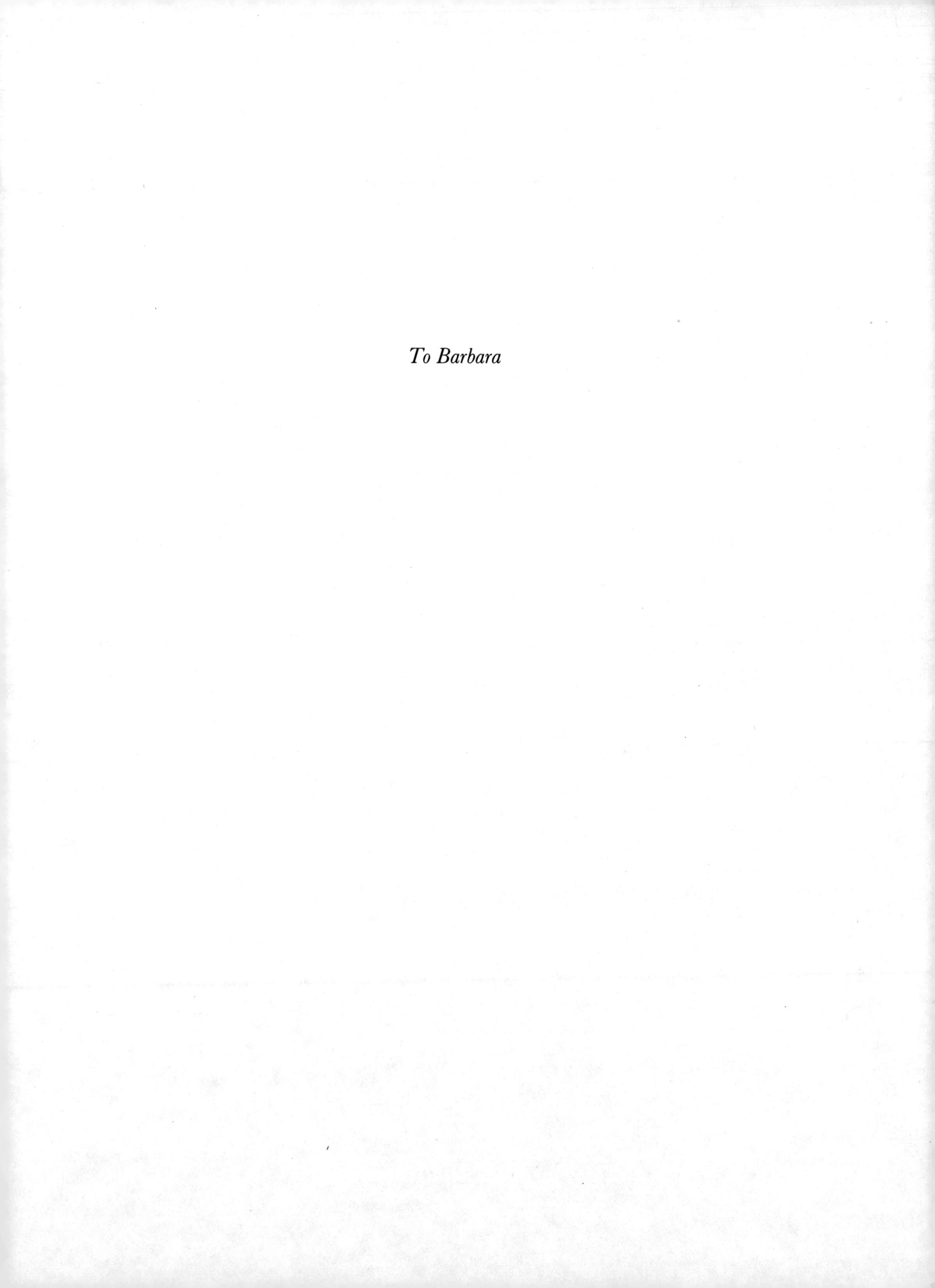

To Barbara

CONTENTS

INTRODUCTION

America is witnessing a return to crafts. Craft suppliers, do-it-yourself companies, and kit manufacturers are all reporting a record year. What is most startling is that this boom period comes during a recession. What accounts for this tremendous growth? There are a number of significant reasons:

Need to create: Automated, bureaucratic, and depersonalized jobs have left people with little sense of fulfillment. The joy of seeing a completed project at the end of a work day is gone. More than ever before every strata of society must obtain the feeling of accomplishment outside of the workday.

More leisure: The four-day week, the thirty-day holiday year, the six-week vacation are all around the corner. Already Americans have more leisure time. There is a definite need to fill these hours. Although family, games, and television have provided for some of the hours, we all have a mania not to waste time. Crafts offer a tangible reward for hours expended.

Release from tension: The pressures of today's society require an escape. Working with one's hands has provided that release. Some of the joys of escaping to a commune are offered by a greenhouse garden.

Demand for quality: You can't complain about shoddy workmanship when you do it yourself. The continual complaints about assembly-line production can only be solved by the return to the craftsman. Unfortunately the only way to craftsmanship is frequently to do it yourself.

Price considerations: Although not all kits are less expensive than finished products, this is most often the case. Areas like furniture, elaborate musical instruments, and certain types of needlepoint offer savings as much as 80% over the finished article! Our tight economy provides that one must build it or in some cases do without.

Educational experience: Building a boat will provide more maritime knowledge than all the sailing imaginable. The knowledge explosion around us makes us want to know, to question even our hobbies.

Kit availability: It may seem strange to say that more kits are being sold because more kits are being made. However, that is exactly the case. Historically, if one wanted to build his own chair he would seek out a master carpenter and study with him. Even making needlepoint required hours of visiting with an expert often two towns away. The ability to buy a prepackaged kit with complete instructions, all needed materials, even required tools makes it a more viable idea.

This book is a response to the growth of this industry.

Why "A Catalog of Kits"

The craft industry is burgeoning. However, two problems existed. First, to find out if a particular item desired was available in kit form. Second, where to obtain the item if it was produced by a kit company. This book seeks to be a directory to the thousands of companies in the industry and the over fifty thousand kits they sell.

How to use this book

It would, of course, be impossible to list every kit made because such a volume would be impossible to compile and produce.

This book is arranged in broad categories. You can therefore leaf through the book to find items that would be of interest to you. The company information (in italics) following the item gives you more details about the company and how to obtain their catalog. There would be little sense in reproducing the hundreds of items that a company produces. The representative sample and the information that follows will help you to decide whether you'll want more details.

The Other Sources section provides more places to write if a particular type of kit interests you. For example, some readers will find a description of one plane kit too many, while others will want exact details on all that exist.

Therefore the book attempts to fill not only the information gap but the directory goal as well.

In addition, there is an index that lists the items mentioned in this book and the companies that make them.

How to order

If you read no other information in the introduction we hope you'll read this: *Please don't order from this book.* The *Catalog of Kits* took over eighteen months to complete. In normal times some prices would be inaccurate, but during the inflationary seventies, most prices will be inaccurate. They are provided for guidelines only. Also, many of these firms are small businesses. Some will survive and grow—others will (unfortunately) be out of business on the publication date. In short, *before ordering anything write for complete details.*

Where a catalog is mentioned, it's a good idea to write for the catalog first. If a charge is indicated (usually 10¢ to $1) be sure to include it. It becomes prohibitively expensive for many small manufacturers to send catalogs without charge.

One last note on ordering. Many of the firms listed are exclusively mail-order ventures. Some actually operate part time. Therefore if you live near an address listed, don't drop by unless you call first!

Who is included

Specifically, almost everyone who sells kits by mail. To compile this book we sent letters to over six thousand companies, made hundreds of phone calls, and in the final hours sent five hundred telegrams asking for last-minute details. The company names were derived by researchers who pored over magazines in every field, talking to trade associations, mail-order firms and in some cases friends and acquaintances who had happily built kits.

We also ordered and built (to various degrees of completion) hundreds of kits. At various times we inflicted wines that were kit-made on our friends. In addition, there were conversations with almost a hundred people who routinely build kits. In cases where we constructed a kit, we naturally had more information. In some cases, we relied on manufacturers' statements. It may seem that we are more critical of some kits than others, but this opinion may reflect only that we had much more information than the typical buyer. We emphasize that buying any kit that's more elaborate than a balsa glider should be done with care. If you think this catalog or the advertisements don't give you full information, you should not hesitate to write for further details or even to call the manufacturer (especially on large kits). Most are extremely helpful.

Finally, nobody paid to be in the catalog. People who receive a good deal of space we felt warranted it.

Who is not included

If your favorite kit or kit company is not included it is for one of the following reasons.

We didn't find them: After poring over magazines by the ton, sending all the letters, and visiting stores everywhere, we are still sure we missed some people. A book of this nature can never be complete. Chances are if somebody is missing it's simply because we missed them. We will remedy that in future editions. We require your help to keep this book up to date. If you have ideas for listings (or you're in the kit business yourself) please write to me. (For address, see "About future editions," p. 12.)

Items widely available at retail: We did not include kits widely sold in retail stores. For example, in the Toys and Models section we eliminated national toy companies that seldom sell mail order but prefer to retail items through toy stores. There are examples in many sections. Under needlepoint we eliminated Bucilla and Columbia-Minerva, two fine large yarn manufacturers. Anyone interested in these items probably knows of them and would be better to purchase them locally.

People who did not reply: Many firms simply did not answer our series of requests for information. We felt if a request for free publicity goes unheeded a customer's request would be similarly ignored. Sometimes we were able to purchase one of their kits or otherwise obtain information. Barring this, we simply excluded them.

Firms that asked to be deleted: Several firms stated that "they had more business than they could handle." One firm wrote that they were true craftsmen and wanted no part of a commercial venture. And a few wrote simply that they were glad our book was being produced but they were afraid the number of inquires it would generate would be too much for them to handle.

Firms with really inferior products: These comprise only a dozen or so companies. Our experience indicates mail-order operators to be very ethical and more than fair. However, like every other profession there are unethical practitioners. We have eliminated anyone who was selling inferior merchandise, or in any way made representations that they didn't live up to.

About mail order

Many of the firms here could not survive in any other way but mail order. Their prices frequently reflect no middlemen, no sales clerks, no expensive downtown rents. They are also able to offer items that have a limited potential market.

About listings

This book is intended as a guide. We have used sources we believe to be reliable. However, listing in the book is not intended to be an endorsement. The rules of fair play and the rather strong hand of the postal authorities should assure you of honest dealing. However, we cannot guarantee any source, the address, or the information.

About suppliers

Kit suppliers tend to be smaller firms. Most were craftsmen first who started producing kits for friends and neighbors, then graduated to mail order. We mention this only so you'll understand. Some may be inundated with requests from this catalog and unable to answer. Other times you'll be required to wait longer than you'd like to receive the item you've ordered. Please be patient.

About future editions

The future only points to more and more kits. Almost every supplier we spoke with had planned additions to the line. We count on our readers' help in the updating process. Readers are asked to submit ideas and comments to Jeffrey Feinman, Ventura Associates, 40 East 49 Street, New York, N.Y. 10017.

Now begin

You can build a whole house—and most everything that's in it. The joy of creativity has no qualifications. We wish you the exhilarating feeling of saying, "I did it myself."

The Catalog
of Kits

The earliest musical instruments were the hands and feet, clapped and stomped to mark rhythm. After that came drums made from logs, rattles, shakers, scrapers, and membrane drums. Once man had begun to make music with instruments, he expanded fast. There were twig flutes, conch-shell horns, and gut guitars.

The modern orchestra dates from about the 16th century, when the harpsichord began to dominate the scene. The harpsichord and clavichord are actually keyed dulcimers—successful attempts to systematize string playing by using keys and hammers. During the 16th, 17th, and 18th centuries, the harpsichord was the king of the keyboard instruments. All of Bach's "piano" pieces were actually composed for harpsichord or hammer klavier. The development of the pianoforte (the "loud-soft") changed all that. The more expressive piano took over the keyboard field, and opened up the door for such masters of expression as Beethoven.

Among the strings, the violin reigns supreme, as she always has. A few famous handmade instruments, hundreds of years old, are still the most sought after among musicians. But homier stringed instruments like the dulcimer and the banjo have been gaining popularity ever since the 1930s.

All this interest in instruments and how they work has spawned many musical kits. You can make anything from a little thumb piano to a full-sized harpsichord. Some are just for fun, and the family band. Others are quality instruments that rank with the best of their kind anywhere.

THE DULCIMER SHOPPE
Drawer E—Highway 9 North
Mountain View, Ark. 72560

DULCIMER SHOPPE DULCIMERS

There's something about an entire shop devoted to one product that inspires confidence. In fact, this shop sells other folk instruments as well, but their main enterprise is the manufacturing of dulcimers and dulcimer accessories. And since the dulcimer is an intensely personal instrument, this small operation is a good source for dulcimer kits. Two kits are available, both selling for less than half the usual price of a fully assembled model. The three-string dulcimer has a sweet, musical tone and laminated walnut face, back, and sides. The scroll and fretboard are made of solid walnut. The four-string dulcimer is the same as the three-string except that one extra peg, string, and tail pin nail are included and four holes are drilled in the scroll. Both kits include the shop's own instruction booklet, "Four and Twenty," which will get a beginner actually playing in ten or fifteen minutes. As for assembly, all it takes is "a few hours of loving labor." Three-string: $31.95. Four-string: $34.50.

BURTON HARPSICHORD
Box 80222
Lincoln, Nebr. 68501

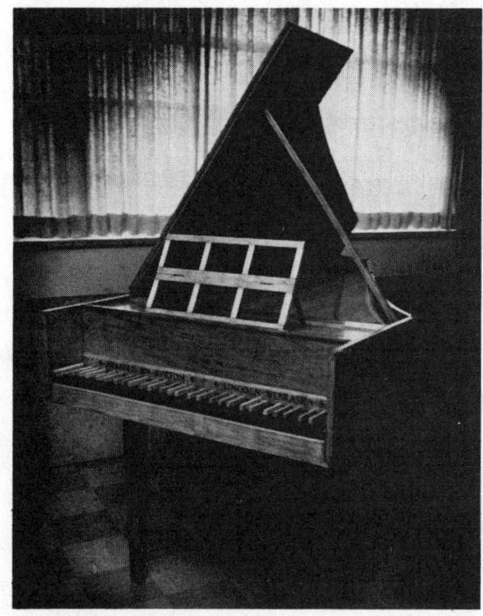

HARPSICHORD

We list several harpsichord kits but our favorites are from Burton. They offer two kit formats. The "Basic" Burton harpsichord kit is for the builder who has a good knowledge of woodworking. Included in the basic kit are those parts you would have a hard time making yourself or finding in your home-town—things like the keyboard, soundboard, and tuning pins. You do the carpentry work on a basic kit, with the selection of woods done at your local lumber yard according to the Wood Tables, and the cutting of parts according to the detailed plans and specifications included in your Manual of Instruc-tions. The builder of a basic kit should have access to a radial arm saw and/or a table saw, and a drill press.

The "Complete" Burton harpsichord kit in-cludes everything you will need to complete your harpsichord, except some common tools such as a hammer, screwdriver, and your choice of finishing materials. All wooden parts are carefully cut and fitted, and even such small items as glue, an X-Acto knife, and cheesecloth are included. The wood parts of all complete kits are of beautifully grained birch, ready to be painted or stained. Again, we suggest you approach either kit with eyes wide open. This is not a rainy Sunday afternoon project. If you are willing to put out the work and have the needed skills, you'll be pleased with the result. The resonant musical instrument (the favorite instrument of Bach) will bring hours of playing pleasure, and it's truly a lovely piece of furniture. Basic kit: $255. Complete kit: $500.

EDMUND SCIENTIFIC

555 Edscorp Bldg.
Barrington, N.J. 08007

MUSICVISION KITS

For some people, hearing music is not enough—they have to see it, too. MusicVision is for them. It is a system of small mirrors that react to sound vibra-tions, which in connection with a light source and speakers somehow produce twirling, dancing, un-dulating shapes of circles, bands, dots, orbits, and waves of ever-changing colored light. All of these keep time to the music, of course. If you get your jollies from this sort of business, you'll want to try one of the MusicVision kits.

The "Starter" kit contains mirrors, a special rubber membrane, color filters, and instructions for using these to build a MusicVision system with a speaker from an old radio or tape recorder. The easy-to-build "Do-It-Yourself" kit supplies every-thing you need to make an 8″ motiondizer and a 9″ color wheel, speaker, membrane, seven front-sur-faced mirrors, motor, and instructions. Note that this kit costs more than three times as much as the Starter kit. You'd best be convinced you really want a MusicVision system before you mess with this one. Starter kit $6.00. Do-It-Yourself kit $18.75.

INTERNATIONAL VIOLIN CO.

414 East Baltimore St.
Baltimore, Md. 21202

VIOLIN OUTFIT

A Stradivarius it's not, but then again, you're not Heifetz! The sound is remarkably good, all things considered. This kit will undoubtedly have some violin makers who spent decades studying their craft a bit upset. However, with a little dedication, you can make a worthwhile instrument at an un-believable price. Your kit includes the following:

1 two-piece spruce top wood
1 two-piece flamed maple back, with set un-bent ribs
1 set of corner blocks
1 set of spruce lining, not bent
1 carved neck with scroll, without peg holes
1 bottle of neck stain
1 ebony fingerboard
1 set of fiber purfling, easy to bend
1 ebony top nut
1 ebony saddle
1 ebony end pin
1 fifteen-in. length of spruce for sound posts
1 #180/4 bridge
1 #16/8 ebony tailpiece with gut attached
2 #925 bass bars
1 set 22/8 ebony pegs
1 set Chieftain violin strings
1 #3600 E string adjuster
1 peg soap
½ lb. violin glue
1 varnish brush
1 three-oz. pumice stone
12 pieces sandpaper, assorted
1 two-oz. bottle Luigi Nicoseco oil varnish

Plus a set of instructions, and you're on your own. $44.

International Violin offers kits of violins, violas, cellos, basses, and drums at competitive prices. They offer a free leaflet that explains their firm and varied offerings.

ZUCKERMANN, INC.
160 Ave. of the Americas
New York, N.Y. 10013

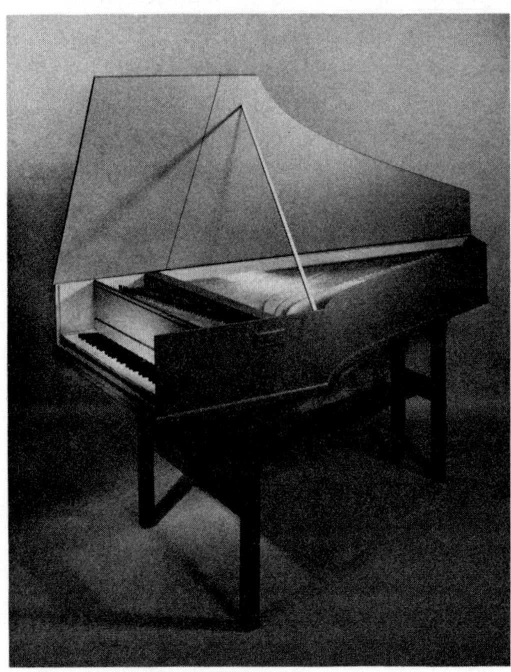

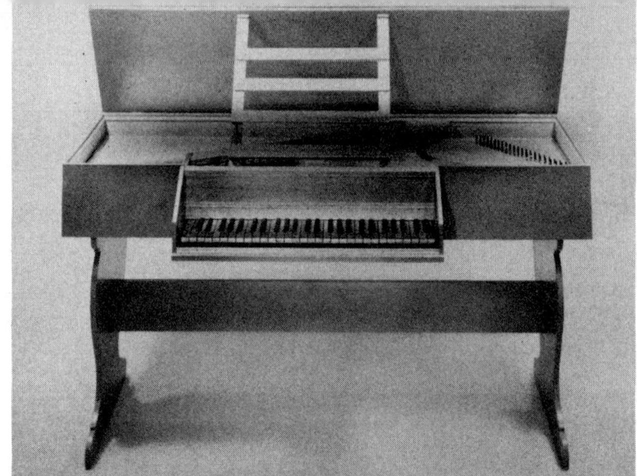

FLEMISH HARPSICHORD

A fine harpsichord developed on the model of a 17th-century instrument expanded to 52 notes. Zuckermann's has long been the standard harpsichord kit and there is no doubt that you can build an instrument which, as they advertise, is worth several times the kit price. On the other hand, they are not "easy to build." You need good power tools, a lot of space, and patience. If there are many homes and conservatories with Zuckermann harpsichords, there are also many basements with unfinished kits. In fact, one of our staff was once offered a job by Zuckermann to go around and finish kits that could not be completed. This is still a fine kit—just make sure you know what you're getting into.

The instrument has one choir of strings at normal pitch, and another that plays an octave higher (8' and 4' disposition). The longer strings are rich enough in tone to carry the burden of the music; the 4' choir can be added at will for contrasting passages. This was the normal disposition for the old Flemish instruments. However, for those who prefer the 2' x 8' disposition, the 4' bridge and strings can be omitted, and another set of strings at normal pitch added, to give the 2' x 8' ensemble.

The keyboard features the "short octave" (GG/BB). That is, the lowest note, which appears to be BB, is actually used to sound the lower and very useful GG; the low C and D sharps sound respectively AA and BB. Complete kit: $595.

ITALIAN VIRGINAL

The virginal is a harpsichord—it plucks its strings—but instead of having the strings run from front to back, as in a harpsichord, they run from side to side. This kit is of the Italian type, with moldings and veneers that give the inside of the instrument a complex appearance. The kit is complete, including old-fashioned cut nails and pearwood natural and dull black sharp keys. Construction is easier than the harpsichord, but the same advice might apply. Complete kit: $350. Cabinet parts: $175. Musical parts: $175.

DOUBLE-STRUNG CLAVICHORD

The clavichord is a solo instrument since it does not have sufficient volume to compete with other instruments, but it is extremely expressive. The kit can be bought complete or as a "basic kit" in which you supply wood and cut parts for the cabinet. Complete kit: $350. Basic kit: $195.

Company has a showroom in New York (address above) where you can see completed kits or pick up kits to save transportation charges. They will also send you the name of a professional builder or firm near you who can help. As mentioned, you should discuss the kind of work involved. Zuckermann also makes a Double Harpsichord and a Concert Five-Octave Harpsichord. If you live near New York, visit their showroom if possible.

MASON & SULLIVAN
39 Blossom Ave.
Osterville, Mass. 02655

MINIATURE PIANO MUSIC BOX

If a tinkly "Let Me Call You Sweetheart" emanating from a cherry-wood miniature piano is your idea of paradise, you'll want this easy, inexpensive kit. All parts are preshaped, and keyboard and loud/soft pedal are completely assembled. Finished size 8" × 5" × 3". Swiss movement has a choice of tunes for every taste—from "Edelweiss" to "Born Free." $13.25.

RADIO SHACK
2615 West 7 St.
Fort Worth, Tex. 76107

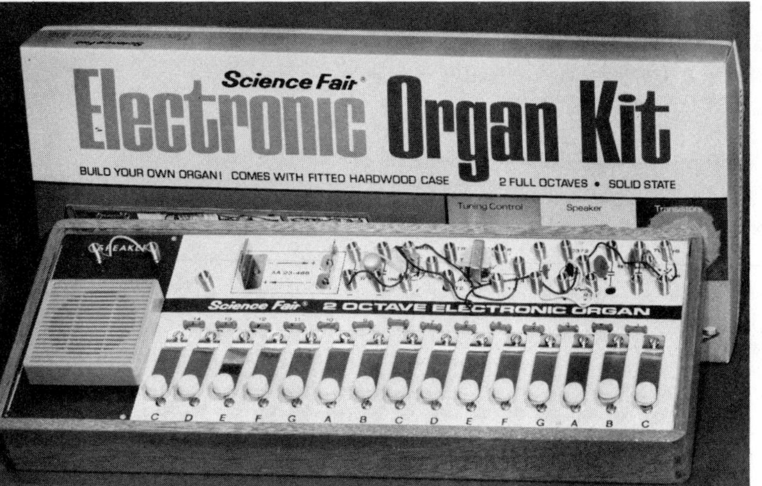

ELECTRONIC ORGAN

Here's an inexpensive electronic and music project that will bring you enjoyment in the building and playing phase—your own tunable organ in a 15″ × 5″ hardwood box. Plays natural major scale through two octaves. All spring-clip assembly—no soldering. With speaker, batteries, and songbook of popular melodies. $12.95.

THE SCHOBER ORGAN CORP.
43 West 61 St.
New York, N.Y. 10023

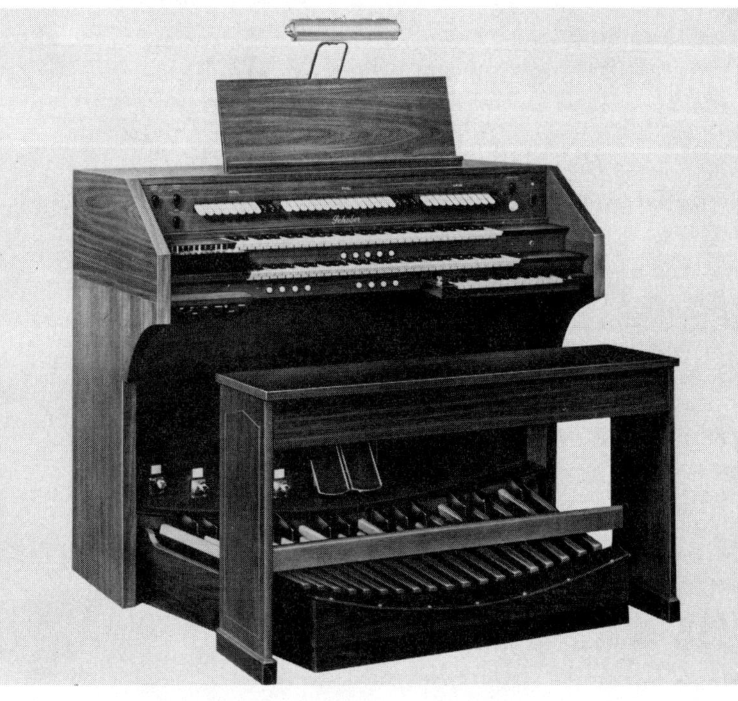

SCHOBER RECITAL ORGAN

This instrument is the equivalent in size and musical capability of a good pipe organ. Advanced electronic techniques, employed by musician-engineers, have produced in the Recital Organ a truly musical instrument containing every facility required by the professional organist and the completeness that makes the Recital easiest for the beginner to learn on. This organ meets American Guild of Organists specifications; its appearance, essential dimensions, and playing facilities are identical to those of a pipe organ. The Recital sound is extraordinarily pipelike. Especially when it is played through the Schober Revertape Unit or in a good auditorium, the average listener finds it hard to believe that the tones are produced electronically. Kit with console: $2,299. With console plans, but no wood: $1,954.

To assemble a complete organ, ready to play and enjoy, you might possibly have the additional cost of an amplifier and speaker system, also available from Schober.

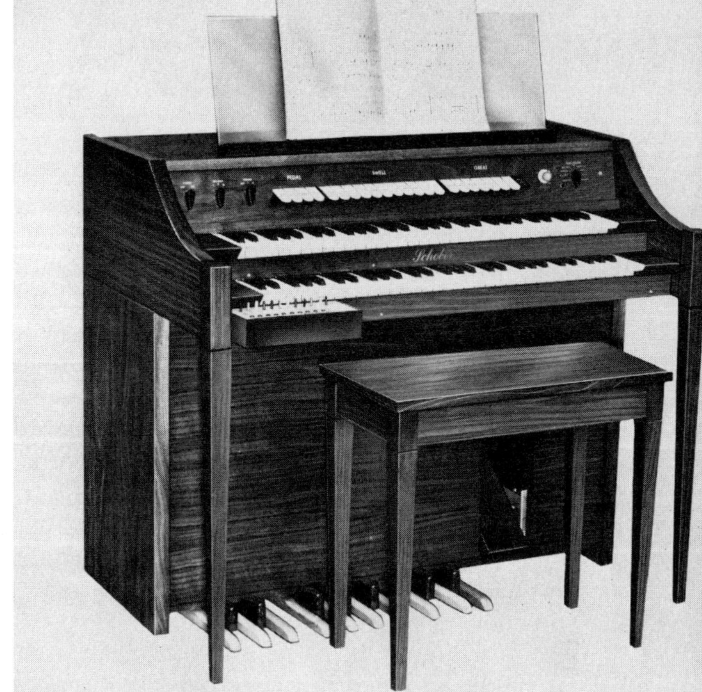

SCHOBER CONSOLETTE II ORGAN

If you cannot find room for a full-sized organ, the Schober Consolette II is the outstanding choice among "home-size" instruments. It takes no more space than the usual spinet, but far outstrips most smaller organs in musical capabilities. Its two keyboards have the same 61 notes as on large organs. It has 17 pedals instead of the usual 13. And its 22 organ voices present a most unusual variety in three pitch registers for each manual and two in the pedals. Built of beautifully grained genuine walnut. Kit with console: $1,283. With console plane, but no wood: $1,064. If you purchase amplifier and speakers from Schober, typical total cost is $236.

Can an organ designed to be assembled by inexperienced people equal or exceed the musical and technical quality of those built in factories? Schober answers, "Definitely yes!" The quality of the modern electronics kit is amply proved by the quality of hi-fi and stereo equipment assembled every year by amateurs. Anyone who can read and who enjoys working with his hands can build a Schober organ. Whether for home, school, or church use, the fact that you furnish the labor, instead of paying for it, means that your money buys more, so that you can have a much more complete, interesting, and useful musical instrument than is available anywhere else in comparable size and price.

Schober's Time Payment Plan permits you to order and receive Schober kits and accessories when you send in a down payment of only 20% of the total with your order. You can then pay the remainder in twenty-four monthly installments over a two-year period. Complete catalog free.

HEATHKIT
The Heath Co.
Benton Harbor, Mich. 49022

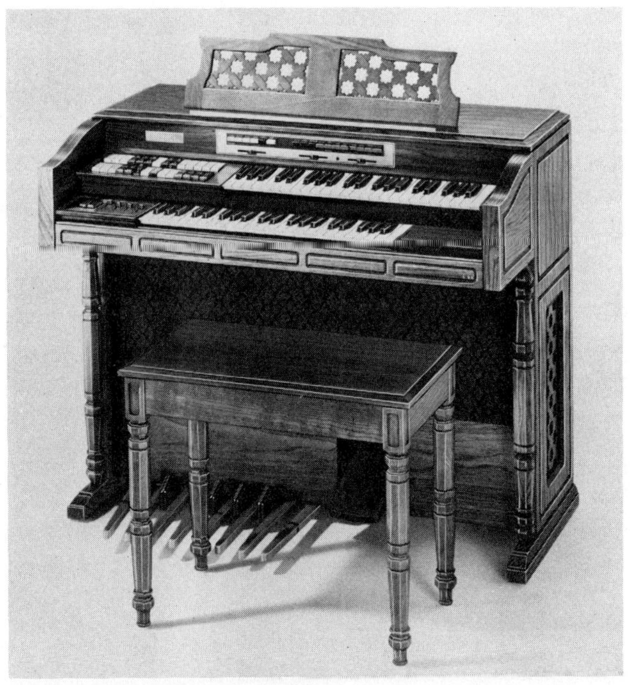

HEATHKIT/THOMAS SPINET ORGAN

Electronic Organ featuring piano, guitar, banjo, or harpsichord accompaniment, alternating bass pedal tones, percussion on both manuals. Convenient accessory panel allows for quick installation of cassette recording equipment, earphones for silent practicing, and connection of an external tone cabinet. Cabinetry available in your choice of Contemporary (our preference) or Spanish Mediterranean. Kit, contemporary: $1045.00. Kit, Mediterranean:

$1095.00. Automatic rhythm section device: $279.95.

Heathkit has several kits of interest to musicians including guitar amplifiers, metronome, and a distortion booster. For full discussion, see Electronics section.

J. WITCHER
ANCIENT INSTRUMENT
17715 La Rosa Lane
Fountain Valley, Calif. 92708

HURDY-GURDY

If you have a pet monkey and a tin cup, all you need is a hurdy-gurdy. Once an expensive proposition, now an ex-engineer has put out this quality hurdy-gurdy kit. Includes all the pieces and complete assembly instructions. $75.

The company for unusual musical kits. Among the offerings are flutes, cornetti, and citterns.

ROBINSON'S HARP SHOP
Mount Laguna, Calif. 92048

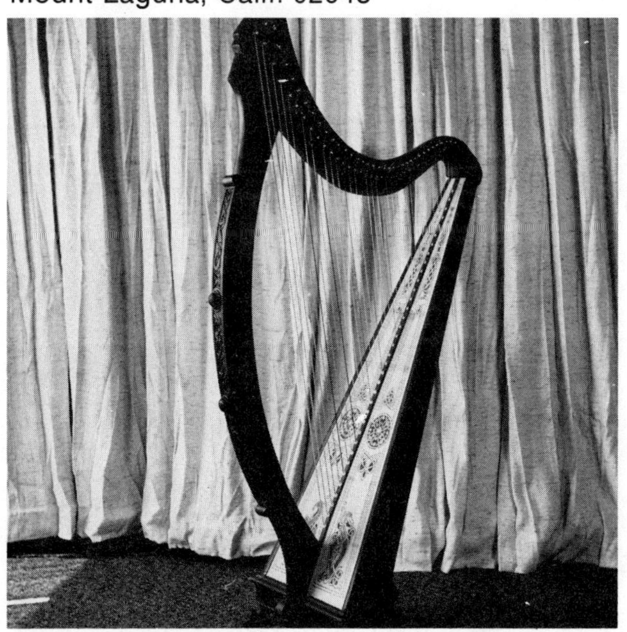

TARA HARP

This harp is an authentic replica of the instruments made by James McFall of Dublin at the turn of this century. The sound chamber is made of five-ply hardwood shell, which produces superb full tones. The neck and column assembly is constructed of 25 to 30 layers of hardwood ply. The spruce sound board is hand engraved with original Celtic design. Column and box are intricately carved, as are the lion-paw feet. Semi-tone levers are installed at each string. Tuning key is provided. (Kit prices vary with the availability of materials. Estimate on request.)

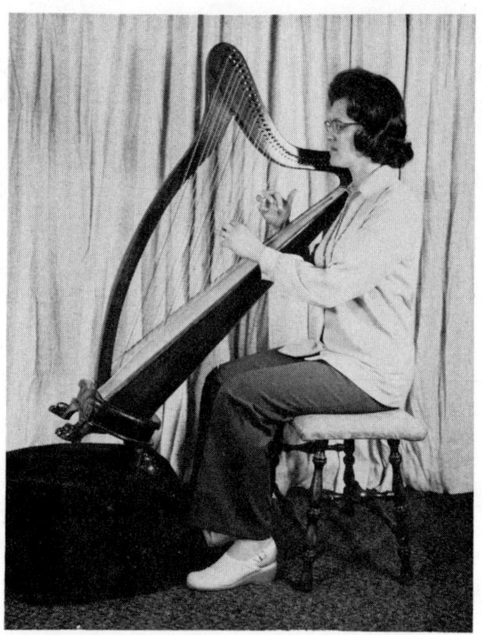

IRISH HARP

Since the early 1800s most Irish harp craftsmen have settled on a more or less common design that bears almost no resemblance to the harps in use in earlier centuries. The very distinguishing features of the ancient Irish harp are gone. Instead, the design includes features of harps which evolved in France, Italy, and Bavaria. These harps weigh from 12 to 15 lb., have from 30 to 36 strings, and are finished in natural wood tones or antique colors. Often shamrock decorations are used, although in some cases, gold-leaf floral designs or Irish Celtic dragons are applied. Because of the recent upsurge of artist costs, small harps are more often undecorated. Kit price on request.

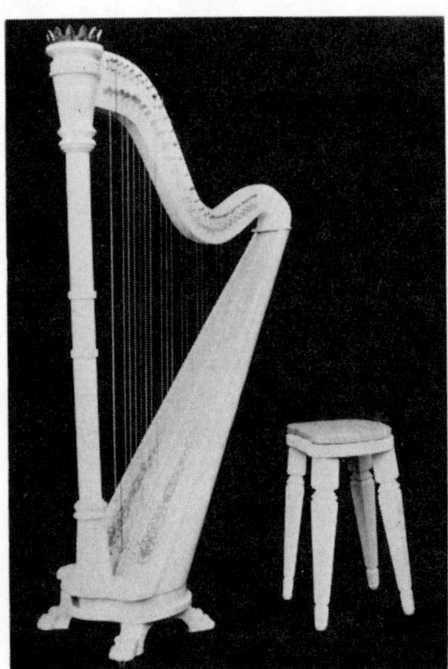

MINI-CONCERT

This harp has a spruce sound board with exterior vertical grain and optional gold-leaf decoration. A cast bronze crown caps the hand-turned column with a regal touch. It also features the carved lion-paw feet base. Semi-tone levers and tuning key are included. Kit price on request.

There are very few harp makers in the world, and manufacturing costs for harps are high compared to those of more common instruments. Robinson's Harp Shop acknowledges this to be so, and wants you to have the best harp at the lowest price possible. Proof of their sincerity is that they'll send you, if you want, "a list of all the other harp makers they know, so you can buy your harp close to home and save." It's enough to make you want to go out of your way to buy from Robinson's. They carry all types of harp kits, including Mexican harps, Paraguayan harps, and another Irish harp called the "Leprechaun."

CAPRITAURUS
Box 153
Felton, Calif. 95018

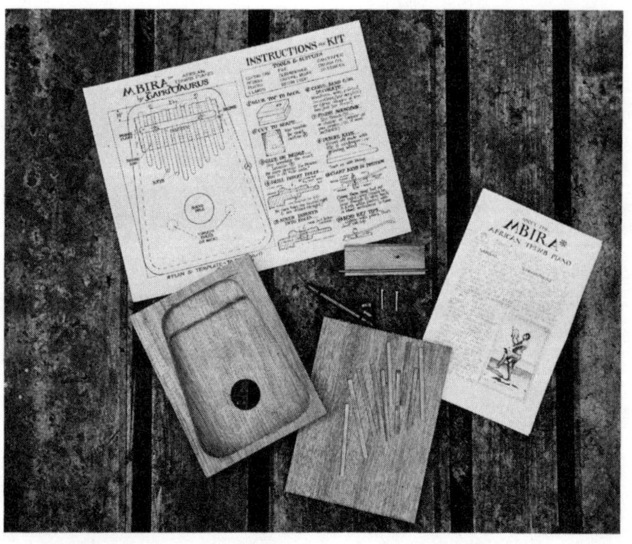

MBIRA THUMB PIANO

An entertaining musical kit that can be assembled in a single afternoon, even by the novice craftsman. A "Mbira" is an authentic African instrument dating back to the 16th century. It is called a thumb piano because it is held in both hands while the thumbs pluck the metal reeds. The actual construction of this model is mahogany and ash spring steel. Complete playing instructions are included. Very fairly priced at only $8.95.

Capritaurus' free, 8-pp. catalog features kits as well as traditional instruments. We are impressed with their lower than usual prices and their better than usual kit instructions.

HERE, INC.

410 Cedar Ave.
Minneapolis, Minn. 55404

PSALTERIES

The psaltery is a twelve-string instrument that can play an astonishing number of folk tunes when tuned to match the open string and first eleven frets of the dulcimer. It may be plucked, hammered, or bowed to play. The kit has an oak frame, cedar soundboard, and Philippine mahogany plywood back. It measures about 20″ × 12″ × 2″ and costs $20.

Here, Inc. has a small free catalog with a variety of dulcimer, banjo, and other string instrument kits.

AMBIRA

Ambira is one company's name for a thumb piano, a westernized version of West Africa's most popular musical instrument. Made of Philippine mahogany plywood and solid wood, it features reeds that are flipped to produce a rich thumping sound. This is a delightful assembly project—easy to put together and even easier to play. $6.

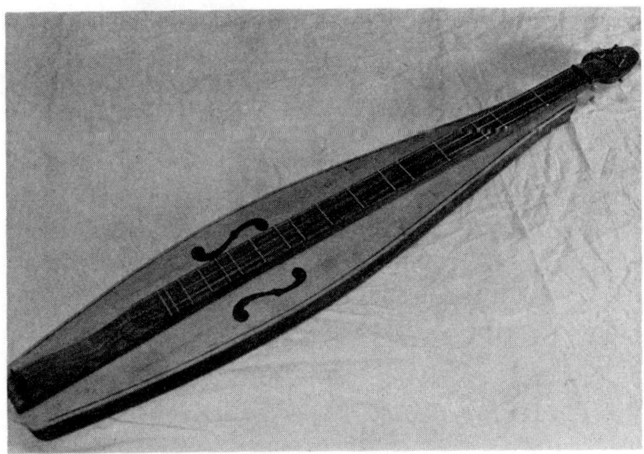

DULCIMER KIT

If you're tired of throwing away money on your children's piano lessons, try an instrument they'll really enjoy—the dulcimer. You'll love the beautiful tunes. Here, Inc. kits are the answer. The manufacturer tells us, "Our reported failure rate on kits is less than one half of a percent," adding that even if you fail "you will know you are a part of a very small, select group." With that kind of moral support you can hardly go wrong. Pictured is one of their simplest kits. It is a three-string dulcimer available in Philippine mahogany and spruce, and

includes all parts but no tools, glue, or finish. You'll find the sound from this product as good as from those that are three times the price. In general, the cost differences are more in appearance of the wood and shaping. Dulcimer in photo above, $30.

HUGHES DULCIMER CO.

8665 West 13 Ave.
Denver, Colo. 80215

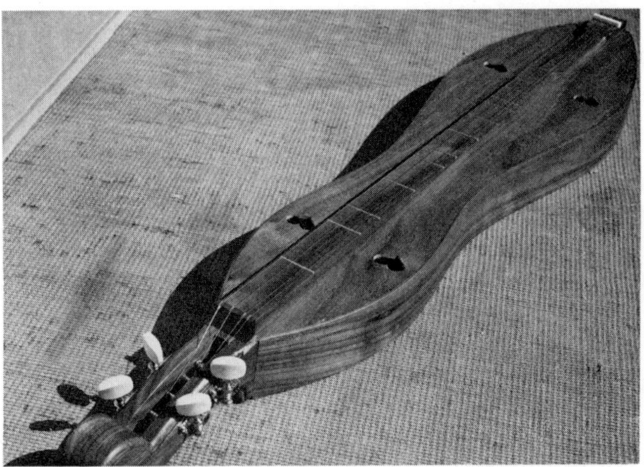

DULCIMERS

In the race for dulcimer power, Hughes is clearly the winner, having no fewer than sixteen separate dulcimer kits. The "Musician's" model comes in four versions: a four-string 31″, a four-string 37″, a three-string 31″, and a three-string 37″ model that has machine-gear tuning like a guitar. Hughes says it is the best starting dulcimer for most people, particularly the four-string 37″ model. They estimate assembly time at four to five hours.

Their "Central City" model features friction peg tuning, which is very authentic but difficult. This model also comes in four versions: four-string or three-string, 38″ or 28″. Six to seven hours is the estimated time for assembly.

If you have eight hours available you can assemble the "Hourglass" model, a traditional-shaped dulcimer with a rich tone. This four-string instrument comes in walnut, mahogany, or spruce in either 39″ size or 29″ size. The 39″ mahogany version is the best starting kit.

Hughes also sells a six-string "Church" dulcimer that has a rich bass sound but is a little more complex. Courting couples may enjoy the "Double" or "Courting" dulcimer, a sort of musical chaperon —as long as the dulcimer can be heard, the couple can be up to no mischief. (Twentieth-century musicians undoubtedly find new interpretations and uses.) The Double and Church dulcimers require about ten hours to build. All of the Hughes dulcimer kits cost less than half the fully assembled price. They are also, incidentally, considerably cheaper than any of their competitors. Cost: In the following list of code numbers, the first letter indicates the model; the pair of numbers indicates the length in inches; the second letter indicates the kind of wood (W = walnut, S = spruce, P = pine, A = ash, and M = Philippine mahogany); and the last number indicates the number of strings. Thus M37M4 is a Musician's model, 37″ Philippine mahogany four-string dulcimer.

Musician's Model		*Hourglass Model*	
M37M4	$11.95	H39W4	$25.95
M37M3	10.95	H39M4	17.95
M31M4	9.95	H29W4	23.95
M31M3	8.95	H29M4	15.95
		H29S4	23.95

Central City Model		*Church Dulcimer*	
C38M4	$10.95	X44M6	$16.95
C38M3	9.95		
C28M4	8.95	*Double or Courting*	
C28M3	7.95		
		D40W8	$26.95
		D40M8	18.95

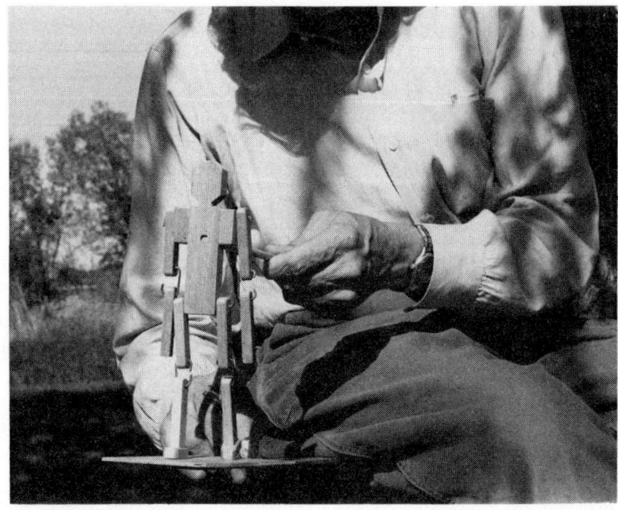

LIMBERJACK

This whimsical rhythm instrument has long been a favorite plaything of Appalachian children, and urban youngsters might take a fancy to it too if they can be torn away from their battery-operated Batmobiles. The limberjack is a loose-jointed little man who dances a jig when you tap the paddle that he stands on. It can be assembled in about an hour (younger children will need an adult's help). A rewarding project, bargain-priced. $6.95.

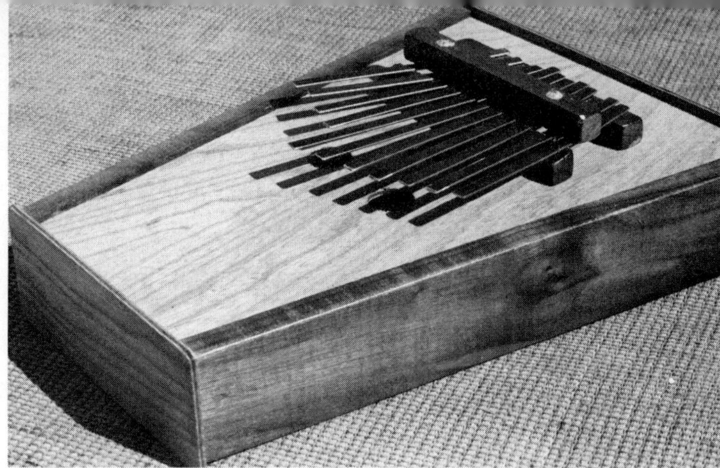

KALIMBAS

This is the larger version of the mbira, the African thumb piano. The kalimba has a rich history—tribal dances and then slave caravans were led by it. Later it was used by the slaves as an instrument of revolt (they sent drumlike messages to tell when to break their chains). Today kalimbas are used by rock groups and the more esoteric folk musicians, no strangers to revolt themselves. It is also effective as a combination pitch pipe and incidental rhythm instrument and can be used with rhythm band instruments. The kalimba, which is about the size of a shoe box, can be assembled in about five hours and is quite easy to play. Priced at a reasonable $5.95 in walnut.

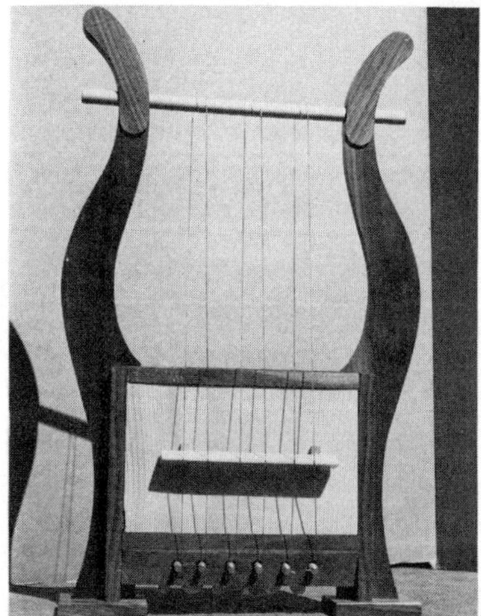

LYRE

Not too many people have actually seen a lyre, the stringed instrument of ancient Greece. This particular version has 6 strings and can be used as a simple accompaniment to folk singing. But its main appeal is the charm of actually building and playing an ancient instrument. Building time is about six hours. The sound board is spruce and the body walnut. $19.95.

IRISH HARPS

So easy to play that no one has bothered to write an instruction book, this instrument looks like a regular harp but is held on the lap. It produces a melodious, liquid tone and is relatively simple to assemble. It is available in mahogany at $24.95.

SITAR

Build your own sitar and play the music of India. The frets are adjustable to accommodate the many scales of Indian music. This sitar is a particularly good value—the fully assembled model costs three times as much. $24.95.

GUITARS

Hughes offers four remarkably inexpensive guitar kits, each of which builds a trapezoidal shape, which is much easier to build than the usual curvy models. (The original shape—which looks like the body of a woman—comes from the 16th century, when a serenading gentleman tried to convince a cloistered lady that he would rather stroke her than the guitar.) Although the trapezoidal shape is easier, it's no cinch. Allot at least forty hours. The mahogany model is easier to build but isn't as good a guitar as the spruce model. Also available is an acoustic bass guitar, used only with other instruments to provide the bass background. Prices from $9.95 to $25.95.

CONSTANTINE
2050 Eastchester Rd.
Bronx, N.Y. 10461

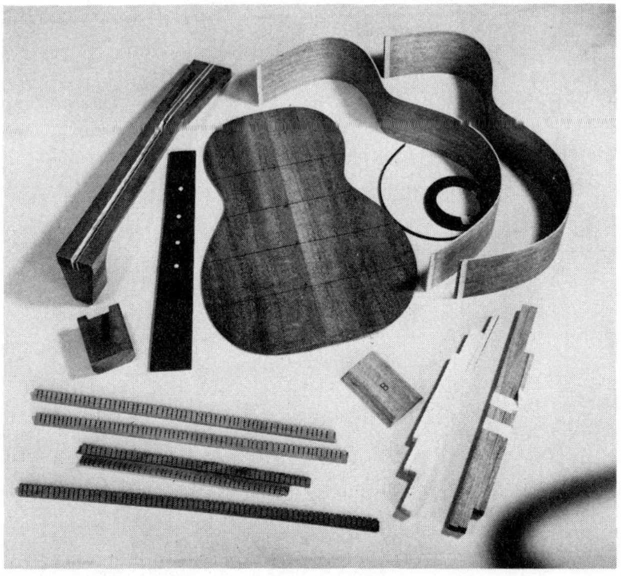

FOLK GUITAR

A good buy and relatively easy to assemble. All parts are precut of the finest materials (Constantine is known for its fine woods and wood products) and require only hand planing, knife trimming, and sanding. Kits contain all materials and components, including sandpaper and glue. Folk guitar has steel strings and measures 4½″ × 15″ × 37½″. (10 lb.) $94.49.

OTHER SOURCES

Appleseed John's General Store
Box 332 Heritage Sq.
Golden, Colo. 80439

Source for musical kits with an emphasis on dulcimers. Catalog (25¢).

Artisan Organs
128 East Wheeler Ave.
Arcadia, Calif. 91006

Large organ kits and components for church, theater, or huge living room. Information (free).

B. W. M. Benn Harpsichords
4424 Judson Lane
Minneapolis, Minn. 55435

Harpsichords, clavichords, spinets for the professional kit builder. Fine-priced, fine-instrument kits. However, do not attempt unless you have a full workshop and a real ability at this type of project.

Big Instrument Workshop
318 North 36 St.
Seattle, Wash. 98103

Catalog (16 pp., 75¢) has a variety of musical instruments in kit formats. Of particular interest is their Italian harpsichord kit. It is favorably priced with a number of interesting options and extras.

Craftsman Wood Service Co.
2727 South Mary St.
Chicago, Ill. 60608

Dulcimer and guitar kits. Catalog (50¢).

Lee Music Mfg. Co.
525 Venezia Ave.
Venice, Calif. 90291

Tired of pumping your old player piano? Lee Music offers kits for electrifying your player piano or reed organ. Easy to install. Brochure (free).

W. P. Ratajak
1636 Brook Lane
Corvallis, Oreg. 97330

Clavichords and harpsichords in kit and semi-kit form.

The String Shop
8432 High Ridge Rd.
Ellicott City, Md. 21043

Easy-to-assemble string instrument kits, including banjos, dulcimers, psalteries, and thumb pianos. School discounts. Catalog (free).

The Williams Workshop
1229 Olancha Dr.
Los Angeles, Calif. 90065

In case you like the harpsichord look but live in a studio apartment, Williams has the answer. Complete kits of small-sized harpsichords.

E. O. Witt
Route 3
Three Rivers, Mich. 49093

Harpsichords and clavichords in semi-kit form. That is, all the hard tricky work is done but plenty left for you. By completing yourself you still save up to half on usual finished price.

"Do-it-yourself" is becoming the motto of the gourmet set as never before, especially if those gourmets don't happen to be fabulously wealthy. People are growing their own vegetables, baking their own bread, and making their own yogurt and wine. Homemade products are often superior to their supermarket counterparts, and often cheaper, too.

Sometimes a kit is the perfect way to get started on a long-term enterprise such as wine-making, which will end up brightening all your leisure hours. Food kits are also a good way to discover just what you can and like to do.

Of course, in these days of chemical additives, there's another good reason for doing it yourself. If you make it, you know pretty much what's in it. Many people are doing more work in the kitchen because they feel the food they make for their families is more wholesome. Bread is fresher, yogurt tangier, bean sprouts crunchier, spices more flavorful when they're produced by you.

You'll find that some of the kits reviewed here require some initial investment. But usually you can use the equipment over and over, so the more you make, the less the cost per batch. Other kits are obvious money-savers from the start. Try to buy samples or small sizes if you're not sure how often you'll use them. Very likely, you'll be so pleased when you eat the results that you'll be back for the large economy-size.

WALTER T. KELLEY CO.
Clarkson, Ky. 42726

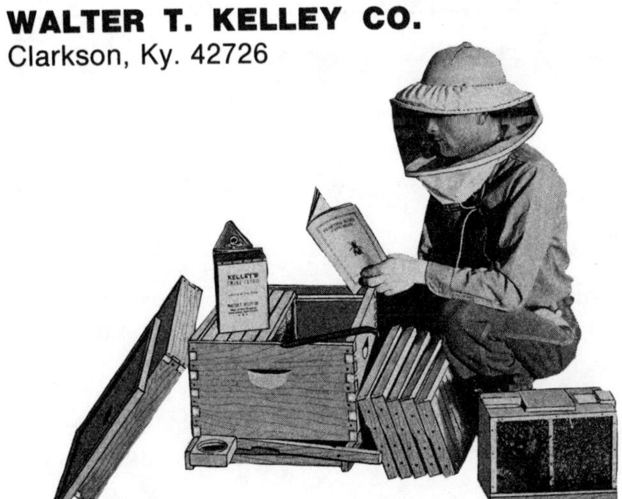

BEEKEEPING KIT

Why pay high supermarket prices for honey? At last, you need not put off getting into beekeeping any longer. A complete kit includes a hive which is shipped knocked down with complete instructions and nails for assembly. You get bee gloves, 10 sheets of ready-wired comb foundation, and a book on how to do everything right. The kit is also available with a swarm of Italian bees and a select young queen ("Write us when you are ready for them"). Beginner's Outfit: $33. Beginner's Outfit with Bees: $55.

SOMERSET HOUSE
Box 1786
Poughkeepsie, N.Y. 12601

YOGURT MAKER

Yogurt consumption has increased twenty times in ten years. Once a food of the old, the health devotee, and the sick, it has grown in popularity. In fact, it is today a widely accepted dessert, snack, and even a meal. You can make exceptionally good-tasting yogurt yourself. Never pay 39¢ a cup again. It even works with powdered milk. Complete kit is well designed and contains everything you need. Homemade yogurt in just three hours. $9.95.

PICKLEMASTERS
Box 65036
Los Angeles, Calif. 90065

PICKLE MAKER

All the right spices, all the right salts, all the right sugars and you can pickle it right in your own home. Here's a kit to turn cucumbers into pickles just like "at the factory." You can also make great relishes and it even pickles watermelon rind. Price is a little steep, but then how can you put a value on a good pickle? $10.

PFAELZER BROTHERS
4501 West District Blvd.
Chicago, Ill. 60632

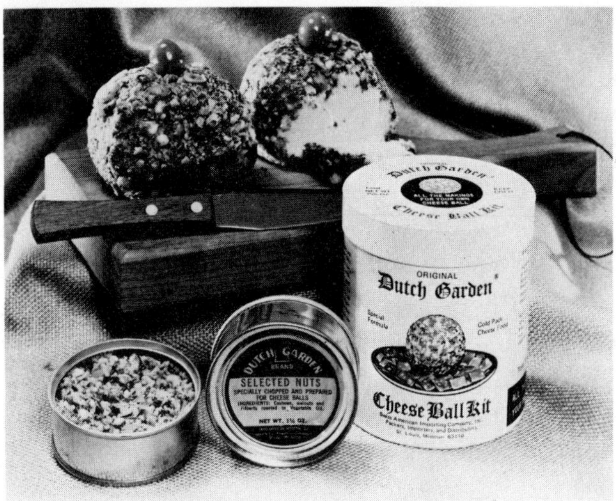

CHEESE BALL KIT

Pfaelzer Brothers are the purveyors of fine mail-order foods. They ship out those four-inch-thick steaks that big shots get at Christmas. Now they've come up with something for the little guy. It's delicious and easy to prepare, two sure pluses in food. In fact, it's the one kit in this book no one can mess up. The kit includes a pound of club cheddar. You roll the cheese into ball form, add the secret spices, then put the specially prepared cashews, walnuts, and filbert nuts on the outside. Real easy. And if it's not too aesthetically pleasing, feel free to eat the evidence. $4.95.

ACCESSORIES
437 Hyde St.
San Francisco, Calif. 94109

SOURDOUGH BREAD

San Francisco is popular for more than cable cars and Fisherman's Wharf. Tourists and residents acclaim the fine sourdough bread. This favorite food is served in most good Frisco restaurants. Visitors line up at the airport bread store to take home samples. It's so well liked, in fact, that in the early 1960s two brothers formed a business flying it airfreight to New York restaurants.

Now, you can have the real thing . . . well, almost. The Sourdough kit actually makes an excellent product. Kit includes yeast (which will last forever if cared for), a stoneware crock, and instructions. $7.95.

VINO CORP.
80 Commerce St.
Rochester, N.Y. 14623

BRANDIED FRUIT MAKER

Dessert, dessert, dessert! Probably left over from childhood, dessert remains everyone's favorite part of the meal. Now you can create your own special toppings or desserts with this new kit. Kit includes one half-gallon rumtopf jar, special brandied fruit yeast, rum flavoring, and a traditional rumtopf ladle. Included is a special recipe book of exotic treats you can make. $7.99.

WELCH'S FOODS, INC.
Westfield, N.Y. 14787

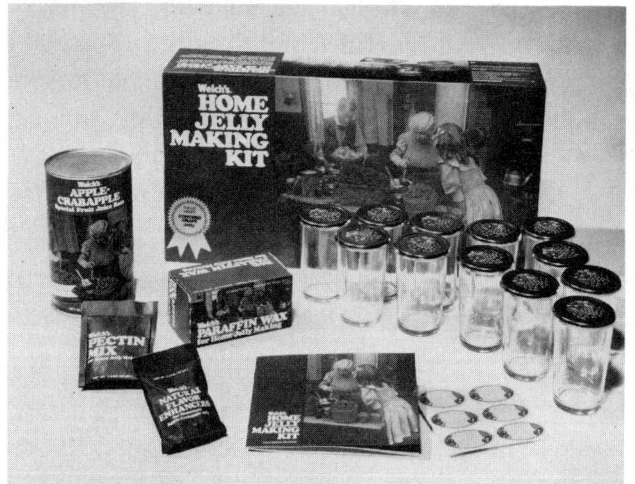

JELLY-MAKING

Somehow it seems a little odd to us that this country's best-known factory-made jelly company would try to sell a kit like this. The kit, you see, teaches you how to make jelly at home. Maybe the strategy is that after you see how much trouble it is you'll return to the A & P and buy the on-shelf variety.

Anyway, the commercial folk give you a chance to do it yourself, and that's exactly what you can do with the complete kit. The jelly-making kits come in a deluxe variety (with 12 reusable jars and caps). Each kit contains the following items: 1 information booklet; 1 can special fruit juice base; 1 envelope natural flavor enhancer; 1 envelope pectin base; and 5 paraffin cakes. The kits may be ordered in the following flavors: Concord grape; apple-crabapple; and American cherry.

Homemade baked bread and real jelly is everyone's memory of a trip to grandma's. Now you can re-create it all for $8.99.

WAGNER PRODUCTS

Riverview Dr.
Hustisford, Wis. 53034

HOME SAUSAGE KITCHEN

A new-fashioned way to make old-fashioned sausage. And although the finished product won't win any county fair prizes, the sausage-making process itself is easy and pleasant and economical. Ideal for teen-age parties. We recommend the "basic" sausage kitchen rather than the more expensive "gourmet" sausage kitchen, since the only difference is that the latter contains a "deluxe sausage stuffer" instead of an "economy sausage stuffer." Basic kit: $10.95. Gourmet kit: $14.95.

HOME CHEESERY KITS

If you have a yen to create your own cheese, Wagner's kits are easy to use and can make for family or company fun. But as for the cheese, be warned—you are likely to find a more palatable product at your local delicatessen. The "Basic" kit contains everything you need to make cheese at home, including rennet and coloring tablets, cheese press, thermometer, recipes, and instructions. The "Gourmet" kit is much the same, except that it features an earthenware-colored crock that holds 20 oz. of cheese and a "decorator-styled" cheese press. The "Deluxe Electric Home Cheesery" contains all of the above plus a "specially calibrated hot tray." All three kits are slickly packaged and attractively designed, making them good for gift-giving. Note that all kits require a few kitchen ingredients and do not include utensils. Basic kit: $7.95. Gourmet kit: $9.95. Electric kit: $14.95.

HOME COTTAGE CHEESERY

Cottage cheese is a little easier to make at home than other cheese and you may find the product more acceptable than the cheeses turned out by the other Home Cheesery kits. Although you're not likely to give the Breakstone people any competition, you'll find the cheese-making process enjoyable and economical. Kit contains water-jacketed cottage cheese vat, thermometer, and complete instructions and recipes. A good gift possibility. $9.95.

PUCKIN HUDDLE

Oliverea, N.Y. 12462

LOLLYPOP KITS

Grandma made lollypops and now you can, too. Our favorite food kit. You get six decorative molds of a bunny, a heart, a soldier, a four-leaf clover, a funny face, and an elephant. Plus sticks, recipes, and instructions. A "can't miss" food project. Really simple. $6.75.

A most delightful catalog (24 pp., 50¢) of what the owners call "Craftskills from the Catskills," features charming items and a number of interesting kits.

MANNA SUPPLY CO.

Box 3006
Santa Monica, Calif. 90403

SPROUT-EASE

Even a Biology 1 student knows the health value of sprouts. They contain the B-complex vitamins, minerals, and proteins. Only problem is they cost 89¢ for a little bag in the health food store. Now you can grow your own. Most amazing is that no soil is needed, only moisture and air. You can eat sprouts in salads, soups, omelets, or right out of the fridge. The Manna kit includes 3 standard-size open end jar tops, 3 drain screens, and 3 trial bags of seeds and instruments. In terms of value, 1 tablespoon of alfalfa seed makes a quart of fresh sprouts. The entire kit for your kitchen farm is $2.25 postpaid.

SPEL SALES

14 Slingerland Ave.
Pequannock, N.J. 07940

POLISH-STYLE SAUSAGE KIT

Wagner Products (above) offers one style of family-fun sausage kit. Spel offers a more sophisticated product that makes Polish sausages! Now you can have fresh sausage with the right amount of seasoning to your particular taste. Each kit includes a sausage-stuffing horn, freshly cured and salted hog casings, an old-world blend of spices and seasoning, complete instructions, and our favorite sausage recipes. $5.95 postpaid.

Company also offers a cold cut kit and other food kits. Send 10¢ for a brochure.

OTHER SOURCES

J. T. McCarthy Co.
P.O. Box 7012
Milwaukee, Wis. 53213

Water filter and water softener kits that will save you 50% by assembling them yourself. Catalog ($2—credited to your first order).

American wine consumption has climbed from 250,000,000 gallons in 1965 to an impressive 350,000,000 gallons in 1975. With numbers like that the kit makers can't be far behind.

The kits have refined the earthy, messy, complex endeavor into an antiseptic, speedy, family-fun activity. The only drawback is that this must be considered an afternoon's relaxation rather than a gastronomic adventure as our experience indicates the process leaves much to be desired in terms of quality production. But perhaps your luck will be better!

A word of caution: If you really start liking the stuff, we suggest a visit to your nearest office of the Federal Alcohol and Tobacco Tax. You are required to file Form 1541. It allows you to make up to 200 gallons of wine a year for your own consumption.

Wine-making is no longer the exclusive property of Tennessee backwoodsmen, nor that of old maids squeezing the elderberry bush, nor the Gallo family. You'll find this an enjoyable hobby and a perfect gift (the kit that is, not the wine).

WELCH'S FOODS, INC.
Westfield, N.Y. 14787

WELCH'S WINE COUNTRY KIT

The overall analysis at a recent homemade wine-tasting party was "sort of grape juice with a kick." With that as an analysis, it's only natural that Welch's should get into the game. Welch's, for the nonsupermarket shopper, provides this country with much of our grape juice. Now they've put together a kit that includes everything you need to make ten bottles of wine, right down to the labels.

It's all attractively packaged and will perform about as well as the others outlined in this section. The Welch's name may give the wary some confidence. The kit is actually in wide distribution at retail. J. C. Penny, for example, stocks it at many stores. Or you can order by mail directly from Welch's. $9.95.

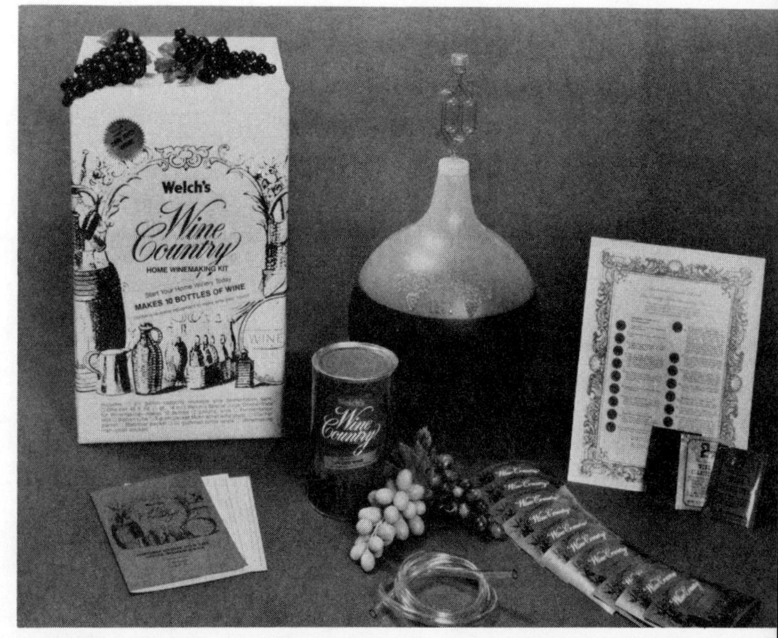

SEMPLEX OF U.S.A.
4805 Lyndale Ave., North
Minneapolis, Minn. 55412

SEMPLEX KIT

For the most serious wine enthusiast there is the Semplex Company kit. The "Starter" kit contains all that's needed (sans sugar and water) for only $11.95 postpaid. Their back-up catalog allows you to choose from some dozen other concentrates, eight types of yeast, fifteen books for the advanced, packages, and six kinds of sugar. There's also a complete list of all you need from champagne bottle stoppers (8¢ each) to a grape press ($174.).

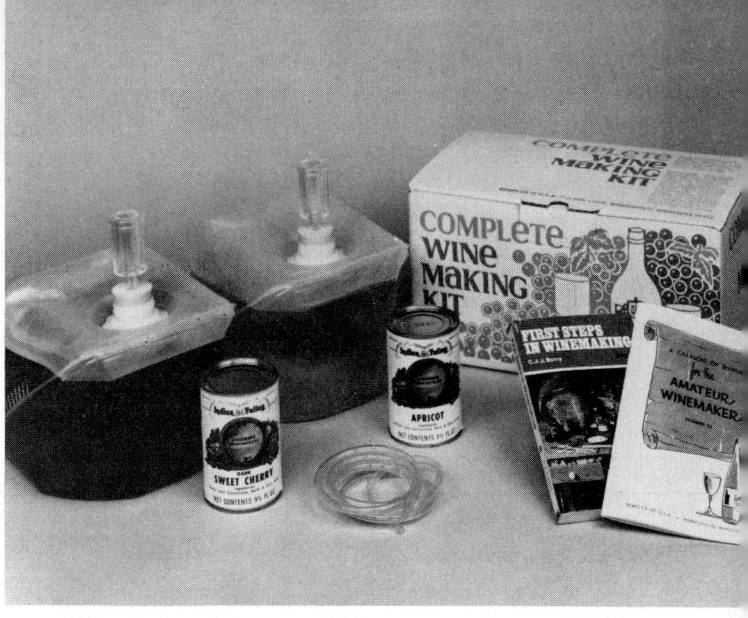

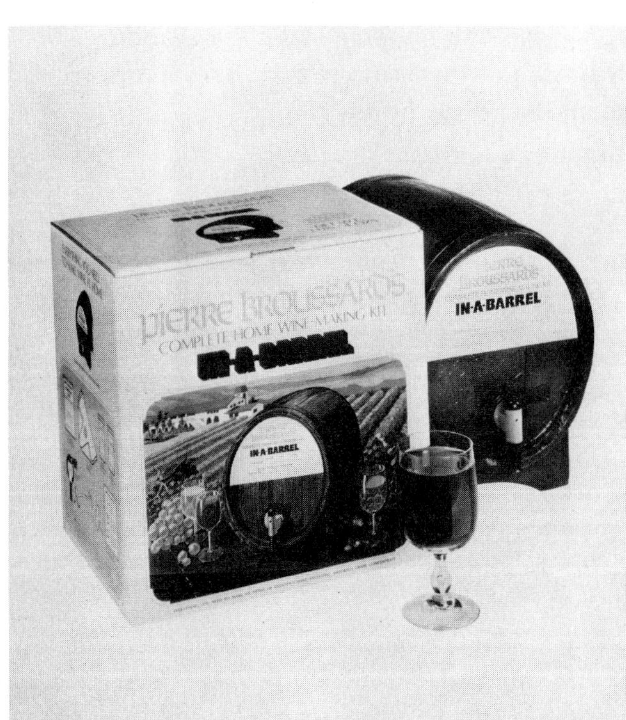

PRODUCT SPECIALTIES
900 Jorie Blvd.
Oak Brook, Ill. 60521

PIERRE BROUSSARD'S COMPLETE HOME WINE-MAKING KIT

Don't let the French name fool you—the company stands no chance of driving Lafite Rothschild out of business. However, this is the best of the wine-making kits we've tried. It's quite simple and involves only two steps, no siphoning, no straining, no filtering, no bottling, no sterilization, no scrubbing, no large space. They offer a choice of five wine varieties—Burgundy, Sherry, Rosé, Chianti, and Chablis.

It's in-a-barrel packaging adds to the fun. You not only "manufacture" it in an attractive barrel, but it becomes a perfect serving device. Complete kit includes: imported concentrate, wine skin and spigot, decorative barrel, yeast and yeast food, clarifier settler, air-lock assembly, and easy-to-read instructions. $11.99.

OTHER SOURCES

Bacchanalia
273 Riverside Ave.
Westport, Conn. 06880

Barrel Winery
1201 University Ave.
Berkeley, Calif. 94702

Brant's Wine Rack
Box 3256
Orange, Calif. 92665

Continental
Box 18223
Indianapolis, Ind. 46218

Jim Dandy Wine Supplies
8454 Beechmont
Cincinnati, Ohio 45230

Hobby U.S.A.
43 North 9 St.
Allentown, Pa. 18101

In the early part of the 19th century, the Industrial Revolution began to make handcrafts obsolete. Most people came to prefer and value machine-made or "store-bought" goods over those made at home. This is not surprising, considering the novelty and slickness of the new mass-produced items.

But machines and assembly lines have not been the perfect solution we once thought they would be. In the first place, no machine can produce the effects of a hand-rubbed piece of furniture or a one-of-a-kind necklace strung just for you. Even more important, we have been missing the sheer *pleasure* of making and using something ourselves. Working with his own hands is a spiritual need that man, with all his machines, has not outgrown.

In the last decade or so, we have realized that hand-crafted objects are functional, expressive, and more beautiful than just about anything we can afford to buy. Most people would rather have a box decoupaged by you than an expensive inlaid one made at a factory. Whether you prefer to work with fiber, metal, paper, or wood, there is a craft, and very likely a kit for you in today's market.

TANDY LEATHER CO.
2727 West 7 St.
Fort Worth, Tex. 76107

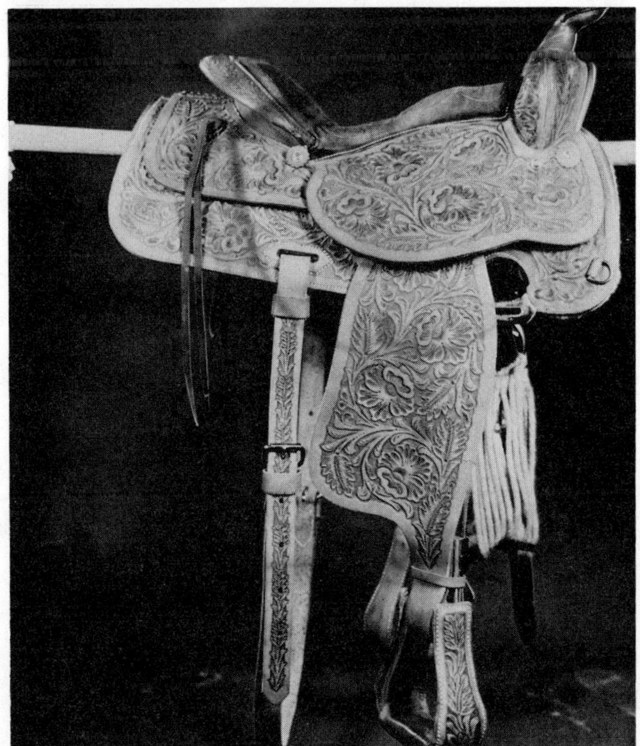

WESTERN SADDLE

Here's a leather craftsman's dream. Experience and a fair amount of determination will provide you with an impressive result. It features a 15″ seat with padding. Rigging is steel-plate reinforced. Its square skirts are sheepswool-lined. The stirrups feature quick-change leather buckles. Assembly instructions are easy-to-follow. Allow lots of time to complete. $235.

BILLFOLD KITS

You may think a billfold is a billfold is a billfold, but to the Tandy Leather Company a billfold is something that comes in no fewer than twenty-three styles. All kits contain real leather parts and all materials needed, plus complete instructions. They are available with tooling designs that you can engrave or stain (scrolls, flowers, even initials and full names) or in elegant black Moroccan grain leather. Most styles are intended for men, but there are a few women's billfolds and a boy's kit that just fits small pockets. Any of these can be put together by someone with little or no experience in such things and an experienced leathercrafter will find them a breeze. The following are some of the kits available; for full descriptions of the entire line, see Tandy catalog.

A mere $1.95 buys a preembossed man's billfold kit that includes lacing and can be finished or dyed. The same price buys the "Baron," a child's billfold kit that contains precut, prepunched parts, pocket coin holder, window pocket, carving pattern, lacing, and easy-to-follow instructions. Unlike other children's leather projects on the market, this one does not require that a child have a 160 I.Q. The "Trucker's Wallet" kit is a huge 4½" × 9¼" and has a chain to attach it to a belt. We haven't noticed too many truckdrivers with wallets hanging on their belts, but it's a good idea nonetheless. The "Pocket Secretary" ($3.95) holds papers and cards as well as money. The "Spiral Line Triplefold" kit ($4.95) actually folds only twice, but is simple, elegant, and compact.

MOCCASINS

Easy-to-make moccasin kits for both kids and grown-ups. These are good family projects (nothing like sitting around the fire lacing up moccasins!) and practical money savers. All kits include precut, prepunched leather or suede parts, preattached insoles, laces, and instructions.

The "Tuffy" mocs are palomino-colored (pale beige, to nonhorse folk) with plaid linings, and are available only in children's sizes. The "Indian Scout" kit makes women's or men's moccasins in an amber suede. The adult version is called the "Kuffy" and costs $1. more. Unfortunately, the "Komfy"—the ultimate in indoor footwear—is available only in adult sizes. We say unfortunately because kids would love the fluffy wool lining and cuffs. The "Bullhide" kit, like its name, is sturdy, rugged, and, predictably, for men only. Tuffy: $2.95. Indian scout: $2.95. Kuffy: $3.95. Komfy: $4.45. Bullhide: $4.45.

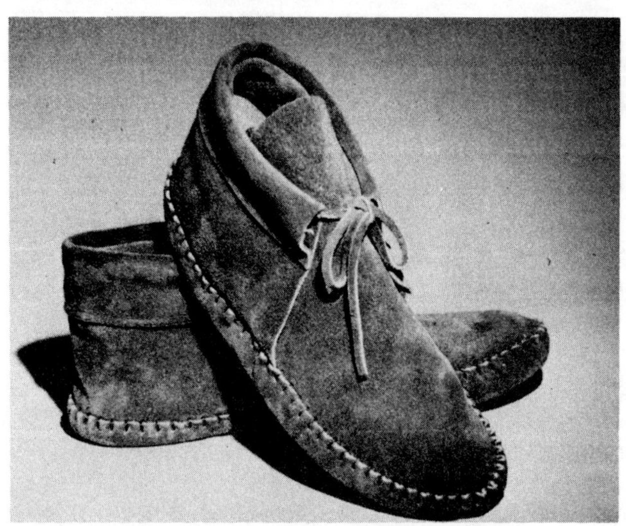

INCA BOOT KIT

The Inca boot is not a boot at all, nor does it have much connection with the Incas. It is a soft, high-rise, laced and fringed moccasin that is so comfortable and good looking you'll want to abandon all your other shoes. Kit contains all necessary equipment and directions. Specify men's, women's, or children's size. As it happens, these kits sell for only slightly less than a similar shoe in finished form, but think of the satisfaction of making your own. Child's Inca boot (4609): $4.95. Adult's Inca boot (4611): $6.45.

INDIAN LORE

Tandy offers a full selection of what they choose to call "Indian Lore" kits. Whether a ticktacktoe game played with cowhide symbols on a miniature suede skin actually qualifies as "Indian lore" is open to question. And we've seen as many cowboys in the suede "Chief" vest as we've seen Indians. But most of the kits (there are about twenty) seem reasonably related to Indian crafts. And all are easy to make and easy to pay for. Good gift choices. The following are among the highlights. See Tandy catalog for full selection.

The unfortunately named "Indian Skin Plaque" kit (honest, kids, no Indian lost his skin to make this) is actually a hunk of leather ready to decorate and lace to a frame. It sells for $1. For $5.95 your son can make himself a 21" high feathered and beaded "War Bonnet," but less adventurous parents may prefer the less expensive "Indian Headdress" kit. The "Peace Pipe" kit is an appealing wood and feather affair that costs only a dollar. Equally inexpensive is the expansively named "Buffalo Horn Trophy Plaque" kit, on which your child can tool his own name. The manufacturer claims that the heavy leather "blade" of the "Tomahawk" kit is safe for children, but steer clear of this one if your kid is more warlike than average. Get him instead the "Mini-Drum" kit, an easy lacing and assembling project and a bargain at 69 cents. For the more serious drum fan, there is the "Tom-Tom" kit for $9.95, with plumes, drumstick materials, and six decorating patterns.

Tandy is the foremost leather kit company in the country. They literally offer shoestrings to saddles. Dave Tandy started the company some fifty years ago with a single kit. Today there is a kit to fit every age and skill level. Some of their beginner items are little more than lacing projects, while the more elaborate kits can require many days of work. Free catalog.

KAYEFF, INC.
511 Campesina
Los Angeles, Calif. 91006

SHELL ART ON SILK

Another adventure in crafts. Depending on your taste, it will either delight or depress you. We know art but we may not know what you like. The kit includes one prepainted 12" × 18" piece of silk, assorted natural sea shells, bonding material, and a wood applicator. The "idea" is to take the tiny sea shells and glue them to the picture to "create" an art piece. $10.

THE SAND CATS
P.O. Box 15084
Lakewood, Colo. 80215

BEGINNER'S PRACTICE SAND PAINTING KIT

Sand—that ubiquitous mineral you've sifted through your fingers so many times or built castles with at the beach. Cal and Nita Simmons, the "Sand Cats," have developed a way of using sand artistically; they have collected sand grains from all over the U.S.A., for apparently not all sand grains are alike. Some are fine, some medium; there exists natural sand, crushed rock, artificially colored natural sand, or crushed marble. Did you realize that many different minerals, rock fragments, shell fragments, whole shells, gemstones, etc., can be found in sands? The "Sand Cats" have collected over 250 different sands.

Sand paintings themselves are made by fastening the sand to a baseboard with a diluted mixture of glue. The glue is applied with an artist's brush and the sand is sprinkled on. Of course, it sticks where the glue is and the surplus can be poured off. Sand painting can also be done on suitable cardboard for greeting cards, Xmas cards, or whatever.

Cal and Nita feel that sand painting can be a great hobby and they admit that the sand painter is more of a "glue technician" than an artist. Actually, the art, which involves sand collecting, can turn you into an amateur geologist or minerologist as well as a painter.

The Beginner's Practice Sand Painting Kit contains materials and sands to make six 5″ × 7″ sand paintings on pressed board; also included in the kit are brushes, glue, sand, and instructions. A small financial investment for a hobby that could mushroom into a whole scientific endeavor. $3.

KALEIDOSCOPE
288 The Prado, N.E.
Atlanta, Ga. 30309

STRATAVARIUM

A natural art form, the Stratavarium is a combination of a plant and seashell in a sand base. You create the entire effect with this interesting kit. The kit includes a plexiglass container, a rare tropical plant, an unusual seashell, and varied-color sands that you layer. 4″ × 4″ × 7″. $20.

OLDSTONE ENTERPRISES
77 Summer St.
Boston, Mass. 02110

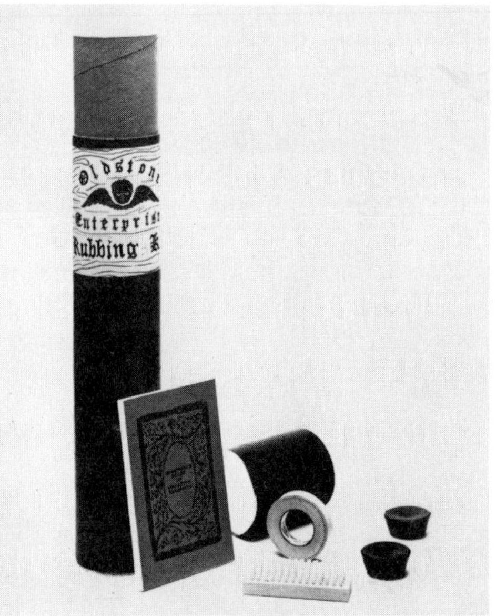

THE ORIGINAL OLDSTONE RUBBING KIT

Here is a project for those who enjoy the outdoors, who like to be artistic on occasion, and who desire inexpensive ways of pursuing the first two ideas. What could this hobby be? Why, it's rubbing, the art of transferring the design of any textured surface to a piece of paper or fabric using a special wax or crayon. What you end up with will be an exact, life-size reproduction of the textured surface.

The outdoor materials necessary for working on this endeavor include a local graveyard filled with very old gravestones (being a resident of New England is a definite asset) or a decorative manhole found just about everywhere, or even an historical marker, which no state is lacking.

In the process of working with rubbings, you obtain a little history (the tales that are told on epitaphs!), you are a participant in a popular art form, and you're bound to have lots of fun. This is actually a quite serious and popular hobby in England.

The Original Oldstone Rubbing kit contains five sheets of 24″ × 36″ Aqaba hemp rubbing paper, also ideal for block printing; two 2-oz. cupcakes of Oldstone Rubbing Wax (one black and one brown—a plastic bag is provided for holding wax when not being used); a roll of tape for holding paper securely to the surface being rubbed; a bristle brush for clearing a surface of undesirable particles; and the new 1973 edition of *Oldstone's Guide to Creative Rubbings*. All this comes in a black leatherette carrying case, which the company calls "the last word in gravestone rubbing equipment." $6.50.

SPENCER GIFTS

Spencer Bldg.
Atlantic City, N.J. 08411

STAINED GLASS KIT

This is not a stained glass assembly kit, but rather sort of a painting set. We're not sure you'll want the "cathedral glass" look all over your crystal stemware (or your front windows), but it might be a good way to keep your kids out of your hair on a rainy afternoon—and you can always give them jelly jars to work. Kit includes four jars of glass dye, simulated leading, thinner, and easy instructions. $4.99.

OPEN DOOR ENTERPRISES, INC.

1249 Dell Ave.
Campbell, Calif. 95008

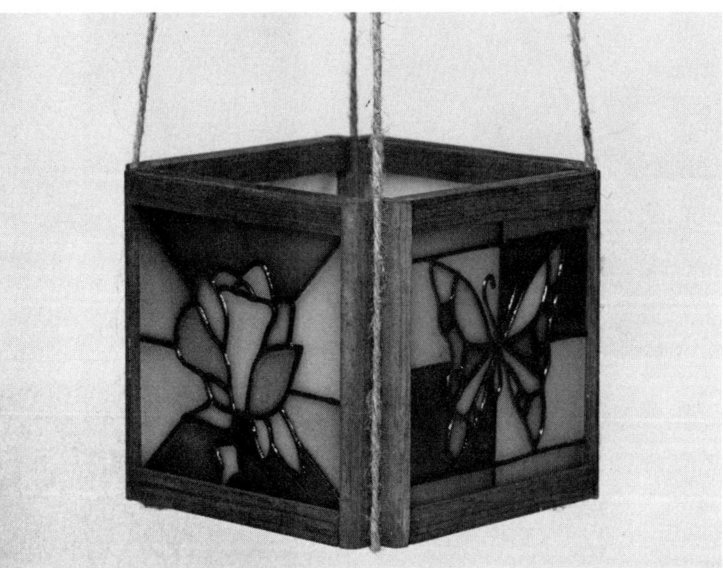

STAINED GLASS HANGING LANTERN KIT

A building with stained glass windows is bound to receive an appreciative look, for stained glass has a beauty totally its own. A Tiffany lamp is treasured because of its stained glass, and few religious edifices are constructed without stained glass windows.

With the appeal of stained glass and with an eye to fuel consumption, the Candlelantern should prove to be a popular kit. Safe, simple, and creative "stained glass" patterns are produced on clear plexiglass with easy-to-use liquid lead and colorful glass stains. The Stained Glass Hanging Lantern kit supplies you with suggested artwork, but original designs can be used as well as tracings from photographs, prints, etc. The decorated panels are mounted into prefinished woodwork and a metal base is installed. A lighted candle glows through the stained panels. Each kit contains 2 oz. liquid lead,

three ¾-oz. bottles of water-base glass stain, four 4⅜″ × 4⅜″ plexiglass panels, precut, walnut-stained wooden frame pieces, metal base, paint brush, glue, cord for hanging, and simple instructions. Completed size: 5″ × 5″ × 5½″. $10.

GLASS HOUSE STUDIO

Box 3267
St. Paul, Minn. 55165

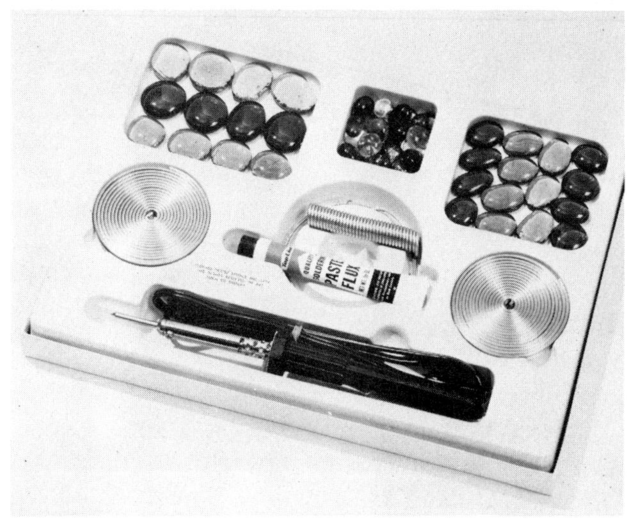

STAINED GLASS-MAKING KIT

Create a variety of stained glass designs with this master kit. The designs are up to you, but all the materials are right there for assembly. Will take some fooling around until you get anything worthwhile; however, once you get in the swing, you'll be doing cathedral windows in no time. $12.95 postpaid.

QUINCRAFTS CORP.

184 Washington St.
Quincy, Mass. 02169

"STAINED PLASTIC" KIT

If the work outlined in the stained glass kits seems too hard, here's an easy substitute. Place the Makit frame on a foil-covered cookie sheet. Fill the space in the frame with the kit's plastic cooking crystals. Process in kitchen oven at 375° for 20 minutes. Cool, then peel off foil. The results are delightful. This is, of course, a children's project and we usually object to any child project that involves ovens and cooking. However, with adult supervision you'll be pleasantly surprised with the creations. Mini-kit (1 mold), plus a supply of crystals: $1.98. Complete catalog of a hundred-plus molds included with order.

PLUME TRADING CO.

155 Lexington Ave.
New York, N.Y. 10016

INDIAN WARSHIRT

Next time your husband shows up at 3:00 A.M., slip into your homemade Sioux Indian warshirt. These authentic shirts are made from fine suede. Four skins are supplied, two for front and back panels and two smaller for sleeves. You also receive binding for the collar. Complete instructions show you how to make any reasonable-size shirt with material supplied. $18.95.

Plume produces a catalog (34 pp., 25¢) of every conceivable type of Indian headdress, clothing, moccasin, and jewelry kit. They are in varying degrees of authenticity. It seems strange to have the kingpin of Indian crafts on New York's Lexington Avenue; however, we really haven't found another good source for this type of product. Most Indians sell only the finished product. The firm originally sold Scouts Indian craft projects, but now sells to "everyone," including—according to the owner—some Indians!

POURETTE MANUFACTURING CO.

6818 Roosevelt Way, N.E.
Seattle, Wash. 98115

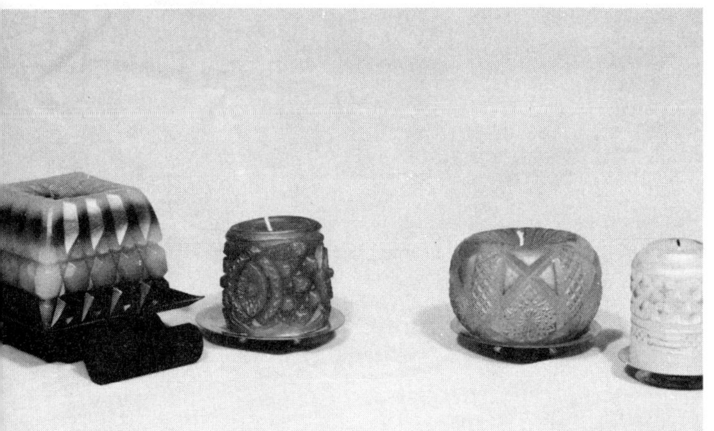

CRYSTAL-ETTE CANDLE-MAKING KITS

Colonial Americans made and used candles because candles were the only source of light within the home in the evening. These early Americans probably never thought of making a practical, functional candle that would look both formal and elegant—a candle with a cut-glass look.

Each of these kits features 2 Crystal-ette molds that are constructed of flexible vinyl plastic, 2 lb. wax, 1 yd. wicking, 1 wick rod, mold sealer, 1 tube of Rub 'n Buff antique gold, 3 color chips (red, blue, yellow), carnation-scented rosette, and complete instructions. $6.75.

LEATHERCRAFT SUPPLY CO.

25 Great Jones St.
New York, N.Y. 10012

HANGING CANDLE HOLDER KIT

·Leather—the ideal complement to the natural beauty of candles (equally attractive with plants and flowers). Adaptable to many candle or flower pot shapes and sizes. Strap lengths easy to adjust. Straps and bottom piece cut from sturdy cowhide. Kit complete with durable metal rings and rivets, plus easy-to-follow instructions. Choose natural cowhide (can be tooled, carved, and dyed any color) or toned latigo (easy to tool, may be stained or antiqued to chosen shade of brown). $4.50.

"ALL-PURPOSE" BAG

A sportsman's unique and useful leathercraft project. Ideal for servicemen, perfect for hunters, etc. Kit is cut from fine-grade carving leather with care and precision. Styled with a clever carrying handle and a full opening zipper. Includes moisture-proof lining, die-cut leather, hardware, lace, photo, tracing, and complete instructions. Measures 9¾″ × 4¾″ × 5½″. $8.30.

Send $1. for a super catalog of leather goodies.

PAT ENTERPRISES

770 Northwest 197 Terrace
Miami, Fla. 33169

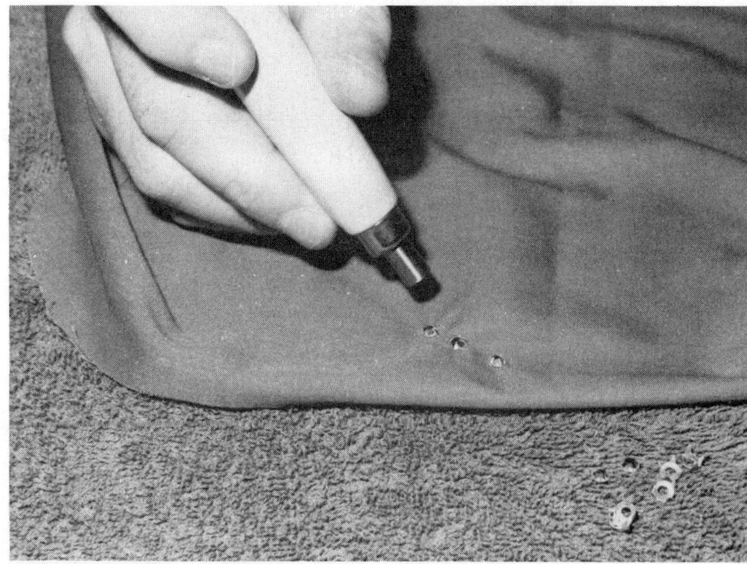

RHINESTONE SETTING

The in-fashions today have the sparkle and glitter look. You can fashion your own design on jeans, dresses, sweaters, and T-shirts. Kit includes a quality tool made of solid wood with steel tip, instructions, plus a supply of rhinestones. $4.95.

GALLAGHER-FOSTER HOUSE
6523 Galena Rd.
Peoria, Ill. 61601

COTTON AND FELT CLOWN

Third graders used to make these by cutting out circles of fabric scraps, sewing them, and stringing them together to make a colorful dangling toy. This kit supplies all precut pieces and includes padding, yarn, and thread, but otherwise the principle is the same and your efforts result in a 15″ clown with woolly hair and a pointed hat. Youngsters can make these for themselves or younger children; adults will enjoy making clowns as gifts (they look charming hanging from a newborn's carriage). $4.99.

FRIENDS INDUSTRIES, INC.
40 Gazza Blvd.
Farmingdale, N.Y. 11735

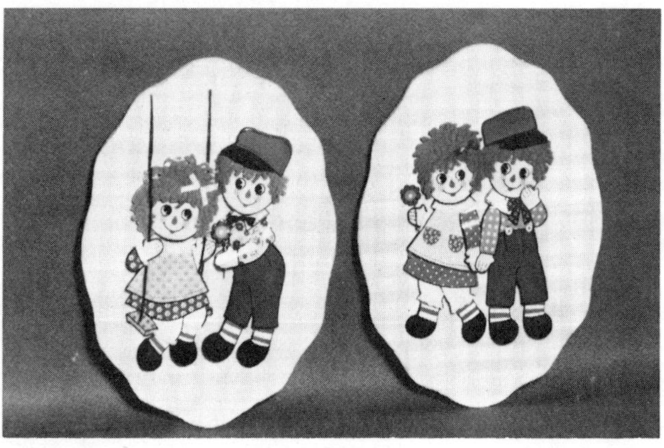

RAG DOLL DIMENSIONAL KIT

Raggedy Ann and Andy are as much a part of the American scene as Mickey Mouse and Donald Duck. These rag dolls—residing in almost every home—can now be found on 2.5″ × 7″ scalloped wood plaques, looking as appealing as ever.

The complete rag doll decoupage kit contains four prints for dimensional effect, gingham background, glue, stain and rickrack trim. Rag doll advocates now have a novel way of displaying their favorite "people." $4.50.

THE CRACKER BOX
River Rd.
Point Pleasant, Pa. 18950

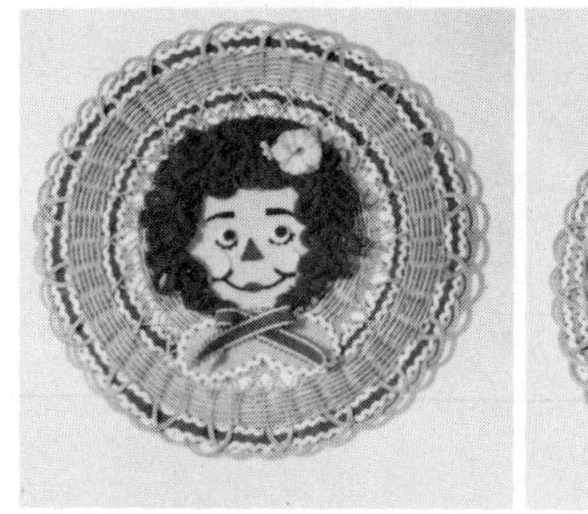

ANN & ANDY

Every child will delight to this pair of familiar smiling faces. They are done on a 14″ rattan mat and have flesh-colored faces with red carpet yarn hair. All complete with Andy's gingham cap, blue velvet tie, and Ann's hair flower. $2.75 each. $5.00 for the pair.

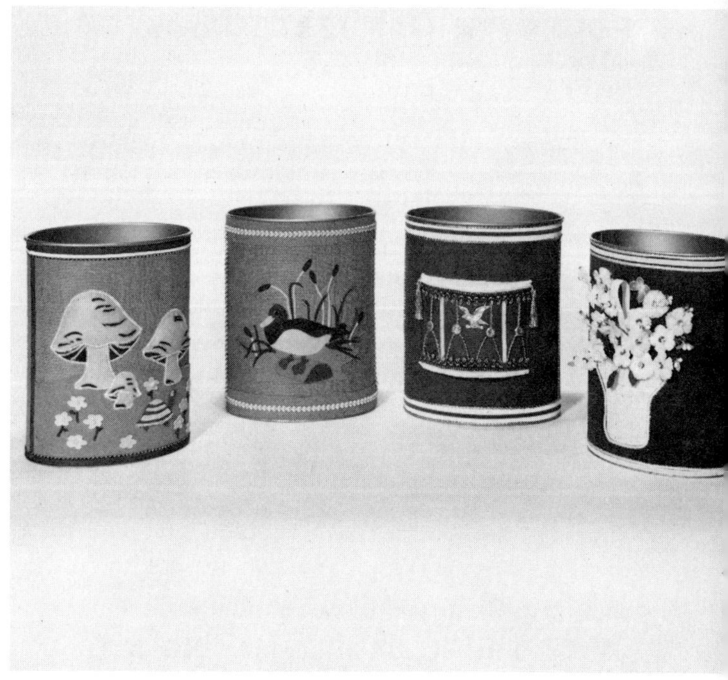

WASTEBASKET KIT

Why have dull wastebaskets? The last undecorated item in a household comes to life with this fun project. Everything is top quality in each kit. First-line felt, burlap, velvet, or braid is used. No plastics or vinyl. Even the 12″ basket (included) is of sturdy metal. $5.98.

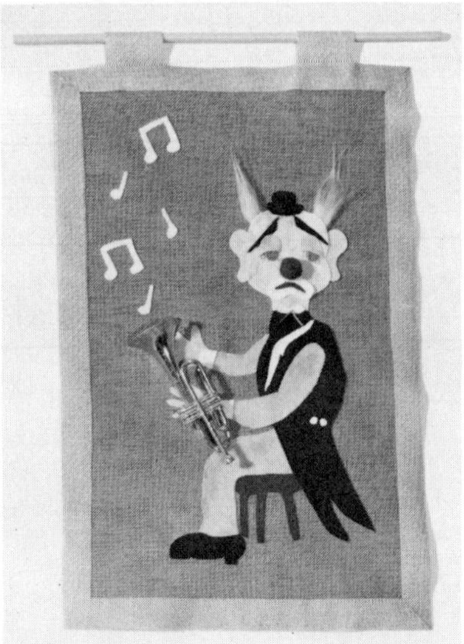

WALL TAPESTRY

The sad clown seems to delight us all. This large wall hanging kit can become a nice addition to any child's room. He'll enjoy seeing it again and again, but most of all, he'll enjoy making it. It's a nice size—18″ × 27″. Felt backing on green burlap. Even the wood pole is supplied. $3.50.

Don't miss the Cracker Box catalog (32 pp., $1.50) for a variety of interesting craft projects. Although not always our taste, there is a varied selection of products. The owners, Paul Caine and Walter Williams, are personally involved in the creation of each kit, right down to writing the instructions. Their attitude is best expressed in their answer to our form letter asking "tell us about your business." Paul wrote: "The crux is we like to create beautiful things, and we love our work, so it isn't all that hard." Needless to say, it's a pleasure to deal with a company like that.

SHILLCRAFT

500 North Calvert St.
Baltimore, Md. 21202·

RUG-MAKING

"Even if you've never done handwork before, you can make a lovely rug on your first try." So says the manufacturer. Although it may not be as easy as all that, it is not a complex process. Shillcraft is the largest manufacturer of ready-cut rug kits in the world.

The "secret" is precut yarn. Each pack contains 320 pieces of moth-proof 6-ply rug yarn cut to uniform length (2½″). It is simply knotted in the canvas, no cutting or winding is required.

The kits also include the following. Color-stenciled canvas: The design is stenciled in color on the strong 100% cotton canvas; you simply match the colors of the yarn to the colors on the canvas. Latchet Hook: Easy-knot steel hook of Shillcraft's own special design. Knots each piece of yarn perfectly and so firmly, yarn cannot pull out. It allows you to keep your hands free of the part already

worked. Complete instructions, binding tape, needle, and thread.

Catalog (48 pp., $1.) shows all the designs and gives full information. The following are some representative prices for 100% Wove rugs. (Wove/nylon blends are somewhat cheaper.)

14″ × 32″	$18.50
22″ × 36″	30.50
27″ × 54″	54.00
60″ × 84″	169.00
80″ × 120″	293.00

HALTER CORP.

32123 Winona Rd.
Winona, Ohio 44493

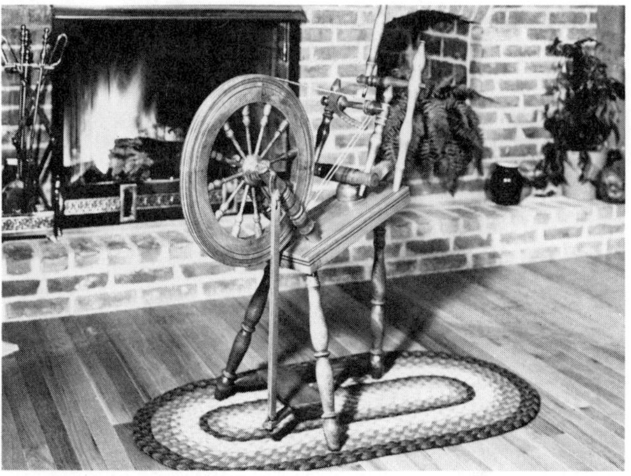

SPINNING WHEEL

Be the first one on your block to spin your own cloth. This authentic reproduction of a Saxony-type spinning wheel is not only a decorative and unusual collector's item, but it really works. There is probably nothing you can think of that is more representative of early America and this particular piece is a faithful reproduction of the style widely used.

The spinning wheel is not difficult to build, as the wheel itself comes to you completely assembled. The wood is all fine-grained solid maple, with no glued parts. All fittings are solid brass and wrought iron. The flyer bearings and drive belts are genuine leather. The flyer is also preassembled to the flyer shaft and the bearing holes are prepunched. The turned parts are all sanded and drilled or slotted for easy assembly; however, light sanding may be necessary depending upon the desired finish. The solid maple can easily be finished in a honey-tone finish to match much of the Early American maple furniture, or it can be stained dark to more nearly match a walnut finish. When completed, the spinning wheel stands 42″ high. Included with all materials is a hand-bound book on "Spinning." $81.50.

SCHOOL PRODUCTS

312 East 23 St.
New York, N.Y. 10010

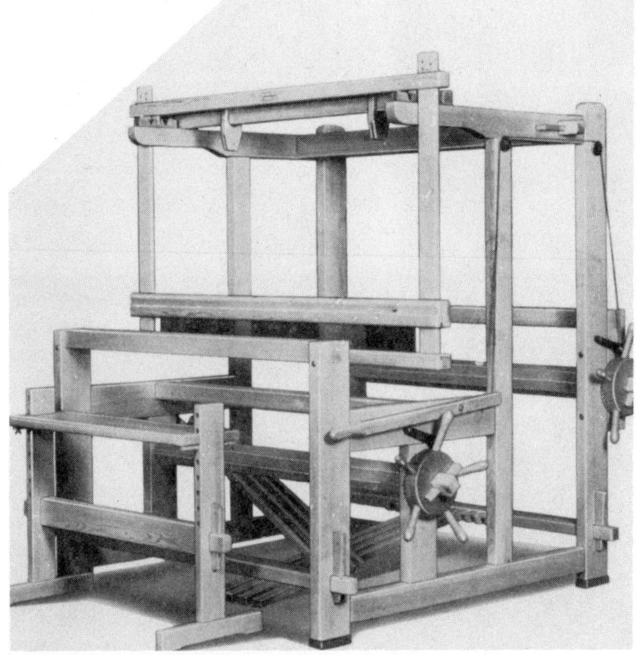

SWEDISH LOOM

Tired of that nine to five job? Put together a Swedish loom and you're in business for yourself. Actually, if you like weaving, this simple project will bring you hours of joy. All wood construction, it's pegged for easy assembly. Sturdy wheel-type rachets with strong teeth that make this suitable for rugs as well as fabric weaving. A thousand string heddles for ultimate performance. $330.

HOMESTEAD WOOLEN MILLS

West Swanzey, N.H. 03469

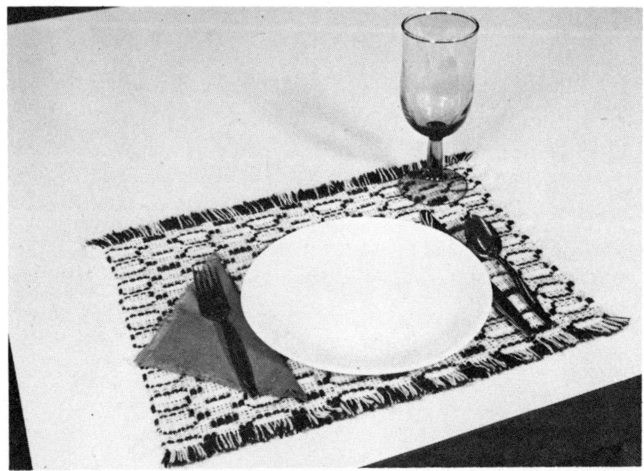

HOMESPUN PLACE MAT

How nice to eat on placemats you made! This kit is a winner for three reasons. First, it's simple. Second, it's inexpensive. Three, you can tell your friends your homemade dinner is served on homemade placemats!

All you do is fringe their homespun fabric. It's reversible, washable, and fits most any table style. Colors to match your color scheme. Two for $1.95, six for $4.95. Catalog 10¢.

ARTEN

P.O. Box 2241
Fort Collins, Colo. 80521

REDWOOD CANDLE HOLDER

Delight your family and friends and brighten your home with this unique redwood candle holder! The brushed, burnt finish highlights its natural beauty. Holds candle up to 2¾″ diameter (candle not included). Overall dimensions: 5⅞″ × 12½″. Kit includes: all redwood pieces, cut and brushed; channeled redwood base; center nail; and complete instructions for a professional job. Very modern design. $4.95.

POURETTE MANUFACTURING CO.

Seattle, Wash. 98115

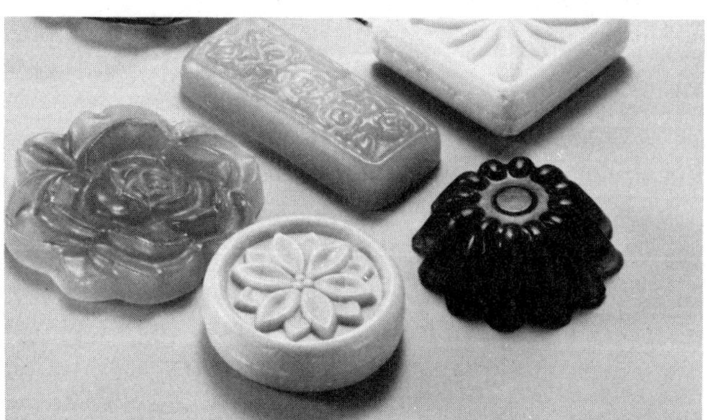

SOAP-MAKING KIT

Soap is nothing but a rectangular bar sitting on a sink waiting to clean anyone who picks it up. But now, no longer does soap need to conjure up such a bland image; after all, there is no decree stating that soap cannot take on novel shapes such as footballs, trains, flowers, shells, little ladies and gentlemen . . . or even feet! Soap can be noticed and admired and not just be part of the sink and the water.

Pourette Manufacturing Co. has developed three soap-making kits that contain all the ingredients for making several novelty soap shapes. Besides the glycerine soap, the kits offer you various soap molds, mold stands, color buds, scent rosettes, cotton cords, and instruction sheets. Every soap dish, every sink, and every dirty hand will want one, two, three, or more. $4.75.

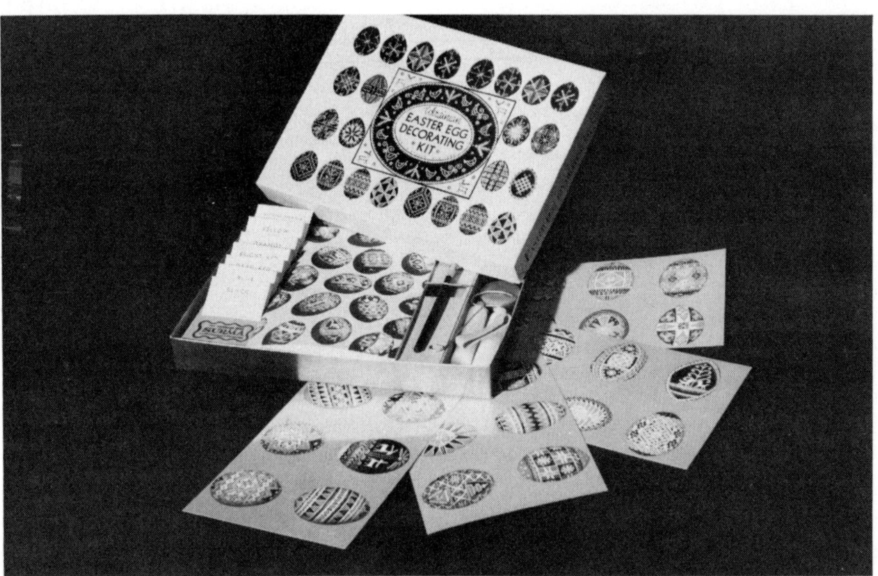

EASTER EGG DECORATING KIT
(Ukrainian)

In the Ukraine, egg decorating is a very important custom. Each province, each village—indeed, almost every family—has its own special ritual, its own symbols, meanings, and secret formulas for dyeing eggs. By contrast, Easter egg decorating in the United States is primarily enjoyed by children who then hunt the dyed eggs. The decorated Easter egg became an important symbol in the Ukrainian rituals of the Christian religion. The American Easter egg became a symbol of the Easter bunny and baskets filled with colored eggs.

Of the various types of Easter eggs in the Ukraine, the "pysanka" and the "krashanka" are the most widely known. "Krashanka" is a hard-boiled egg, dyed a solid brilliant color, which may be eaten. "Pysanka" is a raw egg with designs actually written on the egg, which is dyed in several colors. The "pysanka" may not be eaten.

Among the colorful Hutzuls in the Western Ukraine, there is a belief that the fate of the world depends upon pysanky; as long as egg decorating continues, the world will exist. Throughout the whole of the Ukraine, the custom of egg dyeing is observed solemnly and with great ceremony and the Hutzuls are, perhaps, most noted for their intricately decorated eggs.

When a Ukrainian woman sat down to her solemn task of decorating "pysanky," made the sign of the cross, and whispered "God, help me!", she believed He would. Using age-old symbols familiar to her village or province, she would begin her basic design as had been done a thousand times before. And though she used the same plan, she always achieved variety.

Geometric motifs are the oldest and most general form of ornamentation. There are a few geometric motifs with curved lines that are a transition to plant ornamentation (plant motif). On "pysanky," plant ornamentation is closely allied with geometric form, supplementing it and forming a harmonious whole. And then there are the animal motifs, which offer technical difficulties. The shape of an egg favors geometric or plant ornamentation. In representations of animals, the work must be in miniature and requires great skill. For these reasons, "pysanky" of this type are rare.

The beauty of Ukrainian Easter eggs has long been recognized. Yet, it is only recently—with the increased study of folk arts and the realization of their importance—that artists and scholars have sought to study and analyze their designs. What once seemed to be an ancient tradition is now recognized as a distinct and well-developed branch of folk art. Perhaps nothing better illustrates the Ukrainian feeling for beauty and form.

Included in the Ukrainian Easter Egg Decorating kit are dyes (pure certified colors available) in a variety of colors and shades; setting solution (add a little powder to each dissolved color); beeswax; and kistka, a type of pen used to apply beeswax to the egg. Pysanka and krashanka aside, we feel you'll find this an interesting project that's different from most craft kits available. $7.50.

BOYCAN CRAFT SUPPLIES
1052 East State St.
Sharon, Pa. 16146

LUSTRE-FILM BUNNY

Lustre-Film is another new material for craft use. It's a special poly film in bright colors that is easy to work with. A little practice will make you an expert in design. The bunny kit is made using a gallon plastic bottle as a base. You supply the base (an empty bleach bottle is fine). Kit includes multicolor Lustre-Film, bunny head form, bunny face, wires, ribbon, and bunny ears. Once you get the knack of working with this material, you'll find any number of rewarding projects. $2.79. Additional Lustre-Film: 69¢.

Boycan deserves special note in this section. They publish one of the most complete craft catalogs available (68 pp., free). It includes kits and materials for a lifetime of crafts projects. Mostly, they carry standard kits (string art, candle kits, etc.). However, if one-stop shopping interests you, we highly recommend them. Their prices are competitive and in some cases extra-reasonable.

EDMUND SCIENTIFIC CO.
Barrington, N.J. 08007

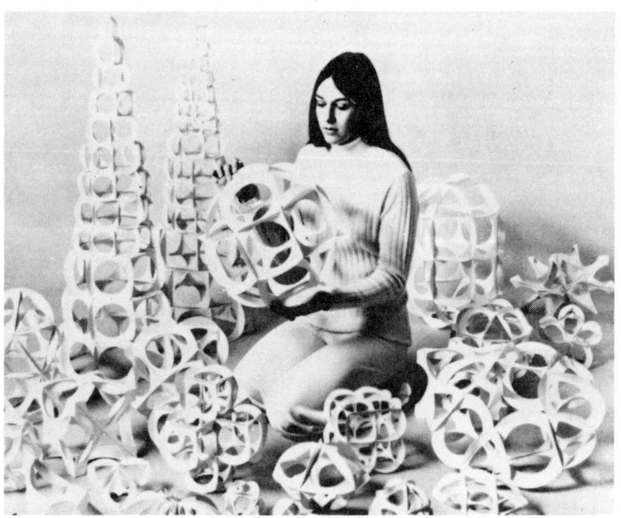

SPACIAL ART KIT

Spacial art is not finger painting in a lunar module, it's forming decorative, three-dimensional forms from two basic two-dimensional modules. Kit consists of ten 12½″-square sturdy white paper sheets on which 140 separate rings (3″, 4¾″, and 7¼″) have been perforated and scored for folding. Simple enough for kindergartners and challenging enough for artists—or so the manufacturer claims. We think his claim is true after trying a few of these. Color and texture can be added. $3.50.

SUSAN PRESCOTT
40 East 49 St.
New York, N.Y. 10017

INSTANT FIREWOOD

Beat the high cost of firewood with this unique kit. Imagine a hundred hours of fireplace heat for only four bucks! Best of all, you use your old newspapers rather than cutting down trees. Sturdy kit converts any old newspapers into tight log-like bundles. Special ties hold the papers together. You don't need lighter fluid or even kindling wood. The kit makes "logs" in which air circulates for easy lighting. Kit with enough ties to make a hundred logs $3.99. Extra ties 100 for $1.

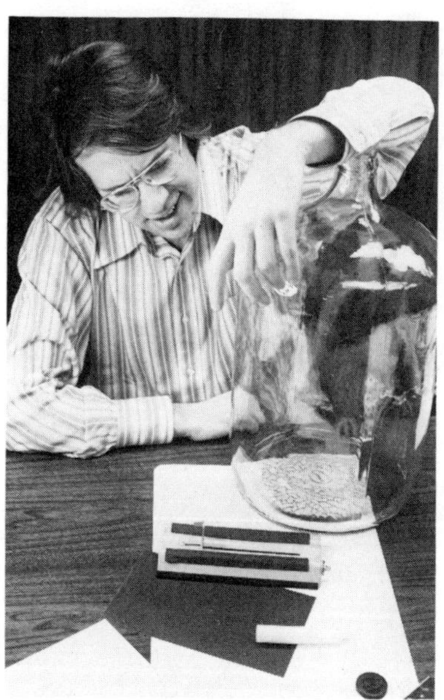

BOTTLE CUTTER

There are at least a dozen versions of this recycling device on the market today—a testament to the popularity of anything even remotely connected to the magic word "ecology." In fact, bottle cutting—that is, making decorative or useful glass objects out of old bottles—is fun, easy, and thoroughly satisfying. It's also a little scary, and should not be tackled by young children except with close adult supervision. This one is really a bargain. Not a saw, not a hot wire, but an easy-to-assemble kit that works with almost any size bottle. The one pictured may be slightly too ambitious an undertaking, but the kit will comfortably handle any old beer bottle. $5.

THE BUTTERFLY
48-52 Clearview Expressway
Bayside, N.Y. 11364

UNITED STATES RELIEF MAP

An enjoyable learning project for fourth, fifth, and sixth graders. Through the use of art materials, the student uses his hands to learn while creating a physical map of the United States. Kit includes supplies for a detailed map: instant papier-mâché, glue, paint, brush, and labels. The house did get a little messy when we put in our papier-mâché Rocky Mountains. But on the whole, the project was most worthwhile. $5.

CHILDCRAFT EDUCATION CORP.
52 Hook Rd.
Bayonne, N.J. 07002

CELLUCLAY CREATIVE KIT

Celluclay is a ready-to-use instant papier-mâché for making jewelry, wall plaques, trays, and a myriad of practical and decorative items. Dries to a permanent hard finish. The kit contains all the Celluclay, modeling tools, acrylic paints, plastic molds, and brushes to make 101 perfect gifts, plus a 32-pp. illustrated instruction book. A fine, practical creative art and a fascinating hobby for six years and up. $4.50.

STAMP PAD ART KIT

Twenty-four die-cut designs on clear plastic cubes create an endless variety of designs. Imaginative, dimensioned to combine interesting repeat patterns, or free form. Four stamp pads are included: colors can be "mixed" by overprinting right on the paper. Use them to make posters, collage designs, book covers. Four to ten years. $5.95.

TWISTASCULPT
5555 Carlton Way
Los Angeles, Calif. 90028

TWISTASCULPT

A new approach to creative, three-dimensional paper sculpture. Thousands of interesting sculptures. Really quite ingenious. You receive instructions and materials for two original masterpieces. All you add is imagination, some glue, scissors, and paper. $2.98.

THE HANDCRAFTERS
1 West Brown St.
Waupun, Wis. 53963

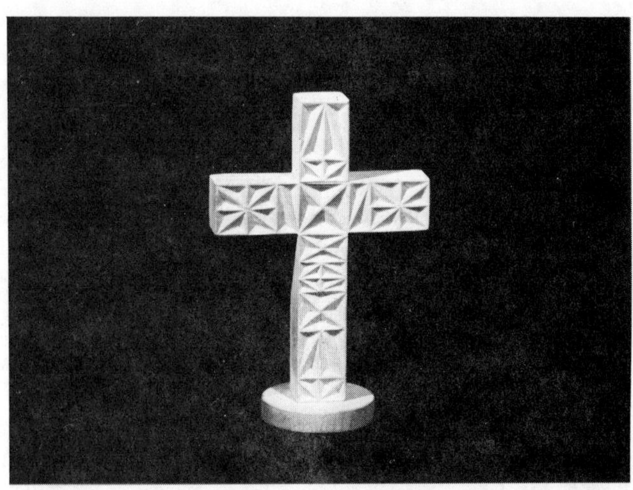

BASIC CRAFTS CROSS

A simple craft project that teaches gluing, decorating, and finishing.

Because these crosses offer so many ways to practice good craft procedures, they have been extremely popular in schools, summer camps, and occupational therapy departments. After assembly, they can be chip carved (as shown in the illustration) painted, or decorated with many other materials. Only 50¢.

You'll find these people an excellent source of child craft kits. They have such simple items as a recipe holder, an easy-to-assemble clothes pin, and a few wood dowels. And if you're buying for any hobby groups, their wholesale division offers exceptionally attractive prices. Leaflet free.

STEWART CLAY CO.
133 Mulberry St.
New York, N.Y. 10013

KICK WHEEL KIT

Another entry in the kick wheel category is from Stewart Clay. The frame is built from kiln-dried two-by-four and two-by-six spruce. The wheel has a sturdy footrest, an adjustable seat, and a 3 sq. ft. working surface. With the frame is a 12″ aluminum throwing head, steel shaft, 2 heavy-duty, self-aligning bearings, and a 150 lb., steel-reinforced concrete flywheel. Once complete, you'll have a product worth three times the price. In kit form: $60.

WESTWOOD CERAMIC SUPPLY CO.

14400 Lomitas Ave.
City of Industry, Calif. 91744

MOLD MAKERS

Now you can make a mold out of your favorite toy, sculpture, plaque, model, or whatever. Perfect for teachers, designers, or even a hobbyist. Included in the kit are: 1 qt. Westwood Latex, strips of cheesecloth, a 4-oz. bottle of Plastilube, and a 1″ and a ½″ application brush. Also included in the kit is a complete instruction booklet on making latex molds and using them for casting and reproducing in plastic or wax. $5.

SOLDNER POTTERY EQUIPMENT, INC.

P.O. Box 90
Aspen, Colo.

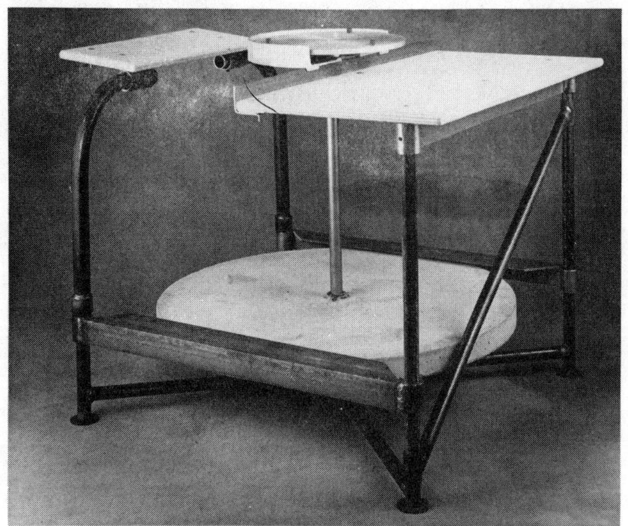

KNOCKDOWN KICK WHEEL KIT

Could it be that children are not the only ones who enjoy touching and manipulating mud and wet clay? Does this childhood pleasure remain in some of us through the adult years? Working with a material such as clay has become a very popular vocation and avocation, and produces beautiful results once your labor is finished. If you want to create pottery with an economical kick wheel, you should investigate the kick wheel kit that the Soldner Company has put together. Here are listed the Soldner Kick Wheel kit specifications: a wood seat with changeable height and angle that can be moved forward and back (¾″ × 8″ × 19″); a throwing head (12″ aluminum alloy with concentric centering rings); 1″ heavy-duty, self-aligning pre-greased, ground and polished ball bearings; 2″ × 3″ angle iron foot rests; a splash pan (13″ aluminum alloy half pan with "snap-on features"); reinforced concrete flywheel, 30″ diameter; a ¾″ ×

16″ × 32″ table; welded steel pipe frame; "X" truss in shape, 32″ × 32″ × 26″ high. This kit comes complete with instructions and with an Allen wrench for assembly. $190.

CRAFTOOL

1421 West 240 St.
Harbor City, Calif. 90710

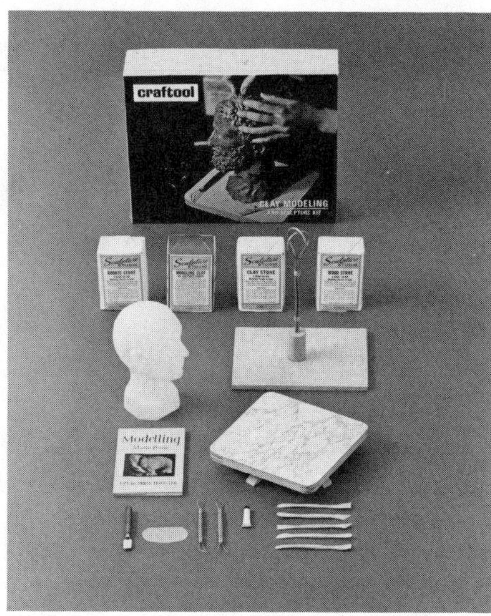

SCULPTURE KIT

Throughout the ages, the challenge to the sculptor has been to capture the elemental meanings of form. Sculpture has always been one of the most popular ways of satisfying the creative impulse to shape with your hands, and it still attracts those who seek both knowledge and the creation of beauty.

Thousands of books have been written that outline sculpting technique, but it is only by persistent effort and constant practice with sculptor's tools that true creative expression can unfold.

The interesting fact about this sculpture kit is that even a first-day beginner will begin seeing exciting results. Although all one really needs is a hunk of clay, the kit provides the professional, satisfying results. Priced at $24.95, the kit includes:

    4 lb. modeling clay
    4 lb. wood stone
    5 assorted boxwood tools
    1 steel tool
    1 revolving model stand
    1 sculpture armature
    4 lb. bronze stone
    2 wire tools (double end)
    1 palette scraper
    1 sure-sculpt head
    1 tube patina coloring
    1 illustrated Instruction Manual

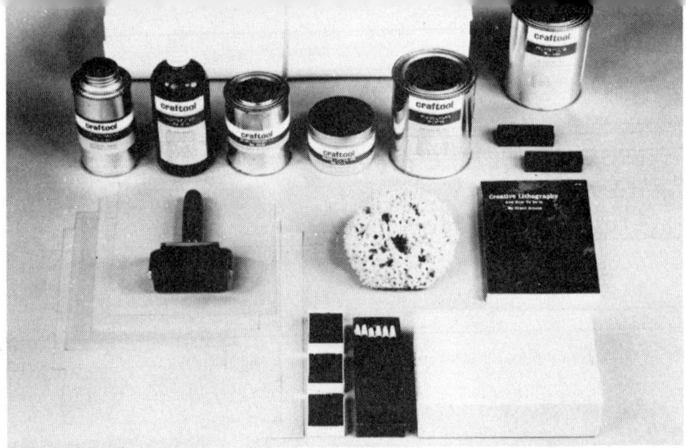

LITHOGRAPHY KIT

With Warhol lithos fetching huge sums, it's time for any developing artist to try this growing medium. The process is more involved than smearing oils on canvas, but the results are often impressive. In addition, a single zinc plate will yield many prints. This can supply all your Christmas gifts or your more commercial desires!

"The Lithography Kit" costs $180. and contains the necessary materials, papers, inks, and tools for doing fine lithographic work, including:

    6 zinc plates—8″ × 10″—grained
    1 zinc plate—10″ × 14″—grained
    3 dozen litho crayons
    1 lb. crayon ink
    1 lb. quartz powder
    2 sticks rubbing ink
    1 pt. litho varnish
    1 doz. assorted crayon pencils
    1 gum arabic
    1 pt. Liquid Tusche
    1 sponge
    1 litho stone 10″ × 12″
    1 ink brayer
    20 sheets 19″ × 26″ Rives paper
    1 lb. Carbo-Rubbing grain
    1 Instruction Book

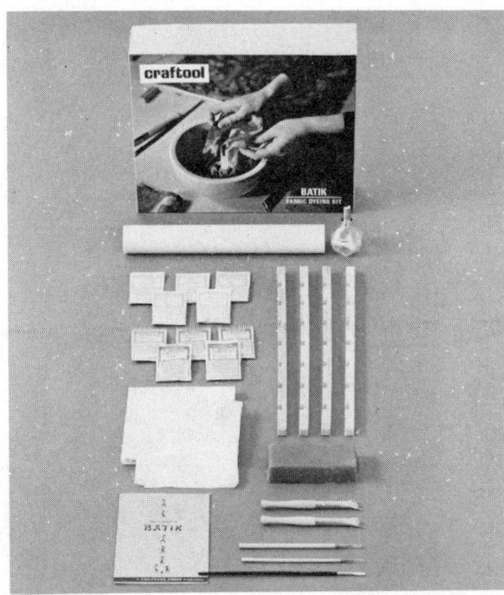

FABRIC-DYEING KIT

From Egypt to Persia, and then to India and Indonesia, batik spread with the migrations of early civilization. A "written batik" of old may have taken a year or more to reach perfection. while today the work takes only days.

Five basic steps comprise the batik dye method: Washing the fabric, waxing the designs on the cloth, dyeing the waxed fabric, fixing or setting the dyes, and removing the wax. Batik designs were originally derived from nature symbols. Gradually, other figures were added from various cultures and religions of Asia. After hundreds of years, these design elements have been formalized and each has a name and meaning. Batik is basically a freehand art and much has always depended on the skill of the artisan, writing with the "tjanting" for a faithful execution of the traditional designs.

Color is basic to batik design and enchants the eye with innumerable subtle blendings. Historically, in Indonesia, the first color used was indigo blue—a plant dye—on white bleached cloth. In the 13th century, red and yellow were introduced and these three were the traditional colors for centuries.

A complete kit ($24.95), containing everything you need to do batik work with professional results, includes:

    1 large tjanting needle
    1 medium tjanting needle
    5 one-oz. packages of silk batik dye
    1 lb. batik formula wax
    1 package of waxed paper
    2 Chinese bamboo brushes
    1 wooden stretcher frame set
    1 alcohol lamp
    1 yd. pure cotton
    1 bristle brush
    ⅓ yd. pure silk
    1 illustrated Instruction Manual

The finest craft catalog (150 pp., $1.) available. Advanced kits and supplies for the serious craftsman. Includes sculpture, weaving, printing, and many other art forms. Fast service on mail orders.

GEMINI PRODUCTIONS

R.R. 2, Box 167 B
Plainfield, Ill. 60544

PLAQUES TO DECORATE

Kind of a cop-out in the crafts project area. The plaques are all done, you simply paint to complete. Reminds us of those cake mixes where the housewife adds the eggs and says the cakes are homemade. However, some do-it-yourself beginners may find this a pleasant first project. Kit is in Early American style, and Country Kitchen, Lobster Sign, Seafarers Inn, and Old Oak Tavern are the four designs offered in this line. Plaque, instructions, paint, and brushes included. Each kit is $5.98.

STANLEY TOOLS
New Britain, Conn. 06050

SURFORM SHAPER

Stanley, one of the fine old names in quality tools, has a crafts kit. It's a Surform Sculpture set. Sculpturing with Surform tools is a new form of creative expression that is ideal for everyone from beginner to skilled professional. Surform tools are safe and easy to work with since they require no adjusting or sharpening. They work on a wide range of materials, wood of all kinds, plastics, plaster, soft metals, and stone.

Stanley's 21-005 Surform Sculpture kit contains everything you need to launch a new hobby: a Surform round file (297); a flat file (295); a pocket plane (399); a coping saw (39-106); an outlined piece of wood; and a 24-pp. instruction book that explains Surform sculpture in depth and has additional sculpture ideas. Write for more details. Complete kit: $12.99.

TITAN PRODUCTS
320 East Alton St.
Santa Ana, Calif. 92707

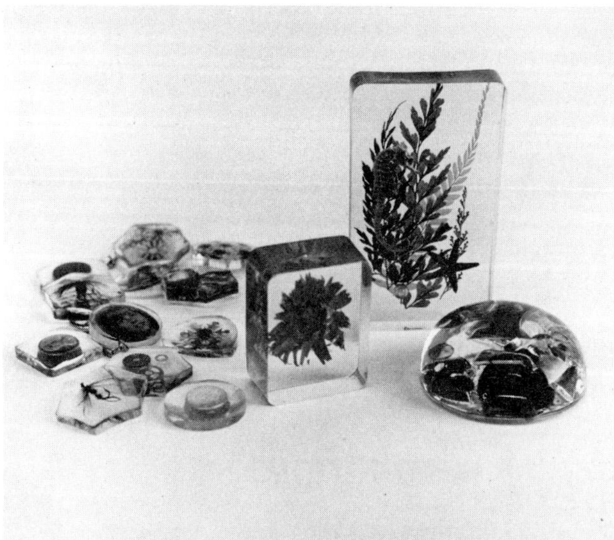

"PRESERVE FOREVER" CRAFT SET

At last, an answer of what to do with cherished mementos like baby's first tooth, the key to the summer cottage, and the shell from Coney Island. Just pour Liquid Plastic in the mold and add your priceless souvenirs. Within the hour your artifact is preserved forever in a block of solid plastic. It's a simple craft but lots of fun. Kit includes Liquid Plastic, catalyst, seven reusable molds, and polishing materials. Even includes unusual embedments to get you started. $11.

OPEN DOOR ENTERPRISES, INC.
1249 Dell Ave.
Campbell, Calif. 95008

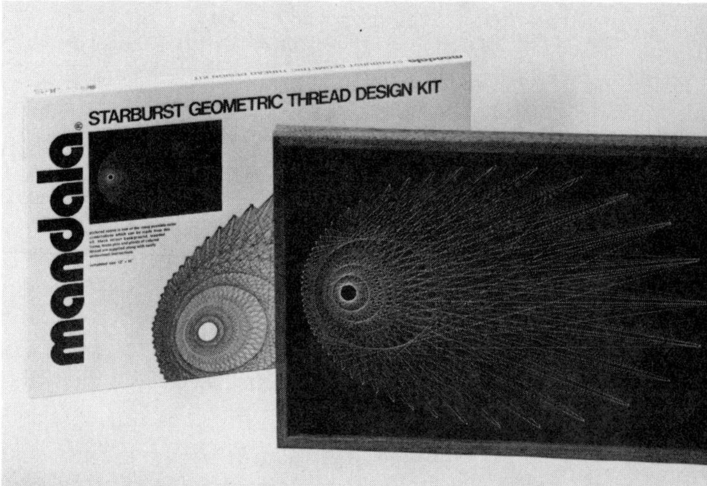

STARBURST GEOMETRIC THREAD DESIGN KIT

Man's ingenuity in the art field knows no bounds. For years, the common thread has been used to make cloth, to sew garments together, to patch holes, and to fasten buttons that have fallen off.

In bypassing the usual utilitarian function of thread and by borrowing geometric shapes from Euclid, a colorful design made with threads has evolved.

The Starburst kit contains Open Door's famous Mandala geometric design. The kit supplies you with a rich black velour background, along with a walnut-stained hardwood frame, brass pins, plenty of colored thread, and simple instructions. Finished sizes: 12″ × 12″ and 12″ × 18″. $10.

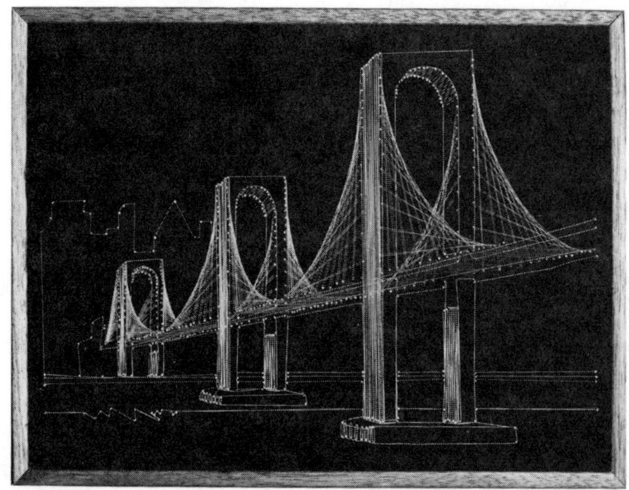

THREADCRAFT DESIGN KIT
(Suspension Bridge)

Still life in thread is what this bridge is all about;

amazing that the threads can be made to resemble steel girders and the gold lamé cord employed can be so effectively used that the bridge really appears to have many lights scattered all about it.

Threadcraft has combined simple techniques of thread artistry with classic representational subjects and made it available in kit form. In the Suspension Bridge kit you will find a black velour background, walnut-stained hardwood frame, plenty of colored thread, gold lamé cord for accentuating highlights, pins, and detailed instructions. Completed size is approximately 12″ × 16″. $10.

SPACE LOOM THREAD MOBILE KIT

Famous for his unusual sculptures and mobiles, Calder probably never thought of using household thread as part of his mobile designs. Well, Bill Hand of San Rafael, California, did think of it and thereby invented the Space Loom mobile. The many variations (and they do look very complex and intricate) employ maple dowels, thread, and space to create a suspension of hyperbolic curves in three dimensions.

The Space Loom kit (called Angelfish) includes unassembled wooden framework, thread, special glue, hanging hardware, and detailed instructions. $5.

SYNERGISTICS RESEARCH CORP.
30 West 22 St.
New York, N.Y. 10010

COPPER "REAL LIFE DESIGN" WIRE ART KIT

The kit is complete with a fully assembled imported frame of polished metal, felt-covered wood panel, pins and wire for your choice of Spad biplane, two-mast schooner, or penny-farthing bicycle from the one basic kit. 9″ × 13″ black felt panel. $11.95.

Wire Art Kits are also offered for abstract geometric design and some of these give an interesting complex design. The actual kit construction on these is very simple. Two frame finishes are available (with matching pins and wire) and three background colors (black, blue, or red). 9″ × 9″: $7.95. 9″ × 13″: $9.95. 17″ × 17″: $14.95.

SUBURBIA
366 Wacouta
St. Paul, Minn. 55101

WIRE SCULPTURE KIT

Why should kids have all the fun? This kit is often found in toy departments, but it's really a great crafts hobby for adults as well, especially those with not too much time on their hands. Square metal frame and complete set of wire and escutcheon pins lets you make attractive three-dimensional wall decorations in no time. Hobbyists light on imagination will appreciate the "suggested patterns"; more creative souls will enjoy making up their own. Available in gold or silver. $14.95.

AMERICAN HANDICRAFTS
1330 East 4 St.
Fort Worth, Tex. 76102

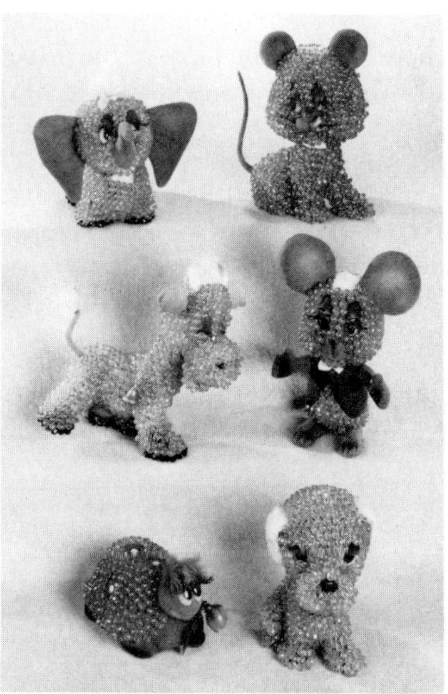

BEADED ANIMAL KITS

Little beaded animals are easy to make, even for beginners . . . and so low-priced that you can try selling them for fun and profit. They make great gifts and are excellent projects for bazaars and other fund-raising events. American Handicrafts offers a choice of cow, cat, elephant, mouse, turtle, donkey, and poodle—all whimsical and cute with long eyelashes and other anthropomorphic details. $3. each.

DECOUPAGE

With American Handicrafts' assortment of decoupage kits, you can decorate everything in your house, including the kitchen sink. In fact, this company has systematized this centuries-old artform so that it's simple, quick, and tidy. And if a little of the creativity is lost in the process, who will complain?

Each of the following kits contains a variety of prints—all the crafter has to do is prepare a plaque or other surface with paint or stain, glue the print on it, seal the picture for protection, and coat the entire project with finish. The "Deluxe" kit is actually a starter kit containing twelve prints and all other necessary equipment and materials. With "Torch Lamp" kit you can mount and decorate a 6″ wall globe. Choice of prints—Dutch Delft or ornate flowers. The "Mini" kit makes thirty decorative plaques, and the "Micro" kit makes ten plaques. Deluxe: $13.95. Torch Lamp: $15.95. Mini: $11.95. Micro: $14.95.

MACRAME

Macrame, the art of creative knot tying, burst on the scene a few years back and it looks like it's here to stay. There's almost no limit to the things one can make with this technique—from decorative wall hangings to belts, vests, and necklaces. American Handicrafts sells nine inexpensive macrame kits, ranging in price from $1.95 for a tiara choker, to $4.95 for a coronet belt or a Cherokee purse. Each kit includes all necessary materials and instructions. All are easy and fun. $1.95 to $4.95.

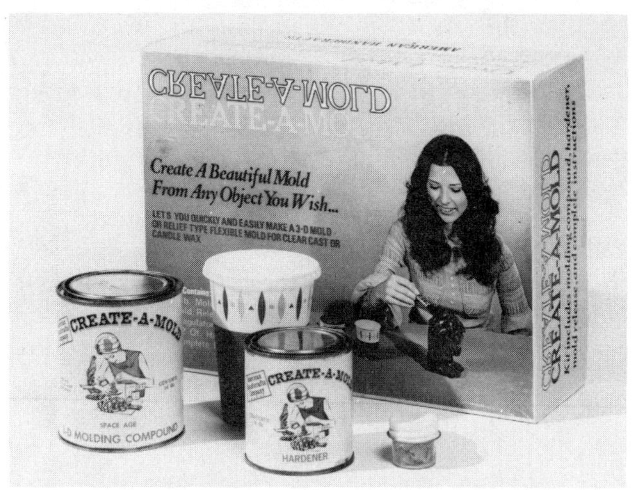

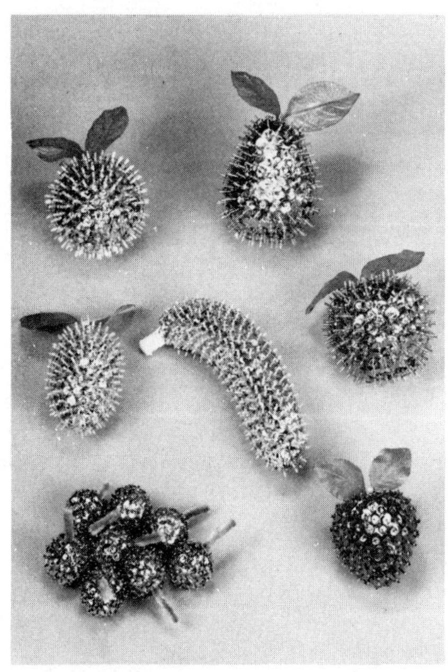

CREATE-A-MOLD KIT

Remember those little rubber molds that you played with as a kid, the ones that made funny little statues of Mickey Mouse or Donald Duck? Now there are kits available that let you make your own molds from any object you wish. The create-a-mold kit contains ½ gal. molding, coagulator, mold release, and instructions. It can be used with wax or plaster and makes flexible, reusable, heat-resistant molds. $24.95.

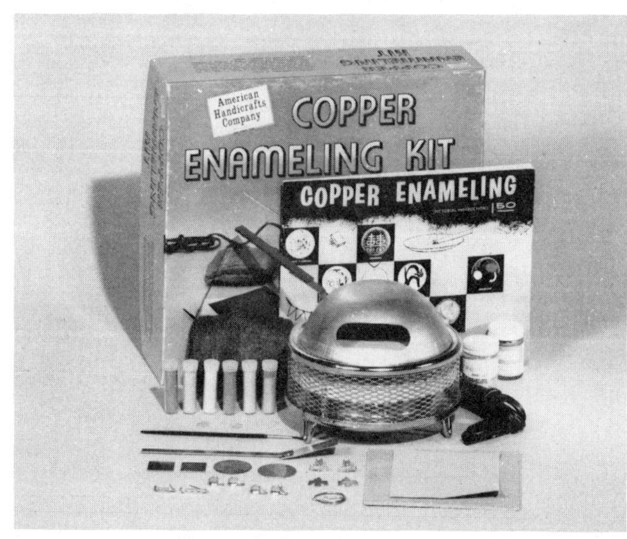

SEQUIN FRUIT

If you think that sequins belong on scarves and fruit belongs on the vine, stay away from these sparkly kits. Actually, a sequin grape cluster has a certain flashy charm, and a glittery banana might just be the height of seventies pizazz. These little baubles are a cinch to make and can be worn, hung, or displayed in a bowl. Choose a pear, orange, grape, apple, or banana at $2. per fruit.

COPPER ENAMELING

Copper-enameling jewelry is fun and relatively easy, but it's usually a hassle to do at home because of the need for a kiln. American Handicrafts has solved the problem by putting together a kit complete with a small but good-quality kiln (6″ × 7″ × 4½″). Easy-to-follow directions and all materials let you make one pair of cuff links, two pairs of earrings, pendants, etc., with six other assorted copper shapes. $19.95.

CONSTANTINE

2050 Eastchester Rd.
Bronx, N.Y. 10461

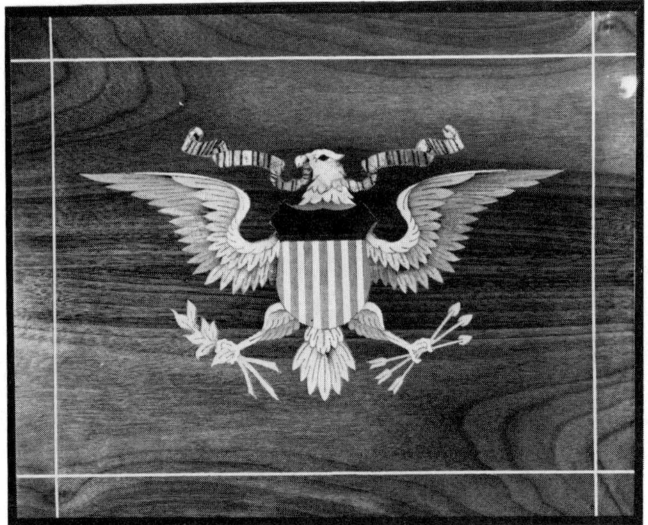

MARQUETRY PICTURE KITS

Marquetry is the art of making pictures out of various woods, and Constantine seems to have cornered the market on marquetry designs. They offer no less than thirty-five different marquetry picture kits depicting a variety of subjects. Don't look for Picasso abstracts or Warhol soup cans; these are all familiar scenes of wholesome country life . . . from Old Glory itself to bucking broncos, Hawaiian hulas, sleigh rides, and church spires. There are also a few stylized drummer boy and clown pictures that would be charming in a child's room. For the ethnic-minded, Constantine offers a bullfighter and a Spanish dancer. For the earthy, they have a Garden of Eden scene—13″ × 16″. Each kit contains colorful veneers 1/40″ thick, veneer borders, panel of hardboard for mounting, mahogany backing veneer, inlayer's crack filler, carbon paper, sandpaper, adhesive, finishing material, full-size patterns, and easy-to-follow instructions. $8.95.

PRECUT INLAID "LAST SUPPER" PICTURE KIT

How you see this 21″ × 38″ inlaid reproduction of Leonardo's masterpiece depends on your point of view. Many traditionalists will not like the technique, but by any standards, it's beautiful. Constantine has used twenty-three different rare woods—577 individual pieces!—to recreate the "glow and richness" of the original work (and there is no question that they have succeeded in capturing perception and depth of facial expressions and body postures). Sort of a cross between a paint-by-numbers set and a jigsaw puzzle, but more challenging than either, this is a kit for an experienced craftsman. All equipment is included; no cutting or pressing is required. (12 lb.) $45.

VENEERING

Everything you need to get started in veneering without clamps is included in this introductory kit. Eight square feet of fine veneer, a one-pint can of special glue, and a complete set of instructions let you get the feel of covering old furniture or objects with new wood. Believe it or not, covering furniture with wood veneer costs just pennies more than covering it with Contac paper—and think of the difference in appearance! $3.75.

WOOD INLAY PICTURE KITS

If you fancy a picture of the Cornish coast or a Swiss lake adorning your wall, you can make one easily and cheaply with these inlay kits. All you have to do is cut out parts from wood veneer, following a printed pattern, and glue them to a 5″ × 7″ hardwood panel. In addition to the two subjects given above, Constantine offers "Village Inn" and "Bavarian Castle." 99¢ each. Set of four: $3.75.

LAZY SUSAN TURNTABLE

This is no ordinary lazy susan. It has a distinctive three-roses veneer face in the center, which you glue on to walnut backing. Complete kit can be made by even a beginner in about two hours. It contains rose veneer, a 14″ composition disc, flexible walnut edging, lazy susan 3″ bearing, walnut base block (¾″ × 5½″ × 5½″), cement, finishing materials, and instructions. Practical and pretty, especially if you like roses. $9.90.

WOOD SHAKER SET

For less than two bucks, you can make a set of salt and pepper shakers for yourself and one for your best friend—the kit makes two sets. Simple design, simple to make. Available in rosewood or teak. $1.55.

hardware, prefinished picture frame molding, hundreds of one-of-a-kind carving blocks from pocket-size to car trunk-size, picture kits for tabletop assembly, professional wood finishing supplies, and whatever else you need to put more zest in your woodworking.

BASIC CRAFTS CO.

312 East 23 St.
New York, N.Y. 10010

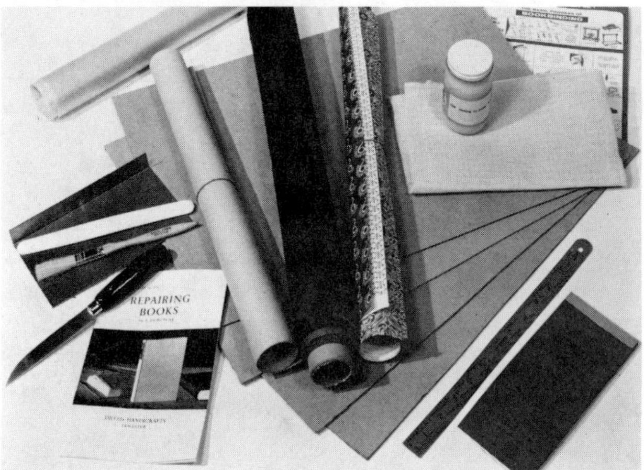

BOOK REPAIR KIT

A simple way to get into bookbinding and repairs, this kit contains sufficient material for rebinding about twelve books, and is particularly suited to rebinding paperbacks into hard-cover form. Kit includes swatchbook, waxed paper, backing paper, ruler, bone folder, knife, and a copy of "Repairing Books." $13.95.

BOOKBINDING SUPPLIES KIT

Having mastered the basic kit, you will want to set up a little factory to redo all your books. You now need the supplies kit. $19.95.

- 1 cake beeswax
- 1 half-cone Irish linen thread
- 1 qt. bookbinder's glue
- 1 ball soft 3-ply twine
- 1 qt. flexible padding glue
- 1 pt. quick-setting glue
- 10 yd. red headband material
- 10 yd. green headband material
- 10 yd. blue headband material
- 5 yd. 36″ binding super
- 9 yd. plastic-coated bookcloth, assorted colors, 20″ wide
- 10 sheets 15″ × 20″ binder board
- 3 sheets plain backing papers
- 10 sheets assorted imported French and English end papers
- 4 rolls waxed paper, 12″ wide
- instruction sheet
- catalog

Complete supplies for bookbinding presses, cutters, tools. Interesting free catalog that contains description of the steps in binding a book.

AVALON INDUSTRIES, INC.

95 Lorimer St.
Brooklyn, N.Y. 11208

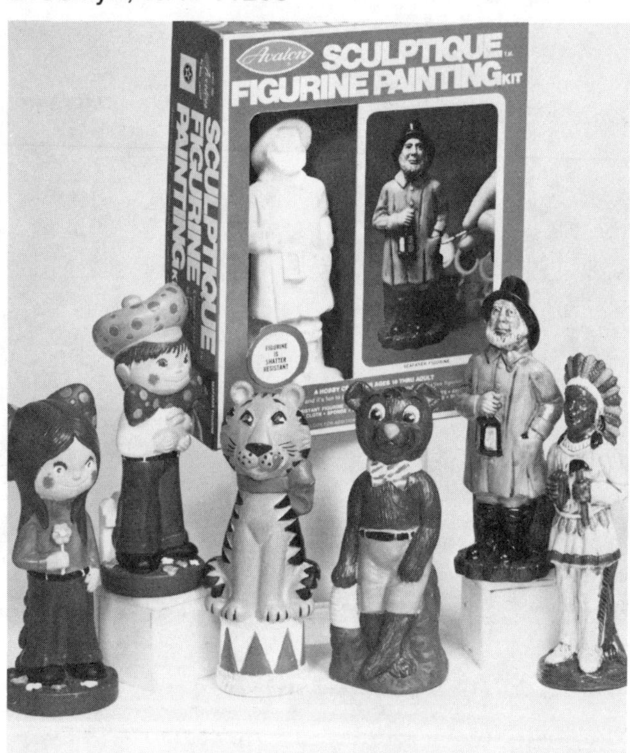

Each kit contains an undecorated, shatter-resistant figurine and all painting supplies. Figure is approximately 6″ high. Choose from six figures including Old Seafarer, Cigar Store Indian, Boy, Girl, Tiger, and Bear. $4.50.

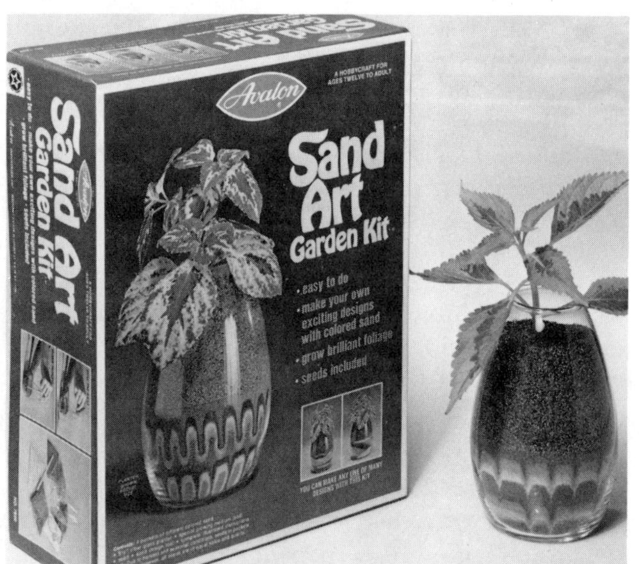

SAND ART GARDEN KIT

Create a unique poured sand design and then grow

a plant on top. The seeds for your foliage plant are included in the kit, as well as colored sand, soil, planter, sand-art tool, and instructions. $6.00.

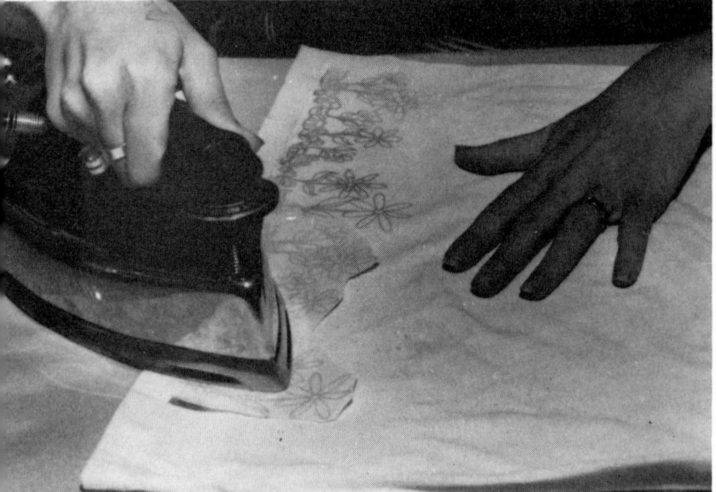

PAINT 'N' WEAR CLOTHES PAINTING KIT

Popular with teen-agers and chic matrons alike, clothes painting lets you turn ordinary jeans and T-shirts into hand-painted originals. The painted tie may even be making a comeback. This kit includes iron-on transfer patterns, paints, brush, and acrylic fabric to practice on. $6.00.

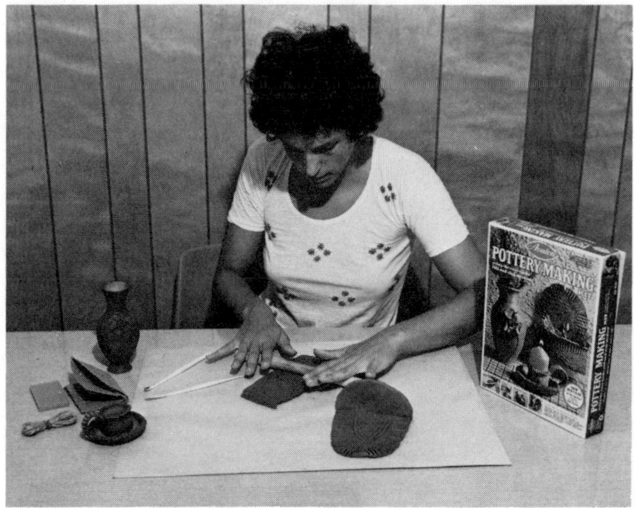

POTTERY-MAKING KIT

Complete kit for handmade pottery using slab and coil methods. Contains Avalon's self-hardening clay plus tools and instructions. No pottery wheel or firing needed. $6.00.

Avalon makes more kits than any other manufacturer. Their selections include crafts, painting, food kits (such as wine and sourdough bread), bottle cutting, decoupage, novelty candles, soap-making, glass staining, weaving, embroidery, stencils, paper dolls, leathercraft, and practically every other household amusement craft.

PRIMA EDUCATION PRODUCTS
A Division of Hudson Photographic Industries, Inc.
Irvington-on-Hudson, N.Y. 10533

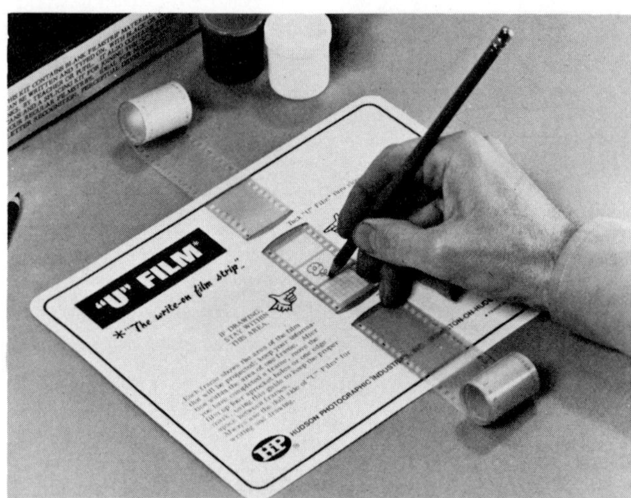

"U-FILM" FILMSTRIP KIT

"U-Film" is a tough plastic film made to the exact size of standard filmstrips (35 mm. single frame) and slides (35 mm. double frame, 2″ × 2″ mounts). Its important and exclusive feature is its blank-treated surface which can be written, drawn, or typed on. In addition, most materials are erasable so that it may be used over and over again. It will also accept a lacquer fixative spray (like Krylon) for protection of its surface—when this is done materials upon it may not be smudged or erased.

Intended primarily for classroom use, "U-Film" kits might also be of interest to businessmen, clubs, scientists, and artists. In fact, if your business is information in any form, you might find a use for "instant film." Each kit contains filmstrip, guide, storage cans, and splicing tape. Replacement film is available from the company, as well as slide mounts (for turning each "U-Film" frame into a 35 mm. slide). $13.

THE BEADERY
Hope Valley, R.I. 02832

BEADED FLOWER KIT

Susan Johnson is currently on the design staff of the Beadery and she feels that "working with beads is like painting in oils." Ms. Johnson loves to find new combinations that work well together. According to her, there's not a spot in her home or her wardrobe that wouldn't look better with beads.

Using beads to create flowers is an attractive idea, because whether the flower is a daisy, tulip, daffodil, or rose, the beaded shapes exhibit a refreshing colorful glow because of the way the individual beads reflect light. Indeed, there are probably many spots in your home that would benefit from having these eye-catching accent pieces.

Each beaded flower kit contains everything needed to complete one unique jeweled flower. $2.50.

CRAFTSMAN
2727 South Mary St.
Chicago, Ill. 60608

PRECUT INLAID "CHRIST IN GETHSEMANE" PICTURE KIT

Constantine has no monopoly on religious inlaid pictures (see "Last Supper" above). "Christ in Gethsemane" is equally inspiring but far less tiring. At less than half the price (and almost half the size) of Constantine's picture, this "Christ" is a good starting project. Also available are "Wintertime" and "Swan Scene." Christ: $15.95 (4 lb.). Wintertime: $16.95 (6 lb.). Swan Scene: $15.95 (5 lb.).

CALIFORNIA TITAN PRODUCTS, INC.
320 East Alton
Santa Ana, Calif. 92707

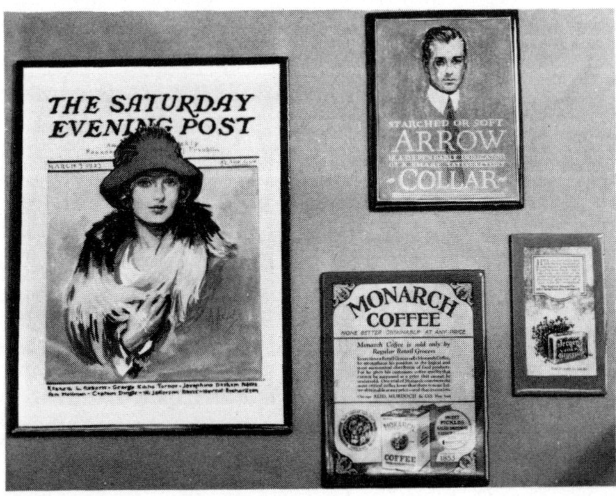

ONE-STEP DECOUPAGE KIT (NOSTALGIA PRINTS)

The interest in nostalgia has reached its height in popularity. This decoupage kit with nostalgia prints is aptly titled, "When Mother Was a Girl"; a glance at these advertisements, posters, and magazine covers from yesteryear are bound to evoke sentimental thoughts of those days that were. Turn-of-the-century memorabilia for you who were part of that time and for us who may wistfully wish we were.

The unique plaque kit provides a one-step decoupage that can be completed in one application. It is easy to use and easy to mix—a high-build polymer that gives a fabulous finish. The kit contains a coordinated grouping of memorabilia (as seen in photo), fine wood and hardboard plaques, accent paints, glue, mixing supplies, and complete instructions. Everything is old-time, except the price. $7.75.

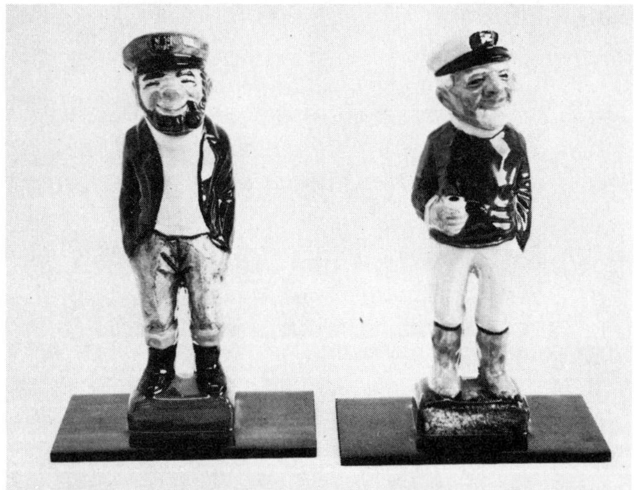

CERAMIC DECORATING KITS (BISQUE CRAFT)

"The Flower Children" are what these adorable little figures are called, and they are lovely. Four miniature girls (each measuring 3″ high), waiting to be displayed and admired, are real ceramic art pieces decorated by you. Each figure can be finished to permanent high gloss or satin finish.

"Captain and His Crew" is the name for these two pleasant-looking fellows. With the appearance of carved wood perhaps whittled by an old fisherman, the captain and his crew certainly would be a pleasant pair of genuine bisque ceramic figures to paint and glaze.

Each kit contains kiln-fired ceramic objects, acrylic cake underglaze colors, one-step glaze finish, steel wool, brushes, mixing supplies, and complete instructions. Flower Children: $10.00. Captain and His Crew: $7.75.

BRONZE CASTING KIT (HISTORICAL MEDALLIONS)

The ancient Romans seemingly perfected the art of bronze casting; bronze artifacts were produced in great quantity and are still being found at the sites of pre-Christian Roman ruins. Admiration for the craftsman of bronze pieces has induced the Titan Company to develop a kit that enables you to experience this ancient art form. No heat is necessar' and the castings have a surface of 100% bronze.

The Historical Medallion kit includes Bronze Craft liquid, catalyst, preshaped mold, mixing supplies, and complete instructions. Bronze Craft offers a new concept in metal casting. $7.95.

LILLIAN VERNON
510 South Fulton Ave.
Mt. Vernon, N.Y. 10550

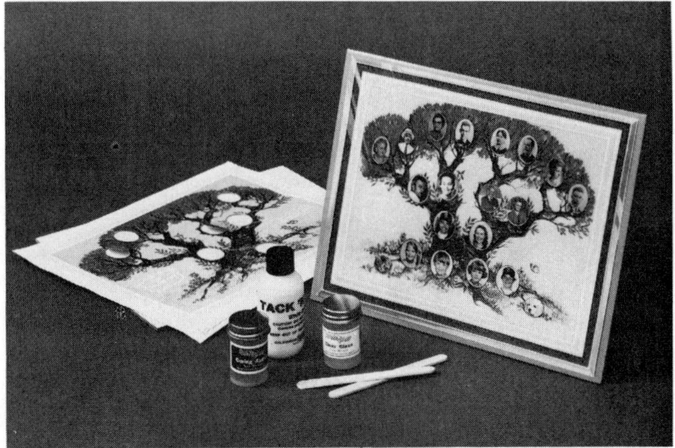

DECOUPAGE FAMILY TREE

Make a family photo-tree. New decoupage kit creates an heirloom to be treasured. Everything's included except your own photos—8½ × 11" frame-look masonite plaque, full-color tree print, paint, glue, glaze, hanger, mixing needs, applicator, and instructions. Tree is cleverly designed so you only punch out as many 1" ovals as you need for photos, adapts perfectly for any number up to twenty. Fabulous one-step decoupage glaze preserves them forever. $5.98.

BEEHIVE CRAFTS
P.O. Box 244
Winnetka, Ill. 60093

DECOUPAGE BEATRIX POTTER PRINTS

Mother Rabbit, Peter Rabbit, Jeremy Fisher, and Jemima Puddleduck all get together to form a kit with joy. Just put together the Beatrix Potter characters and you're on your way to fun. These prints are full color for *vue d'optique* (or decoupage as its more commonly known). Complete kit contains four prints plus a fifth print for the background, a 3½" × 4¼" unfinished frame with a brass-plated hanging hook, clear plexiglass cover for the frame, all burlap trims in yellow, and instructions with cutting guides. $4.

ARTIS, INC.
9123 East Tunas Dr.
Temple City, Calif. 91780

SHRINK-ART DESIGNER KIT

For some, the word "shrink" should relate to the field of science rather than art, but no professional help is needed when working with the Shrink-Art kit. Indeed, all the interested artist is required to do is trace, color, cut, and bake and the art object shrinks to miniature size. The completed piece of art can then be framed, made into jewelry, or displayed in some other way.

Artis, Inc. has many kinds of Shrink-Art kits. The Shrink-Art "Designer" kit contains: 2 books, 3 special sheets opaque—11" × 17", 3 sheets clear—11" × 17", Magic Print, 5 pens, jewelry findings, instructions for painting and sketching, and more. $9.98.

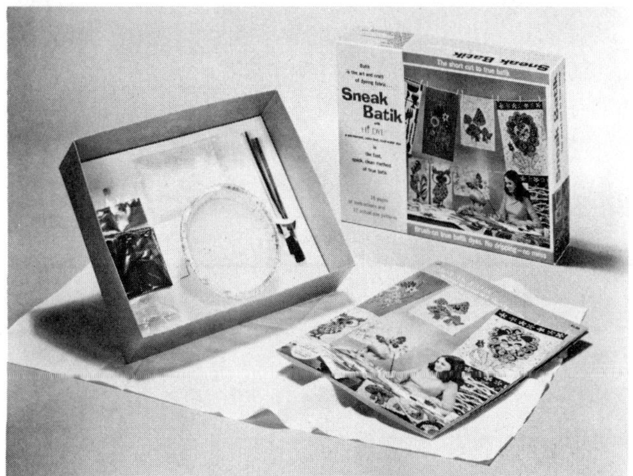

SNEAK BATIK WITH HI-DYE

For those of you who are curious as to what Hi-Dye is . . . Well, it's a high-intensity dye for natural fibers—a permanent, colorfast, cool water dye that dries in thirty minutes. And for those of you who enjoy the hobby of fabric dyeing, the Sneak Batik kit should interest you, for Hi-Dye may be used for the special instant batik system called Sneak Batik, by simply adding a Hi-Dye print base (thickener) and using the brush-on method.

The Sneak Batik kit is the easy, clean method of batik. The kit contains all necessary materials, instructions, and twelve actual-size patterns. $6.

PERMA-TECH MARKETING ASSOC.
P.O. Box 24506
Los Angeles, Calif. 90024

ETCH ON METAL

Take a 3" × 4" brass plaque (supplied), follow the

simple instructions, and voilá . . . a metal master-piece. The results are really quite impressive, and the work required is really quite simple. Well-designed kit with everything required included. $7.95.

TANDY LEATHER CO.
2727 West Seventh St.
Fort Worth, Tex. 76107

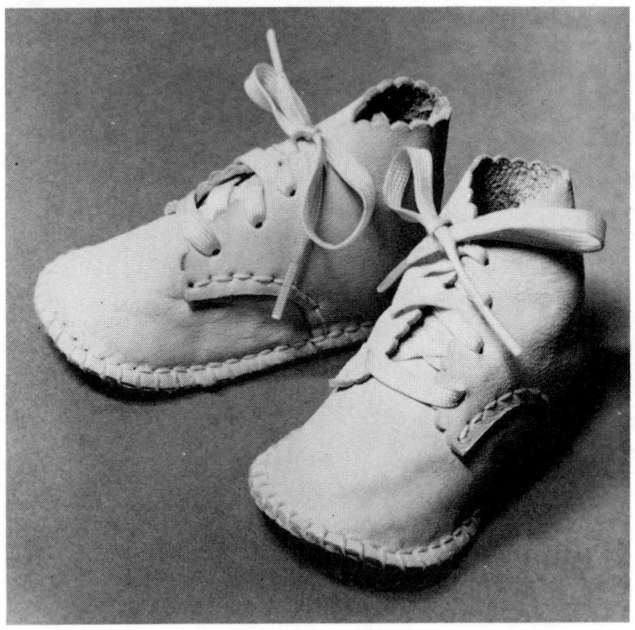

BABY'S FIRST SHOES

This is not as far out as you might expect. For one thing, these are really glorified booties, even though they look like the real thing. Made of precut lambskin parts, they fit babies up to six or eight months. Of course, at that age few children are actually walking. The First Shoes kit can be made in less than an hour—a perfect activity for a parent while the baby is sleeping. In addition, this item makes a perfect baby gift at a reasonable price. $1.98.

PDC.
3713 Highland Ave.
Manhattan Beach, Calif. 90266

BABY HAND PRINTS

If you can't be permanently enshrined in cement at Grauman's Chinese Theater, this kit may be a solution. Perfect for nonmovie star immortality. It's called Baby Paw Prints. Doting Grandmas will love it! The kit contains everything needed to easily make and frame a permanent impression of baby's handprints or footprints. It includes decorative wood frame in lemon, lime, or orange color; frame backing; decorative hook; ornamental brass name plate; and two picture-size "Magic Foam" pads for impressions. The technique is simple and mess-free. $4.98.

NATIONAL HANDICRAFT INSTITUTE
Des Moines, Iowa 50337

STITCH STAND

Terrific Mother's Day gift. All her sewing needs on one handsome stand she'll be proud to show her friends. Two-tiered with center post in a rich walnut finish, it holds five regular and seven large-sized spools and is topped by a golden braid-bound, tricot-covered pincushion. She will have hooks to hang her scissors and measuring tape. Kit has all materials and is quickly assembled. 9½" tall. $1.49.

COFFEE MILL PLANTER

A planter with nostalgia built in. Remember Grandma and her old coffee mill? They've made it into a beautiful redwood planter (the coffee mill, not Grandma), accented with black knobs and a shiny 3"-deep black pot. Kit has precision-cut parts, all materials (including lush parsley and pert, red-capped mushrooms in case you don't want to use your own plants), and measures 4½" square, 5¾" high. Complete kit: $2.29.

TURTLE TRIVET

Clever creature, this. Hang on kitchen wall when he's not working and he's just decorative. Whip him out and under that hot dish you bring to the table. Party time he will carry your snack-holding toothpicks on his back to your guests and just sit there enjoying their compliments. Thick redwood body, sturdy wooden feet give stability. Has natural cork shell design, jewel eyes, and a tapered tail. 7¼" long. All materials: $1.25.

CHEF'S SHELF

Spice up your kitchen with a homey Colonial rack that holds cans, jars, and bottles on two shelves 9" wide and 2½" deep. Kit contains precut parts, materials for satiny walnut finish, and measures 13⅞" × 9¾". Great kitchen organizer and room beautifier. $4.49.

NOSTALGIA NICHE

A lovely wall hanging or tabletop display. Fill with treasured family or personal mementos. Precision-cut pine, nut-brown color, octagon-shaped, and 12½", divided into sections 2" deep. A brown burlap background accents and enhances each keepsake. Easily assembled. A real decorator's item. $2.59.

These are just a few of the oodles and oodles of do-it-yourself kits that National has for every gift-giving occasion. Make something for yourself. You deserve something nice! This is the company that has the crafts club (see Clubs section for details).

MIDWEST MAIL SERVICE

P.O. Box 1148
Elkhart, Ind. 46514

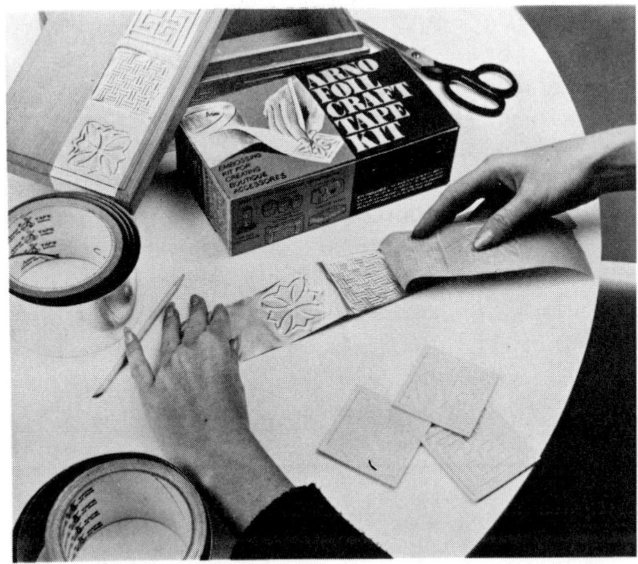

FOIL CRAFT KIT

Remember when you were a kid and you put paper over a penny to get a raised image of Mr. Lincoln? That's the idea behind Foil Craft. The kit includes silver and gold pressure-sensitive tape, a stylus, an instruction sheet, and—so you aren't limited to Lincolns and Jeffersons—four attractive abstract designs. You emboss a raised design onto the tape, then apply it to cannisters, candle holders, jewelry boxes, picture frames, even doors and walls. The tape can also be applied directly to a raised surface and then rubbed down. This is a pleasant decorative project, although we wish the price were a little lower for what is essentially a small set of craft equipment. But then, we wish all prices were lower. $5.95.

FRIENDS INDUSTRIES, INC.

40 Gazza Blvd.
Farmingdale, N.Y. 11735

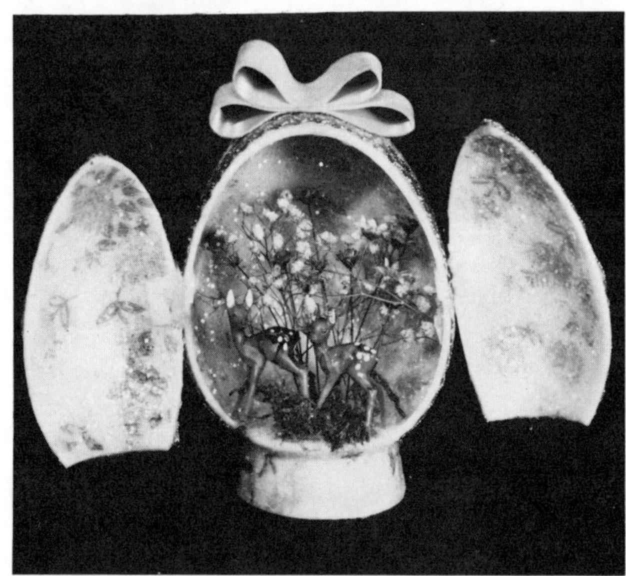

EGGCRAFT WITH DEER KIT

You needn't wait until Easter to appreciate this decorative egg containing two gentle deer. To view the colorful egg as a whole, you simply close the doors.

The kit contains diamond glitter, ribbon, and gold trim, self-contained stand, real dried flowers and deer ornament, and easy-to-follow instructions. $6,

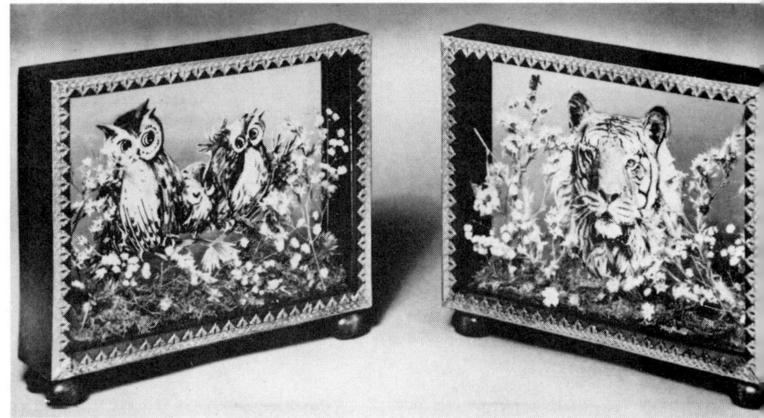

WILD LIFE SERIES KIT

The owls and the tiger seem to be just sitting there, hoping to be admired. You can create a realistic natural setting with this craft kit.

In the kit, you get pine frame, acetate "windows," dimensional prints, real dried flowers, simulated gold trim, your choice of tiger print or owl print, and easy-to-follow, illustrated instructions. Once completed, you have a permanent decoration for any room. $5.

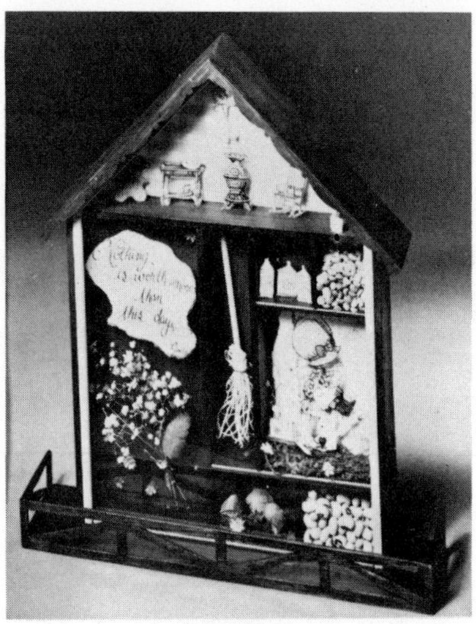

COLLECTOR'S HUTCH KIT

The design here is charming and rather interesting, for collected in the compartments (with an attic compartment under the roof) within the frame is a potbellied stove, a rocking chair, "Li'l boy" taking a rest, some mushrooms, beans, a few containers, a broom, and some dried flowers. An air of old-fashioned days seems to surround the entire hutch. Kind of fun to look at, discover, and build.

Included in the craft kit are all wood parts (note the unique fence design), real dried flowers, dried vegetables (may vary with seasonable availability), dimensional and single prints, glass facing, and easy-to-follow, illustrated instructions. (Measures 13″ × 11″ × 2½″) $9.

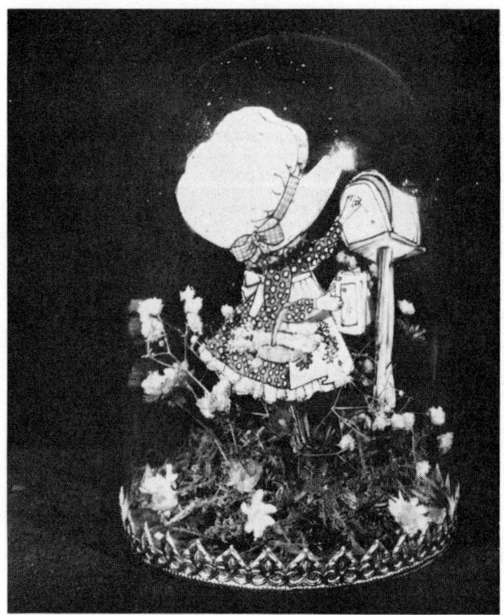

MINI GLASS DOME WITH LITTLE BOY

An endearing little boy reaching toward the mailbox, "Li'l boy" stands within a real glass dome. He actually is a dimensional print captured under Corning glass. The kit also includes real dried flowers, gold trim, cork base, and easy-to-follow, illustrated instructions. You do all the arranging. An unusual idea in a boxed kit. $5.

Friends produces a variety of decoupage and construction box kits. They are of good quality. Free color catalog available.

HOUSE OF MINNEL
Deerpath Rd.
Batavia, Ill. 60510

MEMORY BOX

Create your own display center for cherished memorabilia. Now, at last, a solution for how to display the stubs from your first movie together, the key to your first car, a favorite photo, or whatever in the little memory category. The 8¾″ × 14¾″ box has a dozen little compartments, plus a glass cover. You assemble, stain, fill, cover, and hang on the wall. Your treasures are protected and shown off. $8.98.

CAROUSEL CRAFTS MFG. CO.
P.O. Box 42549
Houston, Tex. 77042

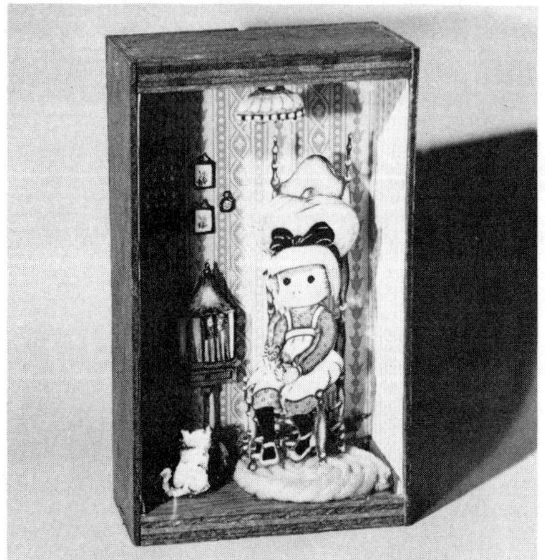

MINI-CRATES

A box or crate, rectangular in shape, whose inside dimensions are rather petite (6⅞″ wide, 4⅜″ tall, 2½″ deep), but which contains adorable little people situated among authentic-looking scenes of life. That's what the Carousel Crafts Mini-Crate is all about. By fitting the many delightful scenes into the empty mini-crates, you create almost instant charm from a bygone era.

The kit is complete with full-color prints that have multiple elements for a layered, three-dimensional effect in figures as well as accessories and decorations. Room scenes contain authentic wallpaper, yarn for rugs, prestained moldings for chair rails and baseboards. A variety of different scenes is available. $5.95 for each crate and scene.

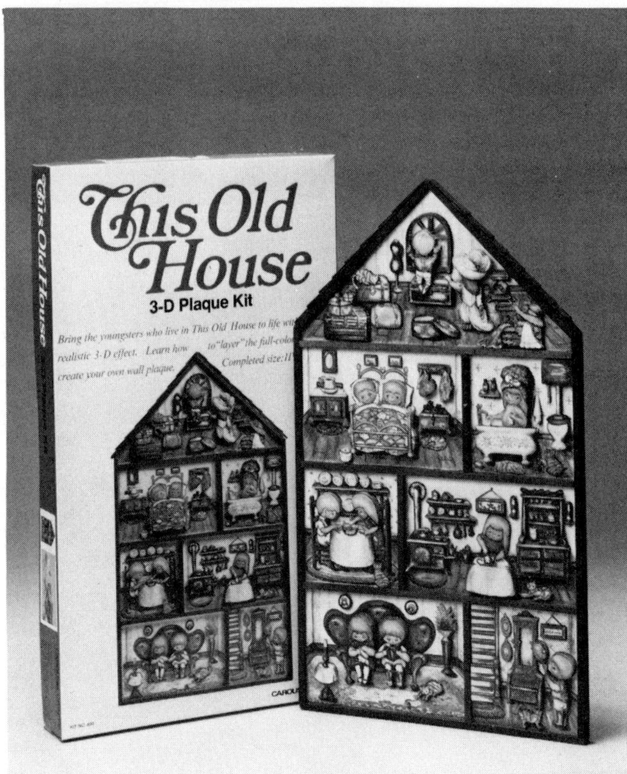

3-D PLAQUE DOLLHOUSE

The charm and lure of dollhouses, with their miniature inhabitants and furnishings, can be found in a Carousel Crafts dollhouse with a title that befits its interior rooms: "This Old House." For inside this modular dollhouse, you can fit in full-color prints (in dimension) of furniture and little characters reminiscent of the way things were ... a Colonial hutch, a Victorian overstuffed sofa, a brass bed, a bathtub with legs, Tiffany lamps, etc. A most charming plaque for your wall.

Utilizing the idea of crates, very small and of various sizes placed on top of one another, you can build the dollhouse a room or floor at a time, using the two-room Maxi-crate with matching attic (as shown in photo) or the Mini-crate with its own matching attic. Available are prestained moldings for baseboards, chair rails, and rafters. $8.95.

OTHER SOURCES

Activa Products, Inc.
7 Front St.
San Francisco, Calif. 94111

Manufactures a variety of ceramic kits, many of which would be of special interest to young people.

American Toy Co.
6130 North Clark St.
Chicago, Ill. 60660

Well-made woodburning kits.

Bergen Arts and Crafts
Box 381
Marblehead, Mass. 01945

Huge collection of craft kits including enameling, sculpture, batik, beadcraft, and aluminum etchings. Giant catalog (175 pp.) worth owning ($1.).

Dick Blick
P.O. Box 1267
Galesburg, Ill. 61401

Blick leads the craft-source parade with a giant (236 pp.) catalog ($1.). There are craft kits and supplies of every description. The range is from beginner toys to materials for advanced artisans.

Craftsman Wood Service Co.
2727 South Mary St.
Chicago, Ill. 60608

Wood inlay and precut veneer picture kits. Catalog (50¢).

Heidi-Craft
P.O. Box 159
Jamestown, N.C. 27282

Source for lovely wall decorations that you assemble yourself. A variety of styles and subjects.

Handicrafts Co.
Box 395
Sioux Falls, S.D. 57101

As the name implies, a variety of handicrafts. Catalog (free).

Lemco
P.O. Box 40545
San Francisco, Calif. 94140

Single biggest supplier of macrame kits and supplies.

Sangram Corp.
Box 2275
Pueblo, Colo. 81004

A variety of photo transfer kits. Turns your photos into decals and print transfers.

Shop Supply House
476-A First St.
Encinitas, Calif. 92024

Salt and pepper shaker kits. Brochure (self-addressed, stamped envelope).

Westone Craft Co.
P.O. Box 1181
Atlanta, Ga. 30301

Source for frame-making kit.

Willis Glass
Box 3460
Anaheim, Calif. 92803

Glass-blowing kits and supplies. Leaflet (free).

Every year, more Americans are coming back to the "old-fashioned Christmas"— the traditions that made the holiday season so precious when we were kids. And what is an old-fashioned Christmas? Why, home-baked cookies and handmade, personalized presents. What we've been missing in this mechanized, commercial time is the homey pleasure in doing things, rather than buying things for each other.

Since not everyone is a master craftsman, kits can be a big help at this do-it-yourself holiday. A wide variety of Christmas items is already available, and the list grows every year as designers catch on to the new trend. Imagine building a Hansel and Gretel gingerbread house with your kids, rather than buying one at the bakery. Or think of the pleasure your handmade ornaments will bring to family and friends. It hardly compares to an outing to the local department store to buy a box of breakables.

Like a lot of old-fashioned things, the handmade Christmas takes a bit more time and planning. If you think back, though, that was a part of the excitement, too. Remember the growing anticipation from Thanksgiving to Christmas as the house filled up with fruits, flour, sugar, butter, chocolates, fabric, glitter, and glue? And if somebody was doing a little sawing and hammering in some off-limits corner of the cellar, the kids were probably delirious with curiosity.

We hope that the kits included here will give you a start on planning your own holiday time. There's probably no other season when doing-it-yourself can make such a fundamental difference.

DONALD KNOOB & FRIENDS

85 Fourth Ave.
New York, N.Y. 10003

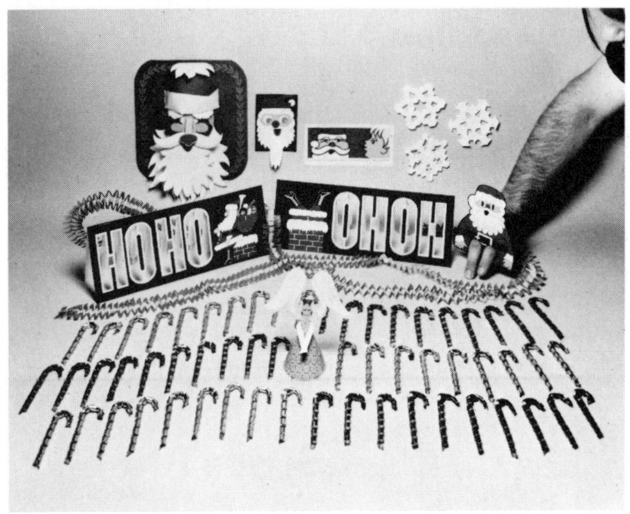

CHRISTMAS CRAFTS

Five dozen things to make for Christmas in minutes . . . with just scissors! What a nice surprise. Twist an aluminum strip around a plastic tube, bend over the top, and you have a beautiful Tinsel-Cane for the family tree. And this new Christmas Fun kit includes five dozen of these 4″ ornaments, all kinds of bright decorations for the home and stocking stuffers for the kids.

There's a Santa Claus paper sculpture for your door, snowflake cutouts for your window, a self-standing angel doll for your table, and two colorful 6′ streamers for your tree or wherever your home needs a dash of color. Another happy surprise is a 12″ decoration with cutout letters. With a jolly Santa on one side, it reads "HO HO." But the same letters become "OH OH" on the other side, which shows a not-so-jolly Santa stuck in a chimney.

For the kids, there's a Santa puppet that uses your fingers for legs, a visual trick that shows Santa getting a big kiss, and a bubble pipe for blowing "the nicest ornaments in the world." Another cutout toy is called the Jiggle-Wiggle. As the instructions explain, "You jiggle Santa's beard and his eyes wiggle. Pull too hard and his mouth opens wide. Ouch!"

Best of all, everything in the kit can be made quickly and easily, with just a pair of scissors. The price is great also, only $2. postpaid.

HANOVER HOUSE
Hanover, Pa. 17331

NEEDLEPOINT CHRISTMAS ORNAMENTS

What could be prettier than a handmade needlework plaque hanging on the Christmas tree? Three handmade needlework plaques. Each of these kits contains materials for three 4½″ needlepoint ornaments. Easy to make and lovely to hang. Includes holly, angel, and candle. $7.98.

THE CRACKER BOX
River Rd.
Point Pleasant, Pa. 18950

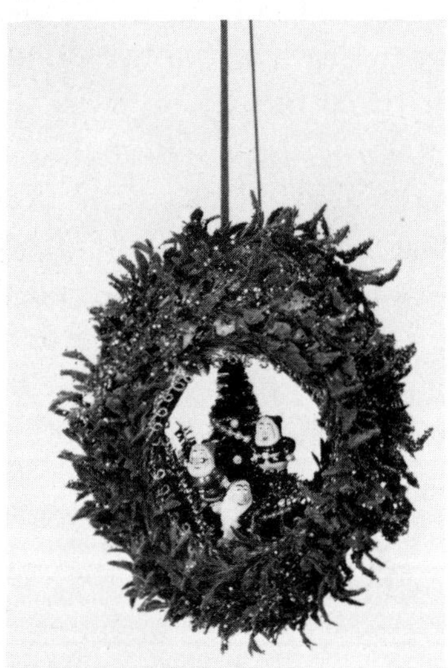

CHRISTMAS ORNAMENTS

If ornate Christmas balls and tree hangers intrigue you, look no further. The Cracker Box people (see Crafts section for more details) have put together a remarkable array of Christmas tree cheerers. Every possible Christmas motif is incorporated into the offerings and the kits are complete, except for the glue. The idea of homemade ornaments may be just the kind of project you're looking for to make Christmas a little more real. The kits are competitively priced. Illustrated above is Santa's Here: $1.85. Under the Mistletoe: $6.75. Santa and the Elves: $3.75.

RANTALA CRAFTS
Box 87
Wadena, Minn. 56482

ORNAMENT WOOD CURLS

The first time I saw wood-curl ornaments it was very impressive. What excited me even more was that they had been made from wood shavings that a carpenter was about to throw away. Leave it to some smart marketer to turn this all into a business. Rantala supplies you with thirty-two feet of wood curls and a booklet on making decorations. This old-fashioned craft is fun and easy. Reasonably priced at $1.

JUNE ZIMONICK'S STUDIO
840 Cook St., Box 113
De Pere, Wis. 54115

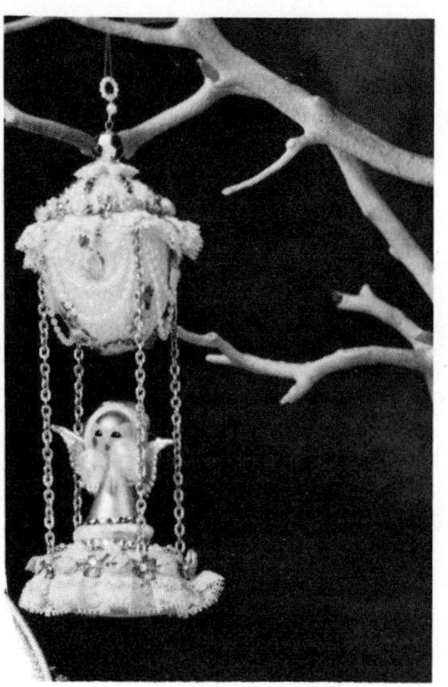

CHRISTMAS DECORATIONS FOR TREE AND HOME

Christmas decorations tend to run to the elaborate in many kits. The "Sugar Plum Fairy" illustrated above is a project quickly put together. Some call it garish, others call it beautiful. If you do decide to order, you'll find the materials first-rate and the instructions well done. $5.95.

Zimonick's offers a free catalog of over 200 other such Christmas items, some with a good deal of imagination in design. Some nice ideas for different decorations.

ALDEBARAN EDUCATIONAL
P.O. Box 21132
Woodhaven, N.Y. 11421

MACRAME SNOWFLAKE KITS

Make beautiful snowflakes in gold and silver metallic braid. Perfect tree hangers or simply as window decorations. Kit makes ten snowflakes in gold and silver. Interesting designs in unusual style. $8.

GREENLAND STUDIOS
Greenland Bldg.
Miami, Fla. 33059

PAINT-BY-NUMBER
CHRISTMAS ORNAMENT KITS

Kind of high-camp cheapies, these kits are, but they are not without charm. How else could you manage to obtain more than a dozen two-sided ornaments for a dollar and have creative satisfaction besides? No artistic talent needed. Kit includes brush, glitter, glue, and golden cords for hanging ornaments. Ornament kit: $1. Wood kit: $1.98.

YULETIDE FELT KIT

A typical mail-order goodie, but good value and good quality. Kit includes all materials needed to make twelve ornaments—yarn, needle, braid, sequins, glitter, glue, padding, and golden cord hangers. Ornaments are bell, Santa Claus, Christmas tree, wreaths, and other relatively nonreligious items. A nice Christmas season project for all those kids home from school. $3.98.

LILLIAN VERNON
510 South Fulton Highway
Mt. Vernon, N.Y. 10550

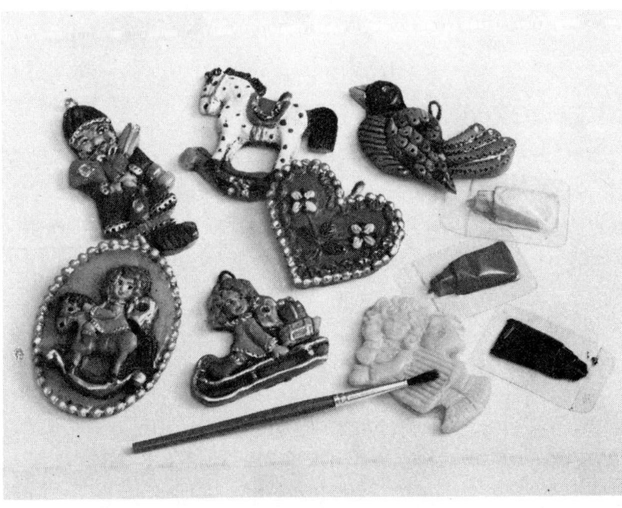

WAX TREE ORNAMENTS

Wax ornaments have been traditional in Europe for centuries. These are imported from Germany. Old-World charm and all you do is paint. Kit includes six different ornaments, complete with hang cords, three primary colors plus white to mix your own rainbow of hues, brush, and gilt to set them asparkle. Sizes range from 2½″ to 3½″. $4.98.

FRIENDS INDUSTRY
200 Fifth Ave.
New York, N.Y. 10021

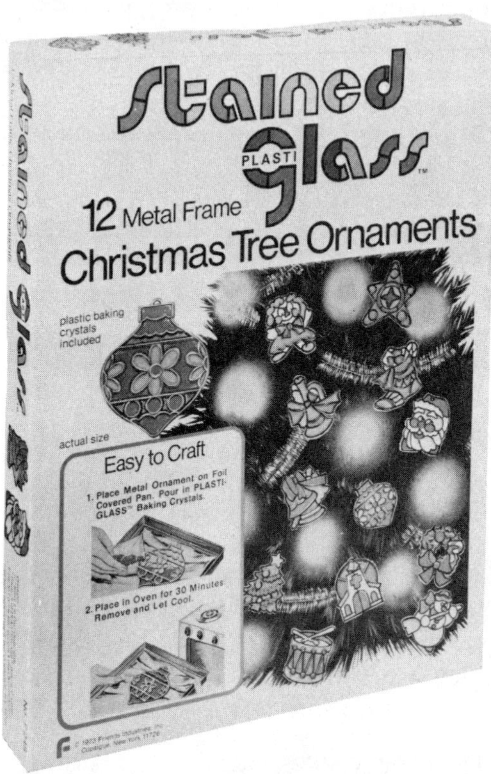

STAINED PLASTIC-GLASS
CHRISTMAS TREE ORNAMENTS

You'll bake up some Christmas joy with this attractive kit. Simply fill the molds with plastic baking crystals and place in oven for thirty minutes. After cooling, you have attractive tree decorations. A complement to any tree. $6.

WHITTEMORE-DURGIN
Box 2065
Hanover, Mass. 02339

STAINED GLASS ORNAMENTS

The basic glass kit (No. 11) is at $12.95 a true bargain. This company, the largest supplier of materials, tools, and patterns for the stained glass craftsman, would have to charge $18.48 if they sold you all the kit's contents separately. The kit includes complete instructions and preformed glass to make three hanging ornaments (which the manufacturer colorfully calls the Ambidextrous Butterfly, the Fecund Whale, and the Nonchalant Orange), plus loads of bulk materials with which you can design at least a dozen more ornaments. Kit comes with all necessary equipment and tools as well as their booklet, "Getting Started in Stained Glass," which gives step-by-step instructions.

Not the least of the pleasures of ordering this kit from Whittemore-Durgin is receiving their literature—twenty or more pages of closely typed lists, copious descriptions, and chatty discourses—all written in an arch, intensely personal style. Comments like "Our intention is that our dealings together shall be pleasant, interesting, mildly exciting, and nontoxic," are interlaced with curious old illustrations and complicated listings of their many wares. $12.95.

GALLAGHER-FOSTER HOUSE

6523 Galena Rd.
Peoria, Ill. 61601

GINGERBREAD HOUSE

This precut mahogany, paint-by-number gingerbread house, complete with separate boy and girl figures, is meant to be a Christmas centerpiece decoration, but there is no reason why it can't function out of season. It's 7″ × 9½″ and features nontoxic acrylic paints. A good project for kids, and a lot less messy than baking a gingerbread house. $4.99.

CLOTHESPIN CHRISTMAS ORNAMENTS

Making your own Christmas ornaments is a nice tradition and a good way to engage the kids in a noncommercial aspect of what has become a veritable orgy of merchandising. Unlike many such ornaments, these simple-to-make wooden clothespin people are neither tacky nor glittery. And, although you may long for the day when Grandma gave the children sewing basket scraps and a bag of her best clothespins, a prearranged kit is not to be sneezed at, especially at this price. The kit includes twenty wood clothespins, plus all materials and tools needed to make Santa Claus, soldiers, cowboys, clowns, and for some reason, doctors and nurses. $4.99.

"SEASON'S GREETINGS" GUEST TOWELS

While everyone is "nestled all snug in their beds," you can be embroidering guest towels for Christmas morn. As you might expect, one of these linen towels says Merry Christmas, and the other Happy New Year. Kit includes towels with stamped-on pattern, threads, and full instructions. $2.99 for both towels.

ARTS OF NOW

1884 Forge St.
Tucker, Ga. 30084

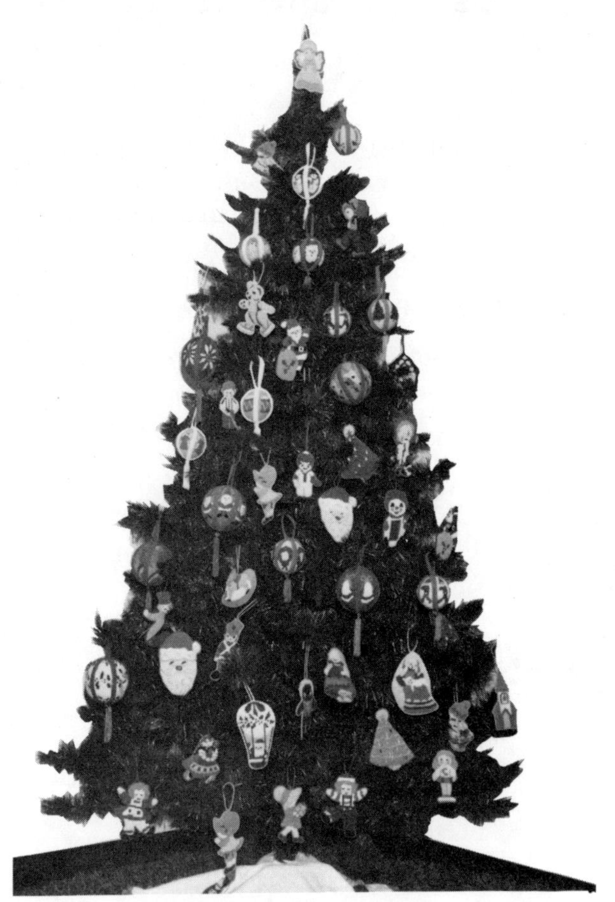

NEEDLEPOINT TREETOPS AND ORNAMENTS

In these times of disposable everything, here is a welcome change in decorations. They are unbreakable, mothproof, and will be handed down from generation to generation. They are the gifts that say "I care." On the top of the tree is an extra-large decoration, 7″ × 9″. They can also be placed inside a wreath, on a felt banner, in a centerpiece, or as a picture with additional yarn to fill in the background. An added attraction is that these are learning tools, each incorporating up to six different needlepoint stitches to add dimension and interest.

The ornaments have an average finished size of 4″ × 5″, a perfect size for a beginner. You can choose from dozens of ornaments including such designs as Santa Claus, Christmas Bell, Angel Cookie, Snowman, Teddy Bear on Ice Skates, Church, and a Rocking Horse. Write and ask for Christmas brochure for detailed list of designs available. Tree toppers: $10. each. Ornaments: $4. each.

BAHLSEN, INC.

34–39 56 St.
Woodside, N.Y. 11377

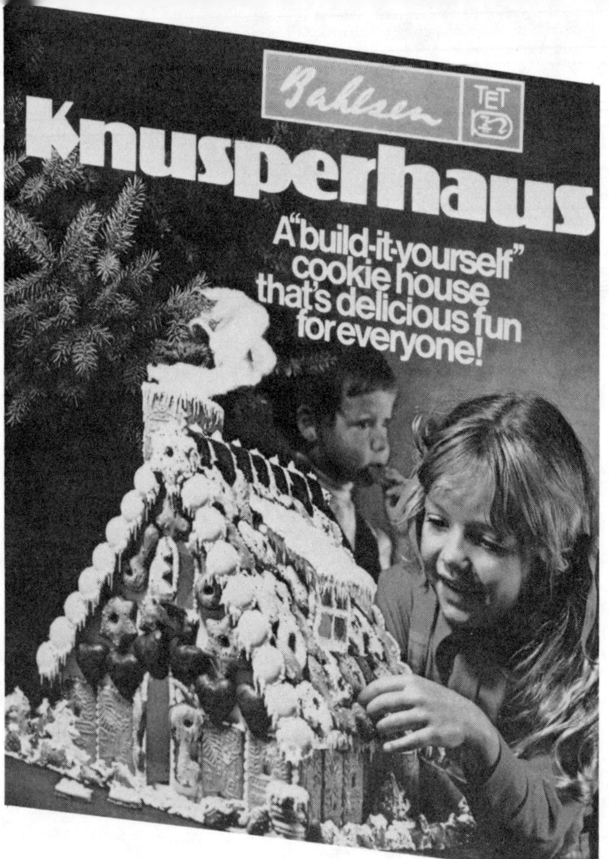

CHRISTMAS COOKIE HOUSE

Hansel and Gretel never had it so good. Watch your kids' eyes light up as they see this magical do-it-yourself *Knusperhaus*. It's the original old-fashioned cookie house. Combines a fun project with a delightful eye-catching Christmas centerpiece. Best of all is eating the results afterwards. Everything to build a big 18″ × 15″ *Knusperhaus* included: house forms, red paper for windows and doors, powdered sugar, easy-to-follow instructions, and four bags full of delicious cookies—from Bahlsen, importers of baked goods. $10.95.

THUMBELINA NEEDLEWORK SHOP

1685 Copenhagen Dr.
Solvang, Calif. 93463

DANISH CHRISTMAS CALENDARS

An interesting sewing project. According to Danish custom, each child should have a Christmas calendar at Christmas. Small, inexpensive gifts are wrapped and hung on the rings, one for each day of December. The calendar is hung up on the first day of December, and each day until Christmas, the child opens the gift for the day. When filled with tiny packages, the calendar is a most attractive Christmas decoration, and the prospect of a surprise gift each day delights the children. The calendars are both fun and easy to make. They are done in cross-stitch, and only the colorful design is embroidered, following a count-out chart. The design is not traced on the material. 14″ × 29″. $9.50.

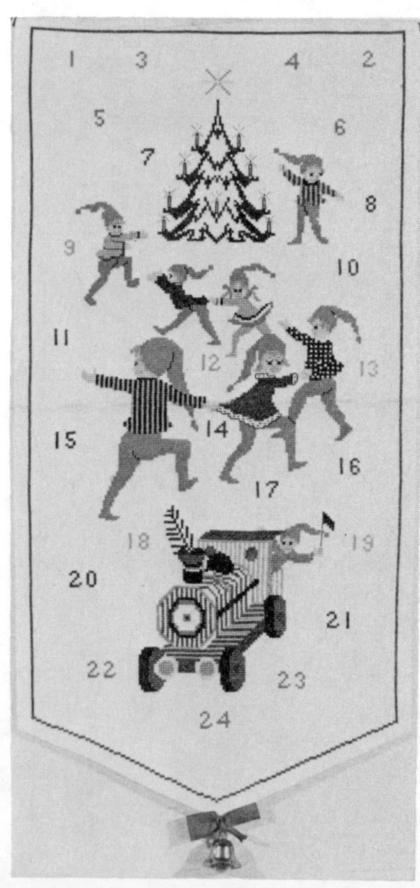

Keeping track of the passage of time is one of the most human of activities. As far as we know, no other animal marks the changes of the seasons or the phases of the moon. Recent anthropological work has shown that the calendar, in some form, is one of the oldest artifacts of mankind.

The clock is just a more detailed calendar, keeping track of the movement of the sun through every day and parts of the day. The oldest clock is the sundial, found in Babylonia between 3000 and 2000 B.C. Around 200 B.C., the clocks started turning up in the same region, including water clocks, striped candles, and burning knotted ropes.

Since then, our clocks have become mechanized, electrical, electronic, and almost as accurate as anyone could want. And probably from the first moment clocks had moving parts, someone developed the passion for tinkering with them. So widespread is this love that it has passed into the language in the expression, "what makes it tick?" Today, thousands of people are united by their hobby of fixing or building or restoring clocks. There are specialists in Early American standing clocks or Dutch wall clocks. Whatever your preference in period and style, you'll be able to find a kit to make one. Modern manufacturing has given us back some lost time.

HEATH COMPANY
Benton Harbor, Mich. 49022

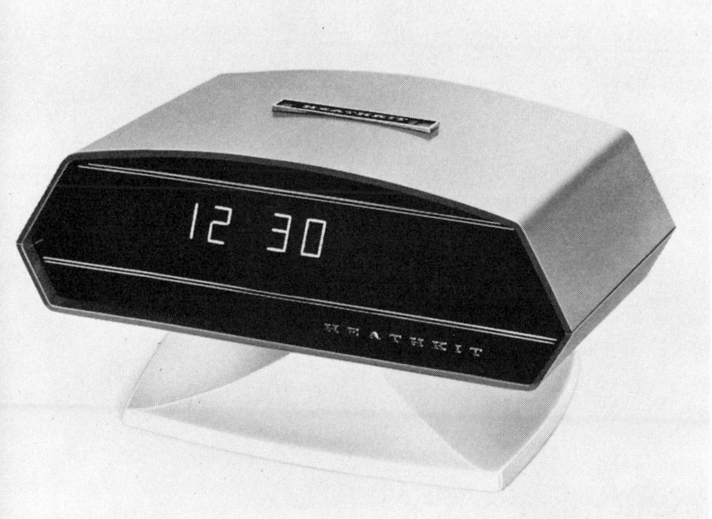

DELUXE ELECTRIC CLOCK

The time in hours, minutes, and seconds and also a touch switch for the day and date! Built-in stand. Big orange digits that you can see from across the room. But the best feature is building the Heathkit precision instrument. $82.95.

WALLY'S WAGON
P.O. Box 111
New Kensington, Pa. 15068

CUCKOO CLOCK

From the Black Forest comes the classic cuckoo clock. This 10″ clock is in the traditional colors, complete with moving bird. The movement is weight and pendulum-style. Fun to put together, fun once completed. $22.

EDUCATIONAL DESIGNS, INC.
47 West 13 St.
New York, N.Y. 10011

CLOCK AND PENDULUM KIT

The design of this clever device is elegant in its simplicity. The box becomes the body of the clock to which the pendulum and hands are easily attached. Youngsters can build a timing clock and metronome, construct a simulated stopwatch, and carry out Galileo's famous pendulum experiments —all with no tools at all. No batteries or outside power sources required. $6.

GENERAL TIME SERVICE

170–08 Jamaica Ave.
Jamaica, N.Y. 11433

SOLID-STATE CLOCK

You can make your own Isotron 100 Battery Clock.
Once complete, use it with a picture, needlepoint, or
model boat. Its uses are limited only by your
imagination. You receive solid-state movement, two
sets of decorative hands, and complete, well-written
instructions. No special tools, and easy to
complete. $9.95.

NEWPORT ENTERPRISES

2309 West Burbank Blvd.
Burbank, Calif. 91506

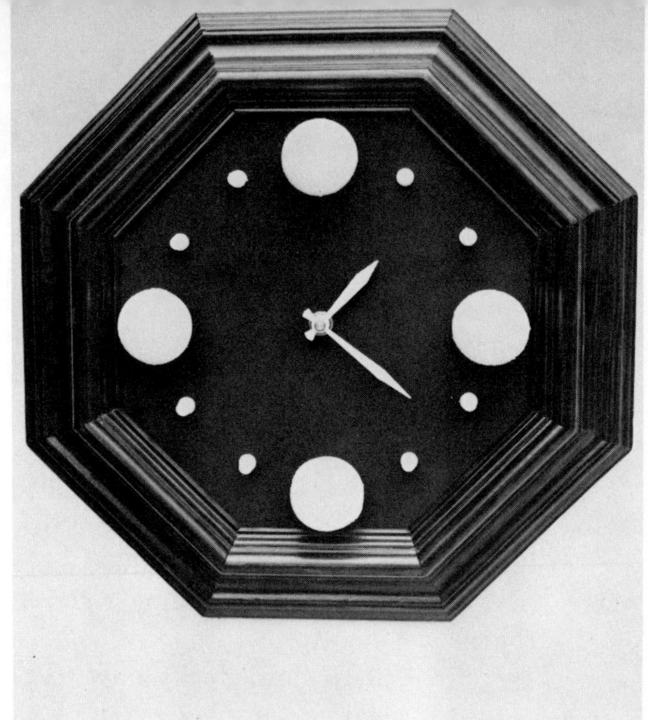

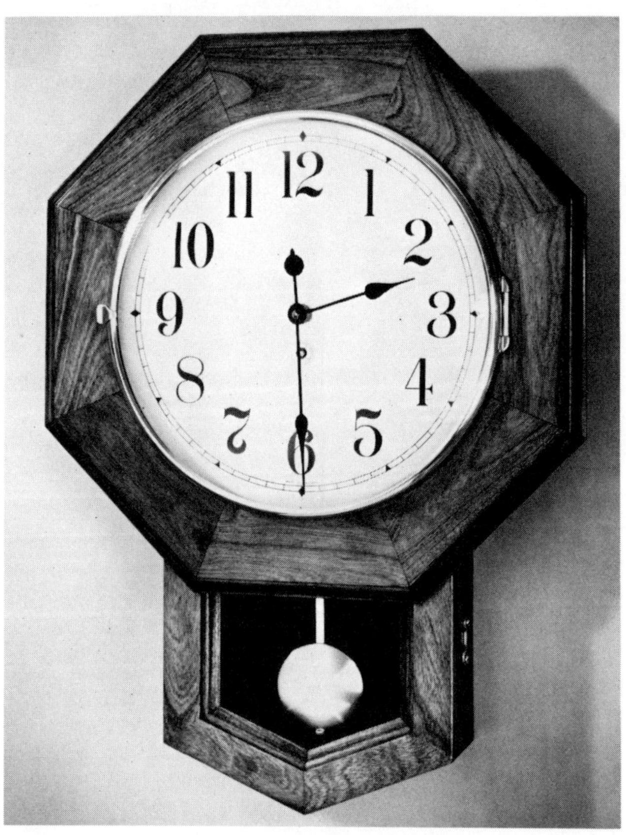

SCHOOL CLOCK

Here is the original school clock styled for today.
The antiqued dial is mounted on hardboard and
installed in a massive 18″ octagon frame. The glass
door with a screened design on the inside is
mounted with brass hinges and has a brass knob
and hook. All wood parts are premium white pine
and may be stained or antiqued any color. You
simply assemble wood parts. Nails and hardware
supplied. $39.95.

GOLFER'S CLOCK

What golfer wouldn't love this for his game room or
den! Golf clock using four practice-type golf balls
and eight tee-type white push pins as markers. Fasten the golf balls with screws and push the markers
into the predrilled panel for quick and easy assembly after finishing the frame. Install the panel with
push points. 14¼″ × 14¼″ overall. Kit includes
unfinished frame, movement and hands, golf kit,
panel, velour. $18.

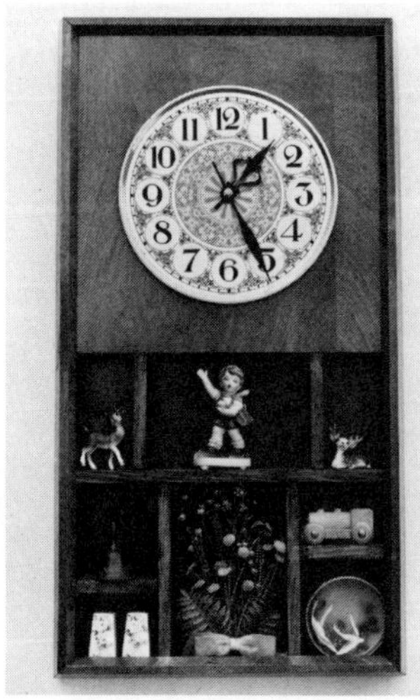

EVERYTHING CLOCK

All the family keepsakes are easily displayed on
these shelves. Use your imagination to finish this
clock in any number of ways. Display your small
keepsakes or miniatures on the shelves, or make an
ecology clock using beans, corn, rice, or other
kitchen items by installing glass.

Kit includes frame, clear birch veneer dial panel and bottom panel, movement and hands, and dial. Note: If glass is installed in the bottom, the shelves must be cut down to the thickness of the glass. 12½″ × 23½″. $39.95.

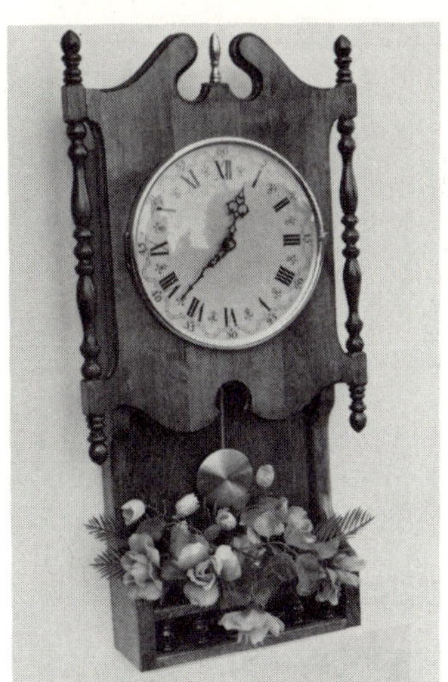

PLANTER CLOCK

Here is a beautiful hardwood clock for Early American or Provincial decor. Wood parts are solid hardwood, back is birch veneer. Takes a natural stain finish in any color to produce a beautiful wall piece. Place your own ferns or flowers over the bottom railing. Miniature figures may also be used. $48.

H. DeCOVNICK & SON

P.O. Box 68
Alamo, Calif. 94507

ELI TERRY CLOCK

One of America's most famous clock designers, Eli Terry of New England, sold many thousands of these clocks during its period of manufacture in the past century. The Eli Terry kit authentically reproduces the original design from the shape of its brass finials to the beautifully hand-painted dial and tablet. Truly a clock kit that will provide a sense of pride and satisfaction to the craftsman. Complete with hardware and movement. $131.50.

DeCovnick has one of the best selections of clock kits available. The catalog (50¢) will provide the winner with many choices. Our inability to obtain photos precluded our showing more, but we suggest you write for their worthwhile catalog.

EMPEROR CLOCK CO.

Emperor Industrial Park
Greeno Rd.
U.S. 98, Truck Route
Fairhope, Ala. 36532

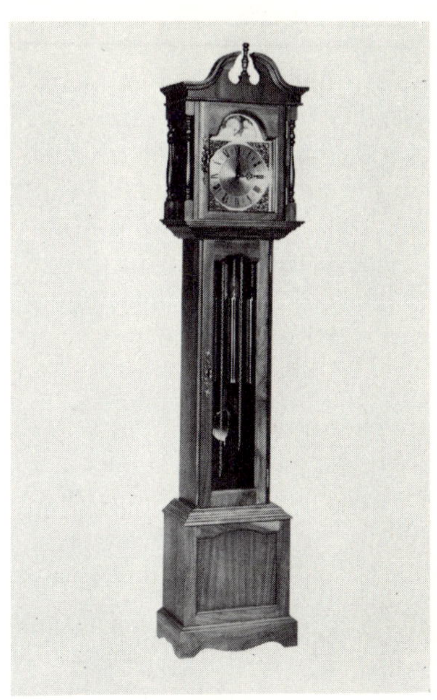

GRANDFATHER CLOCK

This elegant grandfather clock is very attractive and attractively priced. The knowledge required is a little carpentry rather than clock-making (the movement is fully assembled and only needs mounting). All pieces precut and presanded at the factory. Breakfront swan neck crown and finial, waist and dial doors, dial frame and sculptured base-front factory assembled. Complete hardware and assembly instructions included. Each piece may be reordered separately. No woodworking experience necessary according to the manufacturer. The wood is solid ¾″ cherry, which truly has a rich look. A good buy at $89.50.

Emperor claims to be the largest manufacturer of grandfather clocks. They have a number of interesting kits. Details free.

B & F ENTERPRISES

119 Foster St.
Peabody, Mass. 01960

LOW-COST DIGITAL CLOCK

Digital clock, capable of 12- or 24-hour display in hours, minutes, and seconds. Intended as a beginner's kit (only screwdriver and soldering iron needed). Guaranteed success (maximum repair charge $10.). $47.50.

AIRCRAFT AUTO BOAT QUARTZ CRYSTAL CHRONOMETER

Measuring only 2½″ × 2½″ × 2⅜″, and accurate to ten seconds a month, this chronometer "promises to entirely replace mechanical clocks in cars, boats, and airplanes." Fits a standard 2¼″ instrument panel cutout. The displays are bright L.E.D. displays. Setting controls are recessed and operate from a pointed object such as a pencil point or paper clip, in order to keep unauthorized hands off. The clock should only have to be reset at very great intervals, or in the event of power loss (i.e., replacing battery in car). The clock is wired so that the timing circuits are always running, but the displays are only lit when the ignition is on (negligible power drain). Operates on 10 to 14 v. d.c. Kit: $69.50. 24-v. adapter: $10.

B & F deals primarily in surplus and discount electronic components and equipment (see Electronics section). The company offers several other clocks as well as components and subassembly kits for rolling your own.

RADIO SHACK
2615 West 7 St.
Fort Worth, Tex. 76107

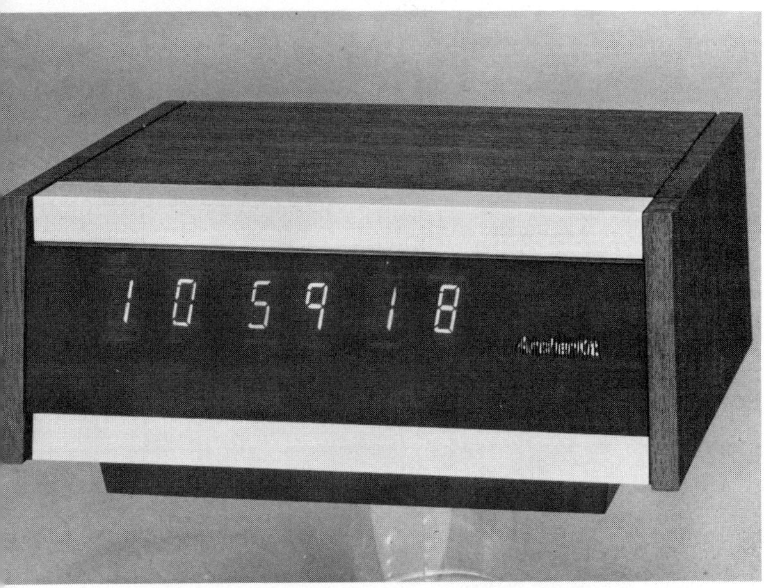

ELECTRONIC DIGITAL CLOCK

If you have the feeling time is slipping away, just watch this electronic clock for a few minutes. Shows hours, minutes, and even seconds. All electronic, absolutely silent. A fascinating timepiece! Features 12- or 24-hour operation, fluorescent tube 6-digit readout, hi-low brightness switch, "hold" button for synchronizing with hourly "beep" on radio-TV stations. Premounted for easy assembly. Smoke-tint panel, woodgrain case. 3¼″ × 7¼″ × 4½″ $59.95.

GENERAL CRAFTS CORP.
3031 James St.
Baltimore, Md. 21230

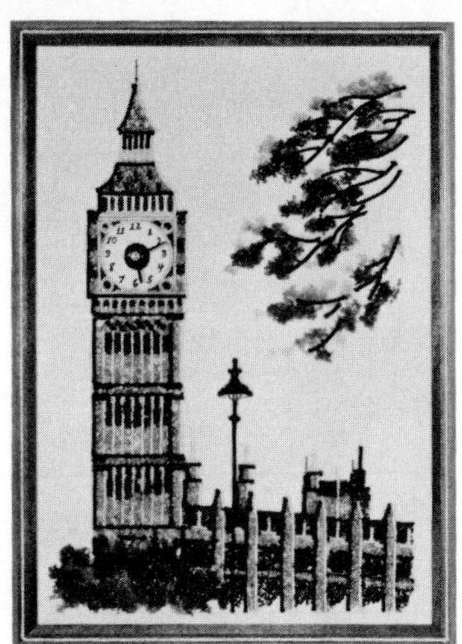

BIG BEN DECORATOR CLOCK

The world's best-known clock can now grace your home. A functional, cordless wall clock kit that can be created-by-number and can be a work of art at the same time!

You mosaic it, and after following the included instructions, you just insert the battery-operated electronic movement and you have a clock set in a lovely mosaic design on textured, neutral panels. The frame is included, but not the battery. Big Ben would surely be pleased in his new setting. $25.

MASON & SULLIVAN CO.
39 Blossom Ave.
Osterville, Mass. 02655

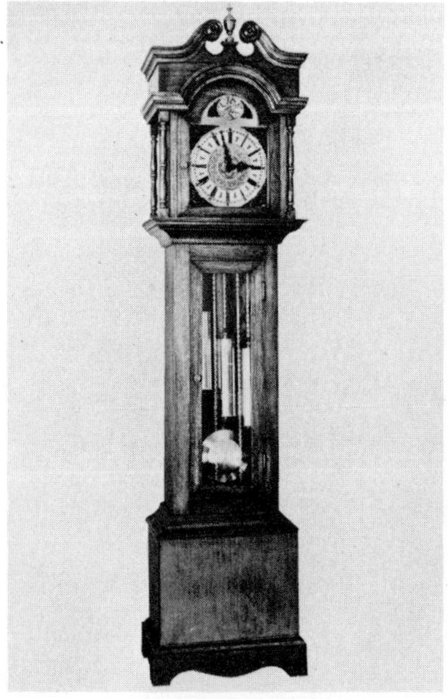

GRANDFATHER CLOCK CASE

This authentically detailed grandfather clock case

was inspired by a museum piece, and you can build it in mahogany, cherry, or walnut. Although you can buy a complete kit, parts are ordered individually. Some experience in woodworking, plus good tools, are obviously necessary to build this case. The simpler wood pieces are not cut out for you, and you have the option of buying the lumber for these locally. The more difficult moldings and turnings are done for you at the factory. Prices vary according to whether you purchase the extra lumber, and which wood you choose. 84″ high, 19″ wide, 12⅛″ deep. Catalog free. Price for moldings, turnings, and hardware for case only. Mahogany: $60.25. Cherry: $68.75. Walnut: $82.85.

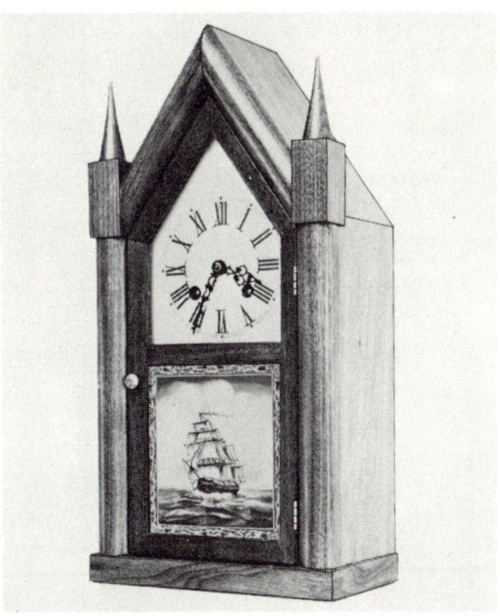

STEEPLE CLOCK

An authentic replica of an American steeple clock made in the mid-19th century. This is one of the most popular clocks in the company's catalog. Because of this, it is available in a complete kit with fully precut wood parts. Complete kit (movement not included): Cherry: $42.00. Walnut: $44.24.

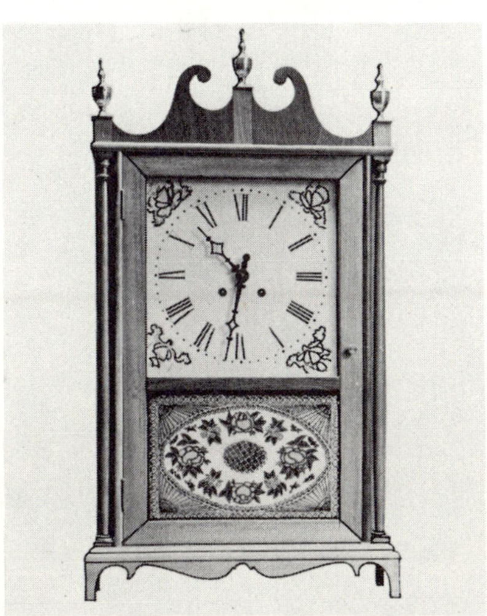

ELI TERRY PILLAR AND SCROLL CLOCK

Eli Terry designed this beautiful pillar and scroll

clock in 1808. It was one of the most popular timepieces in 19th-century America and has become a classic that will endure for generations to come. Originals are rare and expensive. 30½″ high, 17¼″ wide, 5″ deep. Kit includes lumber for case (movement not included). Mahogany: $61.50. Cherry: $64.90. Walnut: $70.34. Complete blueprints: $1.00.

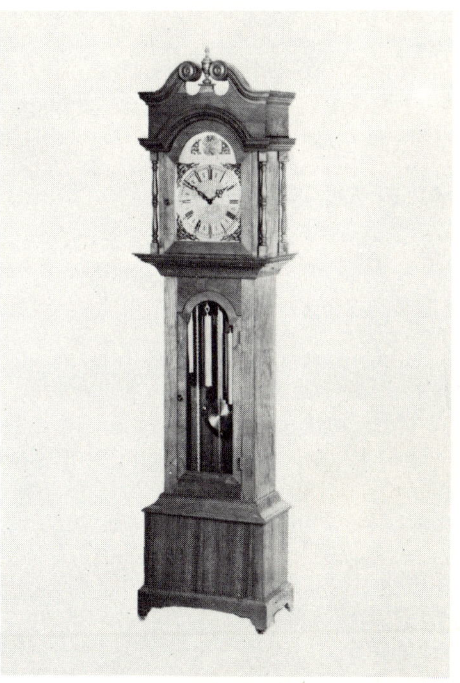

GRANDMOTHER CLOCK CASE

Early American styling in a smaller clock of the grandfather type. As with all their clocks, Mason & Sullivan also sell kits for the movements and make recommendations about which works to use with which clock. 74″ high, 19″ wide, 10″ deep. Kit price includes moldings, turnings, and hardware (movement not included). Mahogany: $58.85. Cherry: $67.10. Walnut: $80.95.

This company sells kits for making grandfather and grandmother clock cases. You can buy one of several separate kits to build the clock movement. Case kits include the more difficult moldings and turnings, plus instructions about how to cut the easier pieces yourself out of plain wood. (This requires a good saber saw plus woodworking experience.) You can also order the lumber for these plain pieces from Mason & Sullivan. In most cases, you can order complete blueprints for clock cases without buying the full kit. Pieces can also be ordered individually.

Mason & Sullivan also sells complete kits for smaller clocks, as well as the individual pieces. In addition, there are barometers, Swiss music boxes, even a design for a needlepoint clock. Catalog free.

THE GALLERY
Div. of Amsterdam Co.
Amsterdam, N.Y. 12010

VISIBLE CLOCK

If you want to watch time go by and have some time on your hands, you'll enjoy assembling this attractive see-through timepiece. But be warned: this is not an evening's work. It has more than fifty parts, including gears, and must be assembled with care and precision. The finished product sits inside a lucite case 4″ × 4¼″ × 2¾″ and has elegant, prestamped Roman numerals. $18.50.

ALPHA ELECTRONICS
P.O. Box 1005
Merritt Island, Fla. 32952

DIGITAL WATCH

The watch industry finally has a new product—the quartz-timed digital watch, which displays time in numbers. Now it's available in kit form at considerably less than the made-up version. Complete kit includes the stainless steel case (which also must be assembled). $68.90.

BARBARA ELENA
136 East 57 St.
New York, N.Y. 10022

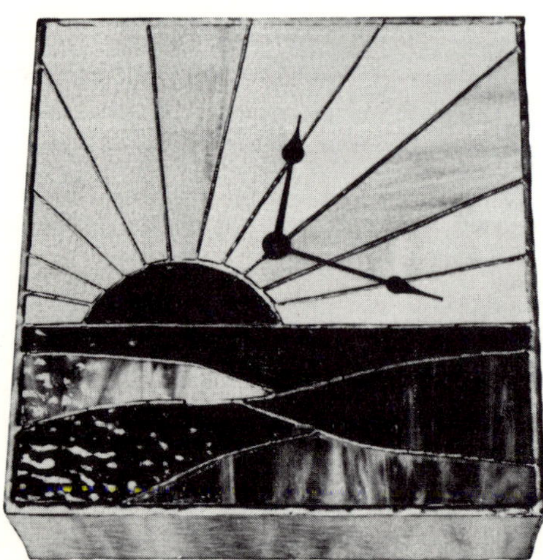

STAINED GLASS CLOCK

The ancient craft of stained glass work combined with a modern timepiece. This classic timepiece will be admired in the den, living room, or playroom. Kit includes first-quality UL-approved clock, 2 light bulbs; wire and plug; hanging brackets; 24 pieces of distinctive precut stained glass; flux and flux brush; patina, solder, and a carefully detailed and illustrated craft manual compiled especially for this kit. $40.

CRAFT PRODUCTS CO.
North Ave. and Route 83
Elmhurst, Ill. 60123

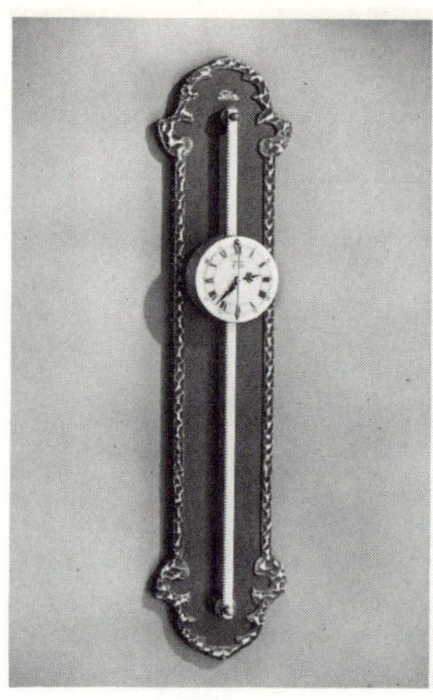

ORNAMENTAL SAW CLOCK KIT

Typical of clocks made around 1750, this fine reproduction of an ornamental saw clock is 25½″ long by 4¼″ wide. Its background is wood, painted in dark antique red or green and bordered in antique gold. The well-executed clock with porcelain dial and delicate black hands runs by gravity. Raise it to the top of the saw track and it will slowly and quietly descend over a period of thirty-two hours and keep accurate time. The only assembly necessary is mounting the saw track on the wood background. Full instructions are included. Even the most unhandy craftsman can handle this. $76.90.

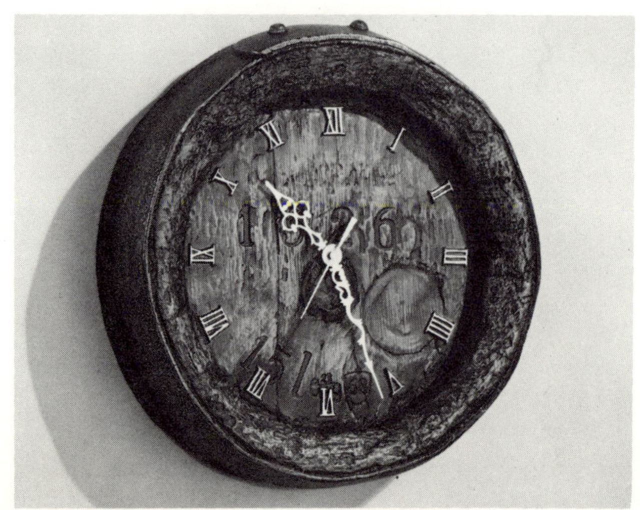

SIMULATED BARREL END CLOCK KIT

This quaint clock is simulated to look like the end of a barrel and is suitable for a den, boy's room, or recreation room. It is 12½″ in diameter, 3¼″ deep, and finished in brown, shaded for a rugged appearance. The date "1326" is embedded in the face, and the Roman numerals are raised and painted gold. The edge is encircled with a simulated metal barrel hoop. All that you have to do to finish the clock is to mount the fine German battery movement, which is equipped with brass serpentine hands. Simulated wood. $49.50.

SCHOOL CLOCK KIT

This should touch off memories of childhood. How many hours did you spend gazing at a clock like the one shown? This popular school clock in oak or cherry is easy to assemble for a touch of nostalgia in your home. It is 24″ high by 16½″ wide. Included in the kit is the fine thirty-one-day Ansonia "C" gong-strike movement, which chimes on the hour and the half-hour. Also included in the kit are the bezel, dial, and hardware. $45.50.

Well-produced (100 + pp.) catalog ($1.), featuring many different clocks and movements that will add charm to your home and satisfy the amateur horologist within you. However, as most are 50 to 95% assembled, they are more for clock fanciers than kit makers. We do recommend their catalog.

CALDWELL INDUSTRIES
Luling, Tex. 78648

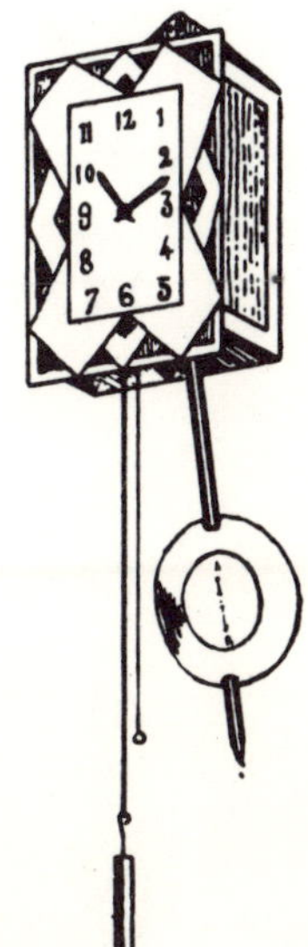

CARDBOARD CLOCK

This clock is a great exercise in horological engineering. Constructed entirely out of paper, with an occasional piece of string or a toothpick for added strength, it develops into a working model. The design for this clock originated in France in 1933, and the parts are printed on sheets of 14″ × 18″ #60 paper—accompanying instructions are in French! The diagrams are clear enough, so this is no handicap. Finished size, 7″ × 10″ × 3″. The construction techniques using cardboard to produce gears and surprisingly rigid structures are fascinating. $4.25.

WOODEN CLOCK KIT

Twenty-eight prepared components, hand-painted dial with wooden gears and frame. You collect two stones for the weights. 6″. dial. running time, 17 hours. $37.50.

Caldwell offers about ten different clock kits, including a lucite visible clock, wooden kitchen clock, and several plastic antique re-creations. They also offer an interesting steam engine and tool kits (see Toys and Models and Tools sections).

OTHER SOURCES

Craftsman Wood Service Co.
2727 South Mary St.
Chicago, Ill. 60608

Grandfather clock kits. Catalog (50¢).

Gaston Wood Finishes
3630 E. 10 St.
Bloomington, Ind. 47401

Assorted clock kits. Catalog (50¢).

Held Products
9 Lakeview Dr.
Farmington, Conn. 06032

14th- and 15th-century-style wooden wheel clock kits that include premachined parts. Catalog (free).

House of Clermont
525 Skyview Dr.
Nashville, Tenn. 37206

Choose from two wall clock kits. Brochure (10¢).

JHS Enterprises
Box 81
Point Clear, Ala. 36564

Easy-to-assemble, hand-painted cuckoo clock kit. Catalog (25¢, refundable with order).

Kuempel Chime Clock Works
21190 Minnetonka Blvd.
Excelsior, Minn. 55331

A variety of kits for construction of classic-type grandfather clocks.

Old Bedford Clock Co.
555 Old Bedford Rd.
Westport, Mass. 02790

Two clock kits offered, "Old Bedford" and "Sheraton." School discounts. Catalog (25¢).

Selva Company
487 Armour Circle, N.E.
Atlanta, Ga. 30324

Casual and modern clock kit designs. Catalog ($2.).

Have you ever wondered what the difference is between costume jewelry and "real" jewelry? It used to be just the preciousness of the materials used. Diamonds were used in genuine jewelry; rhinestones, paste, or glass were used in costume jewelry. But these days, both kinds of ornaments are as likely as not to be made out of lucite or stone. So what's all the fuss about? Usually, it's a question of design. The more sophisticated the designer, the higher the price. This is especially true when the piece is a one-of-a-kind design.

If you wear jewelry much, you've probably had the experience of putting on your favorite pair of earrings, only to have your friend turn up in the very same ones. Of course you don't drop dead from embarrassment, but somehow it diminishes the specialness of those earrings. But how can you afford the custom designs that make a piece of jewelry really your own? One way, perhaps the best, is to become your own designer.

Making jewelry for yourself isn't as hard as you may think, particularly if you have the help of some of the kits presented here. No matter how little experience you may have had, there is a kit that will make jewelry design easy and pleasurable for you. Once you've had a little practice with a kit or two, you may branch out to new materials such as natural objects, treasured keepsakes, even common things you find around the house. If you find you enjoy the work, you'll soon be giving your creations as gifts. But whether or not jewelry-making becomes a consuming interest, you're sure to get lasting pleasure from your personalized designs, especially when you're the only one at the party who isn't wearing the same earrings.

MARY WALES

Box 1487
San Mateo, Calif. 94401

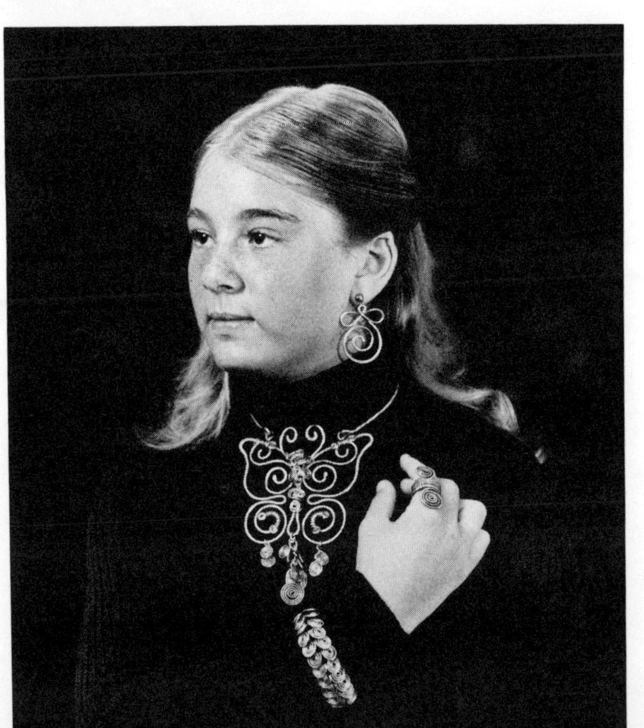

WIRE JEWELRY

Some of the earliest jewelry in the history of the world was fashioned from wire; a visit to just about any museum will bear out this fact. Mary Wales, who devised the wire jewelry-making kit, has spent many years studying and adapting methods of the ancient Greek, Egyptian, and Byzantine craftsmen to the modern tools and materials of today. The names of some of her original designs are intriguing: butterfly, sunflower, Grecian necklace, Ionic neck ring, dragonfly wings.

Earrings, bracelets, rings, neck rings, and necklaces can be fashioned by you from Mary Wales' kit; yet part of the fun of making wire jewelry is expressing your own ideas. You can vary the several basic methods in many different ways according to your taste.

The kit contains materials for six to twelve pieces, and includes step-by-step illustrated directions, make-easy templates, 78' brass wire (4 gauges), pointed nose pliers with cutters, metal file, and 2 sets of earring backs and beads. $12.

PLUME TRADING CO.

155 Lexington Ave.
New York, N.Y. 10016

INDIAN COWRIE SHELL NECKLACE

Cowrie shells have long been popular among American Indians. Recently, they have caught on here. In fact, one investment service reports a number of Cowrie shell investors. You can be ready for the return to the shell/bead economy with this (and other) kits from Plume. Plume sells a variety of Indian jewelry and crafts (see Needlepoint and Sewing section for details). This particular kit includes 100 tubular beads, 7 Cowrie shells (drilled at the top), string, and simple instructions. This is a simple child's project, but the result is a pretty necklace. Some Indian groups attribute strange powers to Cowrie shell wearers, so you're on your own once you complete this kit. $6.00.

ZYMEX

900 West Los Vallecitos
San Marcos, Calif. 92069

TURQUOISE STONE JEWELRY KITS

The Southwest fashion rage of turquoise is catching on everywhere. It seems the Indian-influenced jewelry is suddenly everyone's favorite. It's the perfect fashion accessory with most any outfit. Now, at a fraction of the retail price, you can create your own. You receive manmade turquoise stones and attractive mountings. Earring kit: $1.90. Adjustable ring: $1.29. Pendant with chain: $2.10. Others at similar attractive prices.

Zymex publishes a free color catalog illustrated with hundreds of jewelry kits. Includes semi-precious stones, pearls, and cameos.

CAROUSEL CRAFTS

P.O. Box 42549
Houston, Tex. 77042

FAVORITE PERSON PENDANT KIT

You can wear a 2″ oval pendant with any photo serving as the design. It's all made possible by a special kit and a special process.

Kit includes template for cutting any photo into a 2″ oval. This fits into a lovely brooch. Included is a 36″ leather thong. The photo is permanently affixed through the "transfer-it" process. Simply apply the special chemical to the photo. Let set overnight. Then soak the paper as you would a decal. Your photo slides off and onto the kit's brooch. An interesting project. Various-size jewelry kits available. Write for complete prices.

KRICK-KIT CO.

31 North Brentwood St.
St. Louis, Mo. 63105

HEIRLOOM JEWELRY IN NEEDLEPOINT

A quaint bouquet design hand-painted on white canvas. You needlepoint the design, then attach to brooch for wearing. Each kit includes Persian yarn, needle, antique finish metal brooch with jewelry clasp, plus well-written instructions. $8.50.

THE BEADERY

Hope Valley, R.I. 02832

HEIRLOOM JEWELRY KIT

The craft enthusiast can fashion her (his) own necklace today and wear it tomorrow with the Beadery's collection of unique, romantic necklaces and classic cameos. The "Antiqua" in a necklace of amethyst and silver or turquoise and silver; the "Desirade" in coral and silver or jade and silver; the "Margarita" has lapis and silver or turquoise and silver; and the classic "cameo" pendant and bracelet is of hornshell and gold or jade and gold or wedgewood and gold.

Each kit contains Gemocite stones (simulated semi-precious stones) and plated heirloom settings, plus all necessary materials to complete one of the above-mentioned jewelry pieces. $6.

BEADED BRACELET AND EARRING KIT

Whenever you were involved in an arts and crafts class, whether at school, scouts, or camp, you were instructed to work with beads—usually with string—to make a piece of jewelry. With the beaded bracelet and earring kit, you can graduate from stringing beads in a makeshift arts and crafts class to creating beaded jewelry with a professional look.

Each kit features different colors (red-white-and-blue, milk white, clear crystal and crystal jonquil, ice blue and lime) and contains everything to complete one full set. $2.50.

CRAFTOOL CO.
1421 West 240 St.
Harbor City, Calif. 90710

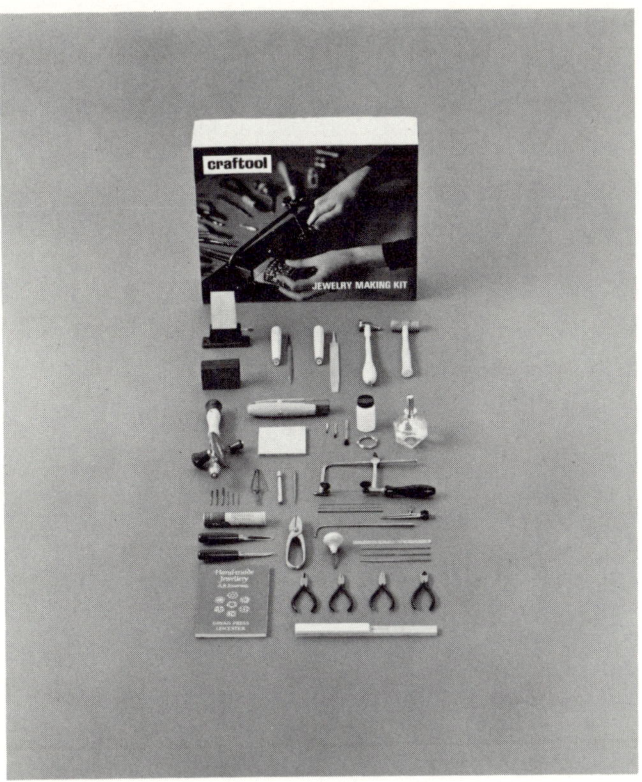

JEWELRY-MAKING KIT

If you're beyond simply gluing a stone to a tie clip, you may be ready for this superkit. All the advanced materials for real jewelry-making. The tools are handy for most types of jewelry setting and work. However, it's perfect for instantly turning sheet copper and silver into delicate jewelry. The price is a steep $119.95 . . . but worthwhile if you're serious.

 bench pin with holder
 jeweler's sawframe and blades
 jeweler's shears
 2 files with handles
 3 assorted needle files
 divider
 scale, 6″
 double end pin vise
 ring vise
 1 curved burnisher
 1 stone pusher
 hand drill
 6 assorted twist drills
 soldering tweezers
 4 assorted professional jeweler's pliers (round-nose plier, chain-nose plier, flat-nose plier, diagonal cutting plier)
 ball peen hammer
 rawhide mallet
 felt hand buff
 red rouge
 blowpipe
 alcohol lamp
 charcoal block
 asbestos soldering pad
 scraper
 soldering flux
 3 assorted flux brushes
 silver solder
 jewelry metal
 scriber
 illustrated Instruction Manual

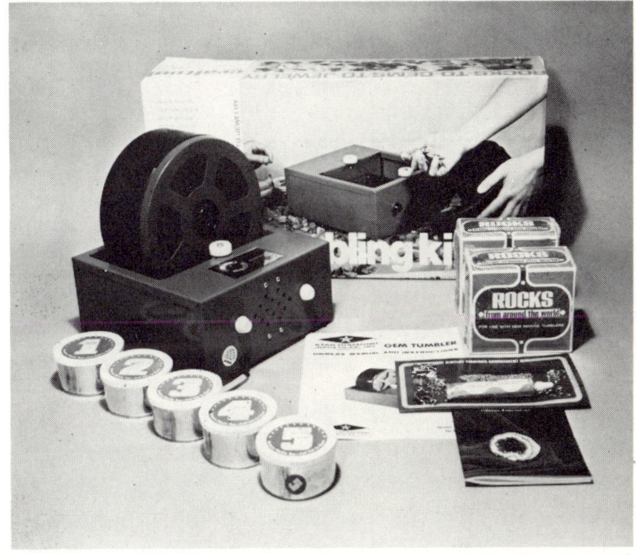

JEWEL STONE-MAKING KIT

Perfect stones for your jewelry pieces. The kit provides all the ingredients to process rough rock into gemstones for setting. Kit includes: heavy-duty, 6-lb. Rolling Star Tumbler with rubber barrel; abrasive grits—course, medium, and fine; polishing compound and polishing pellets; two boxes of assorted rough rocks (2½ lb. per box); Hamilton gold finish jewelry findings; cement and complete Instruction Manual. Simply put the "rocks" in your tumbler with polishing compound and pellets, and out come "gems." $69.95.

ARTIS, INC.
9123 East Tunas Dr.
Temple City, Calif. 91780

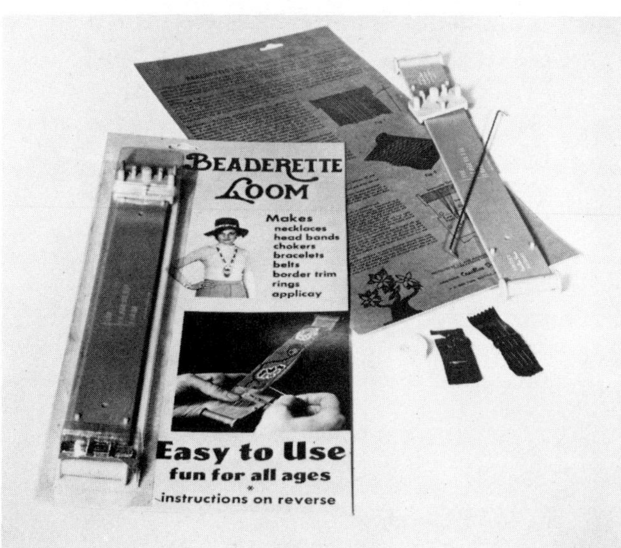

THE BEADERETTE LOOM

How interesting that the American Indian has become a source of imitation through the years. Tents for the contemporary camper, bows and arrows for the hobbyist, herbs for the pharmaceutical companies and, most common, Indian artistry and craft work for those who wish to create. Beaded ornamentation is worn even today among the American Indians; for example, necklaces, belts, headbands, and rings.

Now the Artis company has packaged a bead and loom set (inspired by the age-old native bow loom originally made from tree branches) that not only has a loom but a slider attachment that allows for making continuous bands up to 20″ long. Easy to use, the finished work can be a necklace, belt, headband, ring, choker, or border trim. In addition to the loom with slider, the Beaderette Loom kit contains polyester thread, thin steel needles, needle threader, design ideas, construction manual, and 40g. beads. $4.

SUSAN PRESCOTT
40 East 49 St.
New York, N.Y. 10017

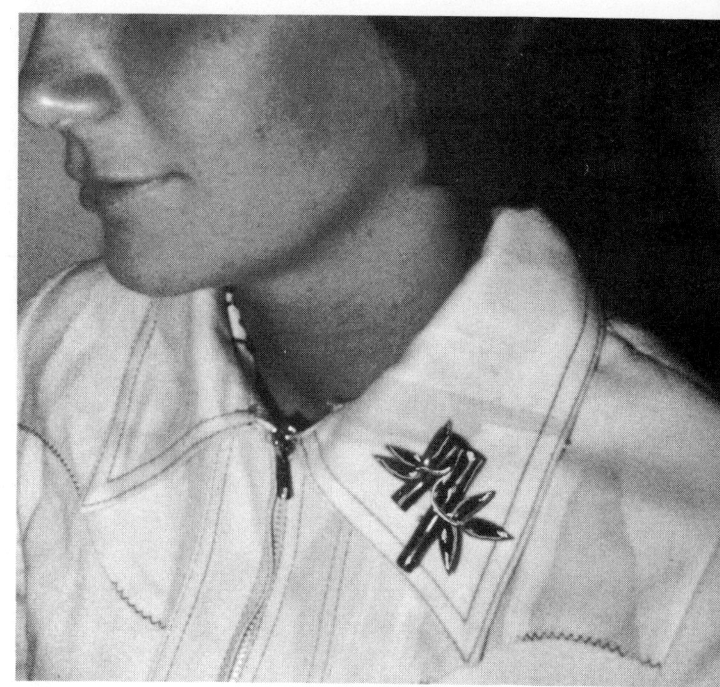

JADE PIN

Make this attractive jade pin and save as much as 75% over retail price. It's an easy assembly job. All of the "Petals" and "Bamboo Woods" are made of genuine jade. These stones are hand-cut in the Orient from selected jade. Pin itself is gold electroplated. You simply glue. $6.

OTHER SOURCES

Bead Game
505 North Fairfax Ave.
Los Angeles, Calif. 90036

Catalog (46 pp., 25¢) lists everything for jewelry-making. Page after page of beads, hoops, hooks, rings, and the solder or glue to put it all together. Prices average to high.

Del Trading Post
Mission, S.D. 57555

Indian jewelry kits. Catalog (50¢).

Donbar Co.
2934 West Fullerton
Chicago, Ill. 60647

A variety of jewelry kits. Plus information on how to sell what you make.

Man or, more often, woman has been sewing cloths together ever since she was ousted from Eden. Until the 18th century, all clothing or decorative sewing was done by hand. In 1755, an Englishman invented the first aid to hand sewing, the double-pointed needle. This eliminated the need to turn the needle around before pushing it back through the cloth. But it was almost a hundred years more before the first sewing machine lightened the burden for all those millions of needle-scarred hands.

Today, with over 2,000 kinds of sewing machines on the market, and the ready-to-wear industry a major global force, a lot of people are rediscovering making their own. In the last ten years, sales of patterns tripled in this country. People (and not just ladies, either) are making clothes, sweaters, blankets, decorative embroidery, cushions—even tapestries—as never before. Many kinds of art needlework have come back into fashion, including needlepoint, knitting, weaving, and crocheting.

Why is everybody sewing? For quality, economy, and satisfaction. As labor becomes more costly, fine handwork can hardly be bought at any price. Not only that, but people in this post-industrial age have discovered all over again that it feels good to make something well with one's own hands. For beginners, there's nothing better than a kit to help you get started. Even experienced needleworkers may prefer kits for the time and money they save. Luckily, the sewing kit explosion parallels the explosion of new interest in needlework. A good sewing kit is like a lesson from an expert, and the tuition is low.

THE STITCHERY

204 Worcester Turnpike
Wellesley Hills, Mass. 02181

CREWEL CALENDAR

The upper part of this crewel calendar shows a basket of strawberries and a pitcher of daisies on a red-checked table cloth. You embroider only the cheerful berry and blossoms design. The lower part is a complete calendar. When the year is over, you can cut away the calendar and have a lovely and lasting embroidered picture. The kit includes design and calendar printed on parchment-colored homespun, embroidery yarns, needle, and directions. Finished size is 14″ × 22″. $6.95.

LEO LION RYA PILLOW

Shaggy Rya yarns and rug yarns are combined on this pillow cover, using the latch hook technique. The pillow cover is a 22″ square canvas, and it is the head and face of wistful, lovable Leo the Lion. The kit includes design in color on rug canvas, yarns for complete pillow top, corduroy backing, and complete directions. (Latch hook not included.) Finished size is 18″ square. Perfect for a den or child's room. $24.95.

BABY OWL TOTE BAG

An adorable baby owl sitting on a grouping of fall leaves, acorns, and weeds decorates the front of this handsome tote bag. The completely assembled tote is made of sturdy brown duck with vinyl lining and inside zipper pocket. The front panel of natural linen-cotton blend fabric zips off completely to make it easy for you to work the design. Handles are an adequate length for hand or shoulder carrying. The kit includes tote, crewel yarns, needles, and directions. Size about 12″ × 14″ × 3″. $34.95.

CREWEL BOOKEND

Here's a clever new embroidery project to make for yourself or for a gift. Each kit includes design on linen, crewel yarns in appropriate colors, needle, sturdy wood bookend with metal base, and instructions. Finished size is 6″ × 6½″. Floral design: $6.95. Birds in a Tree: $6.95.

CREWEL EVENING SKIRT

Flowing embroidered blossoms and leaves flourish on this elegant wraparound evening skirt that can be worn with any number of tops. Kit includes design on wrinkle-resistant, sand-colored polyester-rayon blend fabric, embroidery yarns, needle, and directions for embroidering and assembling skirt (no sewing machine required). Designed by Yvonne Young, the skirt is adjustable to fit any size from 8 through 18. Kit #40-008, rust, gold, green: $27.95. Kit #40-010, blue, gold, green: $27.95.

THUMPER ™ CRIB SHEET AND PILLOW CASE

Here's a colorful gift to make for the new baby. Worked mainly in cross-stitch, the kit includes design on permanent-press polyester and cotton crib sheet and pillow case; embroidery floss in yellow, pink, blue, brown, and green, and instructions. $6.95.

NEEDLEPOINT CHESSBOARD

A handsome needlepoint chessboard that you could also hang on the wall or use as a pillow top. The kit includes 10-mesh canvas, tapestry yarns, needle, and directions, including easy-to-follow chart. Finished size is 16″ × 16″. $7.95.

The Stitchery has one of the largest selections of needlepoint kits and they are constantly adding new items and ideas. Catalog (25¢) is highly recommended.

MARK-ANN MFG.
69 Warren St.
New Rochelle, N.Y. 10801

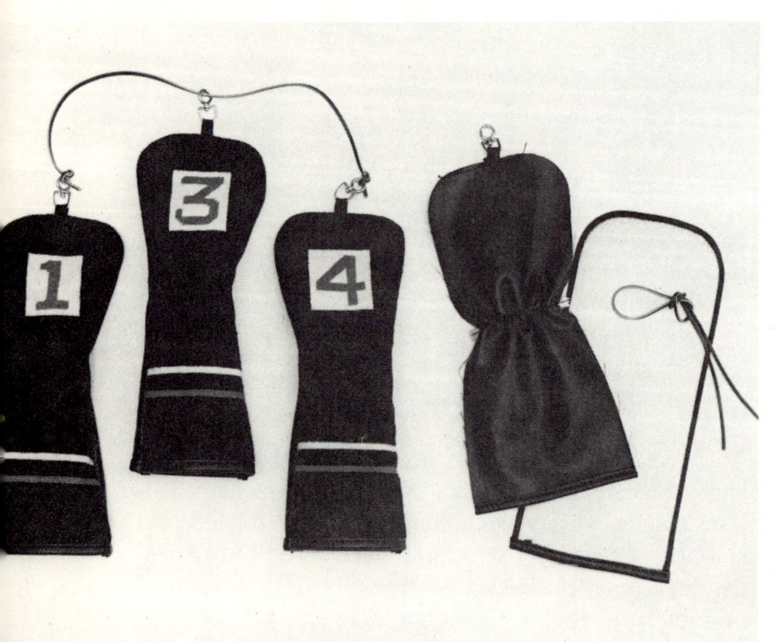
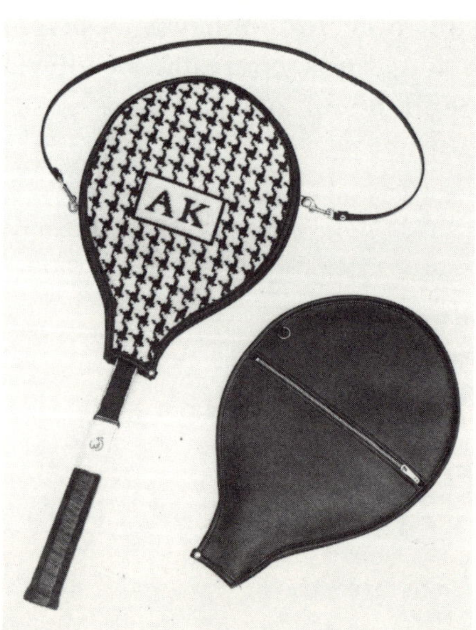

GOLF CLUB COVERS

A perfect project for the weekend golf widow! Show him you care. It may not save your marriage, but it will brighten up his golf clubs. It may even improve his game as he unnerves the competition.

Complete kit consists of three covers. Needlepoint, block, face together, sew (hand or machine), and turn inside out. A quality product. $9.

TENNIS RACKET COVER

The match to the golf covers. As tennis is a social outing as well as a sport, it's important to dress right. That, we assume, should also include your racket. Houndstooth needlepoint pattern with his or her initials. Paternayan wool, needle, instructions, and vinyl backing included. $11.50.

Mark-Ann publishes a small brochure with needlepoint totes, belts, portfolios, and other tennis racket covers (4 pp.). Available free.

YIELD HOUSE
Dept. 262
North Conway, N.H. 03860

PATCHWORK QUILT

We're a little put off by the idea of mail-order patches—traditionally, one accumulated patches from years of sewing leftovers—but we'll admit this is an easy and pleasant way to jump on today's patchwork bandwagon. Yield House's inexpensive kit consists of bright-print cotton squares, which you sew together to make a quilt. Quilt kit requires stuffing. $14.95.

NED ENTERPRISES, INC.
6530 East Spring St.
Long Beach, Calif. 90815

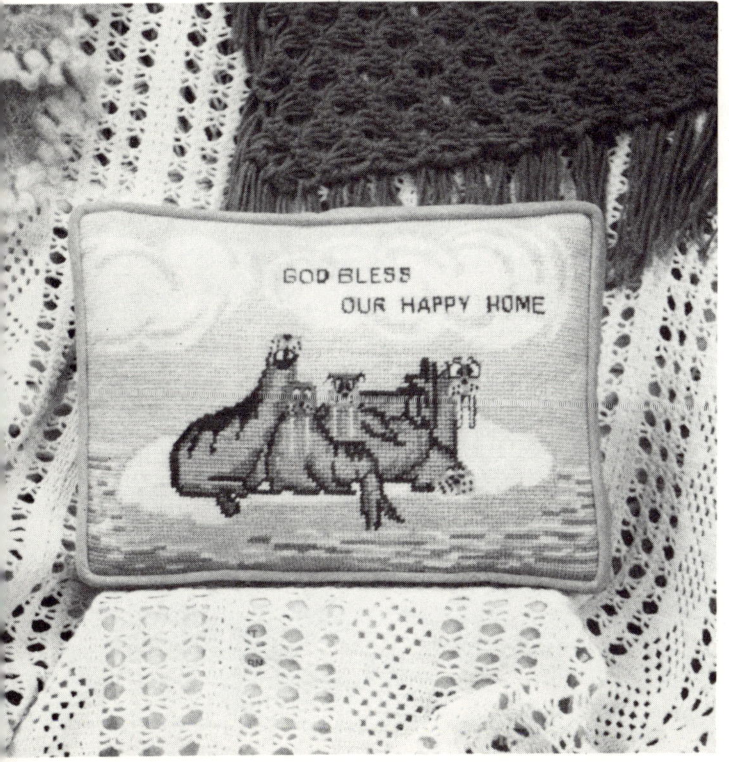

ME MA WALRUS

The walrus is a humorous-looking mammal whose habits are family-oriented. This interesting needlepoint design is sure to bring a grin of pleasure and the hope that your home is as happy as that of the walrus family.

The kit itself comes packaged with Paternayan Persian yarn (the real Persian yarn—no imitations), needle, instructions, all of which is placed in a plastic carry-all bag. $15.

SIGN OF THE PEACOCK
Cashiers, N.C. 28717

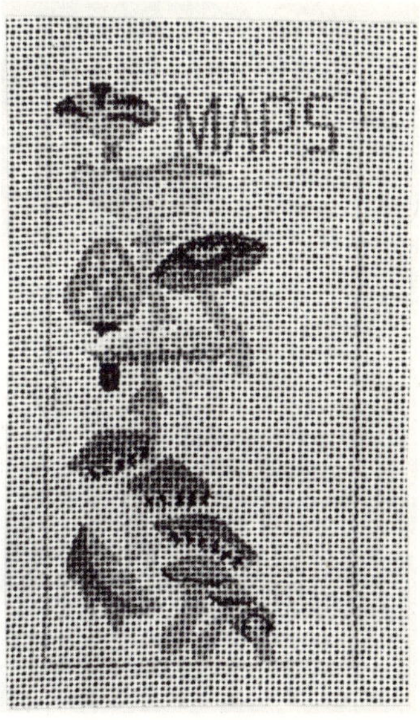

MAP CASE

As you know, there is a wide choice of needlepoint kit designs to cover pillows, to frame and hang on the wall, to decorate a tennis racket cover, to make tote-bags, coaster bottoms, and the like. But you probably never thought of covering those maps, which are strewn about in your auto's glove compartment or the car's back seat, with a charming needlepoint design. Sign of the Peacock has come up with the idea of a map case kit for all needlepoint enthusiasts.

The designs on the case are either orange and yellow mushrooms or a seashell design, and you can choose the background color to complement your car's interior. Suitable backing is included as well as instructions for mounting. $8.50.

A small leaflet (free) of tasteful needlepoint.

DESIGNS BY MEMORY LANE
1015 Liberty Lane
Stillwater, Okla. 74074

DESIGNER NEEDLEPOINT PILLOWS

The "Eye of the Tornado" pillow will add a nice designer note to many a home. Hand-painted canvas in the color of your choice and enough 3-ply Persian yarn to complete a 14″ square pillow. Company has a number of other unique pillow designs to offer. $25. each.

PEACOCK ALLEY

650 Crosswell, S.E.
Grand Rapids, Mich. 49506

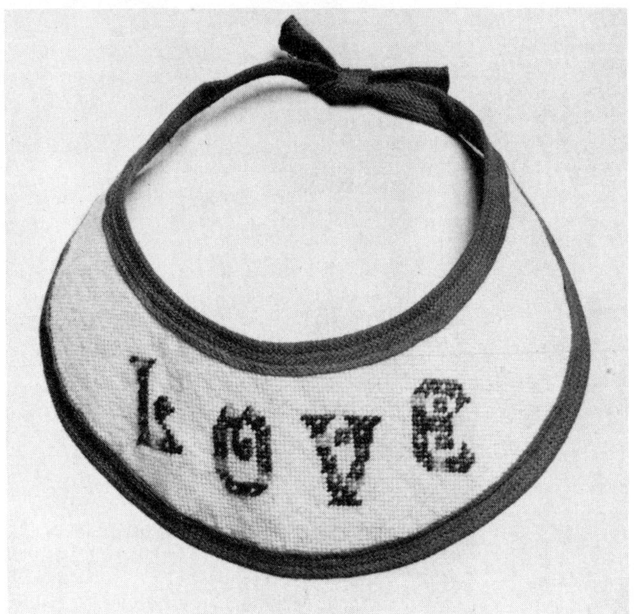

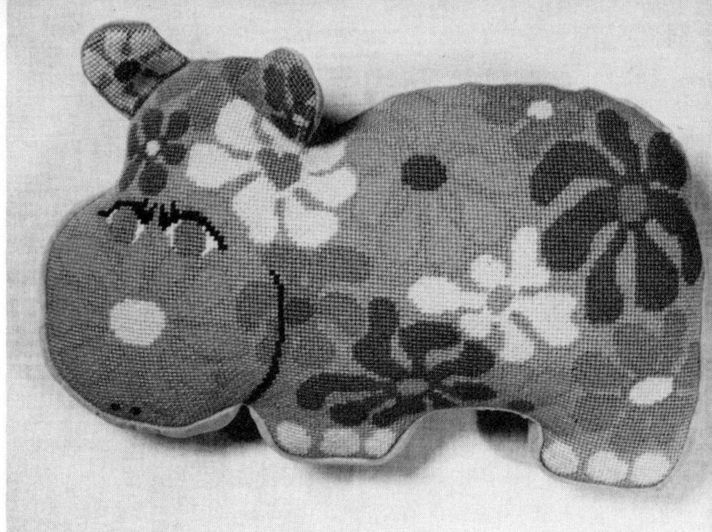

HAPPY HIPPO

A friendly version of the Hippo. Our friend is 15″ × 9″ (12-mesh) in wild color flowers on a hot pink background. The matching fabric background is included. Certain to scare away any sadness. $25.

SPORTS VISOR

What better way to keep the sun out of your eyes? This visor can be a message to your tennis partner or simply a utility eye saver. It comes prefinished with cotton tape on 13-mesh interlock canvas. Kit includes backing material but no yarn. $8.25.

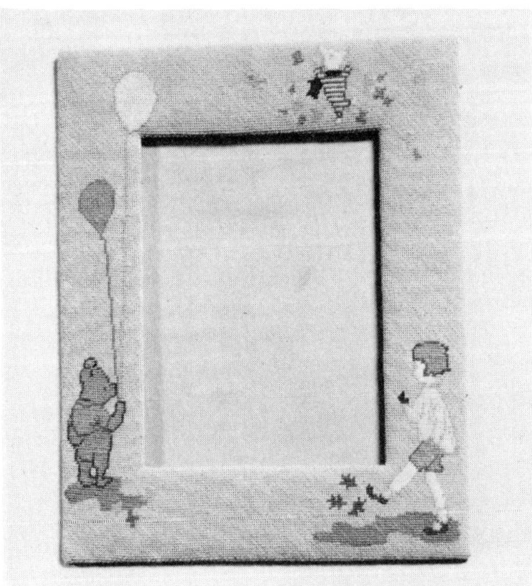

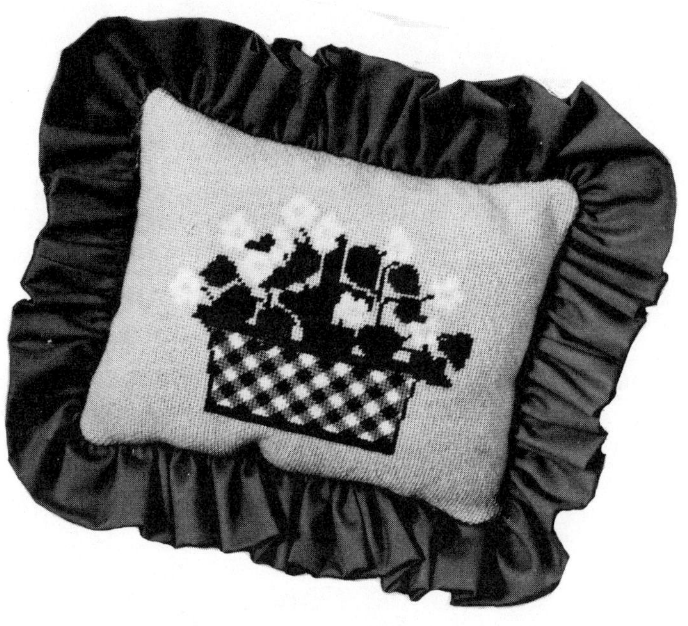

POOH PICTURE

It seems the older we get, the more we delight in Pooh. Now you can combine the Pooh charm in needlepoint with your own picture. The completed Pooh picture is 14″ × 16″ around the outside. The opening is fine for your 8″ × 10″ picture. Your own young Christopher Robin will adore it. $26.50.

STRAWBERRY BASKET

Green, gingham-patterned basket is heaped with dainty strawberries, leaves, and blossoms. Pale green background. Charming when finished with ruffle as shown—8″ × 9½″—14-mesh. Perfect for living room or any young lady's bedroom. $17.50.

Peacock Alley has two catalogs (16 pp. each, $1. for both) with original designs of fine ideas. All their products have been hand-painted on single-mesh, white French canvas. All designs come with fine Persian yarns in good color selections. All kits include needle and complete instructions. They also offer custom designing.

GENERAL CRAFTS CORP.

3031 James St.
Baltimore, Md. 21230

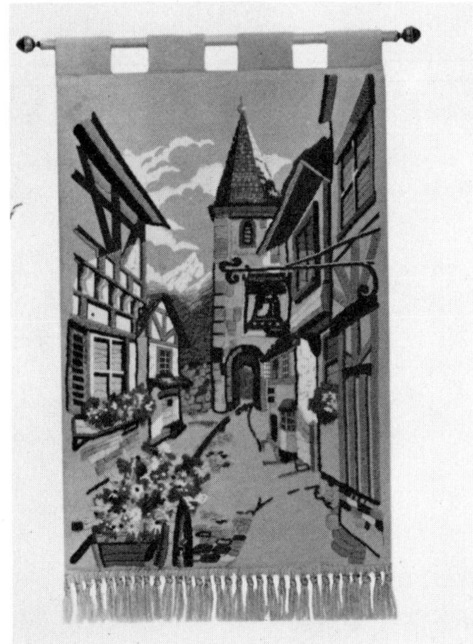

CREWEL TAPESTRY KIT (Swiss Village)

A different crewel project. No need to live in a castle in order to own your own tapestry . . . nor do you have to live in the days of knights.

A crewel tapestry depicting a Swiss village scene will look as attractive on the wall of your home as on the wall of a castle. General Crafts offers a crewel tapestry kit that is complete with everything you need to create your own beautiful and imaginative wall hanging. Simple instructions are included. Design is screened on the fabric background. Six different scenes available. $20. each.

HORCHOW COLLECTION

Box 34862
Dallas, Tex. 75234

NEEDLEPOINT ACRYLIC PARSON'S TABLE

What do you do when you run out of room for needlepoint pillows? You needlepoint a table—an acrylic Parson's table, to be exact. It measures 16″ × 16″ × 16″ and comes complete with its own needlepoint kit, containing a hand-screened canvas, imported wool yarn, a needle, and clear, easy instructions. Kit also includes a wood board on which to mount your finished needlepoint. The board is predrilled, ready to fasten onto the table with small brass nails. Beautiful. $125.

SALTER PATH

Box 346B, RFD 3
Shandy Lane
Wilmington, N.C. 28401

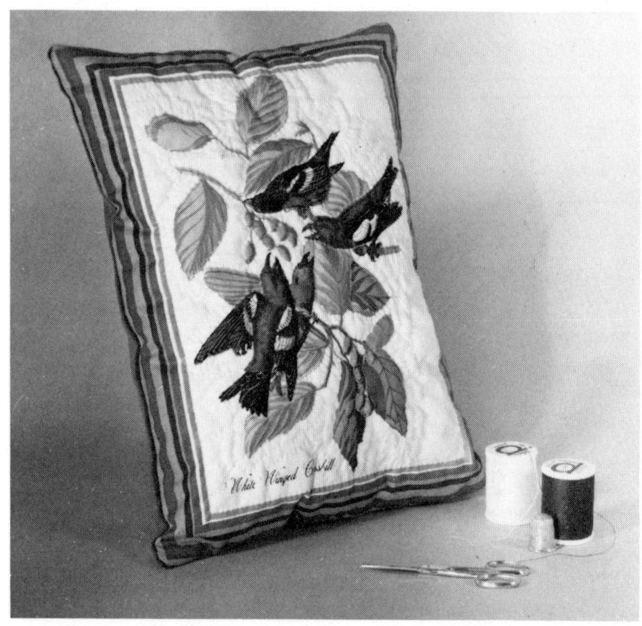

QUILTED PILLOW KIT

Spelling bees, cold New England nights, quilting parties . . . All these situations evoke images of ladies in log cabins with needles, thread, and yards of materials endeavoring to create practical beauty with the art of quilting. This art has never been lost; indeed, a homemade quilted article is always appreciated by giver and receiver alike.

The quilting parties of Colonial times would have been more successful if the participants could have worked with the Salter Path Party Pillow kits. A kit for each lady, complete with everything necessary for quilting: quilting needle, thread, thimble, scissors, and material. The fabrics are hand-screened in England and the backing is velveteen.

Audubon Bird Series or Golfer Series are the kit designs. The completed pillow measures 11″ × 15″ and would look good sitting anywhere in your home. The colors are turquoise, blue, moss green, and brown. $9.50.

THE PATIO

550 Powell St.
San Francisco, Calif. 94108

STITCH-A-NOTE

Now needlepointers can produce their own cards, which certainly shows a great deal more personal thought than a Hallmark card selection. Viewed as making a greeting card, it's a lot of work. But conceived as a needlecraft picture, it's really simple to produce a card that will certainly be kept and that's perfect for framing. Greeting cards come screened, with yarn, needle, instructions, and envelopes. Set of six cards: $13.50.

SUSAN PRESCOTT
40 East 49 St.
New York, N.Y. 10017

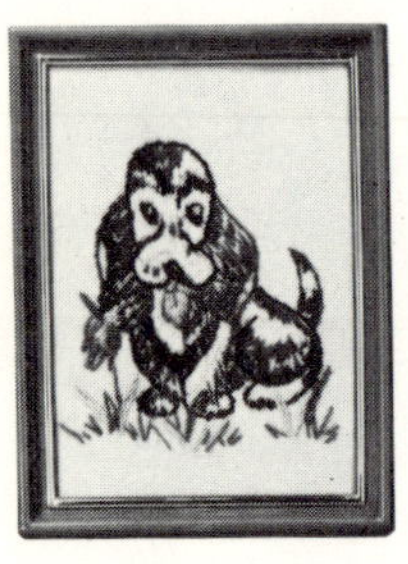
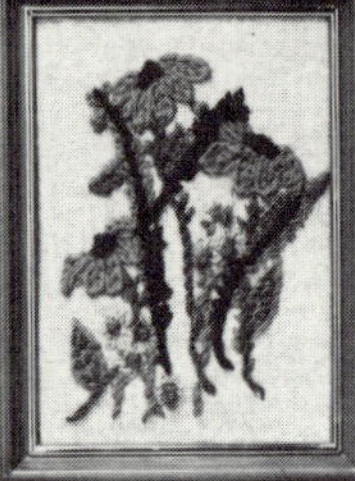
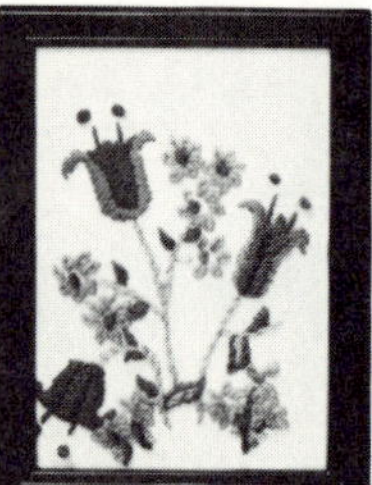
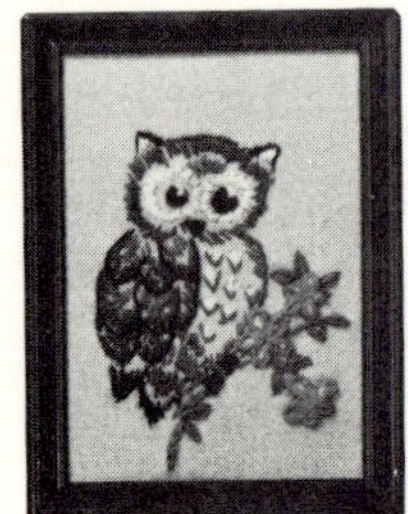
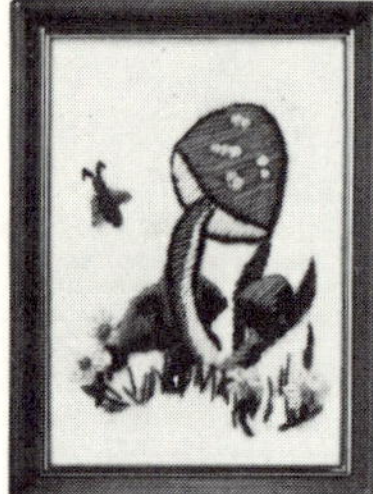
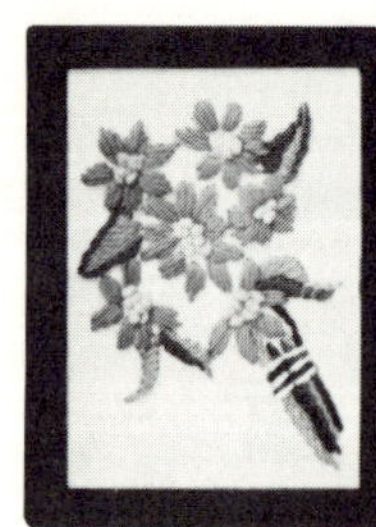

BARGAIN CREWEL KITS

Old American ingenuity in action ... When the crewel/needlepoint boom started, it was only a matter of time until the low-priced competitors jumped in. Prescott makes a line of interesting crewel kits. Each kit includes the screened material, thread, needle, and instructions. Mass production makes it all possible. The firm supplies wholesalers as well as retailers. Lest you think they are selling price only, check out the quality. The designs are interesting (if not award winners) and the product quality is surprisingly good. It's all American-made in good old Brooklyn, New York. Finished canvas, 6″ × 9″. Choice of designs: $1. postpaid (yes, a buck postpaid). All six: $5. postpaid. Schools, summer camps, organizations, write for even bigger savings!

Small catalog (6 pp.) free for postage stamp. Prescott offers a limited line of low-priced crewel kits.

HOUSE OF BELLS
Rustburg, Va. 24588

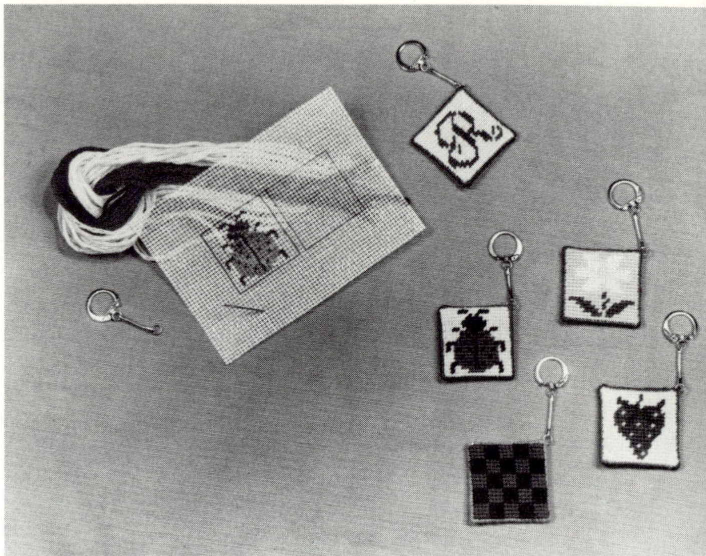

KEY CHAIN KIT

Your common keys take on new beauty when attached to a needlepoint key chain. A simple project and one that will make a nice, inexpensive gift. Your choice of a brightly colored ladybug, strawberry, checkerboard, daisy, or your initial. Completed canvas measures 2″ square. Kit includes painted canvas, yarn, needle, stiffener, and instructions. $3.

JANE SNEAD SAMPLERS
Box 4909
Philadelphia, Pa. 19119

"HARDER I WORK" SAMPLER

The ethic of an earlier age reproduced in a simple kit. Done in cross-stitch using two shades of green and red. $2.60.

American samplers date back to the Pilgrims. In the early days they were small in size as linen looms turned out small cloths. The linen was the wide-mesh variety as early Americans counted threads to create designs. The new samplers, of course, have printed designs or messages, but the basic concept has not changed. Samplers offer a delightful way to create an heirloom with a message of importance to the maker. Catalog free (40 pp.) contains reasonably priced samplers with messages of (perhaps) a better time. Typical samplers include "Give us this day our daily bread" ($3.15); "Character, like embroidery, is made stitch by stitch" ($2.30); "Do unto others . . ." ($2.80); and "God bless America" ($3.50 in red, white, and blue, of course).

MUSEUM SHOP
PHILADELPHIA MUSEUM OF ART

Box 7646
Philadelphia, Pa. 19101

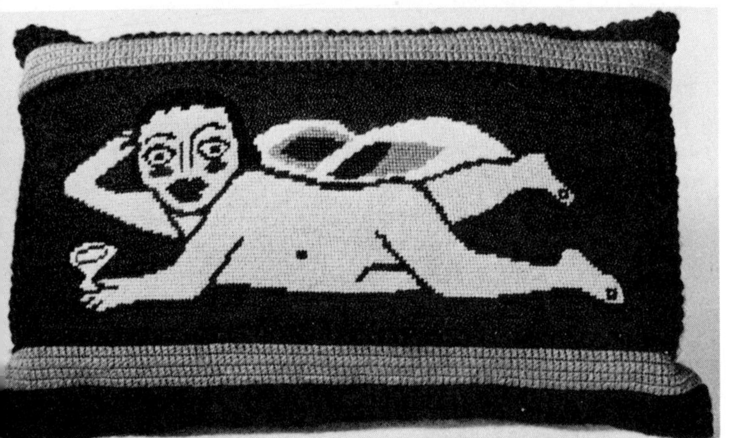

EGYPTIAN COPTIC ANGEL

A pillow kit taken from a tapestry woven circa 4th century A.D. that shows the Greco-Roman influence. Any relation to *Cosmopolitan* magazine's centerfold is purely coincidental. The kit (no backing included) is hand-painted and of excellent quality. $25.

Complete catalog ($1., 24 pp.) of unusual kits including such items as Art Nouveau alphabet patches from 1900, baptismal certificates, and Guatemalan textile designs. Strongly recommended for those interested in kits not usually available at retail.

COULTER STUDIOS, INC.

138 East 60 St.
New York, N.Y. 10022

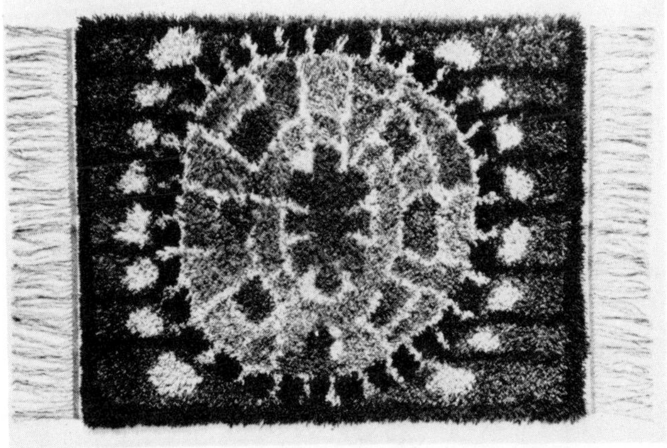

RYA RUGS

At direct-from-importer prices, Coulter Studios offers beautiful Rya rug kits that you can make on your lap, no frames or looms needed. Just thread your large eye needle and begin to make ghiordes knots (the same knots found in precious Oriental rugs). The knots cannot pull out and the rugs can be dry cleaned or vacuumed with complete safety.

Each kit contains: a woven wool and linen backing; all the wool you need to complete the pattern of your choice; a chart of wool colors and an easy-to-follow graph of the artist-designed pattern, needles, and full instructions. As a bonus, Coulter starts the first five or six knots for you. If you would like to choose your own pattern and individual colors, Coulter will make a custom graph at a slight cost.

Kit designs range from graphics to flowers in bright to subtle colors in a large variety of sizes. And if you want to start off slowly, why not pick a Rya Pillow kit and give your couch a face lift.

24″ × 27″ Rya rug kit	$ 65.35
79″ × 118″ Rya rug kit	582.00
39″ × 59″ Rya rug kit	157.20
Pillow kits	20.00

LILLIAN VERNON

510 South Fulton Ave.
Mt. Vernon, N.Y. 10550

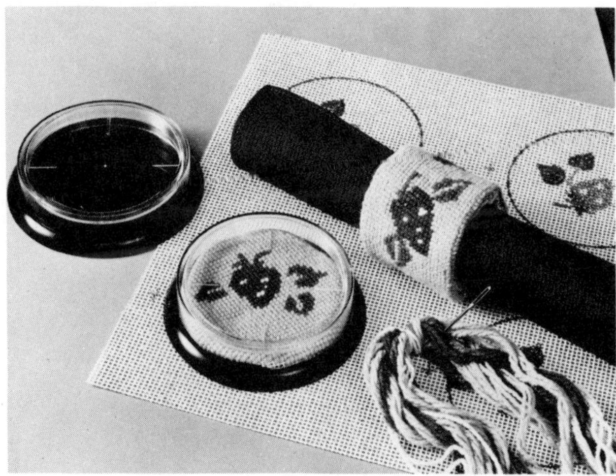

NEEDLEPOINT HOSTESS HELPERS

Strawberry-sweet coasters and napkin rings—easy enough for a beginner, lovely enough for an expert to give with pride. Everything is included—hand-painted canvas, Persian-type yarn, needle, instructions. Coasters are 3¾″ and have clear plastic tops. Needlepoint kit for four coasters: $5.98. Needlepoint kit for four napkin rings: $4.50.

HALBERTS

Bath, Ohio 44210

FAMILY COAT OF ARMS

The ultimate needlepoint project. Tell Halberts

your name and they send back a needlepoint canvas with your coat of arms. Kit includes 11″ × 14″ canvas, needle, and yarn in the proper heraldic colors. $14.95.

CONTEMPORARY QUILTS
5305 Denwood Ave.
Memphis, Tenn. 38117

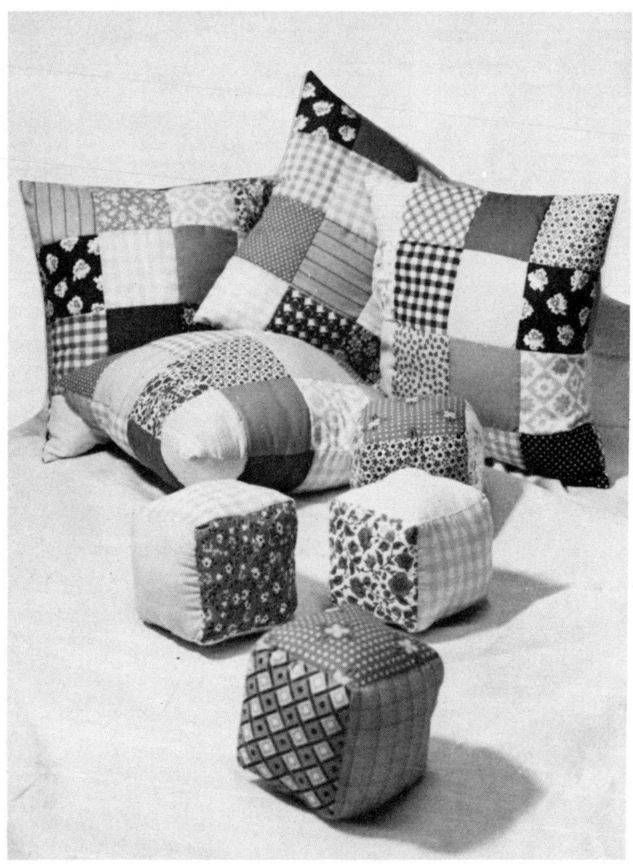

THE QUILT LADY'S PATCHWORK KIT

A popular and appealing motif of late is the return to the past when life and its values were supposedly more simple and meaningful. This interest in yesteryear has generated a desire for patchwork things, particularly those with old-fashioned patterns, timeless in their beauty and design quality.

Even though the company's name, Contemporary Quilts, denotes modernity, the Quilt Lady's Patchwork Kit picks up this theme of the past. The kit includes 96 precut 4″ squares of cotton calico, gingham, and broadcloth; 1 yd. lining; 1 spool thread; needle; cord; and complete, easy-to-follow instructions. With the old-fashioned patchwork patterns you can make toys, pillows, aprons, and/or a tote bag; you can create these lovely items by hand or machine. The instruction book includes lots of patch ideas. $8.

IN-STITCHES
325 East 18 St.
New York, N.Y. 10003

KEYBOARD NEEDLEPOINT

Look no longer for that extra key—attractively display them. You receive a board, 5 hooks, No. 10 canvas, yarn needles, and directions. When complete, you have a decorative and useful wall accessory. $7.50.

SIGN OF THE ARROW
9740 Clayton Rd.
St. Louis, Mo. 63124

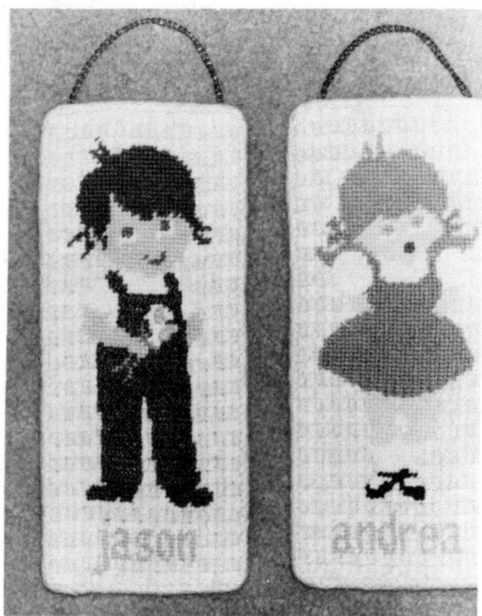

PERSONALIZED DOG TAG

Stitch this personalized dog tag for the little people in your life. Imported canvas with a gingham backing. Alphabet for any name. Available in red on blue—you choose the hair color of your little one. $3.95.

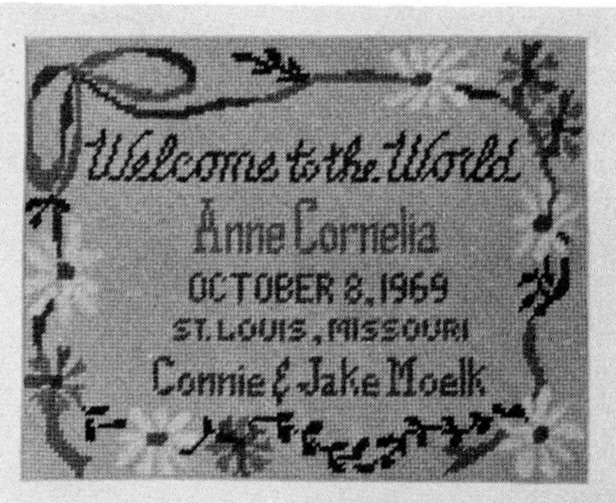

BABY'S BIRTH CERTIFICATE

This "Welcome to the World" birth certificate will look lovely in any child's room. Bordered by daisies

and batchelor buttons, it is the ultimate baby gift. Complete kit with yarn, mesh, etc. Finished size 8″ × 10″. $10.

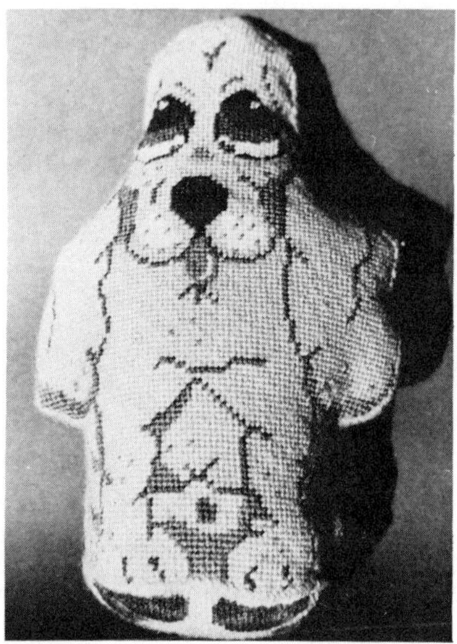

PUPPY DOG

"Clancy" is a lovable pup. He makes a fine pillow, handbag, or toy. Fourteen-mesh canvas for front, back, or base. Easy to assemble. $10.

Sign of the Arrow is a nonprofit needlework shop staffed by volunteers. Proceeds from the store and mail-order business go to sponsor a craft school (Arrowmont) in Gatlinburg, Tennessee, and a mental health service (Cure and Counseling) in St. Louis. Their catalog (8 pp., free) is black-and-white but contains many worthwhile items. The cause, of course, is worthwhile as well.

NEEDLEPOINT, INC.
2308 Halmson St.
Kansas City, Mo. 64041

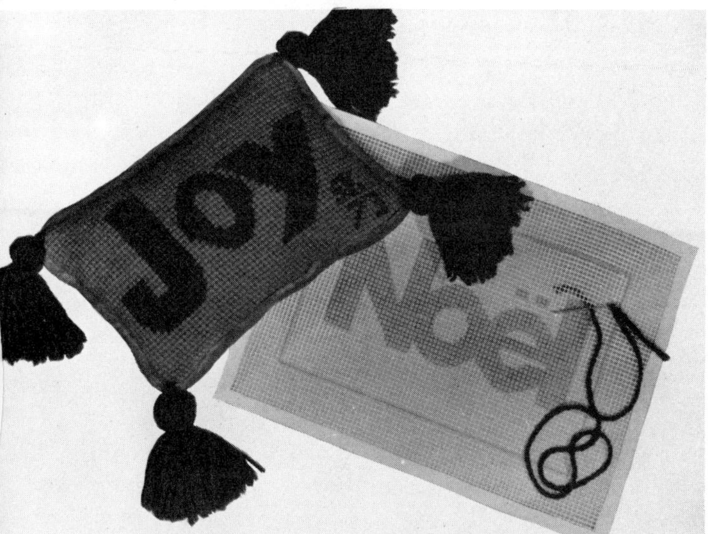

CHRISTMAS TASSEL PILLOW

A lovely Christmas gift that shows your thought-fulness all year long. A truly first-quality product. Only 100% pure virgin long staple wool (4-ply construction) is used, and the canvas itself seems exceptionally well made. The red velveteen backing, cord, and tassels complete this interesting project. $22.50.

Needlepoint, Inc. offers an array of monogrammed canvases including:

> *1. Contemporary letters, in contemporary colors.*
> *2. Old English, in traditional colors.*
> *3. Western, Gay Nineties style.*
> *4. Art Deco, stylized twenties and thirties.*
> *5. Shadowed contemporary letters.*
> *6. Shadowed twenties and thirties stylized letters.*
> *7. Hebrew letters.*
> *8. Chinese letters.*

On special order (in 48 hours) they can make up any 3-letter monogram such as initials, school name, etc.

STITCH WITCH
P.O. Box 228
Old Greenwich, Conn. 06870

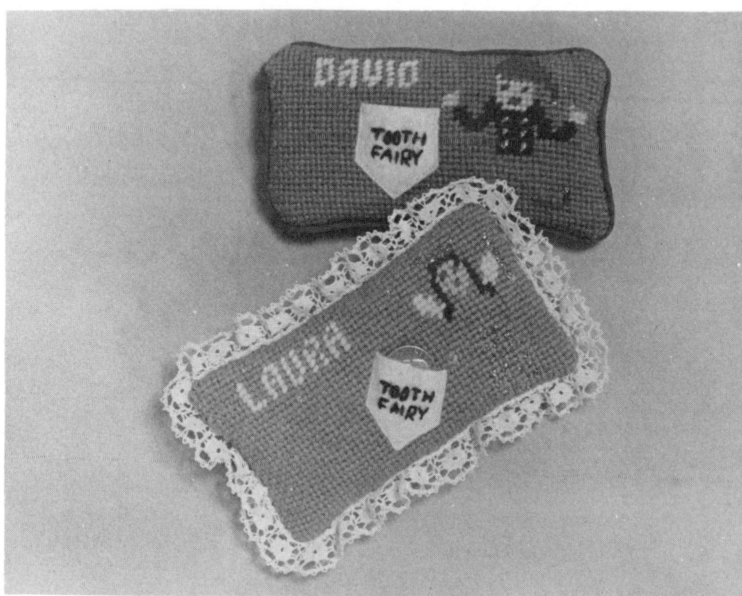

TOOTH FAIRY

Tiny needlepoint pillow with pocket that holds tooth and replacement money. For girls, fairy with metallic gold polka dots on dress, metallic gold crown, wand, and slippers. For boys, green elf, red hat and shoes, metallic gold buttons, shoe and hat tassels on blue background. Approximate finished size 3″ × 5½″. Kit includes No. 10 mono canvas, yarn, needle, design graph, alphabet chart, detailed instructions, lace or piping, and pillow backing. You supply the cash from the tooth fairy. Specify boy or girl when ordering. $4.75.

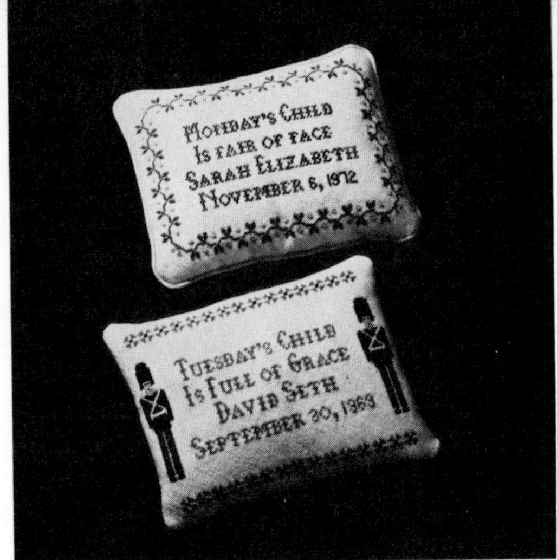

YOUR FAVORITE CHILD (of any age)

For personalizing your favorite child's or friend's name and birthday, Stitch Witch has fourteen kits available for boys or girls that specify Monday through Sunday in a needlepoint for framing or pillow. Finished size 9″ × 12″.

Kit includes No. 13 mono canvas, yarn, needle, alphabet guide, and detailed instructions with enlarged graphic design for easy following. Floral pink and green for girls, blue and red-jacketed guardsmen with a touch of red in the blue border for boys. Both with off-white background. Specify girl or boy, and day of week when ordering. If day is unknown, send month, date, and year and they can supply the correct day. $13.95.

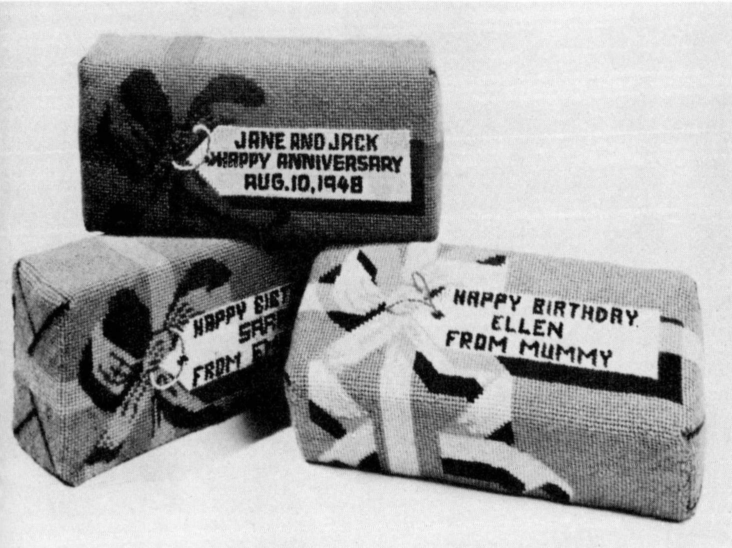

THE PRESENT (for all occasions)

Needlepoint cover for a common brick—it becomes a doorstop, bookend, paperweight, or just a pretty thing. It can say "Happy Birthday," "Happy Anniversary," or "Merry Christmas." Six color combinations—blues/greens, rusts/oranges, reds/pinks, silvery blues, warm golds, or reds/greens. Kit includes No. 13 mono painted canvas, yarn, needle, detailed instructions, alphabet guide, and felt bottom. Specify color choice when ordering. $13.95.

BUTTERFLY CO.
48–52 Clearview Expressway
Bayside, N.Y. 11364

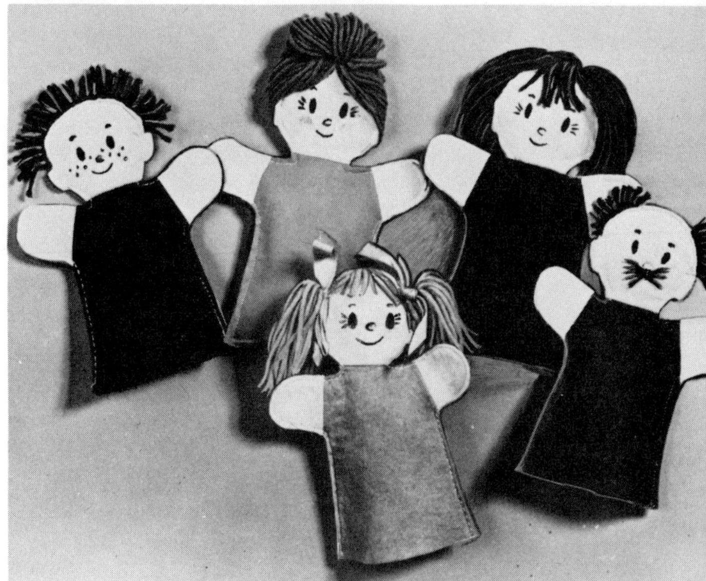

PUPPET PEOPLE

A world of fun as varied as your imagination. The kit combines simplicity of design and construction. Each is a two-faced figure (Happy/Sad) that will delight any child and many an adult. The set of five is made in brilliantly colored felt with printed faces and yarn hair. Sure to bring hours of joy. $7.98

Butterfly is a small business venture of some lovely people. They make first-rate products at fair prices. Catalog (16 pp., 25¢) has some unusual sewing ideas.

HISTORIC HOUSE
1810 Mackenzie Dr.
Columbus, Ohio 43220

FAMILY TREE KIT

Now you can display your family heritage to all. The multi-color design is worked in cross-stitch and is sure to become an instant heirloom. Kit includes floss, printed linen, and instructions. $4.95

HOLUBAR CO.
Box 7
Boulder, Colo. 80302

CARIKIT ROADBAG LUGGAGE

You can pack a lot of clothes or gear in this bag—it's a roomy 26″ × 12″. Although it looks small, the duffle shape accommodates more things with every shove. You make it all yourself. Kit includes precut material, thread, and step-by-step instructions. The material is long-wearing, durable nylon fabric. $16.95.

TONI TOTES OF VERMONT

Route 100
South Londonderry, Vt. 05155

BRASS BUCKLE BELTS

All ready for stitching and ready-to-wear when the last stitch is in. Your choice of men's or women's belts with interesting needlepoint designs. Everything is complete—you simply do the stitchery. Just let them know your waist size. What better way to show off your work than around your waist? $13.

Company catalog (free) has a variety of interesting purses, portfolios, totes, and belts at realistic prices.

MAGIC NEEDLE

44 Green Bay Rd.
Winnetka, Ill. 60093

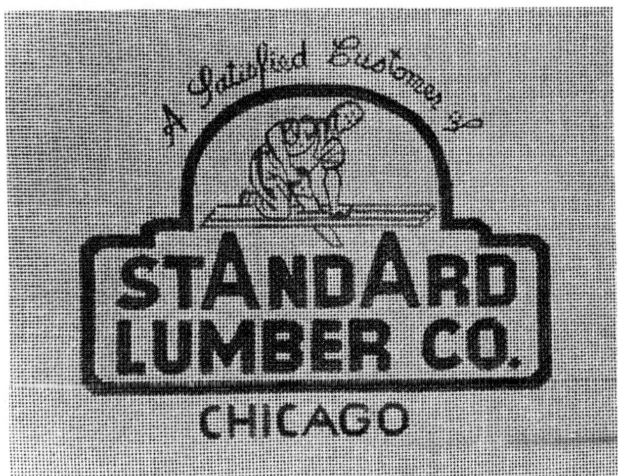

CORPORATE LOGO NEEDLEPOINT

What hard-working businessman could resist his company logo in needlepoint? Perfect for junior executive out to impress the boss who's coming to dinner. Simply send the logo from letterhead to Magic Needle. They paint on No. 14 screen and supply materials. $5.

Magic Needle has an interesting catalog (free) of hand-painted kits and many original designs that we have not seen elsewhere. Especially impressive are their postage stamp reproductions that would warm the heart of any philatelist.

F.A.O. SCHWARZ

Fifth Ave. at 58 St.
New York, N. Y. 10022

PATCHWORK PILLOW

Combine the whimsy of patchwork with the richness of needlepoint in a giant 12″ square pillow. Most needlepoint pillow kits as attractive as this one cost a good deal more and many are harder to fol-low. This is a bargain project that is easy enough for a ten-year-old. Kit contains Orlon yarn in six colors, hand-screened canvas, cotton backing, needle, and instructions. (3 lb.) $7.95.

ELSA WILLIAMS, INC.

West Townsend, Mass. 01474

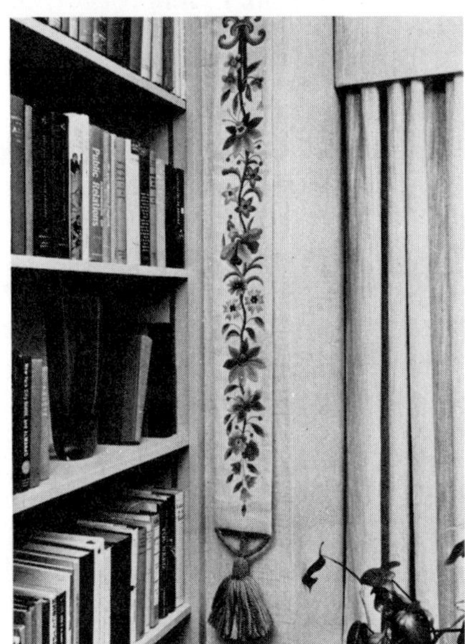

HANG IT THERE!

For a touch of nostalgic charm, this crewel-embroidered bell pull, in classic garland-of-flowers design hand-printed on linen, adds a note of yesterday's elegance to today's home. It's 7½″ × 48″ and comes with genuine crewel wools, needle, and directions. $8.50.

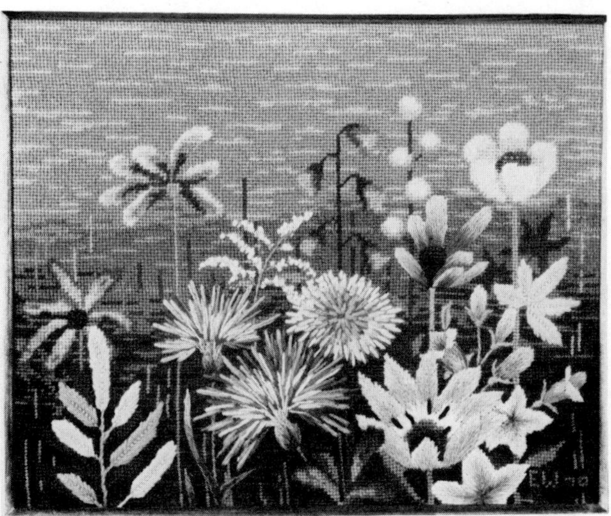

FOREVER IN BLOOM

A field bouquet captured on canvas. The design by Elsa Williams calls for both crewel and tapestry yarn. The combination of surface embroidery stitches for the flowers and canvas-worked tent stitches for the background give this flower picture an exciting three-dimensional quality. Finished picture size is 14″ × 9″ and comes with genuine crewel and tapestry yarn, needle, and directions. $35.

Elsa Williams is one of the great names in stitchery. One of the first to foresee the current needlework explosion, she founded her own company in 1949 and has been supplying needlework buffs in fifty states with quality crewel and needlepoint kits and designs ever since.

As an artist she is deeply rooted in tradition. Whether it's an Elsa Williams original or a piece she has meticulously interpreted from a museum treasure—such as the crewel embroidery adapted from an antique screen which hangs in the White House—she prefers classic, timeless designs that mellow with age.

Elsa Williams is the author of three best-selling books on the needle arts: Heritage Embroidery *(New York: Van Nostrand Reinhold, 1967), a glossary of stitches and valuable reference for crewel devotees;* Creative Canvas Work *(1971), an introduction to needlepoint techniques; and* Bargello Embroidery *(1967), with directions for doing more than fifty geometric needlepoint patterns.*

Long a popular lecturer at professional needlework seminars across the country, Ms. Williams recently established the Elsa Williams School of the Needle Arts at West Townsend, Massachusetts, where novices as well as experienced students learn all aspects of creative needlework in concentrated, one-week courses. Anyone interested in knowing more about this unique live-in school can write for a descriptive folder to: Elsa Williams School of the Needle Arts, West Townsend, Mass. 01474.

For a catalog of her needlepoint work, write to Elsa Williams at the above address.

PATCH-IT DESIGNS
Waitsfield, Vt. 05673

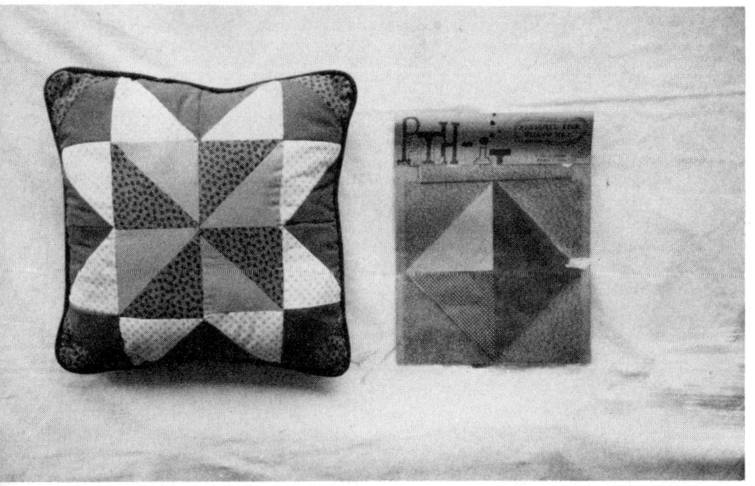

PATCH KITS

In the heart of the Green Mountains, everyone's cutting up patches—calico, polka dot, stripes, and solids. Patch-it Designs offers a delightful variety of reasonably priced patchwork kits. Choose from four quilt designs—pinwheel star, giant tumbling blocks, crescent, and star in cradle size ($6.95) to king size ($46.95). Also available in single, double, and queen. You provide the body and filling.

PATCH-IT has a selection of lovely puffy pillows, including their bicentennial "Spirit of '76" ($6.00). And for the children, a collection of patchwork cuddlies: Calico bird ($2.50), Bossie the Cow ($5.00), Timothy the Turtle ($5.00), or Happy 'n Sad Teddy ($4.50). For the kitchen: An apron kit ($6.50) and potholder kit with enough patches for two potholders ($2.50). And, if you're bored with your favorite striped tie, why not sew fifty precut patches together from their tie kit ($6.50), and do something mad in your new Patch-It tie? All kits contain well-written instructions.

CROSSROADS
P.O. Box 1372
Burbank, Calif. 91507

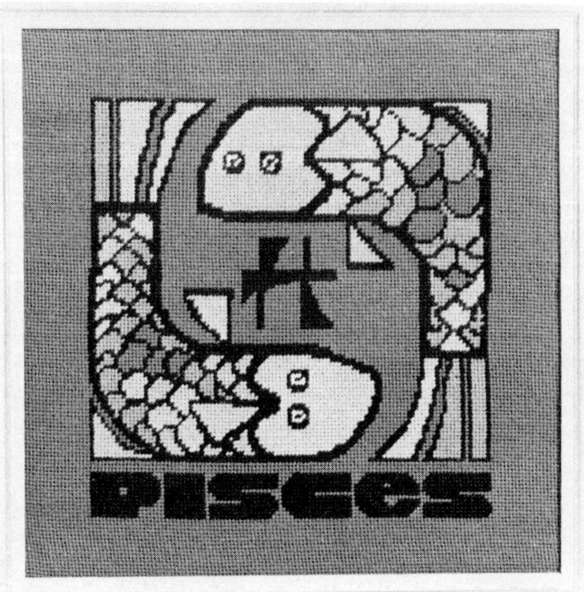

ZODIAC NEEDLEPOINT

Show your sign. If you're a dynamic Scorpio or a determined Virgo, tell the world. Kit includes all materials with highly stylized zodiac symbols. 9″ × 9″: $8. 15″ × 15″: $16. Catalog (free) is 4 pp. of fine four-color photography of interesting needlecraft items.

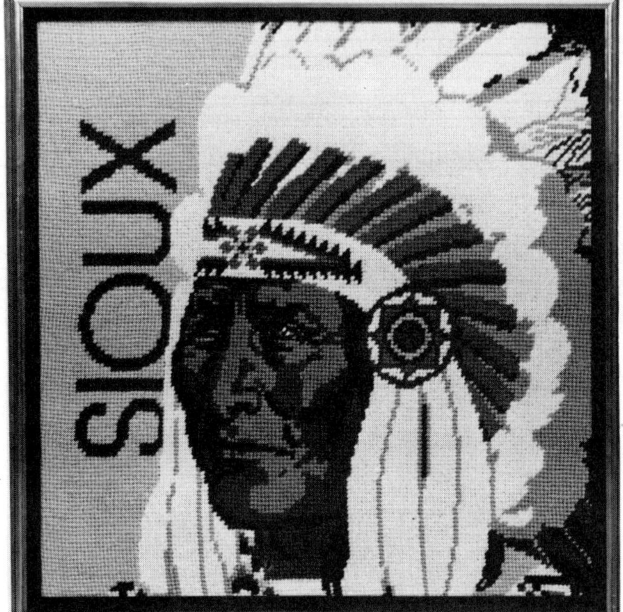

INDIAN NEEDLEPOINT

The majestic American Indian in his finest wardress colors. From his intense eyes to the flowing feathers, this is a fine picture when completed. A popular subject well crafted. $16.

STUDIO KNITTING, INC.
129 West 22 St.
New York, N.Y. 10011

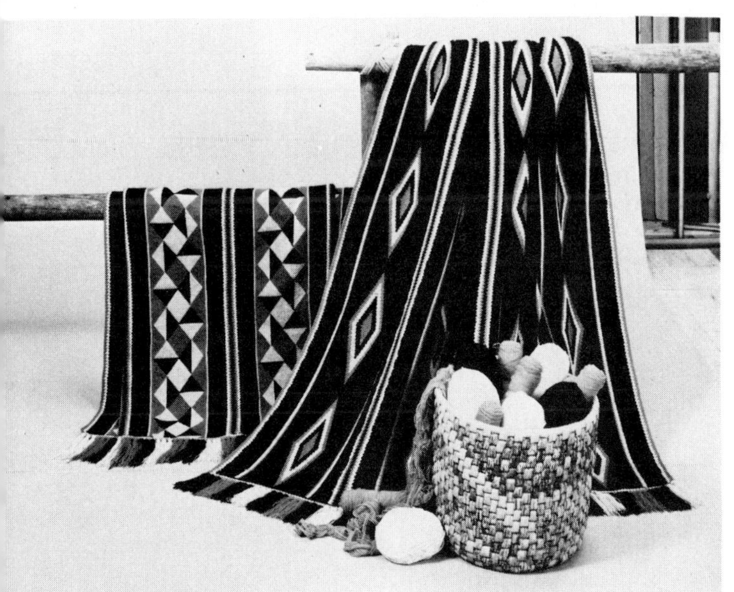

AFGHANS

American Indians used blankets for many purposes, and with today's interest in Indianlore and knitting, it's no wonder that this afghan kit has become a great success. It would take an Indian weaver months to make an afghan like this, you can make it in a few days. When finished, the afghan measures 48″ × 60″ with 4½″ tassels. Available in Mohawk or Navajo patterns, the kit includes 100% Dupont Orlon yarn, which means it is machine-washable and machine-dryable. With the cost of yarn today, it's a value at $28.00.

NU-VENTURE
9610 East 29 St.
Tucson, Ariz. 85710

INDIAN DESIGN NEEDLEPOINT

A fine collection of traditional American Indian designs in needlepoint kits. Assortment includes colorful patterns such as Hopi Indian rain bird and Acoma Indian water bird. They are all original designs. Each kit contains first-quality No. 10 penelope canvas, and fine tapestry yarn. Also included are complete instructions necessary for easy completion of kit and needle. All designs are hand-screened on the canvas. (14″ × 14″ when finished.) $14.95.

THE RUG HUT
6 University Ave.
Los Gatos, Calif. 95030

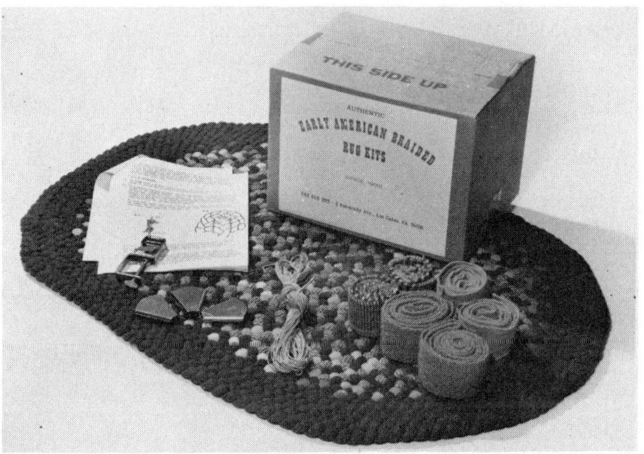

RUG BRAIDING KIT

Make a 2′ × 3′ braided rug to add color to any room in the house. All too many kits require extra parts and much experience, but this is not the case here. The Rug Hut has truly put it all together. You get 6 lb. New Heavy Coat Wool in 2″ strips, 2″ braid-aids, 2 lacing needles, twine, and clamp. The most complete kit we've looked at in the braided rug field. Available in orange/brown or red/brown. A value at $21.50 postpaid.

KRICK-KIT CO.
31 North Brentwood
St. Louis, Mo. 63105

ADDRESS BOOK COVERS

Throw away those leatherette address books, here's one you'll be proud to keep by the telephone. A brightly colored pink carnation cover. The complete kit, with Persian yarn, $7.50. Catalog ($2.) includes dozens of exciting different designs.

CREWEL WORLD
Box 303
Huntingdon Valley, Pa. 19006

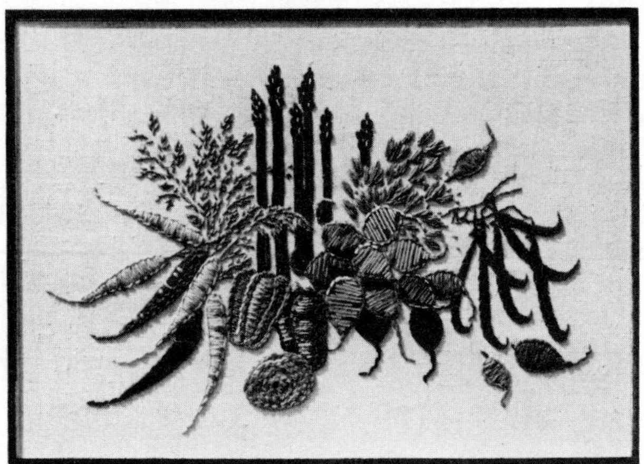

CREWEL PICTURES

A wonderful feeling for form, design, and color exists in these truly exceptional quality kits that are still in the reasonable price range. Crewel World kits are all produced and designed in their own studios. The patterns are clearly stamped for ease of embroidery and instructions are particularly well written. Cardinal, fruit, or vegetable kits: $9.95 each, complete. Catalog is free. Company has interesting designs and offers exceptionally quick order fulfillment.

ERICA WILSON
717 Madison Ave.
New York, N.Y. 10021

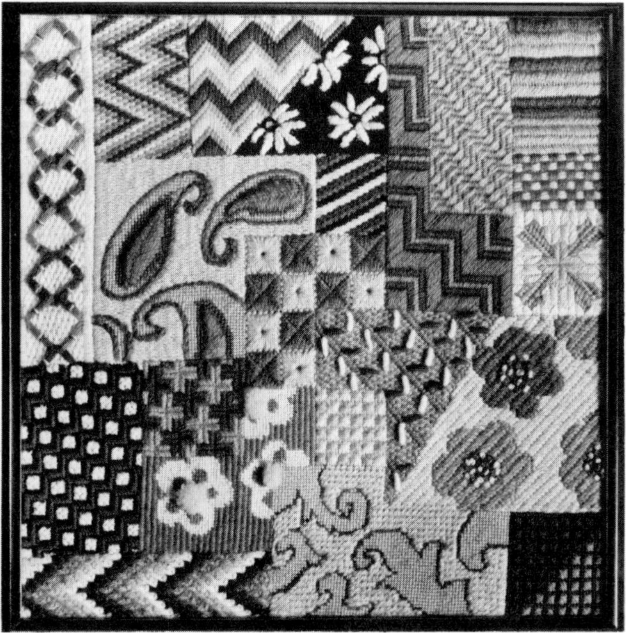

CREWEL POINT COURSE

Erica Wilson is the country's acknowledged leader in the field of needlework. She also happens to be a best-selling author, an originator of imaginative needlework kits, the head of a thriving mail-order business, a creative designer, and a television star on her own show of needlework instruction.

In fact, she deserves much of the credit for reviving the popularity of needlepoint. The "course" illustrated is but one of the five correspondence courses (others: Beginning and Advanced Crewel, Bargello, and Stump Work). You learn thirty different techniques of crewel and needlepoint on canvas, plus you return your sampler (16" square) for criticism. Materials included: Persian yarn, imported canvas, and step-by-step course book. $61 including handling.

KALEIDOSCOPE BARGELLO

This geometric design is worked four ways. The kit includes Persian yarn in shades of gold with white, imported canvas (14" × 14" when completed), and complete instructions. $22.

TIMMIE WILLIE IN A PEA POD

Erica's delightful adaptation in crewel of a Beatrix Potter animal. Design in pale greens and yellows on 8" × 10" linen with instructions. $11.95.

Catalog free. No one can be serious about needlepoint without an Erica Wilson catalog. Although the prices are higher than usual, they are quality products. First-quality right down to the instructions. Erica says she still writes all the instructions herself, with the help of her husband, Vladimir Kagen (the world-famous furniture designer). If you like Erica's styles but the price seems high, she also designs budget-priced kits for Columbia-Minerva, widely available at retail stores. (See Clubs section for details on her Creative Needlework Society.)

SPENCER GIFTS
Spencer Bldg.
Atlantic City, N.J. 08411

MONOGRAMMING KIT

Just in case you forget who you are, it's nice to have your initials on towels, linens, even clothing and baby things. This simple and inexpensive kit includes stamper and ink pad with complete alphabet of cross-stitch initials, plus threads and needle. The Regular kit has letters ¾" high; Deluxe kit, letters 1½" high; Twin kit, letters in both sizes. Regular: $2.99. Deluxe: $3.99. Twin: $5.99. No additional items required.

THE ORANGERIE

P.O. Box 472
South Laguna, Calif. 92677

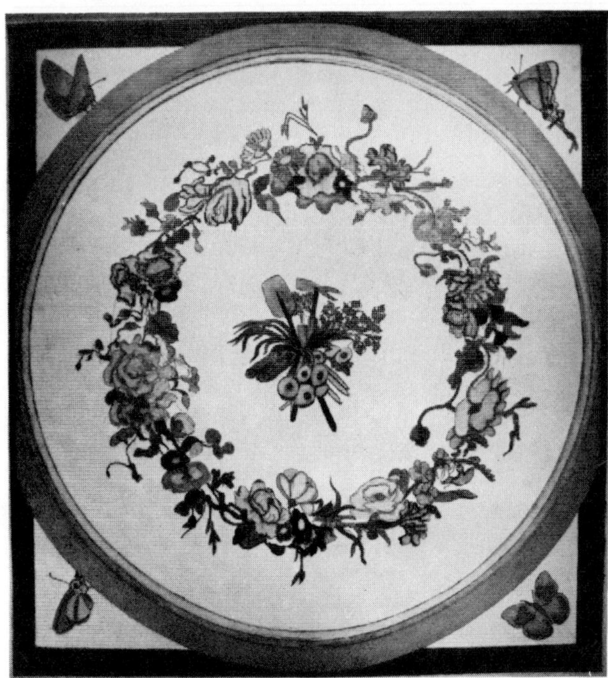

RUG CANVAS

A most attractive rug. The black-and-white photography cannot capture the design beauty of this piece. Its gentle floral wreath is in garden colors. The center is a medallion of garden vegetables. The border is in brown and blue. Hand-painted on canvas, 4′ × 4′. $250.

The Orangerie has a number of rug and needlepoint kits, all hand-painted on canvas. We are impressed with their unique copyrighted designs. Leaflet (free).

HANOVER HOUSE

Hanover, Pa. 17331

NOT-SO-EARLY AMERICAN SAMPLERS

This mail-order house offers five folksy messages that you embroider and hang on your wall or give as gifts. The "be" in "To have a friend you must be one" is a little embroidered bee: ditto for the "umbrella" in "Let a smile be your . . ." Get the picture? Also available are: "If mother says no—ask grandmother"; an attractive birth certificate with a vaguely Pennsylvania Dutch flavor, a good baby gift; and a "God give me the serenity" prayer. Each sampler has delicate flower decorations and other appropriate doo-dads adorning the message. Bee and Umbrella: $2.50 each. Grandmother: $2.95. Birth certificates: $3.95. Prayer: $3.95.

OTHER SOURCES

Barnes & Blake
148 East 28 St.
New York, N.Y. 10016

Free catalog with many interesting and charming kits.

The Creative Needler
Box 158
Orient, Ohio 43146

Hand-painted originals.

Greengage Design
P.O. Box 9683
Washington, D.C. 20016

A collection of hand-painted needlepoint kits with special grace and charm. These kits are expensive (average $35. to $60.) and their brochure is expensive ($2.), but you will be impressed with the distinctive product.

Heritage Hill Patterns
Box 624
Westport, Conn. 06880

Delightful collection of needlepoint kits. Catalog ($1.).

Kalico Kits
Box 25922
Los Angeles, Calif. 90025

Unusual catalog of kits (50¢).

Mary Maxim
2001 Holland Ave.
Port Huron, Mich. 48060

Offers a catalog (64 pp., free) of interest to sewing kit fans. Needlepoint, crewel, crocheting, etc.

Museum of Fine Arts
479 Huntington Ave.
Boston, Mass. 02115

Unusual needlepoint kits based on historic New England. Catalog (25¢).

Needlepoint Design
P.O. Box 316
Kennebunkport, Maine 04046

Catalog with wool samples available ($1.).

Nimble Thimble
Box 713
Aptos, Calif. 95003

Catalog with over 100 designs plus needlepoint supplies ($1.).

Quilts and Other Comforts
5315 West 38 Ave.
Denver Colo. 80212

Source for various kits.

Spinnerin Yarn Co.
230 Fifth Ave.
New York, N.Y. 10001

Rugs, pillows, and wall hangings. Many striking designs. Original ideas on easy-to-work, printed canvases. Colorful catalog (56 pp., free).

Titillations, Ltd.
211 East 60 St.
New York, N.Y. 10022

Catalog ($1.) shows their Art Nouveau and sometimes art outrageous designs. Kits range from $10. to $2,000.

The Yarn Barn
19 South Park Place
Newark, Ohio 43055

Unusual Christmas ornaments and other items.

There was a time when most women had lots of handbags—at least one for every pair of shoes. Your mother, or was it your grandmother, was forever switching her keys and lipstick from one pocketbook to the other so that everything would match. Nowadays, we're much more concerned about good design and fine craftsmanship than whether the purse matches the shoes.

Alas, as with most other products, quality of handbag workmanship seems to be going down as the price goes up. And as with many other products, now may be the time to start thinking about making your own. Leatherwork isn't for pioneers these days, it's for designers who command big fees for their efforts. And of course, leather isn't the only material suitable for a handbag. How about silk, or even canvas?

If you like the idea of having a purse that works for you without having to pay a queen's ransom, you'll be interested in the kits in this section. Depending on your talents, some of these kits are quite easy, others will take some time. Many of them will teach you lasting skills you can carry over into a whole new area of pleasurable activity and personalized design. If you want to, you can even make yourself a bag to go with every pair of shoes, just like Grandma!

TANDY LEATHER CO.
2727 West 7 St.
Fort Worth, Tex. 76107

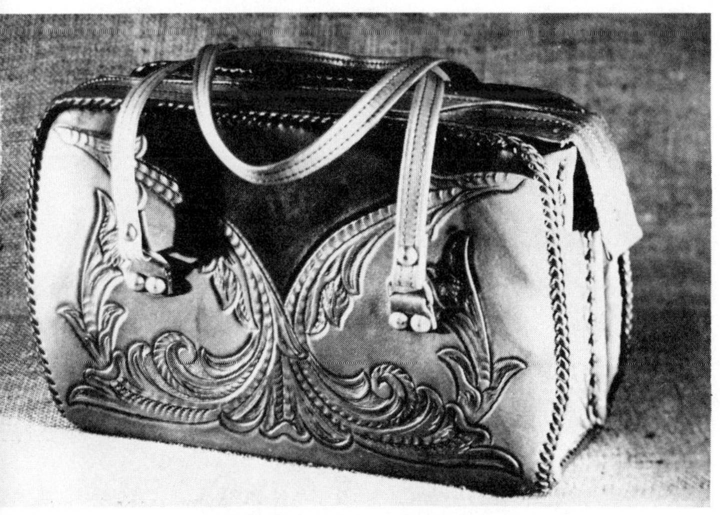

SAFARI HANDBAG

Exciting fashion with a dash of sophistication . . . plus a luxurious lining, a full-length zipper (specially constructed for durability, prestitched to gusset). Kit includes two prestitched pockets (one zippered), double-stitched handles, leather lacing and needle, tooling pattern and instructions. Parts are cut from natural tooling leather, punched and ready to lace! 14″ × 10″ × 5″. Worth over $50. as a finished product. The hand-tooling gives the bag a truly handmade look. A buy at $18.95.

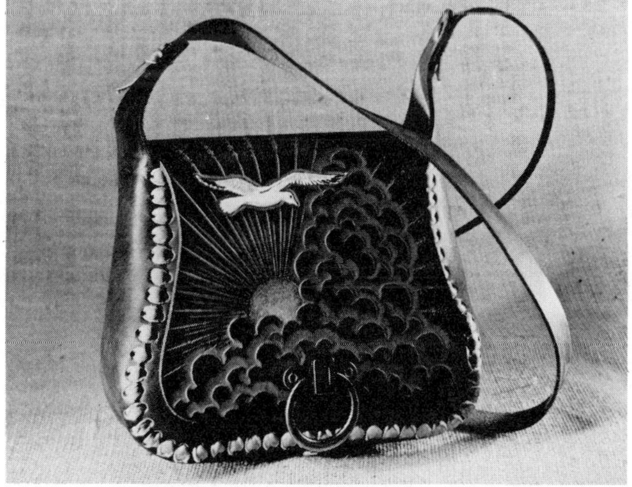

NEW DIMENSIONS HANDBAG

Everything's coming up Seagulls these days. A snappy modern look that will delight almost any gal. From the hardware to the lacing, it's all complete. Finished size is 8″ × 7″ × 3″. $13.95.

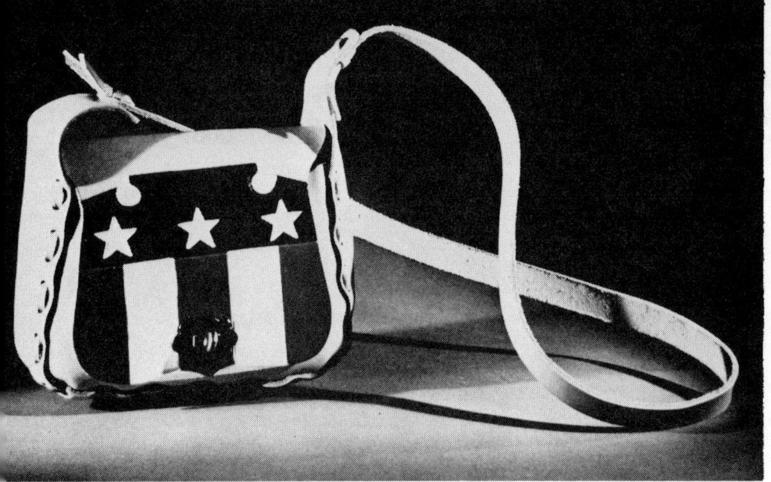

U.S.A. HANDBAG KIT

A very popular item with many groups, this fashion accessory is the perfect gift for your friends of whatever political leaning. Cut from all-American real oak leather, it will wear for years to come. In addition to the design, the slim lines are fashionable with today's style of dress. Everything included to complete this 7″ × 5½″ bag. $8.95.

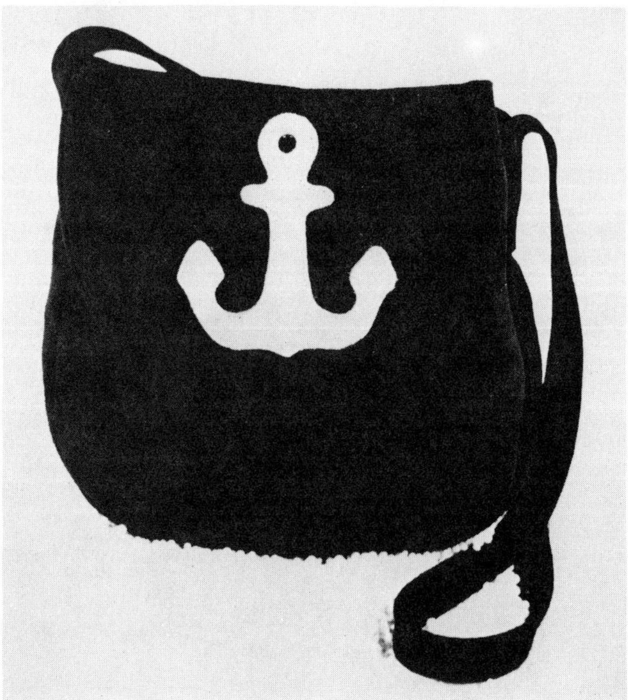

SUEDE SAILOR BAG

The new look of suede, and you can assemble it with your own sewing machine. Precut pieces are deep nautical blue with bright white anchor. Follow instructions to complete. Even the thread is included. $6.95.

Tandy is the largest manufacturer of leather kits in the country. They offer over two dozen handbag kits. (See Tandy Leather Co. in Crafts section for complete company information catalog.)

MUSEUM SHOP
PHILADELPHIA MUSEUM OF ART
Box 7646
Philadelphia, Pa. 19101

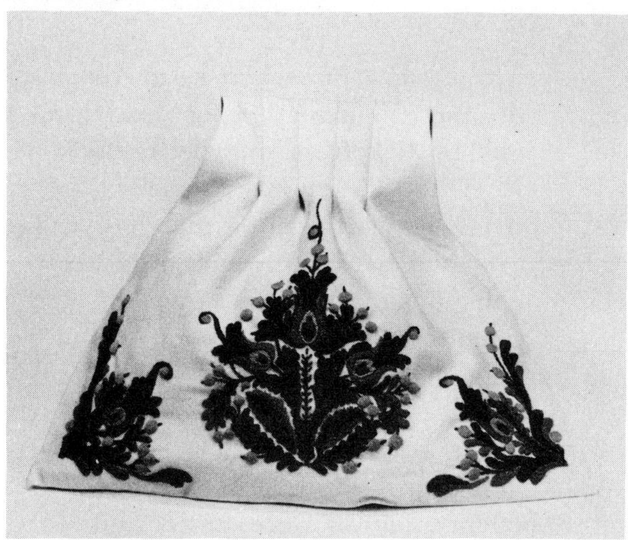

TOTE BAG

The border of an embroidered Hungarian coat provided the inspiration for this crewel tote-bag kit. Includes silk-screened, white permanent-press fabric, red colorfast lining, yarn, needle, and complete working instructions. $10.

SEWING CORNER, INC.
Box 412
Whitestone, N.Y. 11357

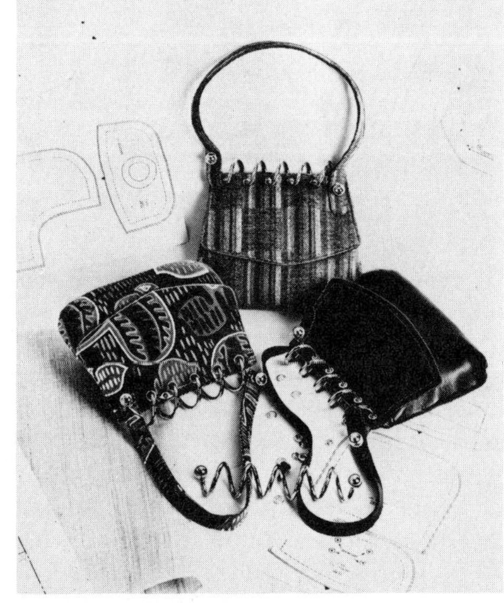

CURLI-Q HANDBAG

Our fashion consultants like this—and our kit makers like it, too—so it must be a winner. A simple project at a reasonable price. Golden spiral winds through easy-to-insert eyelets. Comes with felt, suede, or tapestry fabric. Completed bag 11″ wide by 9″ deep. $6.55.

Catalog of sewing projects (36 pp., free). All reasonably priced and nicely illustrated.

PURSENALITIES

1619 Grand Ave.
Baldwin, New York 11510

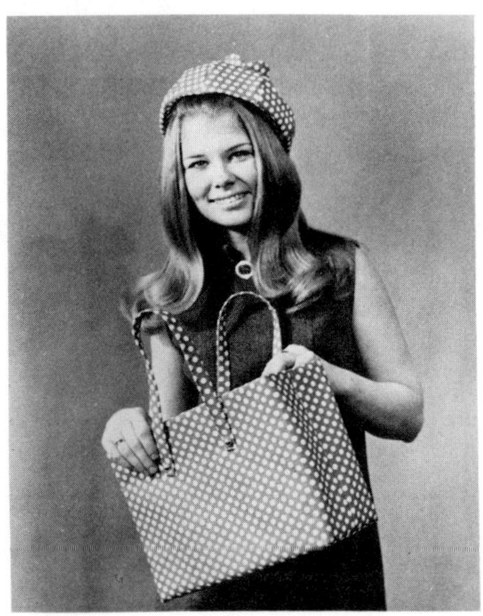

TOTE BAG

The tote is the fastest-growing fashion accessory. Now you can have a collection of them to match any outfit. Simple enough that even a novice sewer can make one. All you do is add your own fabric. Kit has die-cut processed stays (to preserve shape), die-cut 100% polyurethane foam (firm but supple), brass legs that attach easily (use like a thumb tack), handle filler, and patterns and instructions. A reasonable $3. in shopper size (14″ × 10″) or $2. in cocktail size (6″ × 6″).

Publishes free catalog (16 pp.) with lots of low-priced handbags, purses, and related items.

The doll is perhaps the oldest plaything known to man. Anthropologists believe that the only reason dolls are not found in prehistoric graves is that they were made of perishable materials such as cloth and fur. Dolls have been found in abundance in Egyptian tombs that are more than 5,000 years old, and it's easy to see why. A doll is modeled on the human form. It represents ourselves and our kind. Like all creatures, we are interested most of all in ourselves.

Dolls also often represent babies, the new generation. In Africa, in the Orange Free State, each Tingo girl is given a doll to keep for her first child. When the first child is born, the mother gets a new doll to save for the second child. In this custom, the doll stands for the people's faith that there will be children and the human race will go on. In traditional Japan, a new bride always brought her doll collection to her husband's house. Dolls are used by witches, priests, and doctors.

The doll, in short, is a profoundly important symbol for mankind. Americans have often thought of dolls as girls' toys, but lately we've begun to realize that boys want and need dolls, too. And the act of building your own doll is especially satisfying to most people. A handmade doll is a gift that usually remains close to the heart of a child long after he has grown up. Jean Ritchie, the folksinger, tells of being given a wooden doll carved by an old relative. This was in the middle of the Depression, and little Jean was bitterly disappointed that the doll wasn't a big shiny one from the Sears catalog.

Today, of course, the hand-carved doll is priceless, both in monetary value and for what it means to that one-time little girl.

THE ENCHANTED DOLLHOUSE
Manchester, Vermont 05255

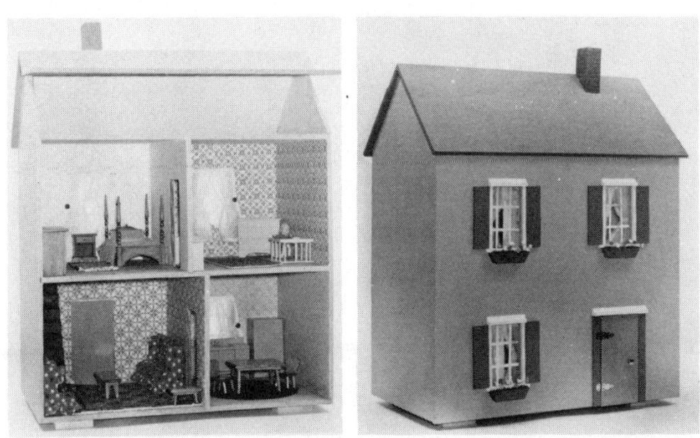

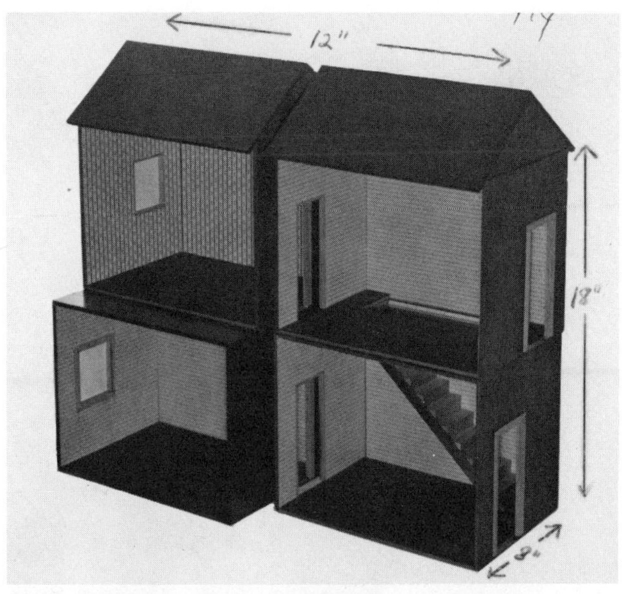

FOUR-ROOM DOLLHOUSE

Be your own builder and let the Enchanted Dollhouse Company be the contractor. Made in America by New Hampshire craftsmen. Four nice-sized rooms. Kit comes with birch plywood precut parts. Unpainted with acetate windows, white pine window trim, and hinged doors. Curtains, wallpaper, furniture available in separate kits. $26. ppd.

THE HOUSE THAT GROWS

Perfect for today's growing doll families. These rooms are made to attach. Any size house can be constructed. All the pieces are interchangeable. The wood constructed pieces can be painted, stained, or wallpapered. Kit #1 (room with roof): $12. Kit #2 (one room): $10. Kit #3 (two story/stairs and roof): $25.

Best catalog (32 pp., $1.) in the dollhouse field. Full color with every kind of assembled and unassembled house imaginable.

THE H. H. PERKINS CO.
P.O. Box 1601
New Haven, Conn. 06508

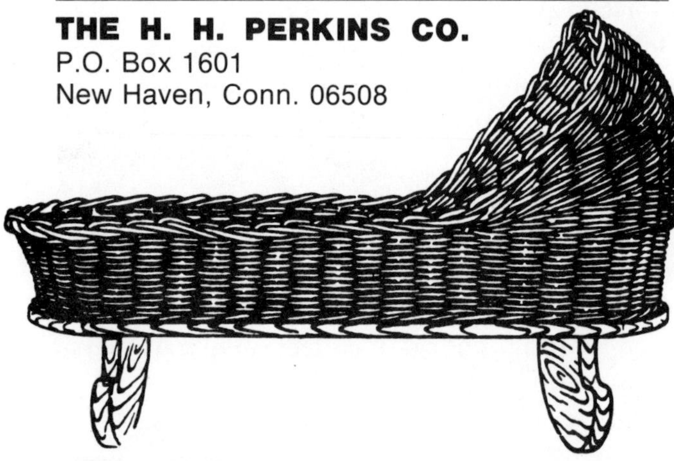

DOLL CRADLE

Make your own old-fashioned doll cradle with this reed kit! The cradle base is 7″ × 15″ and enough reed material is included to complete the kit. A simple weaving project that returns hours of joy. $3.50.

THE BUTTERFLY CO.
48–52 Clearview Expressway
Bayside, N.Y. 11364

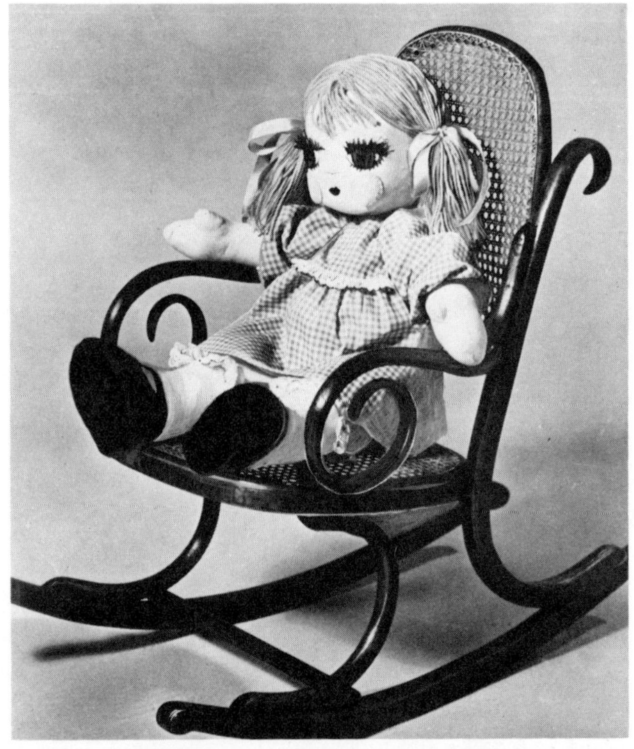

TURN-OF-THE-CENTURY DOLL KIT

The most beautiful doll in the world wears a gingham dress. You'll love "Amanda." Complete she's over 2½′ tall. She's a perfect size 1 and can take all your child's hand-me-downs.

Amanda is patterned after dolls made in the early 1900s that have been handed down from generation to generation with tender loving care, and comes to you with easy-to-follow instructions, plus all the materials you will need to make your own family heirloom.

Kit includes premarked muslin for doll body, precut dress, pantaloons, felt, shoes and facial features, elastic, eyelet ruffle, snaps, embroidery thread, wig yarn, tissue for wig, ribbons for hair, heavy-duty cord, and reinforcement stick (stuffing not included). A good buy at $13. postpaid.

SCIENTIFIC MODELS
340 Snyder Ave.
Berkeley Heights, N.J. 07922

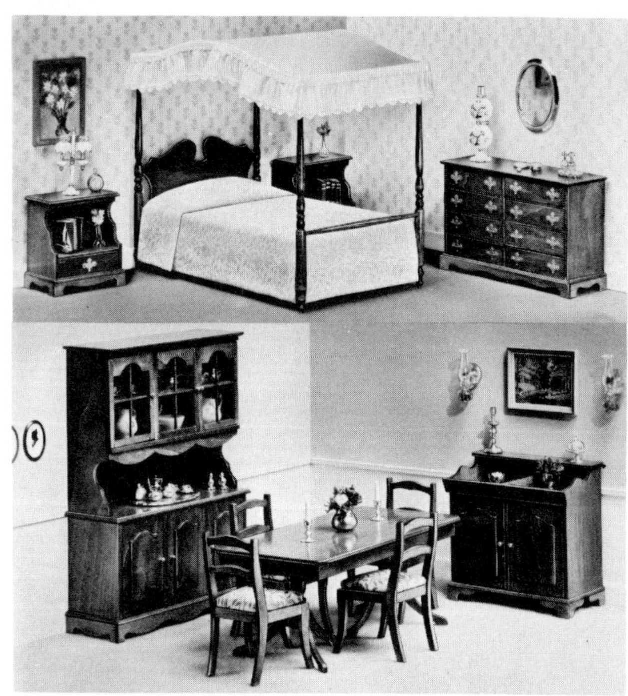

DOLLHOUSE FURNITURE

Fantastic quality with everything ready for you to assemble. Each piece (Scale: 1″ equals 1′) is a charming, perfectly detailed replica. Kit includes quality precut basswood parts, turned wood parts, complete brass hardware, printed miniature upholstery fabric, foam material, wood stain, glue, paint brush, sandpaper, and step-by-step instructions. Made by Scientific Models, who have been in the ship kit business for many years. Living room (sofa, chair, secretary, two tables): $12. Dining room (buffet, dry sink, table, 4 chairs): $12. Bedroom (bed fully dressed, foam mattress, dresser, two night tables): $12.

CRAFT PATTERNS
AND CRAFT PRODUCTS
Elmhurst, Ill. 60126

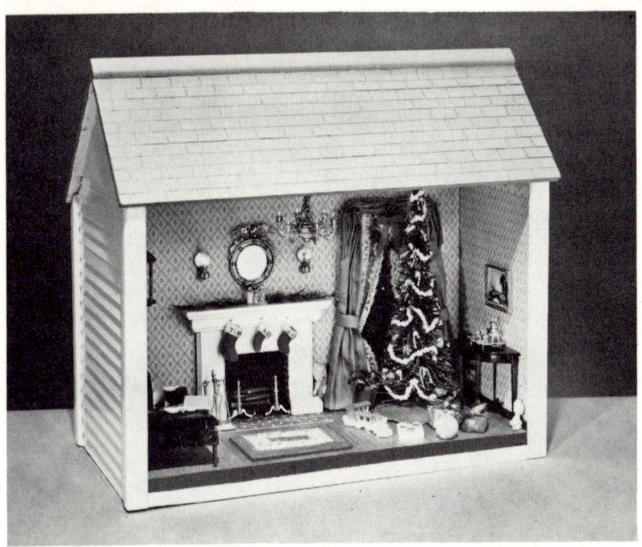

MINIATURE ROOM KIT

This complete kit for a little room all decked out for the holidays is a recent addition to the products of a well-known maker of dollhouse patterns. The entire room is made and furnished in a scale of 1″ equals 1′. A miniature white fireplace mantel is mounted on the back wall, and a little red light under the logs simulates the fire. There's a chandelier, candle sconces on the wall, and real colored lights on the Christmas tree.

Like a lot of big house kits, the complete kit for the miniature room is only a shell. If you want to furnish it as in the photograph, you'll need a few more of the tiny kits made by Craft Patterns. Send for the catalog. Miniature room shell kit: $12.95.

Just to give you an idea, here are a few of the other miniature items available in kit form from Craft Patterns. Prices at the time of writing are listed.

Colonial chair kit	$4.14
Pedestal table kit	5.90
Colonial dry sink kit	6.60
Colonial secretary kit	8.15
Slant-top desk kit	6.60
Chippendale chair kit	8.15
Hepplewhite table kit	5.90
Chippendale sofa kit	9.15
and more . . .	

KRISTAN HELBERG TOYS
Town Square
Nicasio, Calif. 94946

DOLLHOUSE KIT

A very young lady's delight—or even a very young man—for both boys and girls love to play house and to cut out and put together. And that's what this doll kit is all about; in actuality, a book that opens into a Victorian dollhouse (in the shape of an X—in each of the four unfinished triangles is a room), plus twelve sheets of furniture to cut out and put together.

This kit seems ideal for those young people who want to role-play as mommy and daddy and who also wish to make use of their manual dexterity by cutting out and putting together. The price appears to be rather steep, but then the kit idea is rather unusual. $6.75.

BRUMBERGER
200 Fifth Ave.
New York, N.Y. 10010

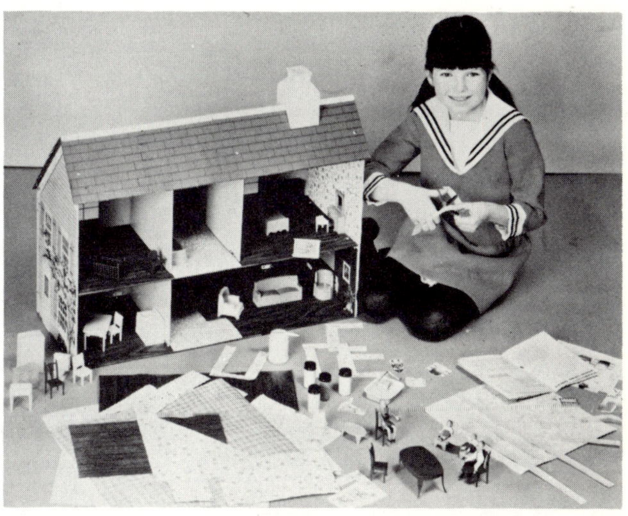

GIANT DOLLHOUSE

A beautifully designed wooden dollhouse over 2½′ wide with a complete do-it-yourself decorating kit. A budding young homemaker has a perfectly wonderful time creating the decor of her house, while she painlessly soaks up a world of knowledge about proper color and design coordination.

There are six rooms of beautifully detailed plastic furniture that can be spray-painted any desired color. Kit includes a complete grouping of decorator materials (assorted wallpapers, vinyl floor coverings, drapery and picture kit) with nontoxic paste and brush, plus four unbreakable bottles of nontoxic washable paints in popular colors along with pan and paint roller. A complete book of decorating hints and tips about color schemes and coordinations, as well as templates for wall accessories, table coverings, and other fascinating creative ideas compiled by the well-known Adrienne Designs, is also included.

The dollhouse, beautifully and realistically lithographed, is constructed of top-grade composition wood for endurance and is complete with steel corner caps and roof caps for greater strength. The young houseowner will revel in such authentic touches as plastic windows, chimney, and a door that opens and closes. Special bonus feature is a completely bendable 4-figure doll family scaled to fit perfectly with this house. Decorator dollhouse size: 30″ long, 13″ wide, 29″ high. $25.

YIELD HOUSE
North Conway, N.H. 03860

DOLLHOUSE TOWNHOUSE

This is a lot of dollhouse for the money and a lovely project for a little city child who can relate better to a 3-story, 6-room "townhouse" than to those bay-windowed, treed, garaged suburban models one usually sees in the stores. It is scaled 1″ to 1′; measures 35″ high, 24″ wide, 12″ deep, and features strong pressboard walls, floors, and roof, 6 shuttered acetate windows, magnetic door latches, and all necessary hardware. Easy-to-follow instructions and carefully constructed parts make this an easy kit for the older youngster to assemble alone and the younger one to enjoy doing with a parent's help. Kit can be stored in closet when not in use. Note: If you've discovered the dark, well-kept secret that little boys love dollhouses too, this is a good kit for the male child since it is less "cute" than most. $29.95.

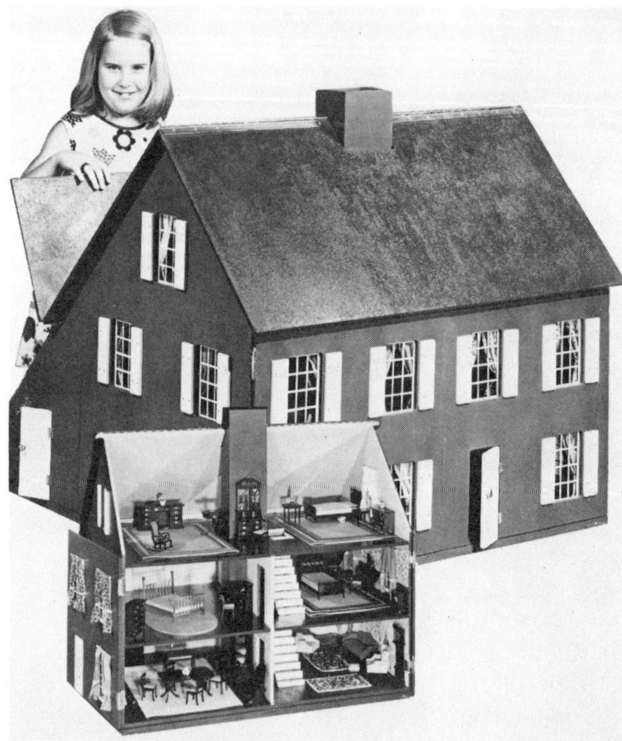

NEW ENGLAND SALTBOX DOLLHOUSE KIT

A veritable Colonial mansion—3 floors, 6 rooms, 17

shuttered windows, 2 staircases, 2 passways, and a chimney. This little girl's (or boy's) dreamworld is made of strong, high-density pressboard, with acetate windows and all doorknobs and hardware. Kit includes easy-to-follow directions, hints, decorating ideas. House is 33″ high, 38″ wide, and 38″ long. It is easy for an adult to assemble, a bit harder for a child under twelve. Paint is not included, nor is furniture. If you're going to spring $49.95 for the house, you should look into Yield House's fabulous collection of authentic scale-model furniture.

CHINA DOLL KIT

An old-fashioned doll from Victorian days. Complete in every detail, right down to her high-button boots. Head and arms of china, plus material and body for pattern. This enchanting doll is 16″ high. $7.95.

CAROUSEL CRAFTS
P.O. Box 42549
Houston, Tex. 77042

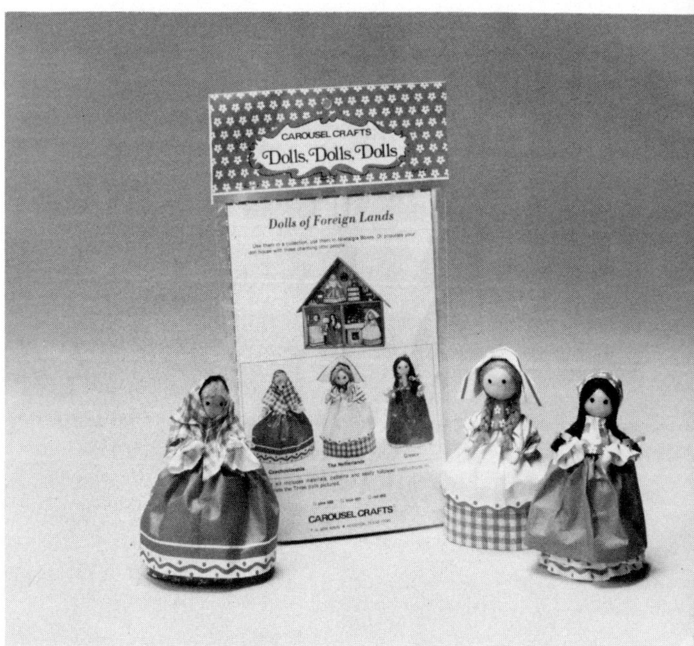

DOLLS OF FOREIGN LANDS

Make a collection of dolls of foreign lands inexpensively with Carousel Crafts kits. Each kit contains materials, patterns, and cloth to make three dolls. The dress charmingly reflects the native country. They can be assembled quickly. As you start your collection, you'll find a mini-world unfolding in little time. Favorably priced at $2.95 per kit of three.

INTERNATIONAL IMPORTS
Box 201D
Toluca Lake, Calif. 91602

VOODOO DOLL

Someone giving you trouble? Simply sew up a voodoo doll, attach a bit of the bad guy's clothing, and insert pins. Lest you think this is all a gag, International Imports publishes a 96-pp. catalog (25¢) with occult, magic, metaphysical, psychic, and spiritual merchandise. They are quite serious about their business; reading the catalog is a weird experience. In any event, back to the kit. They offer a make-it-yourself voodoo doll kit that comes complete with fabric pattern, name tag, "how to do voodoo" instructions, and, of course, a large pin. We don't suggest the kit for children, it's sure to give them nightmares. In fact, we're not sure whom we suggest the kit for. But if the ancient art of voodoo is your thing, you can order the kit for $6. postpaid.

CRAFT CHEST
Box 453
Murray Hill Station
New York, N.Y. 10016

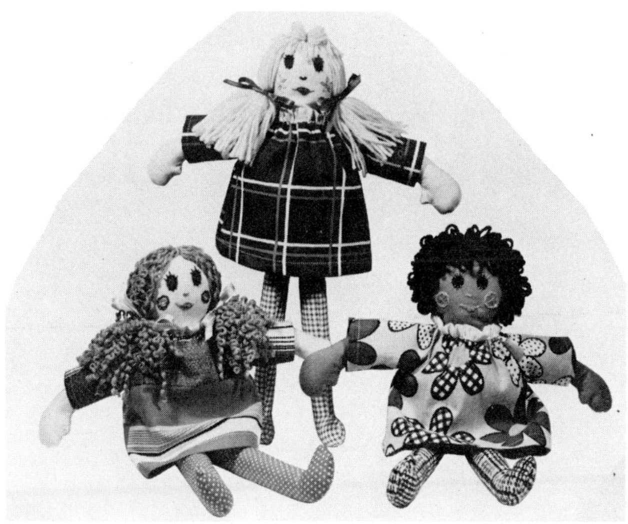

RAG DOLLS

Charming rag dolls that are quick, easy, and fun to sew. Each doll comes in a complete kit with step-by-step instructions, pattern, and materials. Sixteen inches tall when completed. Choose from blond, curly redhead, or Afro. $3.98 each.

MONTE MODELS
P.O. Box 2391
New Bern, N.C. 28560

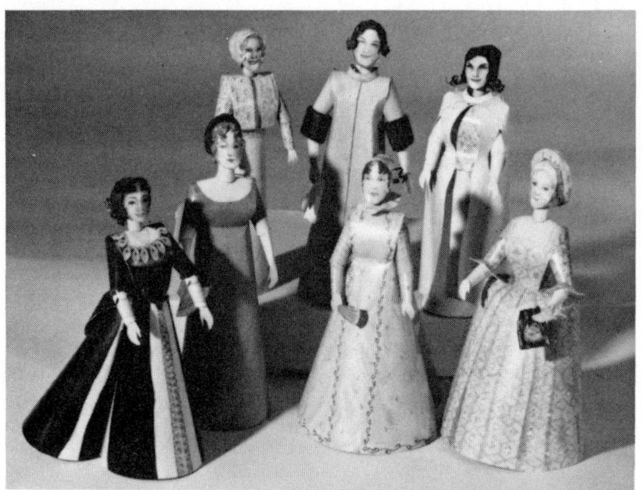

FIRST LADIES OF THE WHITE HOUSE

Three-dimensional paper dolls in full color of President's wives or official hostesses dressed in their Inaugural Ball or formal gowns. Dolls are six inches high. Included are: Martha Washington, Dolley Madison, Martha Jefferson Randolph, Frances Cleveland, Jacqueline Kennedy, Claudia Taylor Johnson, and Patricia Nixon. Complete set of seven. Kit: $3.

Special offer for collectors: First edition of 1000 numbered, uncut sheets of the First Ladies. Each sheet $10. Please advise name to be entered in registration book.

Complete line of card models (see Toys and Models section).

MUSEUM SHOP
PHILADELPHIA MUSEUM OF ART
Box 7646
Philadelphia, Pa. 19101

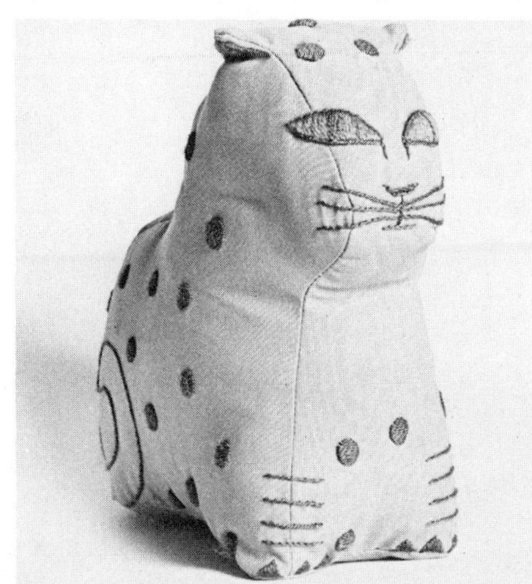

STUFFED CAT DOLL

Crewel kit inspired by a 19th-century Pennsylvania-German cast-iron doorstop. Includes silk-screened fabric, yarn, needle, and complete working instructions. $5.00. Stuffing of nonallergenic polyester fiber is $1.50 extra.

THE ENCHANTED DOLLHOUSE
Manchester Center, Vt. 05255

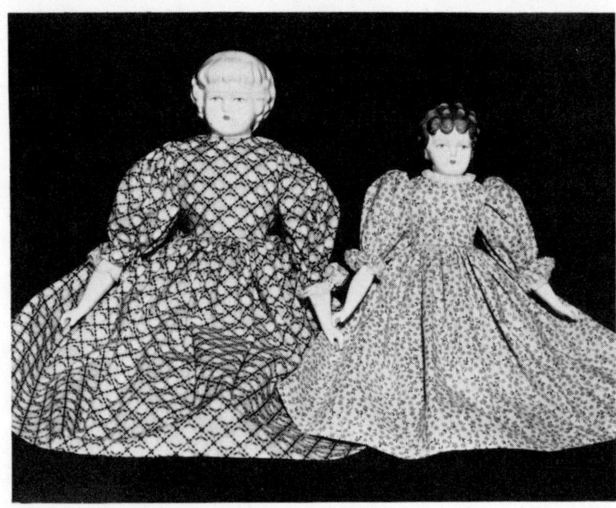

OLD-FASHIONED DOLL KIT

These are the collector's items of the future. Kit furnishes china head, arms, and legs, muslin cloth for body, tape for attaching doll head, and pattern for body and clothes. Fun project sure to please any little girl. "Emma" (blond, 15"): $9. "Meg" (auburn, 12"): $7.

Delightful catalog (32 pp., $1.) for every dollhouse and miniature fancier. Lots of kits and prefinished products. Everything we've seen from them is first quality.

OTHER SOURCES

Dolls and Dreams
454 Third Ave.
New York, N.Y. 10016

Exclusive doll and dollhouse kits. Catalog (free).

Marie Farmer Co.
36 Washington Ave.
Port Richmond, N.Y. 94801

A variety of doll kits. Catalog (50¢).

Standard Dolls
23-83 31 St.
Long Island City, N.Y. 11105

From rag doll kits to antique replica kits. Also lots of parts to create your own kits. Catalog (50¢).

Wood Designs
Box 143
Hawthorne, N.J. 07506

Has a noteworthy collection of all-wood dollhouses. Standard models or custom kits created for you. Brochure (free).

There's a fine line between work and play. It's not at all clear, for example, that building a toy is any less fun than playing with one. For some of us, making it is more fun. Toys built from kits are a natural. You can make personalized, one-of-a-kind toys for the children you love . . . older children can make things for themselves.

In animals, it's easy to see that play is practice for survival in adult life. A kitten playing with a ball is practicing the fine art of mouse catching. Little lions racing and wrestling are really preparing for the day when they'll join the hunt. In humans, too, using toys has a serious purpose underneath. Sports, such as hockey, football, soccer, originated as a kind of mock warfare. In the times when most boys grew up to be soldiers, sports were indeed practice for survival. In our time, they can serve as a necessary outlet for competitive feelings.

Toys serve two basic purposes. One is imitation. A child playing with a doll imitates the way his parents or other adults treat babies. In this way, he teaches himself how to be a parent. The other purpose is instruction. A toy car helps a child learn how cars are made and how they work, especially when he builds the toy car himself. Building a toy can be very instructive for a grown-up, too, and will make a unique gift when you're finished.

Are toys in kits less expensive than toys from a toy store? Usually, but not always. If the major selling point of a toy is workmanship, as with some wooden toys, for instance, you can probably save money by making it yourself. If the outstanding feature is design, probably not. But, once again, you are buying the pleasure of craftsmanship as well as a product. To those with the inclination, it's worth the price.

ELENA CO.
136 East 57 St.
New York, N.Y. 10022

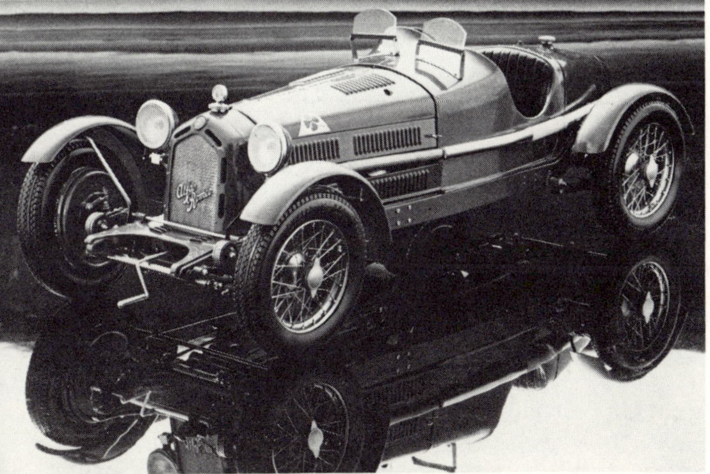

POCHER CLASSIC CARS

The ultimate automobile model kits. The cars which can be built from them are museum-quality reproductions, authentic to the tiniest detail. However, let us warn you at the outset, this is no rainy afternoon project. The kits contain from 823 to 2,199 parts. You are looking at well over a hundred hours of work. Once complete, the project will bring you real kit builder joy.

Reproducing one of these automobiles in miniature is much like building the full-size car. The design of each part, even the smallest, is taken directly from the original factory blueprints and engineering drawings, Many of the same materials are used: brass, iron, copper, stainless steel. Tires are real rubber and upholstery is genuine leather. The parts are put together with bolts and screws; no special tools needed and no painting necessary.

There are four kits available, each a classic in automotive history and styling: the 1907 Fiat 130 h.p. (Grand Prix de France); the 1932 Alfa Romeo Spider Gran Sport Tourismo; the 1932 Rolls-Royce Phantom 11 Drop Head Sedanca Coupe; and the 1931–34 Alfa Romeo 8C 2300 Monza. Each of these kits will test not only your skill but your patience and ability as well. The people who merely admire the finished models can't see it all.

The magneto attached to the engine block of

the Rolls, for instance. To the eye this appears genuine enough, down to the little brass plate on the case. But what can't be seen is that this piece of peripheral equipment is *itself* a perfect scale reproduction—real inside, armature and all. Practically everything that moves on the full-size cars is operational on the models. The brakes work when you press the pedal. The suspension and steering work. The headlights switch on from the dashboard on three models. The doors open, close, and lock. Side windows on the Rolls-Royce roll up and down.

The models are difficult and intricate, but not tricky. Instructions and diagrams are complete and clear; all parts are numbered. And virtually no cementing is necessary. Which means that if you do something wrong the first time, you can take it apart and do it again. The price is steep by model standards, but these are really different from a child's toy hobby kit. Fiat Grand Prix: $100. Alfa Romeo Monza: $125. Alfa Romeo Spider: $150. Rolls-Royce: $200.

Company offers a lavish color brochure with photos and details ($1.).

HERKIMER TOOL & MODEL WORKERS

P.O. Box 191
Herkimer, N.Y. 13350

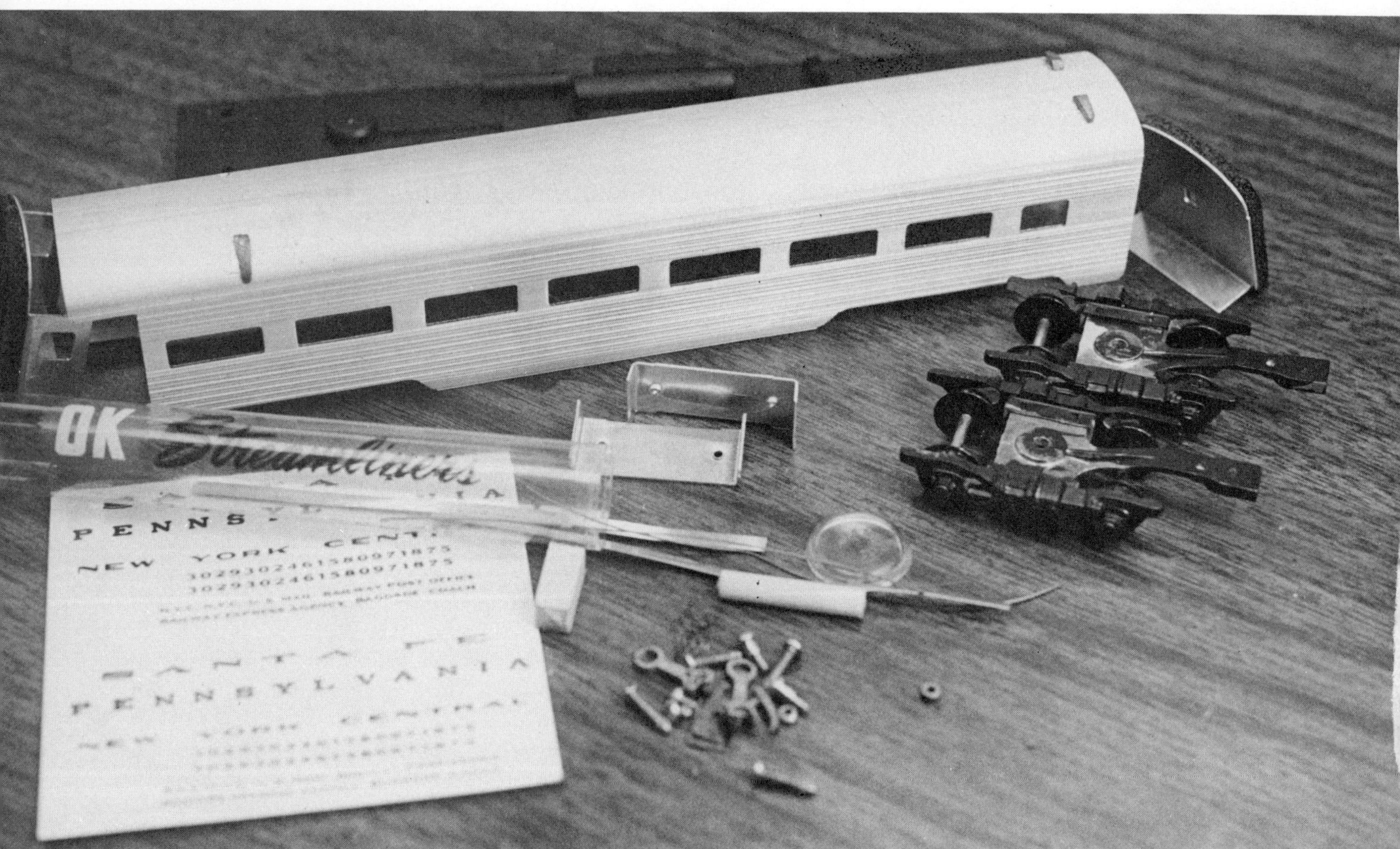

HO "SHORTY" STREAMLINE PASSENGER CAR

A real "blast from the past." The prototype (kit is also available in a scale 80′ version), the kit, the box it comes in, and the company's ads—"Modernize your railroad with the new OK streamliners"—are out of the fifties. We love it. Nice extruded aluminum kit. Not a high detail, but a good-quality model; easy to assemble though it does require drilling. Swift, thrilling action and life-like realism. Kit includes trucks. $6.95.

Complete line of passenger cars in 60′ shorty or 80′ scale version. Car lighting kit available for 95¢.

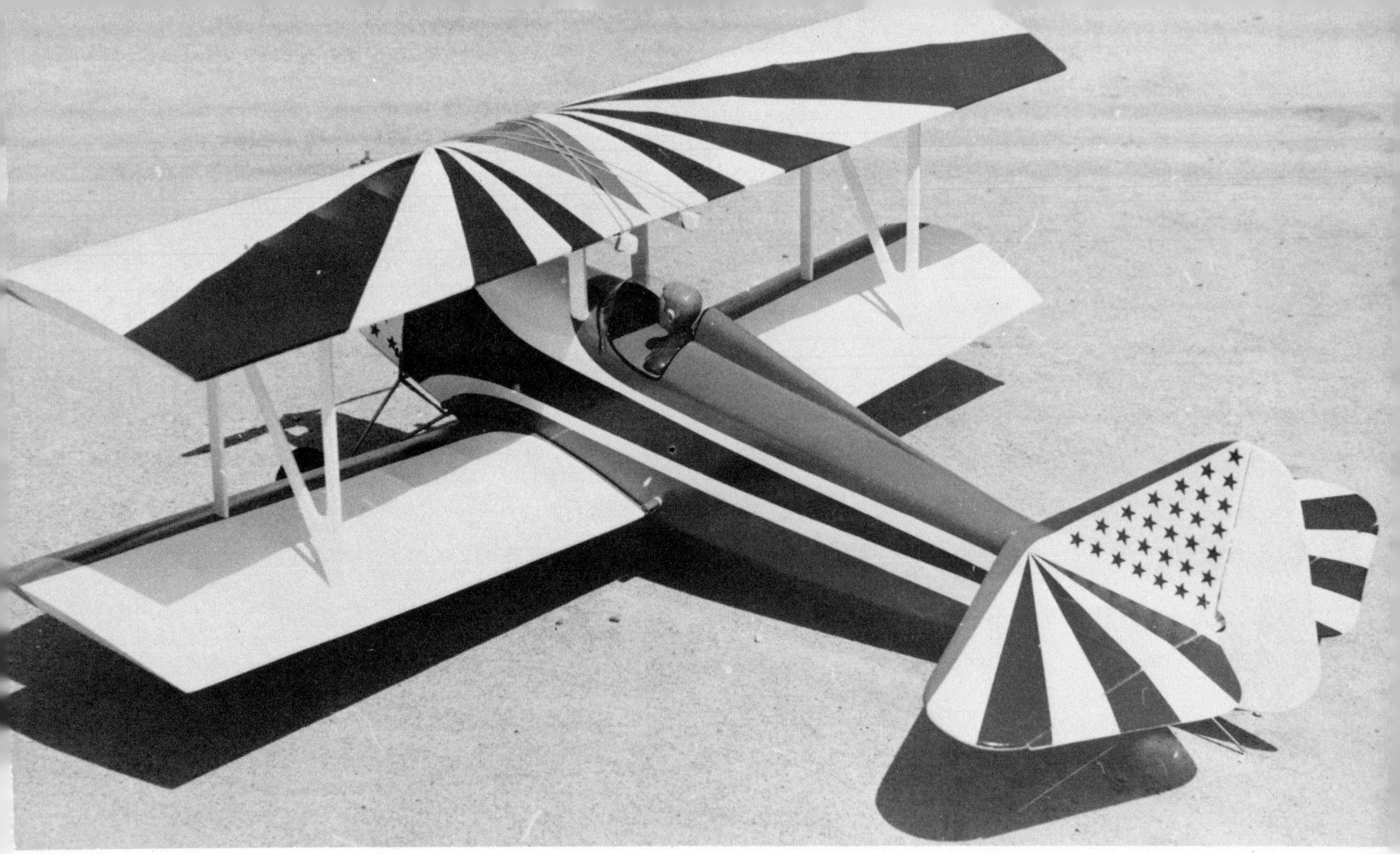

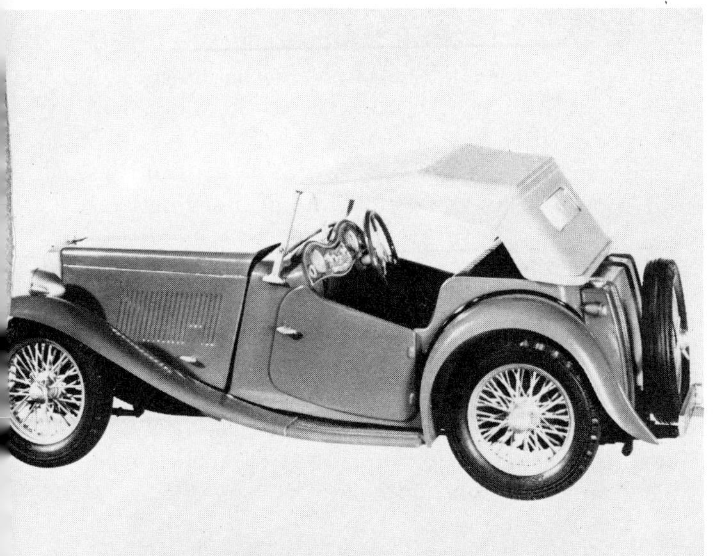

SOUTHERN R/C PRODUCTS, INC.
Rt. 3, Box 47, Nims Lane
Pensacola, Fla. 32503

DELUXE RADIO-CONTROLLED TIGER TAIL

Here's Rod Chidgey's award-winning plane. A super design with first-quality deluxe kit. Includes balsa wood production plus all preshaped parts, foam wing, and complete hardware package. $99.50.

Makes a line of quality radio-controlled models. Catalog free.

ENTEX INDUSTRIES, INC.
1016 East Burgrove
Carson, Calif. 90746

SCALE-MODEL KIT OF THE M.G.T.C.

Perhaps constructing the model of the M.G.T.C. is a healthy substitute for owning the legendary classic sports car. The actual car is a collector's item and no one would be chastised for wanting to own one. Still, you wouldn't have been involved in building the real one, so in a sense the model M.G.T.C. belongs to you in a more meaningful way.

The M.G.T.C. kit is superbly detailed inside and out, and includes fine-spoke wheels, rubber tires, precolored parts, engine, cockpit controls, bonnet hinges, a top in the up position, a top folded down, vinyl weather stripping for the fenders, and much more! For a sportscar that was introduced to America right after World War II, it's come a long way. This scale model measures 8½″ long, 1/16 scale. $9.00

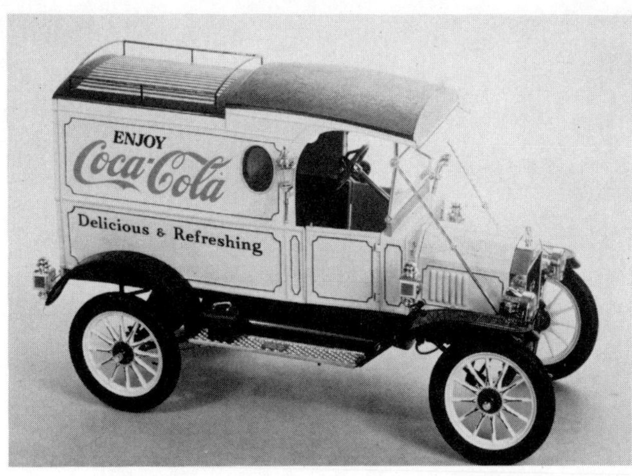

SCALE MODEL OF THE 1913 FORD "T" VAN

Reminiscent of the days when the local tradesmen delivered almost every household commodity. Vans of this type were in use throughout the world. It had a pedal-controlled transmission with two forward speeds and reverse, and a fuel consumption of approximately 30 mpg. It was very economical to run.

The Entex model is approximately 9½″ long, has real wood trim, precolored plastic, rubber tires, and Coca-Cola decals. Perfect engine and chassis detail! $15.

in storage in Los Angeles Harbor. It has flown once for a total distance of one mile. It is now leased by Howard Hughes from the General Services Administration, shrouded in mystery, and the subject of much publicity. Enthusiasts wonder what will be the fate of this fabulous machine.

Faithfully reproduced by Entex from numerous press photographs in 1/200 scale, the model has a wingspan of over 19″. Complete with display stand and marking decals. All parts are precolored. $15.

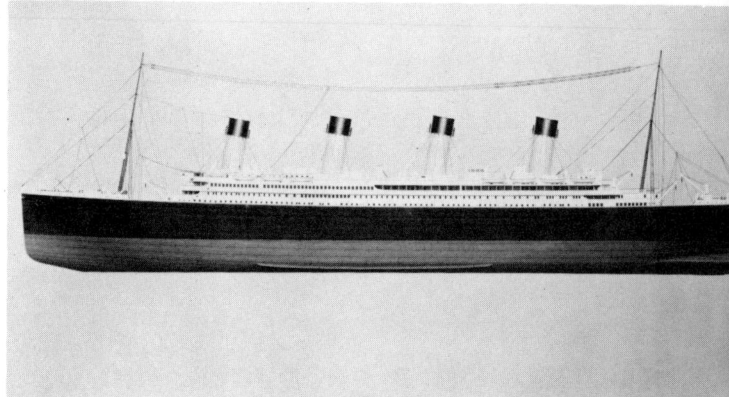

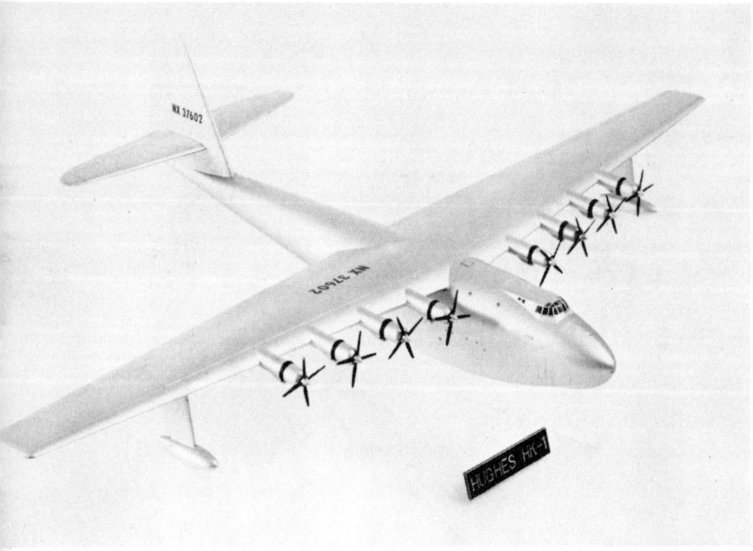

SCALE MODEL OF THE "SPRUCE GOOSE" (HERCULES)

The world's largest airplane and the most unique seaplane ever built, the "Spruce Goose" was built at a cost of $18 million during World War II, and was officially named *Hercules* and dubbed by the press "Spruce Goose" because of its wood construction. This mammoth seaplane, with a wing span of 320′, is

SCALE SHIP MODELS - THE *TITANIC*

Working with models has involved numerous serious-minded people at various stages in their lives. To labor on a project with such intricate detail, such as a scale ship model, you have to feel nothing but superb satisfaction and pride upon its completion. That model and all its many parts become a part of you; while you're assembling the model, you become so familiar with it that few other objects in life are ever that well known to you.

The *Titanic*—the history of this great ship is as well known today as on that fateful morning over sixty years ago, April 15, 1912, when the sinking of the unsinkable made the world's communication systems buzz. Because the builders' original drawings of the *Titanic* were destroyed and their model disappeared during the Senate investigations in 1912, the Entex model was constructed from original drawings, photographs taken by survivors, and other technical journals and is indistinguishable from the original ship.

The *Titanic* model is over 30″ long and 8½″ high; its large size makes it an unavoidable conversation piece of considerable value. This 1/350 scale model kits includes all the usual Entex extras—molded-in color, brass parts, and the ultimate in detail. $30.

LITTLE ENGINES
Box O
Lomita, Calif. 90717

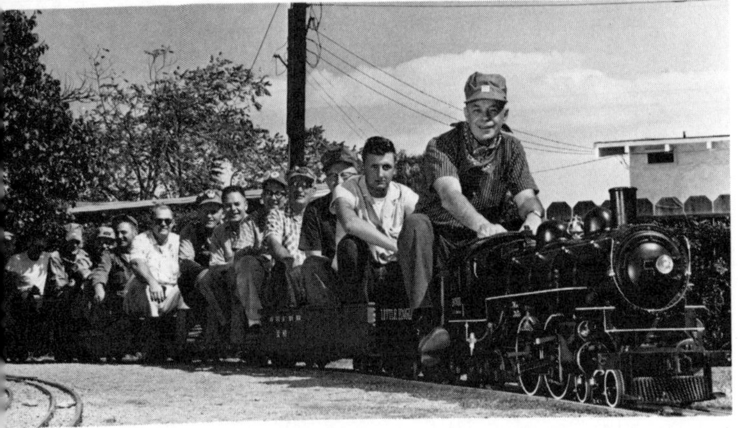

"C. P. HUNTINGTON" LIVE STEAM LOCOMOTIVE

1½″ scale model of the first engine ever owned by the Southern Pacific. The picture says everything. If you can afford it, have the space, and don't own one of these, you must not like trains. The engine can be coal- or oil-fired. Main frame is steel bar stock and you can make your own or buy precision-cut, drilled, and tapped frame ready to assemble. Boiler shells are cast. Kits are sold by single parts or in sections (main frame, boiler, cylinder-piston assembly, etc.). All parts may be purchased "in the rough" or machined. Estimated cost for C. P. Huntington (rough parts): $1,300. Additional charge for machining: $1,200.

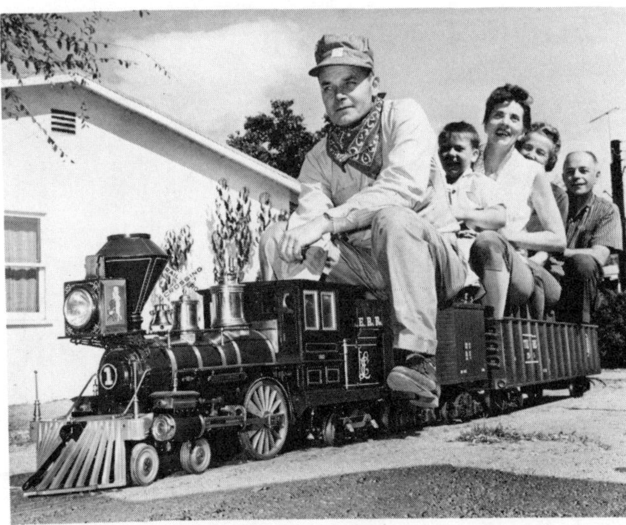

ATLANTIC 4-4-2 LIVE STEAM LOCOMOTIVE

This 1½″ scale 4-4-2 Atlantic engine is a take-off of the Southern Pacific #3000 Series A6 Atlantic. The Atlantic-type is one of America's most beautiful locomotives. With these parts offered, you can fol- low just about any railroad's Atlantic Series engine. We use the square-type tender tank, although a Vanderbilt-type may be used.

The main drive wheels are finished to 10″. A bar stock frame is used in conjunction with castings, which cuts down the size of machinery required. With the machined parts we offer, you can build this engine with a limited amount of tools—a drill-press, hand drill, grinder, and the usual hand tools. You need not worry about being a machinist to do this one.

If you wish to purchase prints ahead during construction, or a complete set of prints before starting an engine, you will be given credit in each section, when you purchase the castings. May we suggest, if you are buying machined parts, you order the first two sections together. Approx. cost for all parts in the rough: $2,500. Additional charge for machining (approx.): $3,000

Company makes parts and fittings for live steam ½″, 1″, 1½″ and 0 scale railroad equipment. (The boxcar that the engineer is sitting on in the C. P. Huntington photo would cost you about $150 to $200 with trucks, depending on how much machining you want done.) Their catalog ($2.) makes an excellent daydream kit if that's your financial bracket. The company is associated with the Lomita Railroad Museum.

QUALITY CRAFT MODELS
177 Wheatley Ave.
Northumberland, Pa. 17857

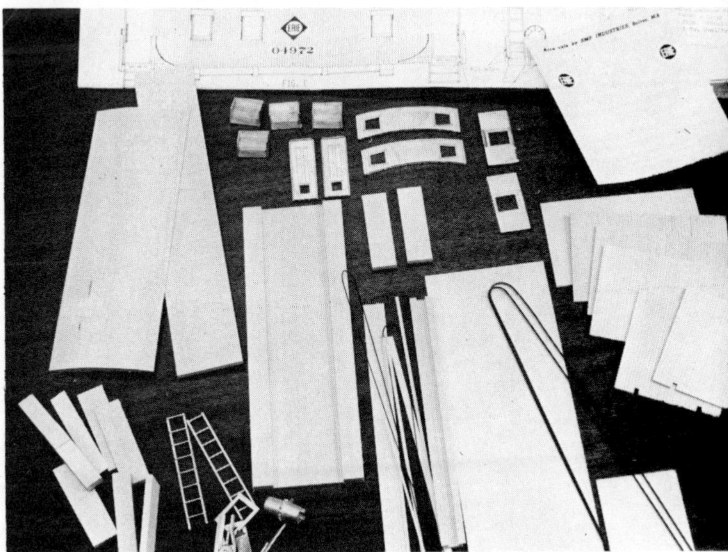

O SCALE ERIE CABOOSE

All-wood caboose. Kit includes precut, color-coded, polished scale wood, metal castings, and all necessary parts and hardware. This is a classic caboose and the construction is of the classic type. Careful work makes a handsome model. No trucks or couplers. $12.95.

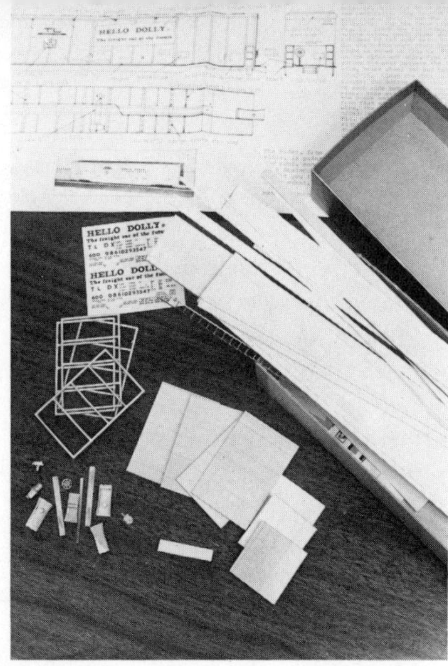

HO SCALE 70' "HELLO DOLLY" BOXCAR

Modern-style giant boxcar (no catwalks, high volume) for the new look in railroading. Straightforward construction from precut, color-coded wood with good castings. Requires care and patience, which will be rewarded. Nice kit. $5.95.

Several interesting kits in the HO, O, and HOn3 are of the "craftsman" type with emphasis on modern rolling stock. Especially interesting are the tri-level auto rack cars and an 87 Flex-i-van flat car. Other models include hi-cube boxcars and a bathtub gondola. Also a "Prestige Series" of classic freight cars.

NORTHEASTERN SCALE MODELS, INC.

Distributor: Wm. K. Walthers, Inc.
P.O. Box 16623
Milwaukee, Wis. 53216

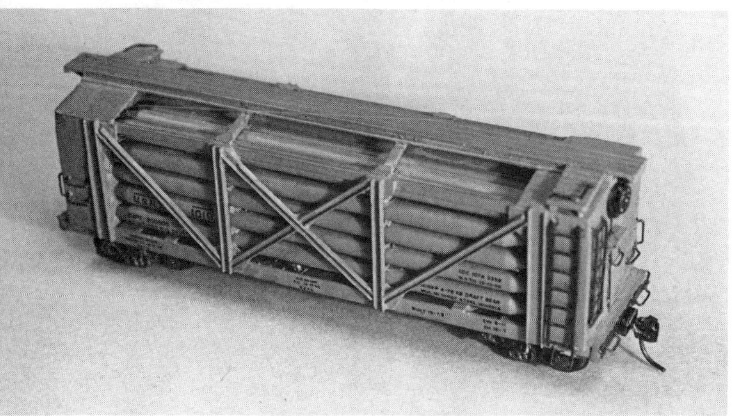

HO SCALE U.S. NAVY HELIUM TANK CAR

A rare piece of rolling stock from the forties, the helium tank car—presumably for dirigibles—is a fascinating kit. The construction requires great patience, but is not really difficult. Makes a beautiful model. Trucks and couplers not included. $5.95.

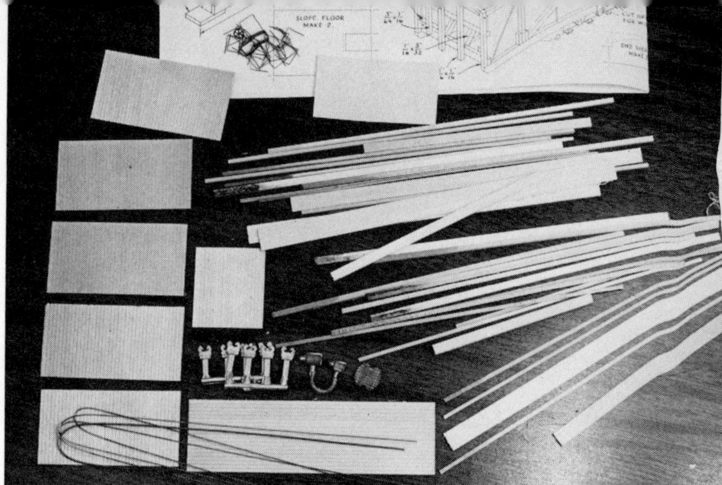

HO SCALE NORFOLK & WESTERN WOODEN HOPPER CAR

Norfolk & Western Railway designed this car during World War I to use as little steel as possible. They succeeded so well that it is practically a classic in wooden car structure. Except for such obvious items as trucks, etc., the only metal parts are tie rods, bolts and nuts, and a few cast fittings. Later modifications replaced the wood-center sills, bolsters, and some bracings with metal. In all, 1,368 of these cars were built. The design was finally cancelled out as obsolete in 1937. Manufacturer says model follows the basic structural design practically timber for timber. Color-coded wood and all hardware, less trucks and couplers, included. $4.95

A complete line of rolling stock, including classic cars and a good selection of the unusual, two kinds of snow plows, poultry car, 1913 insulated tank car, and the 95' Southern Tobacco Hogshead. The company is the manufacturer of an extensive catalog of wood parts, structural shapes, and sheetwood for modelers.

CALDWELL INDUSTRIES

Luling, Texas 78648

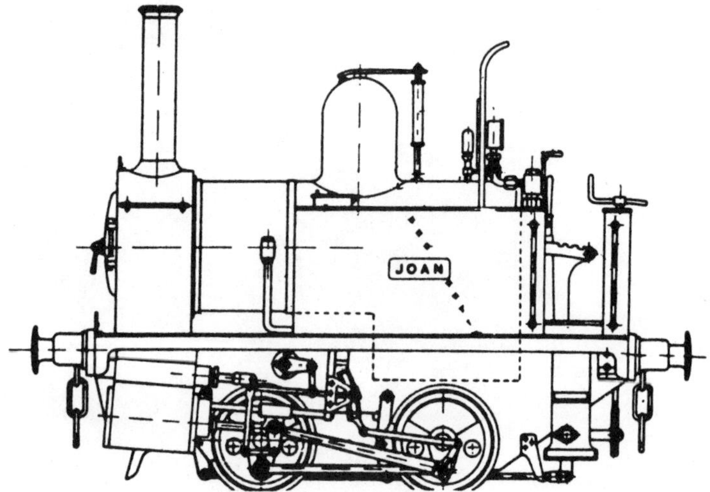

TICH STEAM LOCOMOTIVE

There is no doubt about it. TICH is an ugly little locomotive. There is also no doubt that it is the most popular model locomotive ever built. Designed to be easy to build, TICH has been the start of many a man in the hobby. This tiny engine, given reasonable workmanship, will haul the builder and still have power to spare, while its speed will have to be seen to be believed.

The model is designed to allow the builder to choose what he wants and still have a well-running engine. Two boilers have been designed, one larger than the other for those who insist. Either may be fitted. TICH is 13″ long and 7″ wide, and has cylinders 11/16″ × 1⅛″ and 2″ diameter wheels. It can be built on the smallest of lathes. Drawings (11) and castings for large boiler: $93.50. Drawings and small boiler castings: $90.00.

Caldwell sells many beautiful scale models of steam engines. You buy drawings, castings, and gears from them (sold separately). For most, machining can be done with a Unimat (which they sell). They also have several working gasoline models. Other kit products are clocks (see Clocks section) and machinery tools (see Tools section).

ULRICH
WM. K. WALTHERS, INC.

P.O. Box 16623
Milwaukee, Wis. 53216

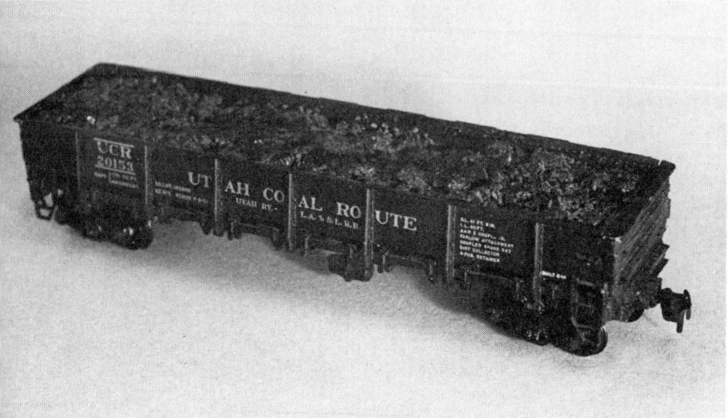

HO SCALE 40′ GENERAL SERVICE GONDOLA

All-metal kit comes with painted and lettered die-cast sides, die-cast ends and underbody, end-number decals, and metal trucks with Delrin wheels and working hopper doors. This model has a triple hopper that can be activated by a track ramp; the hopper doors give a complex appearance to the underbody. The kit is relatively simple and can be assembled in a couple of hours. Available in several road names in black or Tuscan red. $5.50

ULRICH has manufactured excellent all-metal rolling stock for a long time. It's nice to see a good all-metal kit in the plastic age!

TRAIN MINIATURE
La Mesa, Calif. 92041

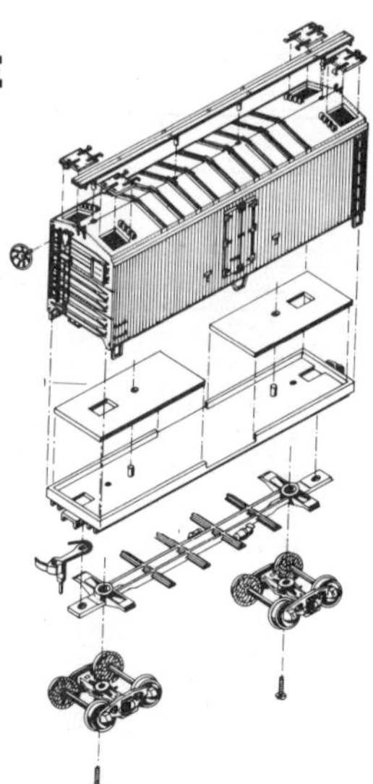

HO SCALE A.R.A. DOUBLE-SHEATHED REEFER

Part of the "car spotter" series, kits are hi-impact styrene, complete with trucks and couplers. Typical, brightly decorated billboard names available—Pluto Water, Domino Sugar, Prima Beer, Goetz, Country Club Beer, and (possibly no longer produced) the Old Dutch Cleanser. New "car spotters" are released continuously, but some are not reissued and may be hard to find. $2.98

Also available: convertible gondola, flat car, bay window caboose, and boxcars in the "car spotter" series.

ATHEARN COMPANY
11919 South Western
Los Angeles, Calif. 90036

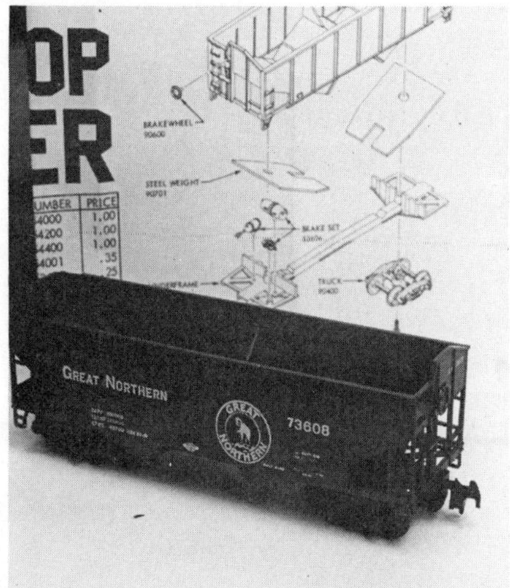

HO GREAT NORTHERN OFFSET SIDE HOPPER

The mechanics (or economics) of plastic production has made possible a tremendous variety of railroad rolling stock of the type that wasn't available several years ago because it wasn't common enough (or bizarre enough to be considered unusual). The offset side hopper of this type is interesting. The kit can be constructed with a simple screwdriver and contains couplers and trucks. Not the ultimate in detail, but for building up a backlog of rolling stock, you can't beat the price. $1.98.

Complete line of rolling stock, all of the simple screwdriver construction-type. Interesting examples: heavy-duty flat car (4 trucks), pickle car, wide-vision cabooses, high cube boxcars. They also sell a good line of diesel locos and shells for "kit-bashers." Good example: GE V28C 12-wheel diesel (powered, $17.98).

TYCO INDUSTRIES
540 Glen Ave.
Moorestown, N.J. 08057

HO MIKADO 2-8-2 STEAM LOCOMOTIVE AND TENDER

The Mikado is one of the classic American locomotives and this is a good beginner's kit. Although it is not highly detailed, the price is right and detailing can be added later. $9.95.

Tyco is an old name in model railroading. They joined the move to plastic with a good-quality, inexpensive, ready-to-run series, but they still offer ten old-time and steam locomotive kits. Although one regrets the inclusion of plastic in these kits, they have certainly held the line on price. Company also has an HO racing car series as well as the elaborate antique car kits.

ABBEY PRESS
St. Meinrad, Ind. 47577

PAPER AIRPLANES

Some years ago the *Scientific American,* an august journal hardly known for its levity, ran a paper airplane contest in which contestants were asked to submit designs for aeronautically sound paper airplanes. From out of the closet came scores of airplane addicts and what may have started out as a tongue-in-cheek affair turned into a fantastic and quite serious series of trials that tested the flying ability and ease of handling of a variety of engineer-designed, aerodynamically perfect paper airplanes. This kit includes six die-cut rigid-stock 8" × 12" planes in high-flying colors with full insignia and weights. Also included is *The Great International Paper Airplane Book,* which gives a day-to-day account of the finals plus designs, data, and time-distance records. We can't think of a dandier gift for anyone who ever sailed a page of his notebook across the classroom. And at under $7. this may be the bargain of the 1970s.

DUMAS PRODUCTS, INC.
790 South Park Ave.
Tucson, Ariz. 85719

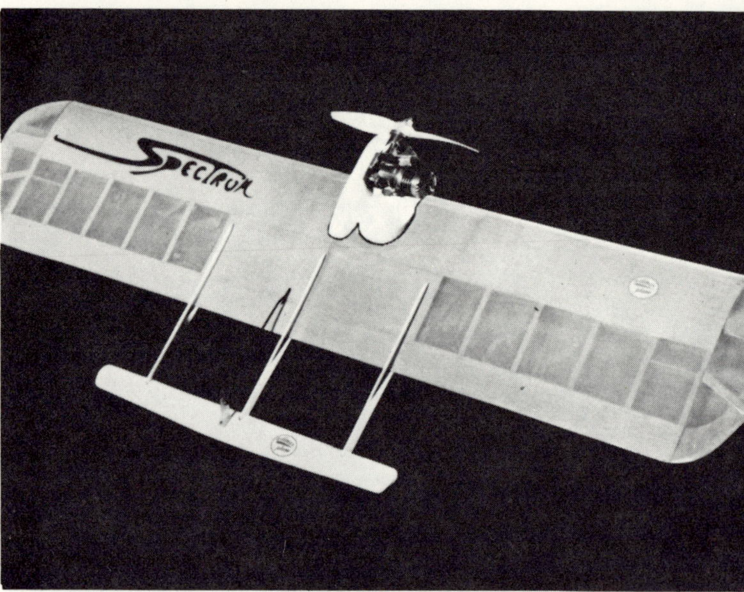

"SPECTRUM" COMBAT PLANE

Extremely maneuverable competition plane. Three shaped spruce booms, spruce leading edge doubler, and molded plastic bubble for fuel tank. 0.35 engine recommended. $8.95.

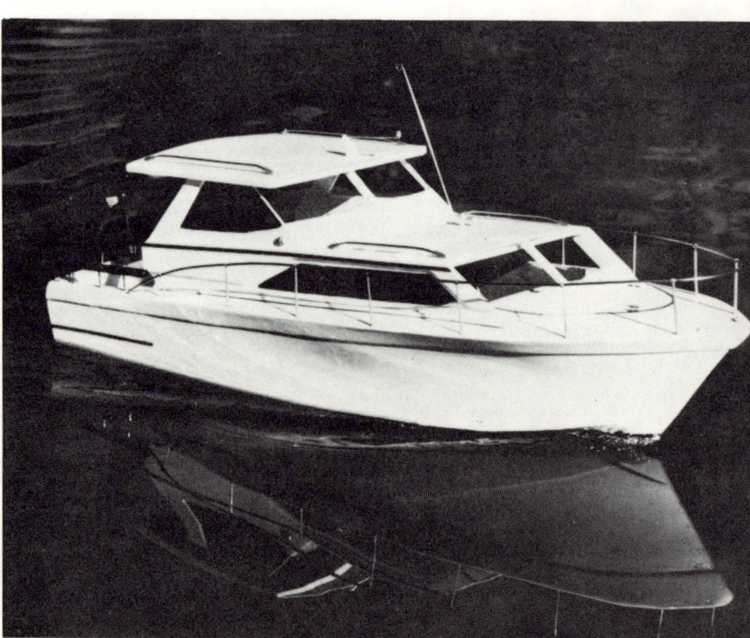

"TROJAN" 31' CRUISER

Plywood construction makes this suitable for free running, radio control, or simply display. Electric power of 0.19 gas engine. Kit includes all deck hardware. $45.75.

"ATLAS VAN LINES" HYDROPLANE

A scale model of the famous unlimited hydroplane driven by Bill Muncy, three-time National Champion. Eighteen inches long, mahogany construction, with formed plastic cowl for 0.049 engine. $7.75. Hardware kit (for running with ½ A engine): $5.95. Same prototype in 36″-long mahogany, birch, and plywood for 0.40 displacement engine: $37.95.

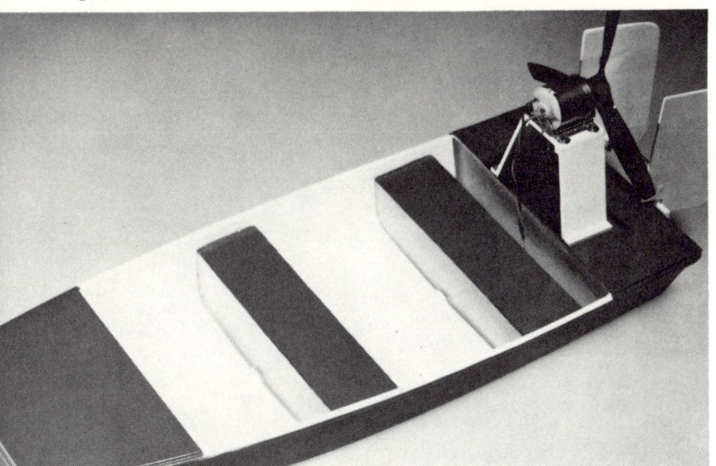

"LITTLE JON" AIR BOAT

For the swimming pool or small lake. Easy to build—all precut mahogany. Run with .020 powered air prop. Length, 15″. $4.95. Kit, with underwater power pod (battery not included): $6.85.

Dumas offers an impressive line of racing boats, hydroplanes, power boats, sailboats, and extensive accessories for running. They also sell several radio control, control line, and free flight models; some are semi-scale, but accent is on performing models.

JOHN HATHAWAY
410 West 6 St./Box 1287
San Pedro, Calif. 90731

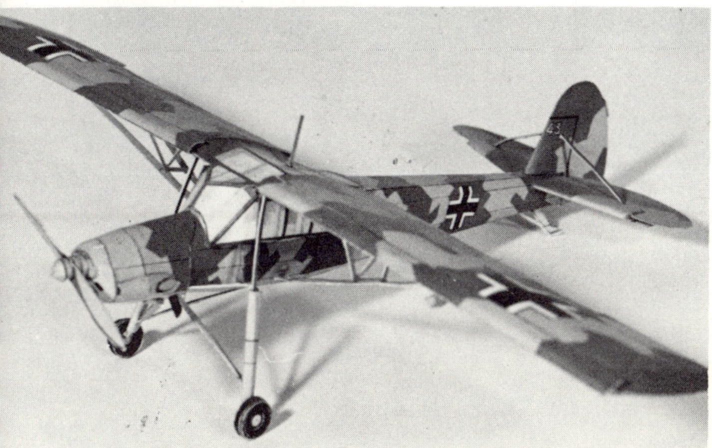

FIESELER STORCH CARD MODEL

Slatted-wing detail, fine-line detail, fairly complex construction. 1:50 scale. $1.84.

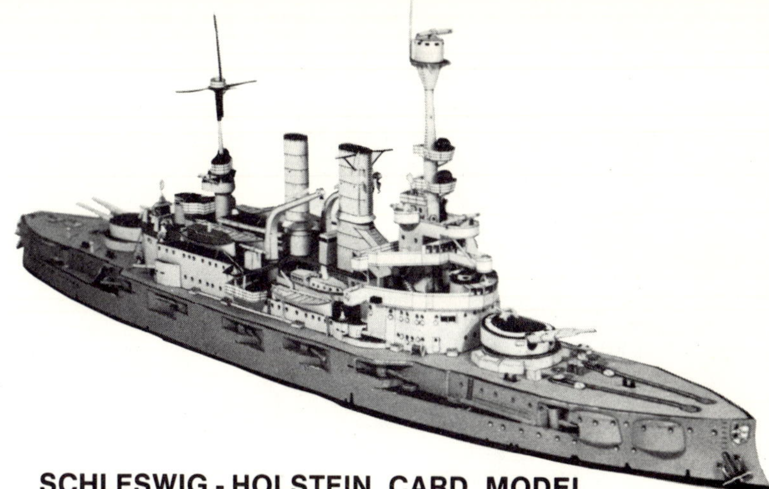

SCHLESWIG - HOLSTEIN CARD MODEL

High-detail card model of World War I German warship 20″ long. $6.50.

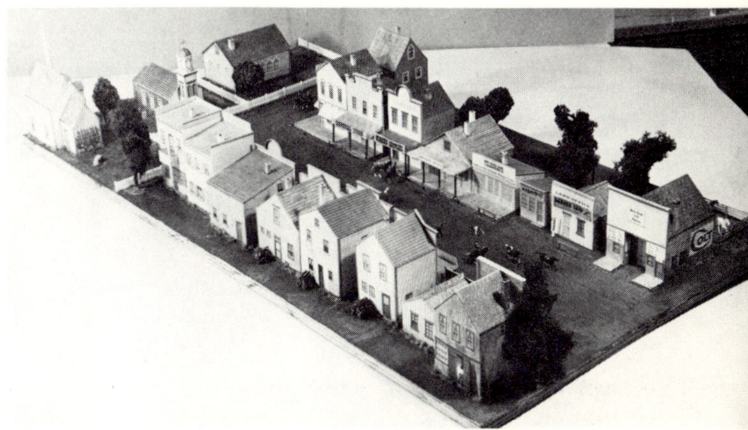

CANYON CITY MODEL

Western Mining Town of 1880s includes 20 card buildings in HO scale. (Figures and landscaping materials can be obtained at hobby shops.) $7.15

A complete line of card models, mostly from Europe, of trains, planes, boats, buildings. Models are supplied on printed sheets and although care in cutting, folding, and joining are needed, work is not difficult. Some complex models can require great patience. Detail obtained can, however, be very impressive.

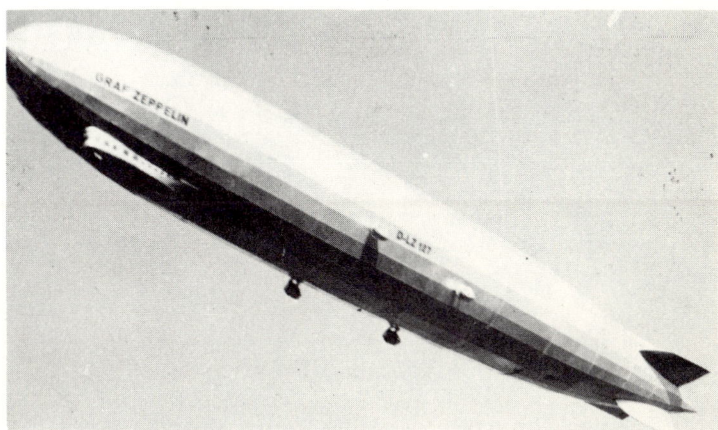

GRAF ZEPPELIN

Giant, 4′ long card model. In book format, simple to construct. $6.95.

FLITELGLAS MODELS
R.R. #1
Neoga, Ill. 62447

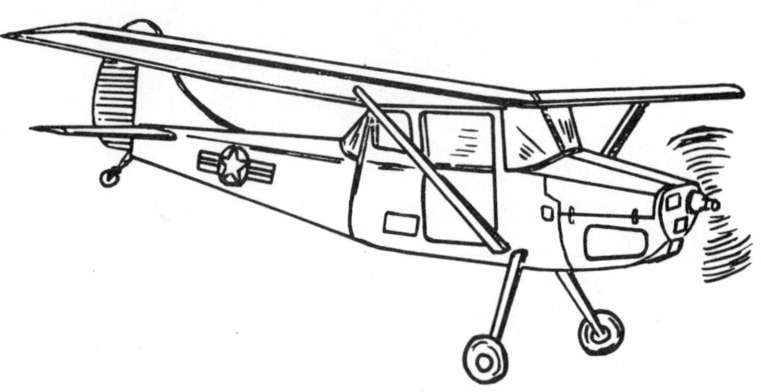

CESSNA O-IE *BIRD-DOG* BASIC TRAINER

Model of the famous *Bird-Dog* used as liaison and Forward Air Controller by the Air Force. This model can be flown with 3-channel radio and is designed as the first trainer for the newcomer to radio control. The plane can be built on the kitchen table with a minimum of tools. Assembly consists of joining wing halves, attaching the tail surfaces and landing gear, and installing engine and radio. Wing is precovered foam core, which requires either Monokote or paint finish. "When properly built and aligned (all outlined in the instruction booklet) this plane can be flown by anyone with only a couple minutes of instructions," says the manufacturer. Wing span 51″; power 0.15-0.25, gas engine. $64.95.

SCIENTIFIC MODELS, INC.
340 Snyder Ave.
Berkeley Heights, N.J. 07922

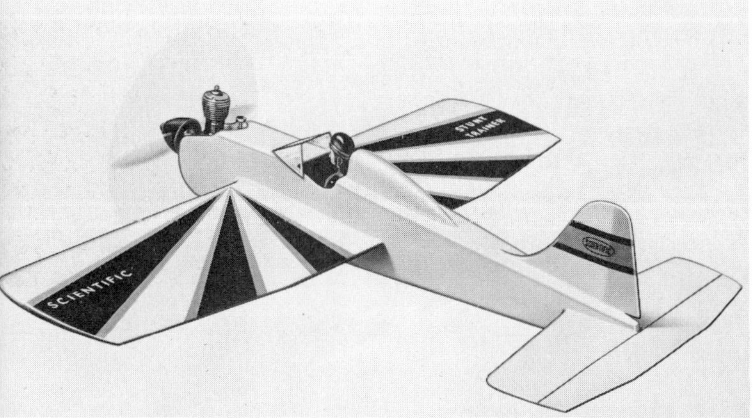

"STUNT TRAINER" FLYING MODEL

Another balsa control live model, this is from the "built-up series"—for the model builder who enjoys the fun of "building" as well as "flying," these

models are ideal. Most of the models shown feature rib-construction wings, as well as leading and trailing edges. All kits include preformed metal parts and easy-to-follow, step-by-step assembly instructions. $5.49.

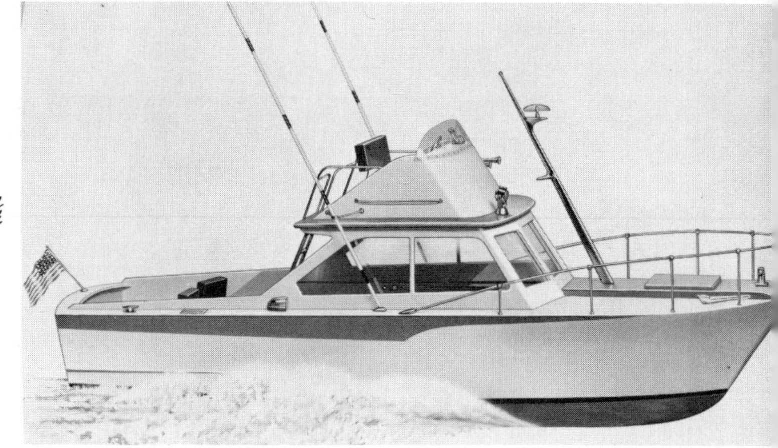

"SPORT FISHERMAN" MODEL KIT

Model of the world-famous Sport Fisherman is loaded with extras not found in any other kit. It has all the necessary marine hardware and cast-metal fittings—including a highly efficient nylon propeller, a neoprene universal, welded 1-piece brass rudder and tiller, cast metal anchor, horn, searchlight, rail stanchions, etc. Other features include die-cut plywood bulkheads and keel, number-coded die-cut balsa materials, plastic windshield, decals, flag and full-sized plans with radio control installation shown. Model can be powered with 6–12 v. electric motor or a ½ A gas engine. Overall length: 27″. Beam: 8½″. $29.95.

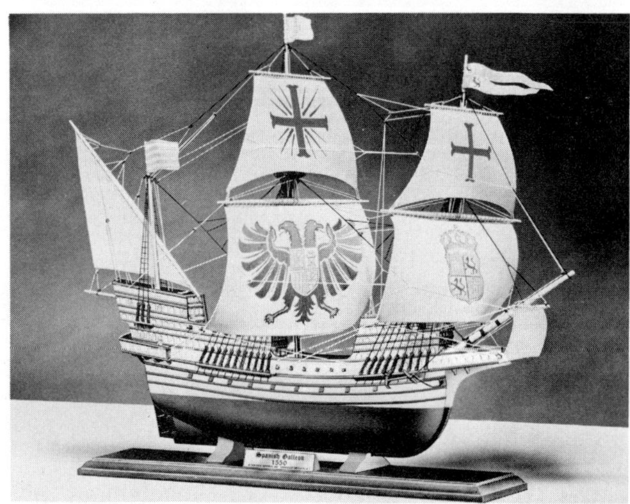

SPANISH GALLEON 1550

A colorful model of the Spanish galleons that ruled the oceans from Europe to the New World carrying supplies and men to the Americas and returning with gold. Lavishly decorated and well armed, they were Spain's naval elite until the Armada's defeat in 1588. Kit includes precarved wood hull, precision-cast metal fittings, cannons, anchor, figurehead, preruled basswood decking, and cloth sails and flags printed in color on antique finish material. Length: 19½″. Height: 14½″. $32.95

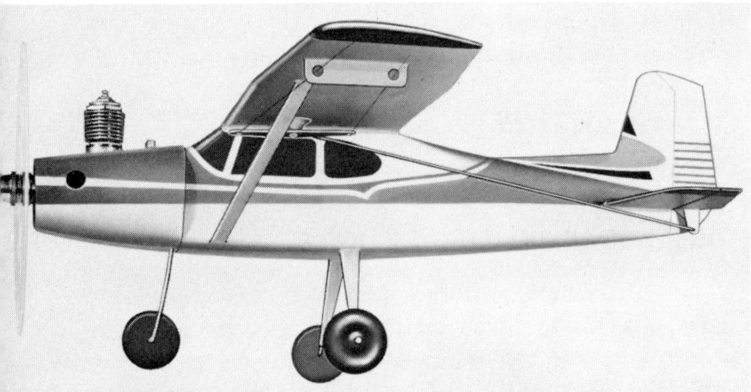

CESSNA 182 TRICYCLE CONTROL LINE FLYING MODEL

This 18″-wingspan flying model is part of Scien-, tific's "carved body series," which, according to the manufacturer, "are designed to get you flying F-A-S-T . . . with a minimum of model building time! All kits shown below feature a fully carved balsa body (fuselage) that eliminates the more time-consuming "tissue covering" method of construction. Kits have preshaped, 1-piccc wings and many have formed cowls and canopies as well. All models include preformed metal parts and easy-to-follow, step-by-step instructions." For 0.202–0.049 gas engines. $5.49.

Scientific has an extensive collection of historic wooden ship models, gas- and rubber-powered flying models, as well as the Realife series of miniature furniture (see Dolls & Dollhouses).

JAMES BLISS & CO., INC.
Route 128
Dedham, Mass. 02026

"TAURUS" EAST COAST TOWBOAT

Few vessels of 1900 were as gracefully functional as this type of towboat. Tugs of today are similar in design—though dieselized. Kit includes 10″ machine-carved waterline pine hull and cabin, printed cabin and pilothouse sides, die-cut plankscored decks, wood materials, fittings, plan and assembly instructions. Ideal for HO gauge rail fans. Can be built in about ten hours. Overall model specifications: Length, 9″, HO gauge (slightly over ⅛″ equals 1′). $13.

STEAM CANAL BARGE—*CITY OF PEKIN*

Originally built as the mule-drawn *City of Henry* in Chicago in 1875, she was converted to a twin-screw tow barge in 1911, and her name changed to *City of Pekin*. Before railroads pushed through at the turn of the century, the Illinois and Michigan Canal carried large tonnage of grain, lumber, coal, beef, etc., between LaSalle and Chicago. The canal linked by water the Great Lakes with the Mississippi River via tributaries.

This barge was typical of those working the canal. Folding rudder permitted close fit in locks and small propellers avoided wash damage to canal banks. Built of white pine and white oak, she was afloat at Channahon, Illinois, in 1936, though forty feet of her stern had been removed.

Complete kit includes plans, instructions, machine-carved hull, wood material, and white metal castings pine hull. Overall model specifications: length, 13½″; height, 3½″; scale, ⅛″ equals 1′. $9.50.

BLISS sells a complete line of model boats including wooden classic ships from Denmark, "Constructo" series imported from Spain, as well as several domestic lines. They also have brass cannon models, working steam engines, fittings for boats, and modeler's tools.

VENTURE AERO-MARINE
Box 5273
Akron, Ohio 44313

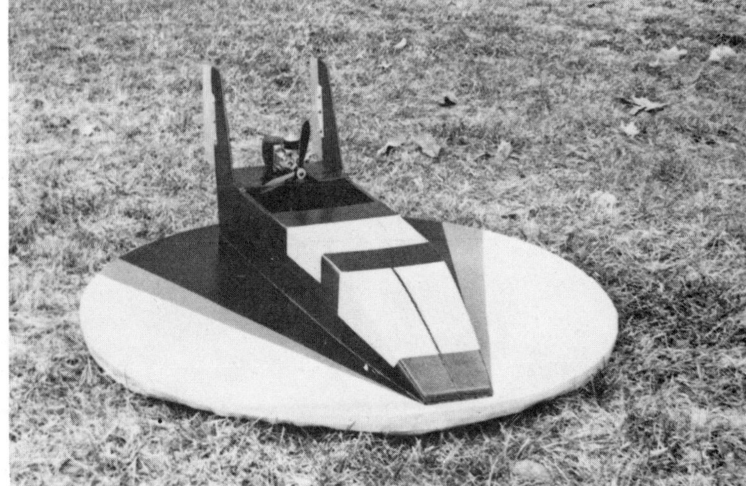

HOVERCRAFT

Before you look into this model, read our section on vehicles. You'll see that "hovering" is a new fad travel form. Now you can build and "hover" with a Hovercraft model kit. These models work on the same principle as the real thing. That is, the featured principle is the air-cushion ride. The models will operate over any reasonably smooth terrain (ice, water, concrete, asphalt, dirt) and will clear obstacles up to 2″ high. The "Air Raiser" illustrated is relatively simple to construct and is more fun than most traditional planes. Also an excellent science fair project. Impress the neighbors. $15.95.

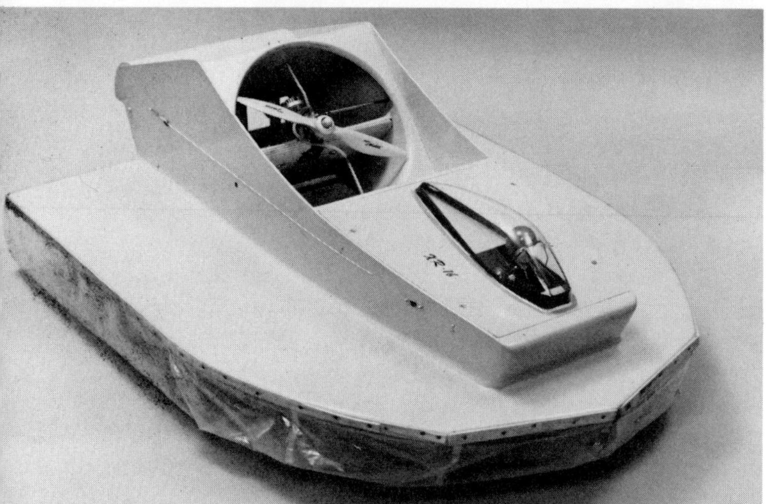

HOVERCRAFT—RADIO OPERATED

The "air cushion machine" above is also available radio operated. This is a super-model by any standards. It has all-plywood-and-foam hull construction for strength and flotation. This model is 40″ long and weighs 7 lb. Use any standard .40 to .78 cu. in. model airplane engine. Price: $54.95 (does not include radio, engine, or hardware).

BANDAI CORPORATION OF AMERICA
1014 East Burgrove
Carson, Calif. 90746

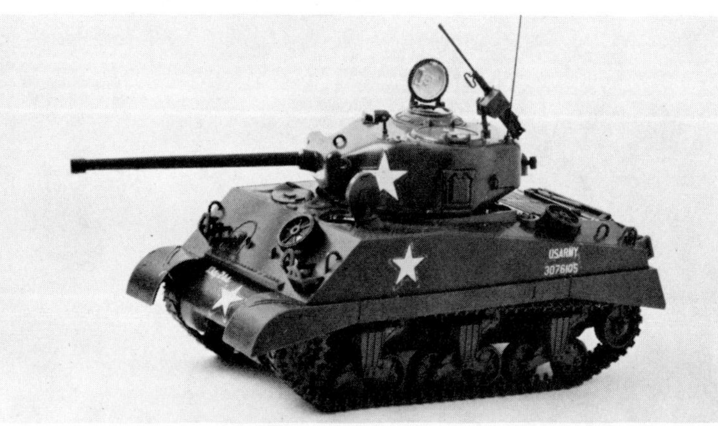

SCALE MODEL OF A SHERMAN M4A3 MEDIUM TANK (76mm)

The fascination with weaponry, ancient and modern, will one day attract some kind of scholarly scrutiny. The preschooler bang-bangs his way through the day and the adult is annually presented with a new choice of war books. Replicas of modern warfare implements and machines are owned by many very young children. For the mature person who has a keen interest in man's battle weapons, there can be no better replica on the market than this scale model, produced by the Bandai Corporation. The Sherman M4A3 medium tank is an excellent example of Bandai's pinpoint series. This tank was commissioned following the Battle of the Bulge. It is generally credited with the victory of the allies on the Western front. $24.

CONSTANTINE
2050 Eastchester Rd.
Bronx, N.Y. 10461

HISTORIC SHIP MODEL KITS

Constantine, an honored name in woodworking materials, offers three well-priced, decorative ship model kits. All kits include carved wood hull, cast metal fittings, anchor, lifeboats, capstan, winch, fife rails, display stand, and full instructions. These are not the simplest of projects, but you certainly don't have to be a retired shipbuilder to do a creditable job. And the results are fabulous looking. The *Cutty Sark,* the most famous of clipper ships, features cloth sails and full rigging. It is 15″ long and 9½″ high. The *Flying Cloud,* launched in 1851, is 13¾″ long and 9″ high. Famous Old Ironsides—the U.S.S. *Constitution*—winner of forty battles, loser of none, has twelve cannons and is 14½″ long and 10″ high. $9.95 each.

BLUEJACKET SHIP CRAFTERS
145 Water St.
South Norwalk, Conn. 06854

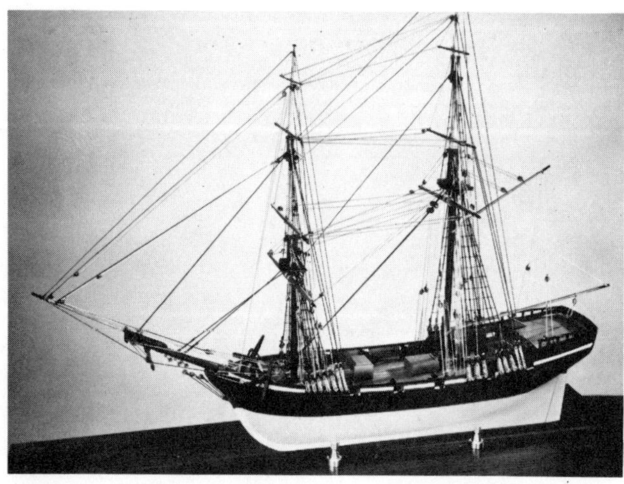

CABOT—MODEL OF EARLY AMERICAN BRIG 1775

Recommended by the manufacturer "for those wanting a small model, overall length 15″, ⅛″ equals 1′ scale." Kit includes machine-carved hull, materials cut to size for keel, rudder, rails, masts, spars, deck houses, etc., plus blueprints, instructions, and the necessary fittings. $29.95.

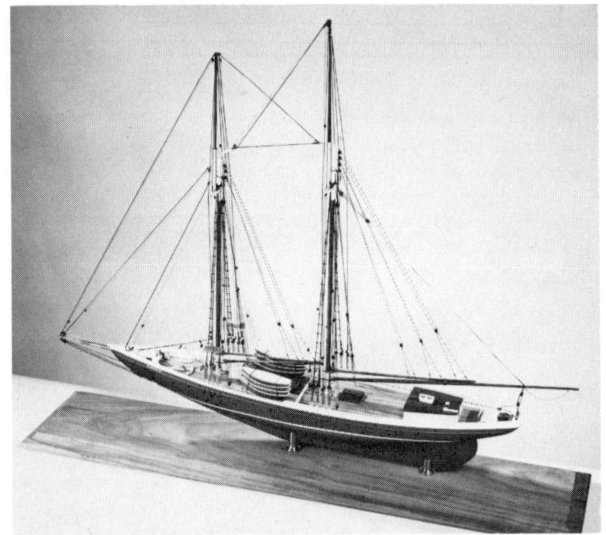

BLUENOSE

Such is the affection Canadians hold for the *Bluenose*, they've struck her likeness on the reverse of Canadian dimes. And good reason. She was built in 1921 at Lunenburg, N.S., as a Banks fisherman, working the rough waters off Newfoundland, and her speed was soon apparent. In her first years she won the International Fisherman's Trophy Cup and in challenges over the next seventeen years she never lost it. She was lost on a reef off Haiti in 1946.

The kit has machine-carved hull, materials for all super-structures, masts, spars, etc., plus detailed plans, instructions, and necessary fittings. Overall length, 22″. Scale, ⅛″ equals 1′. $35.95.

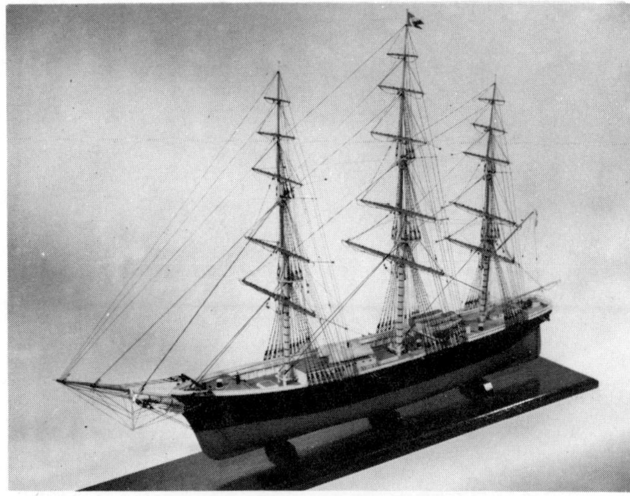

FLYING CLOUD MODEL CLIPPER

Kit has fully carved hull of clear sugar pine. Included are blueprints, instructions, materials for keel, spars, masts, rudder, rails, and fittings. Overall length, 37″. Scale; ⅛″ equals 1′. $72.95.

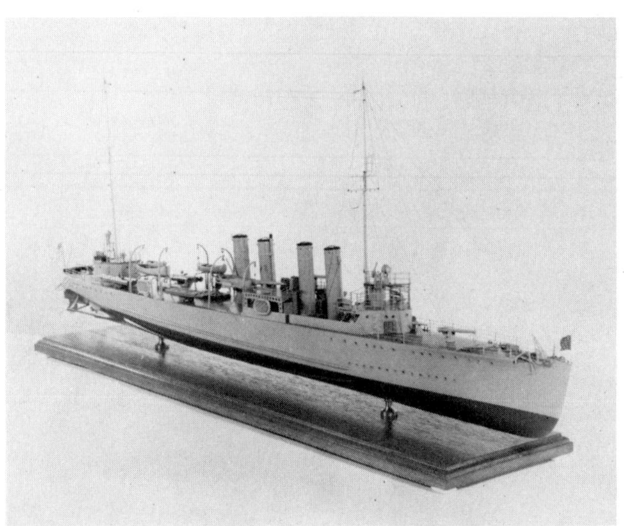

310′ DESTROYER

Carved wood hull, and complete parts and instructions. Model is of the open bridge type. Modifications are possible for any specific vessel. Destroyers of this type were U.S.S. *Ward*, U.S.S. *Reuben James*, and H.M.S. *Campbelltown*. Overall length, 39½″. Scale, ⅛″ equals 1′. $78.75.

Small company offering many ship models, fittings, marine books, tools, and gifts. Catalog (75¢, 64 pp.) offers the following good advice on choosing ship models; "Only you can make the choice. The experienced modeler needs no advice. And the novice doesn't want it. But a beginner is well advised to consider the following: 1. Scale: ¼″ scale demands less intricate workmanship than, say, 1/16″ scale. 2. Rig: A schooner has far less rigging than a full rigged ship. Several models do not even need ratlines. 3. Available time: Ship modeling asks for your time in generous amounts, measured in weeks or months rather than evenings. 4. Size: Larger models are usually easier to work on and are more impressive when completed. However, some of our models are 40″ long—be sure you have room to display it. But shipmates, if your heart is set on a clipper, be not dismayed. Some of the finest ships you'll ever see have been turned out by beginners—what was lacking in experience was made up in zeal. Remember, there is practically no mistake that can't be corrected. Be patient. Learn as you go."

BRENTANO'S

586 Fifth Ave.
New York, N.Y. 10036

DENNIS MOTOR FIRE ENGINE

A miniature masterpiece, this 1/16 scale model features an operating suspension ladder, steerable wheels, working suspension system, and real rubber tires. The hood raises to reveal the White and Pope engine. Novices take note, this kit has 500 parts! $22.

S. T. PRESTON & SON, INC.
Main Street Wharf
Greenport, N.Y. 11944

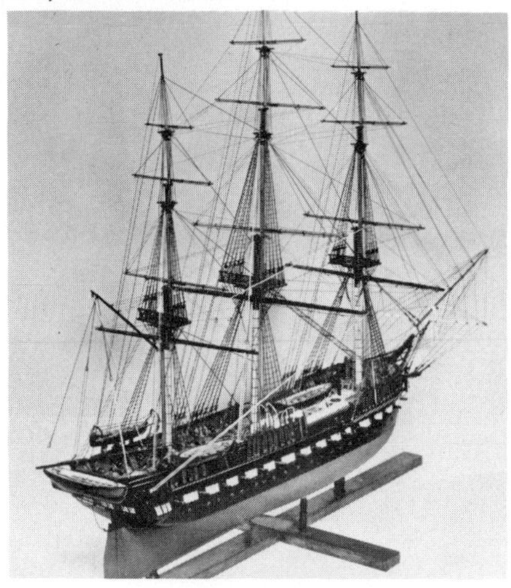

U.S. FRIGATE *CONSTITUTION*

Complete kit includes carved pine hull, shaped spars and masts, complete set of custom fittings, instructions and plans, as well as baseboard and brass mounting pegs. 30" long, 24" high. Scale: 3/32" equals 1'. $69.95.

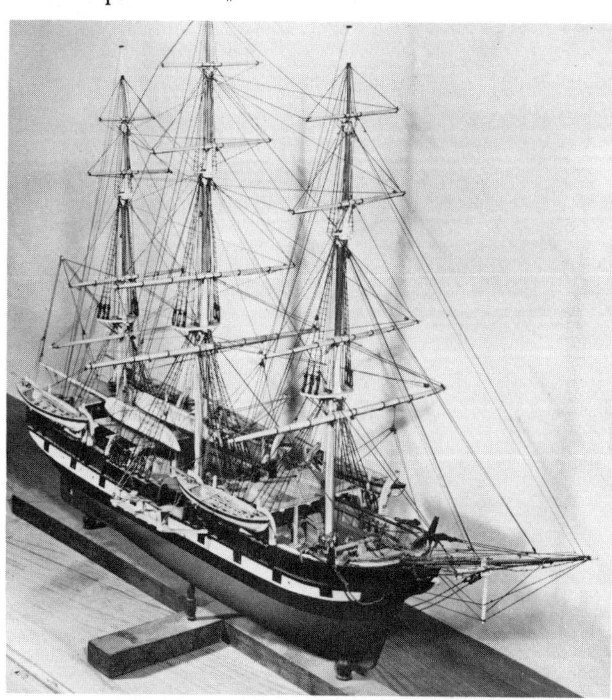

WHALING SHIP *CHARLES W. MORGAN*

The first voyage of the *Charles W. Morgan* began September 6, 1841. Captain T. A. Norton. She was gone for over three years. In her eighty-four years at sea she sailed every ocean and is estimated to have earned over two million dollars. The *Charles W. Morgan* appeared in the motion pictures *Java Head* and *Down to the Sea in Ships,* and now is moored alongside a wharf in Mystic Seaport, Connecticut.

Kit includes carved wood hull, shaped spars and masts, and all riggings and fittings. 26" long, 20" high. $74.95

Preston's sells a complete line of historic ship models as well as brass cannon models and reproductions of ships' figureheads.

MONTE MODELS
P.O. Box 2391
New Bern, N.C. 28560

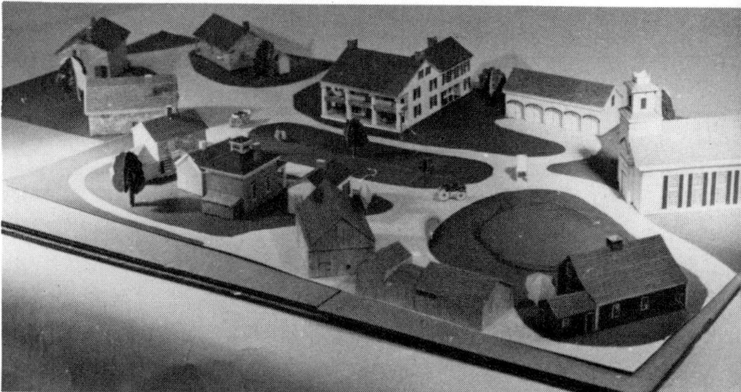

THE VILLAGE CROSSROADS

This card model of Cooperstown, New York, includes ten structures: the homes and shops of a typical agricultural community before the Civil War. Farm animals roam the fields and yards, daily chores are performed, and village craftsmen carry on their trades with old implements in the old way. 40" × 21" × 5½" high. $3.

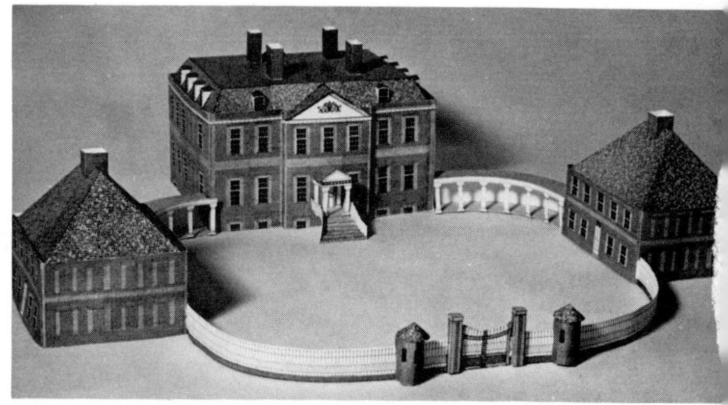

TRYON PALACE CARD MODEL

New Bern, North Carolina—grounds and outbuildings. Originally built in 1767–1770 for the Royal Governor, the Tryon Palace served as the first capitol in the independent state of North Carolina. $1.50.

CLOCK TOWER—GHIRARDELLI SQUARE

An Italian, Domingo Ghirardelli, arrived in San Francisco in 1849 and set up a general merchandise business in Stockton. It flourished so well that in

1893 he purchased the whole block. The Clock Tower was added on to the Ghirardelli block in 1915. $2.

Complete line of card models, mostly from Europe. (See also Dolls & Dollhouses section.)

PAUL J. GRUEN STUDIOS

20 Pleasant St.
Newburyport, Mass. 10950

OLD TOY VEHICLE KITS

A few years ago, Paul J. Gruen, an award-winning toy designer, began to question the shoddiness of many of today's toys and found himself longing for the old days when children and parents built, played with, and repaired toys together. This longing led to the founding of "Old Toy" kits, chosen a few years ago by *The New York Times* as one of the thirteen best toys. Beautifully crafted of precision-cut, predrilled hardwood with peg and glue assembly (no nails, screws, or plastic fixtures), these are wonderful assembly projects that evoke for both parents and kids that nostalgia of finding old toys in the attic. One objection: Many might wish Mr. Gruen's approach were less sexist. Why a doll wardrobe "for girls" and tanks and trucks "for boys"? The Tank is, as a matter of fact, their most popular toy and it's a great-looking item (15″ × 7″ × 7½″). The Freighter is a virtually indestructible cab and trailer (25″ × 7¼″ × 7¼″). The Delivery Truck is the classic old-fashioned model with three-pieced grooved fenders and large maple wheels (18″ × 6″ × 7″). The Pick-up Truck is a classic toy item (12″ × 7″ × 6½″). The company's first kit for girls is a Wardrobe that holds a dozen doll outfits and has miniature hangers. Tank: $12.95. Freighter: $16.95. Delivery Truck: $14.95. Pick-up truck: $10.95. Wardrobe: $13.95.

THE GIFT HORSE

P.O. Box 28902
Atlanta, Ga. 30328

HOBBY HORSE

Toys come and toys go, but sturdy wooden hobby horses are always in fashion. This horse (named Charley) will make your child's eyes light up. Finished size 46″ long × 43″ tall. The wood has been precut and drilled for simple assembly. Natural finish you stain. $44.95.

THE GALLERY

Amsterdam, N.Y. 12010

GIANT WALKING INSECTS

Here's something that will thrill many a youngster and possibly scare Mother. Not for the squeamish! If you're a "bug" about insects, these remarkably (maybe too remarkably) realistic-looking pre-colored plastic and metal 8″ giants are for you! They "come at you" with dramatic action—powered by a wind-up motor—and, they're all members in good standing of the Natural Science Action Series. You receive them in a dormant or "kit" state with easy-to-follow directions for full-scale "hatching," plus a personal history of the insect. Simple to assemble. They're a "dream-come-true" for any "kid" from six to sixty . . . and, of course, do fill an educational bill, too, as each one (Praying Mantis, Rhinoceros Beetle, Stag Beetle, and Long Horn Beetle) is an enlarged, true-to-life replica of its species. Choose them separately or in a set of 4 . . . who knows, they may just walk their way straight into your heart! $4. each.

THE CLASSIC V-8

A fun-to-assemble, ¼-scale, see-through kit of the most popular automobile engine in America today. Battery-powered! Fully operational! You'll see how everything works in your own automobile's V-8 engine and maybe just someday you'll save yourself a bundle in repair bills. The kit includes over 100 moving parts molded in heavy-duty red, black, gray, or clear plastic. Cylinders move in perfect harmony within the chambers. Valves rush up and down, spark plugs fire and light up, gears turn. Everything that moves in a regular full-sized engine moves in this amazing model.

Complete kit comes with everything you need for easy, interesting assembly—including wire, cement, powerful miniature motor (batteries not included)—plus an authoritative "tech manual." $16.95.

GIANT TINKERTOYS

The Tinkertoy grows up . . . and up! Now, no matter how tall a dream or how big a fantasy, any child can build "his thing" into a king-sized reality. He can let his imagination run wild—windmills, spaceships, bridges, a crane with a 9′ boom, a giant truck, a jet can come to life as fast as he thinks! He can create and learn. Constructed of rugged plastic, the Giant Tinkertoy is equally at home in a playroom or on a playground. The brightly colored pieces are color-keyed to an instruction book (included) so that even the tiniest novice construction engineer can "do-it-himself" and come up with a dazzling, almost-real replica. This set includes 52 rods in 5 different lengths, plus 38 spools in 5 distinct sizes—90 pieces in all. All beautifully packed in a rigid, reusable storage container. For king-sized fun for many years to come. $35.

GMB PRODUCTS CO.

P.O. Box 292
Terrell, Tex. 75160

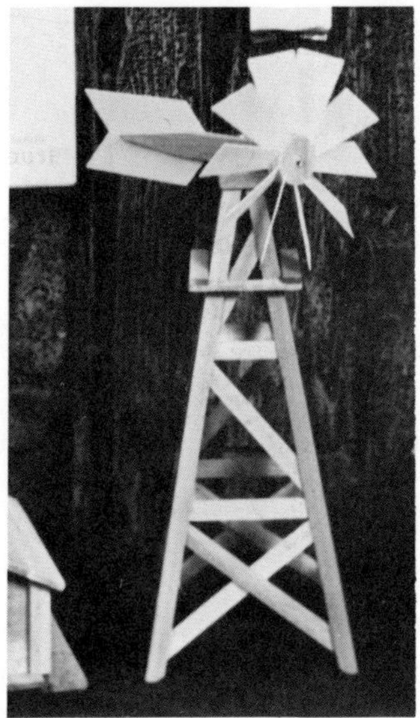

WINDMILL KIT

The true function of the windmill has disappeared, for the most part, from the scene. The windmill, however, can still be seen attached to an old grain mill or water pump (usually no longer in use) or simply a part of someone's antique collection. For those of you who would enjoy owning this symbol of the past, a windmill kit is offered by the GMB Products Co.

The kit has 43 (redwood) pieces, that are assembled with glue and screws (which are included) and easy-to-read instructions. Size of finished windmill is 8″ × 8″ and the base is 24″ high. $8.95.

GMB manufacturers a variety of western red cedar kits, including bird houses and bird feeders.

LAFAYETTE RADIO

111 Jericho Turnpike
Syosset, N.Y. 11791

GILBERT TRI-LAB PAK

An all-purpose, three-in-one science kit—at a very reasonable price. Manufactured by a fine name in educational science, this kit lets the junior scientist perform over 95 experiments in microscope observation, chemistry, and geology. Equipment includes die-cast metal, 75x microscope, slides, chemicals, alcohol lamp, mineral specimens, geologist's hammer, and more. An excellent starter kit. $10.99.

TRANSISTOR RADIO AND PA SYSTEM KIT

An easy-to-build, two-in-one kit. You get a safe, battery-operated, transistorized AM radio receiver plus headphone and microphone for announcing your own radio programs. Kit includes speaker, antenna, and all required parts. (5 lb.) $11.50.

MAGIC-GLO BLACK LIGHT KIT

What youngster doesn't want to write secret messages and learn invisible detection? This kit unravels the mysteries of fluorescence and phosphorescence—and in the process provides hours of fun. Kit contains socket and cord, lamp stand, and all paints, brushes, crayons, inks, and other materials needed to perform experiments. Forty-eight-page booklet explains the use of black light in such fields as minerology, crime detection, medicine, and electronics. $12.95.

ATOMIC ENERGY LAB

This kit will definitely not let you or yours blow up anything, nor will it give the family cat radiation sickness. Rather it will give any interested adult or older child a chance to learn about some basic nuclear physics by experimenting. Instruction booklet tells you how to detect radioactivity with a cloud chamber, how to detect ionization, how to check radioactivity with an electroscope, and more. $10.49.

GILBERT WEATHERCRAFT METEOROLOGY LAB

If Frank Field and Uncle Wethbee are beginning to bore you, try doing-it-yourself. This inexpensive kit, manufactured by a respected name in educational science, includes everything you need to forecast the weather accurately and to gauge relative humidity, precipitation, and all other odds and ends the weatherman tells us. (3 lb.) $10.45.

SKY ROVER CRYSTAL RADIO KIT

A perennial favorite, even with youngsters who think radio is something people listened to in the Dark Ages. Kit is easy to assemble and requires no batteries or electricity. Excellent value. (1 lb.) $3.30.

MINI-LABS
EDUCATIONAL RESOURCES DIVISION
EDUCATIONAL DESIGN INC.
47 West 13 St.
New York, N.Y. 10011

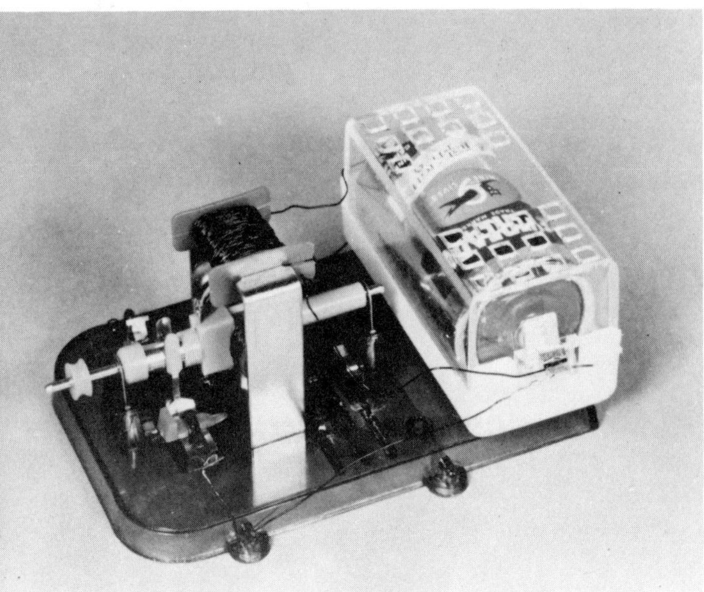

ELECTRIC MOTOR KIT

The builder learns how motors really work by constructing one, winding the armature, adjusting the speed, and running it forwards and backwards. At the price, this is a valuable educational device you should not miss. $3., batteries not included.

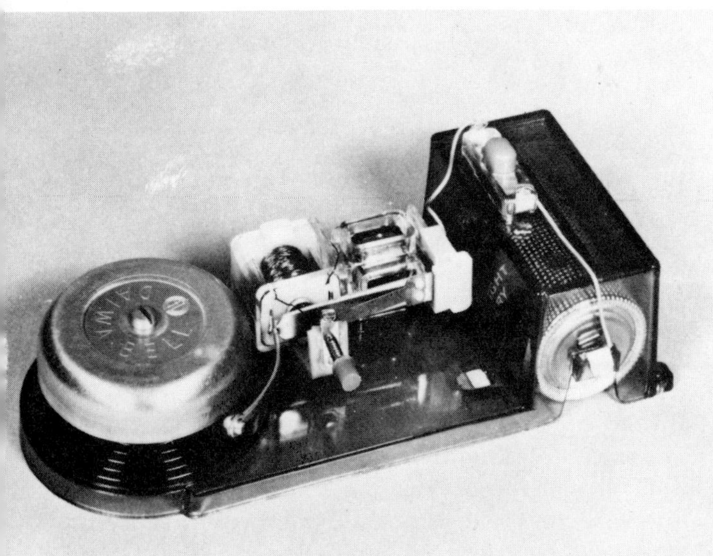

ELECTRIC BELL KIT

Includes all material for an easy-to-make, push-button bell, electrical buzzer, and telegraph key. An interesting and fun way to learn how electricity is used through magnetism to create sound. Morse code and electric magnet activities are also illustrated. Another very good educational toy for very little money. $3., batteries not included.

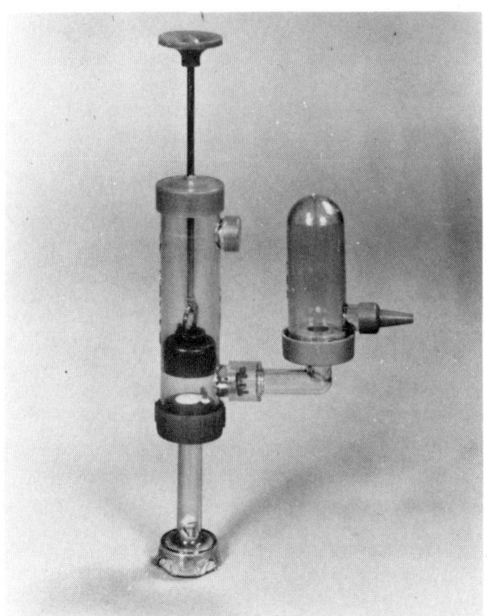

HYDRAULIC PUMP KIT

A complete kit for building many kinds of working pumps: lift pump, force pump, compression pump. The builder assembles cylinder, piston, valves, inlets, outlets, and reservoir. All these interior parts can then be seen while the pump is working. Actually shoots a stream of water 25 ft.

Mini-Labs is a good collection of simple science kits ideal for whetting a young person's appetite for science and machinery, at only $3. Highly recommended.

RADIO SHACK
2617 West 7 St.
Fort Worth, Tex. 76107

OPTICAL LAB KIT

Lenses, prisms, and mechanical parts for construction of a telescope, microscope, periscope, and a 35 mm. camera with interchangeable lenses. The book contains 130 experiments and appears to be a good introduction to optics for youngsters. $19.95.

100-In-1 ELECTRONIC PROJECT KIT

Everything you need to get started in a rewarding electronics hobby. Build radios, amplifiers, computer circuits, strobe lights, photometer—100 projects in all and they really work! All parts mounted on panel—connect, disconnect, reconnect them with no soldering, no tools, no mess. 17½″ × 11″ × 2″ workcase. Requires 9-v and 2 "A" cells. $29.95.

DIGITAL COMPUTER KIT

Gives a great introduction to the world of computer programming and cybernetics—forms a solid base for advanced learning and interests! Teaches binary math in the easy, learn-by-doing way. Program it to predict weather, diagnose illnesses, do translations, and more. With all parts and easy-to-follow instructions. Requires 3 "C" cells. $29.95

Radio Shack has several educational kits in their "Science Fair" series including a color organ, and radio kits (see Electronics section for more information).

ESTES INDUSTRIES
Penrose, Colo. 81240

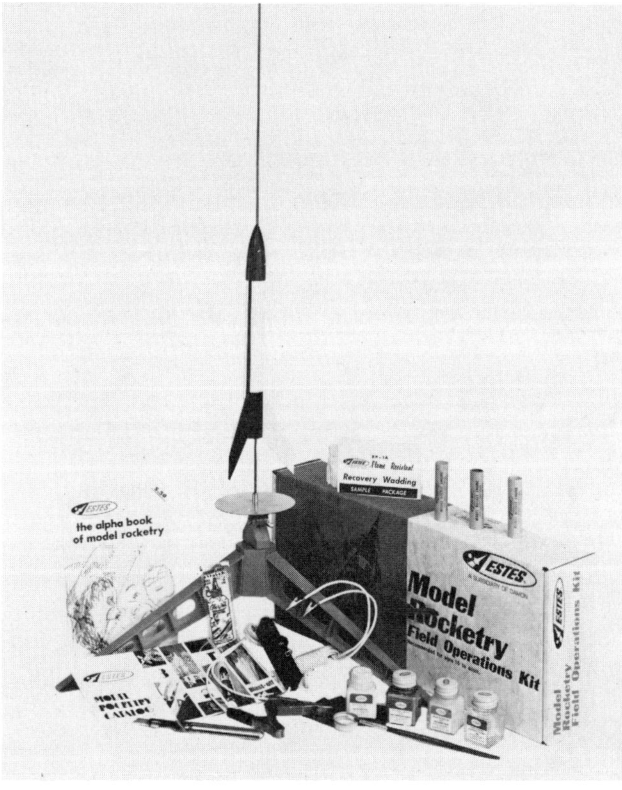

MODEL ROCKET DELUXE STARTER KIT

A complete kit for a beginner in model rocketry. It includes a rocket with balsa nose cone and fins, a launch control system (requires a 12-v. battery, not included), ignition systems, and "Porta-pad" plastic launch pad with blast deflector plate and 3 engines. A nice touch is that all the tools for construction—knife, glue, sand paper, paint, brush, and brush cleaner—are included. Parachute recovery. Complete kit: $9.95.

MARK II SINGLE-STAGE ROCKETS

High-performance, single-stage rocket, 9″ long. Streamer recovery engines not included. Kit K-2: $1.25.

Typical recommended engines: ½A6-2 (max. thrust: 46 oz., thrust duration: 0.2 sec.): 3 for $1.10. C6-5 (max. thrust: 48 oz., thrust duration: 1.7 sec.): 3 for $1.50.

A highly recommended, extensive collection of rockets and rocketry equipment. These range from nonflying demonstrations, fascinating performance models, scale copies of missiles and rockets to crazy toylike models. Skill levels are indicated and a "Model Rocketry Safety Code" is presented, which if scrupulously followed allows a safe and fascinating hobby to be developed by serious youngsters. Catalog (free).

EDMUND SCIENTIFIC CO.
Barrington, N.J. 08007

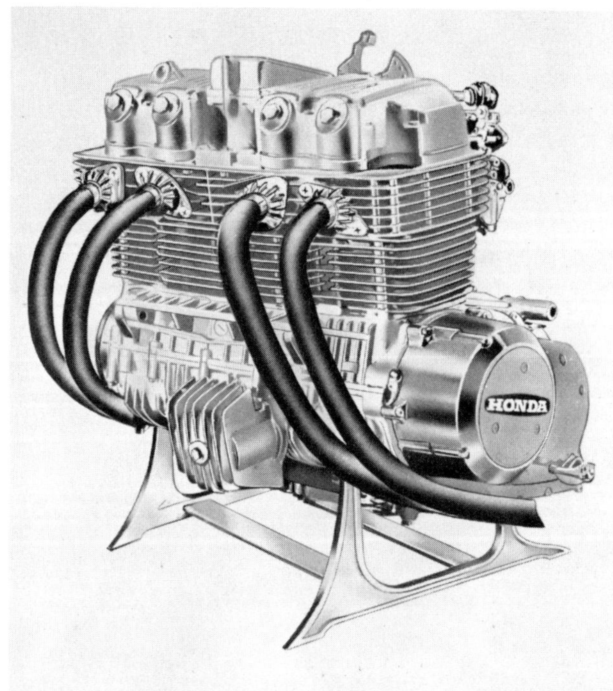

SEE-THRU HONDA ENGINE

Construct a working model of the engine that won the Daytona Grand Prix, the Indianapolis of motorcycle racing. The Honda is the most advanced motorcycle ever offered for sale and the only mass-produced bike with a four-cylinder engine. The model is built to ⅓ scale and does everything the real engine does. With 187 metal and plastic parts, this is not a kit for beginners, but the experienced youngster or adult will find it satisfying and exciting. $13.50.

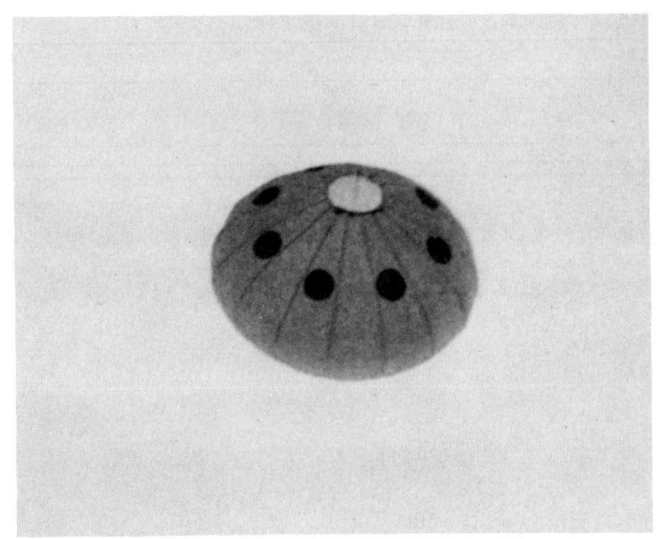

HOT AIR FLYING SAUCER KIT

This may be the answer to all those unexplained UFO sightings. This 9′ flying paper saucer looks like the real thing (whatever that is) and is an inexpensive and simple way to have backyard fun. Objects up to ½ lb. can be lofted in the saucer. Kit includes 16 precut gores of white model paper, 8 red panels for portholes, wire, cord, and instructions. $4.25.

DINOSAUR SKELETON KITS

Every kid loves dinosaurs, especially when they are authentic scale models of the famous American Museum of Natural History skeleton restorations. These quick, easy-to-assemble plastic kits let any youngster (over eight, we think) assemble his own 13″ model of a giant brontosaurus (52 pieces) or a 10″ model of the mastodon elephant ancestor (43 pieces). Each kit: $3.50.

ROCKET KIT

Check this one out with your neighbors before you buy it—they might not be crazy about the idea of a homemade rocket soaring 1,000 feet into the sky. But if you get the all-clear, we can guarantee that your kids (and you) will be fascinated by this unusual kit. Safe liquid propellent gives fantastically realistic lift-off and flight; durable aluminum rocket speeds nearly 300′ per second and returns on parachute of Echo Satellite material. It can be launched over and over again—unless those neighbors get ahold of it. Assembled rocket can be fired manually or electrically. $16.95.

SEE-THRU WANKEL ROTARY ENGINE

General Motors paid $50 million for the rights to use this rotary engine in its cars. For less than $10. you or your kids can build an operating scale model of the engine of the future. Kit features flashing plugs, rubber fan belt, stick shift on-off switch, and prepainted metal and see-through plastic parts. Motor display stand and instructions are included. $6.95.

VISIBLE PUMPING HEART

For every child (or grown-up) who yearns to learn what makes him tick. An easy-to-build, but very impressive working model of the heart's pumping action, complete with red-colored "blood." $8.98.

AMSTERDAM CO.
Amsterdam, N.Y. 02010

WEIGHT MEASUREMENT KIT

Everything you need to assemble an extremely accurate double-platform scale. A full set of gram weights lets you perform interesting experiments in comparative weights and measures. Or you can use small household items like pins and bottle tops, even cards. If you are working with a small child—four- and five-year-olds are fascinated by this type of precision measuring—be sure he or she doesn't try to weigh the dog or a baby sister. Easy assembly for older child or adult. $2.75.

HYDRAULIC PUMP KIT

This is a relatively simple, inexpensive science kit that can be assembled by the older child or adult and appreciated by even a five-year-old. Kit builds lift pump, force pump, compression pump, etc., and can actually shoot a geyser of water 25′ (that's the part the five-year-olds like best). $2.75.

SOUND AND MUSIC LAB KIT

Builder constructs and tunes a two-string musical instrument, and in the process learns a lot about the scientific principles of sound, musical harmony, and melody. A lot of kit for a little money. $2.75.

ELECTRIC BELL TELEGRAPH KIT

For some reason the concept of a telegraph and the mysteries of the Morse Code have always been fascinating to children and perhaps to many adults as well. This inexpensive, easy-to-assemble kit lets you make a push-button bell, electrical buzzer, or telegraph key. A good beginning science kit. $2.75

101 PRODUCTIONS
834 Mission St.
San Francisco, Calif. 94103

MINI-MANSION MODELS

Three-dimensional models of historic buildings in California printed in color on heavy paper, ready to cut out and construct. Authentically rendered to scale by San Francisco architect Roy Killeen. A popular and educational pastime for model buffs. Models vary from 1/16″ to ¼″ scale. You can construct the John Muir house, the Old Plaza Fire House, or the Dickey House of Tiburon, California. $3. each.

ABBEY PRESS
St. Meinrad, Indiana 47577

TETRAKITE

Soar with the winds, lie in the grass, and fly these fantastic kites for hours. Maybe days. The classic TetraKite and SuperTetraKite are, perhaps, the most exciting kites known to man. Alexander Graham Bell created the concept, but it took modern manufacturing methods to bring it to kite enthusiasts. Connoisseurs used to spend days building tetrahedral kites like these by hand. In a 1903 *National Geographic* article, Dr. Bell said, "Tetrahedral kites combine in a marked degree the qualities of strength, lightness, and steady flight." Made today with patented connectors and lightweight sails and struts, these bright red and orange kites are the most spectacular sight in the sky! Easy to assemble and disassemble. The four-sail TetraKite is 2½′ on edge; sixteen-sail SuperTetraKite measures a colossal 5′. Combine four TetraKites and create a SuperTetraKite—or take apart a SuperTetraKites to form four TetraKites (for everyone in the family). Each kite comes with detailed instructions, flying tips, and excerpts from the Bell article. TetraKite also includes a 500′ spool of 25-lb. test multi-strand nylon cord; SuperTetraKite, 1000′ of 50-lb. test. TetraKite: $6.95. SuperTetraKite: $19.95.

DU-BRO PRODUCTS INC.
Wauconda, Ill. 60084

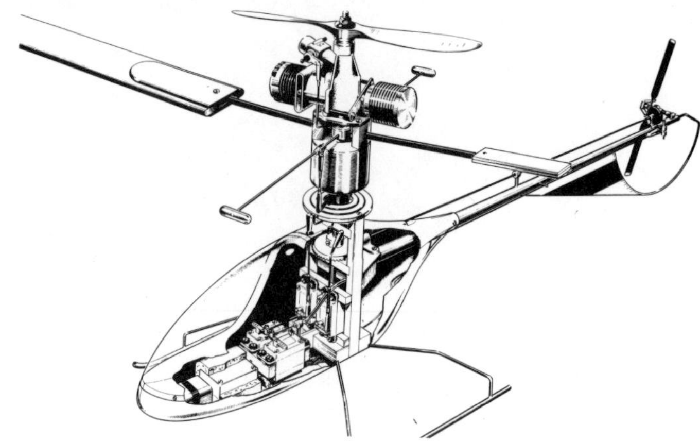

WHIRLYBIRD 505 "QUICK ASSEMBLY" RADIO-CONTROLLED HELICOPTER KIT

Overall length: 37⅝″. Main rotor span: 46½. Main frame assembly parts are precision-cut hardwoods with a rugged fiberglass tail boom. The clean plastic canopy and four fuselage sections are all removable for easy access to radio-control gear and linkages. Main rotors are ¼″ balsa with plywood reinforcing plates. $125.

Also available is the semi-scale Hughes radio-controlled helicopter at $350., and accessories and parts for the helicopter kits. Prices and specifications subject to change.

LENCO PRODUCTS
219 First St.
Buchanan, N.Y. 10511

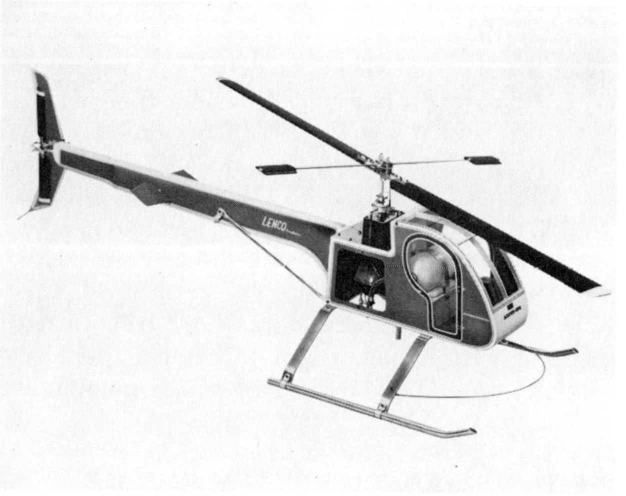

RADIO-CONTROLLED HELICOPTER

Complete kit includes engine, battery, radio, 4 servos, and muffler. Fuselage length, 50″, main rotor span, 59½''. Features completely machined mechanics, all-steel spur gears, no plastic. All prefabricated wood and foam parts. All major mechanical components completely assembled, just bolt in. Kit includes rotor head, transmission and swash plate assembly, tail rotor and drive line. Steers and maneuvers like a pattern plane—aileron and elevator control. $285.

SUBURBIA
Finch Bldg.
366 Wacouta
St. Paul, Minn. 55101

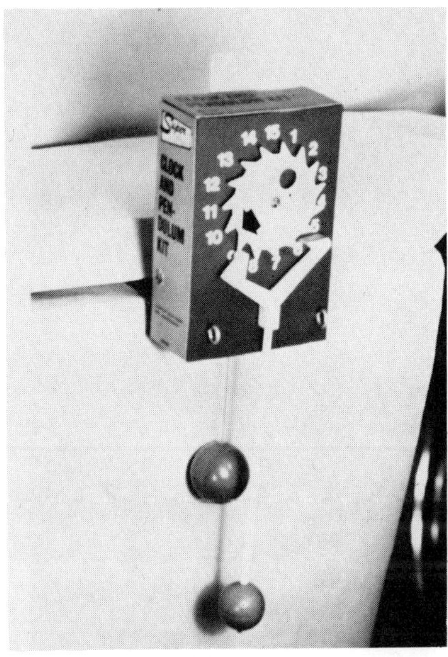

CLOCK AND PENDULUM

The perfect kit to teach children the principles of clock making, for ages eight and up. No tools, batteries, or electricity required. Makes a simulated stopwatch and metronome as well. Simple-to-follow instructions included. $5.

OTHER SOURCES

America's Hobby Center
146 West 22 St.
New York, N.Y. 10011

Another central source for the myriad of plane/boat/train/car kits produced in this country. Catalog is informative ($2.).

Go-Fly-A-Kite Shop
1613 Second Ave.
New York, N.Y. 10028

Probably this country's best-known kite store. An illustrated price list of their kite kits is available (free).

Held Products
9 Lakeview Dr.
Farmington, Conn. 06032

Model Dutch windmill kit. Catalog (free).

H.P.K. Models
P.O. Box 34 Centuck Station
Yonkers, N.Y. 10710

Unusual imported English steam engine kits in castings form for experts and novices. Engines are small but not models. Catalog ($1.).

Model Railroad Corp.
23 West 45 St.
New York, N.Y. 10036

As the name implies, railroad kits. Huge assortment. Enough to thrill the professional kit maker or railroad enthusiast. Detailed catalog (free).

Nautical Americana
Box 949
Plandome, N.Y. 11030

Boats and ships from many countries and time periods. Catalog ($1.).

Polks Hobby Center
314 Fifth Ave.
New York, N.Y. 10001

Every conceivable type of model from every major manufacturer. Large catalog ($2.).

Progressive Edu-Kits, Inc.
P.O. Box 238
Hewlett, N.Y. 11557

Radios, signal probes, and transmitters are among the kits offered in a basic home-training course called "Edu-Kit." Twenty projects can be built in all. School discounts. Information (free).

Reliable Industries, Inc.
34403 Joel St.
New Baltimore, Mich. 48047

Seven steam engine kits in castings form. Power tools required. Catalog ($1.).

Tower Hobbies
Box 778
Chicago, Ill. 61820

Another of the giant model catalogs. Features almost a hundred different manufacturers of models. Bargain prices on many models. Latest catalog (75¢).

Karl F. Wede
RFD 3 Box 344
Saugerties, N.Y. 12477

Quality ship models. Catalog (free).

Woody's Hand Crafts
P.O. Box 3211
Green Bay, Wis. 54303

Miniatures of many varieties, some in kit form. A specialized type of model making. ($1.).

Workshop for Learning, Inc.
5 Bridge St.
Watertown, Mass. 02172

Catalog (40 pp., 50¢) of creative and educational items. A great variety of interesting projects.

Electronics has long been a field in which kits have played a major role in introducing the novice as well as providing economical equipment to the experienced enthusiast. Heathkit has been a major leader in electronic kits and continues to be today. It has the largest selection of electronic equipment in kit form. There is, however, substantial competition and many companies and kits to choose from.

It is wise to remember, in the electronics kits especially, the advice in the introduction to this book—don't assume that because a piece of equipment is in kit form it's a bargain over the built-up item. If you're primarily interested in saving money by buying a kit, be sure to comparison-shop with assembled items. This is not to say that you necessarily get a bad deal if you buy, as a kit, an amplifier worth $200. for $200. Two good reasons for buying a kit are that you enjoy the craft of putting it together and you want to learn about techniques you don't already know. It is not surprising or wrong that you should pay for this. A Heathkit instruction manual, for example, is a carefully planned book that leads even a novice through an extremely enjoyable way to assemble a piece of electronic equipment. Somebody spent a lot of time working this out and it would be unusual if this service were free. On the other hand, if a kit includes a circuit diagram and a bag of components, you should expect a real break on the price. This is not to say that there are not many real bargains in building your own equipment. There are. Only you should not assume this to be so for any given item. It should be emphasized, in any case, that electronics is about the only field we know where quality has improved dramatically with the years and prices have gone down.

If you're completely new to electronics, you might want to try the experimenter kits, such as the Graymark line. These can be quite informative and while the finished product may not be very sophisticated, you can learn a great deal from these items.

Finally, electronics kits sometimes offer items that simply can't be bought elsewhere. These range from the ultra-sophisticated, such as Heath's digital tuner, to unusual designs such as Southwest Technical Products.

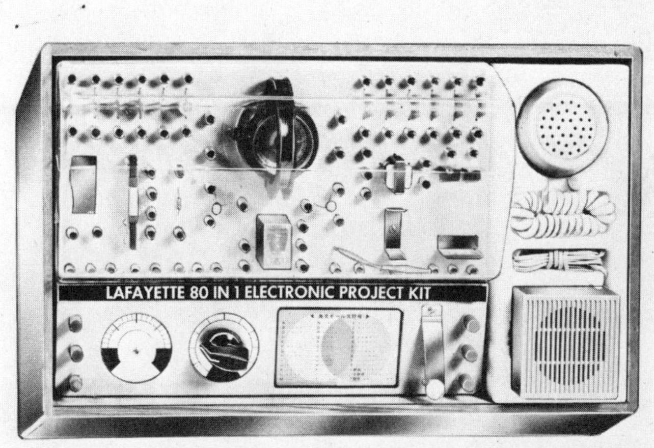

LAFAYETTE RADIO
111 Jericho Tpk.
Syosset, N.Y. 11791

ELECTRONIC PROJECT KITS

"Educational, creative, no technical knowledge necessary . . . Learn while you build." That's what the manufacturer has to say about these experimenter kits. And since Layfayette is famous for electronics, they should know. The kits are offered in four levels of proficiency and ambitiousness. The "10-in-1 kit" builds "educationally stimulating" projects, including circuit testers and communication sets. The kit features an enlarged, visualized, integrated circuit that clearly shows the typical placement of all components. The "20-in-1 kit," as you might expect, lets you build 20 electronic projects, all of which are easily assembled in minutes. Kit contains one transformer, galvanometer, solar battery, two resistors, and three capacitors. With the "80-in-1 kit," you're moving into the big time. Kit includes all parts and instructions for making a variety of useful or interesting items, but considering that the "150-in-1 kit" lets you assemble nearly twice as many projects as the 80-in-1, it is an excellent value at only $9. more that the smaller unit. You may never get to perform 150 experiments, but it's nice to know they're there. Possibilities include radio receivers, solar-powered transistor radio, a metronome, a public address system, muscle stimulator, cat sound simulator, and much more. This kit features the enlarged visualized integrated circuit described under the 10-in-1 kit. All four kits include batteries and none requires soldering. 10-in-1: $9.95. 20-in-1: $12.50. 80-in-1: $20.95. 150-in-1: $29.95.

MYCOM MEDIA
3175 Greenspring Dr.
Timonium, Md. 21093

Mycom Media manufactures for individuals, schools, and camps in the instruction of electrical functions. These are kits in the broad sense of the word. They are expensive because of the high quality, but also because of the highly specialized training manuals that are written to accompany a kit. They are meant truly for teaching rather than as home hobby projects. The number of building experiments are varied. Any educator with an interest in the kits outlined in this chapter should seriously consider Mycom. They publish a (60 pp., free) catalog aimed at college and high school-level educational markets. They are not designed as "make-it-and-keep-it" projects, but rather "make-it-and-learn" projects.

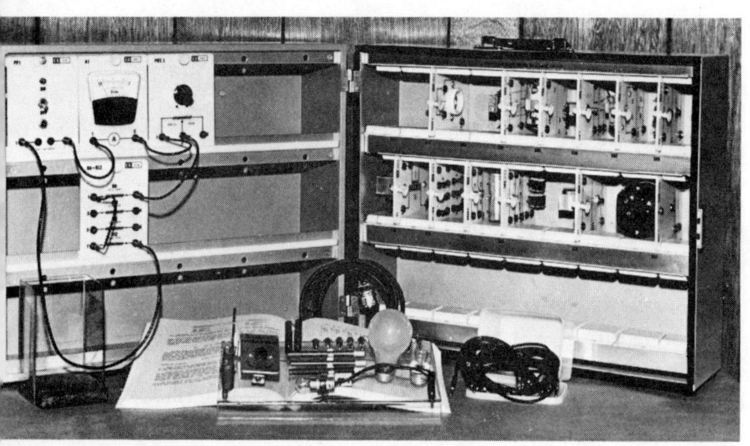

BASIC ELECTRICITY

Basic Electricity offers complete coverage of the information fundamental to the field of electricity in a straightforward and simplified manner. It covers language, laws, symbols, component functions, circuit characteristics, and the application of electricity to the home, business, and industry. Organized for effective learning through efficient experiments, the course helps develop skills and knowledge, paving the student's way for activity in the electrical, electromechanical, and maintenance fields.

Kit includes components depicting the circuits of: protected meter, transformer, motor, variable pot, relay, solenoid, thermistor, rectifying diode, resistors, capacitor, etc. Supplied with all necessary accessories and equipment, such as jumpers, lamps, thermostat, rods, test stand, line cord, and compass, to carry out 53 experiments. $395.

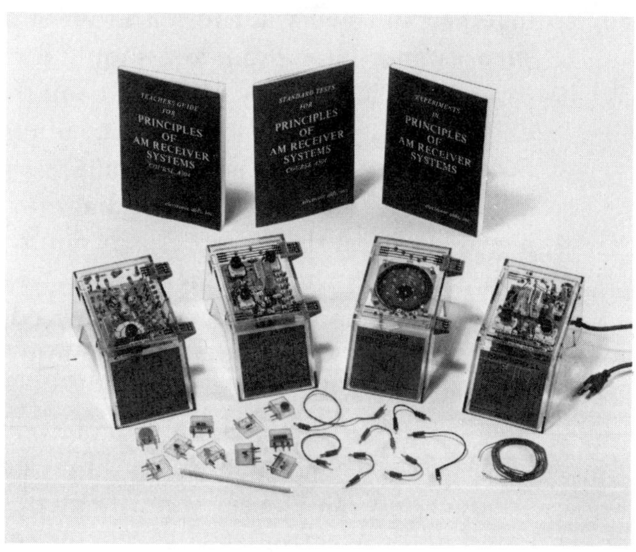

PRINCIPLES OF AM RECEIVER SYSTEMS

A detailed study of solid-state AM receiver circuits, covering oscillators, RF amplifiers, IF amplifiers, detectors, stage alignment, measurements of performance characteristics, and troubleshooting techniques. The kit is designed to assist in teaching the fundamentals of AM receiver technology, with emphasis on contemporary receivers found in commercial radios. Each experiment investigates AM receiver fundamental subsystems, presenting general discussion and a detailed circuit description. $325.

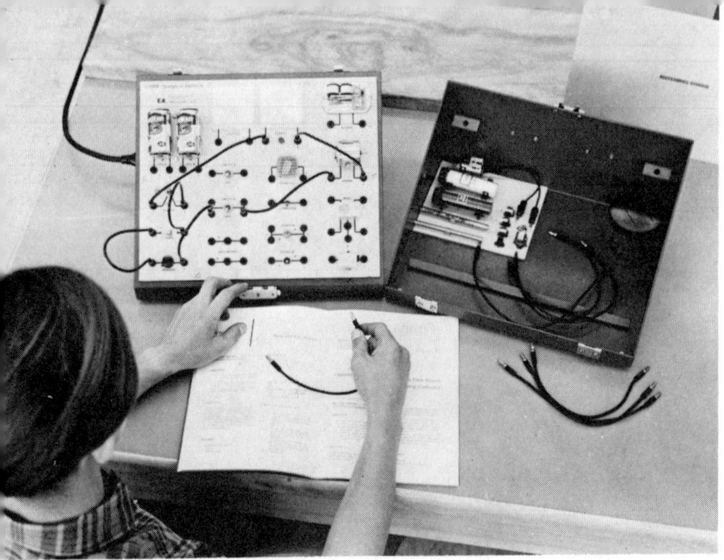

CONCEPTS OF ELECTRICITY

Concepts of Electricity presents a stimulating introduction to the phenomena of electricity and its safe use. By exploring sources and applications of electrical energy, students discover the nature of electricity and experience methods of controlling circuitry. Fifty experiments are grouped in three sections. The first section deals with changing energy from one form to another, the second with applications of various forms of energy, and the third section with the actual principles of electricity. The experiments are performed with components, power sources, and protected meters, all mounted on an unbreakable sloping panel.

HEATHKIT
The Heath Co.
Benton Harbor, Mich. 49022

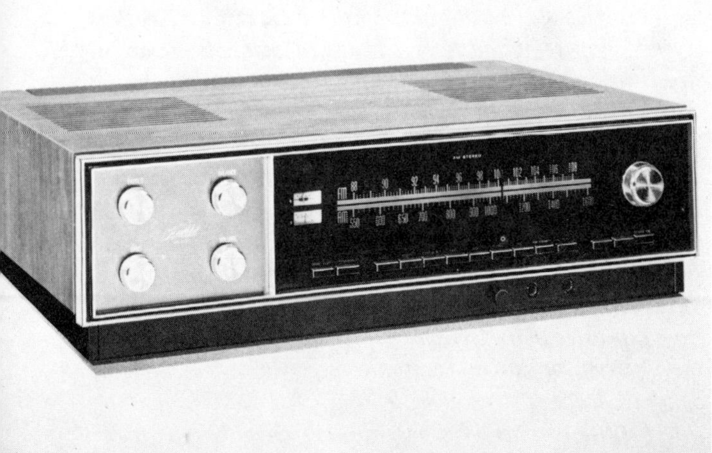

AR-1500 A STEREO RECEIVER

This is a highly acclaimed piece of equipment—a Rolls-Royce receiver at a very good price. Even if you allow for the sizable discounts that are available on built-up equipment, this one is a bargain. The instrument has impressive specifications although for some reason Heath gives IHF (Institute of High Fidelity) standards. IHF is an industry-serving system of specifications that makes everything look better and our tests showed that it lives up to these specifications. In addition to being an excellent receiver, the kit is enjoyable to build and up to Heath's exemplary standards for instructions. In the (new, revised) 1500-A, you first built a "check-out meter," which "gives the novice confidence in his assembly skills." This instrument is then used to check the assembly at various stages. Ninety w. channel (IHF—probably about 60 w. RMS/channel) amplifier; Intermodulation Distortion: Less than 0.1% with 60 w. output, using 60 and 6,000 Hz mixed 4:1, less than 0.1% at 1 w. output. Highly recommended if you want top equipment for stereo. Kit: $399.95. Walnut cabinet: $24.95.

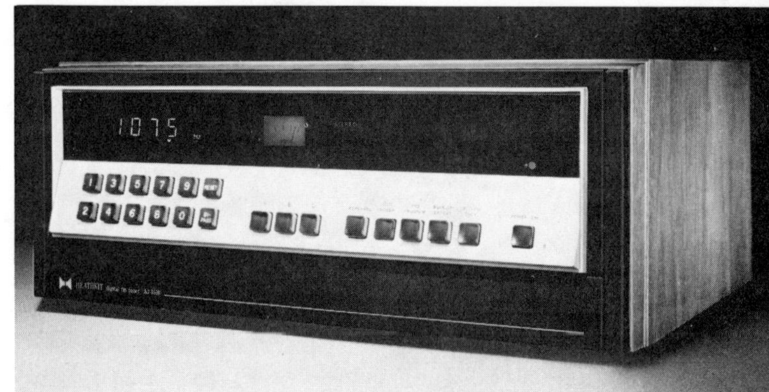

"COMPUTER" TUNER

This is a truly unusual tuner, relying on a digital approach—clearly an intelligent idea for tuning. As described by Heath, it brings "digital computer technology—digital logic, scalers, dividers, decoders, programmers, counters, registers, etc.—to the discriminating audiophile. Now you tune FM and FM stereo via an all-electronic computer keyboard. Lightly touch the keys and a state-of-the-art digital frequency synthesizer does the tuning, with the channel frequency accuracy better than 0.005%! Four glowing readout tubes show you exactly where you are. Touch the Auto-Sweep button and the frequency synthesizer starts counting down from 107.9 MHz, with the readout displaying every available FM frequency through 88.1 MHz, stopping at each station with a listenable signal, or stopping only at stereo stations if you prefer. Depress the by-pass button and the tuner resumes scanning." The instrument has terrific specifications and is an "ultimate" piece of equipment, but it carries a heavy price tag. Kit: $539.95. Pecan veneer cabinet: $24.95.

AJ-14 STEREO TUNER

This is a classic in good, low-priced tuners. You can put it together in one day, it performs well, and is a real bargain. We like this item a lot, for a budget system. It can also be bought as part of the AR–14 Receiver, which we didn't test but has good specifications for a low-power (10 W channel) receiver. AJ-14 Tuner: $59.95. Walnut veneer cabinet: $9.95. AR–14 Receiver: $119.95. Walnut veneer cabinet: $12.95.

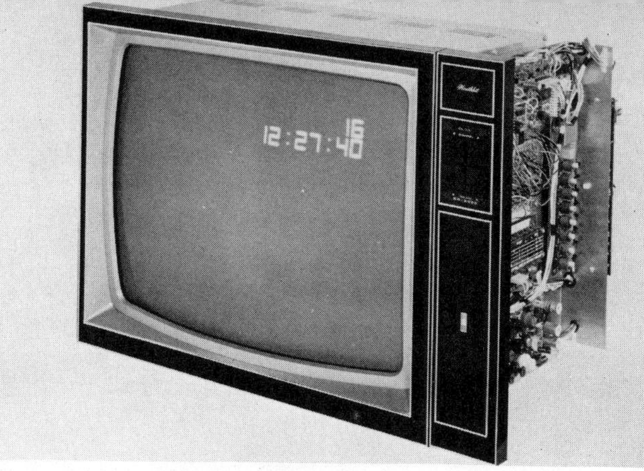

GR-2000 DIGITAL DESIGN 25″ (DIAGONAL) COLOR TV

Heathkit televisions have a reputation for being good but expensive. This is probably the extreme example. Superlative design, great convenience for servicing, many unusual features, and a whopping price of $670. without a cabinet! We suggest you visit one of the Heathkit showrooms and see if the performance is up to the price and your investment of time.

Kit, with one speaker:	$669.95
Remote control unit:	89.95
Digital clock accessory:	29.95
Second speaker:	6.50
Typical Heathkit cabinets:	159.95

There's hardly a worker in the electronics field who hasn't built a Heathkit at one time or other, and although they all swear that the first one they built when they were twelve was the best, this is substantial testimony to Heath's impact on the electronics world. Since the days when the professor of Electrical Engineering built his VTVM, Heath has expanded into an incredibly diverse line of electronic equipment from test equipment to microwave ovens. Like any big leader in the field, you get all kinds of opinions about Heath products. Some of our observations are as follows.

In terms of the actual kit-building experience Heath is beyond compare—beautifully illustrated manuals, clear instructions, great thought in helping you assemble the kit without trouble. With regard to design, although Heathkit has been faulted on some of their test equipment—specifically oscilloscopes—generally design is very good. Heath seems to use quality electronic components, but their mechanical and decorative parts, knobs, dials, etc., don't stack up well against built-up equipment. On the other hand, this can save you money since knobs, incredibly enough, are more expensive than electronic components. This brings us to the question of value. Heathkit is very variable in terms of price. As noted, we believe that $400. for the AR-1500A receiver is a bargain, but anybody who would pay $89.95 for a four-function calculator kit must be a compulsive solderer. Many Heathkits are real bargains, many are competitive with built-up equipment (we actually think that for a hobbyist, the fun of putting it together gives the kit the edge), and some are too expensive. For any given piece of equipment, comparison shopping is called for, but Heath is always a company to check for electronics.

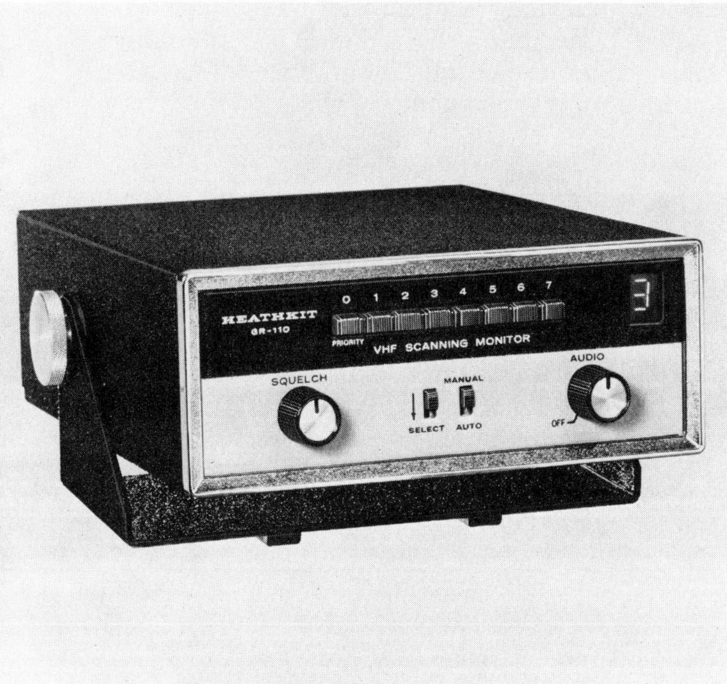

VHF/FM SCANNING MONITOR

Covers any 9 MHz between 146–174 MHz and is capable of automatic or manual scanning. In the manual scanning mode you can manually select any channel from 0 through 7, with bright digital readout. The monitor stays locked on that frequency until you manually select another, or go to the automatic scanning mode. In automatic, the monitor rapidly scans all eight channels and locks on to the first one that starts a transmission. It will remain on that channel as long as a signal is present; when the signal stops, the monitor waits four seconds, then continues scanning. "Easy four-evening assembly," according to the manufacturer. During assembly, the digital monitor can be wired to display the channel number continuously or only when locked on a frequency. Check state and local laws regarding use of monitors in vehicles in your locality. $99.95.

GRAYMARK ENTERPRISES, INC.

P.O. Box 54343
Los Angeles, Calif. 90054

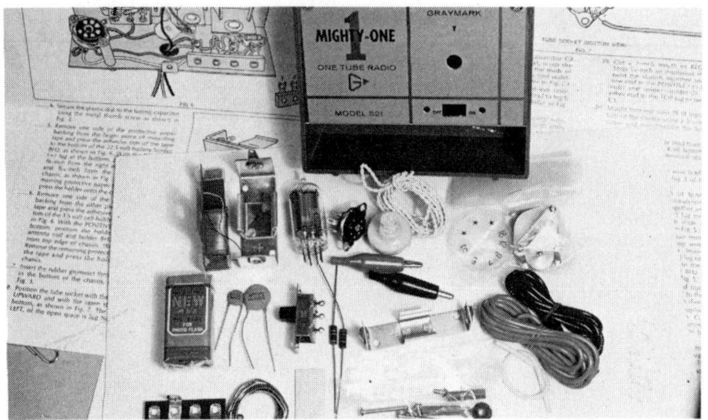

ONE-TUBE RADIO KIT

A simple, battery-operated AM radio that can easily and profitably be built by a teen-ager. The description of how it works is too complex for someone with no knowledge of electronics, but simple enough (because it's a simple circuit) for someone with limited background to understand what makes the radio work. The directions for assembly and hook-up are very detailed and easy to follow. Recommended for youngsters developing an interest in electronics. Battery included. $9.95

Graymark has a crystal radio kit, Morse code, table radio, strobelite, and tachometer kits. They also make a burglar alarm (see Security Systems section) under Lafayette, one of their distributors.

INTERNATIONAL ELECTRONICS UNLIMITED

P.O. Box 1708
Monterey, Calif. 93940

LOGIC PROBE

This kit contains printed circuit boards, all components and hardware, probes, and an attractive metal case for construction of a logic device tester. Building is straightforward, although you must drill the chassis. The instrument is capable of detecting a 10 nanosecond pulse by using multivibrators as "pulse stretches." Dual-slope memory enables detection of pulse which would not be detected visually. This instrument should be useful for "fooling around" with logic as well as for troubleshooting. A good price for the components used. $19.95.

International Electronics has a calculator kit (calculator chip, LED display (9 digits with driver) for $12.95, a stereo multiplex adapter for $6.95, and a couple of clock kits. They also sell electronic components at very good prices—typical: 555 timer for 99¢. Catalog free, 10% discount on orders over $25. (Logic Probe may be included for discount).

DYNACO, INC.

3060 Jefferson St.
Philadelphia, Pa. 19121

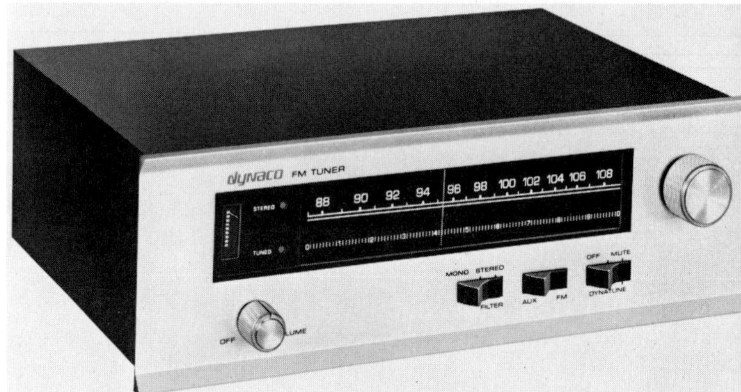

FM-5 TUNER

An easy-to-build kit—factory-assembled and with aligned circuit boards, color-coded wires, etc.—produces an extremely high-quality tuner FET front end, IF amplifier with four integrated circuits and seven ceramic filters. This instrument has impressive specifications: IHF sensitivity, 1.75 mv; Harmonic and intermodulation distortion at 100% modulation 0.5% (max), 0.9% (stereo), capture ratio 1.5 db. This is a top contender in the high-quality tuner field and its extreme ease of construction gives it an edge over several kits, if your main interest is not the actual construction of the instrument. The FM-5 also has a fairly sophisticated automatic frequency control system, "dynatune," which has received good reports. Other features are a mating system (between stations) that works in conjunction with the "dynatune" system, smooth flywheel dial control, and highly accurate dial calibrations. $175.

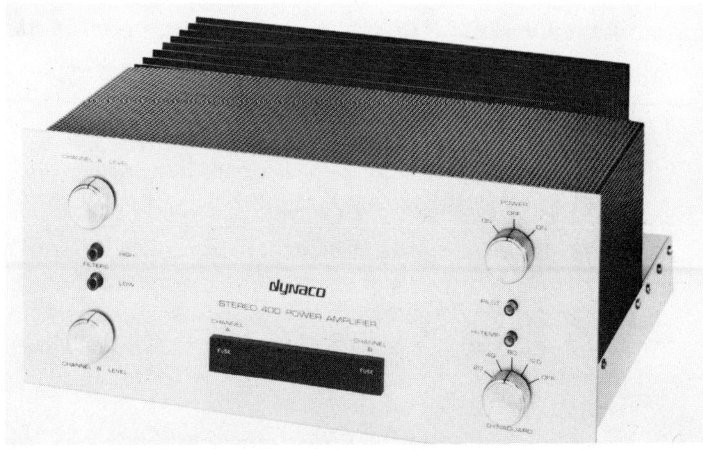

STEREO 400 AND 400M POWER AMPLIFER

The specifications speak for themselves: 200 w. RMS per channel at 8 ohms 1M distortion, less than 0.1% up to 200 watts. If you have to have the ultimate in stereo, you should look into this. The kit is straightforward to build and has very clear instructions. There are several protective circuits and several warnings about connecting this amplifier which you should read carefully before accidentally frying your speakers. You can buy this beautiful monster with two front-panel options: with or without meters. $449. MC-4 illuminated output meters and panel assembly kit for stereo 400: $75.

Dynaco has been making kits for a long time and used to be one of the few outlets for economically priced, superior equipment. There is substantial competition now, but they still are one of the solid high-quality companies. In addition, they still offer the standard vacuum tube power amplifier that some hi-fi nuts swear by. Although, again, you should comparison shop even against built-up equipment, Dynaco is always a contender for hi-fi components.

B & F ENTERPRISES
P.O. Box 44
Hathorne, Mass. 01937

TRANSISTORIZED FLUORESCENT CAMPING/EMERGENCY LIGHT KIT

This transistor inverter-powered camping and emergency light will provide a bright light from a 12-v. d.c. battery. A cigarette lighter adapter is provided for automotive operation, or the unit may be run from other 12-v. lantern batteries. The advantages of this unit over more conventional incandescent lamps is the vastly greater light output for equivalent power input and the superior distribution and color of the light. The camping /emergency light is enclosed in a weather-tight Plexiglass tube, with the electronics built into the tube. Completion time should be less than two hours, making a nice evening's project, even for the beginner. $12.50.

FUNCTION GENERATOR

Twenty Hz–1.5 MHz generator with sine, triangle, square, sawtooth, ramp and pulse waveforms. $99.

Company deals primarily in surplus and discount components and is an excellent delicatessen of component boards, power supplies, readout units, and semiconductors. They offer several kits (see also Clocks section), but even better are their values on parts for kits and components. They also have many surplus pieces of sophisticated junk which you simply must have; for example, a right-ascension circle drive for making the telescope drive you may want some day. Free catalog, but great sales resistance is needed once it is in your hands.

EICO ELECTRONIC INSTRUMENT CO.
283 Malta St.
Brooklyn, N.Y. 11207

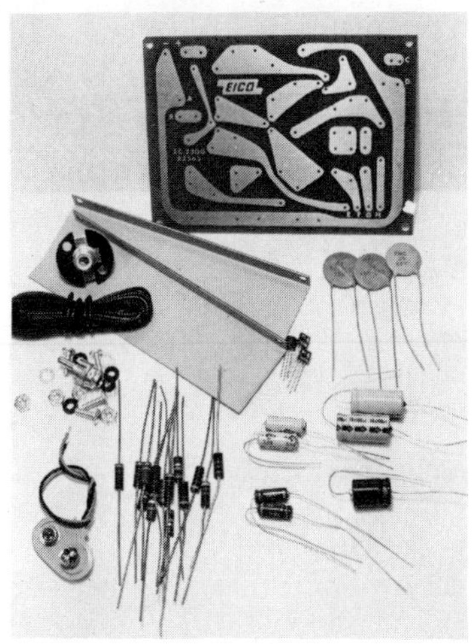

AUDIO PRE-AMP

A three-transistor pre-amp that operates on a 9-w. battery. This is a simple kit with printed circuit board construction. It would be suitable for a beginner in electronics who wanted to have the experience of soldering circuits by working on something simple and inexpensive. As an introduction to electronic theory, however, this is probably not very good. Although the construction details are quite adequate, the description of the theory of operations is too complicated for most who would build such a simple kit. $8.95

EICO has been making kits for a long time and now has an extensive line of test equipment in kit form. Their Eicocraft line for beginners of "the entire family" includes an electronic siren, electronic "bongos," FM radio and a color organ. Their equipment has gotten mixed reviews; the test equipment in particular received high grades. On the other hand, they have been accused of using old transistors and circuits (not necessarily bad in our view). In any case, EICO was uniquely uncooperative in providing us information. We suggest, if you're interested in their equipment, that you find a good dealer since the parent company is fairly unfriendly.

TRIGGER ELECTRONICS
7361 North Ave.
River Forest, Ill. 60305

BOWMAN SOLID-STATE MOD-U-KITS ELECTRONIC STETHOSCOPE

An unusual kit for the electronic hobbyist. Comprises a well-designed three-transistor, high-gain amplifier with sensitivity control. Includes a special stethoscope that shuts out background noises. The printed circuit board is readily assembled in a convenient case. $9.95.

The Bowman kits include an Aircraft Receiver kit ($5.95), Automatic Light Sentry and Alarm Kit ($9.95), and 110-v.a.c. to 6 v.d.c. Converter ($5.95). Trigger has many kits: RCA, Bowman, EICO, TAB Book/Kits, and Graymark, as well as Dynakit and built-up electronic equipment.

RCA CORP.
30 Rockefeller Plaza
New York, N.Y. 10022

SILICON-CONTROLLED RECTIFIER KIT

This Experimenter's Project Kit includes one silicon-controlled rectifier assembly, two transistors, and five rectifiers. Builds ten useful control circuits, including timer, 6-v. and 12-v. battery chargers, flasher, dimmer, speed control for model cars and railroads, time-delay switch, and other equally practical units. $12.95.

RCA offers several project kits in several series. Perhaps most interesting is the Integrated Circuit Series, which offers up-to-the-minute IC's in a kit with drilled and printed circuit boards, and other components and instructions for such projects as audio oscillator, fire alarm, or microphone preamplifier—all in the $6. to $10. range.

LAFAYETTE RADIO
111 Jericho Turnpike
Syosset, N.Y. 11791

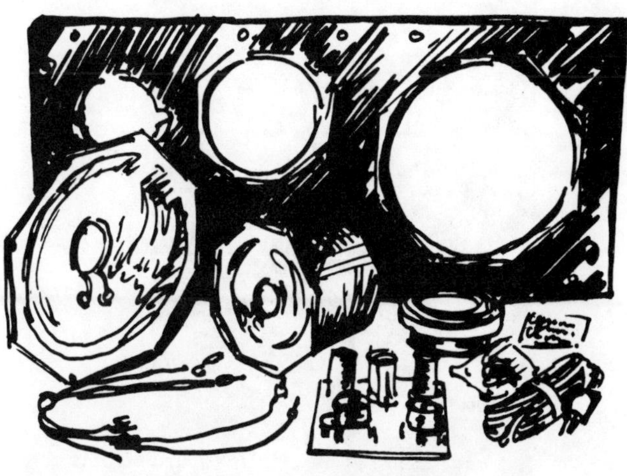

PHILLIPS SPEAKER SYSTEM KIT
ADK 3540 60-W. 3-WAY
HIGH-FIDELITY SYSTEM

Eight-ohm impedance, frequency range 33 to 22,000 Hz. Crossover frequency, 500 to 4,500 Hz. With 10″ woofer, 2″ voice coil, 2-lb. magnet: 5″ midrange; 1″ voice coil, 10-oz. magnet: 1″ supertweeter; 10-oz. magnet, baffle board, and instructions for one enclosure.

You must supply the material for the rest of the speaker enclosure (only the baffle board is included). $79.95.

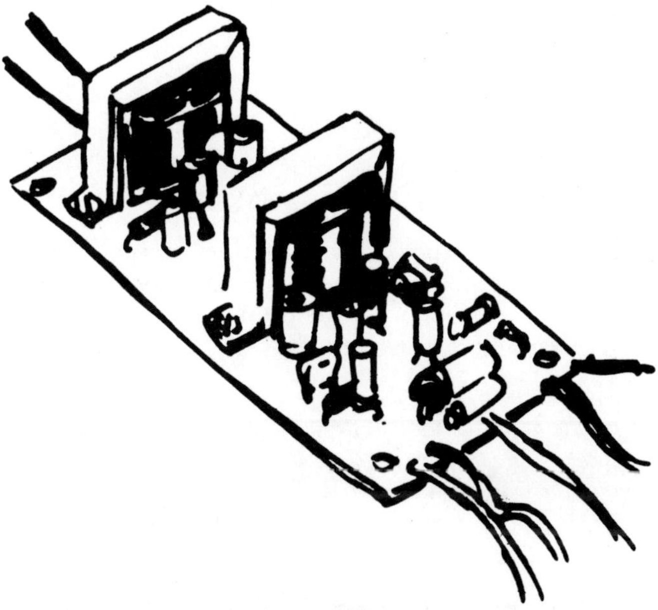

ONE-WATT FOUR-TRANSISTOR
PUSH-PULL AUDIO AMPLIFIER

Powerful miniature amp! Outputs from record players with magnetic cartridge, tape heads, microphones (not exceeding 20 mv.) can be connected directly. Higher output devices connected with resistor in series. Leads for: Volume, On-Off, 8-ohm speaker, battery (1.5 v. "D"). $7.95.

Lafayette sells many kits of their own or of other manufacturers including several educational project kits. Their catalog (free) is especially good on beginner's science and electronic projects.

GRAYMARK LIE DETECTOR KIT

This is really a sweat-meter—it indicates white lies, gray lies, and giant whoppers by the amount of perspiration on the subject's hand. Since even George Washington's hands were known to perspire from time to time, we doubt the accuracy of this device, but it might liven up a party when you run out of conversation and liquor. $9.95.

CTS

1565 North 8 St.
Paducah, Ky. 42001

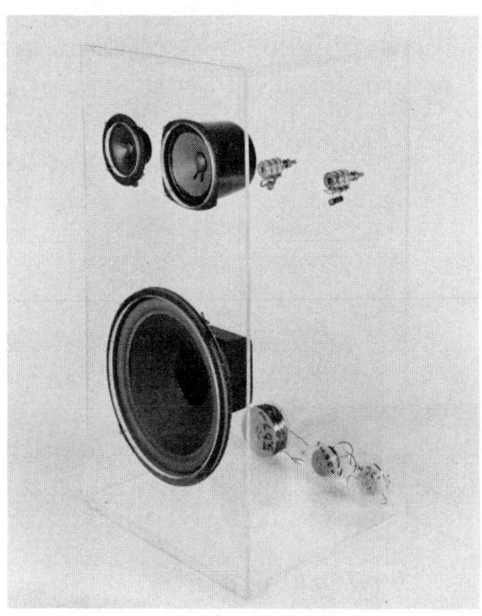

STARRSOND 8 LOUDSPEAKER

High-fidelity speaker kit includes tweeter, mid-range and polyurethane edge bass speaker with crossover networks and controls. You must build cabinet, and details are supplied. $82.21.

This company is primarily a manufacturer of loudspeakers for the high-fidelity industry and you're likely to find their speakers in other equipment you buy. It is undoubtedly true that the major cost of commercial speakers is the cabinetry, which is frequently of the simplest kind.

PAIA ELECTRONICS

Box 14359
Oklahoma City, Okla. 73114

MUSIC SYNTHESIZER —KEYBOARD AND MODULES

If you're serious about electronic music, this certainly seems like an inexpensive way to go. The package kit illustrated includes keyboard and several modules, voltage-controlled amplifier, function generator, filters, and control oscillator band source. The manufacturer suggests it for professional or semi-professional use, and offers an even less expensive version with a different keyboard (see below). Requires hi-fi or instrument amplifier. Complete kit, as illustrated: $218.18.

The company offers, in modular form, the various components for an electronic music synthesizer at low cost. Typical: power supply (100 ma, variable 15v.) $22. Catalog (free) includes other electronic kits—mostly for electronic musical instruments, including electronic wind chimes, surf sounds, and a "solid-state bird."

EDMUND SCIENTIFIC CO.

Barrington, N.J. 08007

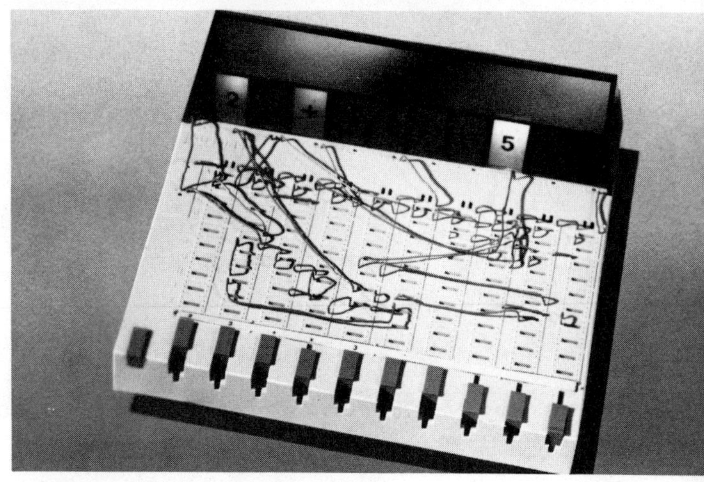

ELECTRONIC COMPUTER

You build it, program it, learn from it. Perform fifty fascinating experiments—play computer casino, predict weather, diagnose illness symptoms, solve mysteries, test intelligence, try to "outwit" the computer, even play miniature chess with it. Readout from illuminated control panel. Includes everything needed except 3 "C" batteries. Informative instruction book leads you step-by-step. It takes a good six hours to build and longer to program, but the results are fascinating. 11″ × 12½″ × 4″. $31.50.

SOUTHWEST TECHNICAL PRODUCTS CORP.

219 West Rhapsody
San Antonio, Tex. 78216

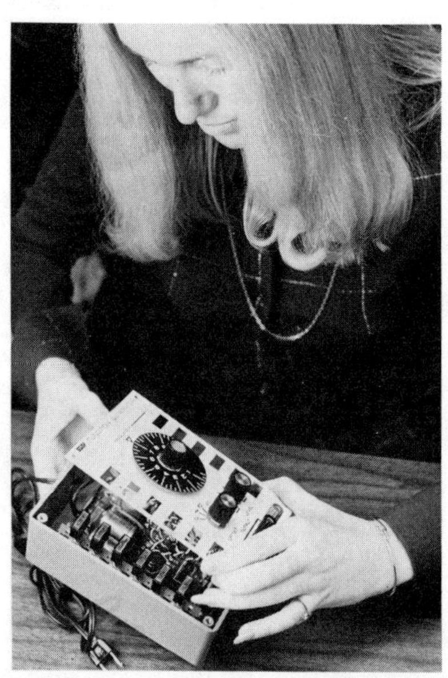

FUNCTION GENERATOR

An a.c.-powered function generator, this instrument

features switch selection of waveform, frequency range, and type of offset. Output amplitude is constant to less than ± 1 db. on any range and with any waveform. Sine wave distortion is less than 1% from 20 to 20,000 cycles. Square wave and pulse rise times are less than 0.25 microsecond. Accuracy is 1% on the range calibrated and better than 5% on all other ranges.

The kit is easy to construct, although it suffers from SWTP's snobbism in giving you minimal instructions. If there are four capacitors, they label three, and, of course, the fourth is the other one called for . . . but, is this kind of stuff really necessary? The constructed kit performs well, however. $39.95.

198/A STEREO PREAMP

A low-distortion preamp based on "op-amp type" circuits using discrete transistors. This instrument has very good specifications.

Frequency Response: Flat ± 1 db. from 10 Hz to KHz. Distortion: Less than 0.05% Harmonic or 1M at rated output. Noise: Phono and Mic, 65 db. down; others 70 db. down. There are push-button tone control settings (-12, -8, -4, 4, 8, 12 db. for treble and base) and a nice-looking front panel. The gain is provided by op-amp circuits, which are available separately, and these plug into "motherboards." Construction appears to be relatively easy. 198/A Preamp: $74.50. 195 Preamp module kit: $8.75.

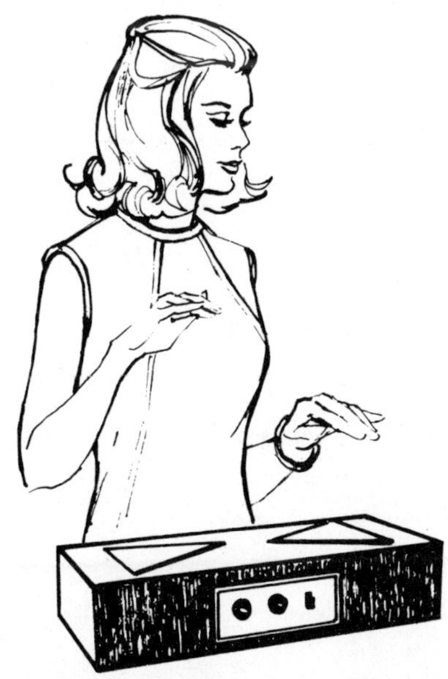

THEREMIN ELECTRONIC MUSICAL INSTRUMENT

A modern, solid-state version of the Theremin all-electronic musical instrument. Two antenna plates, operated by hand capacity, control the pitch and volume of the sound. Can be used with any instrument powered by 9-v. battery. $22.75.

ATV RESEARCH
13th & Broadway
Dakota City, Neb. 68731

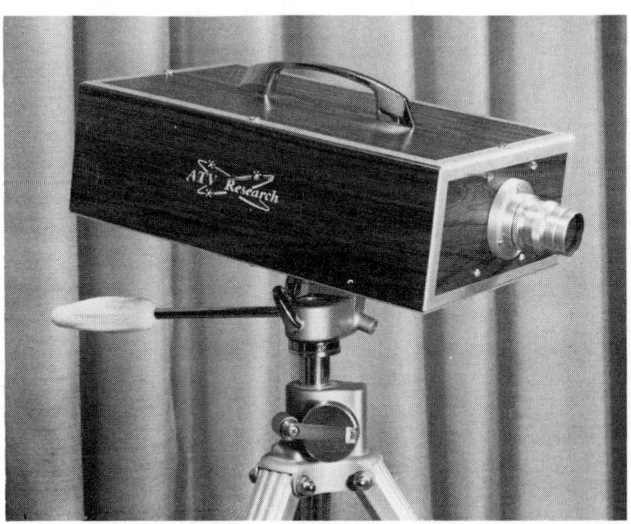

XT-1A TELEVISION CAMERA

For a couple of hundred dollars, a complete closed-circuit television system can be set up using your own television set. The complete camera in photo costs $166. in kit form. With the addition of an audio subcarrier shown below, all you need is a microphone and you're ready to do whatever it is you think you'd do if you got on TV. Can also be used for a surveillance system or to feed a TV monitor or tape system. Kit, less vidicon camera tube: $129.95. Kit, complete: $166.00. Audio Subcarrier kit: $28.95.

Various kits and plans for TV systems, including beginner kits. Free catalog.

THE MACROCOMA CO.

Washington Crossing, Pa. 18977

GIANT TV PROJECTOR

If the thought of a life-size Archie Bunker or a bigger Big Bird turns you on, this is the kit for you. (If it doesn't, you'd better rip out this page so that your fifteen-year-old can't assemble it while you're at the movies.) Although we don't agree with the manufacturer's claim that a 5′ × 6′ TV image projected on the wall has necessarily been "the dream of viewers since the dawn of television," this might be a fun idea, especially for the youngsters. The kit requires no electrical connection to your TV set, it can be used with any TV set, and—amazingly enough—it projects in color when used with a color TV. Easy assembly. $12.95.

FRAZER & ASSOCIATES CONSULTING ENGINEERS

3809 Surfwood Rd.
Malibu, Calif. 90265

GARAGE LIGHT CONTROL

Unit switches when light hits it. Headlights turn on either inside or outside garage lights, which must be turned off manually. Included with the circuit kit is the book *Transistor Projects for Hobbyists and Students.* Kit and book: $9.95.

Company offers ten combination simple circuit kits and book. The kits are simple perf-board construction, and a good introduction to electronics for the novice.

POLLY PAKS

P.O. Box 942
Lynnfield, Mass. 01940

CALCULATORS

Assemble your own calculator. Basic kit includes case, all function flex-key, key board, calculator chip, and display (with built-in magnifier). Instructions included, but they require a fair amount of electronic skills. $59.50.

A variety of electronic kits and parts. Catalog (16 pp., 20¢).

RADIO SHACK

2615 West 7 St.
Fort Worth, Tex. 76107

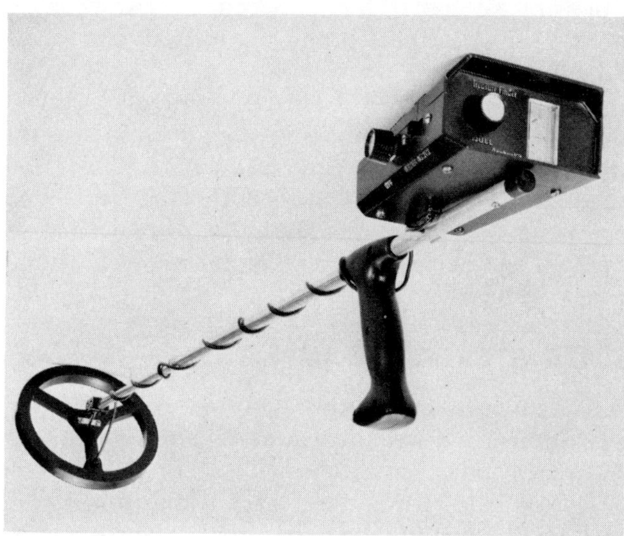

TREASURE FINDER

Looking for buried treasure has become more sophisticated since the days of storybook pirates. You can possibly find doubloons, gold, watches, and the like everywhere from beaches of Coney Island to your own backyard. This build-it-yourself kit detects metallic objects as deep as six feet. Spots anything metallic, even identifies ferrous and nonferrous "finds." Has a speaker and a headphone jack for audible indications and a null meter for visible readings. "FET" search and reference oscillators, IC amplifier, Faraday-shielded pickup coil, adjustable shaft. With all instructions. $34.95.

OTHER SOURCES

Babylon Electronics
P.O. Box J
Carmichael, Calif. 95608
Digital display kits. Brochure (free).

Bigelow Electronics
P.O. Box 125
Bluffton, Ohio 45817
Large selection of inexpensive electronic kits. Flyer (free).

Burstein-Applebee
3199 Mercier St.
Kansas City, Mo. 64111
Very complete catalog (224 pp.) of electronics kits and supplies. Covers stereo, hi-fi, TV categories, as well as other electronic specialties.

Carston Studios
146 Old Brookfield Rd. N.
Danbury, Conn. 06810
Offers discounted kits from Dynaco and EICO electronics.

Digiac Corp.
1261 South Boyle Ave.
Los Angeles, Calif. 90023

School-oriented electronic kits including: radios, walkie talkies, amplifiers, etc. Thirty-five electronic kits in all. School discounts. Brochure (free).

Edie Electronics, Inc.
2700 Hempstead Turnpike
Levittown, N.Y. 11756

Assorted electronic kits.

E.E.S.N.
Box 351
Smithtown, N.Y. 11787

Good source for stereo speaker systems. Save up to 50% over store-bought equipment. Complete kits available.

Environmental Products
Box 1014
Glenwood Springs, Colo. 81601

Easily assembled MOD-kits that perform sophisticated tasks. Catalog (25¢ first class mail, free bulk mail).

Esco Products
171 Oak Ridge Rd.
Oak Ridge, N.J. 07438

Features kits with all the optical components necessary to build a CO2 laser. Also offers Newtonian reflector telescopes and mirror kits. Catalog (free).

Extended Digital Concepts
Box 9161
Berkeley, Calif. 94709

How are your alpha waves lately? Perhaps you can find out by using EDC's EEG monitor kit. When assembled, it boasts of being able to teach you to be calmer and more serene by the method of biofeedback.

Harman-Kardon
55 Ames Court
Plainview, N.Y. 11803

Offers a 120 w. solid-state stereophonic amplifier kit for the novice. Brochure (free).

International Electronics Unlimited
P.O. Box 1708
Monterey, Calif. 93940

Logic probe kits, calculator kits, and a fair range of technical material.

McGee Radio Co.
1901-07 McGee St.
Kansas City, Mo. 64108

Offers a large selection of electronic kits manufactured by companies such as Dynaco and EICO. Catalog (free).

McGraw-Edison Co.
Air Comfort Division
Albion, Mich. 49224

Kit converts forced air furnace to central air conditioner. Takes less than a day to install whole house air conditioning. The only professional help necessary . . . an electrician to make the hookup to outdoor condensing unit. Details (free).

Metrologic Instruments, Inc.
143 Harding Ave.
Bellmawr, N.J. 08030

Choose from five laser kits. Catalog (free).

Micro-Z Electronics Systems
Box 2426
Rolling Hills, Calif. 90274

Kits for digital meters that save you $30. if you assemble them yourself. Brochure (free).

Newark Electronics Corp.
500 North Pulaski Rd.
Chicago, Ill. 60624

Electronic kits.

Phase Corp.
315-A Boston Ave.
Medford, Mass. 12155

Unique electronic kits often unobtainable elsewhere. Catalog (free).

Plasma Systems
P.O. Box 3261
San Jose, Calif. 95116

Laser kits. Catalog (free).

Relco Industries
P.O. Box 10839
Houston, Tex. 77018

Searching for a hidden treasure? Build your own treasure or metal detector. Micro-coil search head and micro-tuner kits also available. Catalog (free).

Telescopics
6565 Romaine St.
Los Angeles, Calif. 90038

Telescope mirror kits. Catalog (free).

Universal Electronics Co.
17811 Sky Park Circle Box 4517
Irvine, Calif. 92664

Choose from 450 models of a.c.-d.c. power supply kits, regulated and unregulated. Catalog (free).

University Optics., Inc.
2122 East Delhi Rd.
Ann Arbor, Mich. 48106

Kits for reflector telescopes, mirror testers, and making mirrors from blanks. Catalog (free).

The most recent statistics from the Justice Department show that crime is up again; and the crime that most people are afraid of is forcible entry, better known as burglary. It seems to be an unfortunate sign of our times that merely locking the door isn't enough anymore. People with drawers full of diamonds have been using alarm systems for years. Now, more and more ordinary folks are getting interested, too.

Some alarm systems work by summoning the police or a private security force. But studies have shown that just the noise of an alarm usually frightens off an intruder before the police come.

One of the earliest burglar alarms were geese. Thousands of years ago in China, property owners learned that a flock of geese makes a tremendous racket. The property owner therefore filled his yard with these geese. When an intruder was about, the resulting noise would alert the household. Unfortunately, geese are too messy for most 3½-room apartments. The electric burglar alarm is the proper substitute.

Technological advancements in electronics have made it possible for the home builder to make very sophisticated alarms. You can have electronic beams that trigger the alarm when broken. You can set an alarm to go off if anybody so much as touches your window. (Watch out you don't scare Mom some night.) Best of all, your peace of mind won't cost you a fortune. An alarm is far better than a weapon in discouraging crime and keeping your family safe. Sleep well.

**MOUNTAIN WEST
ALARM SUPPLY CO.**
4215 North 16 St.
Phoenix, Ariz. 85016

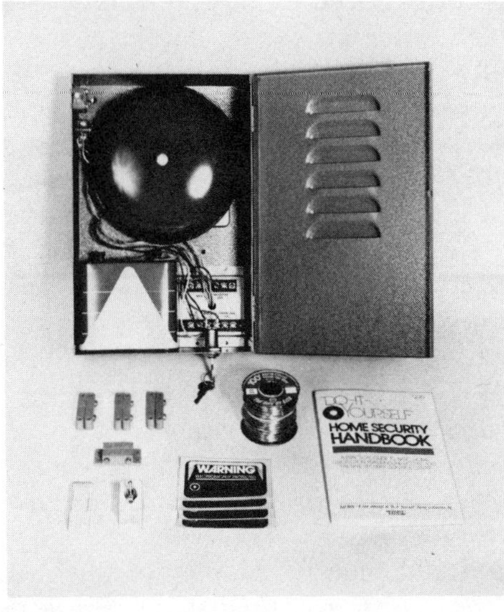

PROFESSIONAL-TYPE ALARM

Small stores, apartments, or offices will find this alarm kit perfect. The extra-loud bell is an enemy of every thief. It's a complete alarm outfit with 4 contacts for doors and windows. The kit has a combination bell box and control instrument, interior on/off switch, panic/battery test button, 100 feet of hookup wire, and an installation handbook.

The alarm system is activated only after you leave premises and close exit door. No need to rush out for fear alarm will ring before you can get out. Twenty-second entrance time delay gives time to shut off alarm upon entering. "Home/Away" switch permits you to cut off entrance door time delay when you are at home for instant alarm. The kit supplies you with 3 closed-circuit magnetic contacts and 1 open-circuit magnetic switch for entrance door. The alarm operates on a standard 12-v. lantern battery. The kit even includes a warning sticker, which may be as great a crime deterrent as the alarm. $95.

MINIMUM WIRING ALARM

One of the kit builder's problems is long-running wiring. The problem is modern buildings often have hard to work with solid walls. This brand new kit features 6 open-circuit magnetic contacts that connect to 3 alarm transmitters. When any of the 6 protected openings is penetrated, an alarm transmitter sends a secure radio signal to receiver located at control up to 200 feet away, and the powerful siren operates. A personal, portable alarm transmitter also will operate siren to handle panic situations. Just carry the transmitter in pocket, purse, or place next to chair when sitting. The kit is designed to handle 3 pairs of openings such as front door and front window, back door and back window, and 2 bedroom windows. Many other combinations are possible with additional open circuit contacts and alarm transmitters. $350. Each kit includes:

   6 open-circuit magnetic contacts
   3 alarm transmitters with batteries
   1 personal alarm transmitter with batteries
   1 alarm receiver, 12 v.d.c.
   1 control with entry/exit delays
   1 electronic siren & tamperproof outdoor
      steel box
   1 power supply 12 v.d.c.
   1 battery 12 v.
   50′ 22/2 wire
   50′ 16/2 wire
   1 set instructions

Mountain West (96 pp., free) catalog bills itself as "space-age security." They have over 500 alarm-type products. Many in kit form, all the latest in technological equipment. Worth reading, sleep better.

PLC ELECTRONICS, INC.
39–50 Crescent St.
Long Island City, N.Y. 11101

COMMERCIAL SECURITY SYSTEM

One of the many versatile systems that can be used to protect the sophisticated retail store downtown or a small factory in a suburban industrial park (and anything in between) with equal effectiveness. True protection is assured thanks to the tamper-resistant features of the rugged, all-steel outdoor bell assembly that is standard with this system.

An additional important feature of this system is its a.c./d.c. operation and automatic switchover to standby reserve power in case of electrical power failure. Installation is simplified with the exclusive PLC plug-in power supply which converts 110 v.a.c. power to low voltage a.c. at the wall outlet, thereby eliminating dangerous and costly electrical wiring.

The security system features 10 sets of Magnetic sensors which will protect 10 single openings or a combination of 4 double-hung windows and 2

standard doors, etc. Two emergency Panic Sensors are included with this system and suggestions for locating them are found in the detailed installation manual.

A unique feature is its exit and entry Time Delay which permits Keyless operation for convenience and greater security since no part of the system is exposed to the outside except the Bell Assembly, which is tamperproof. The Time Delay feature includes an indicator light to remind the owner that he has 30 seconds to turn the system off before the alarm rings, and circuit test and battery test provisions are standard.

Warning Decals, mounting hardware, and a 1-year warranty card are included with a 16-pp., in-depth instruction manual to guide you through the installation. $219.95.

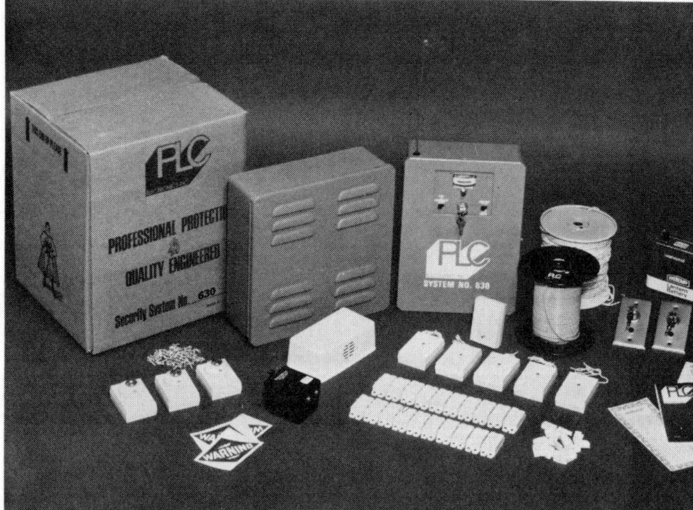

RESIDENTIAL SECURITY SYSTEM

Wireless fire, burglary, and emergency system. You're ready for anything short of a battalion of Marines!

Engineering and design are well represented in this loaded-with-extras system. Complete security and ease-of-operation features such as coming and going time delay; night time instant response; run of the house, hand-held panic transmitter; separate fire alarm; (all wireless) indoor alert horn; dual sound tamper-proof outdoor bell; and a red alarm indicator light are but a few of the many standard features.

And installation is wireless! Twenty single doors and windows or 9 double-hung windows and 2 doors, etc., can be protected with this system and its 20 magnetic sensor sets. Installation time is reduced tremendously thanks to the advanced wireless transmitters that link each protected door and window to the alarm control by a silent radio signal. The heat-sensing fire alarm is also wirelessly connected to the main control and a hand-held panic transmitter can be carried throughout the house as a safeguard against prowlers and unwanted visitors.

It's a.c.-powered with the exclusive PLC plug-in power supply which converts 110 v.a.c. to low voltage at the wall outlet, eliminating costly electrical wiring. Switchover to standby reserve power is automatic, so operation is uninterrupted in case of electrical power failure. Warning decals, mounting hardware, and a 1-year warranty card are included with a 26-p., step-by-step instruction booklet to guide you through the installation. $995.

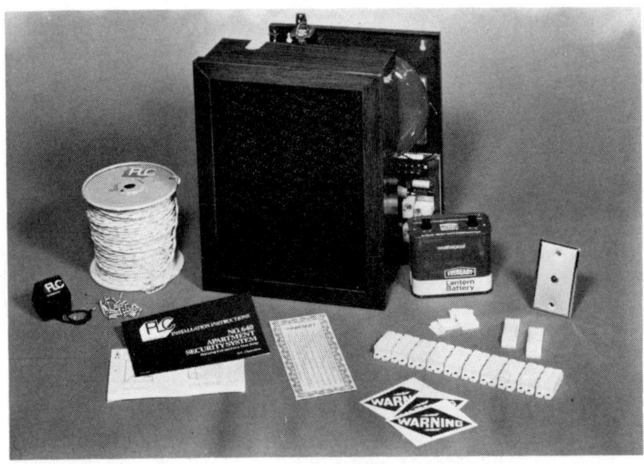

APARTMENT SECURITY SYSTEM

Casual doormen, careless landlords, too few policemen, and our wild times all contribute to the growing need for this product. Even the so-called safest buildings call for such help.

This system features a simulated wood grain control and bell combination and is designed with the tenant and the landlord in mind. Whether the installation takes place in a co-op, condominium, or a rented apartment, the exit and entry Time Delay provision means added convenience and greater security for the tenant and no landlord permission or involvement, because nothing is installed through the door or outside the apartment.

The entire system operates on low voltage. A unique circuit test is incorporated that will be appreciated by the owner and his neighbors, too. By turning the cabinet Key to the "Test" position, the owner is immediately alerted by a built-in buzzer if a door or window has been left open. This step prevents needless and annoying ringing of the actual alarm prior to going out.

Upon entering his or her apartment, the owner is reminded by a Red indicator light that the system has been activated and the thirty-second Time

Delay countdown has started. After turning the system OFF, and if all family members are at home, the No. 640 can be switched over to instant response for the night, for added peace of mind.

Two emergency buttons are included with the No. 640 and either one will activate the alarm whether the system is on or off. All doors and windows in the apartment are professionally protected by the 10 sets of No. 19 Magnetic Sensors that function in conjunction with the supervised alarm circuit. $249.95

ULTRASONIC SECURITY SYSTEM

Ideal for apartments, limited access offices, and certain retail stores, this space-age device protects by creating an invisible wall that "traps" unauthorized personnel at the point of entry. A two-stage alarm system permits convenient time-delayed exit and entry without the bother of additional outside locks and keys, and the owner is always reminded to turn off the system when he comes in, before the actual alarm sounds.

Extra protection is available with this system through the Alarm Circuit Provision, which permits connection of two No. 19 Magnetic Sensors (included) to a door or window not within the protected area of the Ultrasonic pattern. This feature will permit expansion of the protected area to doors or windows that cannot be covered by the 20′ wave pattern created by the No. 740 Ultrasonic. The wave pattern is adjustable down to approximately 5′ and it can be controlled and directed to protect against entry through a roof, a ceiling, or a common wall, as well as to "trap" the area in front of a door or window. $269.99.

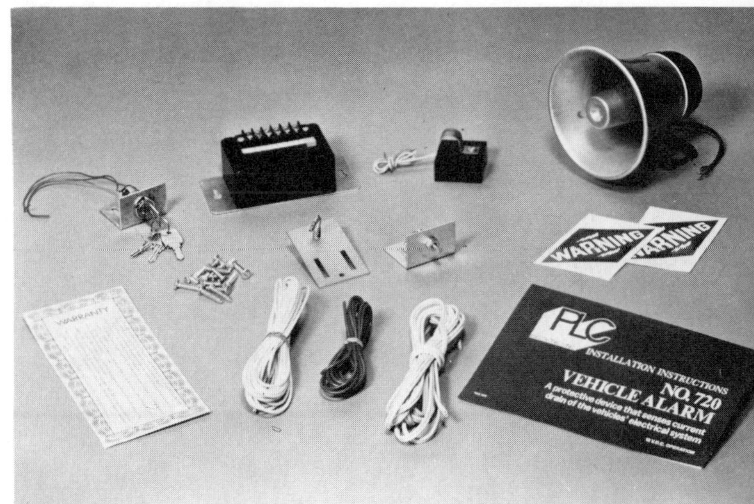

VEHICLE ALARMS

Joy rides of the fifties have given way to organized car theft rings of the seventies. Car thefts are increasing at such a dramatic rate that many big-city police departments have groups that handle this specialized crime. Steering lock devices and Detroit's other marvels help; however, there's nothing like an ear-shattering blast to send the auto thief scurrying. Three hours of installation time is all that's required. $99. Kit includes:

    1 eight-ohm speaker horn
    1 circuit module
    1 key control
    1 hood sensor
    1 trunk sensor
    1 current sensor module
    30' white wire
    10' red wire
    10' white wire (2-conductor)
    2 warning decals
    mounting hardware
    one-year warranty card

FIRE ALARM SYSTEM

Forget about those $5.95 fire alarm kits, they don't work. As corny as it sounds, one shouldn't try and save money when lives are involved. Here's a kit that really works. Designed for both residential and commercial applications, this system will protect a private home of any size or dimension just as well as a retail store, a small factory, warehouse, or private office.

A heavy-duty, all-weather outdoor steel bell assembly is standard as is the ear-piercing indoor horn, which is mounted in an attractive decorator-finished white case. This double feature will signal the neighbors in case of fire, while it alerts or awakens the entire household at the same time. Kit includes bell, horn, wire, heat, sensors, mounting hardware, and instruction book. $249.95.

PLC manufactures a line of quality alarm products. All kits will be shipped through local distributor, who can help you if you run into assembly problems.

KRYSTAL KITS
P.O. Box 445
Bentonville, Ark. 72712

HIGH-VOLUME BURGLAR ALARM SOUNDER

Super-loud sound levels as high as 115 db. can be delivered with both of the "Super Slick" sounders. Battery voltage between 3 and 18 v.d.c. operates the sounder with a peak power output of up to 40 w. All you need to add is a 8-ohm, 30-w. tweeter-type speaker horn. Complete kit of parts including p.c.b. less only the speaker horn. We haven't seen this item, but from the description, the price may be

excessive. This could be a good kit for the novice, but if you know any electronics, you might be able to think of something yourself that will do the same thing for a few dollars. Kit, continuous sound: $10.95. Kit, wavering tone: $12.95.

Many interesting kit projects, and some Experimenter's Kits including integrated circuits and "most needed" resistors and capacitors. These are no bargain (example: "Super Op-Amp Package contains a 741 [50¢ anywhere], plans, info, and resistors and capacitors for "only" $4.95). Some of their circuit ideas may be interesting and they do offer a money-back guarantee.

RADIO SHACK
2615 West 7 St.
Fort Worth, Tex. 76107

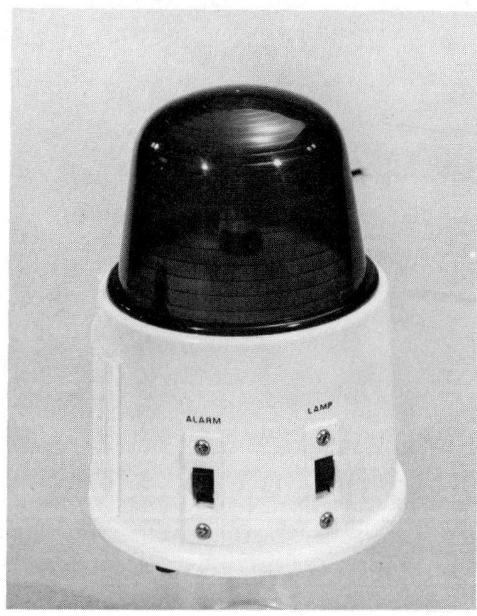

INTRUSION DETECTOR

A low-price defense against the break-and-enter artist. Loud alarm sounds if intruder attempts entry, or set it for silent blinking light warning. Magnetic contact switch attached to door, window, etc. With red dome lamp, ivory-color base. Easy, no-solder assembly. $10.95.

LAFAYETTE RADIO
111 Jericho Tpk.
Syosset, N.Y. 11791

GRAYMARK INFRARED SECURITY SYSTEM KIT

This do-it-yourself anti-rip-off device is about the least costly way of protecting yourself short of stationing a large man with an ax outside your door. A piercing alarm is triggered when an intruder breaks an invisible infrared beam. Alarm sounds inside, but kit includes terminals for installing an external bell or buzzer. The two units—lamp exciter and detector—are housed in streamlined walnut plastic cabinets, and the entire system is easy to assemble, with simplified instruction manual. (4¼ lb.) $29.95.

PEM ENTERPRISES

16 Belmont Dr.
Chelmsford, Mass. 01824

OPEN CIRCUIT BURGLAR/FIRE ALARM KIT

A complete kit that includes the book *How to Build a Burglar Alarm.* Kit contains 8″ underdome bell, metal control box (all holes are predrilled, including hardware), relay, 4 magnetic contact switches, 2 traps, shunt-lock switch, panic switch, and 2 heat detectors. Also includes 100′ wire. $39.95.

WIRELESS BURGLAR/FIRE ALARM

This project will provide any home with complete burglar/fire protection without stringing wires all over the house. Your house wiring system transmits the alarm signals. Each burglar and/or fire sensor is connected by wires to a transmitter, which is plugged into the nearest wall outlet. Your home wiring carries the alarm signal to the remote alarm, which can be plugged into a wall outlet anywhere in your home. Transmitter and receiver kit: $84.95.

OTHER SOURCES

Anes Electronics, Inc.
4112 Del Rey Ave.
Venice, Calif. 90291

Burglar alarms and fire sensors.

Crime Detection Systems
P.O. Box 790
Pearland, Tex. 77581

Complete offerings of home and automotive alarm systems. Catalog (50¢).

Mr. Gasket
4566 Spring Rd.
Cleveland, Ohio 44131

We understand they make superb auto alarm kits. In any event, their name is superb. Complete catalog ($1.).

Informer Alarm Supplies Co.
10 Cherry Hill Rd.
Baltimore, Md. 21225

For home or office. All types of burglar and fire alarm kits. All you need is a spare weekend to put one together. Catalog (free).

King Research Labs, Inc.
801 South 11 Ave.
Maywood, Ill. 60153

Kits for new-style burglar alarm system. Information package ($1.).

McGee Radio Co.
1901–07 McGee St.
Kansas City, Mo. 64108

Burglar alarm kits. Catalog (free).

On-Guard Corporation of America
350 Gotham Parkway
Carlstadt, N.J. 07072

Complete alarm systems of various types and descriptions.

Theft Prevention Co.
Box AE
Cupertino, Calif. 95014

Burglar and fire alarm kits for home or office. Catalog (free).

J.C. Whitney
1917 Archer Ave.
Chicago, Ill. 60680

World's largest supplier of car accessories offers a number of auto alarm kits.

The gun collector is a singular breed. He's very different from the man who just goes out to buy a gun. The collector loves his weapons for their design and workmanship, very rarely for the damage they can do. For him, the logical next step is building the weapon himself.

Nowadays, few of us need to carry weapons for protection. But the years when everybody had to be armed lasted much longer than the few short generations of relative peace and civilization. During those earlier times, men evolved a number of efficient weapons, truly admirable for their beauty and their functional economy. If you feel the power of these qualities in weaponry, you're probably a collector at heart.

Why not try building a weapon from a kit? If you'd like to get into gun or knife making, but don't quite know where to start, a kit can serve you well. Be sure to choose one whose complexity and function are suited to your purpose. If you plan to use a gun that you make for hunting, say, better have some practice first. Needless to say, a badly made weapon is almost sure to turn on you. If the gun will be only for display, on the other hand, it need not be such a professional job. In either case, you'll improve your skills and the finished product with every kit you build.

CONNECTICUT VALLEY ARMS, INC.
Saybrook Rd.
Haddam, Conn. 06438

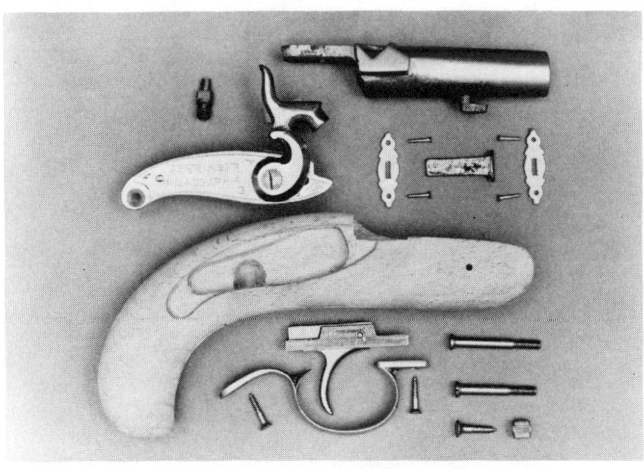

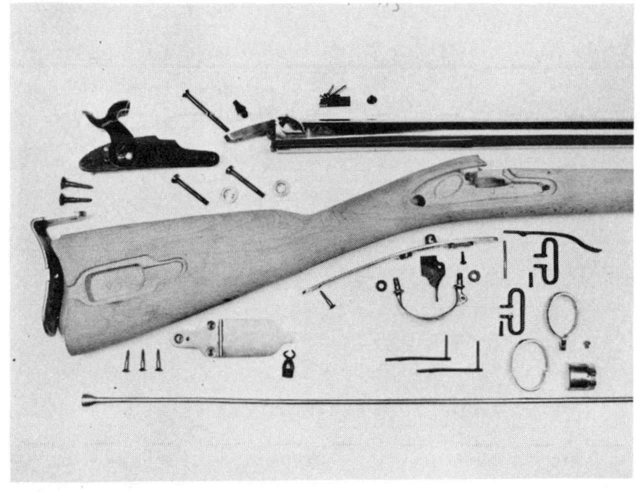

PHILADELPHIA DERRINGER

One of the most famous guns is now in kit form. It contains all parts needed to build an authentic replica of Henry Deringer's famous pistol. The ideal first gun kit as all of the hard work has been done. Requires only final putting together and finishing. You can use home workshop tools. This is the only kit we know of that will let you build a good shooting, truly authentic reproduction of the Philadelphia Derringer—right down to the engraving on the back action lock. $19.95.

ZOUAVE RIFLE KIT

The Zouave .58 caliber rifle was without doubt the high point of percussion rifle development. After extensive use in the Civil War, it has been used ever since as an accurate and highly effective hunting weapon, adequate in knockdown power for even the largest of American game. The barrel comes expertly rifled and polished—complete with three-leaf rear sight, authentic front sight, and threaded breech plug. The authentic Zouave lock is smooth and dependable with authentic "V"-type mainspring. All fittings are solid brass. The stock is fully formed and 90% inlet, requiring only final inletting and finishing. Comes with complete, illustrated instructions. All metal screws and screw holes are drilled and threaded and only home workshop tools are needed. The kit offers the reasonably skillful craftsman the opportunity to reproduce one of the classic weapons of American history. $89.95

An impressive collection of guns all available in kit form. Appears to be very fine quality. Catalog $1.

GOLDEN AGE ARMS CO.
Box 82
Worthington, Ohio 43085

GOLDEN AGE FLINTLOCK PISTOL KIT

Kit contains premium-plus precarved pistol stock; 13/16, .45, .40, .36, or .32 caliber barrel with breech plug; Hamm or Conn. Valley Maslin flintlock; single trigger; trigger guard and butt cap; front and rear sights; front and rear ramrod pipes; fore-end cap; underpinning strip; lock bolts; side plate; and the book, *Building the Kentucky Pistol*. A very impressive kit. Kit with Hamm lock: $106.50. Kit with Conn. Valley lock: $89.50. Silver, instead of brass, hardware: $2.00.

Several fine precarved stock kits for muzzle-loading rifles, shotguns, and pistols, as well as an extensive line of equipment, accessories, and decorations for muzzle-loaders. Very nice catalog ($1.50). This stuff is not cheap, but it is of connoisseur grade.

CUSTOM KNIFEMAKERS SUPPLY
P.O. Box 11448
Dallas, Tex. 75223

KNIFE-MAKING KIT—THE BOWIE

Cavemen fashioned knives from rocks and branches. Before modern technology manufactured knives in great quantity for the consumer, the only method of making knives was by hand. The world was once filled with knife carriers. For the interested hobbiest, there is now a kit that will enable you to make your own bowie knife.

The bowie knife-making kit contains the blade, which is an old pattern in high carbon forged steel (made of a Rockwell hardness, it is fully 5/16″ thick and blade length is 10″), and a true English bowie handle. Complete knife is 15″ long and weighs 1½ lb. $32.50.

Company offers a variety of blades, handles, and sheaths in a number of fine materials. Another case where you'll pay top-dollar but receive quality merchandise.

NUMRICH ARMS CORP.
West Hurley, N.Y. 12491

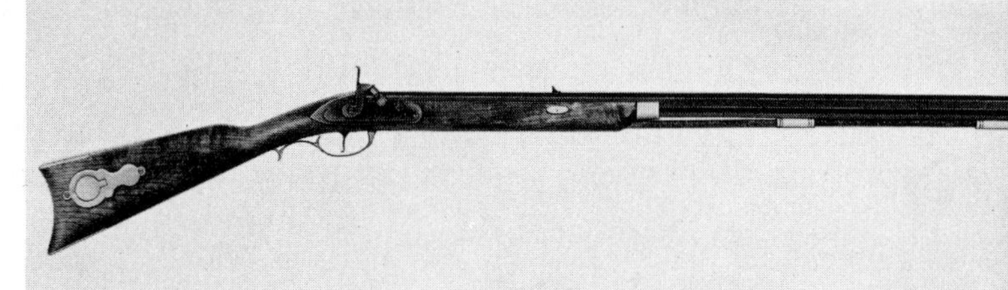

AMERICAN MUZZLE LOADER

Build your own replica of an American muzzle loader. A different touch of Americana. All-metal parts with only a wood rasp and a little sandpaper to finish the job. Stock is fully machine finished and contoured. All parts needed are furnished in the kit. Specify flint or percussion .31, .36, .45, or .50 caliber. No machine or power tools required to complete. $109.95.

Numrich has elaborate (100 pp., $2.50) catalog of every possible gun kit. Also offers sale of individual parts priced separately. Examples are line drawings; catalog has matching price for every component. Also complete kits of Mausers, Colts, Derringers, rifles, and submachine guns. Company stocks 38 million individual parts.

DIXIE GUN WORKS, INC.
Union City, Tenn. 38261

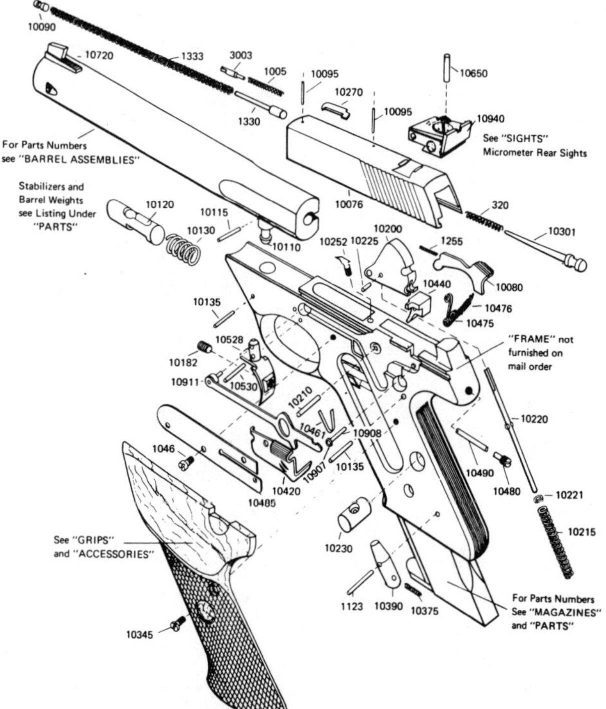

SPILLER & BURR REVOLVER KIT

The Spiller & Burr revolver is today one of the rarest Civil War Confederate revolvers. The original Spiller & Burr revolver production totaled a questionable 1,451 guns, which was a far cry from the contract commissioned by the "Confederate States of America," for 15,000 guns. The firm of Spiller & Burr, Macon, Georgia, produced approximately 700 of these revolvers. The remainder was produced by the Confederate government after it purchased the firm in 1864. There were two models of the Spiller & Burr, and the kit is designed after the conventional approved and accepted later model.

This revolver kit has a solid brass trigger guard and frame with the backstrap cast integral with the frame. Two-piece unfinished walnut grips. All screw holes have been drilled and tapped in proper positions. All major parts are left unfinished and require polishing and gluing the appropriate pieces. One deviation from the original is that the barrel in this kit has 6 lands and 6 grooves, whereas the original had 7 lands and 7 grooves. (This makes it impossible for the finished gun to be faked for an original). $39.95.

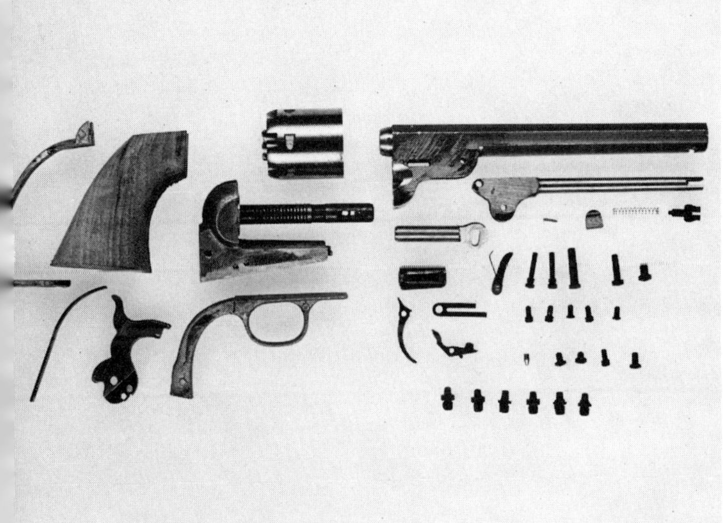

BABY DRAGON REVOLVER KIT

Another Dixie Quality Gun Kit. All metal parts have been left in the white with milling marks still on them. Will require very light filing, buffing, and the required finish that you desire. The .31 caliber octagon barrel has been rifled. You will have to case harden the hammer, trigger, hand, and loading lever. Since the screws in this revolver are all of metric size, all screw holes in the wax-cast brass frame have been drilled and tapped.

Dixie really takes their gun making seriously. They put out a lavishly illustrated catalog (400 pp.) for $2. The company has hundreds of kits and a feeling of the Old South. Even if guns are not for you, you'll enjoy leafing through the catalog.

OTHER SOURCES

Bingham Archery Co.
Ogden, Utah 84403

The Bingham Archery Co. is owned and operated by an industrial arts teacher. This is a business designed to meet the needs of teachers and scout leaders who desire to include archery in their shop programs. Students can now construct modern bows at a very low cost. For those archery enthusiasts who do not have shop facilities or have limited time, there are many designs in semi-finished bows to choose from at different stages of completion. Catalog (free).

Coladonato Bros.
Hazleton, Pa. 18201

No guns, but the largest selection of gun cabinets imaginable. All rugged and durable, easy-to-assemble wood with Colonial ornamental hardware.

Crossbowman
P.O. Box 723
Manteca, Calif. 95336

"Jayhawk Crossbow" kit. Catalog (25¢).

Fernwood Gun Supply
1725 Springbrook Rd.
Walnut Creek, Calif. 94596

No special skills required to assemble the three pistol kits offered: a .44 caliber Derringer, a four-barrel Derringer and a .36 caliber pistol. Brochure (free).

Golden Age Arms Co., Inc.
Box 82
Worthington, Ohio 43085

For antique arms buffs, antique rifle and pistol kits as well as hunting knife kits. Catalog ($1.).

Kittridge Bow Hut
P.O. Box 598
Mammoth Lakes, Calif. 93546

Bow and arrow kits. Catalog (25¢).

Van Sickle Cutlery Co.
P.O. Box 3688
San Angelo, Tex. 76901

Hunting knife kits. Catalog (50¢).

Man has often been called the tool-making animal. Although this is probably not strictly accurate, we are certainly far and away the biggest makers and users of tools. As anthropologists like to say, human culture really depends on our ability to design and use more and more sophisticated tools.

There's certainly no doubt that present-day technological society is based on highly specialized use of tools. Maybe for this reason, more people are discovering the satisfaction to be found in making and building things for their own use. Often our personal use of tools involves woodworking and tools like saws, lathes, wood screwdrivers, and specialized turning instruments. Besides the pleasure derived from such work, there's the joy of making and owning a really fine handmade piece of furniture.

If you use tools for reasons of pride and pleasure, you might want to consider building the tools themselves, as well. For the true builder, craftsmanship extends beyond the products to the implements. This idea has led some manufacturers to offer tool-making kits. Many of these are related to woodworking, probably because tool-building appeals to the same taste as woodworking does. If you are a craftsman—whatever your level of expertise—consider the added pleasure of building with your own handmade tools.

This section will help to suggest some kits you can find to get you started.

AMERICAN MACHINE & TOOL CO.
Fourth Ave. and Spring St.
Royersford, Pa. 19468

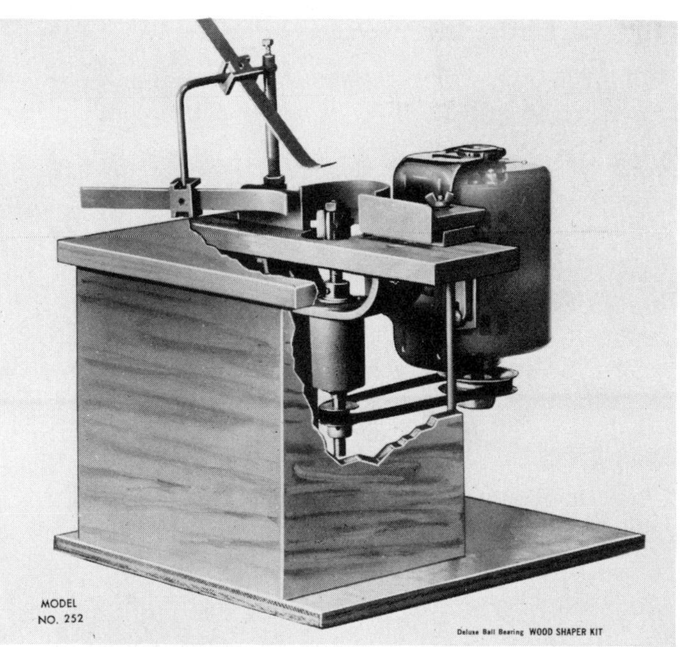

SPINDLE-SHAPER

If you do any kind of woodworking, more com-plicated than whittling a walking stick, you probably need a spindle-shaper—which can set you back about $100. if purchased fully assembled. This device lets you make decorator edges on furniture, form beads, coves, moldings, tongue-in-groove joints, etc. This is not a beginner's project, but instructions and patterns are unusually clearly stated and arranged, so that anyone with some experience and average intelligence can assemble the spindle-shaper in a few evenings. $19.95.

CALDWELL INDUSTRIES
Luling, Tex. 78648

LIGHT VERTICAL MILLING MACHINE KIT

Easily the second most useful major machine tool after the lathe. A uniquely designed milling machine by Edgar T. Westbury. It is intended for home construction. As far as possible machining of large and complex castings have been eliminated through the use of tube construction. The only problem likely to cause trouble is the smoothing off of the 15″ × 15″ base, which requires a fairly large machine and the machining of the dovetail slides and working surfaces of the compound table. Ideally this requires a vertical mill of at least 15″ travel. They offer these parts machined but still leave the remainder for you. The tube construction produces a machine with an almost unlimited flexibility as the milling head can be positioned almost anywhere. Drawings, casting, bearings: $173.25. Partial machining: $75.00 additional.

ROTARY TABLE KIT

For rotating work on mill, drill press, or lathe. Drawings and Castings: $19.

Also offered are a compound Milling Table (castings, feed screws, handles, and plans: $42.95) as well as assembled shop machines (lathes, shapers, and milling machines). See Toys and Models and Clocks sections for other products.

GILLIOM MANUFACTURING CO.
1109 North 2 St.
St. Charles, Mo. 63301

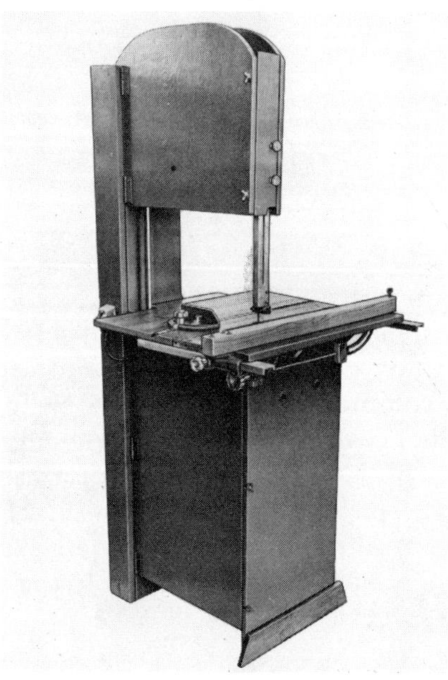

18″ BANDSAW

A real bargain for the home workshop. Although this instrument is not suitable for heavy-duty work (continuous ripping of hardwood or aluminum thicker than ½″), it can make a drastic improvement in do-it-yourself capabilities at home. It will take a ½ h.p. motor and blades up to about ⅜″, and the 18″ throat is extremely convenient. The kit

is offered with aluminum wheels (recommended) or in a cheaper version with hubs for homemade plywood wheels—we don't see the point of saving $13. on a critical part of the instrument. The kit is relatively easy to build (one 4′ × 8′ sheet plywood needed), although it's easier with a good bandsaw. Kit with aluminum wheels: $69.99. Kit with hubs for wood wheels: $56.99.

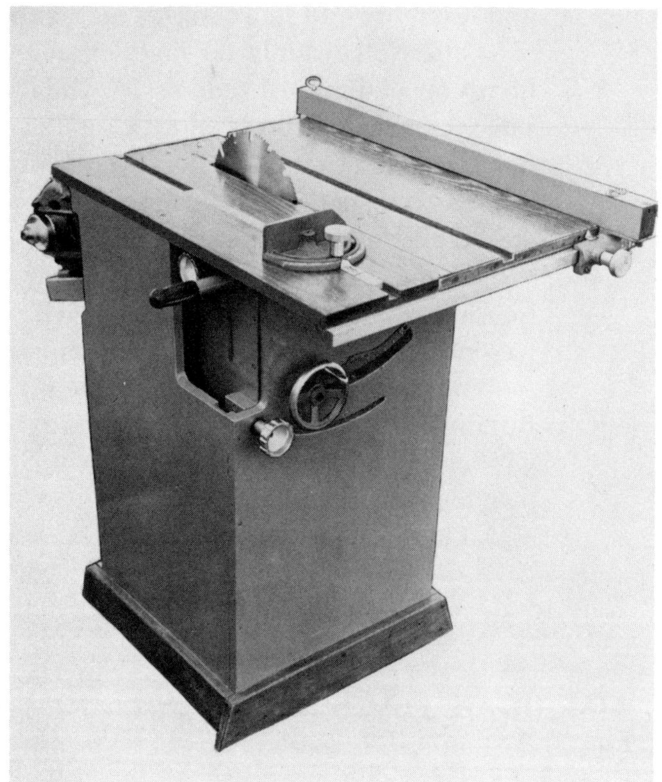

10″ TILT/ARBOR SAW

Kit includes all parts except blade, motor, and wood. Arbor tilts full 45 degrees. Tilting unit is supported on 2 steel hinges, locks rigidly at both front and back at all degrees of tilt. Graduated scale shows angle of cut. 27″ × 29″ table stays at natural level position. Constructed of two pieces of 13/16″ hardwood or plywood, table is reinforced at front and back with aluminum rails. 10″ combination blade cuts from 0″ to 3¼″ with depth of cut controlled by 4½″ diameter handwheel and jackscrew mechanism. Floor model, sets directly on floor, requires no bench or stand. Motor mounts integral with tilting arbor. Belt tension is constant for all cuts. High-speed ball bearing arbor for long, efficient service. $33.99.

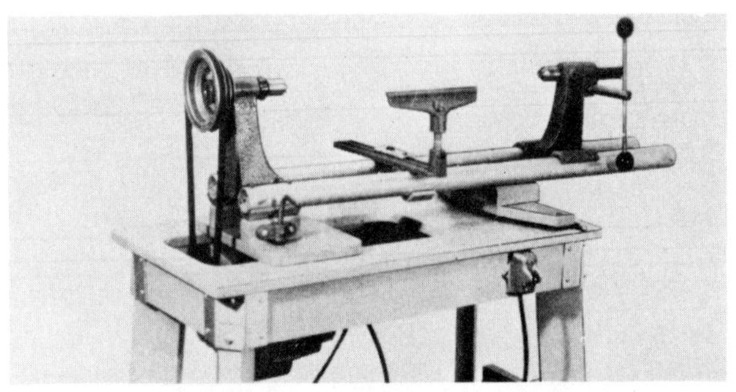

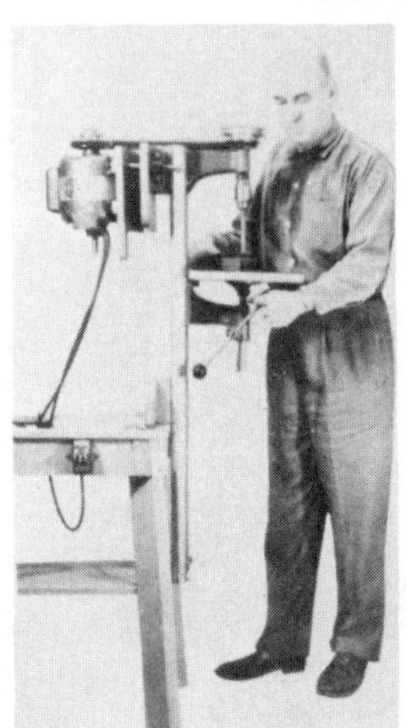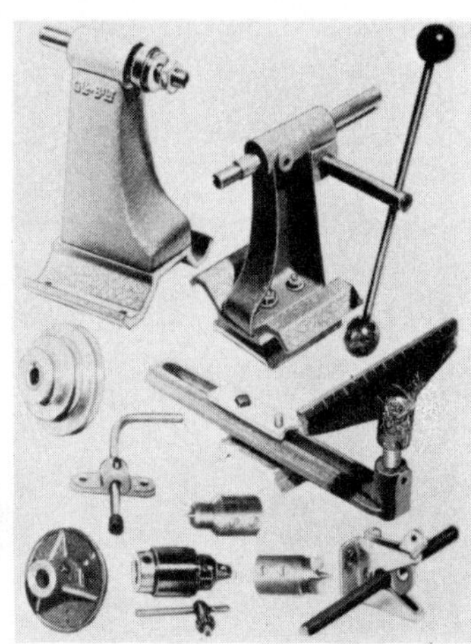

12" COMBINATION PRESS-LATHE

All parts (less motor and switch) for combination drill press and lathe. The drill press will handle a ½" bit in steel. Lathe, 12" swing over bed with 31" distance between centers. Can also be used as a tool grinder or disc sander. Kit: $44.99. Pipe for bed: $5.99.

Several other kits for power tools and a substantial line of accessories and motors (discounts for ordering with power tool kit).

OTHER SOURCES

Casting Specialties
Div. of C.F. Struck Corp.
Cedarburg, Wis. 53012

Large selection of tool kits ranging from simple screwdriver to a heavy-duty air compressor. Catalog (50¢).

Microm Co.
P.O. Box 2313
Santa Ana, Calif. 92707

Milling machine kit. Brochure (free).

The art of decoration and furnishing is the indispensable companion of architecture. Each age in history has had a distinctive way of building, and a distinctive way of furnishing those buildings. Today, we can choose one or many of the styles left to us by our ancestors: the enduring simplicity of classic Japanese style, the complexities of the baroque, the clean lines of Scandinavian modern.

Along with the rediscovery in recent years of handcrafts and do-it-yourselfing has come the realization that handmade furniture is often superior to the factory product. The Shakers, an almost vanished American religious sect, are thought of more for their fine homemade furniture than their pious ways. Original pieces are now nearly priceless.

But for those who want to work in wood, authentic Shaker reproductions are available in good kits, as are reproductions of Early American, French Provincial, and modern furniture. You can build your kitchen cabinets from a kit at half the price and twice the quality of what you can buy. Woodworking has become so popular that there are several monthly magazines devoted to this subject alone. We have no doubt that with inflation and zooming labor costs, doing your own decorating and furnishing will grow even more in the years to come. Love of wood and working with it seems to come naturally to most people. There's no better time to indulge that love than now.

BARZI INTERNATIONAL, INC.

P.O. Box 2178
Memphis, Tenn. 38101

BENTWOOD ROCKER

This is the original bentwood rocker with all the graceful lines and beautiful curls. Seat and back are already hand-caned. Wood parts are finished. Easy assembly, hardware and everything included. $119.95 postpaid.

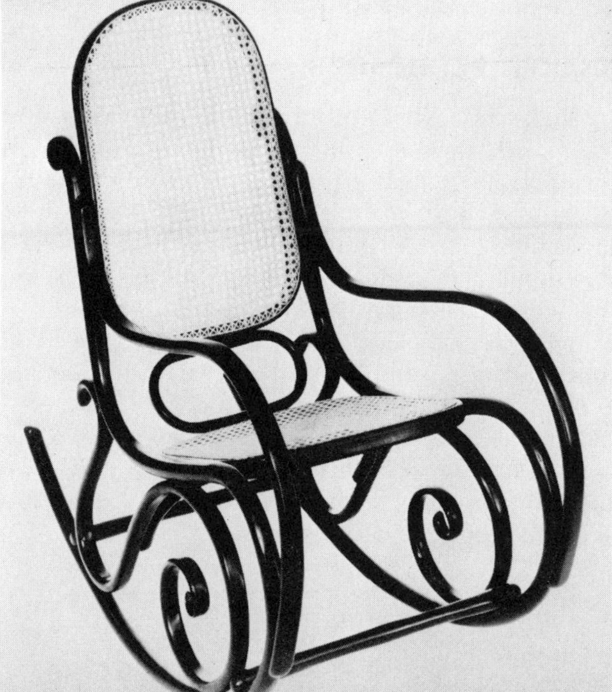

DOOR STORE

210 East 51 St.
New York, N.Y. 10022

ARGENTINE CHAIR

Mahogany with leather cover. An impressive and surprisingly comfortable chair. 29″ high × 26″ wide. Relatively little work with rewarding results. $75.

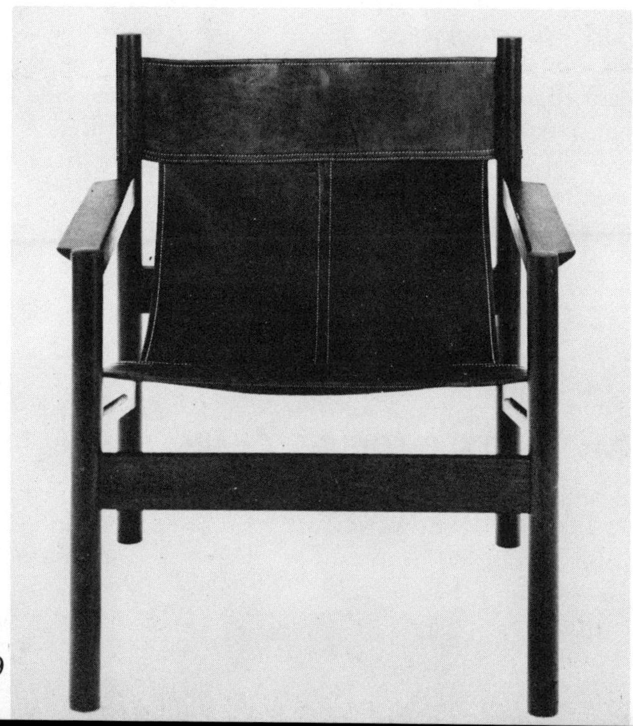

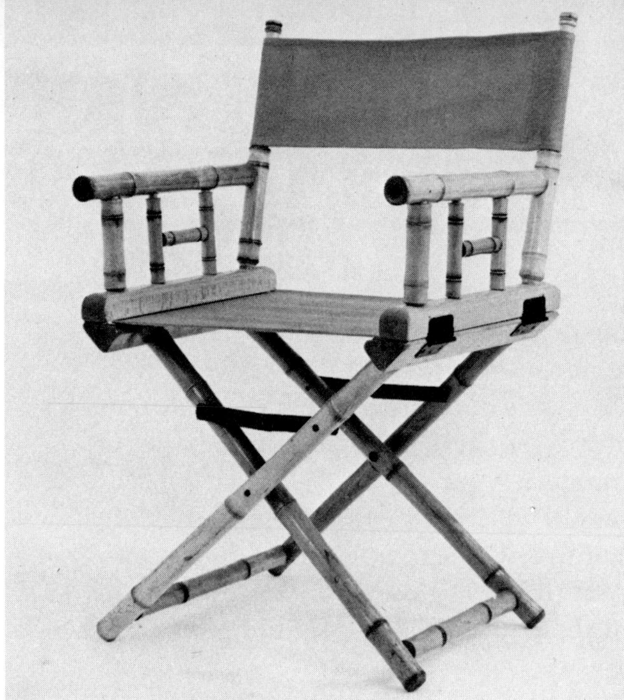

BAMBOO DIRECTOR'S CHAIR

The classic director's chair in a bamboo styling. This functional chair has been designed to incorporate modern styling with an interesting new look. Standard (33″) height. Natural finish, canvas seat, and back. Simple assembly project. $32.

Associated with Door Store of Washington, D.C. Some different items, but basically the same. Catalog available ($1.).

JRM CO.
1912 South Ridge Ave.
Kannapolis, N.C. 28021

EARLY AMERICAN WAGON SEAT BENCH

Jim Martin makes only one kit. Like many kit companies, he started in business to fill local demands. Some twenty years ago, he found an Early American wagon seat in an old barnyard near his North Carolina home. Many of his friends wanted a seat like it. Soon he developed a kit: Solid oak parts, hardware, and instructions. At first, it was only sold locally, but now it's available by mail. It makes a perfect bench or coffee table. Fairly priced at $85. A true piece of "Americana."

GENEDA IMPORTS
Box 204
Teaneck, N.J. 07666

DANISH-STYLE LOUNGE CHAIR

A sturdy chair with sharp lines at a realistic price. Here's a first-rate product. European-imported solid hardwood frame. The design is authentic Danish and has a thick poly-foam fabric seat cushion. The kit can be put together in fifteen minutes. $34.95.

Geneda Catalog (15¢) shows a variety of easy-to-assemble furniture at reasonable prices.

COHASSET COLONIALS
Cohasset, Mass. 02025

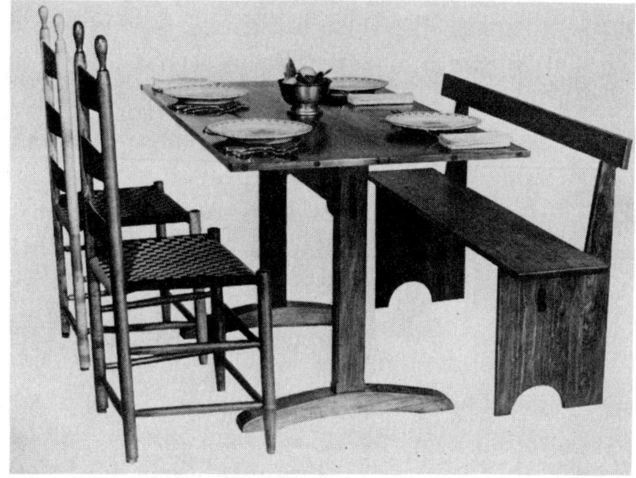

SHAKER TABLE AND BENCH

Traditional Shaker styling. Fine dining room table of pumpkin pine. Exceptionally fair price. 30″ × 54″ × 30″ high.

The bench, used next to the trestle dining table, exemplifies the Shaker's sense of practicality. Children can easily slide along its seat, since it is not encumbered by arms. Because it is relatively narrow, it may serve as a hall seat. 31″ high, 13½″ deep. Seat is 10¼″ × 52″. Table: $79.95. Bench: $29.95.

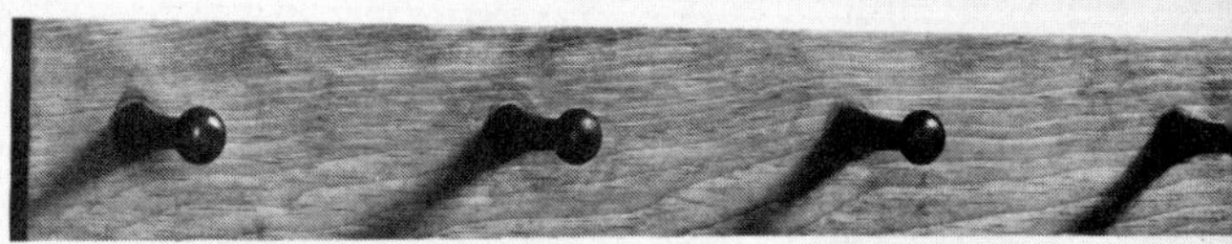

SHAKER PEGBOARDS

In Shaker homes and meeting houses the walls were lined with pine and maple pegboards on which furniture, tools, clothing, and other household items hung when not in use. The look was surprisingly attractive, besides being utilitarian. Although you may not be inclined to hang up your dining room set, you'll find these pegboards ideal for clothing. Hung at a child's level, they encourage neatness and independence, and placed in an entry hall they are a good-looking convenience for coats. Positioned end to end, they can even go across a whole wall or around a room. The pegboards come in two sizes: the 25″ has four maple pegs, the 46″ board has seven pegs. Very easy assembly. 25″: $6.95. 46″: $8.95.

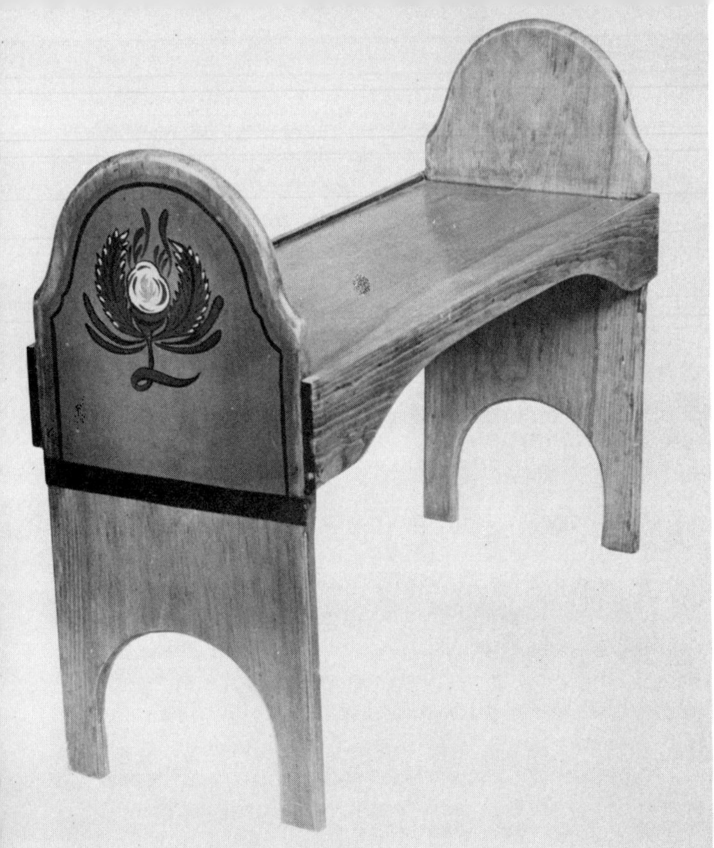

SLEIGH SEAT

A reproduction of the original in New York's Metropolitan Museum of Art, this is a graceful pine heirloom piece that can be used as a decorative bench or as a little snack table. Of particular interest is the stencil design on the ends. Directions and a pattern for reproducing this design are included with the kit. The color pack for the design is not included. Easy assembly. $23.95.

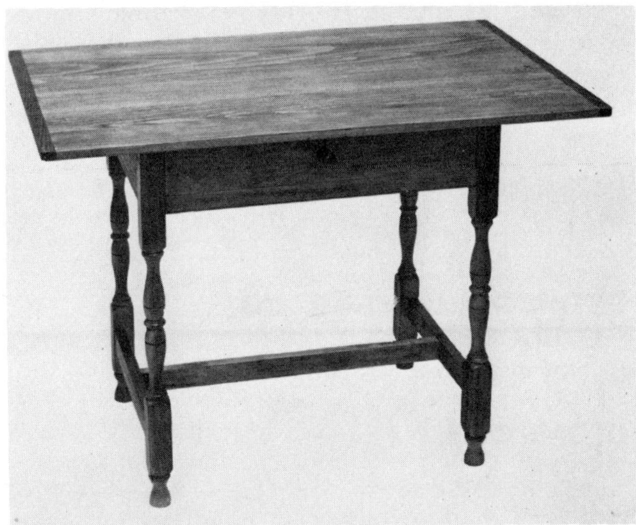

WRITING TABLE

A copy of the original in the Henry Ford Museum, this gracefully proportioned writing table would be attractive in the kitchen as well as the library. It has

a spacious drawer underneath its clear matched maple top (42″ × 36″). $84.95.

TUB COFFEE TABLE

This reproduction of an 18th-century original on display in Gore Place, Waltham, Massachusetts, is very easy to assemble and is elegant in its simplicity. It is 46″ long and 23″ wide and has a solid 1″ top. Perfect for entertaining in a country-style living room. $36.95.

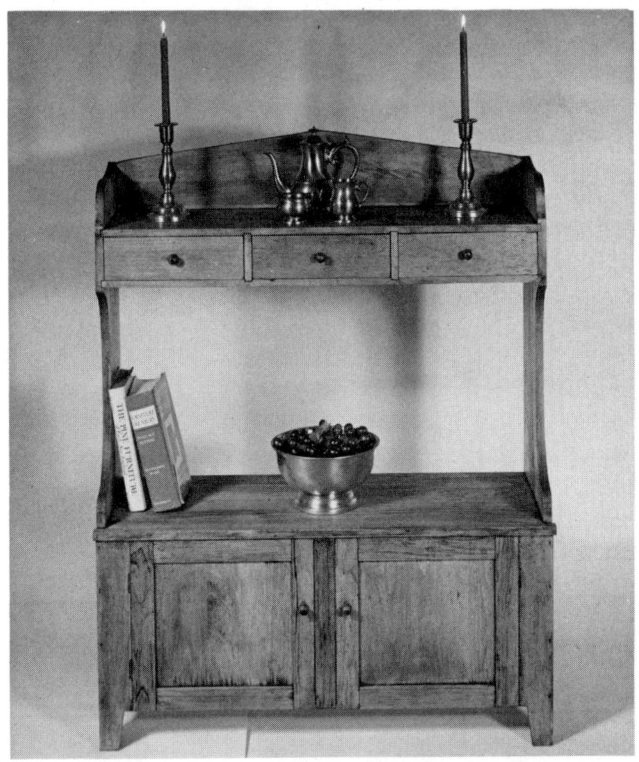

LINCOLN WATER BENCH

This "bench" is not a bench at all, but a spacious and gracious hutch, a reproduction of the original in the Samuel Lincoln House in Hingham, Massachusetts. It has a roomy lower cabinet, which can be used for storing linens, hi-fi equipment, or record albums. Made of clear pumpkin pine throughout, it stands 49″ high and is 40″ across. It has two shelves, the upper one 11″ deep and 45″ from the floor; the lower one 15½″ deep and 19¼″ high. The kit includes brass butt hinges. We think this is Cohasset's most outstanding and unusual piece, and certainly one of the finest examples of kit furniture available. It certainly cannot be assembled in an evening, but the care you devote to putting it together and applying stain and wax will reward you with a beautiful and practical addition to your home. $154.95.

LOW BED

Platform beds and loft beds are standard do-it-yourself projects these days, but who would think of assembling a Colonial-style bed? Cohasset Colonials, that's who. And they've taken care to adapt this copy of an original in New York's Metropolitan Museum to 20th-century sleeping habits. While retaining the holes in the foot rail, through which the early settlers attached their rope mattress supports, they've altered the rails to accommodate a modern box spring and mattress. The kit includes a wrench, glue, all necessary hardware, and six angle irons to hold the box springs. Not for the beginner. Twin: $94.95. Full: $109.95.

FOUR-POSTER CANOPY BED

The ultimate in romance, the four-poster is enjoying a revival these days, and Cohasset's version is truly beautiful in its simple, unadorned, and well-proportioned design. The headboard is double-arched in pumpkin pine, and the posts are solid maple. Available in full-size only (no kings and queens for Colonial Americans!), it includes a straight canopy frame measuring 58″ by 80″. Posts are 77 in. high. $129.95.

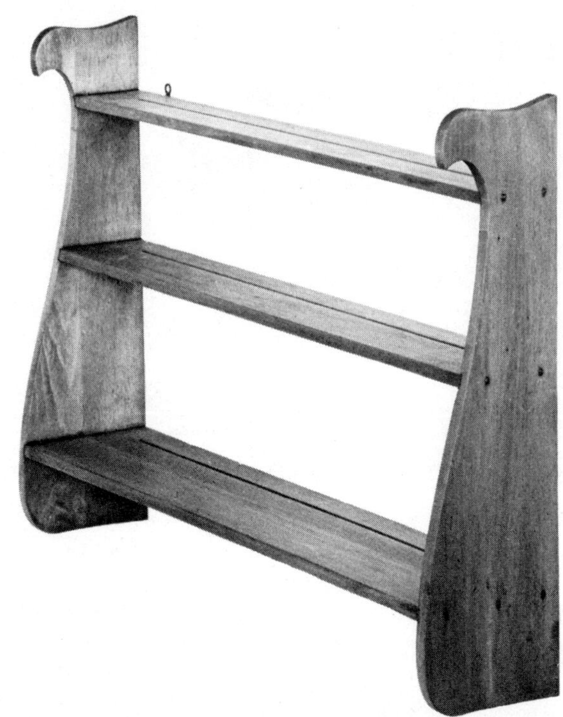

SOLOMON RICHARDSON SHELF

This useful shelf, whose unusual ends show an imagination and flair for handling pine, is a replica of the original in the Solomon Richardson house at Old Sturbridge Village. Designed to hold a wide range of attractive objects, it offers ample shelf space to the collector. 22½″ high by 32¾″ wide with shelves varying from 3½″ to 6½″ wide. Complete with hand-wrought nails and wall hangers. $20.95.

Francis Hagerty, the president of Cohasset Colonials, in our conversations and letters impressed us as a true craftsman. He writes: "Each of our kits is meticulously handcrafted from pumpkin pine and New England hardwoods; all join-

ery, drilling, and sanding is done under my personal supervision. This attention to detail is an assurance that your kit will be easy to assemble and will be a thing of beauty when finished." Their catalog (50¢) and their kits are fine quality.

BANNER BILLIARDS MANUFACTURING CO., INC.
4208 Commerce Ave.
Fairfield, Ala. 35064

TRADITIONAL-STYLE POOL TABLE

Solid, heavyweight (510 lb.) pool room-style table, features 44″ × 88″ playing area, commercial quality live rubber cushions, regulation size, full-depth, high-density plastic pockets, 1½″ shale aggregate bed, and all-wood base. The playing surface is made flat to ± 0.02 inches. Kit includes shaped and precut pieces and all hardware and comes complete with two cues, balls, rack, and cover.

> Standard Kit (unfinished): $259.
> Black walnut finish kit: $279.
> Unfinished with deluxe trim, kit: $279.
> Black walnut, deluxe trim, kit: $289.

SHIP'S WHEEL
Nottingham Square Rd.
Epping, N.H. 03042

LOBSTER TRAP TABLE

Lobster lover or not you'll want to decorate with this unique table. It's a re-creation of a lobster trap. You use it for a table. It's easy to assemble and it's complete with all parts; even net and the nails. Leave out in the back yard to "weather." At $34.95, it's about the cost of a good lobster dinner these days.

Catalog (80 pp., 50¢) has a good showing of furniture, ship models, and gifts—many in kit form.

BEDFORD LUMBER CO.
P.O. Box 65
Shelbyville, Tenn. 37160

CEDAR CHEST

The chest that was part of every household. Young girls used them as hope chests, and families used them to store quilts and blankets. Nothing matches their strong, rugged style. Always bug-free. A true proud possession. Bedford offers the real thing in the original style, and prices are from $30. to $75. depending on size. An easy-to-complete project.

THE H. H. PERKINS CO.

P.O. Box 1601
New Haven, Conn. 06506

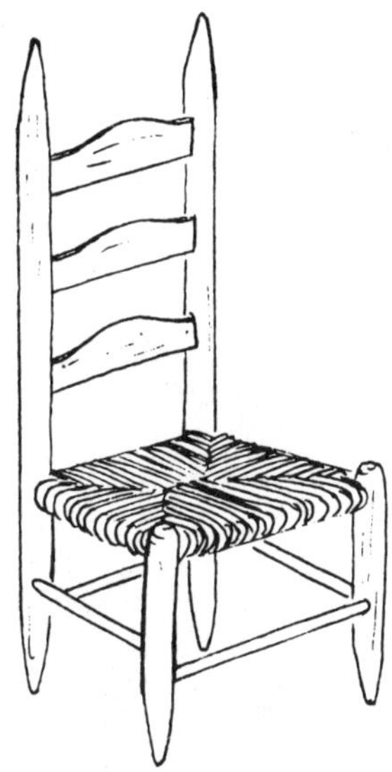

CATHEDRAL LADDER-BACK CHAIR KIT

George Washington must have sat on one just like this. Select solid ash frame, smoothly finished, ready for staining. Fiber rush seat. The frame is partially assembled. Elmer's glue as well as instructions included. Approximate dimensions: 43″ × 16″ × 17″. $15.95. A junior edition of the adult chair kit is also available. Everything is the same except dimensions: 29″ × 15″ × 12″. $10.60.

FOOT STOOL

This is called "Junior #30," but we're sure it's strong enough to hold Dad's tired feet. Kit includes ready-to-assemble, select hardwood framing, fiber rush top, instructions, and Elmer's glue. Approximate dimensions: 13″ × 10″ × 9″. The reeds used for these kits are selected for whiteness, smoothness, and length of strands. All bases are as warp-proof as possible. Sudden changes of temperature should be avoided. $3.85.

Perkins produces a variety of "cane" chairs, footstools, and basket kits at attractive prices.

SHAKER WORKSHOPS, INC.

Box C-1
Concord, Mass. 01742

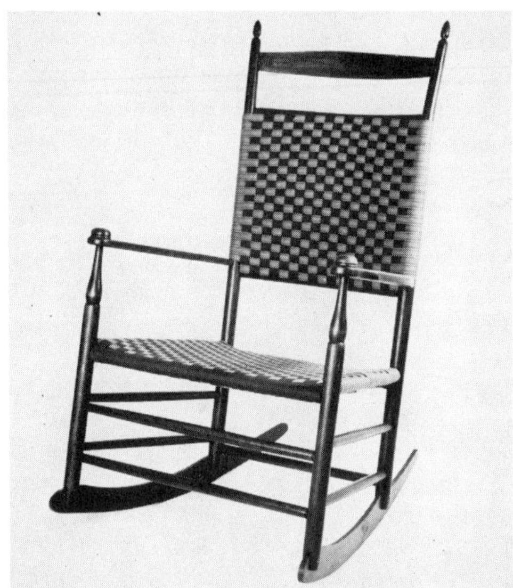

LARGE TAPED-BACK ROCKER

Nothing better exemplifies the functional beauty and strength of Shaker furniture design than this taped-back rocker. This Shaker Workshops reproduction is copied from the largest chair made at the Mt. Lebanon community and the taped back provides extra comfort and an extra area of color to brighten any room. Height, 42″, width (across arms) 25″, width (seat) 23″, depth (seat) 19″. Kit, complete with your choice of Shaker stain (light, medium, or dark) and color choice of tapes for seat and back. $85.

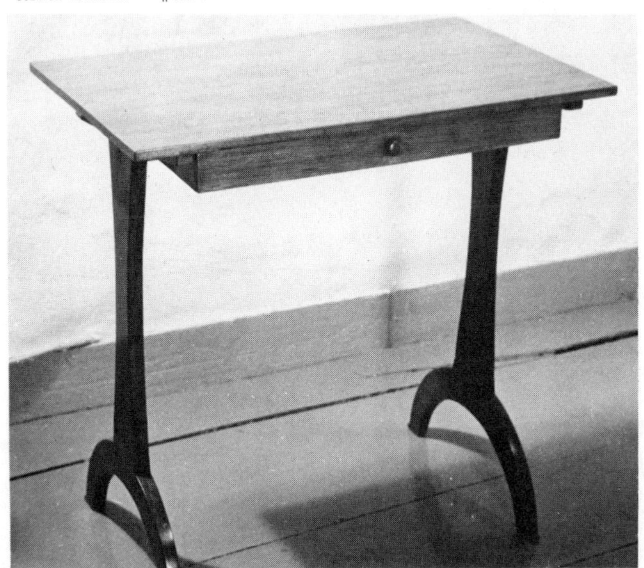

SIDE TABLE

The clean, perfectly functional lines of this elegant side table show why Shaker furniture is coveted today by antiquarians as well as fans of modern design. It anticipates by more than a century the principles behind the best contemporary furniture.

The original of this exact reproduction was made at the Harvard, Massachusetts, community about 1840. The finely profiled trestle legs, unencumbered by a stretcher, and the underslung drawer make it useful as a bedside table, small writing desk, hall table, or as an occasional table for any room of the house. Made from selected hard cherry, available as a kit (with drawer preassembled) including stain. (27¼" high, 28⅜" wide, and 17" deep) $75.

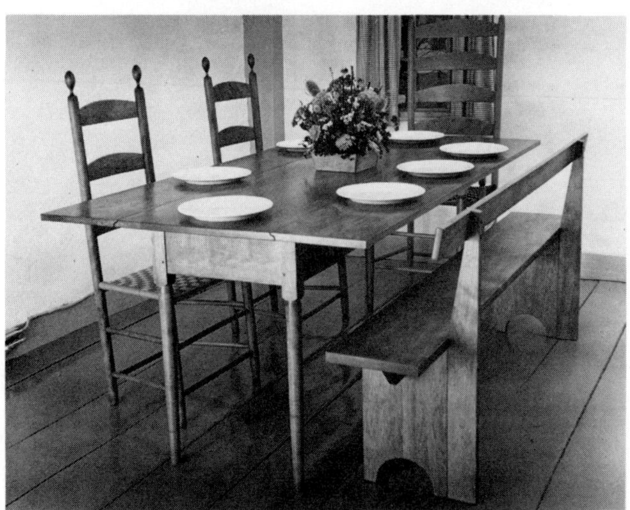

DROP-LEAF TABLE, STRAIGHT-BACK CHAIRS, AND SHAKER BENCH

The table is a copy of a Shaker original made about 1830 at the Hancock, Massachusetts, community. Similar to the well-known harvest table, it is now believed that this type may have originated with the Shakers. The bench, made to the exact same length as the table, has the crisp lines and economy of design that make it undeniably Shaker. Bench kit (8′ long): $50. Straight chair: $40. Table (8′ long): $215.

WEAVER'S CHAIR

Throughout their history the Shakers produced an enormous range of chairs because they realized that the efficiency of their communities depended on artifacts which precisely filled their needs. In many applications, they found that a chair somewhat higher than normal was desirable, and it was perhaps as a weaver's chair, to accompany their huge looms, that the original of this chair was first produced about 1830. Today its classically simple lines fit perfectly with almost any decorating scheme; indeed, its suitability for 20th-century living is perhaps even more universal than even the Shakers would have imagined. As a "counter chair," whether in a "country kitchen" or a modernistic den or bar, this example is, we believe, the perfect answer. Well-made kit. Height: 37½". Height of seat: 24". Width: 18¼". Depth 13¾". $40.

From the late 18th century onwards, the Shakers developed a culture that is still today remarkably fresh and innovative. Deliberately withdrawing from the world around them, the members of this inspired religious communal sect have left us a heritage of simplicity and beauty in their furniture, architecture, and life-style. Shakers were the pacifists and ecologists before it was fashionable. In fact, they were the pioneers in the use of organic foods.

The furniture is one of the only truly American styles of furniture. It's known for its classic simplicity as well as rugged performance. In order to meet the demand for their furniture, they have developed a mail-order business. The kits are all first-rate and require no special tools. Complete catalog (50¢) will give you an insight into this truly American furniture style.

ELENA CO.
136 East 57 St.
New York, N.Y. 10022

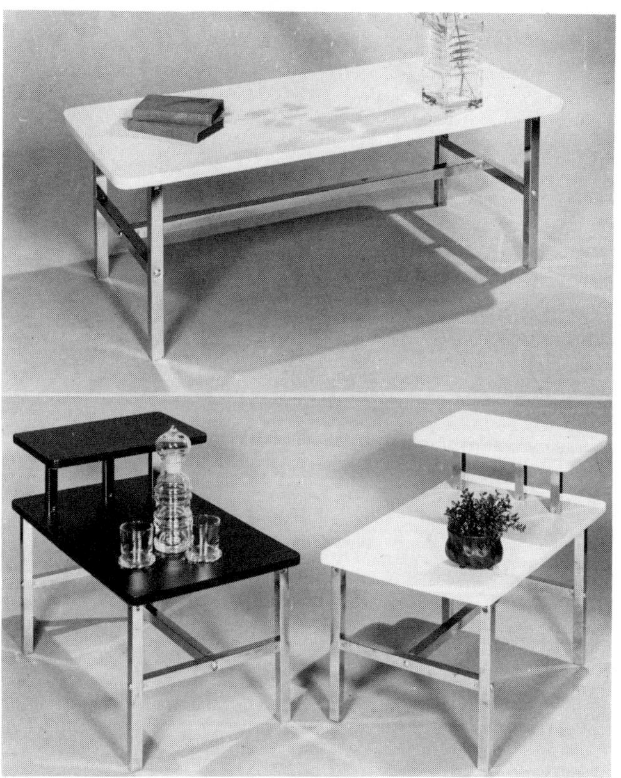

THREE-PIECE TABLE SET

Steel furniture was once known strictly for its sturdiness. Now the chrome look is part of many modern households. With an hour of set-up work, Elena offers a bargain in living room style. The construction is all high-pressure laminated plastics. They offer the advantage of being fire-resistant, stain-proof, and almost indestructible in normal family living. The legs are good quality tubular steel. My secretary assembled a set in the office using only a kitchen knife as equipment. The price for the set of three a reasonable $100.

Elena has a limited line of bargain-priced steel furniture. Mostly coffee table styles, but worth looking into. Leaflet (25¢) brings complete details. Perfect items for a second house or summer place.

MARNCRAFT
Patriot's Crossing
Americus, Ga. 31709

DECORATOR STOOL

Put your feet up and relax after you've made this decorative stool. Wood legs fit into predrilled holes. Then you finish any way you like (stain, antique, paint, decoupage, etc.). 10″ high, 13″ long, 9½″ wide. Fairly priced at $5.95.

CLASSIC CRAFTS
401 North Section St.
Fairhope, Ala. 36532

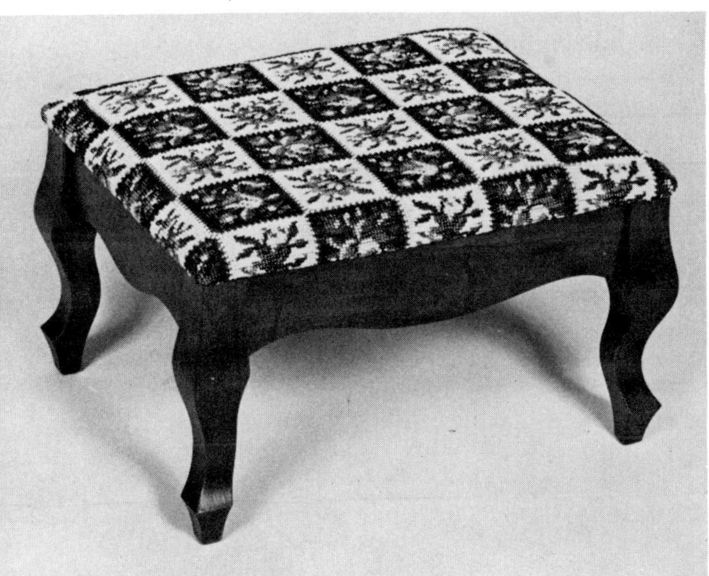

FOOTSTOOL

Constructed of solid Honduras mahogany, this graceful little footstool (11″ × 14″ × 8½″) would make an interesting gift, especially for someone who does needlework (which can be used for the top). It comes with a foam-rubber top, which can be covered with any kind of material. Easy assembly. $13.95.

George DuBrock is the master craftsman behind Classic Crafts, which markets a small line of high-quality furniture kits designed by Mr. DuBrock himself. Some of his other products are shown.

THE CRAFT CENTER
2022 Cunningham Dr.
Hampton, Va. 23666

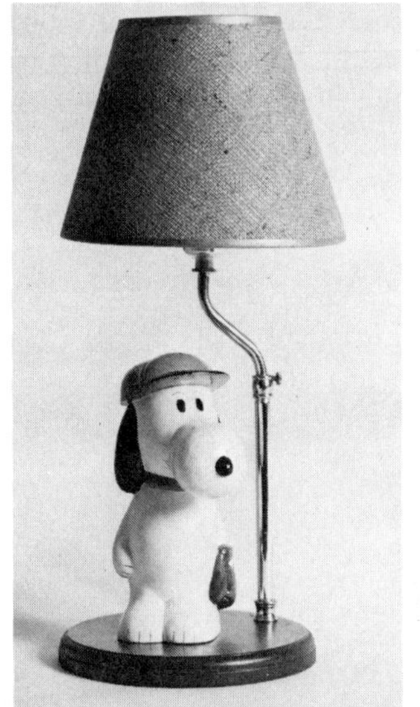
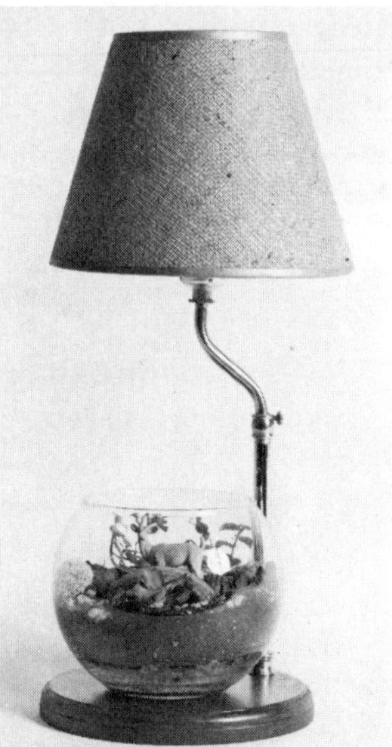

FAVORITE OBJECT LAMP

You can illuminate your terrarium (it helps plants grow) or mount your child's favorite toy. Turns any cherished possession into a lamp. You supply the item and the shade and the Craft Center supplies everything else. Easy to assemble. Unfinished wood base is 7″ in diameter. Brass upright is adjustable from 10″ to 15″ high. A 10″ harp is included for shades that have a center mount, or harp can be left off for snap-on shades. All lamp hardware, including cord and push-through socket, is included in kit. Simply attach object with household glue. Complete kit: $12.95.

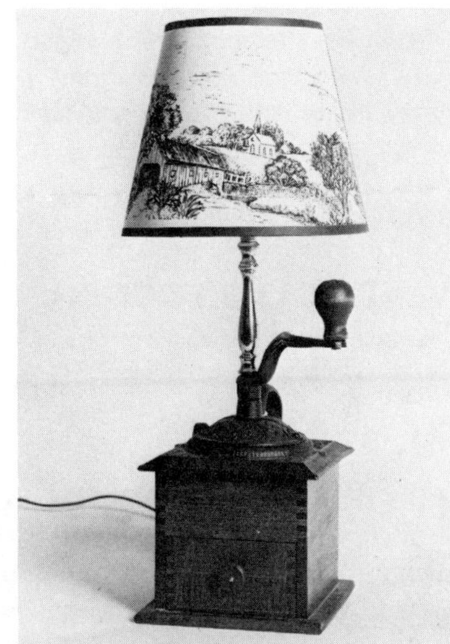

COFFEE GRINDER LAMP

An old-fashioned coffee grinder serves as the base for this lamp. The grinder is a real one (it actually grinds coffee beans). Although we're not sure how practical it is to have your lamp and your coffee grinder together, it does make a conversation piece. The drawer is $4'' \times 4''$ so you can use it to store stamps, jewelry, a few decks of cards, or a packet of instant coffee. The metal parts have been painted in black enamel. The wooden box itself is finished in light walnut. You supply the shade. Everything else to make this kit is included. $22.95.

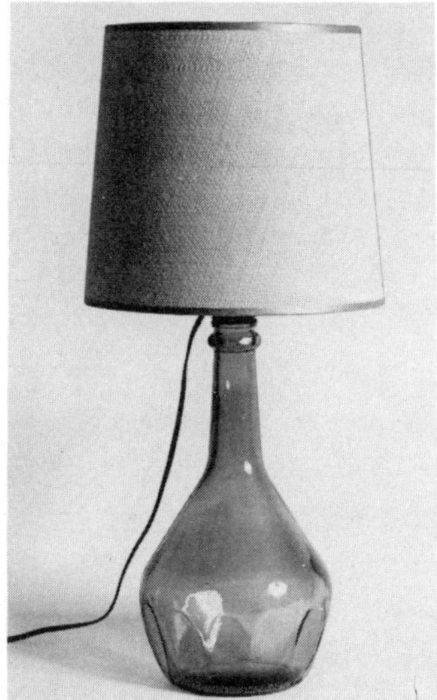

WINE BOTTLE LAMP

A boon to those of us who have those old wine bottles piling up. You can convert them all to lamps and give them away as Christmas presents. Kit contains three rubber adapters to fit any size bottle neck. A push-thru socket, cord, and a 10'' harp (for center-mount shades) are also included. The half-gallon shown here has a 9½'' shade, but the shade is not included. Kit is actually a nice project that's simple enough for any of us. $4.95.

Company at the present time is concentrating on developing lamp kits. They have a number of interesting items. Their prices are in some instances expensive for what you get, but the quality seems excellent. Their next endeavor is to develop children's furniture kits. Send self-addressed envelope for catalog and ask to be put on their mailing list.

RAINBOW ART GLASS CORP.
49 Shark River Rd.
Neptune, N. J. 07753

STAINED GLASS LAMPS

The turn-of-the-century stained glass Tiffany lamps live on. The beauty is hard to reproduce by modern methods, although considerable savings can be made by assembling your own lamp. Rainbow offers a kit with real leaded glass. The glass pieces have been cut to shape (a difficult job for most amateurs). You copperfoil the glass pieces, solder, and assemble. Kit contains everything you need to make a Tiffany lamp sans bulb. $89.50.

The firm offers all types of stained glass kits and forty different types of lamps, pool table domes, mirrors, even stained glass terrariums. Leaflet free.

WHITTEMORE-DURGIN
Box 2065 FE
Hanover, Mass. 02339

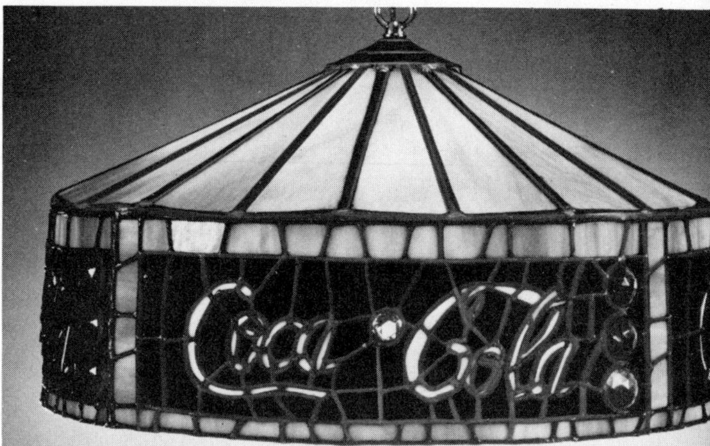

COCA-COLA STAINED GLASS LAMPSHADE

"An original of this lampshade brings $1,500. or more at art auctions," the advertisement tells us. And we have no reason to doubt that this is true. You can produce a replica for less than $70. Whether your reproduction will be of equal quality as the original is open to question, but if it's not, it won't be Whittemore-Durgin's fault. Their kit includes only the finest glass sheets, all the lead necessary, a reusable styrene form, electrical components, and a detailed leaflet of instructions. This is a project only for the craftsman with previously developed skills in cutting glass to pattern and in soldering. $58.

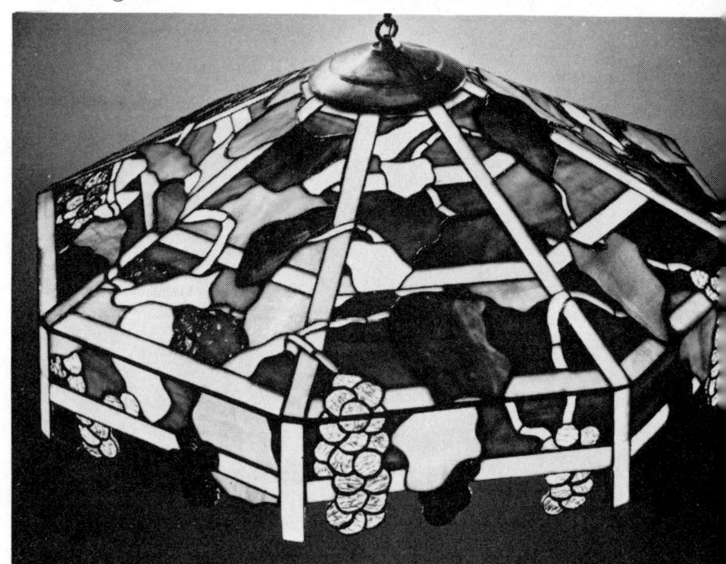

GRAPE-TRELLIS LAMPSHADE

This is a challenging and potentially rewarding

project for an experienced craftsman. Again, definitely not for the novice, who after contemplating the more than 900 pieces of glass might be tempted to use one on his wrists. Whittemore-Durgin, the country's foremost stained glass experts, base their pattern on an original Tiffany lampshade, but have made slight changes so that your product cannot be passed off as an original Tiffany. However, the finished product should be as aesthetically pleasing as the original, since equally luminescent and opalescent glass and techniques have been used. Kit includes color-coded pattern, uncut sheets of all the glass needed, copper tapes, copper sulphate crystals, all electrical components for final mounting, and detailed instructions. Considering the complexity of the project and the beauty of the finished product, we think the price is more than reasonable. $135.

CONSTANTINE
2050 Eastchester Rd.
Bronx, N.Y. 10461

RAINBOW TWIST LAMP

A four-color, twisted, hand-carved wooden lamp that looks like the work of an expert but—and Constantine swears to this—can be built by a beginning woodworker. The hand-carved appearance is actually an amazing woodworking trick, that Constantine shows you how to perform to perfection. Kit includes four woods (walnut, mahogany, padouk, and purple heart) and everything else you need except tools and lampshade. Finished lamp is 20″ high without harp. (12 lb.) $12.95.

DUREL'S
Box 223
Covington, La. 70433

CYPRESS KNEE LAMP

The cypress swamps of the Bayou have always been a place of strange beauty and mystery. Now a native of Louisiana has created a business of selling cypress knees as kits.

A regular lamp kit includes all necessary parts needed to assemble a complete lamp. The 12″ to 24″ cypress knee is machine-brushed to provide a surface which is easily sanded. A Southern yellow pine base, cut and beveled to fit each knee, is predrilled and countersunk for easy assembly. The kit also contains a swivel-top harp, brass finial, tubing cut to proper length and threaded, light socket, slim cord with plug attached, sandpaper, steelwool, and other miscellaneous parts required. $14.95.

CYPRESS GUN RACK

Two cypress knees which when mounted become the bases to hold up any rifle. Kit is two cypress knees and bases. $12.95.

ANTIQUE INSULATOR LAMPS

Remember the insulators high atop telephone poles? They are the latest collector's items. People around the country are buying (borrowing) them and putting them on the mantel. Durel's has turned them into a kit. They supply you with one antique insulator, one weathered cross piece from a telephone pole, plus brass and electric fittings to make a lamp. A conversation piece to be sure! $12.95.

SUBURBIA
366 Wacouta
St. Paul, Minn. 55101

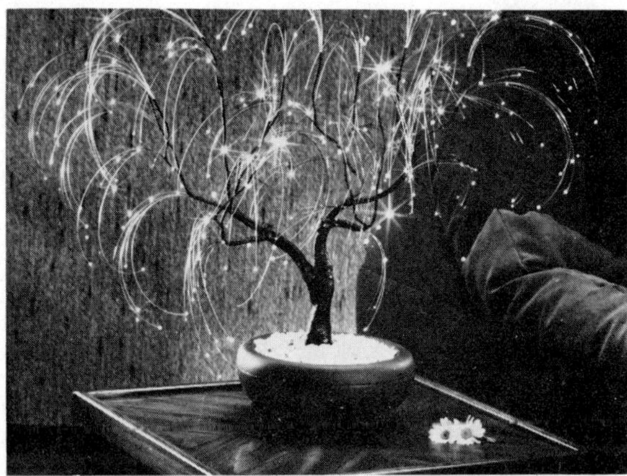

FIBER OPTIC KIT

A new idea in lights and decorating. The Fiber Optics Lamp kit features glowing light transmitted to ends of fibers that fan out from a columnar base. The fibers can be cut and bent to create a variety of effects. The artistic planter bowl combines beautifully with hundreds of delicate points of light to create an elegant decorator piece ideally suited for any home decor. A single light source hidden inside the planter bowl provides the light which shines from each of the fiber tips. The bowl is 8″ wide and is covered with real onyx pebbles. The finished Decorator Tree is about 21″ high. $8.95.

INNERSPACE ENVIRONMENTS, INC.
149 Natoma St.
San Francisco, Calif. 94105

WATERBED KIT

That's right, waterbeds are still "in" and, of course, so are kits—so why not a waterbed kit? Maybe the age of astronauts has inadvertently influenced us here, for one of the main features of the waterbed is that it makes you feel weightless.

A waterbed is soft and swirly, and when you lie down you make waves for ten seconds and then they die away. And despite all the jokes, not one case of seasickness has been reported yet. What makes this particular kit so much cheaper is that you build your own frame; instructions for a frame of two-by-tens put together with steel angle brackets come with the kit. You can go to any lumber yard, buy four boards, and put together a simple, comfortable waterbed.

The Innerspace kit provides everything else you need, including the following. Bag and safety tray: King size (72″ × 84″ × 9″). Heating mat: Fully insulated, 450-w., 110–120 v., 2′ × 4′ sandwich; foil on top for even and broad heat distribution; 1/4″ thick fire-retardant foam backing on bottom to insulate and protect the carpet. Control: A sensitive variable thermostat (± 2°) enclosed within a heavy-duty Bakelite control box for ease of mounting. Faucet and hose adapters, instructions, and patch kit.

You simply attach thermostat sensing bulb. The only tools needed are a screw driver and staple gun for attaching plastic liner. Once built, you may join the devotees who swear it's the only way to sleep. Entire kit: $110.

DOOR STORE OF WASHINGTON, D.C.
3140 M Street, N.W.
Washington, D.C. 20007

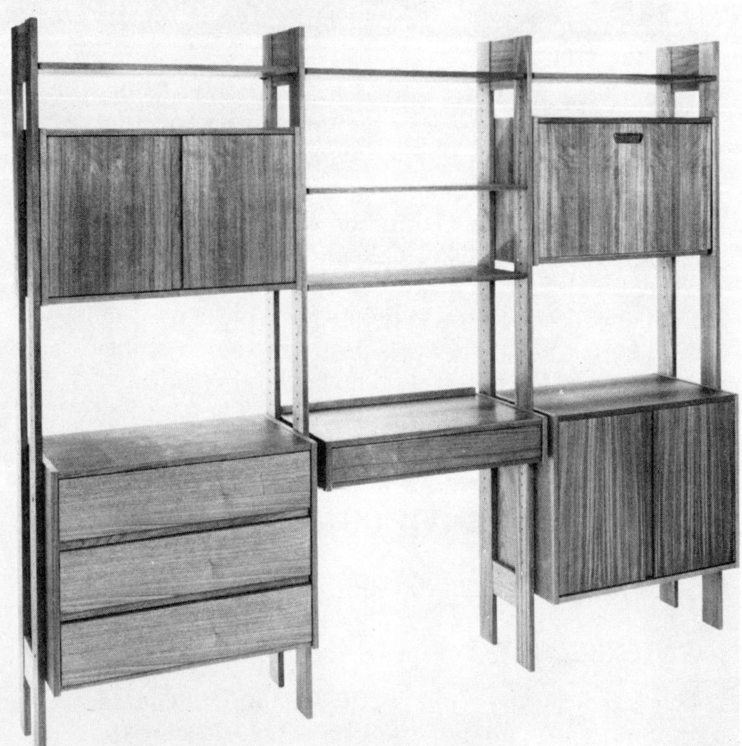

FREE-STANDING STORAGE WALL

How to get organized! Contains: 3-drawer chest; 2-door cabinet with optional interior record dividers; 2-door cabinet with interior shelf; bar cabinet with mica-lined pull-down front that becomes a serving surface; desk surface with wide drawer below; and 5 bookshelves. The tops of the cabinets provide additional useful space for stereo equipment, decorative displays, magazines, telephone, lamp, etc. Base cabinets are 27″ wide, 21″ high, 16″ deep. Top cabinets are 12″ deep. The entire unit is 7′ wide × 6′ high, and is finished front and back, so you can use it as a room divider as well as up against the wall.

Simple put-together project. Instructions and necessary hardware are included. Available in satin-lacquered wood veneers (Walnut: $349. Teak: $359. Rosewood: $389.) or white lacquered finish ($359.).

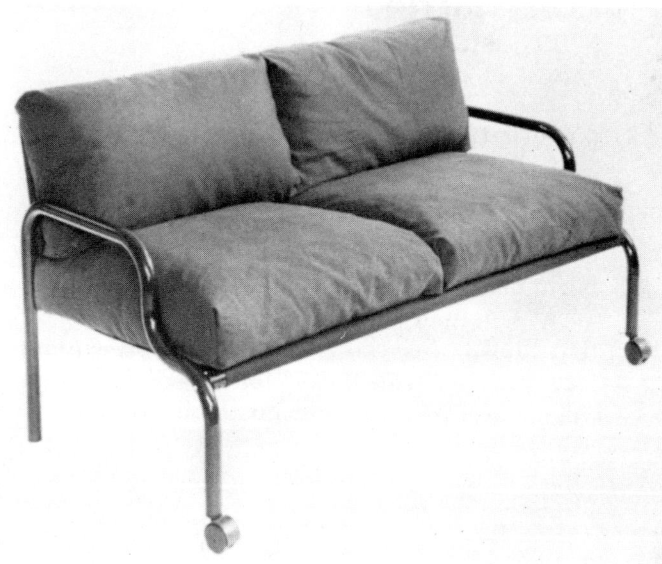

STUNS HI-BACK M-2 LOUNGE CHAIR AND STUNS M-2 SOFA

A new kind of furniture imported from Sweden for you to assemble. Canvas-covered cushions in cheerful, bright colors with matching lacquered steel frames (or in black or natural canvas with chrome frames). Luxuriously comfortable polyfoam-stuffed cushions can be tub washed and hung out to dry.

Has casters for mobility. Instructions and all necessary hardware included. Put together in twenty minutes. Lounge Chair: yellow, orange, green, or brown canvas with matching frame, $90. Black or natural canvas with chrome frame: $100. Sofa: yellow, orange, green, brown, or black canvas with matching frame, $128. Black canvas with chrome frame: $139.

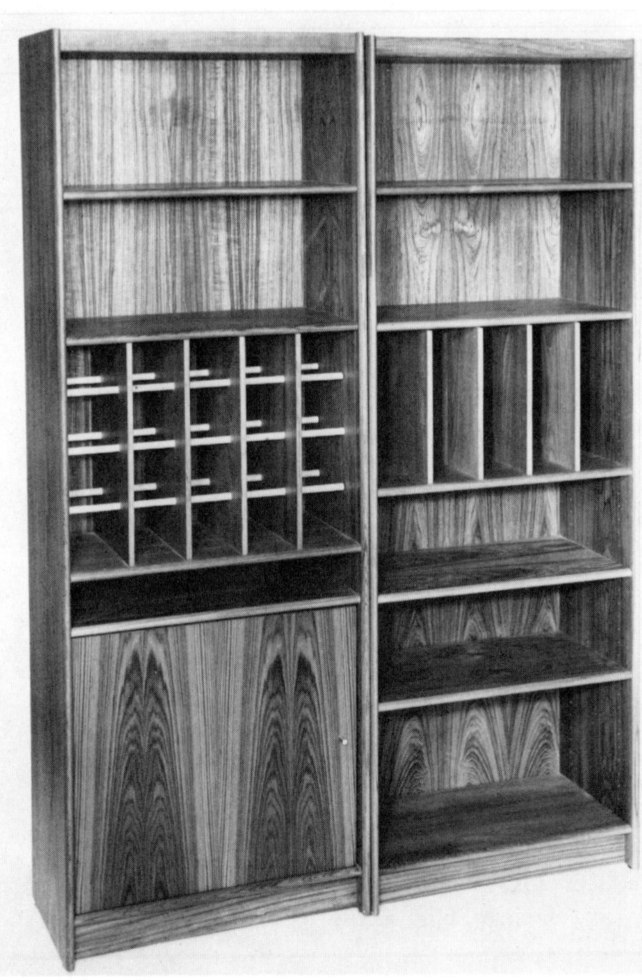

STEREO CENTER AND STORAGE BOOKCASES

An unusual 16″ deep, these handsome teak book-case and storage units hold the largest record changers and stereo components. You can vary their looks and possibilities with generous built-in record racks, wine racks, and doors that enclose the bottom section for storage. Beautifully grained teak veneers with rounded teak edges. Floor levelers to keep your record changer completely level. Magnificent pieces of furniture, used singly or in groups or covering an entire wall. Basic book case unit for you to assemble is 27½″ wide, 78½″ high, 16″ deep (shelf depth, 15″), has six shelves: $210. Additional record rack: $19. Wine rack: $20. Door and hinges: $30.

The Door Store of Washington, D.C., has a fabulous collection of furniture-in-parts, furniture kits, and budget furniture that needs only staining or oiling. Well-illustrated catalog ($1).

FURN-A-KIT
140 East Union Ave.
East Rutherford, N.J. 07073

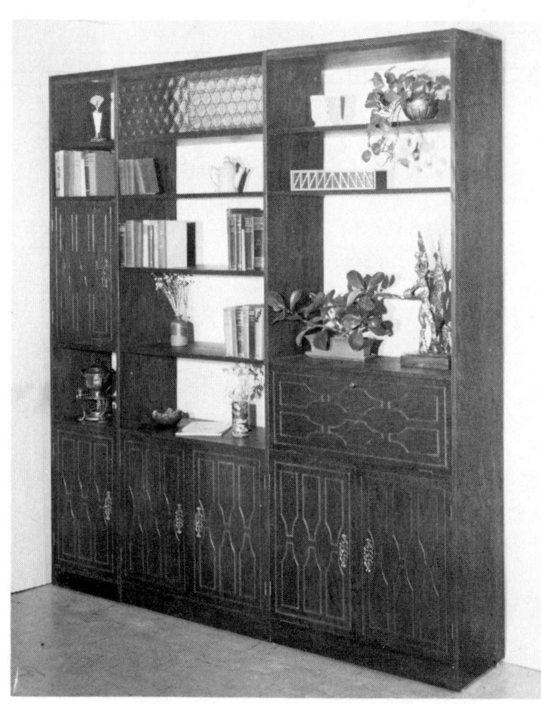

WALL SYSTEMS

What happens when your bookshelves marry your bar and give birth to a chest of drawers? The answer is you have a "wall system," one of the hottest items in today's furniture market. Custom-designed or purchased fully assembled, these systems cost you a fortune. The kit format is a terrific way of getting around this expense. More often than not, by assembling your own, you can save one-third to one-half the cost of fully assembled systems. While many companies manufacture wall systems and components for them, the acknowledged leader in the field of actual kits is Furn-a-Kit, which is certainly to wall systems what IBM is to computers. They offer four basic systems, all of which can then be customized so that there are literally thousands of options.

The systems are available in a wide range of natural finishes and in Furneer, a durable polyester surface that is cheaper than wood. All Furn-a-Kit wall systems are available in a variety of styles (Mediterranean, contemporary, traditional, modern, country), a variety of widths, depths, and lengths, a variety of finishes, colors, and surfaces. They can be had with and without doors, with a number of different valences and bases, with fixed and/or movable shelves, with or without bars, special planters, drop-lid desks, etc. Naturally, everytime you add or subtract another element the prices change—and when you are choosing among the staggering number of elements this ingenious company has to offer, you may feel like forgetting the whole thing and running to your nearest custom-furniture cabinet maker. But resist and persevere, for once you have made your choices and computed the costs, the actual assembly is quite simple and the results are well worth the effort. The following gives a brief description of the wall systems available from Furn-a-Kit, along with some indication of prices and available options.

Living Wall: The Living Wall offers the dramatic impact of built-in furniture and can include storage space, a built-in bar, a desk, bookshelves—all designed by you. Depths are 12″, 15″, and 18″. Widths are 12″, 18″, 24″, and 35″. These, of course, can be combined to fit almost any size wall. Basic units are 94⅝″ high. The following indicates the price range. A 12″ deep and 12″ wide section is $54.50 in wood, $38.50 in Furneer. A section 18″ deep and 35″ wide is $135.50 in wood, $94.50 in Furneer. Individual shelves range from $2.50 (12″ × 12″ Furneer) to $17.50 (18″ × 35″, wood).

Executive Wall: This is the same as the Living Wall, except that its upper sections can be either 12″ or 15″ deep, and its bottom cabinets are 18″ deep. This additional flexibility is supposed to be necessary for the "executive" office, but we think it's equally useful at home. In fact, since "flexibility" is Furn-a-Kit's middle name, they are willing on this system—and in fact all their products—to include as much customizing as possible and to help you design the units for maximum use. The Executive Wall can accommodate a desk, a chest of drawers, filing cabinets, and even a wardrobe closet. Prices are comparable to Living Wall prices and are best determined by consulting charts of options and elements in the Furn-a-Kit catalog.

Hanging Wall: This one hangs (or more correctly, is mounted) on uprights, which have holes all along their length and are grooved so that wires can be concealed. Uprights are available in any length up to 7′. Again, this unit can be used with magazine shelves, bookshelves, planters, desks, bars, and myriad other goodies. Shelves for this unit vary from $6.75 for a 9″ × 24″ shelf in Furneer, to $43.25 for a 18″ × 60″ shelf in wood. Hanging wall cabinets range in price from $23.00 for a 24″ wide, 12½″ high, and 12″ deep doorless cabinet in Furneer, to $105.00 for a 36″ wide, 15″ × 15″ wood cabinet with "sliding sunburst doors." Uprights are $1.60 per foot. For additional prices see Furn-a-Kit catalog.

Freestanding Wall: This sort of thing used to be called a room divider, and it still serves that purpose well, although it can also be used up against the wall. Again, cabinets, bars, and the like are features of this system. They are mounted on

tension poles, which can accommodate ceiling heights of from 7′ to 12′ (you must specify your ceiling height when ordering). Prices are similar to the Hanging Wall prices, except where back finishing is involved (obviously cabinet backs must be finished if they are to stand in the middle of a room).

DINING CHAIRS

Sturdy, simple, contemporary-style dining chairs available with black or white Naugahyde upholstery or your own custom fabric. These chairs won't win any design awards, but they have that inoffensive young-modern look and are quite comfortable. Like all Furn-a-Kit's merchandise, they assemble easily with the aid of a screwdriver and mallet. Naugahyde seat and cane back: side chair, $65.00; arm chair, $74.00. Naugahyde seat and back: side chair, $81.; arm chair, $90. Your fabric on seat and cane back: side chair, $65.00; arm chair, $74.00. Your fabric on seat and back: side chair, $81.; arm chair, $90.

A variety of wall systems, chairs, tables, and other furniture kits at attractive prices. Catalog (48 pp., $1) worth looking into.

YIELD HOUSE
North Conway, N.H. 03860

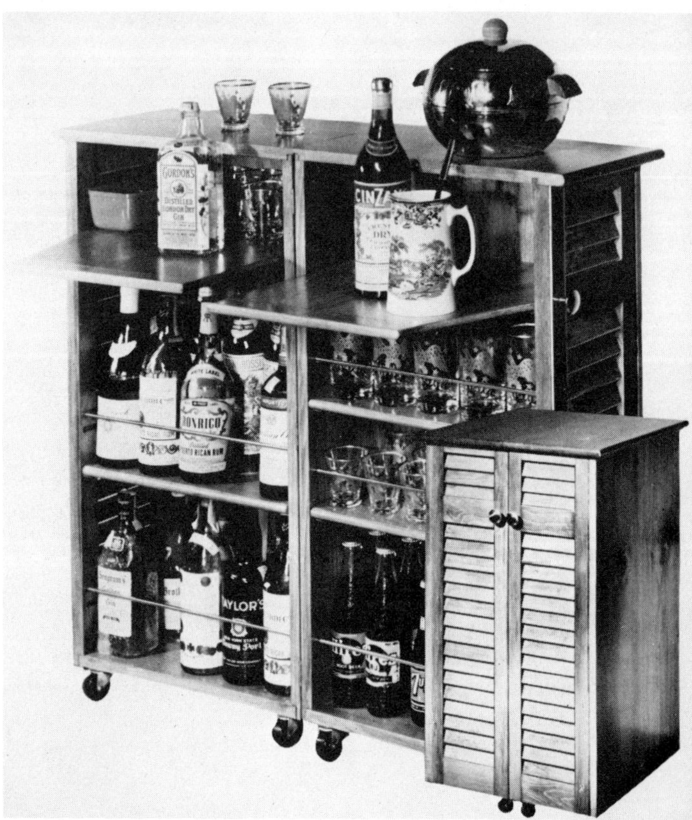

HIDEAWAY BAR
Why must bars serve more than one purpose? It's as

if people are too ashamed to admit that the little pine cabinet over there is simply where they store and serve their liquor. To cover their shame, they make sure it also has at least two (better, three) other functions, preferably totally unrelated to alcohol. This particular item not only has a multiple function (it's a storage cabinet as well as a stand-up bar), but it "hides away" as well. That is, it closes up behind louvered doors, going from an open size of 38″ wide, 19″ deep, 36″ high, to a closed size of a slim 21″ wide. It also locks, has roll-about casters, and is fitted with well-designed shelves and compartments. $89.50.

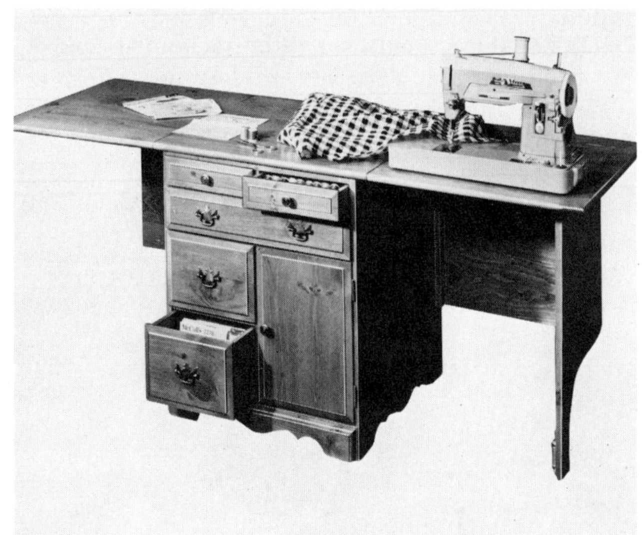

SEWING CABINET

This is a Yield House specialty—and a particularly good value in kit form. The "Total Sewing Center," as its name suggests, holds the machine (and everything else but the kitchen sink, it seems). Yield House calls it their "runaway best seller" and it's not hard to see why. It's compact (only 28¼″ wide when closed); it opens to provide lots of work and storage room (72″ wide when open); it holds all sewing needs neatly and conveniently; it has a protective bin for your portable sewing machine; and it rolls about on casters that can be locked when unit is in use. Made of pine, with brass hardware and colonial styling. Easy assembly. $179.95.

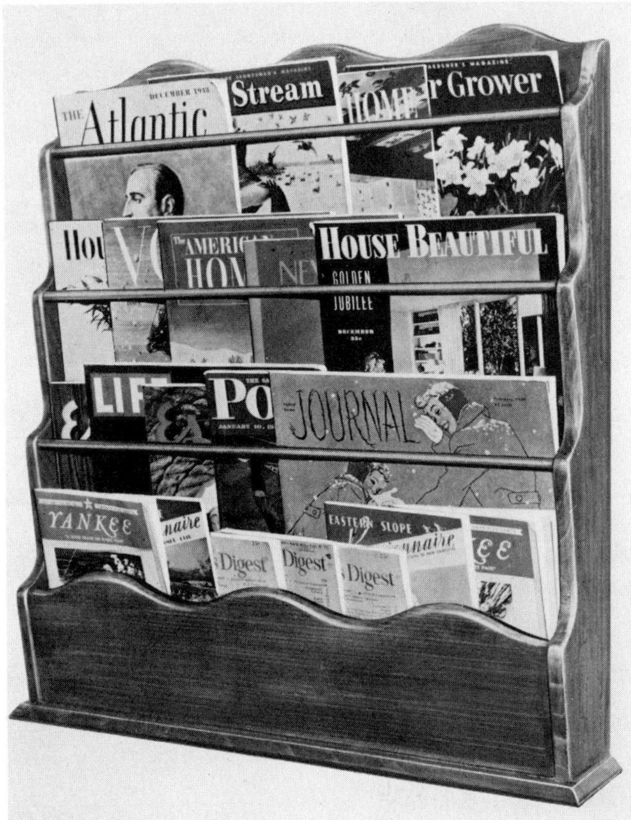

MAGAZINE RACK

You've seen this rack at your dentist's or doctor's office, especially if their waiting rooms are Early American. Yield House calls them their "most famous invention," a questionable designation since the racks don't seem as clever or versatile as some of the other items this reputable firm has to offer. However, there's no question that they are practical. And they are easy to assemble. Yield House intends them for use in offices, reception rooms, and homes, and we think they're best kept out of most homes (lest your living room start to look like your doctor's reception room). Add your own copies of *Life* magazine and *Look* magazine to complete the effect! The Space-Saver holds thirty magazines neatly and compactly. It is 23″ wide, 27″ high and 4¾″ deep. $19.95.

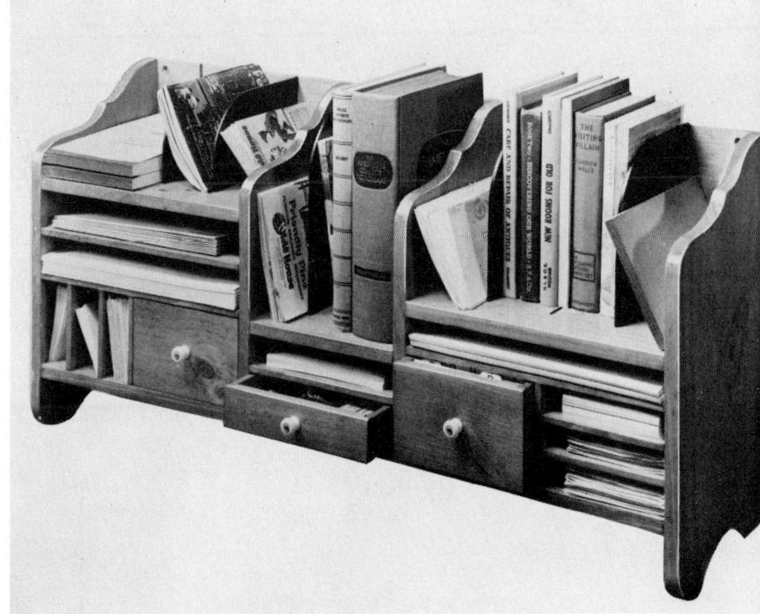

COMPLETE DESK ORGANIZER

"So easy, his secretary could do it," claims the manufacturer. Not only simple to assemble, but extremely practical in design, this desk-top organizer is an efficient clutter fighter for home or office, although its Early American styling may interfere with some modern office decors. It is 33″ long, 16″ high and 9¾″ deep. It fits most desks and stores 3″ × 5″ cards, stamps, clips, rubber bands, paper, books, and reports in assorted slots, drawers, and stand-up compartments. $49.95.

TV CABINET FOR PORTABLES

If you long for the good old days when the TV set was truly a piece of furniture instead of a metallic eye staring at you from a shelf, this is a good kit project to try. For less than $35. and a few evenings' work, you can fake that console look and slip your 19″ or 20″ portable into a solid pine, Early American cabinet that has a lower shelf, 3 small drawers for odds and ends, and a top surface for a plant or photograph. $54.95.

ALL-PURPOSE FOOTSTOOL

Watch out for that "all-purpose" . . . such versatility rarely exists. But if you want a footstool-magazine rack-storage bin (doesn't everybody?), this is the kit for you. It is 17″ wide, 13½″ deep and 14″ high, has a vinyl-covered seat, and, if not gorgeous, it's at least inoffensive, considering its multiple functions. Easy assembly. $29.95.

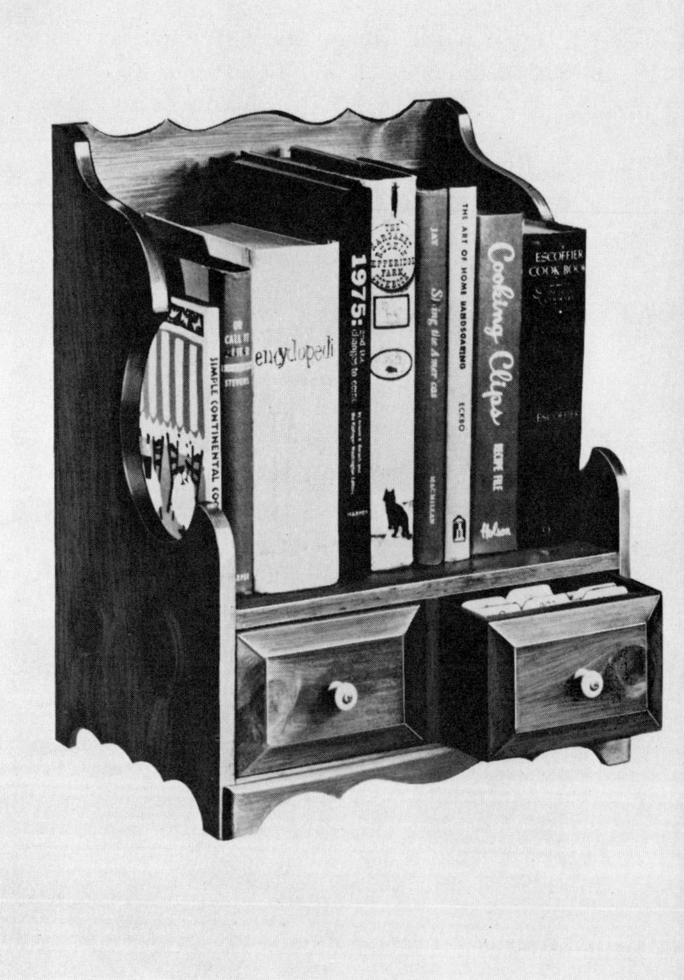

COOKBOOK RECIPE RACK

We don't know how Julia Child stores her recipes (in her head perhaps?), but we bet she'd appreciate this handy item. Not only do two little drawers hold a thousand 3″ × 5″ recipe cards, but also such potential mess-makers as coupons, box tops, and supermarket stamps (which you've been either throwing out or stuffing in with your silverware, right?). Eight to ten cookbooks sit on the upper shelf. Solid pine with white drawer knobs (7 lb.). $15.95.

Yield House is the largest manufacturer of assemble-and-finish furniture. It's all precut and presanded. All the hardware is included. Simply put together and save 50% or more on local products. Catalog (48 pp.) is free.

MYLEN INDUSTRIES

650 Washington St.
Peekskill, N.Y. 10566

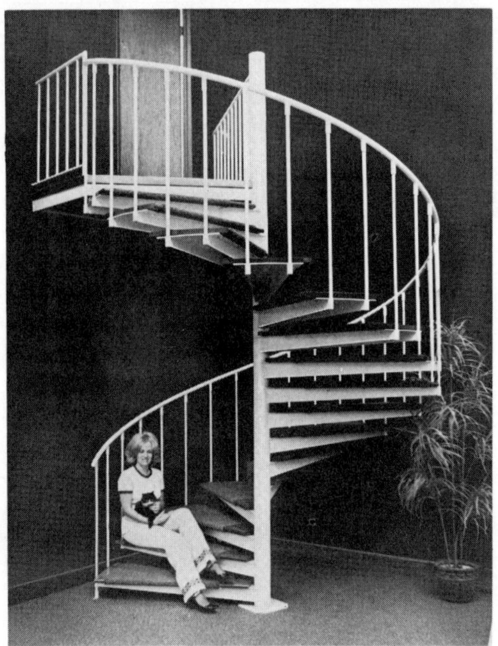

SPIRAL STAIR KIT

For your elegant entrance, it's a spiral staircase. Spiral stairs are a practical solution in many cases where no other stair can be used. The proper use of space is an extremely important factor which architects, builders, decorators, and homeowners are constantly trying to achieve. In many cases even the professional planner is forced to make concessions due to a stair that detracts from the total design and decorative concept.

The Mylen kit is relatively simple to assemble. It is designed for both beauty and safety, and no special tools or major skills are required. A dozen different stock kits are available, and start at $295. (FOB N.Y.—350 lb.). Every kit includes treads, platform, risers, and oak stairs. They can be installed with left-hand or right-hand rotation for indoor or outdoor use.

NATIONAL HANDCRAFT SOCIETY

1425 Grand Ave.
Des Moines, Iowa 50337

COLONIAL READING RACK

At last, à place for all those magazines. There's traditional Early American charm in this handsome and necessary room accessory. The heavy redwood base and top have smoothly rounded edges and are solidly supported with sturdy birch dowels. One-inch diameter ball feet are attached with rugged screws. Easily assembled—includes all precut and shaped parts and hardware, plus everything you need for the mellow Colonial finish that's buffed to a polished and perfect sheen. Base is 6″ × 14″; rack stands 12¾″ high. $4.69.

Company sponsors a membership club (see Clubs section) and offers various kits in annual catalog (free). Most of these products are of the hobby type. Their entry into furniture kits is mostly with smaller pieces such as stools, collector's cupboards, and planters. All very reasonably priced.

THE SWAN CORP.

721 Olive St.
St. Louis, Mo. 63101

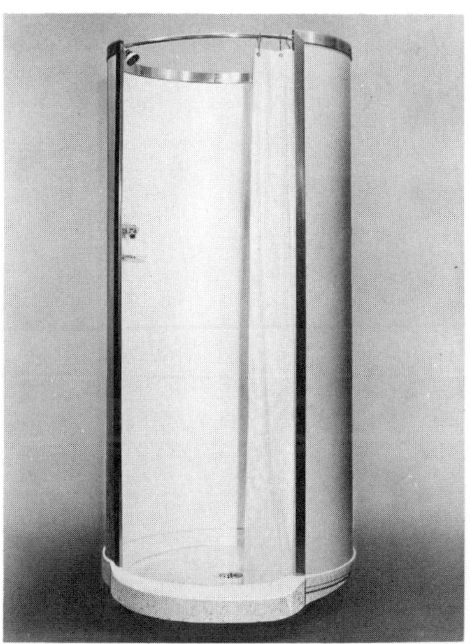

DO-IT-YOURSELF SHOWER

A fiber-reinforced plastic circular shower. A freestanding unit, it comes complete with curtain and soapdish. For small bathrooms, beach houses, etc., it is also weatherproof and can be used out of doors. Construction is simple, but because position of controls is a matter of preference, holes must be drilled. Available in pastel blue or yellow. $95.

The company also makes other shower stalls and an easily installed fiberglass bathtub enclosure that surrounds a standard (57″ to 62″) bathtub.

LESSER STUDIO
156 East 52 St.
New York, N.Y. 10022

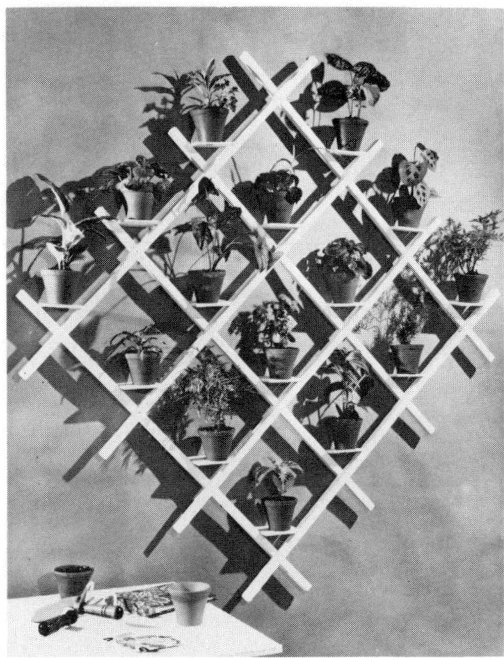

HANGING GARDEN

In Babylon it was called one of the wonders of the ancient world, but this "Hanging Garden" is designed for Now living and enjoyment in a house, apartment, or condominium. Made of wood and 43″ square, it holds 15 pots of 4″ diameter, which can be planted with your favorite greenery and then mounted on the wall. Perfect for today's crowded apartments and houses.

The "Hanging Garden" is mailed as a kit, with a detailed instruction sheet, unpainted, for $29.95 plus postage. It can be ordered painted white for an additional $7.50. Pots are not included.

DOUBLE M MARKETING
P.O. Box 8500
Fountain Valley, Calif. 92708

MURALS

You can be a mural artist. Add style to any room with a mural motif. Choose from action, pop, or zodiac designs. You paint a full-sized mural (up to 10′ wide × 3′ high). Kit includes pattern, brush, paints, instructions. Really professional-looking results. A little harder than using a roller, but worth the effort. Large size: $49.95.

Double M offers kits from $2.95. Catalog with decorator chart and color guides (32 pp., 35¢).

OPEN DOOR ENTERPRISES, INC.
1249 Dell Ave.
Campbell, Calif. 95008

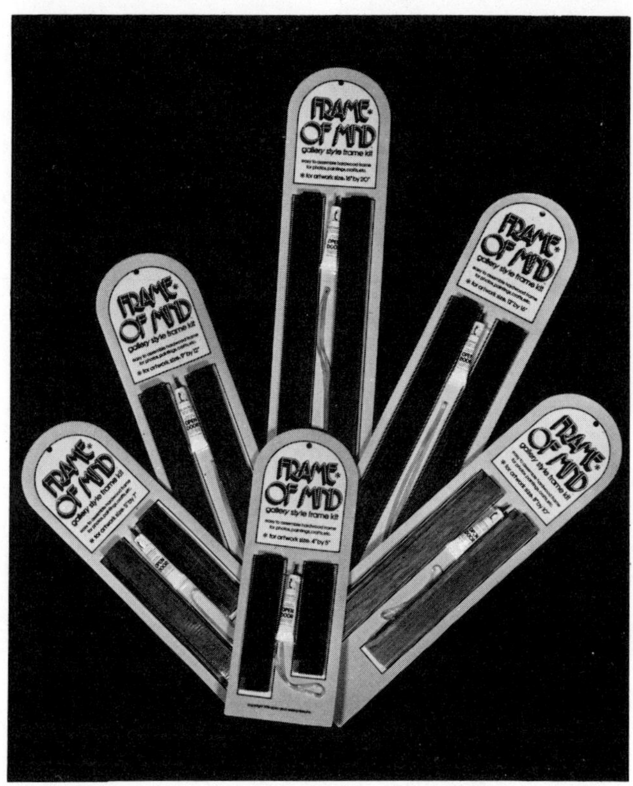

GALLERY-STYLE FRAME

How many people have paintings, a child's favorite coloring, needlepoint works, or etchings that have been lying about in drawers instead of hanging up on walls and all because they have been frameless? A rhetorical question, of course, since almost every home has an artwork or two hidden from view due to avoidance of high-cost frames purchased at art stores.

Now those unexhibited art works can be framed and exhibited. Open Door Enterprises has packaged a framing kit that enables you to frame your pictures at a very low cost. The picture frame kits come in all the standard sizes. Each kit includes walnut-stained hardwood frame pieces with mitered ends, tight-bonding glue, rubber band, and assembly instructions. Attractively priced. (8″ × 10″) $2.50.

LITTLE GIANT PUMP CO.
3810 North Tulsa St.
Oklahoma City, Okla. 73112

LITTLE WATER FALL

Re-create the pleasure of woodside rocks and rills in your home, apartment, or office with the unique

Little Waterfall. Eleven in. high, 18″ wide, and 25″ long, the Little Waterfall weighs less than 10 lb. including a dependable Little Giant Pump that gently recirculates water over three tiers of realistically simulated rock. No plumbing required. Simply assemble, add a gallon of water, and plug in. Perfect for the executive too busy to get outside. Combine with the terrarium kit and you never have to leave your room. This is one of those items that the interior decorating magazines call a "conversation piece." $49.95.

SEARS, ROEBUCK AND CO.
Philadelphia, Pa. 19132

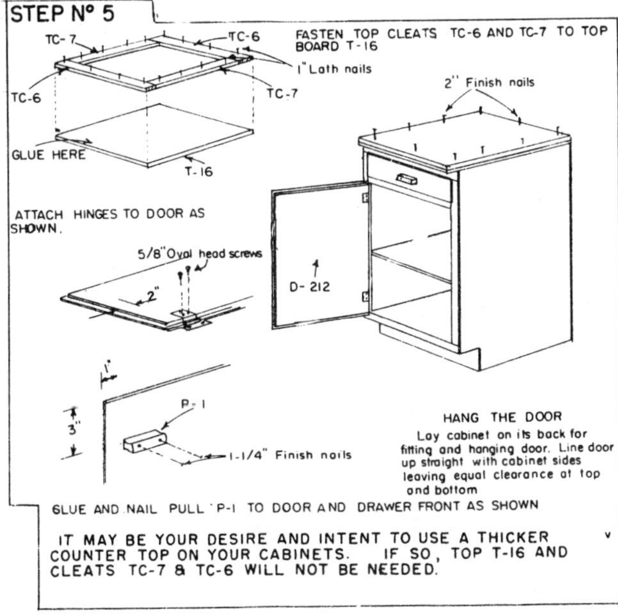

WOOD KITCHEN CABINET

These are very nice, simple, unassembled and unfinished kitchen cabinets. Good joints allow glue and nail construction to provide a very strong and stable cabinet. Painted or finished, these provide attractive and inexpensive ways to provide storage space. Plywood sides and shelves; semi-concealed, sprint-action metal door hinges. The grain on the various wood parts (doors, drawers, sides), although good, is somewhat haphazard with respect to shade and if you choose to finish it, it will have a somewhat rustic look (which we actually like), not always suitable. Available in 18″ one-door, one-drawer and several more elaborate styles, including a corner cabinet. Everything is included—nails, hardware—even glue (not quite enough.) 18″ cabinet, one drawer, one door: $25.00. 60″ cabinet, five drawers, four doors: $72.75.

PLAN-IT-KIT CO.
Box 429
Westport, Conn. 06880

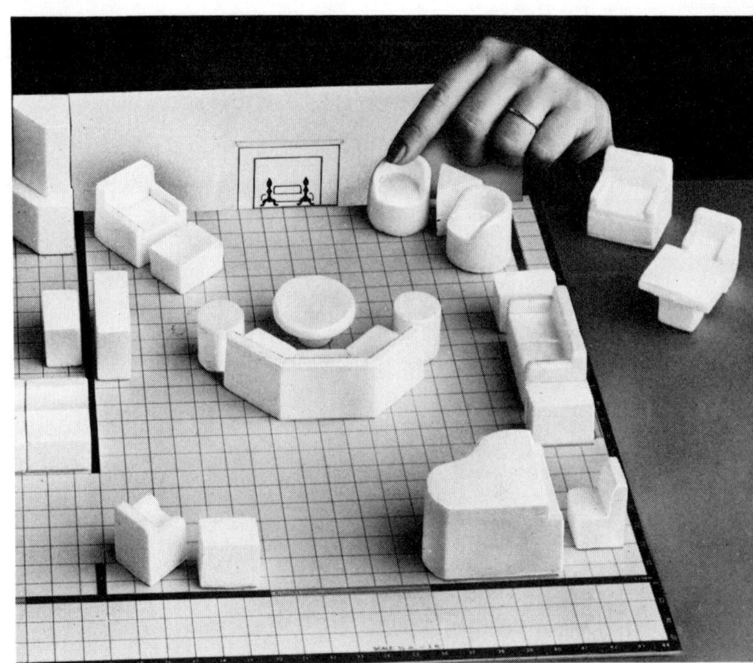

PLAN-IT SET

A great deal of time and effort is spent on home interior design today, and a tremendous amount of work is wasted on unnecessary mistakes—the incorrect purchase and placement of valuable furniture pieces, those color combinations that seem so right when you first think of them, but simply "don't work out" when they're realized in wood, fabric, and paint.

By careful planning—not just with fabric swatches, paper, and pencil, but with the actual three-dimensional, scale-model furnishings and room layouts provided for you by the Plan-It-Kit Company—you can evaluate the "total effect" of a dining room, living room, bedroom, or any room and realize your planning ideas in terms of substance, height, volume, and color.

The kit was designed by a professional Interior Designer, member of the National Society of Interior Designers, especially to meet demand for flexibility and creative inspiration without limiting your imagination in any way. Cast in neutral white, each of the versatile furniture pieces can be painted or fabric swatch-covered; placed on carpeting or other flooring materials; stacked, arranged and rearranged, and put into different combinations until you arrive at the final perfect solution to your decorating problem.

There are sofas, curved, corner and octagon sofa sectionals, loveseats, upholstered chairs of different shapes and sizes, side chairs, dining tables, beds. There are storage and cabinet pieces that can be combined to form triple dressers, stereo cabinets, high chests, low chests, bookcase walls, armoires, breakfronts, bachelor chests, lingerie chests. There are pianos and cocktail tables, side tables, night tables, lamp tables. Over 150 different pieces of furniture can be created with the miniatures in this kit.

> Paint and upholster the 3-D furniture with color and fabrics of your choice.
> Paint and wallpaper the walls.
> Hang drapes and curtains in fabrics of your choice.
> Place pictures and paintings on the walls.
> Lay out furniture and complete rooms on your actual carpet flooring samples.

The 3-D Plan-It-Kit includes:

Over 150 possible furniture combinations.

Furniture pieces based on the average size of furniture manufactured today by all major companies. Each furniture miniature is imprinted with description and size in inches.

Made of durable, lightweight styrofoam to the exact scale of ½″ to 1′.

Walls: Sturdy cardboard, easy to paint or wallpaper.

Windows and doors: Gummed on back for easy application on walls. ½″ to 1′ scale.

Graph Paper: ½″ to 1′ scale has the equivalent space of 27′ × 44′. As many as three rooms can be arranged at one time.

Eight-page illustrated book includes design principles and instructions. $8.98.

HEATILATOR FIREPLACE
Division of Vega Industries, Inc.
Mount Pleasant, Iowa 52641

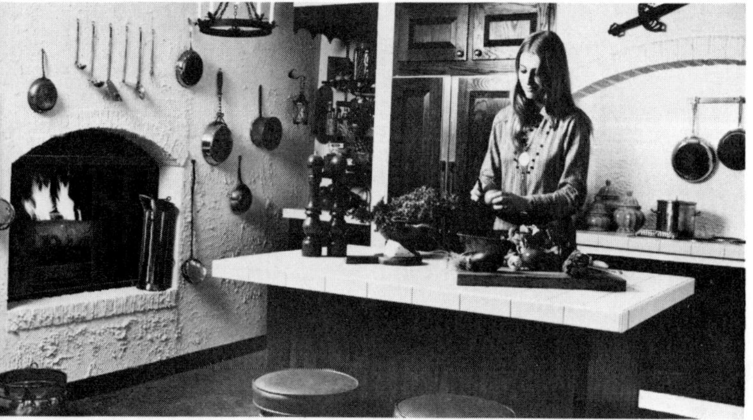

FIREPLACE INSTALLATION

Fireplaces have a universal appeal. Their warmth and coziness have no substitute. A house with a fireplace seems to become, automatically, a home. Of course, at one time in our history, fireplaces were so commonplace that they were rarely fussed over, for when an object is a functional necessity, there is barely time to view it in any aesthetic sense. Heatilator Fireplace is a fireplacing firm that offers 1-2-3 simplicity of installation, versatility, and flexibility of placement, with no special support foundation or masonry. You can face the fireplace with marble, glass, brick, stone, or any natural facing to complete the room decor, and it is guaranteed smoke-free, a feature our colonial ancestors would have envied. Easy to assemble and install. Prices vary widely with type of fireplace required. Write for free details.

THE GARLINGHOUSE CO.
2320 Kansas Ave.
Topeka, Kans. 66611

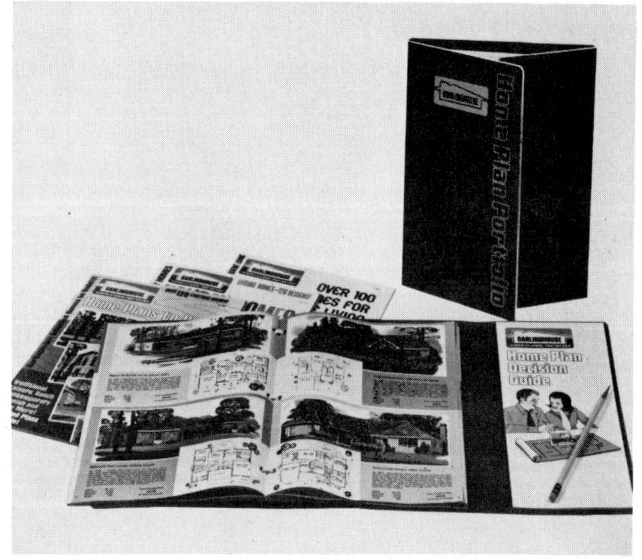

HOME-PLAN PORTFOLIO KIT

Over 300 home designs you can build. Again, a kit in the nontraditional sense, but certainly a help in planning for your dream house. Portfolio includes page after page of home designs. Also a home-plan decision portfolio that helps you look at the variables. The "Kit" helps you tailor your plans to your family needs. Covers contemporary, traditional, leisure, ranch, hillside, multi-unit . . . to name a few. Reasonably priced at $2.95.

NATIONAL PLAN SERVICE, INC.

435 West Fullerton Ave.
Elmhurst, Ill. 60126

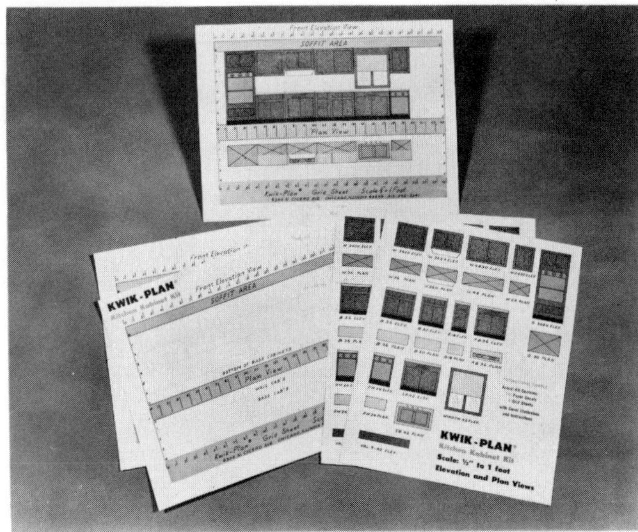

KWIK-PLAN KIT

A most unusual kit. Most kits, when complete, leave you with a tired back but a beautiful product. This kit is the opposite; it will save your back and once complete, you throw it away. "Kwik-plan" is a design kit that saves you moving around lots of furniture to "see how it looks." Now you can get a bird's-eye view of how a room actually looks. The kit is in proportion (scale: ½" equals 1'). Each kit contains 140 peel-off decals that one places on the master grid sheet to create an organized effective room. The kitchen kit, for example, contains wall cabinets, stove, sinks, dishwasher, refrigerator, even windows. You plan for step-saving, efficiency, and beauty. Kits available for many rooms at a cost of $3.

J. W. HOLST

1005 East Bay St.
East Tawas, Mich. 48730

HOME-A-MINUTE

Where should you put the window? Now, live in your new home or remodeled home today with this kit. Plan ahead, see how layout will look before you build or remodel. Here's everything you should have and know to help save many dollars. Dozens of windows, kitchen cabinets, doors, fiber partitions, etc., at ¼ scale. Put your home ideas in three-dimensional form. Arrange furniture fixtures to fit your scheme. Build, dismantle, and originate any number of floor plans. Kit also includes 65-p. book to help estimate actual costs, financing, etc. Only $3.95.

OTHER SOURCES

Charlie F. & Others
5657 Mill St.
Erie, Pa. 16509
Walnut display and wall case kits. Brochure (free).

Creative Corner
910 North Marshfield Ave.
Chicago, Ill. 60622
Features sixteen different Tiffany-style lamp kits made with authentic leaded stained glass. School discounts. Information (free).

Creative Education Services, Inc.
Box 663
West Caldwell, N.J. 07006
Wrought-iron furniture kits that require no heat and need little space to assemble. School discounts. Brochure (free).

Country Workshop
95 Rome St.
Newark, N.J. 07105
Not truly a kit house, but they offer a variety of durable hardwood furniture with some assembly needed. Many of these products need only a coat of stain to finish.

Designer Kits
39-06 Crescent St.
Long Island City, N.Y. 11101
Easy-to-assemble kits for making chrome steel furniture. Catalog (free).

Florida Waterbed Corp.
148 North Brevard Ave.
Cocoa Beach, Fla. 32931
Waterbed kits.

Giles & Kendall
P.O. Box 188
Huntsville, Ala. 35804
Ready-to-assemble cedar bookcases, chests, hi-fi/stereo cabinets, gun racks, coffee and cocktail tables. Catalog (free).

Held Products
9 Lakeview Dr.
Farmington, Conn. 06032
Medieval lantern kit. Catalog (free).

The Iron Shop
400 Reed Rd.
Broomall, Pa. 19008
Stair kits from $355.-up.

Minnesota Woodworkers Supply Co.
925 Winnetka Ave., North
Minneapolis, Minn. 55427
Small selection of furniture kits. Catalog (50¢).

Studio Stair
1735 Holmes Rd.
Ypsilanti, Mich. 48197
A number of stair kits, many with unique designs.

T. C. Industries
P.O. Box 71
North Dayton, Ohio 45404
Simple lamp kits. Information (free).

Wood-Mosaic Corp.
P.O. Box 21159
Louisville, Ky. 40221
Parquet floor kits featuring teak wood materials.

Can you really build a house from a kit? The answer is, yes and no. The word "kit" is a little misleading in the case of homes. When a prefabricated cabin arrives as a truckful of logs, it doesn't fit the common notion of a kit. Nevertheless, it does the things a kit is supposed to do; namely, give you the premeasured parts and the instructions you need to build something. There's another thing you should know about house "kits." When you've put the kit together, what you have is a finished shell. That means no plumbing, wiring, heating, or insulation. In some instances, the kit doesn't even include the roofing and flooring.

When you decide to build a dwelling of any kind, consider the advantages of prefabrication. You save a substantial amount over a custom-built house because all the parts are standard and interchangeable. If you have a few talented friends and are handy yourself, you can put the house up on your own and save an enormous amount on construction costs. Most of the manufacturers included in this section say that their homes can be put up by experienced do-it-yourselfers. But unless you've done some actual construction work, you may have an exaggerated idea of how much you can do. Consult a local builder or contractor to be sure you're aware of what you're getting into.

All of the house "kits" here were designed as vacation cabins or homes. But more and more people with an eye to savings have been buying prefabs for permanent homes. Remember you can be quite happy in a wilderness cabin with no plumbing or lights. As a year-round home, your house will obviously require more extensive finishing. One company estimates that your finished house will cost you three to four times the purchase price of the "kit." It should be mentioned that one house, the Shelter Kit, can be assembled by two inexperienced workers in four days. All companies will send more detailed information by mail.

SHELTER-KIT, INC.
332 Central St.
Franklin, N.H. 03235

UNIT ONE

Shelter-Kit is the clear champion in the field of shelter kits. Unit One is the standard module sold by the company. You can build one for a 1-room cabin, or you can build four together and have a 3-bedroom house. Unit One has been planned to give a feeling of spaciousness far beyond its actual size. One whole wall is made of sliding glass doors, and high ceilings are built right into the design.

Although uninsulated, Unit One is completely weather-tight and habitable, at least in summer, just as it comes to you. The cabin is designed to sit on posts that rest on concrete footings. This kind of foundation is easy for even the novice to build. The shelter itself can be carried by two people in its kit

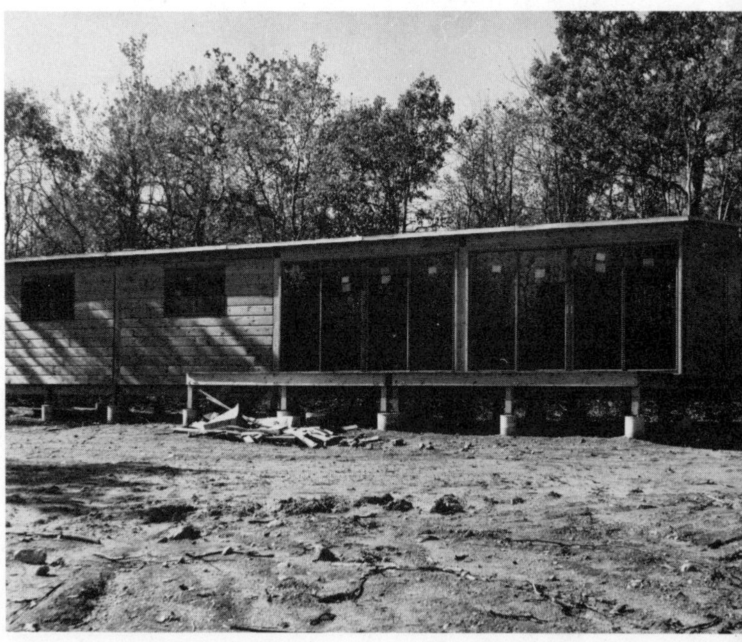

form, and assembled by the same intrepid two—with no prior experience—in four days. This is the most portable, buildable house we've seen. It wouldn't even be very difficult to move, if you wanted to take it to another site later.

Unlike some others, Shelter Kit is a complete kit. You get roofing, flooring, windows, doors, hardware, tools, preservative, sealer, and instructions—not to mention frame and walls. You could take it up to that great piece of inaccessible wilderness property you got such a bargain on, put it up, and be sleeping in your cabin in four days. Terrific.

If the prices listed don't quite make you faint from low altitude, keep in mind that you'll have almost no construction costs and builders' fees. If you pick up the kit at the factory, there aren't even any delivery costs. Sample prices:

Single Modules

Unit One (144 sq. ft.)	$2,145.
Unit One with deck (198 sq. ft.)	2,332.
Unit One with porch (198 sq. ft.)	2,640.

Standard Combinations

Deluxe camp (306 sq. ft.)	2,889.
1-Bedroom plan (450 sq. ft.)	4,748.
Economy 2-bedroom plan (633 sq. ft.)	5,564.
Economy 3-bedroom plan (723 sq. ft)	7,043.
2-bedroom plan (816 sq. ft.)	8,681.
3-bedroom plan (1068 sq. ft.)	10,916.

STANDARD HOMES

U.S. Highway 169 and I-35
P.O. Box 1900
Olathe, Kans. 66061

STANDARD HOMES PACKAGE

A large, substantial new home in a kit? Can such a thing be possible? Well, it is a rather large-sized kit; three or four truckloads of Standard Home's basic package, as a matter of fact. The first truck might carry your new home's rim sill, floor joists, sub-floor, etc; number two truck will deliver to you the exterior and interior panels and roof framing, windows, doors; load three may carry the plasterboard, interior doors, kitchen cabinets, and other essentials to complete your home. Exterior walls come to you already insulated; window and door trims come in packaged sets.

Depending on your situation, you have three choices as to what to do with the material once you've ordered it and it has been delivered: (1) You could hire a general contractor or professional home builder; (2) You could subcontract the house yourself; or, (3) you could do it yourself. This last choice requires experience and expertise, but of course, it is the most economical way to build your own home.

The styles of the homes offered include bi-level, split-level, colonial, ranch, duplex, and apartment building with four units; there are homes with family rooms and some without. The number of bedrooms varies with each plan. There are more than fifty models to choose from. Standard Homes publishes a catalog that furnishes you with detailed information about their basic package, their materials, delivery, basic prices, methods of payment, etc.

BELLAIRE LOG CABIN MANUFACTURING CO.

Box 322
Bellaire, Mich. 49615

LOG CABINS

The difference here is split-log construction, so that the inside walls are flat and have the look of paneling. While this produces a more traditional finished interior with no extra work on your part, it also reduces the insulating power of the logs. Bellaire has its own fleet of trucks, so you're saved the problem of outside delivery. The company claims that "any layman can do the job" of erecting one of the precut log buildings. You can, of course, arrange to have help locally. The estimate does not include foundation, cement floor, or fireplaces. Bellaire does not do plumbing, wiring, heating, etc. Note that erection is not part of the log cabin package, but must be separately arranged. Sample costs:

	Materials	*Wood Floor*	*Erection*
2 bedrooms	$4,757.99	$1,089.57	$1,975.00
1 bedroom	3,530.09	679.41	1,456.00
large single room	2,169.57	447.33	850.00
2-bedroom chalet	8,938.07	1,524.84	3,800.00
3 bedrooms	7,184.61	1,259.02	2,675.00

L. C. ANDREWS, INC.

South Windham, Maine 04082

LOG CABIN HOMES

More log cabins, this time made out of cedar logs. Each manufacturer has his reasons for preferring whichever kind of wood he uses. It's probably a matter of what's available, but if you have strong ideas about wood color, check into how each kind weathers. White cedar turns silver gray. Pine has a warmer cast, and spruce ages more slowly than other woods.

L. C. Andrews logs are put together with the tongue-in-groove method rather than spline-and-gasket. It's up to you to get independent advice about which is better protection against the wind and weather. More than ten models are available from Andrews, and they will customize any design to your needs. This company sensibly warns against thinking of prefab log cabin packages as "kits" in the usual sense. These houses can be built successfully only by the *very* experienced do-it-yourselfer or by a contractor. Prices are not available from L.C. Andrews except by individual request, since cost depends on the building site.

R-J INDUSTRIES, INC.

Box 237
Readlyn, Iowa 50668

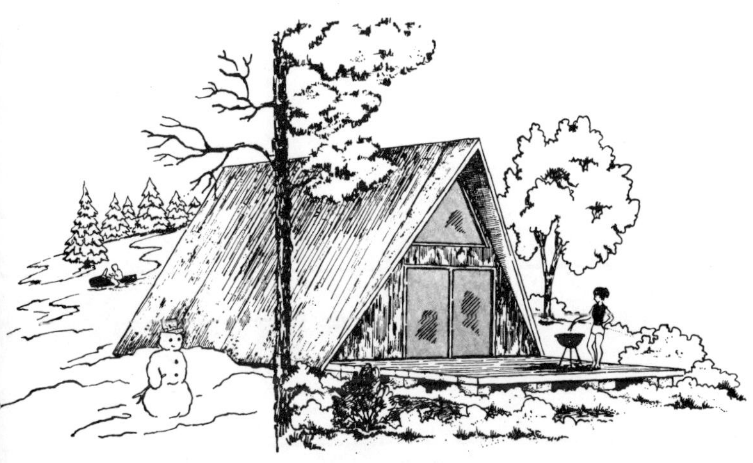

NORTH LODGE PREFABRICATED CABIN

Suitable for all climates, can be heated by electricity or gas, 2″ foam insulation. This cabin is available in a 16′ × 16′, 16′ × 24′, and 16′ × 32′ model. Interior can be divided as you choose. Kit does not include wiring, fixtures, or decor. Kits: 16′ × 16′: $3,495. 16′ × 24′: $4,495. 16′ × 32′: $5,745.

NEW ENGLAND LOG HOMES, INC.

P.O. Box 5056
Hamden, Conn. 06518

LOG HOUSES

This Connecticut company offers log home models ranging up to over $10,000. Those logs are hand-paled, rather than tooled by machine, for whatever difference that might make. This outfit also takes on the job of seeing that your log home kit is delivered to the site. They send you the stairs along with your logs, spline, polyurethane gaskets, second-floor joists, and any extras like porch posts that may come with your package. You supply the foundation, plumbing, wiring, partitions, dimension lumber, flooring, roofing, heating, and masonry. New England Log Homes does have supplementary materials, such as roofing, for sale at extra cost. Sample costs:

2 bedrooms, 1 level	$3,600.
2 bedrooms, 2 levels	4,960.
4 bedrooms, 2 levels	8,150.

GREEN MOUNTAIN CABINS

Box 190
Chester, Vt. 05143

LOG CABIN DESIGN KIT AND MANUAL

This item is a *design* kit, not the logs and joists themselves. You get a set of instructions on how to draw a floor plan, and a list of the parts sold by the company (porches, walls, roofs, etc.). You can compare the prices of parts the company sells with local prices, and if you can't design it yourself even with the design kit, Green Mountain designers will do it for you. But this plan does get you away from forcing your needs into one or another prechosen model. Kit: $3.

Prices of log cabins vary according to features and extras that you select. Green Mountain sells both a log package and a full-skill package. Even with the full-skill package, however, you must expect to purchase some building supplies (tar paper, for example) from a local outlet. Sample prices are as follows:

1 bedroom plus sleeping loft (log package)	$ 6,639.
Full-skill	9,506.
4 bedrooms chalet-style (log package)	7,134.
4 bedrooms, dining room, family room (full-skill)	10,534.
4 bedrooms, dining room, family room, den (log package)	17,157.
Full-skill	21,391.

Green Mountain also has a brochure called "Building a Green Mountain Log Cabin." It's free if you actually buy a log package, otherwise the price is $2. This is essentially the instruction manual for putting up the house and you might want to see how it's done before you order the logs.

NATIONAL LOG CONSTRUCTION CO. OF MONTANA

P.O. Box 68
Thompson Falls, Mont. 59873

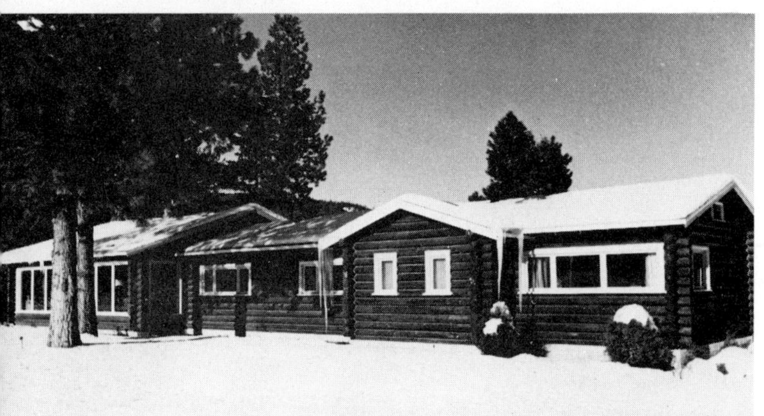

LOG CABIN HOME

Photo shows a fairly elaborate example of log cabin homes you can buy in kit form. "Air-lock" logs are notched and have center holes (better insulation and drying properties). The kit includes logs, window and door frames, rafters, ties, porch material, caulk, and insulation. No fixtures are supplied and, depending on your needs, total cost of a house will be three to four times the price of the kit. Kits available range from "just a cabin" ($3,146.) to a house with 16 guest rooms and a restaurant ($35,627.). The average vacation cottage is about $7,000. Company will design a house to your specifications or needs. Figure one year advance notice on kits.

VERMONT LOG BUILDINGS, INC.

Hartland, Vt. 05048

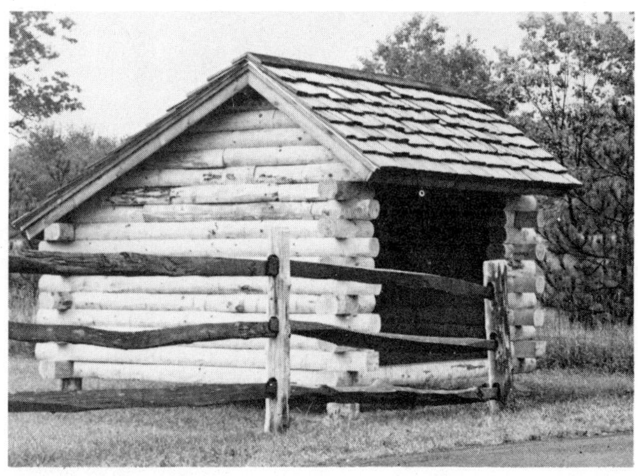

THE LEAN-TO

This is the simplest item in the long line of log buildings from Real Log Homes: the classic saltbox, open on one side. The kit includes precut log walls, precut ridgepole and rafters, hardboard spline, 10″ spikes, and polyurethane gaskets. The lean-to probably doesn't require a foundation, but if you want one, it's up to you to supply it. The smallest size (10′ × 10′) is good for a garden shed or children's playhouse. The largest side (10′ × 16′) would be a great hiker's shelter. For whatever other ideas strike you, there are two intermediate sizes (10′ × 12′ and 10′ × 14′). Since all the logs have been dipped in wood preservatives, the lean-to should be practically maintenance-free. The saltbox construction makes it immune to high winds and heavy snow loads. Prices:

10′ × 10′	$940.
10′ × 12′	1,010.
10′ × 14′	1,060.
10′ × 16′	1,150.

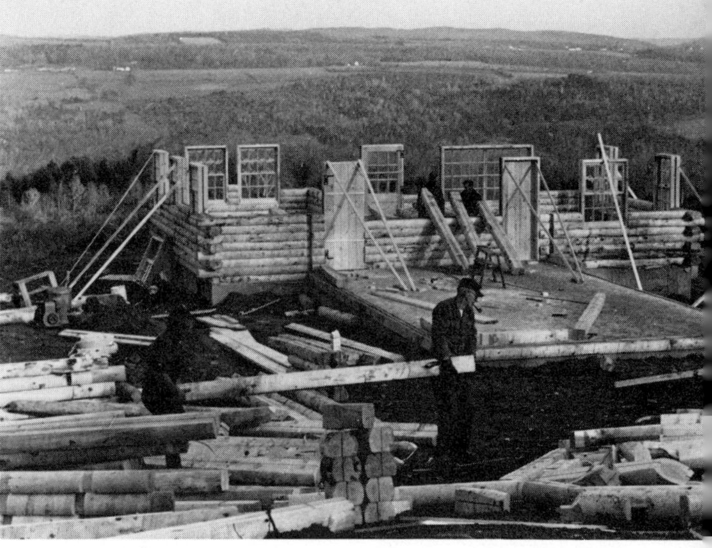

THE TYSON

The Tyson model log home is one of the smaller ones offered by this company, both in price and floor space. Like many Real Log plans, this one comes in an "A" and "B" form. The Tyson "A" is the simple saltbox again, a strong and economical structure with 2 bedrooms and a large kitchen/living room area, plus bathroom. Interior partitioning is up to you, of course, so you can close the kitchen off from the living room if you want to. The Tyson "B," besides an extra bedroom, has an offset living room floor plan to provide a little entry space at the front door. Both are 1-story plans, without basement, unless you choose to build one separately when you lay the foundation.

Kit includes: log walls, prehung doors, windows, and louvers, rafters, snowblocks, ridgepole, collar ties, splines, and polyurethane gaskets. You supply foundation, fireplace, floor joists and girder, interior partitions, flooring, underlayment, stairs, and roofing. What you don't have to supply for yourself are interior walls, interior finish, and insulation. All the logs supplied are 8″ to 10″ thick; which is 8″ to 10″ of the best natural insulation around. Logs should wear and weather beautifully both inside and out. The manufacturer says that their spline-and-gasket construction makes caulking between the logs unnecessary. Four experienced men can erect the Tyson in four days. But note the word "experienced." It will probably take you and your brother-in-law the bookkeeper a little longer. A field man will accompany each kit, but only guarantees to stay around for the first four hours of construction. Tyson A: $4,570. Tyson B: $6,050.

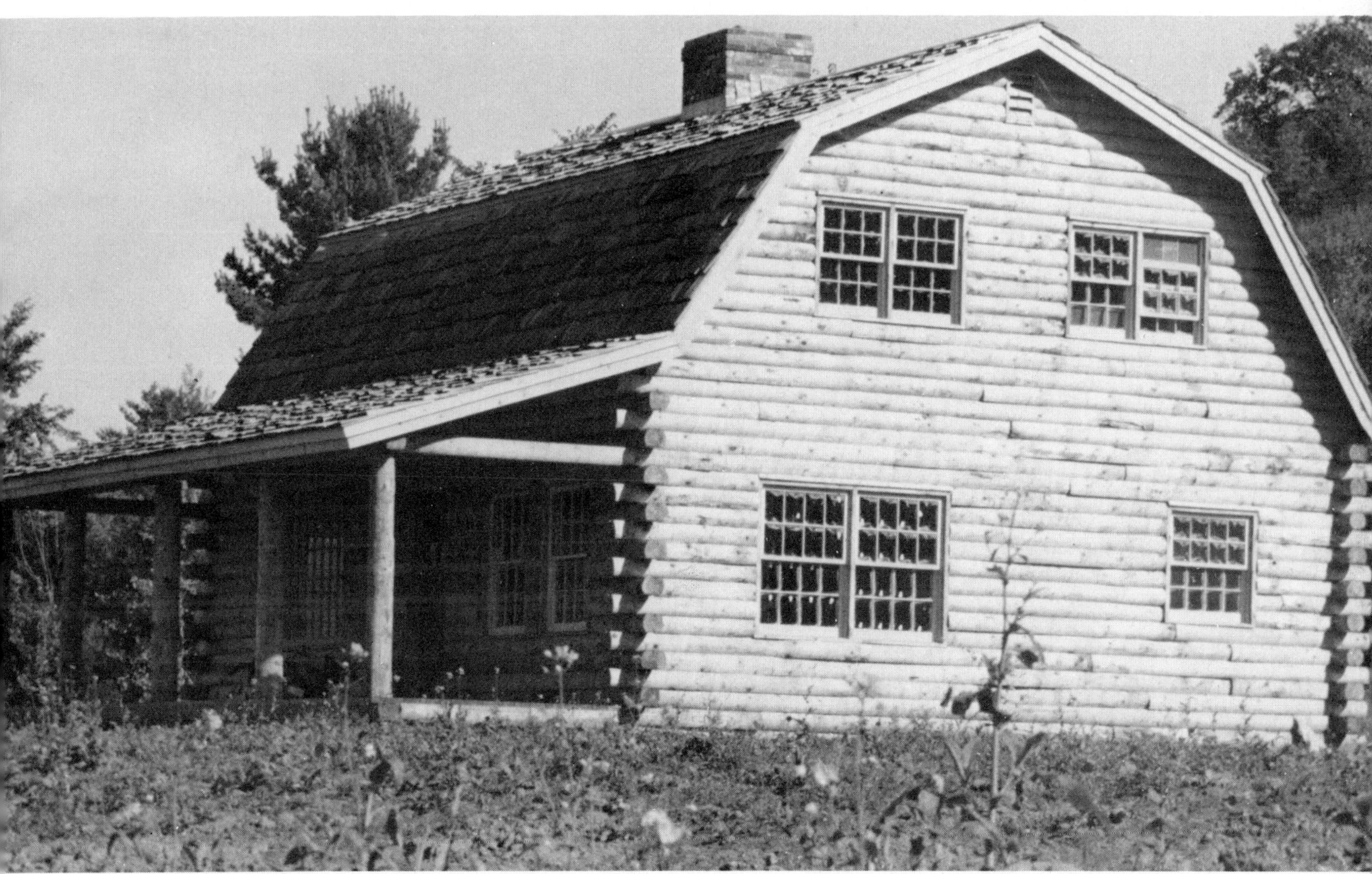

THE PLYMOUTH

This plan seems to be a favorite model with Real Log Homes, judging from the number of variations available. The design is basically like a classic gambrel-roofed barn with a porch across the front. The 2-story floor plan allows ample space for a growing family or weekend guests. All Real Log Homes were designed with vacation living in mind, but they could just as well be year-round homes with proper heating. The Plymouth comes in two variations, with Plan "B" slightly larger (870 sq. ft.) than Plan "A." Typically, this kit includes the logs, doors, windows, ceiling posts, etc., plus the fireplace mantel, and everything for the porch except the flooring. As usual, you supply the foundation and interior finishing materials. Furthermore, the company assumes no responsibility for shipping the kit to you, although they "usually" make the arrangements. That means you have to pay the trucker the moment he pulls up to the door. It also means that if the logs arrive broken, you have no one to yell at but that guy behind the wheel. Shipping may be a minor point when you're ordering a needlepoint kit, but it can be a major hassle when the kit is a whole house. The following prices do not include shipping. Plan A: $7,790. Plan B: $8,660.

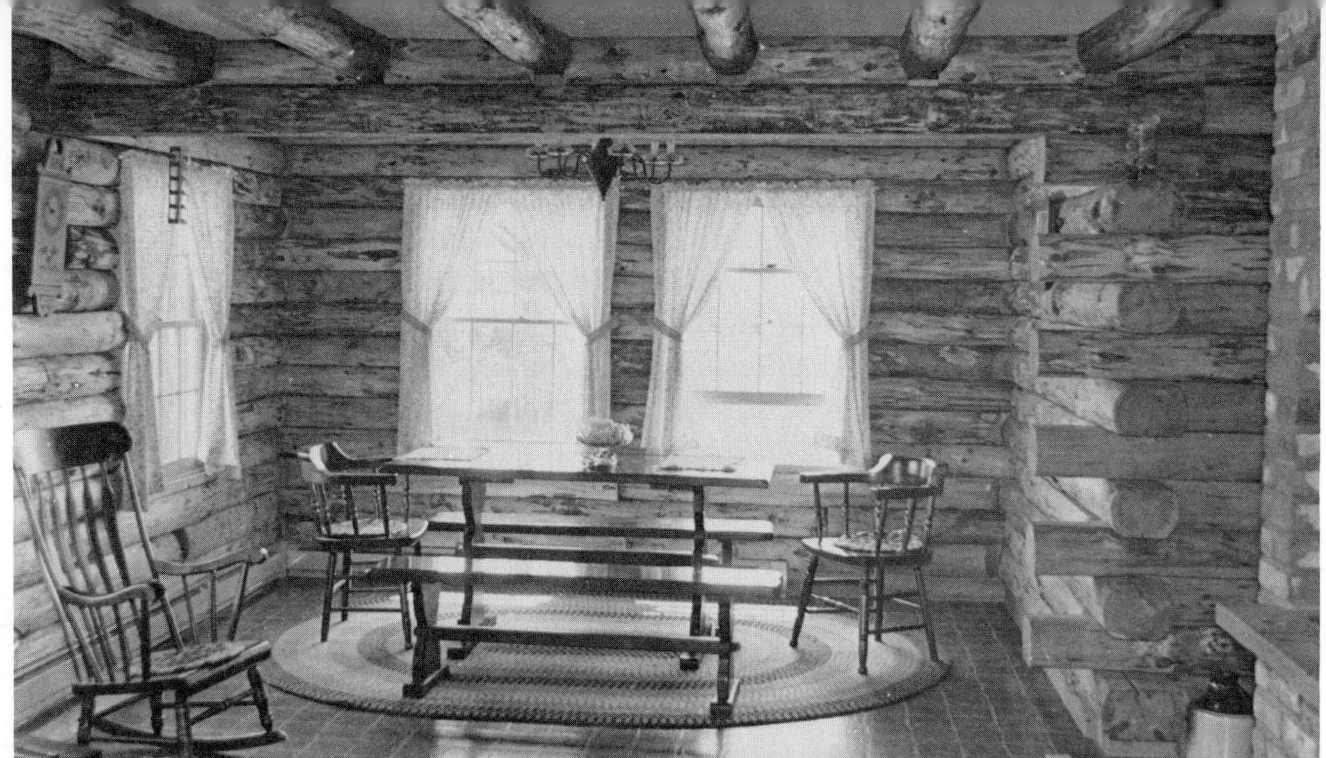

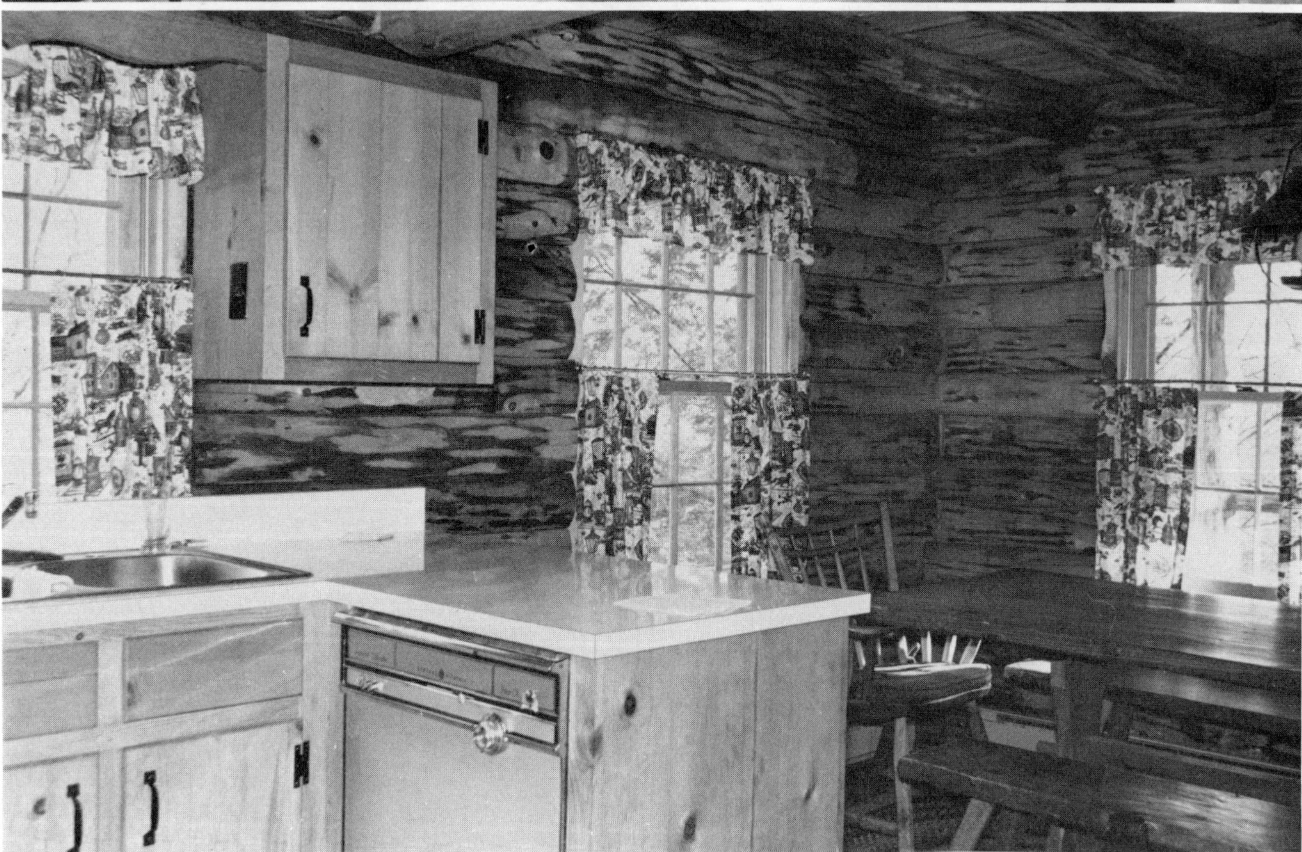

THE SHERE

This is the basic large house in the Real Log line. Plan "H" features a 2-story cathedral ceiling in the living room, 2 full baths, and 4 bedrooms. Plan "W" allows for 1 or even 2 extra bedrooms upstairs in place of the cathedral ceiling. The company describes this model as simulating and typical Colonial "add-on" design. It does indeed have an authentic pioneer exterior.

Outside, there's nothing to prevent you from modernizing a log home. Nor are you bound to Early American decor, although the logs certainly do suggest it. This company was obviously founded during the second-home explosion that rocked the Northeast a few years ago. The boom has eased off now, but the house kit may be finding new customers in people who want an economical *first* home. Model H: $9,850. Model W: $10,330.

*Real Log Homes are manufactured in Vermont, North Caro-
lina, and Montana. Naturally, you should write to the plant
nearest you. If you live in the West: Real Log Homes, Dept.
WM, Box 1520, Missoula, Mont. 59801. In the Southeast:
Carolina Log Buildings, Inc., Dept. WM, P.O. Box 368,
Howard Gap Rd., Fletcher, N.C. 28732. In the East:
Vermont Log Buildings, Inc., Dept. WM, Route #5,
Hartland, Vt. 05048.*

*You must keep in mind that unless you are a very
experienced do-it-yourselfer, you will need the help of a
contractor to build your foundation and to assemble the house
itself. The shipping is basically your problem. The house as
assembled from the kit is still uninhabitable without floors,
roof, stairs, and in some cases, joists and girders. For a
vacation home, you may not need plumbing, wiring, or
heating right away. For a permanent home you will, and this
also adds to the cost. In short, the price of the kit is really just
the beginning. Before you order your log house, be sure you
know the price of the "accessories." Real Log Homes manufactures kits for some 35 models, ranging from the lean-to on
up to a ski lodge with almost 5,000 sq. ft. of floor space.
Some have porches, dormers, and wings. You can build a
3-car garage, a barn, or a breezeway. These are all completely integrated designs, which can't be substantially altered after you've made your choice.*

HEXAGON HOMES
905 North Flood
Norman, Okla. 73069

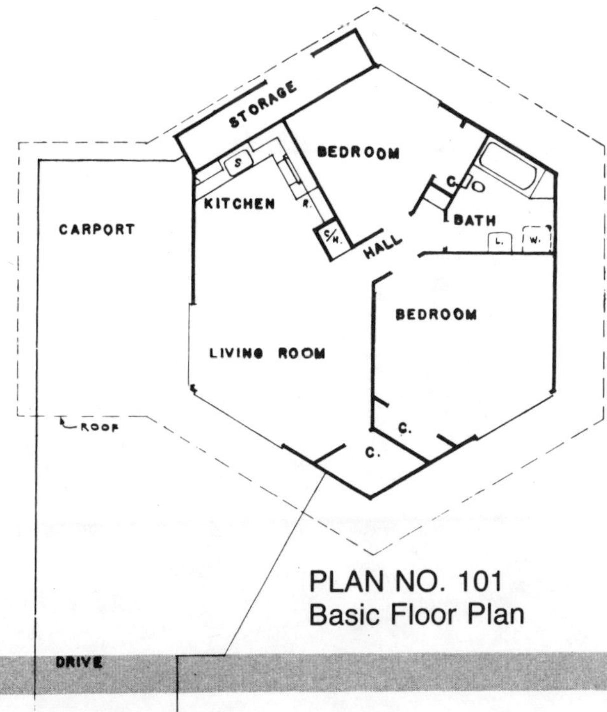

PLAN NO. 101
Basic Floor Plan

HEXAGON HOMES

The Hexagon Home is designed to be as complete
as possible and prefinished at the factory. Most of
the on-site labors of a technical type are eliminated.

This, of course, makes it easier for the nonprofes-
sional. It also enables you to use the less expensive
and less skilled labor that may be more readily
available in your area. The manufacturer states
"one can finish a house in three weeks compared to
three months for a similar conventional house."

Two outstanding features are the factory-built
foundation and the fact that the parts for a house
(up to 1650 sq. ft.) load into a single 40' trailer for
economical delivery.

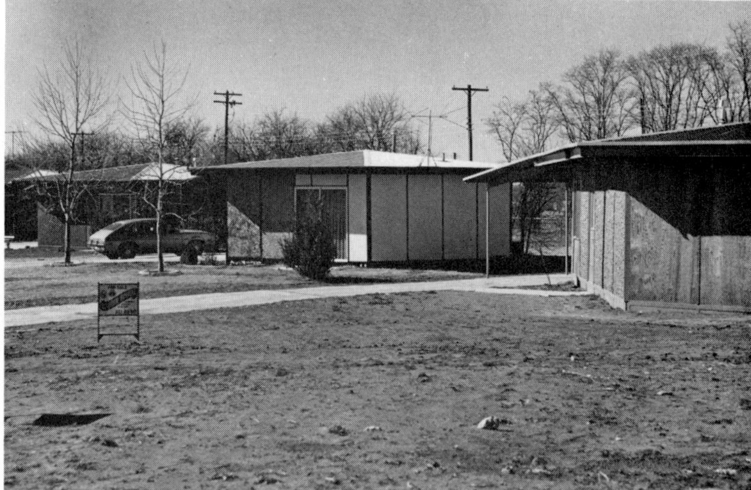

In addition, the truly "kit" nature of this
product means no expensive erection tools and
equipment. Other than the usual carpenter tools, all
you need is a wrench and a caulking gun. The basic
plan illustrated (#101) costs $8,500. Add about
$700. for plumbing and $500. for wiring. Also figure
freight from Oklahoma. Larger plans are available
to customer specifications.

INTERNATIONAL HOMES OF CEDAR
P.O. Box 268
Woodinville, Wash. 98072

PRECUT HOMES

Not exactly prefab homes, the products of International Homes of Cedar are custom-designed buildings. The system involves a patented system of interlock joining boards at corners for walls, foundation, etc. The company says that this joint is so
secure that a complete home could be assembled
"almost without nails." This system claims to
produce weather-tight walls for the same reason
that there are no chinks in a spline-and-gasket log
home.

Because these houses are not predesigned,
you'll most likely need the services of a builder or
architect to work up a plan suitable to you. You, of
course, pay for foundation, plumbing, wiring, and

finishing as well as site development and building costs. Sample costs:

704 sq. ft. with loft	$9,093.
1,128 sq. ft.	11,492.
1,163 sq. ft. with loft and carport	17,640.

THE WICKES CORP.

P.O. Box 3244PG
Saginaw, Mich. 48605

PREASSEMBLED VACATION HOMES

Wickes has close to twenty models, plus options on changing any styles to suit your needs. The standard house package includes all exterior construction materials necessary to build the basic shell or closed-in structure. Whichever package you order, the company will supply materials (including nails) and detailed instructions. Foundations and fireplaces are supplied by you. In addition, Wickes will sell you packages to install plumbing, wiring, insulation, heating, interior walls, interior doors, ceilings, flooring, and kitchen cabinets. You can even buy a set of "Bavarian-style shutters."

This company says that its materials plus the detailed instructions will allow assembly by non-professionals. As usual, we say that if you don't know a hacksaw from a hammer, you should probably start your do-it-yourself career with something a little smaller than a whole house. Prices vary, depending on which package or combination you select.

NOR-WES BUILDING SUPPLIES LTD.

1075 Marine Dr.
North Vancouver, B.C. Canada

PRECUT CHALET

A-frame or mansard roof chalets of western red cedar. The smallest house in this line has 2 bedrooms, a cathedral ceiling in the living room, a kitchenette, a bathroom, and a deck. Nor-wes supplies the lumber, sashes, doors, hardware, insulation, nails, and trim. They *do not* provide foundation, fireplace, plumbing, wiring, heating, erection, finishing, floors, or glass for the front wall. They do send along glass for windows and glass doors. You get a construction guide book, but unless you know what you are doing, you'll need some professional help. A crew of four professionals can erect an A-frame in eight days.

Delivery is by truck or rail from Canada and costs extra. If you want to, you can buy a set of plans and a list of parts separately. The price of plans will be deducted if you buy a whole package later. Sample prices:

2 bedrooms, 645 sq. ft.	$ 7,363.
2 bedrooms & loft, 850 sq. ft.	10,573.
3 bedrooms & dining room, 1,800 sq. ft.	22,228.

YANKEE BARN HOMES

Drawer A
Grantham, N.H. 03753

PREFABRICATED HOUSES

Yankee Barn Homes aren't really kits, or at least, not kits that the owner is encouraged to build by himself. They are prefabricated homes in the traditional sense, although an instruction booklet is included in the package. If you're used to construction, you and your friends could probably do it. So far, most of the Barns sold have been erected by the parent organization, Hanslin Associated. These are real homes, not cabins or lean-tos. The smallest Yankee barn has 870 sq. ft. and up to 3 bedrooms. Prices are for finished houses, including forced air heating and interior painting or staining. Foundation, land costs, and site development not included.
Sample prices:

3 bedrooms, 870 sq. ft.	$25.000.
3 bedrooms, 1,239 sq. ft.	34,000.
6 bedrooms, 1,922 sq. ft.	49,000.

SOLAR ENERGY ENGINEERING

748 Big Tree Rd.
South Daytona, Fla. 32019

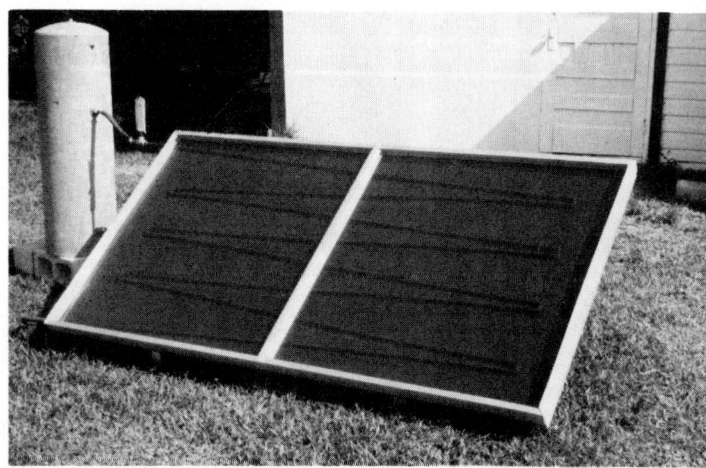

SOLAR HEATING SYSTEMS

Ancient people worshipped the sun. Now, once again, man is turning to the sun in awe. The idea is to use the sun as a source of heat.

The concept of solar heating is not new. It has enjoyed widespread use in Florida and in the Middle Eastern countries for over forty years. Solar Energy Engineering has combined this concept with modern space age materials and "know-how" to develop a modern energy system.

These solar collectors are attractive. The unit looks like a large aluminum-framed picture window. The coils blend into the collector plate and are almost indiscernible. The mounting hardware is designed to complement the rest of the unit. All plumbing and other components can be hidden. Good weight distribution keeps roof loads well below safe limits. This mounting is custom-fitted to give maximum year-round performance.

Solar heating systems are constructed of high-quality materials. Designed and tested to give years of trouble-free service.

Present operating systems have demonstrated a 30% reduction in electrical usage. Some systems require no electricity to function, others require circulating pumps and thermostats that operate at a very low wattage. The kit is relatively simple to construct and when complete will provide 25,000 BTU output per day. $219.95.

OTHER SOURCES

Air-Lock Company Log Co., Inc.
P.O. Box 1073
Prescott, Ariz. 86301

An unusual log cabin design features hollow logs joined horizontally by tongue and groove. Hollow logs are lighter for easier shipping or even airlifting. Catalog ($2.).

American Timber Homes, Inc.
Escanaba, Mich. 49829

White cedar plank houses in full-shell packages. Uses spline construction. Catalog ($1.)

Cedar Forest Products Co.
Polo, Ill. 61064

Western red cedar house kits, cedar plank house and garage kits. Full shell only. Information (free).

Custom Builders Corp.
3739 South Lindbergh
St. Louis, Mo. 63127

Choose from a huge selection of vacation and year-round home kits. Catalog ($1.).

Fab-A-Log of Washington
1400 Interurban Ave.
Tukwila, Seattle, Wash. 98618

A selection of 20 coded and easy-to-assemble home kits. Information package ($2.).

Futuro Corp.
1900 Rittenhouse Sq.
Philadelphia, Pa. 19103

Easy-to-assemble Finnish-style modern roundhouse kits. One large model looks like a flying saucer. Brochure (free).

International Mill and Timber Co.
Bay City, Mich. 48706

Fifty possible designs of home and garage kits. Catalog (25¢).

Lindal Cedar Homes
P.O. Box 8839
Seattle, Wash. 98178

Western red cedar planks. Full-shell (roof, floor, etc.) kits. Catalog ($1.).

Modular Concepts, Inc.
P.O. Box 70
100 Ontario St.
East Rochester, N.Y. 14445

Easy-to-assemble modular home kits. Thirty-five models in all including A-frames, chalets, and cabins.

Momadics Tipi Makers.
Star Route Box 41
Cloverdale, Oreg. 97112

Kits to make very livable tipis. Information (25¢).

National Log Construction of Montana
Box 68
Thompson Falls, Mont. 59873

Air-lock log cabin kits. Fifty-five models to choose from. Catalog ($2.).

Northern Products, Inc.
Bomarc Rd.
Bangor, Maine 04401

White pine log cabins joined by tongue and groove with extension at the corners. Choose from 10 kits. Catalog ($2.).

Pease Co.
900 Forest Ave.
Hamilton, Ohio 45012

Pease offers 3 vacation home kits but they leave the wiring, plumbing, heating, and cooling to you. Catalog ($1.50).

Pierson Home Prefabricators
Rt. 1 Box 114
Eureka, Calif. 95501

Redwood A-frame kits. Information brochure ($1.).

Rondisics, Inc.
527 McDowell St.
Asheville, N.C. 28803

Sells the "Rondette," a sort of combination of the roundhouse and the geodesic dome. Redwood kit is available as both a shell and a complete house.

Standard Homes Co.
P.O. Box 1900
U.S. H'way 169 and I-35
Olathe, Kans. 66061

Choose from 55 models of partially assembled home kits. Catalog ($1.).

Timberlodge, Inc.
105 West 8 Ave.
North Kansas City, Mo. 64116

Log houses and plank houses in kits. Information (free).

Ward Cabin Co.
Box 72
Houlton, Maine 04730

Northern white cedar log houses. Cabins and permanent homes are available. Catalog ($2.).

The geodesic dome is associated with designer-philosopher R. Buckminster Fuller. In 1951, Fuller took out a patent on a method for constructing domes or whole spheres by dividing the surfaces into triangles. As Fuller has pointed out many times, a geodesic dome is the best way to enclose the most space with the least surface area. This means that the dome is the biggest house for the least money, or at least the fewest materials. It also means that less surface is exposed to hot and cold weather, so you should be able to use less energy to heat and cool a dome.

In fact, people have been living in domes for most of human history. Think of igloos, wigwams, and thatched huts. But because of thousands of years of disuse, the dome today has a hypermodern look. It is associated with futuristics and the counterculture. In fact, the dome is for everyone. Its economical advantages can benefit the family with little children, the commune, or even a single individual. Kits are available for domes to shelter swimming pools, tennis courts, and recreation areas.

In general, domes are easier as do-it-yourself projects than are traditional, rectangular homes. Because of the triangular structure, domes are extremely stable and modular. Parts can be shipped as just a pile of similar triangles plus struts, hubs, and covering material. Like traditional house kits, dome kits usually come without interior finishing materials, plumbing, and wiring. But you'll probably have more money left for these things with a geodesic dome than with a conventional rectangular house. Furthermore, interest in domes is running high right now, so you'll find lots of reading material around to help you with your building.

DOME EAST CORP.
325 Duffy Ave.
Hicksville, N.Y. 11801

"POOLDOME"

This is an aluminum frame dome covered by a membrane of reinforced vinyl. Although prefabricated, this is not exactly a do-it-yourself kit. The company will let you build it yourself, but you have to hire a Dome East construction supervisor and Dome East installation equipment.

"Pooldome" and its twin, "Tennisdome," are large structures, obviously designed to shelter a lot of people. Approximate prices here include the frame, membrane, ventilation system, and one entrance. Sample prices:

1,020 sq. ft	$13,520.
2,850 sq. ft.	16,150.
4,460 sq. ft.	24,430.
6,420 sq. ft.	32,700.

"Shelterdome," the related smaller structure, is available from 300 sq. ft. ($2,400).

WOOD DOME

This is the real kit put out by Dome East. That is, it is the one actually designed to be assembled by the purchaser, presumably an amateur. There are three types of kits available.

1. *Connector Kits.* Dome East supplies the hubs

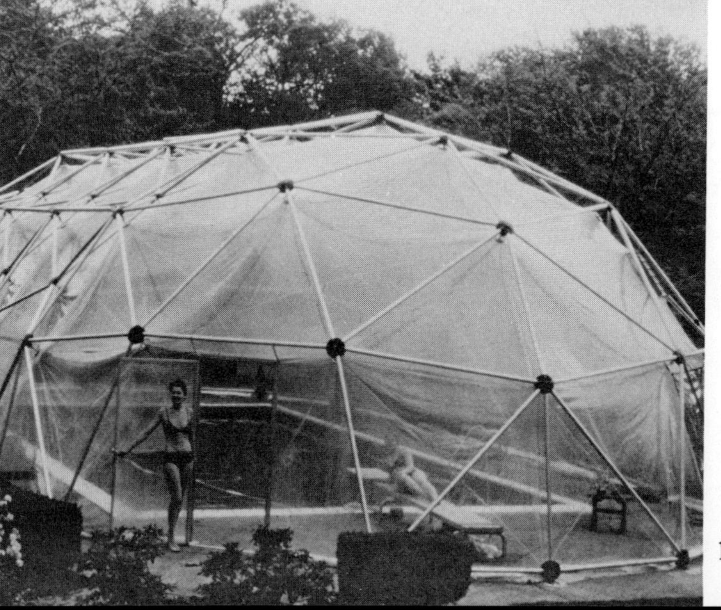

and working drawings. You cut your own struts and panels and assemble them yourself. The hub (patent pending) is made of aluminum. This is the cheapest but the most time-consuming way to build. It is recommended for experienced woodworkers or builders.

2. *Shell Kits:* You buy a Dome East shell and assemble it yourself with the precut and color-coded parts with instructions to assemble. This takes less time and skill and is designed for those who are at home with carpentry or mechanics.

3. *Shell Kits erected.* You can hire Dome East's supervisors to direct and assist in your dome erection or have a Dome East crew assemble your entire shell for you.

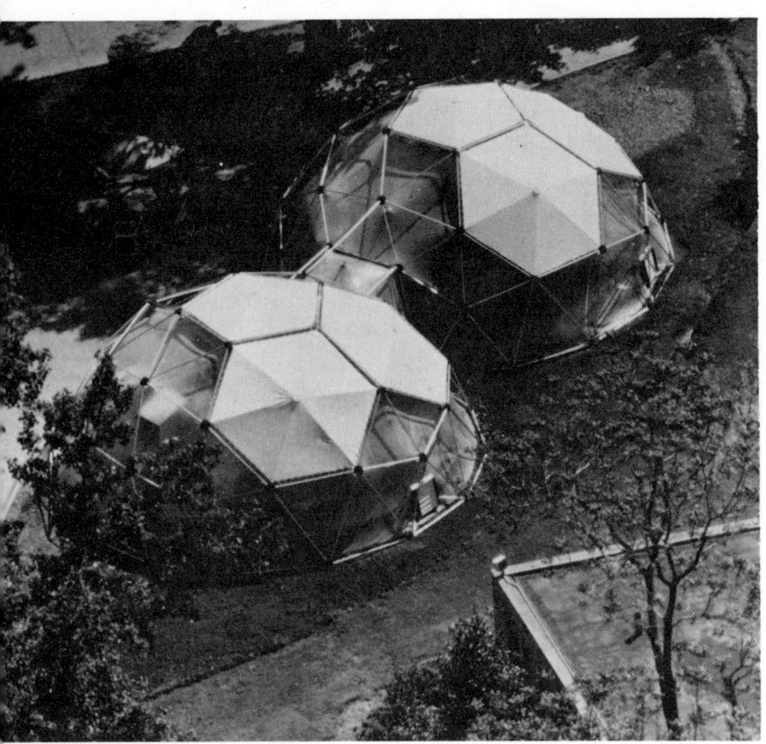

Materials supplied (depending on which kit you buy) include aluminum hub, wooden struts and panels, sealer, insulation, windows and doors, and finishing materials.

Sealer and insulation not included. Sample prices of complete shells:

Diameter	Price
26½	$2,690.
26¾'	3,960.
30½'	3,890.
39⅝'	7,640.
49⅝'	13,600.
60½'	22,860.

TENSION STRUCTURES, INC.

9800 Ann Arbor Rd.
Plymouth, Mich. 48170

O'DOME

The "O'Dome" is not a geodesic dome in the Fuller tradition, but a "tension structure," something like a cross between a tent and an igloo (a tigloo?). Kits weigh about 200 lb. and can be shipped anywhere. Assembly takes about two days (if you have assemblers). Dome must rest on a foundation or deck. Each O'Dome comes complete with panels, doorway components, sliding glass door, skylight, and all necessary hardware. Structure requires no painting and can be cleaned (outside) with a garden hose. Prices vary widely with styles offered. Write for details.

GEODESIC STRUCTURES, INC.

P.O. Box 176
Roosevelt, N.J. 08555

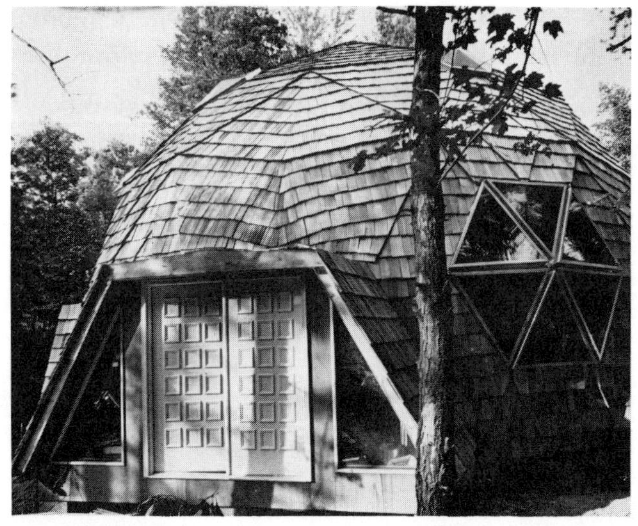

This company has eleven dome models, ranging from small house or vacation cabin-size, up to institutional-sized buildings. Although Geodesic Structures is a little stingy with information (catalog, $1.), it does emphasize ease of erection without special tools and skills. Evidently, individual kits are custom-prepared either from stock plans or personalized designs. Cost estimates and financial arrangements are made when you write for information.

ZOMETOY ZOMEWORKS CORP.

P.O. Box 712
Albuquerque, N. Mex. 87103

ZOMETOYS

Zomeworks does everything from selling you a skeleton to helping build the house for you. A zome? It's a zone-structure dome, based on zonohedron. Although the company dislikes the word "kit" in application to its products, there is one thing they sell which they themselves call a kit. It's the "Zometoy," a zone-structure climbing toy or a model to build. This way you can have some fun and find out what a zome is while you practice. Zometoy sampler kit includes instruction sheet, 15 connectors, 71 #3 sticks (red, white, black), 35 #2 sticks (red, white, black), $15. Large Zometoy kit includes Zome Primer, all sizes of sticks in all three colors, handmade wooden carrying case (901 pieces): $100.

GEODESIC DOMES

10290 Davison Rd.
Davison, Mich. 48423

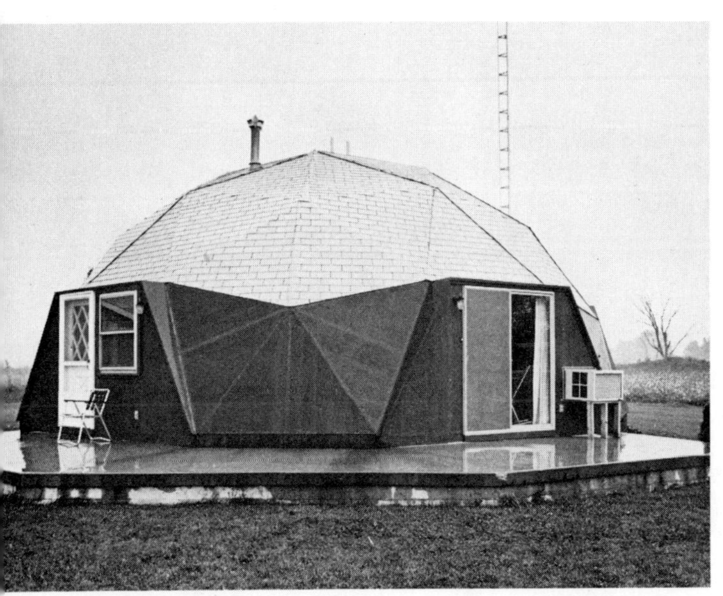

DOME KITS

Geodesic, the company, makes four models of geodesic, the dome. Two are house-sized, one is evidently intended as an institutional building. The Geodesic catalog says that large domes have been sold as offices, churches, drive-in restaurants, motels, ice rinks, and so forth. The fourth dome structure is a canopy on supports, to be used as an open shelter or pavilion.

The same catalog estimates that assembly of the average dome kit takes eighty man-hours. The company also says that three men have erected such a kit in twelve hours. Except for the foundation, the dome exterior can clearly be erected without expert help. Since concrete forms and specifications are supplied with the kit, it seems likely that dedicated amateurs could pour the foundation, too. All kits include interchangeable wood triangles for the shell, plus all the bolts, washers, and nuts needed. Kits are shipped by commercial carrier at your expense, or you can pick the kit up at the factory. All prices are FOB Davison, Michigan. Sample prices:

Alpine, 485 sq. ft.	$ 2,250.
Sierra, 1,100 sq. ft.	4,400.
Solar Canopy, 1,100 sq. ft. canopy	3,000.
Mars, 60′ diameter dome	16,500.

Also available: Skylights, interior finishing panels, insulation in panels, and fir liners. The literature from the company doesn't make it clear whether windows, doors, caulking materials, etc., are included in the package, but one presumes so. Catalog free from the company.

We Americans are a casual people who love to be outside. We are also a practical people who love to find a bargain. Hence the popularity of kits for outdoor living. The return of the backyard vegetable garden has happened with such speed that one scientist estimates we may soon be back to the point where everybody grows his own soup. Ornamental gardening is at its peak, too, and a house isn't a home without a few plants.

Why not broaden the scope of your outdoor life? A greenhouse can extend the life of your cherry tomato plants to twelve months a year. You can propagate and raise house plants that would cost you hundreds of dollars to buy. And you can have the incomparable pleasure of nurturing living things.

And speaking of living things, how about your family's recreation time? In this country, the family that plays together most often does it outside. Have you thought of a swimming pool? Maybe a kit is the answer. Or put together a trampoline and watch the backyard fill up with kids. A kit gives you the double pleasure of building, then using. Have fun.

NATIONAL GREENHOUSE CO.
Pana, Ill. 62557

"EAGLET" GREENHOUSES

These are smaller hobby and home greenhouses produced by a manufacturer of big commercial-sized units for growers and nurserymen. Panels are double-strength glass, and all models require a masonry foundation supplied by the buyer. Construction of one of these greenhouses is not for the inexperienced thumb-banger. The advantage of real glass over polyethylene or fiberglass is, of course, full light transmission. This can be important if your winter sun is limited or if you're trying to grow delicate, sun-loving plants. The following sample prices are the lowest prices. Larger greenhouses or models with doors, two glass ends, or automatic ventilation are higher.

    Freestanding, 12'9½" × 11'4"
                    $ 982. (no door)
    Freestanding, 15'10¾" × 11'14"
                    1,068. (no door)
    Lean-to, 6'4¾" × 11'4"   622. (no door)
    Lean-to, 7'11⅜" × 11'4"   656. (no door)

PANELITE HOBBY GREENHOUSE

This is an economy package available in one size only with no modifications. The Panelite is a free-standing greenhouse with aluminum frame, glass panels, door with screened opening, ventilation window, and cedar sill. It does not require a foundation, making it easy for the hobbyist to erect. Included in the package are 2 plant benches and 2 shelves.

The Panelite is 7'4¾" wide by 8'6 1/16" long. Company ships the whole package at your expense. Allow several weeks for delivery. $613.

Besides home and hobby greenhouses, National is a maker of glass and plastic greenhouses for professional growers. The company also carries a complete line of greenhouse accessories.

J. A. NEARING CO., INC.
100788 Tucker St.
Beltsville, Md. 20705

JANCO GREENHOUSES

Janco is another line of high-quality glass and aluminum greenhouses for the really serious gardener. These greenhouses are houses (or at least rooms) and represent a substantial outlay of money and time. This kind of greenhouse is a real investment, but once you have one, you have it for life! Although not portable, Janco (and other good aluminum and glass) greenhouses are an addition to your home and will increase its value if you sell.

There are many Janco models, ranging from around $600. to around $3,000. You can also get window greenhouses ($135. to $185.) and commercial-size greenhouses. Janco has the most complete catalog of greenhouse kit supplies we've seen, featuring everything *including* the kitchen sink and beyond. Send for their catalog and see for yourself.

PETER REIMULLER GREENHOUSEMAN

980 17 Ave.
P.O. Box 2666
Santa Cruz, Calif. 95063

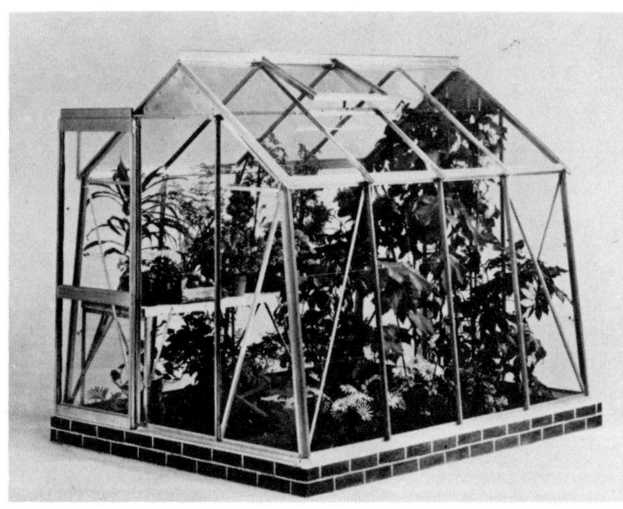

THE "LUMINAIR"

This is the top-of-the-line greenhouse from Peter Reimuller. It has a no-maintenance aluminum frame, glass all the way to the simple base (not poured foundation), and a sliding glass door. The kit is remarkably easy to assemble and you can move the finished greenhouse whenever you want to the other end of the garden or across the country. There is a ventilator window in the roof. The whole kit can be erected without any cutting or drilling. You need only a wrench and a screwdriver.

The "Luminair" is available in two sizes only. Bench supports are extra.

Luminair Six (6′3″ wide × 8′6″ long)
$479.95
Luminair Eight (8′4″ wide × 10′7″ long)
599.95
Bench supports: $24.95 and $32.95

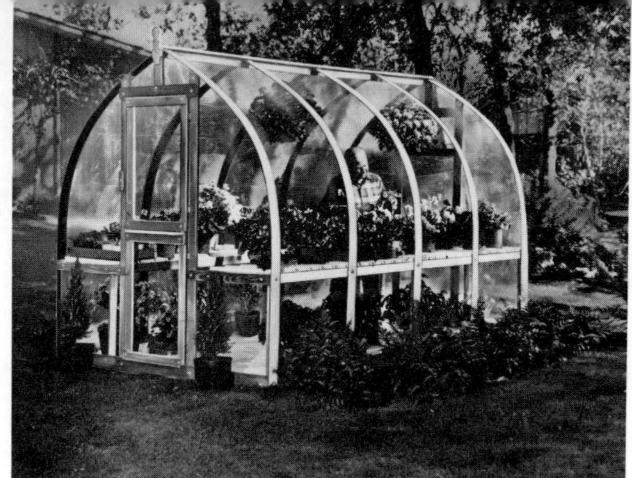

THE "CRYSTALAIRE"

This model has redwood framework covered with plastic greenhouse covering which the company says will last for years. Such coverings usually admit about 90% of the available light. The arch design makes the "Crystalaire" the most attractive of the company's designs, though not the most efficient or durable (not the most expensive, either). Like the other models, this one is really easy to assemble and portable.

Crystalaire, 7′ wide × 12′long $129.95.
Pair of benches: $42.95.

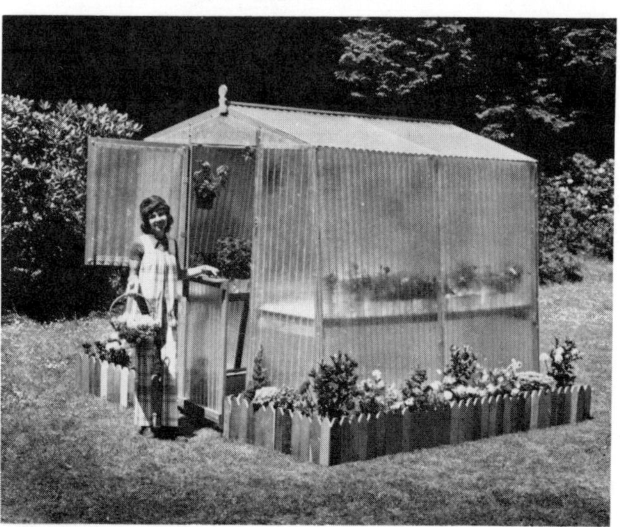

THE "PEARL MIST"

A hobby greenhouse with redwood frame and fiberglass covering. Fiberglass is sturdy and conducts light very well, but is not transparent. This is a disadvantage in appearance, since you can't see your plants from outside or rather you can see them only dimly. Nevertheless, this material is just fine for growing plants and it's both sturdier and cheaper than regular glass. Requires no foundation, easy to assemble, and portable.

Pearl Mist, 8' wide × 8' long $219.95
Pearl Mist, 8' wide × 12' long   304.95
Pearl Mist, 8' wide × 16' long   389.95
Pair of benches: $39.95, $54.95, $66.95.

Reimuller also makes a "Li'l Giant" Greenhouse which is essentially a large cord frame for keeping annuals through the winter or starting seedlings in early spring. In addition, you can order heaters, fans, automatic shutters, thermometers, humidifiers, humidistats, hygrometers, heating cables, and/or a special accessories package.

All of the greenhouses sold by Reimuller are real kits for the do-it-yourselfer. Any hobbyist can assemble the frames in less than a day. The instructions supplied are so clear and easy to read that they're a pleasure in themselves. Prices are good and accessories are reasonable, too. All models are freestanding and portable.

LORD & BURNHAM
Division Burnham Corp.
Irvington, N.Y. 10533

There are two basic L & B models, both with aluminum frames and glass panels. The "Sunlyt" is straight-sided with a pointy roof, just like that classic house you used to draw in kindergarten. The "Orlyt" is arched or slanted. Some have curved glass panels joining the wall to the roof. Both come in freestanding and lean-to styles.

Although designed to be assembled at home, L & B greenhouses are very sophisticated. Unless you're an experienced builder, you'll need the help of a handyman or contractor. All models require at least some concrete foundations and some need walls. This kind of greenhouse is a real investment, and you should give it some thought first. Send for the catalog to see all the models and combinations possible. Prices range from about $500. to $3,000.

TURNER EQUIPMENT CO., INC.
P.O. Box 1260
Goldsboro, N.C, 27530

POLYETHYLENE GREENHOUSE

Cheaper than fiberglass and much cheaper than real glass, these polyethylene greenhouse kits are available in both freestanding models and lean-to models to build against the side of another building. The polyethylene film is 90% light translucent. All freestanding models are 14' wide and 34' high. All lean-to models are 7' wide and up to 30' high. Unfortunately, the polyethylene cover only lasts for a season since ultraviolet light causes deterioration. The company estimates that replacement polyethylene film will cost you about $15. a year.

All polyethylene models can be set on a foundation of concrete blocks and wooden sills, so that you don't need expensive and difficult poured foundations. Detailed foundation instructions accompany each kit. Also available is a special kit for converting a polyethylene greenhouse to permanent fiberglass. And every model can be extended later when you need more room or have more money. All models have a manually operated vent above the door. Doors are polyethylene-covered and are standard equipment. All fasteners, hardware, and assembly instructions are supplied. Sample prices, including estimated BTU requirements (for heating the greenhouse):

Model No.	*FREESTANDING* Dimensions W X L	BTU Factor	Price
1414P	14' × 14'	6,000	$206.00
1434P	14' × 34'	12,000	428.50
	LEAN-TO		
714P	7' × 14'	3,000	$119.50
730P	7' × 30'	5,400	209.50

FIBERGLASS GREENHOUSE

Fiberglass is a permanent greenhouse material, guaranteed by Turner to last fifteen years. The fiberglass panels will not shatter, crack, rust, or rot, and can be set directly into concrete or ground. Fiberglass is 95% light translucent. One fiberglass door and one vent are standard equipment, and panels are precut. You have to drill the holes yourself, however, as you assemble the greenhouse. Hardware, fasteners, and instructions are provided. Turner ships your fiberglass greenhouse prepaid east of the Mississippi River, but there are additional charges for more distant points. Sample prices:

MODEL	*Freestanding* DIMENSIONS W X L	BTU FACTOR	PRICE
1414 FG	14' wide × 14' long	6,000	$552.
1434 FG	14' wide × 34' long	12,000	1,112.
	Lean-to		
714 FG	7' wide × 14' long	3,000	$290.
730 FG	7' wide × 30' long	5,400	512.

ECONOMIZER MODELS

Turner Equipment sells two budget models for those who want a small, freestanding permanent greenhouse. Instead of the manually operated window-vent that is standard on the larger models, the Economizer has an automatic exhaust fan mounted on a shutter. You also get a fiberglass door, a motorized intake fan, and a thermostat. Like all the low-budget polyethylene and fiberglass kits from this company, transparent panels go all the way to the ground or foundation for maximum light and growing space. Sample prices:

Economizer 10, 8′ wide × 10′ long, 3,200 BTU	$432.75
Economizer 14, 8′ wide × 14′ long, 4,000 BTU	$495.75

Turner offers a wide range of kits especially geared to the do-it-yourselfer. Catalog free.

TEXAS GREENHOUSE CO., INC.
2717 St Louis Ave.
Fort Worth, Tex. 76110

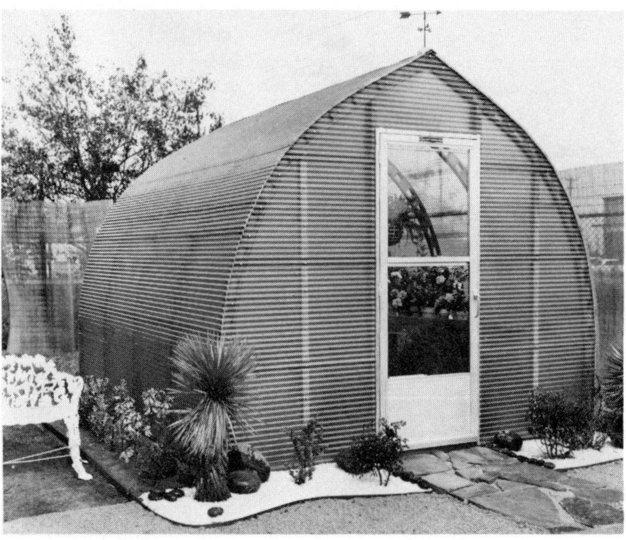

LOW-COST FIBERGLASS GREENHOUSE "THE OASIS"

This and other kits sold by the company offer a relatively easy way to set yourself up for serious plant raising. Construction appears to be relatively easy, but a foundation is required and you must be prepared, at least, to drive two-by-four stakes, or pour concrete. Precut redwood frame, sky green (81% light transmission), or clear fiberglass with shutter fan. (10′ wide × 11′10″ long) $524. Frt. pd.

YIELD HOUSE
North Conway, N.H. 03860

PURPLE MARTIN BIRDHOUSE

In the last few years, a strange rumor has circulated that the purple martin, when housed comfortably in a home of his own, will eat all the harmful insects on your property and thus return your investment in his housing ten times over. This claim, largely unsubstantiated, has led scores of people to install a veritable apartment house for Purple Martin families. Yield House's "Martin House" kit lets you give a home to "fourteen swooping, chortling, frolicking martin families." Whether all this merry making will be accompanied by mosquito eating is still not clear, but you can give it a try. The kit—20½″ high, 16″ wide, and 26½″ long—is easy to assemble and is mounted on a pipe or post. $24.95.

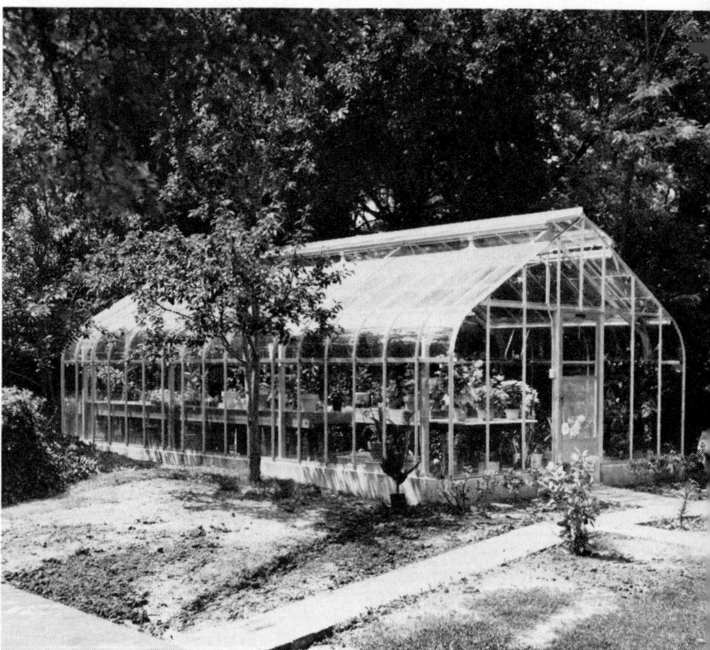

ALUMINUM FRAME GREENHOUSE "ELITE 1500"

Sophisticated aluminum frame, galvanized steel substructure, glass greenhouses. Rustproof hardware, glass-to-ground construction (you can use the area under the benches for growing). Concrete foundation required and you should obviously investigate how much heavy work will be involved. Elite 1500, 15′ wide × 29′ long: $2,472.

A complete line of greenhouse kits and an extensive catalog of accessories. A charming "clearvue" redwood greenhouse (about 8′ x 11′) is offered for $580, which requires no foundation and can be set on a cedar base.

GARDEN WAY RESEARCH
Charlotte, Vt. 05445

GARDEN CART

For large gardens or farms this cart is a handy way to move relatively large loads (substantially larger than a wheel barrow). The kit includes all the hardware, wheels, axle, handle, etc., and complete instructions. You must supply ½″-thick plywood (takes most of a 4′ × 8′ piece). The kit actually only saves you $25. over the completely assembled piece and unless you have a lot of scrap plywood, you may not want to exercise your building skills on such a utilitarian object. Kit price (shipping included): $107. (Vt., N.H.) to $121 (West Coast).

HOWMET CORP.

Box 40
Magnolia, Ark. 71753

PICNIC TABLE

Somehow the fun around a picnic table is greater than around a dining room table. Maybe it's the outdoors and maybe it's the food, but everyone loves a picnic. Howmet has a 6′ sturdy all-metal table. It takes less than an hour to assemble this precision-made kit. The tubular steel is rustproof and washes down with a damp cloth. Everything is in the kit, just add the ants and hamburgers. $99.

RAIN JET CORP.

301 South Flower St.
Burbank, Calif. 91503

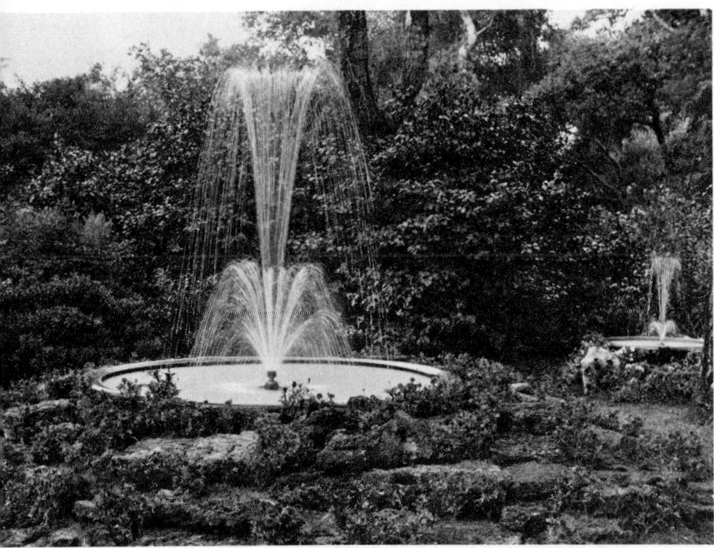

OUTDOOR FOUNTAINS

Everytime Hollywood wants to make someone look rich they put a fountain in his backyard. Fact is, it truly adds a touch of elegance to your home. Rain Jet Corporation has everything in do-it-yourself, save-yourself-money form. No plumbing is required as the water recirculates. The material is fiberglass and aluminum. Instead of tossing coins in the fountain at Tivoli it can all happen in your backyard. The water shoots to five feet. The bowl itself is three feet. Truly charming. $249.50.

Rain Jet Catalogue (16 pp. free) has every type of fountain you could desire. Prices are inexpensive when compared to the custom-built competition.

DUNCRAFT

25 South Main St.
Penacook, N.H. 03301

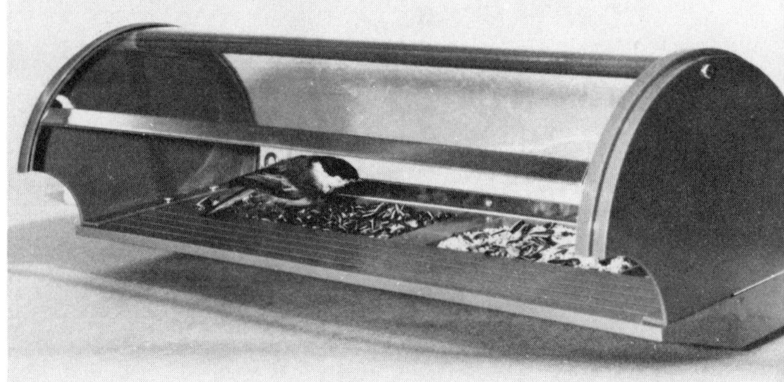

BIRD FEEDERS FLIGHT DOME

Enjoy bird watching at its very best. The engineering secret here is the dome. It provides roofing to ward off pigeons, yet it's transparent so you can watch your grosbeaks and pine siskins at close quarters. The rooftop dome shelters the feed tray and slides forward for indoor servicing. Built-in adapter socket for mounting atop any 1″ outer diameter post. Kit for hanging also available. Feeder is 8″ × 19½″. $9.95 (hanging kit 75¢ extra, and sill extension for storm windows $1.50 extra).

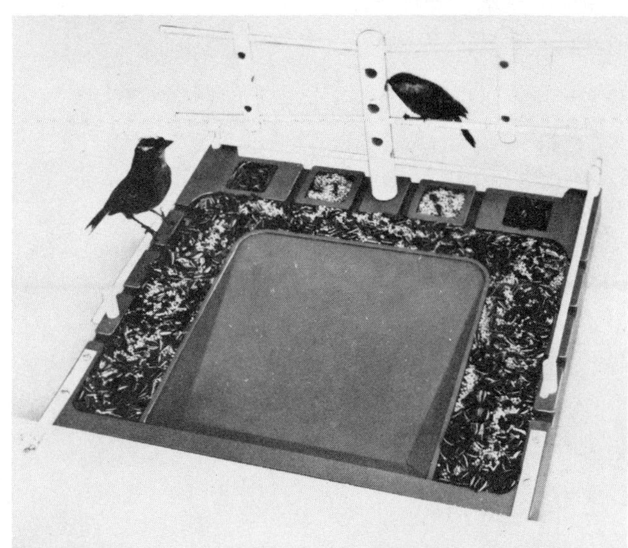

FLIGHT DECK

Offer your birds everything they need: seed, a

drinking and bathing pool, and a dab of peanut butter on the feeding stick. This is a nonrestrictive feeder—you can attract many different species at one time. Clips on or off your sill with no tools. Easy to refill—just open your window. (15″ × 17″) $8.95.

Duncraft catalog (32 pp.) is free and contains everything you need to feed the starving birds of the world (sans food). A shape and style to please every bird fancier, right down to specialized feeders for hummingbirds, thistles, and sapsuckers. Most feeders available in kit form.

CONSTANTINE
2050 Eastchester Rd.
Bronx, N.Y. 10461

BIRD FEEDER

This is a good companion project to the birdhouse listed above. If you are going to give the birds a home, you might as well feed them too. And this is a cheap, easy way to treat a whole flock of birds to dinner. Solidly constructed of basswood, the feeder is simple to assemble and attractive. $1.29.

BRENTANO'S
586 Fifth Ave.
New York, N.Y. 10036

RUSTIC BUFFET BIRD FEEDER

Those birds too elegant for Constantine's bargain bird feeder (see above) will surely flock to this handsome all-weather pine buffet feeder. Kit is easy to assemble, nice to look at, and all-inclusive (floor, walls, roof, glass, suet, nails, instructions). Not bad for $7.

TECO
Box 706, 1122 Industrial Dr.
Matthews, N.C. 28105

TRAMPOLINE KIT

We'll avoid all puns like "Jump for Joy," but you'll enjoy this commercial-size trampoline. A complete 6′ × 12′ pit-in-ground-type trampoline. You receive a black polypropylene net (mat) plus 100 springs and 100 eye bolts. Then start digging a hole in your lawn 3′ deep. Complete installation instructions. Manufacturer offers a 30-day, no-questions-asked, money-back guarantee. However, he does not tell you what to do with the hole in your lawn. Kit is same quality as used at commercial trampoline center. Complete. $165. postpaid.

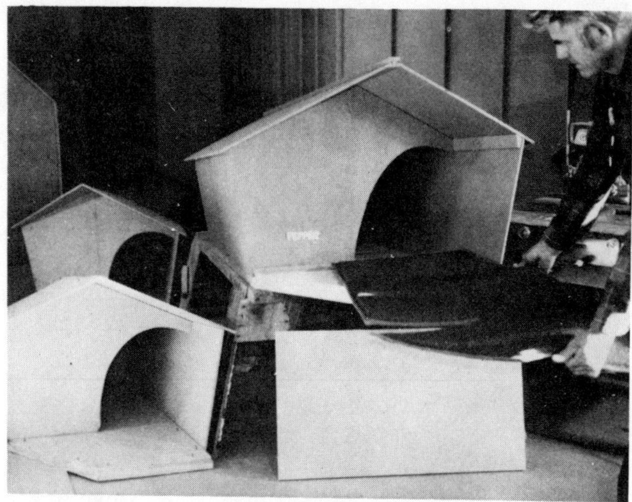

SHETTEL-WAY INNOVATIONS
P.O. Box 12
Twin Falls, Idaho 83301

DOGGY DEN

This is an attractive dog house that is easy to build, although small dogs like miniature breeds will have trouble setting up the heavier pieces and may need some help. It is doubtful, even with the price of wood the way it is, whether this kit is a particular bargain, but the product is nice and enjoyable to construct. Two versions for small and large dogs, several accessories. Small kit: $23.50. Large kit: $29.00. Cedar shingle roof: add $14.00. Floor pad: add $16.00.

HEALD, INC.
P.O. Box 1148
Benton Harbor, Mich. 49022

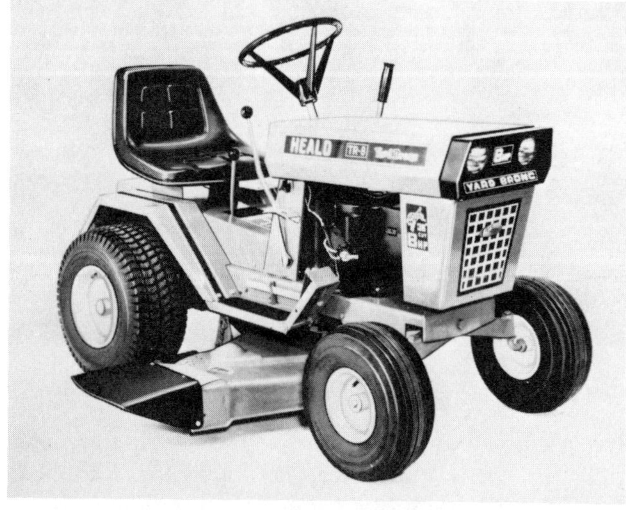

8 H.P. LAWN AND GARDEN TRACTOR KIT

New Yard Bronc TR-8 from Heald, Inc. is powered by 8 h.p. 306 cc. Tecumseh engine. Yard Bronc features 4-speed Peerless transaxle, geared automotive-type steering, disc brake, floating front axle, and $18 \times 8.50 \times 8$ rear and $15 \times 6.00 \times 6$ front tires. Accessories include electric start/headlights; 36" mower deck; 42"dozer blade; snow thrower; larger muffler; chrome hub caps; and rear tire chains. Yard Bronc comes in easy-to-build, semi-kit form. Base kit price: $499.95.

CHILD LIFE PLAY SPECIALTIES, INC.
55 Whitney St.
Holliston, Mass. 01746

KINDER CLIMBER

Children from two to seven will love this outdoor, compact portable gym. Lots of climbing area with a center platform to walk through, chin, or play house. Six feet high, 3'4" long, with 5'-wide base for stability. Child Life is so proud of the quality of their materials that they offer a money back guarantee if you are not fully satisfied with their merchandise. Finest woods and hardware throughout. $42.

THE LADDER JUNGLE

The Ladder Jungle is really the Rolls-Royce of jungle gyms. Four preassembled sections easily bolt together to form a square that is 8' across. Over one hundred rungs are closely spaced for short legs. The center area is open to encourage real gymnastics, and the child can climb through in either direction. A challenge and fun for children from ages three through twelve. $180.

THE FIREMAN'S GYM

The Fireman's Gym is the most complete and varied climbing gym made. Its full 8' height gives playmates a large and challenging area for climbing and acrobatics. Rungs go up 6' on all sides. The gym is 5' × 3'4" with the center entirely open and bridged by two cleated boards. Children can move these about to make a roof, table, or steps in a variety of dramatic play possibilities.

At one end of the gym there is a large net of polyfiber that you climb like part of a commando course. The opposite end of the frame holds a rugged knotted rope for hand-over-hand climbing contests, and two 8' sliding poles that are great for fast trips down to answer the fire alarm.

Preassembled side sections easily bolt together. The wooden frame gives long years of durability. Forest green uprights contrast with maple-yellow rungs to make the Fireman's Gym a fine looking addition to your yard. Ground space is 5' × 8'.

Stakes give complete stability, so you can install the gym in any level area.

The many features of the Fireman's Gym make it appealing to little ones, yet maintain their interest on through the early teens. Happy play combines with sound physical development year after year. Ages two to twelve. Kit #FGK: $156.

The satisfaction of having fine play equipment is increased and there is considerable saving in these Child Life kits. All braces and rungs are factory varnished, ready to assemble, and use. Kit directions are written in detail and have good outline drawings to guide you in each step. Everything you need except hammer, pliers, and screwdriver is included. You can make a fine family project out of your kit because there is something each member of the family can do. Child Life's money-back guarantee assures a quality product. Catalog free.

OTHER SOURCES

American Fence Co.
8205 South 71 H'way.
Kansas City, Mo. 64132

A variety of easy-to-assemble dog runs, pens, and kennels. Brochure (free).

Brinkman Mfg. & Fence Co., Inc.
Rt. 8, Huntoon & Auburn Rd.
Topeka, Kans. 66604

Kits for easily assembled fences, horse corrals, and dog kennels. Catalog (free).

Crest Kennel Co.
2200 South Valentia St.
Denver, Col. 80231

A good assortment of easy-to-assemble kennel and run kits for your favorite pet. Catalog (free).

Held Products
9 Lakeview Dr.
Farmington, Conn. 06032

Bird house kit. Catalog (free).

Sturdy-Built Mfg. Co.
11304 S.W. Boones Ferry Rd.
Portland, Oreg. 97219

Redwood and glass greenhouse kits. Good selection. Catalog ($1.).

Tired of shooting baskets and playing catch? Looking for something new, something different, something more your own? How about a duck decoy kit? Or you could build your own mini-gym. In the realm of sports, kit making should appeal to those who are looking for something a little out of the ordinary.

Sports kits will attract those contemplative types, like fishermen, who like to build their equipment as well as use it. You must have known that type of sportsman whose real pleasure is in the tying of flies. If you understand that turn of mind, you may be in the market for a taxidermy kit or one of the other sports-related kits featured here. Most manufacturers of such kits have other items as well, so write directly to the companies for further information.

MIDLAND TACKLE CO.

66 Route 17
Sloatsburg, N.Y. 10974

CUSTOM FISHING ROD

A variety of fishing rods available in kit form. Choice of ferrules, cork butts, grips, and collars. Catalog features over a hundred styles in a wide range of prices. Write for free catalog.

SPEL SALES

14 Slingerland Ave.
Pequannock, N.J. 07440

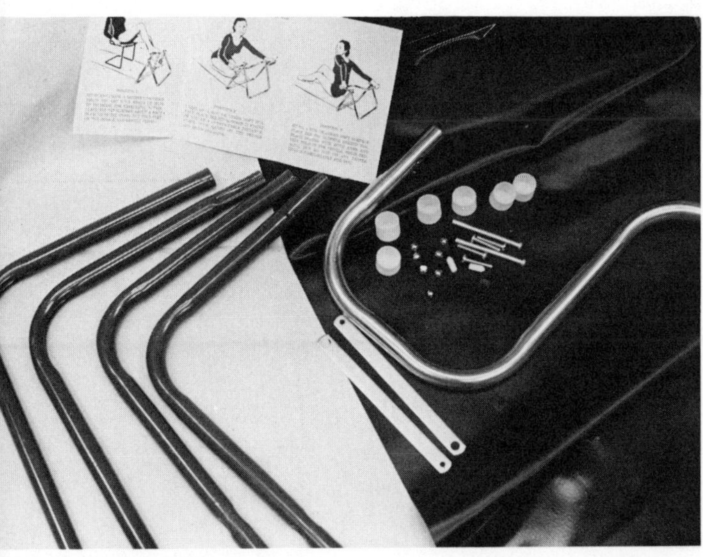

MINI-GYM

Put this little kit together and you have your own little gym. Not exactly all the facilities of the Ath-letic Club, but it will do wonders. Best of all, you can "work out" while you read a book or even watch television. Work out for five minutes a day, just pedal like you would a bike. Tones and slims. Once completed, it still folds to closet size. $10.

BAY COUNTRY WOODCRAFTS

U.S. Route 13
Oak Hall, Va. 23416

DUCK DECOYS

The hunter's friend and the duck's enemy, the duck decoy comes of age. The art of producing your own decoy is a two-fold hobby. First, the hunter can enjoy producing his own decoy. Second, the home hobbyist can enjoy this American folk art.

Duck decoy carving originated with the American Indians in Colonial times. The hobby is now enjoying a revival. These kits bring you the art in such simple form even a beginner will enjoy it.

The decorative duck decoy kits contain parts that are carefully carved from solid white pine, smoothly sanded, and ready for assembly. Included in each kit are a head, body, glass eyes, sandpaper, and instructions. The completed duck is about 10" to 16" long. Kits are $9.95 each, $18 per pair.

Bay Country Woodcrafters offers a catalog (25¢) of various decoy kits. Company is located near a wildlife refuge on the eastern shore of Virginia. It is the largest decoy factory in the world.

DECOYS UNLIMITED

Clinton, Iowa 52732

DUCK DECOY MOLDS

Here's a kit that will not only give you a super duck

decoy, but can put you in business in this growing field. After you buy the kit, you can get extra plastic for $1. a pound. Then it will only cost you about 83¢ for each duck. The kit includes a decoy mold, plastic, Epoxy, repair compound (fastens head permanently), and a gallon of two different color paints.

How do you make a duck decoy? Simply prepare the mold, fill it, cool it, attach head, and paint.

Price depends if you're shooting geese on the Mississippi River or canvasbacks in Canada. But the complete set-up with molds will run about $75. Catalog free.

VAN DYKE SUPPLY CO.
Woonsocket, S. D. 57385

TAXIDERM

This kit contains everything you need to "finish" your prize hunting catch. Definitely not for the squeamish. Complete instructions, plus all needed chemicals: 19.50.

Van Dyke has various materials for tanning, taxidermy, and the like. Complete catalog free.

OTHER SOURCES

Aspen Lures
Box 2918
Aspen, Colo. 81611

Kits for fishing rods, lures, jigs, and sinkers. Catalog (free).

Gold Day Products
Box 305
Lake Forest, Ill. 60045

Price of golf clubs teeing you off? Why not make your own clubs from a kit? Send for more information.

Larand Enterprises
P.O. Box 34
Harbor City, Calif. 90710

Offers a kit to make your own water skis. Brochure (free).

Lure-Craft Mfg. Co.
Bloomington, Ind. 47401

Bait your fish at half the price. Offers kit for making plastic worms. Catalog (free).

Michigan Water Specialties, Inc.
P.O. Box 397
Union Lake, Mich. 48085

Just what you've always wanted—an underwater saucer. It comes in kit form and when assembled you can put on your scuba equipment and be towed in your saucer by a motor boat or lare sailboat. Literature (free).

Sportsman Mfg. Co.
444 11th St.
Clarkston, Wash. 99403

4′ × 8′ pool table kit that will save you over $100, if you assemble it yourself. Brochure (free).

T. C. Industries
P.O. Box 71
N. Dayton, Ohio 45404

Kit for cue rack. Information (free).

The outdoors movement has hit Americans hard. Each summer, more and more of us are driving or walking or climbing farther into the wilderness to get a taste of natural surroundings. Unfortunately, some of our wilderness areas are being hit hard too, by people whose equipment is too motorized, mechanical, and destructive to the forest environment.

We feel that hand-building your own equipment makes more sense for the camper than practically anyone. There is a certain contradiction in setting out to commune with nature in a mass-manufactured camping outfit. In addition, there are real savings to be realized in making your own camping equipment. In some cases, you can spend twice as much for a finished item as for a kit to make your own. The quality is often superior in the kits.

We have included a sampling of camping kits ranging from sleeping bags to a complete camper to fit on your pickup truck. For the dedicated outdoorsman, these kits are the perfect answer to low-priced excellence. For the novice, they are good introductions to the fascinating field of camping gear. To anyone who cares about do-it-yourself and roughing it, equipment kits are a way to make you as self reliant in your preparations as you are on the trail.

ADVENTURE 16

10056 Bert Acosta Dr.
Santee, Calif. 92071

BACKPACK KIT

The company calls this their "kit-pak." Everything you need to make a high-quality backpack. Almost everything, that is. You also need a good sewing machine and the knowledge to use one. Kit includes nylon material, hardware, aluminum tubing, rivets, and fittings. A little experience with cutting and sewing patterns will help a lot. Completed pack is big, well padded, and sturdy. $17.95.

KLIMA KRAFT

316 East Dr.
Oak Ridge, Tenn. 37830

PACK FRAME KIT

An adventuresome spirit and a love of the outdoors are usually the only requirements needed to motivate you to own a pack frame. To enjoy that climb up the mountains, to be able to sprint through the winding trails of wilderness with ease, or to ride that bicycle many miles a day touring rural America, you don't have to feel like a pack mule.

The pack frame that Klima Kraft has assembled consists of a nylon cord that allows full circulation of air under and around your pack, thereby maintaining a cool back, free from sweat. The weight of the pack is well distributed so that you never feel you have, if you'll pardon the cliché, the world on your shoulders. So, no longer do you need to feel like Atlas. The kit comes with complete instructions and should not prove to be too difficult to assemble. $9.50.

GANDER MOUNTAIN, INC.

P. O. Box 248
Wilmot, Wis. 53192

TRAVEL KITCHEN

If camping out's a drag; if you can never find anything, here's the answer. Makes camp cooking a joy—everything handy and in its place. Precision precut parts are select A/C exterior plywood with all necessary hardware, handles, glue, sandpaper, and instructions included. Easily assembled with hammer and screwdriver—no cutting or fitting. Shelves are adjustable to fit your cooking equipment, foodstuffs, dishpan, dishes, etc. Has divided utensil drawer and is drilled for handles and convenient paper towel holder. Framed counter door provides a handy work area—will not warp. Sets firmly on picnic table or folding stove stand. Size is 27" wide, 18" high, and 12½" deep. $19.95.

VIKING CAMPER SUPPLY INC.

99 Glenwood Ave.
Minneapolis, Minn. 55403

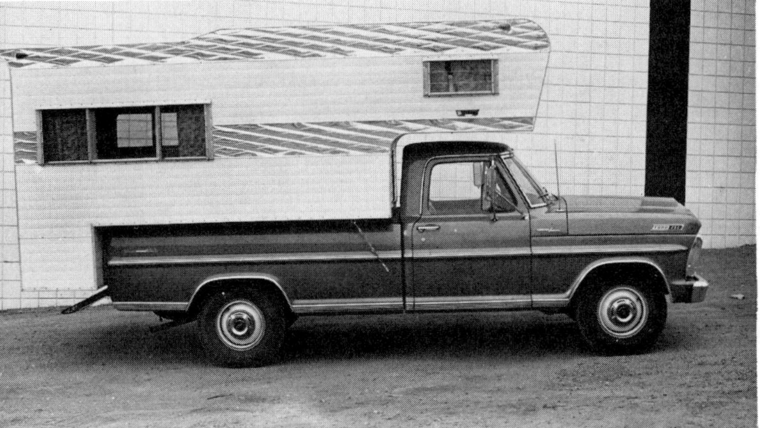

CAMPERS

Rent too high? Hassled by the job? The city got you bugged? Pack up the family in this camper and you're on the way. This camper sleeps six. The dinette is in the rear. The bedroom is in the front (overcab). A bath and closet separate the two giving you, in effect, three rooms. There is up to 8' of cabinet space along one side with room for heater, oven, refrigerator, range hood, etc. All of this plus plenty of safety glass all around. You supply the truck. The kit to construct the camper only: $930.

FROSTLINE KITS

452 Burbank
Broomfield, Colo. 80020

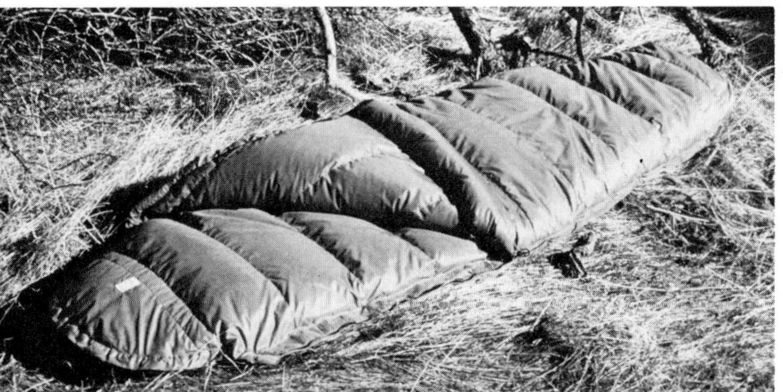

COUGAR SLEEPING BAG

A sleeping bag with a built-in, full-length shredded foam pad, which means you don't have to buy (and carry) a separate pad. The rest of the bag is filled with top-grade prime northern goose down. Slant-tube design to provide maximum warmth by squeezing out cold air spaces around the body. A 70″ zipper opens at foot end to cool feet and will work to another sleeping bag. Available in navy blue, medium blue, or green ripstop nylon. Down filling is accomplished by using a plastic packet. You open the flip-top at one end of the plastic down-filled packet, insert into the compartment, and push in the down, remove the empty packet and discard. Requires only a sewing machine. Standard kit (15° to 65°): regular, $57.95; large, $62.95. Winter kit (-10° to -65°): regular, $62.95; large, $66.95. Stuff sack: $2.25.

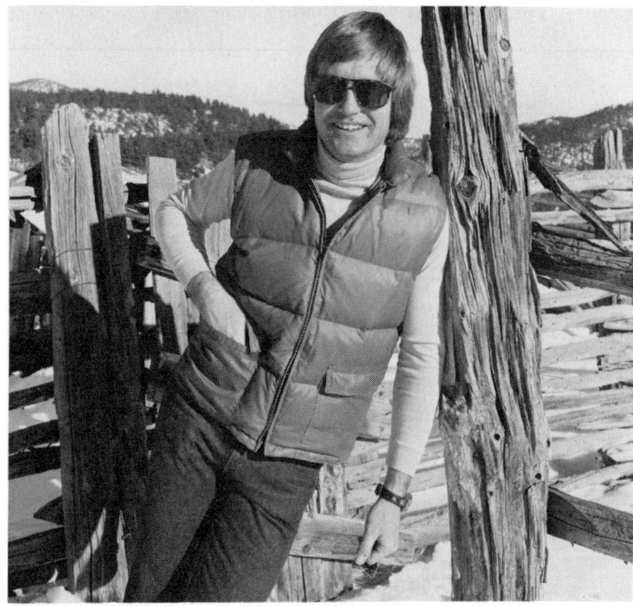

DOWN VEST

Super-compact kit that "will literally fit into your pocket, then rebound instantly to provide extra insulation when you need it most." This kit is cut from 1.9 oz. ripstop nylon and filled with prime northern goose down. Simply stitched-through construction means one or two evenings work. Vest is also available in a reversible hunter's version. Colors: Navy blue, Medium blue, green, red, and International Orange. Sizes: men's small (ladies' medium), men's X-large. Kit: $13.95. Stuff sack: $1.15.

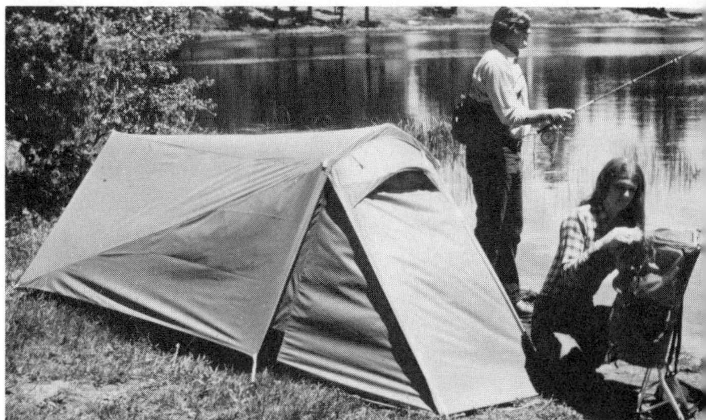

KODIAK TENT

The original no-front-guyline tent. Steep walls and

wide top make more room than in any A-frame style with similar floor area. Three can sleep in a Kodiak in a pinch, two with their heads at the rear, the third between with head and shoulders in the vestibule. Lots of room for two and their gear. Vestibule can be opened at front or from either side or front can be pitched for shade. Self-supporting front vent has mosquito netting and closing flap inside. All zippers are rugged Delrin: Two at front corners of vestibule, two at rear providing a full-opening rear end covered by mosquito netting (no entry) for maximum ventilation, and one at center of front. Mosquito netting separates main tent and vestibule. The floor measures 7½′ × 4½′ and the front hood extends a full 3′ ahead of the floor. The Kodiak is 45″ high at the front and 32″ at the rear. Two floor choices, both nylon: one a lightweight floor of 3 oz. waterproof urethane-coated taffeta: the other a heavy-duty floor of 3¾ oz. waterproof, urethane-coated Oxford cloth; 9 oz. total difference in weight. Tent poles are complete with shock-cord: Just wave them in the air and they snap themselves together. No tools needed for assembly. Poles fold down to 20″. Kit comes complete with carrying sack kit, detailed illustrated instructions, and all necessary parts and materials, including thread. The tent takes seven pegs. $75.95.

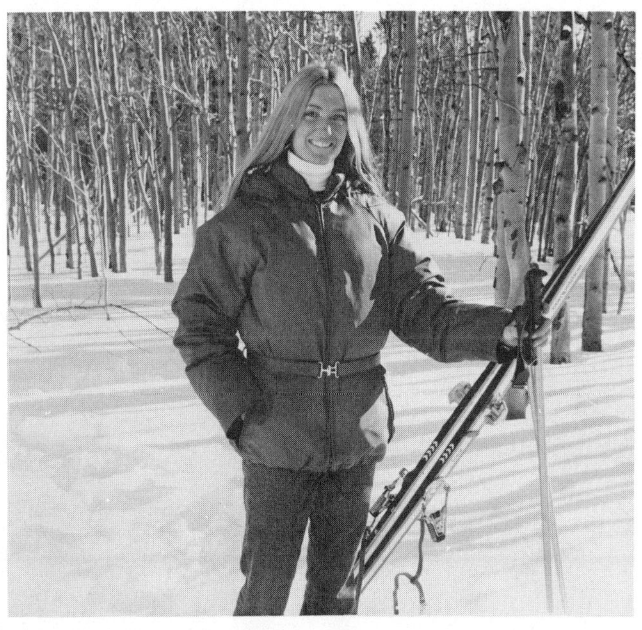

PARSENN SKI COAT

Prime goose down quilted between inner linings (quilt lines do not show on outside.). Kit includes matching belt, concealed knit cuffs in regular sleeves. Colors: navy blue, medium blue, forest green, red, and gold. Weight: 1 lb. 15 oz. (med.). Average thickness 1″ with 9 oz. down (med.). $29.95.

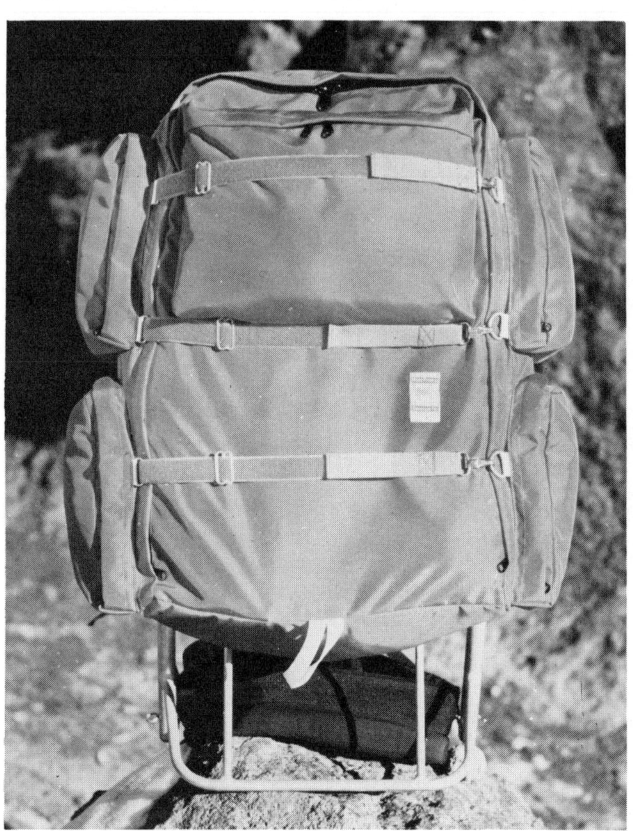

THE HATCH-BACK SACK

An unusual type of backpack; sack does not have an opening at the top. Instead, entire back zippers open for access to any part or all of the contents. Back zippers also open from bottom so you can get to lower part of the pack without opening top. Three adjustable cinch straps allow the pack to be compressed toward the frame as the load diminishes, thereby enabling you to shift the center of gravity closer to your back and/or higher to decrease back pull. Cinch straps easily unhook with snap hooks at one end. Four large side pockets have 15½″ zippers that open from top to bottom. All zippers covered by wide water-shedding flaps. Map pocket behind your head where you can reach it. Kit includes leather accessory strap holders, ice ax holder, grommet tool and hole cutter, toothed grommets and clevis pins for frame attachment. This large capacity sack measures 22″ high, 16″ wide, is 9″ thick at top, 9″ at bottom. Will fit any adult frame up to 16″ wide, with instructions for custom fitting to frame and for drilling new holes when necessary. Made from 7.5 oz. urethane-coated nylon in orange or green. $19.95.

A complete line of camping equipment—sleeping bags, sacks, jackets, parkas, boots, as well as some raw materials. The kits try to provide everything except a sewing machine, which is required. If you have to set a grommet, they give you a grommet setting tool. There are substantial savings over ready-made equipment.

In the old naval definition, a boat is any vessel that can be taken on board a ship. Many Navy men still wince at the sound of people calling a huge liner or destroyer a "boat." But ships are becoming fewer and boats more plentiful. And boats are getting bigger, too. There are a lot of yachts around that could sink that noblest ship.

The most popular pleasure boat, however, is not the ocean-going yacht, but the little versatile runabout. Powered either by an outboard or an inboard engine, runabouts are everywhere a fixture of summertime, U.S.A. They are used for water-skiing, trawling, or just running about. Sailboats run a close second to the small motorboats, not to mention the rising popularity of canoes, kayaks ... even the lowly rowboat.

Can you live on a boat? You can if it's a houseboat. Or maybe if you have a canoe, you can live under it as a wilderness shelter. Can you build a boat? Man has been doing it since just about the time he first saw water. Using some of the kits available, you can make everything from a skiff to a racing sloop. Many serious boaters do eventually begin to build their own craft, a natural next step after repairing. Needless to say, this is not an inexpensive pastime, but one that brings satisfaction and often profit to thousands who must go down to the sea.

TRAILCRAFT
Box 606
Concordia, Kans. 66901

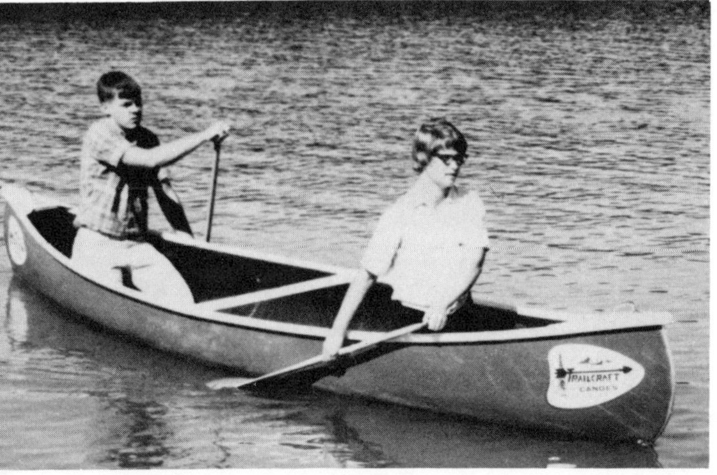

TRAILBLAZER CANOE

Trade one evening of your life for a completed canoe. This performance product is surprisingly low priced. Complete wood and canvas materials with simple-to-follow instructions. Sure enjoyment. 12' size: $59. 16' size: $79.

A variety of other wood canoes as well as fiberglass. Catalog free.

OUTDOOR SPORTS
P.O. Box 1213
Tuscaloosa, Ala. 35401

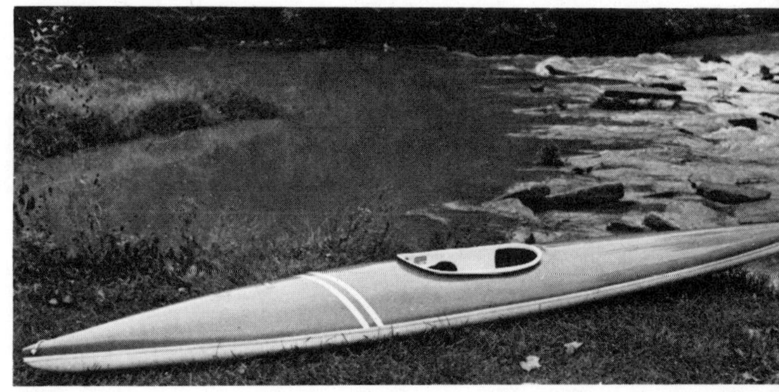

VENTURE 4 KAYAK

Fiberglass hull kayak. Kit includes hull, deck seat, and "H"-form for joining hull and deck and complete instructions. $149. (FOB Indianapolis).

The kit above is also offered with a "big man's hull," and accessories (spray skirts, skegs, etc.) are also available. The Venture kayak is one of their few kits, but catalog (free) is interesting.

DEDHAM KAYAKS
Box 207
West Lynn, Mass. 01905

THE "WANDERER"

Here is a boat you will be proud to own. It is 12′ long, the most popular length ever made. Its width allows for maximum buoyancy without sacrificing ability to paddle easily with double blade paddle. Its extremely low center of gravity and great depth make it the safest kayak of its size yet made. Designed to be ample for two adults, it will easily carry more, yet its light weight makes it possible for even the youngest paddlers to carry it. It is as steady as a rock, very fast under paddle, takes a tremendous load and sails like a champion. Kits contains parts for frame (completely machined), floors, canvas covering, hardware, tape for joints, trim, and complete assembly instructions. 12′ long, 32″ wide, 13½″ deep, and weighs 34 lb. $49.95.

"SQUARE ENDER"

The Square Ender is ideal for hunting, fishing, camping, or sailing. It can be paddled, sailed, rowed, or powered with a small motor to save rowing. It has a maximum capacity in a minimum length while maintaining its valuable all-purpose ability. (12′ long, 35″ wide, 13½″ deep, transom width 28″, cockpit 8½′) Complete kit: $55.95.

THE "CRUISER"

This boat is just the thing for the trip you have been planning. Put on a double bottom for greater security while away from home, load her up, and shove off. Construction kit: $59.95. Nitrate dope: $7.50. Canvas and adhesive for double bottom: $13.95. Paint and varnish kit: $9.95

Dedham Kayaks are safe! Sitting in this kayak you cannot tip over. Your weight is carried on the floor, which is fastened directly to the keel. As a result, you are actually sitting below the water line. This low center of gravity, plus a slightly V-bottom design, make them exceptionally steady. With cut-to-size kits, anyone can build himself a kayak he will be proud to own. You do not have to live beside the water, nor even own a car. A pair of bicycle wheels and an axle make an excellent kayak carriage. Catalog free.

GLEN-L DESIGNS
9152 Rosecrans
Bellflower, Calif. 90706

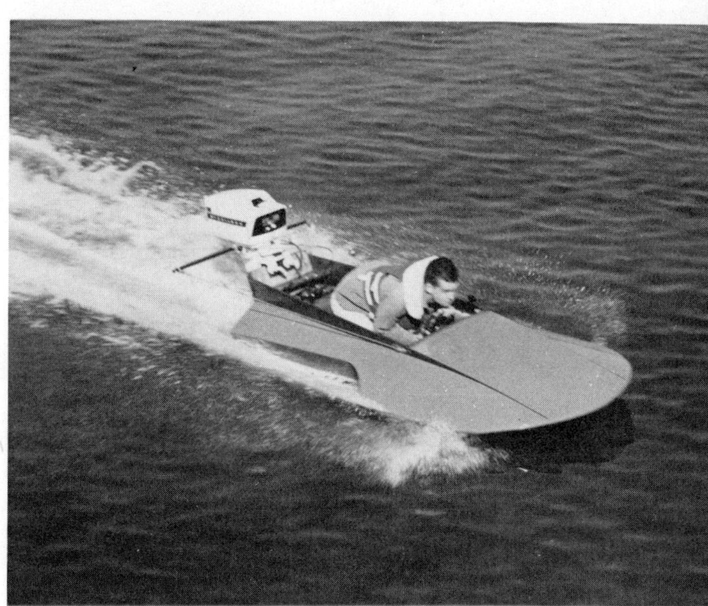

COMPACT 8′ HYDROPLANE

The Tiny Titan is an 8′, three-point hydroplane. Yes, the same type of hull that holds all of the major racing records, but of course this is a compact economy version. The Tiny Titan is especially intended for construction by the amateur builder with little or no experience. Fun and speed on a budget best characterize the Tiny Titan. For straightaway speed on the water, not much can match a three-point hydroplane. In fact, the majority of today's high-speed boat records have been set by hydros. The two sponsons or runners of the hull provide stability at high speeds, while the air rushing under the tunnel provides a lifting force. The hull is semi-supported on a cushion of air so that little, if any, of the transom is in contact with the water while the propeller digs in below. Because hydros are designed to go over the water, they're meant for use only in smooth or protected waters. A good breeze or choppy water will beat the heck out of both the boat and the driver. Plus, hydroplanes are very sensitive to weight. In order to get the best performance, you must hold down the weight, not only of the motor, but the driver, too. That means only one person per hydro. This boat is actually a compact version of a real competition hydro. Kit includes all necessary plans, detailed instructions, photos of procedures, important templates as well as assembled frames, transom, bow pieces, runner chine, deck beam, and motorboard. Plywood planking and longitudinal obtained locally to save shipping. $70. (FOB California.)

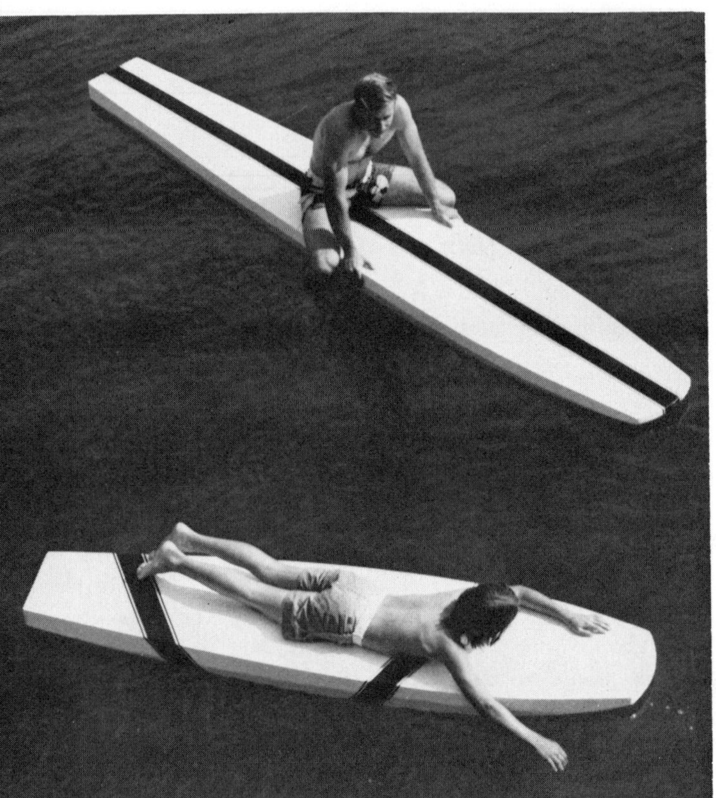

PADDLEBOARD

A fun, safe, simple, boating project. Just about anyone can build this boat. Truly nothing is left to chance. Once complete, it will bring family fun. The unit is lightweight and easily transported. It can handle good loads, up to a couple of adults. It's watertight and therefore virtually impossible to sink. Use it on any body of water or even a swimming pool. Kit includes all of the fastenings, bow pieces, transom, each of the frames, fastening schedule, bill of materials, and complete plans for construction of either the 8′ or 12′ paddleboard. All you need is a piece of plywood, available locally. $19.95.

Glen-L has a complete catalog (68 pp., $1.), which has dozens of different boats in a variety of price ranges. We strongly recommend the Glen-L catalog to anyone who is serious about boat kits.

CLARK CRAFT BOAT CO.
16 Aqua Lane
Tonawanda, N. Y. 14150

CN-112—8′ HYDRO

Sleek lines, low profile, and easy, rigid construction stand out at a glance in this three-point hydroplane. Just visualize your own hydro skipping gently over the water—riding lightly, yet with no tendency to wild running. Remarkable handling and stability with jet-like speed.

Type: Racing class
Construction: Plywood
Weight Approx.: 95 lb.
Beam: 60″
Draft: 6″
Seats: 1
Rec. Power: to 20 h.p.
Rec. Speeds: 45–55 mph

Frame Set (includes all framing material and transom framing): $110.00. Complete Kit (includes all material precut for easy assembly): $225.00. Fiberglass covering kit: $21.30. Screw and fastening kit: $13.50.

9″ TUNNEL RACER

The sleek new tunnel racer, by Clark Craft, can use any outboard engine from 7½ to 25 h.p.r. This boat has been designed with the 25 S.S. Class in mind and should qualify for this class if racing one of these smaller tunnel or hydro designs is your goal. Because of the deeper tunnel sections over the same size hydroplane, these tunnel boats are softer riding and can generally go through rougher, choppier water at higher speeds. In addition, the transom area is generally wider and can carry more weight aft. TU-9 does not set as low in the water (at rest) as some of the other hydro designs.

Complete boat kit, now available for the TU-9, includes all of the parts completely cut out and ready to assemble, all of the fastenings and screws, glue, and a complete set of building instructions.

Frame sets for the TU-9 includes the tunnel frame members only, with a full set of plans and patterns to complete the boat. Complete boat kit: $210.

16′ HURRICANE PB-26

Designed for offshore use on lake, bay, or ocean. Features exceptionally wide beam for soft riding, plus high flared sides for a dry ride. Forward deck is handsomely crowned. Exclusive Tredronic bottom design produces fine forward sections for a smooth, soft ride plus ample dead rise for carrying heavy loads at top speed. Fast and extremely maneuverable.

Boat Kit includes: All frames preassembled from select mahogany, preassembled transom reinforced with ¾″ solid mahogany framing. Rugged 1¾″ thick solid mahogany stem, completely machined and ready to set up. All other frame parts and seats precut from solid mahogany. Side and bottom planking is genuine waterproof plywood. Kit also includes all necessary screws plus complete, illustrated instructions, bedding compound, and marine glue. Complete boat kit: $375.

Length: 16′
Beam: 74″
Forward deck: 72″
Maximum hull depth: 42″
Depth forward: 31″
Depth amidship: 28″
Depth transom: 23″
Transom width (top):   59″
Transom width (waterline):   54″
Aft deck (PB-24) length: 39″
Weight (approx.):   440 lb.
Motors: to 75 h.p.
Bottom planking (plywood):   ⅜″
Side planking (plywood):   ¼″
Transom (plywood):   ¾″
Frames (mahogany):   ¾″
Assembly time: 30 hrs.

10′ PACKETTE—PB-17

A good lightweight boat, under 90 lb., that can be used as a row boat or with a small outboard motor, but primarily as an excellent sailer for the beginner. Advanced sailing skills are not required. This beamy little boat is almost impossible to capsize even in high winds due to the sail area and design of this little sailer. Boat is constructed with ¼″ waterproof plywood over mahogany frames that are included and completely preassembled. Kit for this design also includes all the fastenings, step-by-step instructions, bedding compounds, silicon bronze anchor, fast nails, and all material to assemble the boat kit completely, less paint. $110.

Length: 10′
Beam: 55″
Depth: 17″
Weight (approx.) lb.:   90
Seating: 2–3
Motor size: to 5 h.p.
Assembly time (hours):   9

8-FOOT PRAM

Basic Boat Kit only, includes plans, fiberglass materials, foam, precut seats, gunwale trim, transom stiffeners, screws, and step-by-step instructions. This dinghy is designed to exploit the latest amateur building techniques. Constructed of foam and fiberglass, this hull can be built by one person in just one weekend. Only simple tools including a saw, drill, and screwdriver are required to install the gunwales and seats. Safe for youngsters, this boat cannot sink. It is also useful as a tender to larger boats or as a trial kit to preface the construction of a larger boat on the succeeding pages. $169.

LOA: 7′6″
Beam: 3′10″
Depth: 15″
Seating: 2–3
Motor size: to 3½ h.p.

OUTBOUND HYDROPLANE

This little boat is winning many races both in the U.S. and abroad due to its extremely rugged but light construction and its ability to stay out front in slight choppy water. Complete boat kit: All batten and framing members are completely precut from either spruce or Philippine mahogany. Aft decking panels are ¼″ marine glued plywood. Forward deck is top-grade aircraft linen. Bottom panels and non-trip areas are ¼″ marine glued plywood. Lightening holes are marked only. Kit includes all anchor-fast nails of silicon bronze and screws necessary to build the boat. Glue and complete building instructions for assembly are included with this kit. All parts are completely premarked for easy assembly. $225.

Design No. CU-42
Name: Wetback
Type: Three Point Hydroplane
Construction: Plywood
Weight (approx.):   115 lb.
LOA: 9′10″
Beam: 4′
Draft: 6″
Type Bottom: Fin
Seats: 1
Rec. Power.   7–30 h.p.
Rec. Speeds up to 70 mph
Class: A, Alkie, B, or C stock

Clark Crafts offers four huge catalogs. They cover everything from plywood power boats to hydroplanes. Hundreds of pages of photos and descriptions to fascinate the craftsman or the daydreamer. The catalogs are most informative and well prepared.

TAFT MARINE CORP.
636 39 Ave. N.E.
Minneapolis, Minn. 55421

PENGUIN PRECUT BOAT KIT

A Phil Rhodes-designed racing dinghy for amateurs and experts. Light and fast—an excellent beginner's boat and a favorite of the experts for year-round racing summer series to frostbiting. Popular with man-wife teams as the light weight permits easy transportation on a light trailer or cartop. All frame parts, rails, etc., made from spruce selected from large stock of spar materials. Weight can be held to 134 lb. with mahogany planking (fir planking, 4½ lb. additional). Price (freight included): $274. Mahogany planking: $15 additional. Sail kits for the Penguin are available for $45.

DN ICE YACHT

Since the development by the Armed Forces of comfortable winter clothing, many Americans in the northern states are enjoying the exciting sport of ice boating.

Taft Marine has chosen one of the most popular-class ice boats to offer in kit form. The DN single-class frequently attains speeds of over 80 mph.

There is an instruction book included with this model boat kit. It is available to prospective customers for a mailing cost of $1. (refunded with kit order). Good idea—gives you a chance to determine the clarity of instructions and procedures before purchasing the kit for $149. (Purchase price includes all wood, screws, glue, semi-finished runner plank, mast, and boom).

16′ CATAMARAN

The latest addition to the Taft line of kits is this 16′ Catamaran. It has 120 sq. ft. main sail and optional 48 sq. ft. jib. This carefully designed boat has asymmetrical hulls in order to eliminate the troublesome centerboard. It will daysail four people. Fast, sporty, good looking. All-glass kit form. Complete kit (less jib, vang, trapeze): $870.

SNIPE BOAT KIT

The Snipe was designed in 1931 by Wm. F. Crosby for publication in *Rudder* magazine. Many Snipe fans boast that it's the best all-around small racing craft in existence. This kit does not require any extra jigs or frames and has been assembled for painting in as little as thirty hours (we won't tell if it takes you thirty-two hours). Your Snipe may be registered for national or local competition by applying to SIRA, 655 Weber Ave., Akron, Ohio 44720, after the boat is ready for planking.

Complete kit includes precut wood parts, semi-finished mast and boom, aluminum dagger board, fastenings, and glue (sails, running and deck hardware, shrouds, and halyards not included). $460. (freight included).

8′ PRAM

Primarily designed as a boy's boat, it can also be used as a tender or auto-top boat. The ample beam makes a safe toy for children and will support two adults. This sailing dinghy version makes an excellent sailer for the beginner and includes all parts,

hardware, pulleys, traveler, rudder, pintles, gudgeons, etc. $79. (freight included).

This company offers a wide selection of equipment, accessories, and replacement parts in kit form. Write for their booklet, "America's Finest Boat Kits," for a complete description.

LUGER INDUSTRIES, INC.
3800 West Highway 12
Burnsville, Minn. 55338

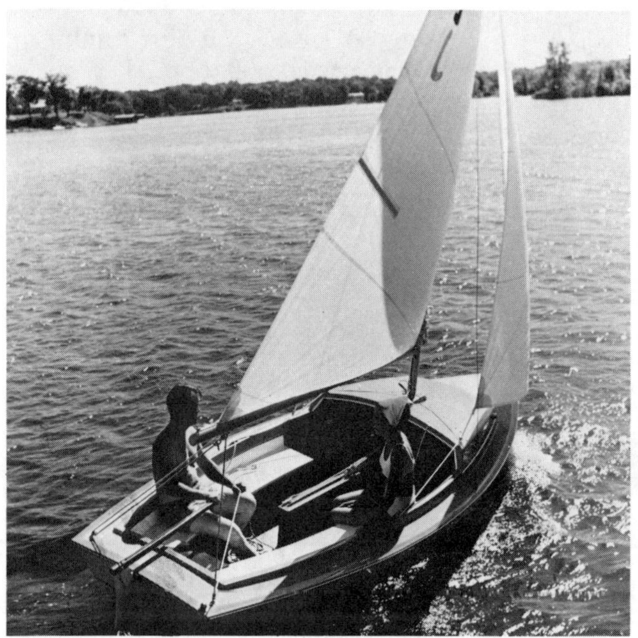

16′ SAILING SLOOP

The 16′ Leeward Sailing Sloop features an all-fiberglass hull and deck, as well as molded fiberglass seats, centerboard well, and shelter cabin. If you can use simple tools and are handy around the house, then you have the ability to assemble this day sailer . . . according to the manufacturer. All the guesswork is eliminated, and your kit comes to you with detailed step-by-step assembly instructions. Featuring clean lines and that factory showroom look, this boat kit is unconditionally guaranteed by the manufacturer and complies fully with the requirements of the U.S. Coast Guard (when assembled in accordance with the manufacturer's instructions). Savings of about 50% over comparable boats in this class that have been factory-finished. The construction, design, and materials are made from exactly the same quality, type, and kind as are used in top-quality, factory-finished boats. The key ingredient is supplied by you—the labor—and by doing so, you can own a boat to be proud of, and at far below the price of a factory-finished boat. Kit price includes: All molded fiberglass sections—deck, cabin top, seats, centerboard well, transom, hull sides and bottom; mast and boom with all standing rigging; rudder, centerboard, all internal hull reinforcing members, fasteners, fiberglass bonding, and instructions needed to complete boat. The "Leeward," priced at $1,000, comes complete with all sails, rigging, etc., and will accommodate up to six people.

22′ SPORT-FISHERMAN

Not a luxury boat, but well designed and a good performer. The Luger's 22′ Newport is specifically designed for owners who want a safe, stable, rugged deep water offshore boat for sport fishing combined with modest cruising accommodations. Perhaps a little more of a challenge to build, but still within the capabilities of the "Handy Man." Available with flush deck cockpit, it has plenty of room for fishing gear and deck chairs, and a live bait well can be installed under the cockpit flooring. If you have a yen for deep water fishing, the Newport can supply the means. It trailers easily at normal speeds, loads and launches quickly. Options include a convertible top (which with side curtains and camper stern cover fully enclose the cockpit) or a windshield kit, with factory-machined and precut solid mahogany frame parts. $1,780.

21′ SAILING SLOOP—THE WINDWARD

This trim craft offers leisure-time sailors the opportunity to take a "cruising summertime vacation." It sleeps four, and has a convertible dinette that seats two or more. The unique cabin design, which utilizes the full width of the hull, provides for generously proportioned interior living accommodations. Once again, this Luger boat kit provides sailors with an opportunity to own a boat above their normal pocketbook reach by assembling a tried and proven boat kit. All you need is common sense, and average around-the-house skills to assemble this professionally designed craft. Explicit instructions in simple language will lead you step by step to completion. No special tools are required, and age is no barrier. Indeed, many sailors who could easily afford to buy expensive factory-finished boats elect to build their own because of the self-satisfaction achieved.

The Windward is available with options in retracting centerboards, an optional swing keel, and an optional fixed fin keel. Additional pluses: roomy cockpit, storage compartment, foredeck hatch, cabin entrance hatchway, and molded fiberglass cabin hatch. With patience and a careful following of the manufacturer's instructions, not even your best friends will know that it's "home-built" unless you elect to tell them. Length, Gunwale: 21′, Waterline: 17′6″. Width, Beam: 84″ (max.). Draft, with centerboard up: 9″, down, 61″. With swing keel up: 22′, down, 61″. Headroom, in cabin: 51″, above quarter berth: 39″, above forward berth: 33″. Cockpit seat to boom: 42″, cockpit well to boom: 54″. Height, waterline to top of mast: 28′. Ballast: with No. 1494 Economy centerboard: 400 lb. (inside hull). With No. 1489 Deluxe centerboard: 240 lb. (inside hull). With No. 1495 Swing Keel: none. Displacement (weight): with centerboards or swing keel: approx. 1550 lb. when ballasted as above. Mast length: 24′6″. Boom length: 11′. Area: mainsail, 134 sq. ft. Working jib: 66 sq. ft. Total area: 200 sq. ft. Area, Genoa jib sail: 102 sq. ft. Max. load capacity (B.I.A.): 2300 lb. (properly located total weight of all persons and gear). Assembly time: 60 to 85 hours. Internal hull reinforcing: precut fir plywood, solid oak. Fasteners: all screws, bolts, etc., stainless steel or brass. Colors: all molded fiberglass sections furnished in standard white. Thickness of molded fiberglass sections: varies from approx. 3/16″ to approx. 3/8″ as required for strength and sound design. Rudder construction: fiberglass with plywood core—can be assembled to be fixed (with quick, no-tools-needed removal) or to "Tip-up." Mast and Boom: polished anodized aluminum. Boom has roller reefing. Standing rigging: stainless steel. Hardware: pulleys, mooring cleats, bow eye for trailering, stay adjusters, etc.—stainless steel, brass, or aluminum. Auxiliary Power: recommended 1½ to 10 h.p. outboard mounted on Luger Hi-Lo Motor Mount No. 10102. Shipping data: sturdy wood framed, cardboard lined, steel-strapped crate measures 22′ × 18′ × 72″, weighs 1,150 lb. If necessary, to facilitate handling on delivery, crate may be opened, parts removed and handled individually by 1 to 3 persons. Kit price includes: All molded fiberglass sections—hull bottom, sides, transom, cockpit, bulkhead, cabin top and hatches; factory-machined and precut internal hull reinforcing members, all other parts required for cockpit well and cabin interior, aluminum mast and boom, standing rigging, rudder, tiller, all screws, fasteners, fiberglass bonding materials, instructions—everything needed to assemble and complete boat as pictured except bow rail, stern rail, and life lines. $2,300.

Luger claims to be the largest manufacturer of boat kits in the world. Your Luger kit comes complete in every detail; nothing needs to be purchased on the outside. The manual for each Luger boat is profusely illustrated with drawings that provide an immediately understandable picture of each assembly step. We are impressed with their good pricing. The complete catalog (22 pp., free) is well designed and most informative.

CANADIAN MULTIHULL SERVICES

2, Thorncliffe Park Dr., Unit 47
Toronto
Ontario, Canada

POLYNESIAN CATAMARAN

James Wharram designed the Polynesian Catamaran because he rejected the city and sought a new life-style; he returned to the sea, sailing his catamaran on four Atlantic crossings. The ancient Polynesians voyaged on their catamarans over a period of 1,000 years. Mr. Wharram seized upon this ancient vessel, studied and designed it for present-day use, and now offers you the joy of sailing a catamaran.

A variety of kits are offered starting at $250. Literature is free. It might be a good idea to send for it and put it into storage for that Monday morning when you can't quite get it "together" for another day in the office!

SEMPLE ENGINE CO., INC.

Box 8354
St. Louis, Mo. 63124

SEMPLE STEAM ENGINES

The romance of the old steam-powered river boats plying the waters can now be yours with the installation of Semple Steam Power in your launch or houseboat up to 35′ in length. Wood or coal is always available, even in the remotest areas, and is much more economical than liquid fuels. Steam boating is safe, dependable, economical—but above all, fun.

Semple engine kits are complete; you need nothing else. Many other kits contain castings only. In addition, they machine the two parts which require elaborate setups and would be a problem in the home shop. They mill and bore the bearing pockets on the base and drill and mill the spiral reverse cam on DL engines. 95% of the remaining work can be done on a 10″ lathe and drill press. Drawings are thorough to the finest detail. All tolerances are clearly indicated. However, should a problem arise, their engineering department is at your service.

Five Horsepower (single), No. 34 = DW 3″ × 4″, wheel reverse. Kit includes: 10 iron castings, 1 steel casting, 7 aluminum castings, 5 ball bearings, 2 lubricators—109 parts total—1 assembly drawing, 2 parts drawing, parts list with matching and assembly instructions. $256.

OSCO MOTORS CORP.

Souderton, Pa. 18964

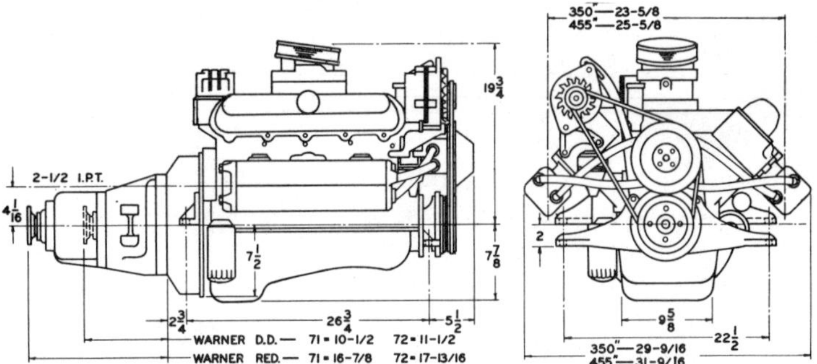

OLDSMOBILE V-8 MARINE CONVERSION KIT

Complete kit for conversion to marine engine includes marine exhaust, manifold, pump accessory and outlet plate, water lines and fittings, front engine supports, vee belt and lifting rings. One-year warranty. $245.20.

More than a dozen engine conversion kits, transmission kits (housing, dive plate, transmission, shaft coupling, supports), and hardware as well as oil cooler and oil line fittings for automatic transmissions (price range: $300. to $500.), hardware, and other marine accessories (instrument panels, propellers, etc.).

STOKES MARINE INDUSTRIES

Coldwater, Mich. 49036

COMPLETE MARINE CONVERSION KIT

Kits are available for most engines including current-year models. Everything is included: manifolds, motor mounts, rubber impeller marine water pump, water fittings, belt, back-fire trap, and all necessary bolts and nuts. Nothing more to buy. To order a conversion kit, send year, model, and displacement of engine information. It is suggested that you include a template of the manifold or a manifold gasket to avoid possible error. Typical prices: Buick V-8: $320. Chevrolet V-8-265-283-327-350: $240. Ford Falcon 6: $210. Ford Fairlane 500: $260.

Marine engines and equipment, manifolds, adapters, and diesel conversion kits.

RICKBORN FLYING BRIDGES

175 Atlantic City Blvd.
Bayville, N.J. 08721

THE MARK TEN FLYING BRIDGE

A flying bridge is a second command station placed

atop a boat. A good bridge is one that is comfortable, large enough to contain the necessary equipage, and will accommodate the operator and a guest or two within the command area. It should also be of a size that will look well and still be small enough to keep the sail area to a minimum.

The Mark Ten is the most popular and comfortable bridge offered by the company. It was designed for 33′ to 40′ cruisers and houseboats. Complete bridge pre-equipped, ready to install, includes the following equipment: flying bridge, storm rails, windscreen, tower tube, complete steering gear, shift and throttle control head, control cables with connectors to lower station, instrument panel, wiring harness with temperature and oil sending units, stainless steel ladder, standard stainless steel deck railing set, stainless steel constellation steering wheel, heavy-duty vinyl bridge cover, snaps riveted to the bridge, and complete installation instructions. You'll save $450. by installing the bridge yourself. Single engine: $1989. Twin engine: $2,244.

Rickborn offers over seven other flying bridges with a good selection of accessories. Literature is free. However, we recommend Commodore Rickborn's manual, "How to Install a Flying Bridge" ($4.50). Established company. Excellent literature.

ARCO MANUFACTURING, INC. OF RACINE

1501 Clark St.
Racine, Wis. 53403

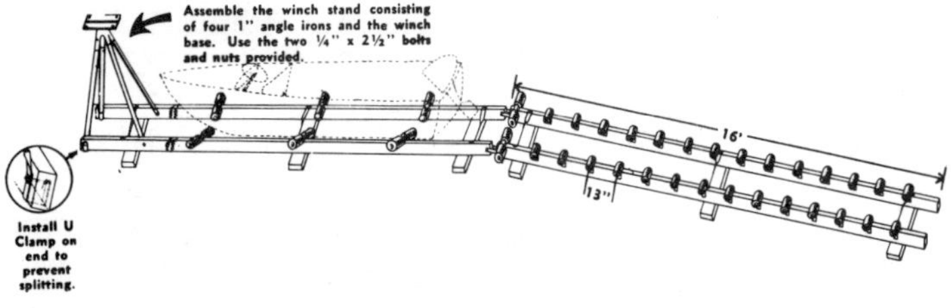

HEAVY-DUTY BOAT RAMP KIT

Sold in two sections: Upper section includes rollers, wrench, stands, steel side braces. Lower section, heavy-duty single rollers, dual tilt rollers, steel tie plates, and side braces. You must supply lumber (2 × 6's recommended for rails). Construction is straightforward. Of course, a boat ramp does not have to consist of two sections. Some people use only the upper section to beach their boat on an incline rather than take it out of the water or tie it up to the dock. Some need two or more lower sections with one upper section to get their boat up on shore. Upper section kit: $58. Lower section kit: $129.

Several styles of boat ramps and dock assembly equipment.

SUPERCRAFT PRODUCTS

6 Cross St.
Monticello, N.Y. 12701

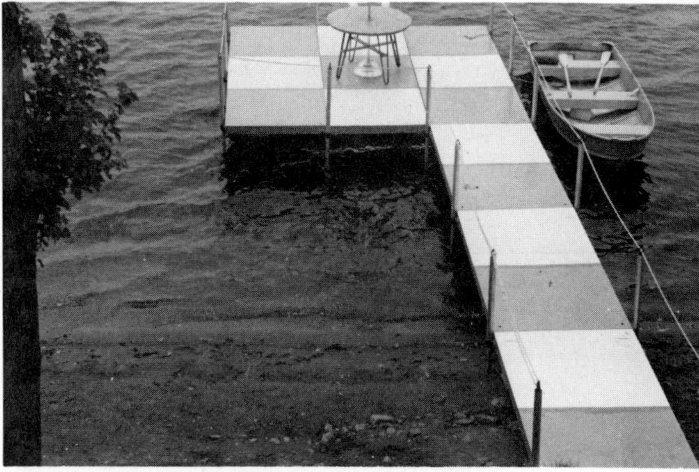

PORTABLE SECTIONAL DOCKS

Simple, nonfloating docks that utilize ordinary plumber's pipe. Assembly is fairly straightforward and manufacturer claims it can even be installed in tidal waters (write for further information). Almost any conceivable shape dock can be constructed for the modular units. Typical prices: 3′ × 8′ module, $69.80. 5′ × 8′ module, $95.25. Dock base brackets, $9.75 pair. Ladder, $42.50 each.

Several options on dock kits are available, including floating docks using 55 gal. drums (not included). A typical 4-section unit (10′ x 10′), which would utilize 6 drums, runs $288. Special sizes or requirements for marinas and docks can be arranged with the company. Write for catalog (free).

ALAN-CLARKE CO.

235 Main St.
Northport, N.Y. 11768

SAIL KITS

Once he has procured a sailboat hull, the owner's most important decision is selecting the sails. The kits below are made up of the core items necessary to construct a sail. In most cases, additional items will be necessary to complete your sail. There is so much variety among most boats that it is best to leave certain fittings out of the kits and let the purchaser select these items individually.

MAIN AND MIZZEN SAIL KITS

All kits include a 4-oz. spool of Dacron thread, a book of instructions, a 1-oz. spool of low twist Dacron thread for hand sewing; and several sail needles. Include a sketch of your sail so that enough bolt rope is included with your kit.

Sq. Ft.	Wt. of Cloth (Dacron)	Amt. of Cloth	Size Rings 2 (tack, clew)	Size hdbd. (Flat Alum.)	Diam. Bolt Rope (Spun Dacron)	price
40	3 oz.	17 yd.	#3	#0	1/4"	$ 31.50
100	3.8 oz.	14 yd.	#4	#1	5/16"	58.00
150	5 oz.	20 yd.	#5	#2	5/16"	88.00
200	6.5 oz.	27 yd.	#6	#3	3/8"	135.00

JIB AND GENOA SAIL KITS

All kits include a 4-oz. spool of Dacron thread, a book of instructions ("Make Your Own Sails" by Howker and Budd), a 1-oz. spool of low twist Dacron thread for hand sewing, and several sail needles. Include a sketch of your sail so that enough Vinyl covered stainless steel wire is included with your kit.

Sq. Ft.	Wt. of Cloth	Amt. of Cloth	Size of Rings (clew tack/head)		Diam. of Luff Wire	Price
30	3 oz.	5 yd.	#4	#2	3/32"	$ 27.00
70	3.8 oz.	10 yd.	#5	#3	3/32"	45.00
110	4.5 oz.	15 yd.	#5	#3	1/8"	68.00
190	6.5 oz.	26 yd.	#9	#5	5/32"	140.00

SAILRITE KITS

2010 Lincoln Blvd.
Venice, Calif. 90291

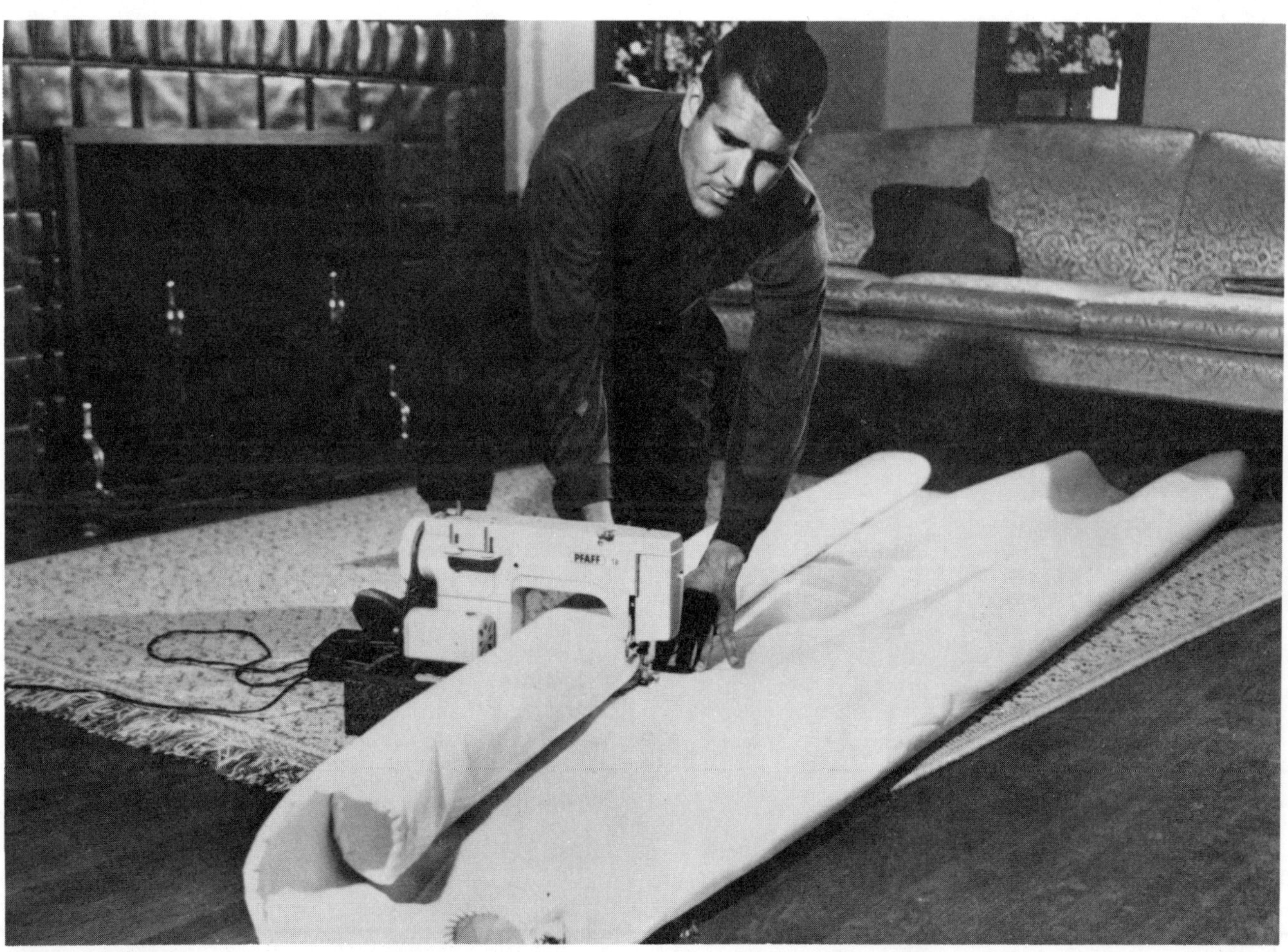

SAIL COVER

Make your own fine quality, custom-crafted sail cover. All thread, material, and hardware is included. The covers can be fashioned with any home sewing machine. Two kit sizes are available: one for booms of less than 10.5', and one for booms to 16'. Both Dacron and acrylic cover cloth are available in white or blue. Prices range from $22.89 to $32.81 for the smaller kit, and from $37.70 to $50.66 for the larger one, depending upon cloth selection.

It is now possible to build your own racing sails with Sailrite Kits. Everything is included: fine Dacron or nylon cloth, Dacron thread, needles, wax, hardware, etc. Portable sewing machines are perfectly adequate for sail making when the procedures outlined in four manuals covering the construction of jibsails, spinnakers and staysails, stormsails, and mainsails are followed.

The Amateur Sailmaker's Catalogue *from Sailrite Kits lists over 100 sail kits for boats to 35' LOA:*

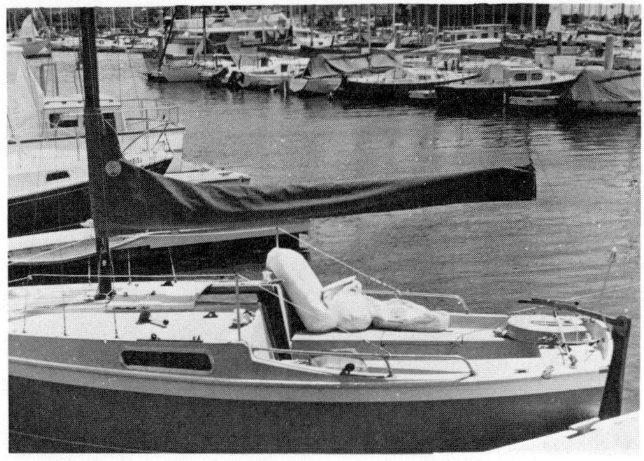

OTHER SOURCES

Arcmarine Corp.
2370 North Flower St.
Santa Ana, Calif. 92706

Kit to convert your trailer or camper into a houseboat. Package includes two fiberglass hulls with engine wells and transoms for single or twin engines and 12′ ×26′ deck. Information packet (free).

Arco Mfg. Co., Inc.
P.O. Box 817
1701 13th Ave. North
Grand Forks, N.D. 58201

Inboard and outboard boat ramp kits. Information (free).

E.R. Butler & Sons
25 Mugford St.
P.O. Box 123
Marblehead, Mass. 01945

No experience necessary to assemble these simple prams and day sailers. Clear out the garage for a mere two weekends and start putting the pieces together. Happy boating. Catalog (free).

Champion Boats of California
13076 Saticoy St.
North Hollywood, Calif. 91605

Selection of eleven different models of racing boat kits. Information (50¢).

W.M. Cookson
James Wharram Designs
1553 Armacost
Los Angeles, Calif. 90025

Offers catamaran kits modeled after ancient Polynesian sailing crafts. Catalog ($2.).

Dak Hydrofoils
P.O. Box 71
Sausalito, Calif. 94965

Aluminum hydrofoil kits for catamarans. Information (free).

Duster Sailplane Kits
P.O. Box 1261
San Pedro, Calif. 90732

Designed especially for the home builder, Duster offers complete glider kits that can be assembled quickly. Brochure (free).

Easterly Yachts
Div. Scheyd-Brennan, Inc.
1729 Lake
Box 9104
Metairie, La. 70005

Two complete racing cruising sloop kits, both with fiberglass hulls. Information (free).

Folboat Corp.
Stark Industrial Park
P.O. Box 7097
Charleston, S.C. 29405

Offers very easy-to-assemble prefab canoe, kayak, outboard, runabout, and day sailer kits. School and institution discounts. Catalog (free).

High Performance Products, Inc.
25 Industrial Park Rd.
Higham, Mass. 02043

Kayak and canoe kits designed by Toni Prijon and Klaus Lettmann often found amongst the winners in whitewater competition. Catalog (free).

Huck Finn, Inc.
8333 Sunset Rd., N.E.
Minneapolis, Minn. 55432

Your choice of 17′ to 42′ pontoon boat kits that assemble easily. Wood decking materials not included. Literature (free).

Kenner Boat Co.
Box 16
Knoxville, Ark. 72845

A number of interesting fiberglass sailboat kits.

Lehman Mfg. Co. Inc.
800 East Elizabeth Avenue
Linden, N.J. 07036

Want to adapt your automotive engine to marine use? "Marine Power," the catalog put out by Lehman, describes various kits with step-by-step procedures. The engines they feature were selected because of their easy economical and seaworthy convertability and their dependability in marine work.

Quicksilver Boats
249 Warfield Ave.
Venice, Fla. 33595

Small boat kits including: canoes, kayaks, and skiffs. Separate kits for sails. Catalog (free).

Quicksilver Canoes
115 McGavock Pike
Nashville, Tenn. 37214

Canoe and kayak kit.

Riverside Fiberglass Canoe Co.
P.O. Box 5595
Riverside, Calif. 92507

Wood and fiberglass kits for a fine duck boat.

Rotocast Products, Inc.
6700 N.W. 36 Ave.
Miami, Fla. 33147

Pontoon boat kits made of high-density polyethylene material. All necessary hardware included. Information (free).

Sailing Kit Kraft
Box 13247
St. Petersburg, Fla. 33733

Catalog (free) of interesting kits on a variety of boats from a 22′ ($3,000.) to a 41′ ($18,000.). All about half the price of a stock boat.

Samson Marine Design Ltd.
540 Minoru Blvd.
Richmond, Vancouver, B.C. Canada

The above company offers designs and fitting kits for home boat builders. At present, over 4,000 boats are being built to their designs and they are supplying the fitting kits to many of these builders. Details and specifications would have to be worked out directly with them.

Seafarer Fiberglass Yachts, Inc.
760 Park Ave.
Huntington, N.Y. 11743

Well-designed fiberglass sailing kits. Kits also available for sailing and rowing dinghies. Company offers to complete the kit for you if you get stuck in the middle. Catalog (free).

Spencer Amphibian Air Car
8725 Oland Ave.
Sun Valley, Calif. 91352

Kit to build four-passenger amphibian. First of its kind. Information package ($4.).

Spencer Boats, Ltd.
1240 Twiggs Rd.
Richmond, B.C. Canada

Fiberglass molded sailboat kits. Catalog (free).

Tri-Star Trimarans
P.O. Box 286
Venice, Calif. 90291

18′ to 65′ trimaran kits designed by naval architect Ed Horstman. Plywood construction. Catalog ($3.).

Vadnestadt & McGruer, Ltd.
Box 7
Owen Sound, Ontario, Canada

Day sailer kit. Brochure (free).

Yacht Craftsmen
1682 Placentia Ave.
Costa Mesa, Calif. 92627

Save 50% on a top-quality proven fiberglass cruising yacht by leading designers such as Lapworth, Crealock, and McGlasson. Low initial outlay. You buy kits (hull and deck kit, ballast kit, rigging kit, etc.) as you progress. 24′ up to 44′. Detailed instructions and full-sized templates.

How long have men been flying? In their imaginations, since the beginning of time. Roger Bacon proposed the hot air balloon in about 1250. Leonardo da Vinci, in the early 1500s, made extensive notes and drawings about the possibilities of human flight, including the design of what is now the helicopter. When lighter-than-air hydrogen was discovered in the 18th century, the means to make balloon flight practical had arrived. And, with the internal combustion engine came the power to keep aloft heavier-than-air craft.

On December 17, 1903, at Kitty Hawk, N.C., Wilbur and Orville Wright made the first true airplane flight. Since that time, less than seventy-five years ago, we have seen that little rickety airplane metamorphose into such miracles as the supersonic jet and the moon rocket. In fact, we may have just about reached the limit of how fast we can fly without doing damage to our planet and its atmosphere.

But we certainly haven't exhausted the recreational and personal possibilities of aircraft. Ballooning and gliding are coming into their own these days for people who want to fly for the pure joy of the thing. Personal airplanes are popular as never before among hobbyists and travelers.

Can you really build an airplane from a kit? Yes, you can, or a glider or a balloon. It's not quite as easy as making a model airplane from a kit, but then, a model airplane won't fly you to Chicago. For anyone who wants or needs to fly, building your own aircraft is something to consider seriously. When you're finished, you'll have an intimate knowledge of flying that you could hardly get any other way.

BENSEN AIRCRAFT CORP.

P.O. Box 2746
Raleigh-Durham Airport
Raleigh, N.C. 27602

BENSEN GYROCOPTER

You need it. If you don't already have a mini-helicopter that parks in your garage, you can get kits in varying degrees of semi-completion. Basic kit ($1,899.) to Deluxe kit ($2,385.). Needless to say, you should discuss amount of work involved with the distributor before purchasing.

The power is a 72 h.p. McCulloch engine capable of speeds up to 80 mph. Capable of gliding without power, the Gyrocopter is therefore a safe machine to fly, even for beginning pilots. The Bensen Gyrocopter is included in the National Air Museum of the Smithsonian Institution in Washington.

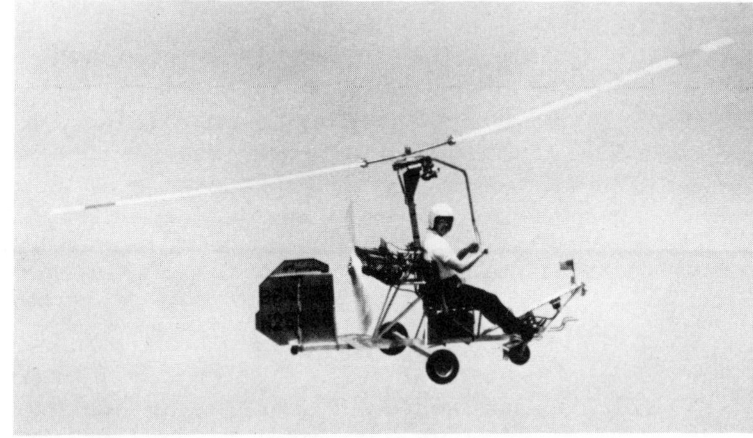

Bensen will also sell you a gyroglider or hydroglider (pulled by motor boat), plans for installation of a VW or other engine, or if you must have a joystick-type control system, plans for this modification.

STOLP STARDUSTER CORP.

4301 Twining, Flabob Airport
Riverside, Calif. 92509

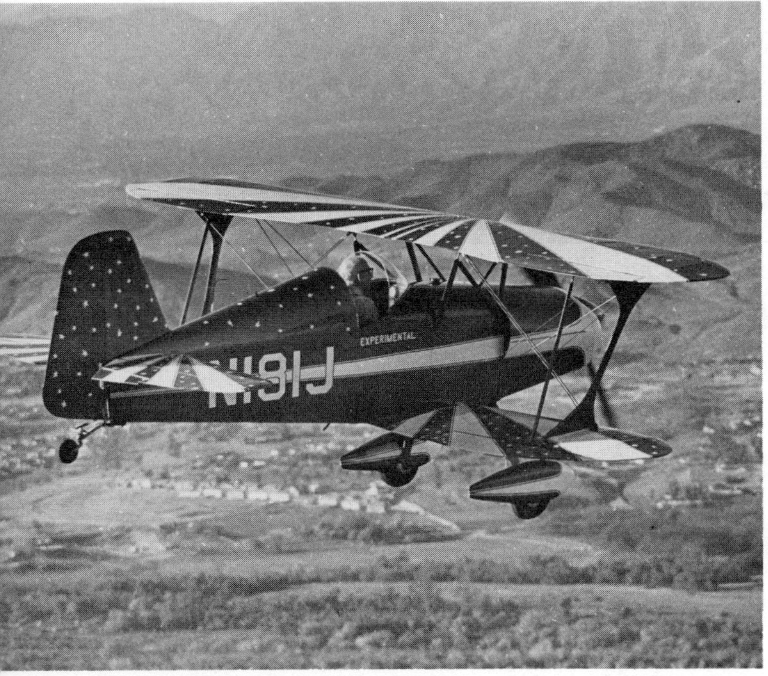

ACRODUSTER I SA700

Designed for unlimited aerobatic competition. It is also a nice sport plane when powered by 125–160 h.p. engines.

The prototype is powered by a 200 h.p. Lycoming, with a Hartzell C/S aerobatic prop. It also has a full electrical system. Empty weight of the prototype is 906 lb. With no electrical system, and a fixed pitch prop, weight would be around 740 lb. Prototype preformance is spectacular. It has a guaranteed roll rate of 240° per second. Time to climb from brake release to 300′ is one minute and 20 seconds, indicated crusing speed is 160 mph at 24-24, power off stall speed is around 75 mph.

Handling characteristics are superb. It has no detectable adverse yaw or left turning tendency. The ailerons are effective all the way through a stall. It spins easily and recovers easily, upright or inverted. Vision over the nose is good. It lands easily and tracks straight ahead. The rudder is effective throughout the roll out.

It can be built easily and quickly, with the complete materials package available from Starduster. The aluminum fuselage skins are sheared to size, and all straight flanges are bent. Landing gear, fuel tank, and motor mount are furnished ready to install. Everything you need to build the airframe, except for engine and propeller, is included. Materials kit: $4,000. With engine: $4,500.

BEDE AIRCRAFT, INC.

Newton Municipal Airport
Newton, Kans. 67114

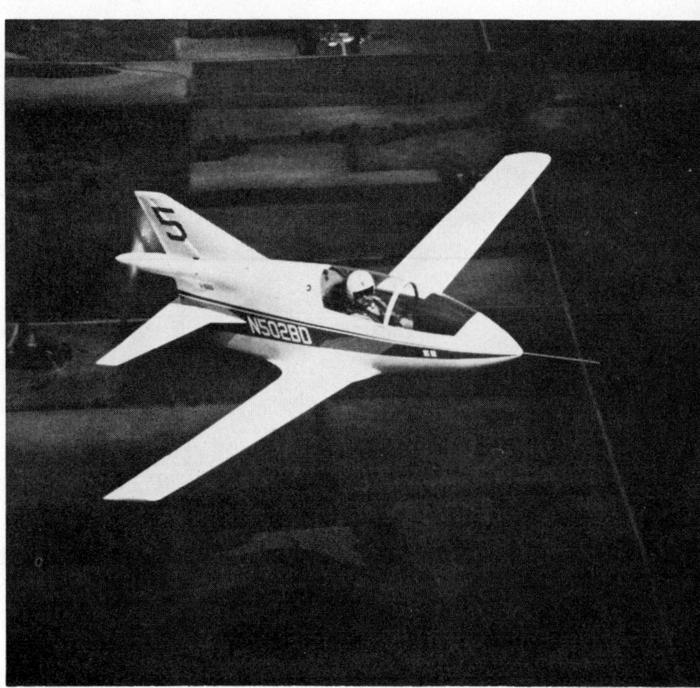

BD-5 AIRCRAFT

BD-5 is a very small aircraft designed to be the optimum configuration to transport a single person comfortably. Every aerodynamic feature known today that could minimize drag, improve speed, climb, range, and takeoff are incorporated in the BD-5. Its cruising speeds are quite fast. But this is not at the sacrifice of stall speeds, which govern the takeoff and landing performance. The wing loading for the BD-5A is comparable to high-performance, single-engine airplanes such as Beech Bonanzas and Cessna 210s. The stalling speeds and therefore approach speeds are comparable. With the BD-5B, which has the longer wings, the wing loading is reduced further. With this configuration, the wing loading is comparable to Cherokee 180s, Beech Musketeers, and Cessna Cardinals. Again, the stalling speeds and approach speeds are similar to these aircraft.

When we compare cruising speeds, however, the BD-5 leaves all the rest behind. Speed is not the only good feature of the BD-5. It is highly maneuverable. It is fully aerobatic. It can perform the simplest and most complicated maneuvers flown. The cruising range, the miles per gallon, the service ceiling, and all other performance figures are quite good. They either equal or exceed other light planes in most every area. The BD-5 has performance in exactly the same way a modern small sports car has performance in its operation.

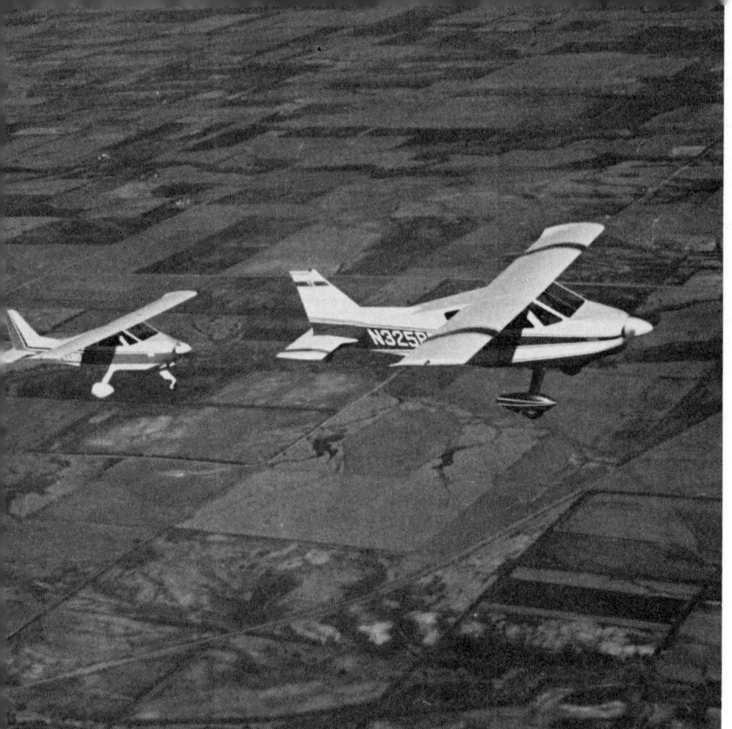

BD-4 AIRCRAFT

This is an extremely popular entry into the home-built aircraft. Some quotes (below) from their catalog explain Bede's point of view and what you can expect in their kits. The plane is constructed of metal and fiberglass and can be built either as a two- or a four-place aircraft.

> Although the BD-4 was engineered to meet or exceed (often by a wide margin) the structural requirements for certified aircraft as specified by the FAA in FAR-Part 23, it is not certified and is intended only for construction and operation as an amateur-built airplane.

> ... We feel that a builder who is fairly capable with hand tools and who uses the plans and prepackaged materials might construct a BD-4 in as little as 900 man-hours. The average will probably be around 1,200 hours. This is still pretty spectacular when you consider that most two-place homebuilts require 3600 to 4800 hours for their fabrication. Whereas, two to five—or even seven—years of spare time labor is required to put most amateur-built airplanes into the air, the BD-4 can be constructed in as little as six months.

> There are some welded parts in the BD-4, but there are not very many and they are all small. Any qualified welding shop in your area will be able to fabricate them for you. The whole fuselage is welded together on many homebuilts and this requires the construction of a complicated jig and the pur-chase of expensive welding equipment. By contrast, all the welded items in the BD-4 can be held at one time by one man. You will find it easy to "farm out" this part of your BD-4 and we will help you locate a good welder if you cannot find one. Eventually, we will be able to supply all welded parts refinished.

Complete Kit (less engine): $3,975.

The May 1973 issue of Playboy *has an article about Bill Bede and his plan for producing an "aeronautical Volkswagen." His vision of a private plane that can compete with other modes of transportation in terms of price seems a little strange right now (who would like to prepare the environmental impact statement for a world with a sky full of BD-5's?), but as an inexpensive start for the real enthusiast, this may be a great breakthrough.*

SCHWEIZER AIRCRAFT CORP.
P.O. Box 147
Elmira, N.Y. 14902

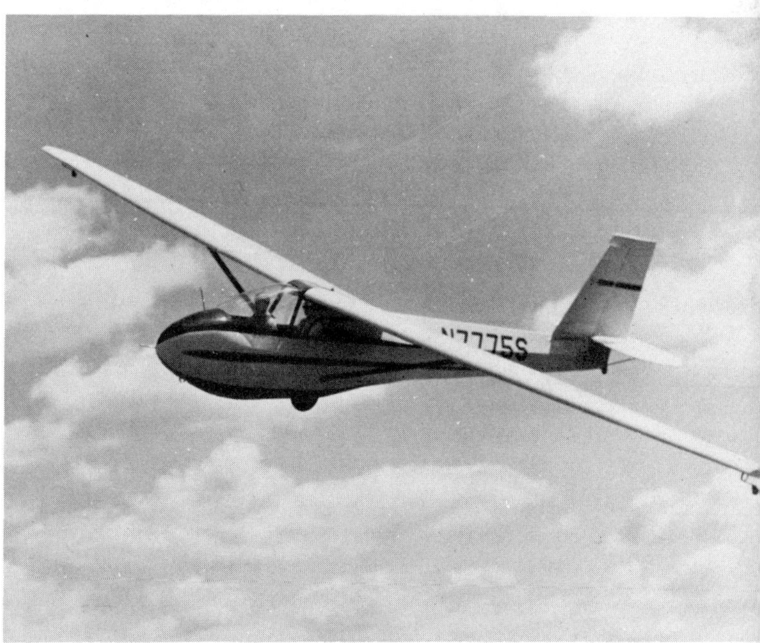

SAILPLANE

Schweizer Aircraft was the first company in America to design and produce a two-place sailplane for student instruction (the SGS 2-8). Before that, training was carried on in single-place gliders. With the advent of dual instruction, standardized training procedures were developed which produced better pilots more quickly and safely.

The 2-33 was developed from the 2-22, which was the first 2-place sailplane specifically designed for clubs and commercial schools. It quickly was recognized as the standard trainer throughout the United States and Canada. The 2-22 played a very important role in the popularity and growth of North American soaring. Many of America's top soaring pilots took their first soaring flight in a 2-22.

The 2-33 is a very worthy successor. Its new features and outstanding flight characteristics made it an instant success. More than 200 were delivered in the first four years.

The 2-33 was developed to provide even greater all-around soaring satisfaction for its occupants, whether they are an instructor and student, or a pilot taking a member of his family for a soaring flight or introducing a friend to the sport. The comfort of the 2-33 cockpit for both pilot and passenger combined with the excellent flight and handling characteristics assures enjoying two-place soaring to the fullest extent.

One of the basic requirements for a sailplane used in training is that it be strong, tough, and easy to maintain. All the components of the 2-33 are constructed of the commercial aircraft steel and aluminum alloys for structural integrity and durability. The 2-33 is designed and built from the ground up to provide the most soaring with the least maintenance for years of service.

The ruggedness and strength of the 2-33 starts with the welded chrome-moly steel tube fuselage and horizontal surfaces. These components are corrosion-proofed with zinc chromate and then covered with Ceconite fabric finished with aircraft dope and enamel. Most of the fuselage features a fiberglass fairing. The wings and vertical surfaces are of all-aluminum construction, including the surface skins. The aluminum frame rudder is Ceconite-covered.

The 2-33 AK Sailplane is now available as a new FAA-approved construction kit. It was specifically developed in response to requests from clubs, technical and vocational schools, and air youth groups.

The 2-33 AK kit, with its composite aircraft construction, is ideally suited for an interesting and rewarding do-it-yourself project or an instructional program for training in aircraft techniques. In either case, the final product is a dual-control sailplane that will take its place on the flight line as an ideal trainer or two-place fun sailplane.

While the price of the 2-33 kit is approximately 80% of the complete model, the lower cost was not the deciding factor in its development. Its greatest initial value is that it can provide the basis for an extremely interesting and rewarding aircraft construction program. One that can provide both education and experience in aircraft construction and a finished product ideally suited for a flight training program. Prices are now being finalized for the new kit. Write for complete details.

BUSHBY AIRCRAFT, INC.
Route 1, Box 13B
Minooka, Ill. 60447

MIDGET MUSTANG

This is the Midget Mustang originally designed by David Long as a high-performance, all-metal sport plane, but incorporating construction changes designed for the home builder. These changes include standardization of materials to make use of the new alloys readily available, and construction simplification. The Midget Mustang's 9-G structural strength and low-power loading give a true high-performance, fully aerobatic sport plane, as well as fast cruise speed for cross-country flying. The cabin size of the Mustang will accommodate persons up to 6'2" and 200 lb.

Techniques developed during fifteen years of Midget Mustang construction make this aircraft the simplest-to-build design available to the home builder today. There are no complicated fittings or parts that the home builder would not be able to fabricate without special tools; no machine work is required. By the use of two simple wood jigs it is possible to build the Midget Mustang without any exacting hole matching or blind riveting. The Mustang design is such as to make all rivets available for riveting in the conventional manner. Total construction cost (excluding engine) can be kept to *less than $1,200.* if judgment is exercised in purchasing materials. All construction materials used are standard aircraft or commercial items. Labor for construction of the Midget Mustang by a person of average mechanical ability is approximately 100 man-hours.

Equipment needed for construction in addition to the normal hand tools includes the following: rivet gun and sets, cleco skin fasteners, air compressor, tin snips, and availability of 8' capacity sheet metal bending brake. The bending brake is usually available at the local furnace or sheet-metal shop. The air compressor required can be a simple ¼ h.p-type capable of 60 lb. pressure, with small volume output. Basic kit: $650.

MAG-AERO, INC.
P.O. Box 181
Lyons, Wis. 53148

ACRO-SPORT PLANE

A proven design—open cockpit flying has always been an inspiration to pilots. The helmet and goggle era will never leave the aviation scene. This has certainly been evidenced by the recent, increasing demands for biplanes and open cockpits. Possibly, it is a bit of nostalgia from the early days—World War I, the twenties, and the thirties.

Of course, industry with its sophistications, its electronics, and its comfortable cabins has taken many of the aviation enthusiasts farther away from the good old days of flying. True, there are disadvantages in winter. However, with such modern innovations as bubble canopies and warm, insulated clothing, these inhibiting factors are resolved.

The EAA Acro-Sport was designed for several purposes: to retain the nostalgia of flying and to provide inspiration and reminiscence of those pioneers who offered so much to make aviation what it is today. But basically the Acro-Sport was designed for use in schools—high school industrial arts programs, Civil Air Patrol groups, or any other similar activity.

Already, many schools throughout the country are showing a great interest in the building of aircraft in the industrial arts program. Many schools consider realistic programs that will offer the young people the opportunity to find their talents and skills, whether it be in woodworking, welding, sheet metal, or design study.

How does a school get started on Project Schoolflight? After your school has decided to proceed with Project Schoolflight, send $20. to EAA for a complete set of Acro-Sport drawings. (Normally these drawings sell for $60. and only schools participating in Project Schoolflight are eligible for the special $20. price). The plans consist of 22 sheets of beautifully drawn, easy-to-follow instructions, with nearly 100 isometric drawings, photos, and exploded views. Full-size rib drawings and a complete parts and materials list are included. In addition, a profusely illustrated step-by-step builder's manual supplements Acro-Sport drawings. A copy of EAA's monthly magazine, *Sport Aviation,* will also be included. This publication is a source of invaluable information on construction techniques and furnishes you with names of advertisers offering materials and supplies. EAA can also put you in touch with EAA members or EAA chapters near you for advice and technical assistance with your project.

Contact the Foundation at the following address: EAA Air Education Museum Foundation, Inc. Box 299, Hales Corners, Wis. 53130

The comprehensive kit of materials, less engine and propeller, will cost less than $3,000. (Engine and propeller costs will depend upon the combination chosen and whether they are new or used.) Many possibilities will exist for funding. Local pilots such as EAA Chapter members might prepurchase the plane, or local merchants and business or service groups might sponsor the project. Since the resulting product, the EAA Acro-Sport biplane, will be highly salable and command a price well above the construction costs, this is one Industrial Arts project that can replenish rather than consume funds. The Acro Sport is already establishing a healthy reputation with sportplane pilots. When finished, the Acro-Sport is a valuable piece of property.

The space required for Project Schoolflight depends upon the number of students and the number of other class projects being worked on concurrently. If the aircraft is adopted as a joint wood shop-metal shop project, the wings can be built by the wood shop classes, while the fuselage, landing gear, and tail are being fabricated by the metal shop classes.

If the aircraft is chosen as the project of a separate Aeronautics class, then a separate Aeronautics shop with a minimum of 2,200 sq. ft. has been recommended to provide room for machine tools, tool racks, work benches, student lockers, and other requirements. This ideal arrangement will avoid conflicts with other classes.

Between classes the aircraft components can be stored adequately in a floor space of 15′ × 20′, or the components can be hung on wall hooks or placed upon racks to make room for other projects.

The calendar time required to construct the EAA Acro-Sport will depend on both the scheduled class time per day and on the adoption of a serial or a concurrent construction scheme. Based upon a classroom schedule of two hours per day, five days per week, with the wings being constructed while the fuselage, landing gear, and tail are being fabricated, the Acro-Sport should be ready for its engine, propeller, and first flight in four semesters.

Armed with the assurance that the money will be returned, the school should have little trouble getting sponsorship financing from local businesses. The airplane can also possibly be presold to a sport pilot who will advance the price of the airplane to the school.

Complete kit of plans, parts, and materials—less engine and prop: $3,000.

MONNETT EXPERIMENTAL AIRCRAFT, INC.

410 Adams
Elgin, Ill. 60120

SONERAI II

The Sonerai II is a Volkswagen-powered sport plane. It uses a minimum of different sizes of easily obtainable materials to reduce the cost without hampering the integrity of the design. The wing is all-aluminum and is composed of two panels that fold alongside the fuselage, enabling Sonerai II to be towed tail first on its own gear. The fuselage with simple built-in engine mount and the tail surfaces are of standard chrome tubing construction. The design allows access to the engine, tank, and instruments. The fuselage rear and the tail surfaces are fabric covered. The landing gear is a formed aluminum spring with 5″ go-cart-type wheels. A taper rod-type tail spring is employed.

Sonerai II is an answer for the individual who wants a high-performance, two-place sport plane that is simple and inexpensive to build and maintain. Its 140 mph cruise and 420-lb. useful load with a 1,700 cc. VW make it outstanding in its class. $2,500.

Specifications:

Span 18′8″	Gross weight 925 lb.
Length 18′10″	Fuel capacity 10 gal.
Wing area 84 sq. ft.	Cruising speed 140 mph
Empty weight 506 lb.	Engine 1,700 cc. VW

MINI-HAWK INTERNATIONAL, INC.
1930 Stewart St.
Santa Monica, Calif. 90404

MINI-HAWK I

The Mini-Hawk I is the result of more than two years of research and design effort, combining the simplest of fabrication approaches, evolved over many years of homebuilt aircraft construction, with new techniques, some innovations, and with outstanding appearance, design, and performance. It is a rare combination of class, quality, simplicity, and economy.

The plane features all-metal construction, tricycle landing gear, positive push rod controls, geared aileron controls, and stability unmatched in its class of sport plane. Its power plant is the highly dependable, yet inexpensive VW engine, modified to aircraft specifications, including up-draft carburetion and dual ignition system.

The Mini-Hawk I is packaged in many different ways, from partial to complete prefabricated kits, to suit the budgets and talents of any and all sportsmen. The Complete Kit Package, without engine, for the engine mechanic who would rather convert his own VW engine. $1,245.

Complete Kit Package, including engine for those who are anxious to fly their own personal plane with minimum effort, time, and money. The average layman, or woman, could complete this man-sized erector set in a dozen weekends. $2,325.

For the first time in the history of aviation, Mini-Hawk International has produced an airplane package priced competitively with foreign compact cars, and with the plane's removable wings, it takes no more space in your garage than a second car. So you can indulge your sporting blood in an atmosphere free as the birds!

BRYAN AIRCRAFT, INC.
Williams County Airport
Bryan, Ohio 43506

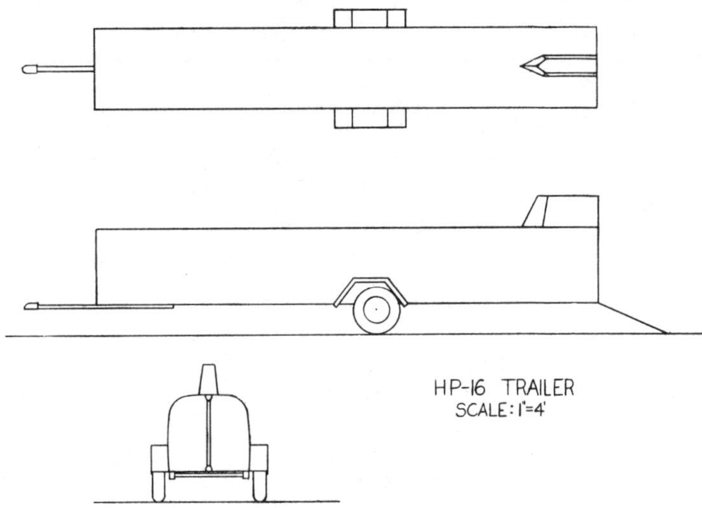

SAILPLANE TRAILER KIT

The Bryan Aircraft Sailplane Trailer is designed for the HP series sailplanes but can easily be adapted to accommodate most current high-performance, single-place sailplanes.

This all-metal trailer is simple to assemble and can be completed in about 75 man-hours by builders with average mechanical ability. No jigs or fixtures are required.

The trailer is lightweight (approximately 600 lb.) and has sway-free stability at all speeds whether loaded or empty.

A large rear door swings down to form a ramp for ease of loading and unloading.

Matching wheels to the same size used on the owner's car eliminates the necessity of carrying a spare tire for the trailer, thereby saving extra weight and cost.

Skins, preformed bows, lights, wiring, coupler, coil spring axle, wheels, hubs, tires, tubes, bolts, nuts, and washers are included in the kit.

A front-wheel jack kit can be supplied. This unit makes trailer ground handling and hook up an effortless operation for one person. $1,000.

RS 15 SAILPLANE

The RS 15 is a high-performance, 15-m. span sailplane designed to meet OSTIV Standard Class specifications. It is designed for simple, rapid assembly by the home builder and is licensed in the Amateur Built Experimental Category.

Special attention has been given to achieving top performance, rugged construction, adequate room for a 6′6″ pilot, and very lightweight.

The following features simplify construction and reduce assembly time to approximately 700 man-hours for a builder with average mechanical aptitude:

1. Main wing spar caps premachined from solid aluminum plate stock.
2. Elimination of most wing skin riveting by the use of precut, structural foam plastic ribs spaced every 4″.
3. Preforming and heat treating of all skins and sheet metal parts.
4. Completion of all landing gear, controls, and other items requiring welding.
5. Preformed canopy frames.
6. Prefabricated control cables.
7. Prefabricated fiberglass forward fuselage pod complete with bulkheads.
8. 6″ diameter aluminum tube tail boom.
9. Complete supply of rivets, bolts, nuts, washers, cotter keys, cement, and all other necessary parts. Paint and instruments are not included in the kit, but can be supplied at extra cost.

No jigs are required. Wings and tail surfaces are built on a table. Templates are provided for checking proper wing alignment. A 24″ hardened steel drill guide is furnished to facilitate drilling accurately spaced holes in wing and tail skins.

The builder needs only hand tools, a rivet gun, an electric drill, and an air compressor. No previous sheet-metal experience is necessary, but we recommend that you have help from a local aircraft sheet-metal man to get started, or spend a few days with Bryan Aircraft to learn how to rivet properly.

Tail kit:	$ 225.
Wing kit:	2,195.
Fuselage kit:	2,695.
Complete kit:	4,995.

SEMCO BALLOONS
Rt. 3 Box 678E
Coeur D'Alene, Idaho 83814

HOT AIR BALLOON KIT

Ballooning is the oldest form of air transport. As early as 1783 Frenchmen were experimenting with hot air balloons. Today the device is more of a sport than a method of transportation. Hot air balloon enthusiasts discuss it with extreme gusto. However, the expense and the required technical know-how have kept the following from growing. Reliable reports indicate fewer than 500 balloons in the sky.

The Semco kit is a three-passenger model that the manufacturer describes as complete in every way and easy to construct. Its diameter is 52′ and it's 70′ high, requiring only 4 minutes inflation time. The gondola is wider. Burners are mounted and operating cost is only $1.50 an hour. (FOB Idaho) $3,200.

SOUTHERN AERONAUTICAL CORP.
14100 Lake Candlewood Ct.
Miami Lakes, Fla. 33014

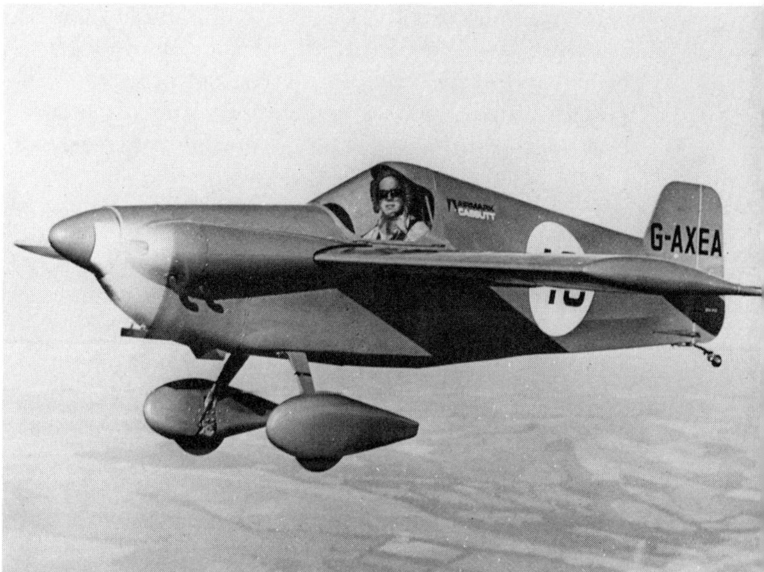

VW-POWERED RENEGADE

This plane fulfills two roles: it qualifies as a competition-class racer and also as an ideal inexpensive sport plane.

FUSELAGE KIT: $288.

Kit includes full-scale plywood template of both fuselage sides, all members marked for easy layout, cutting and welding jig. Full-scale template of seat back, bulkhead, instrument panel, and fuel tank profile. Full-scale pattern of engine-mount bolt centers.

Step-by-step work instruction with diagram. Instructions coded to correspond with details on the plans. Longerons cut to length. All 4130 steel tubing —steel sheet, alum. sheet, alum. stringers, alum. angle to build fuselage, engine mount, fin, gussets, turtleback and fittings for tail spring, stabilizer, landing gear, wing and canopy.

Also includes formed plex, bubble, fiberglass top molded to fit bubble, tubing hinges, and lock to build canopy frame.

LANDING GEAR KIT: $275.

Kit includes: SAE 9260 spring gear formed, drilled, tapered, heat treated, tempered, ready to paint and install. 2 alum. axles, Cessna-type drilled to fit gear, axle nut, 8 axle mounting bolts and nuts, two 5:00 ×5 wheels, brakes, bearings (Cleveland or Goodyear, depending on availability). Also, includes tail wheel, ball bearings, tire, welded fork and tail spring.

CONTROL KIT: $306.

Kit includes: spruce stabilizer with all pieces finish-milled, front spar glued and milled, all ribs built and glued. Includes corner blocks, 4 plywood skin panels, all steel tubing to build elevator, spar ends swaged, horn and 3 hinges completed, ready to install. All tubing to build ailerons with balance arms, actuating arms, 2 actuating links, 4 self-aligning bearings, 4 machined and threaded bearing bushings, and 6 hinges completed, ready to install. Also includes tubing, hinges, shackles, sleeves, thimbles, toe brake pedals, and cable runs. Also includes 2 hydraulic master cylinders (no reservoir required), end fittings, Flex lines and alum. lines for installation to brakes. Also includes material to build rudder, stick, torque column, bellcrank, all hinges required, cable turnbuckles, sleeves, etc., for elevator cable run.

WING KIT: $414.

Kit includes all spruce finish milled. Rear spars, aileron spars, nose section, 3 lamination main spar glued and milled, corner blocks, all ribs completed, glued, and ready to install. Also includes 4 fiberglass wing skins, glue, 2 steel retainers, and 2 rear spar fittings.

FINAL ASSEMBLY KIT: $95.

10-gal. alum. fuel tank heliarc welded with filler, outlet and two vent ports. Flexible fuel line with end fittings, gascolator, sheet for firewall and firewall pattern.

THE TEENIE CO.
Box 3163
Pensacola, Fla. 32506

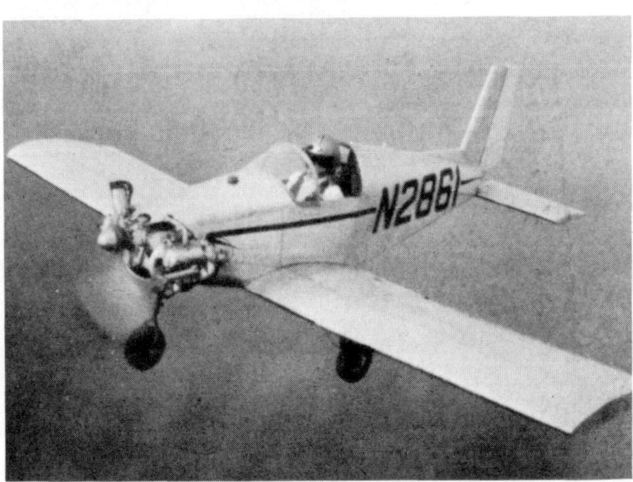

(HOMEBUILT) AIRPLANE KIT

An aluminum airplane with a Volkswagen engine built at home is a project most pilots never thought they could handle. However, here is a small aircraft that is easy to construct. To assist you in this endeavor, the kit even includes an 8 mm movie film showing construction steps!

The finished plane can sit nicely in your backyard ... until you're ready to take off! No metal working or riveting experience needed. $610.

Empty weight 310 lb.
Fuel 9 gal.
Wing span 18'
Length 12'10"
Gross weight 590 lb.
Climb 800 fpm.
Lift off 50 mph
Cruise ¾ throttle 110 mph 2½ gph (up to 140 mph with canopy)
Top speed level 120 mph - as is
Tricycle gear
350 × 4 tires and wheels
Land 50 mph
Wood propeller 50" × 40"
Includes Electronic Tachometer diagram

PAZMANY AIRCRAFT CORP.

P.O. Box 80051
San Diego, Calif. 92138

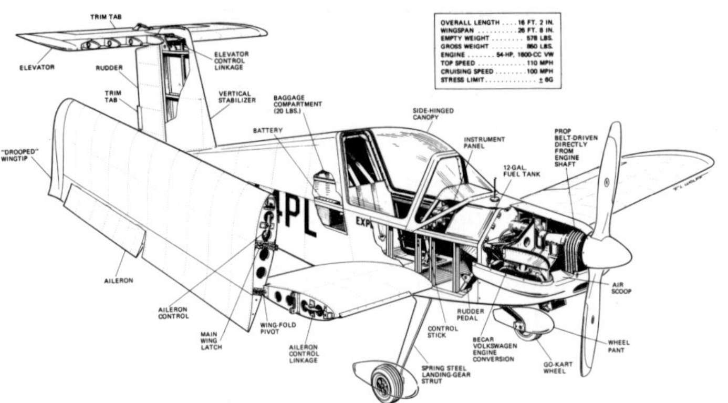

THE PAZMANY PL-4A

The PL-4A is intended to answer the need for a well-designed, all-metal airplane that is easy to build and fly, with low initial and operating costs, and folding wings so that it may be towed behind an automobile and stored at home.

It is a low-wing airplane, VW-powered, with a closed or open cockpit large enough to accommodate even very large persons and a generous baggage compartment. A "T" tail configuration improves effectiveness.

The kit includes:

> molded fiberglass fairings (including shipping)
> fuel tank (molded fiberglass—components not assembled)
> cowl and spinner (for VW with reduction, fiberglass, crated)
> windshield and canopy (molded plexiglass, untrimmed, crated)
> propeller for VW with reduction
> welded engine mount for VW with "V" reduction
> control stick-welded assembly (only 4130 steel parts)
> 2 brake caliper adapters (welded assembly)
> 4 firewall fittings for engine mount (welded assembly)
> 2 rear spar swivel joint fittings (welded assembly)
> tail wheel assembly (complete with wheel and springs)
> 2 aileron mass balance weights
> aluminum wing fittings (not drilled)
> fuselage extrusions (bent and crated)
> brake system (master cylinder, discs, calipers, adapters, tube)
> stabilator trim machined parts, includes plastic wheel
> 2 landing gear aluminum wheels, with bearings

The complete kit including all plans and manuals is $1,320. An introductory package explaining the kit is $3.—well worth it in interesting reading matter!

D.S.K. AIRCRAFT CORP.

Pacima, Calif. 91331

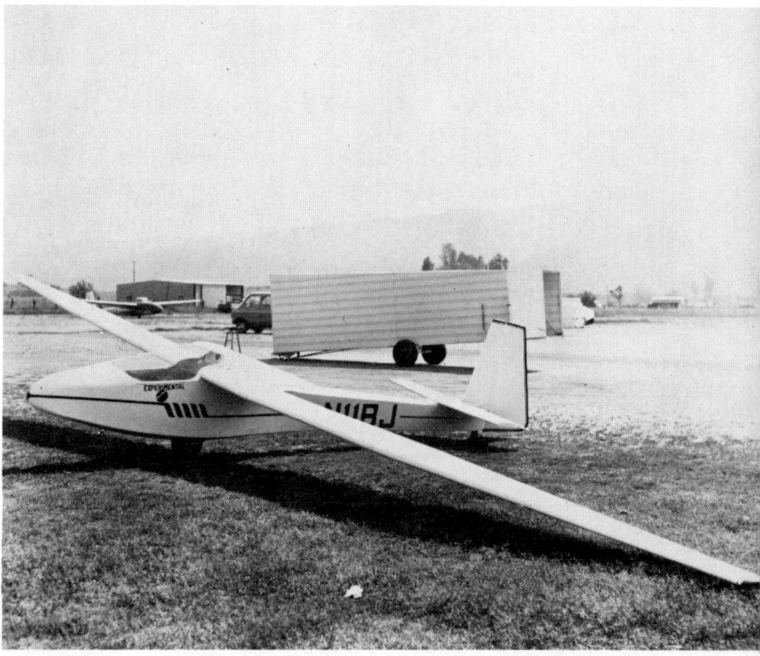

"DUSTER" SAILPLANE

The Duster was designed specifically for the home builder. Using plywood ribs and bulkheads, it goes together quickly. No component is over 18′ long. It can be built and stored in a garage. It is assembled on a simple table made from a 2″ × 12″, 18′ long. If you build from the Woodworkers Kit, the only power tools necessary are a disc sander, a ⅜″ drill, and a saber saw. Flying the Duster is a fun experience; big control surfaces give beautiful response, like a 2½ second roll rate from 45 to 45 bank. An aspect ratio of 17.7 to 1 lets the Duster move out when you put the nose down. 6FPS sink comes at 83 mph. Both the Raw Material and Woodworkers Kits contain everything needed to build the Duster except paint, varnish, glue, and instruments. Raw Material kit: $1,995. Woodworkers kit: $2,995.

EMG ENGINEERING CO.
18518 South Broadway
Gardena, Calif. 90248

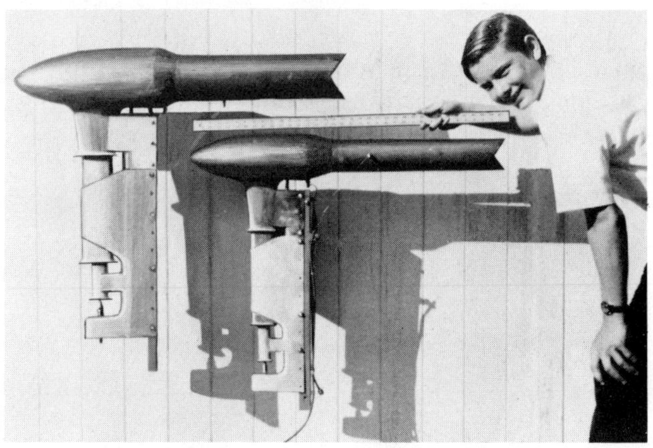

JET ENGINES FOR TEACHING

The jet engines described in the planes section and shown in the photo can be adapted with a teaching stand for demonstrations of jet propulsion for schools and universities. The device demonstrates and teaches the students how to analyze the performance of a jet engine in a simplified manner, by classroom demonstrations, and laboratory experiments by the students. The G8-2 Jet Engine is the simplest pressure jet engine because it has no mov-moving parts. It has push-button starting, 100% throttleable. This makes it extremely easy for the students to comprehend the combustion cycle and the phenomenon of jet propulsion. The kit includes the G8-2-15 Jet Engine Kit, with all necessary component parts. All parts are prefabricated. Valves, switches, lights, instruments, 5-gal. fuel tank, 6 cans of spray paint, and instruction booklet are included. GTS-15 jet engine teaching stand assembly kit: $1,863.50. Technical handbook (general information): $3.

See Planes section.

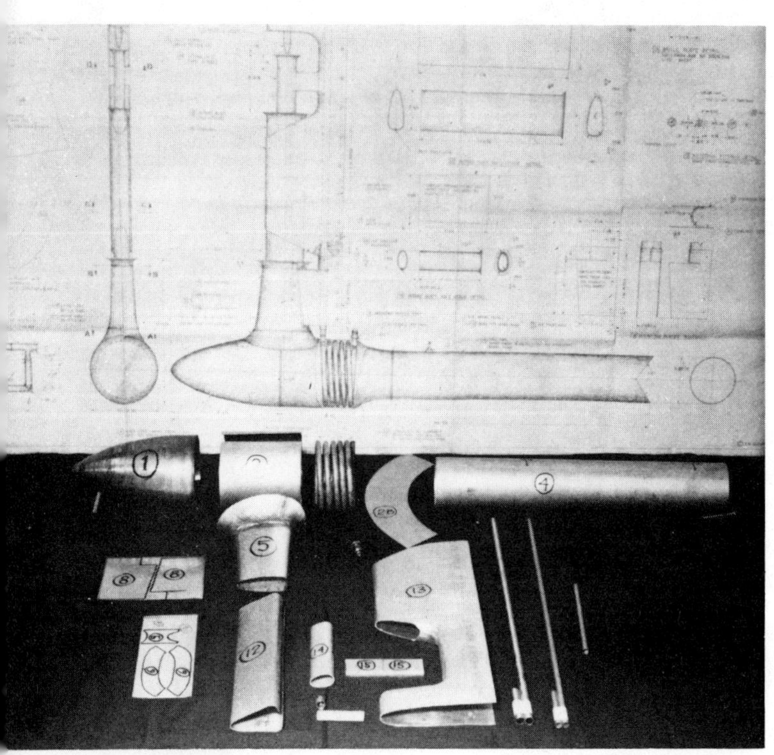

G8-2 PRESSURE JET ENGINE

A small, very inexpensive jet engine that operates on propane. The basic engine is offered in two forms: G8-2-15, which develops a maximum static thrust of 18 lb., and the G8-2-40 with 40 lb. of thrust. The engine can be used for a jet go-cart, flying platform, and other aircraft, including a portable 1-man helicopter for which plans are offered by the company. Two kinds of kits are available: A Construction Package, parts must be finished, trimmed, fit, and welded. The Kit has more of the work done for you but it must be welded by heliarc, too. In addition, you need a fuel tank ignition kit, throttle valve, and spark plug.

	G8-2-15	G8-2-40
Jet engine assembly kit:	$337.50	$395.75
Construction page and plans:	$98.00	$162.00

Started by an aeronautical engineer of great experience, the company currently offers only jet engines, books, and accessories. In production is an 80-lb. thrust engine that will cost an estimated $285. for the construction package and $595. for the kit. A simplified teaching device is available as a kit for schools and universities (see toys and models section).

FREE-FLIGHT SYSTEMS
12424 Gladstone Ave.
Sylmar, Calif. 91342

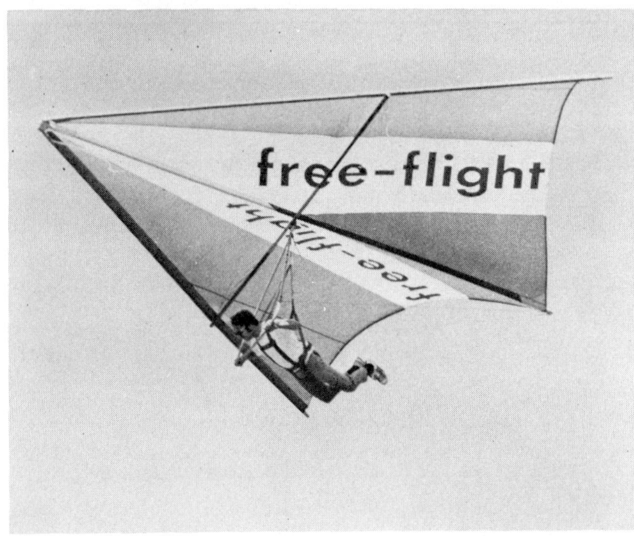

HANG-GLIDER

When was the last time you felt really free? Would you like to really fly? No, not in a 747, but fly like a bird? The answer of course is America's newest sport, Hang Gliding. Although new as a hobby, it probably dates back to Leonardo Da Vinci and man's desire to fly.

Hang gliding simply works on the glider principle. No engine, no wheels, no stewardess, no brakes . . . just you out there flying. Simply run down a hill, take off, and you are on your own. How long you stay up has to do with how good a kit builder you are and how smart you are (the record is 8 hours and 24 minutes by Bob Wills of Santa Ana, Calif.).

The kit contains everything you need: sewn sailcloth wing, prone harness tubing preparation, construction plans, tools, and (of course), flight instructions. It takes about 6 hours to assemble. $485.

OTHER SOURCES

Bushby Aircraft Co.
848 Westwood Dr.
Glenwood, Ill. 60425

Two-place airplane kits for "Deluxe," "Sport," and "Midget" models of the Mustang II. Information packet ($1.).

Cloudman Glidercraft Co.
905 Church St.
Nashville, Tenn. 37203

Produces "Cloudman Glider." Kit is $449. for 19′ sails. Has five other kits available. Brochure free.

Compcop
Box 1267
Redwood City, Calif. 94064

Kit for an easily assembled and disassembled portable one-man helicopter. Terrific for transporting in the trunk of your car. Information (10¢).

Leonard R. Eaves
3818 N.W. 36 St.
Oklahoma City, Okla. 73112

Offers kits for high-wing 2-seater monoplane. Brochure (25¢).

Eipper Formance, Inc.
P.O. Box 246
Lomita, Calif. 90717

Another entry in the hang glider kit contest. They offer both swing seat and prone harness (like superman) kits. They are real enthusiasts and willing to give you a good deal of help. Catalog ($1.).

Mooney Mite Aircraft
Box 3999 Dept XM
Charlottesville, Va. 22903

The M-18 has won a number of world records. It's now available in kit form. Complete details ($1.).

Southern Aeronautical Corp.
14100 Lake Candlewood Ct.
Miami Lakes, Fla. 33014

Two-easy-to-construct, closed cockpit, small sport/racer plane kits. Information ($1.).

Steen Aero Lab
3218 South Cherry St.
Denver, Colo. 80222

Kit for the Steen Skybolt—aerobatic trainer and competition biplane. Information packet ($2.).

Stephens Aircraft Co.
832 North Eldon Ave.
La Puente, Calif. 91744

Kit to build the Stephens AKRO—specifically designed for competition aerobatics. Information package ($2.).

Stewart Aircraft Corp.
Martin Rd.
Clinton, N.Y. 13323

"Headwind" kit. Small, inexpensive, easy-to-construct VW-powered airplane. Information (free).

Sturgeon Air Ltd.
36 Airport Rd.
Edmondton, Alberta, Canada

Largest offering of homebuilt plane kits. General catalog ($3.).

Bill Warwick
5727 W. Clearite
Torrance, Calif. 90505

One-seater sportplane kit. Information packet ($2.).

Western Aircraft Supplies
623 Marketville Rd., N.E.
Calgary, 62, Alberta, Canada

Two-seater light sportplane kits. Catalog ($3.).

Build your own steam-powered bicycle? Why not! If a bike to you is just a way to get to the store when the car's busy, you probably won't be interested. But if you've always been intrigued by the workings of a good machine, you might get to be more interested in putting bikes together than in riding them. Most people who really enjoy vehicles end up taking them apart anyway, so why not make it completely yours by putting it together in the first place?

You can save some money by making your own vehicle, especially a more complicated one like a Hovercraft or a motorcycle. But the real motive of most people who buy such kits is just a desire to be in on the creation of the machine from the very beginning. We should emphasize that this kind of kit isn't for the novice, unless you've had experience in some related field or unless your patience and mechanical skills are high. Of course if you're really determined to do it, you can, but since the investment is usually substantial, it's smart to be sure.

Depending on your needs, you can get a kit for everything from a tricycle to a rocket. We've included what we feel to be a good representative sample. If you want more information, most of these companies will be glad to send you pamphlets, pictures and specific details.

RADIO SHACK

2615 West 7 St.
Fort Worth, Tex. 76107

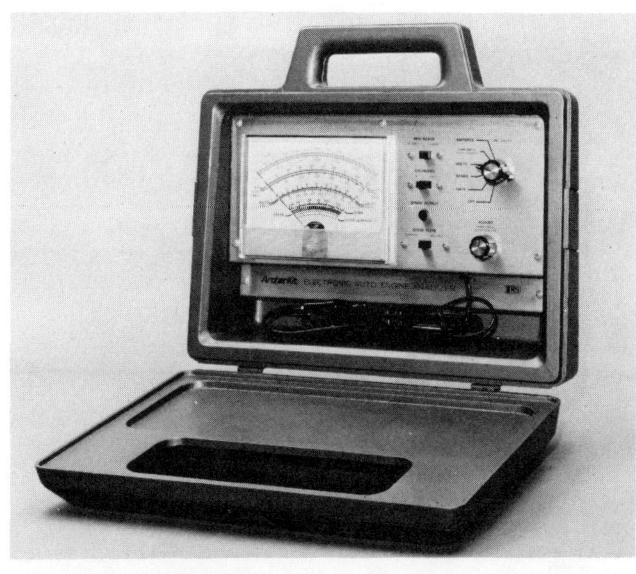

AUTO ANALYZER

A well-tuned engine means more efficient combustion, more power, and smoother running. Performs eight different precision test functions. It's all possible once you put together this simple to build "Portable Auto Analyzer." Tune or troubleshoot any engine for peak performance and economy! Check current and voltage generators, alternator, distributor wear, point surfaces. Also, variation in dwell angle, poor or open ground circuits, coil resistance. Big 3-color meter measures 0-1200-6000 rpm. 0-16 v.; 0-90 amps; 1-20,000 ohms; 0-45°, 0-60°, 0-90° dwell plus spark output and leakage. Single test lead for easy setup. Hi-impact shockproof case, carry handle. For 6 and 12 v. positive or negative grd. PC board for easy assembly. With assembly-operation manual and separate tune-up guides for American and foreign cars. $49.95.

KARR ENTERPRISES

6930 Sylvan Rd.
Citrus Heights, Calif. 95610

PARCEL-SHELF-TO-GLOVE-BOX CONVERSION KIT

The designers of automotive interiors for the Maverick and the Comet are surely hanging their heads in shame. For many Comet and Maverick automobile owners, the parcel shelf on the dashboard has proven to be inadequate. But a remedy has been found, or rather, a kit has been developed. A custom kit that converts the unattractive, untidy parcel shelf into an attractive, tidy glove box with two separate compartments. One up on Detroit.

The glove box consists of two beautiful, professional-looking sliding doors (wood-grain patterned in vinyl) set in a bright, anodized aluminum frame. In the Deluxe model, there is a light in the glove box that automatically goes on when either door is opened and, of course, goes off when closed.

You'll be pleased to know that this kit is simple to install, for no drilling, no cutting, and no special tools or fittings are necessary. Just you, a screwdriver, and a wrench with easy-to-follow instructions included. All of the "labor" can be completed in less than fifteen minutes. Standard model: $9.98. Deluxe model: $12.98.

VENTURE AERO-MARINE
Box 5273
Akron, Ohio 44313

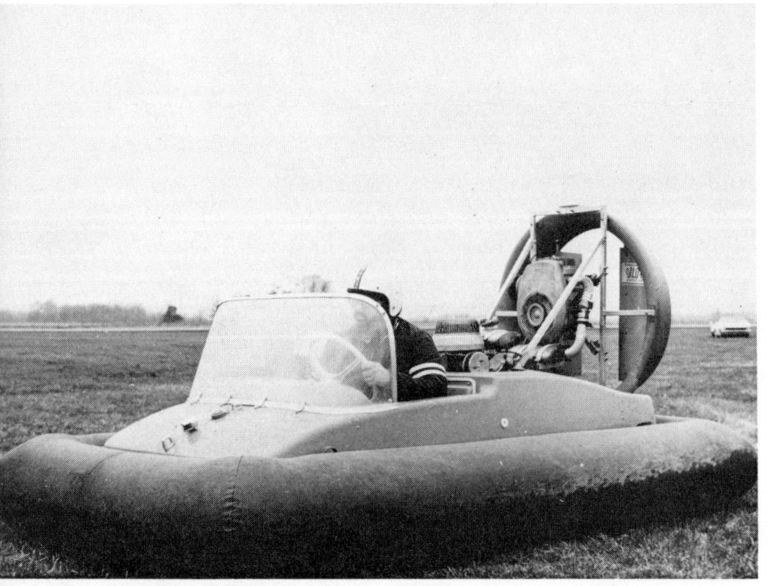

HOVERCRAFTS

The fastest growing new action vehicle is the Hoverbug. There is something exciting, adventurous, flashy, and even utilitarian about the air-cushion vehicle. It has become a cult unto itself. The basic advantage is that "Hover" vehicles operate on land, water, and across snow. You can rip along to the stares of impressed onlookers.

The craft will lift two passengers of average size and carry them over any relatively level surface. It will climb limited grades. However, the Hovercraft more than compensates for its inability to climb hills by its ability to do things that other craft cannot do. For instance, it is the only type of craft that will travel 45 mph over water and continue over land at the same speed.

Primarily, the hovercraft is classed as a marine vehicle in the United States. It is used mostly over water with an obstacle-free surface. The hovercraft is equally at home over ice, so it can be a year-round pleasure craft. The Hoverbug has available, as an option, a top that fully encloses the cockpit. This convertible top may be removed in about five minutes with minimum effort.

The craft is exciting to operate. The air cushion is developed by an 18 h.p. engine driving a ten-bladed plastic fan that develops 6″ to 8″ lift. Forward drive comes from a 25 h.p. engine that drives a 3′ diameter stainless steel-tipped propeller. Both of these engines are controlled by large aircraft-type throttles mounted on a floor console. Steering is done simply by turning a steering wheel in the desired direction. This moves a set of rudders in the slipstream of the pusher propeller. No special license is required other than a standard boat registration. The craft is only 48″ wide at the base and can be carried in the back of a pick-up truck. Hovercrafts do not go over fences and tree stumps. You obviously avoid objects that could do you or the craft harm. Flotation is built in so that the Bug can be parked on the water.

The vehicle has been designed with the home builder in mind and anyone with average shop ability and a few tools should have no problem assembling the craft. The kit comes with very detailed, step-by-step instructions, photographs, and exploded view drawings. Construction time should run between 25 and 30 hours. All holes have been pilot drilled at the factory to help speed up the construction process and to insure proper alignment of certain parts.

The Hoverbug I illustrated is (according to the manufacturer) the ultimate kit. The overall length is 10′ and comfortably accommodates four passengers. The entire kit is $2,495. Options include a recommended bilge pump ($42.50).

DAVID SARLIN
1237 Glen Ave.
Berkeley, Calif. 94708

STEAM-POWERED BICYCLE

As a hobby or as a practical mode of transportation, the bicycle is definitely the rage of the day. All types from a child's sidewalk two-wheeler to the chic, imported 10-speed are now outselling the supply. At last, because of David Sarlin's inventiveness, bicycle devotees can ride a steam-powered bicycle which Mr. Sarlin rather appropriately named "Vesuvius."

Mr. Sarlin designed the steam power unit in 1972. He points out that the boiler is from an 1884 steam velocipede design. This steam bicycle power unit may be attached to any bicycle (or tri-wheeler) with a 24″ to 27″ in diameter wheel in 3 minutes. No modifications are required. The front-wheel mounting allows the rider to view the pulsating engine and check the water level. Rides like a miniature steam locomotive except that no track is needed. The fuel necessary to run this unique bicycle is gasoline and the top speed is 16 mph; the weight with fuel and water is 38 lb.

The kit includes the 23 aluminum, gun metal, and cast-iron castings. Plus a 25-pp. folder that has complete plans and a list of parts to be purchased locally. $57.50.

HEALD INC.
P.O. Box 1148
Benton Harbor, Mich. 49022

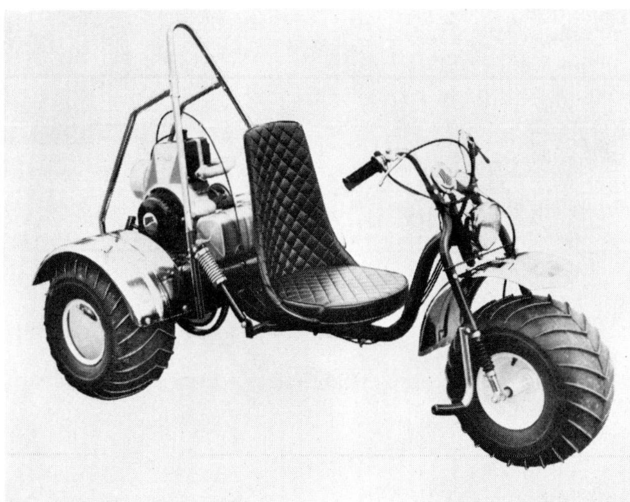

20 H.P. "SUPER TRYKE"

New "Super Tryke" SST has full suspension front and rear, large 21″ diameter × 12″ wide ATV tires and 20 h.p. 295 cc. Kohler engine. Torque Converter drives differential rear axle through No. 40 chain. Options include electric start, front ski, lights, roll bar, and luggage rack. 8 h.p. models also available. Tryke comes in semi-kit form. 8 h.p. kit starts at $369.95.

Company offers several other recreational bikes and other vehicles for farm, home, or gardening (see Greenhouses and Outdoors).

GLEN-L
9152 Rosecrans
City of Commerce, Calif. 90706

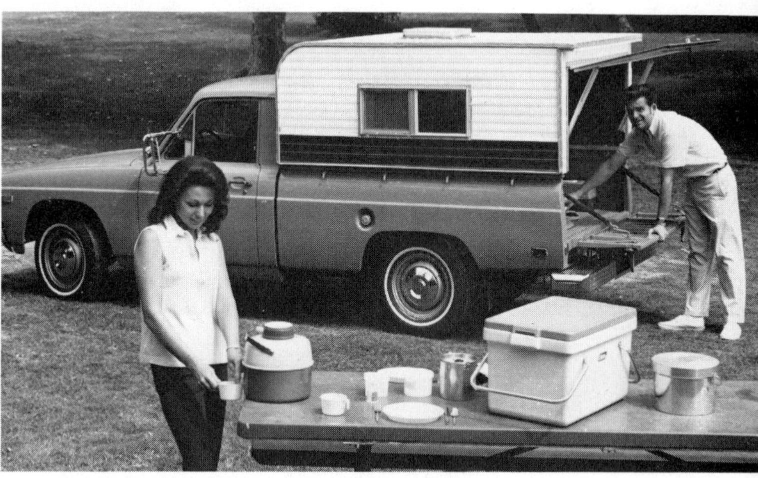

"THE OUTBACK" PICK-UP COVER

This is a pickup cover for small trucks with a nominal 6′ bed: Datsun, Toyota, Courier, Mazda. Although kits are straightforward, needless to say, you need a bit of room to construct it. The basic plans and pattern package is offered and there are various kits for the parts or a complete kit with everything except wood and glue: aluminum skin parts, safety glass screens, and all hardware. Choice of rear doors.

> 20′ Outback kit, complete: $139.00
> 28′ Outback kit, complete: 145.00
> Plans and patterns package (must be ordered
>   separately with kit): 6.95

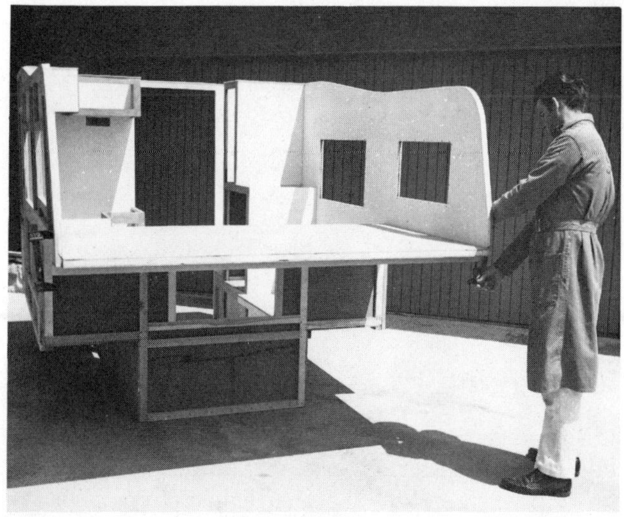

THE IMPORTER CAB-OVER CAMPER

This camper features substantial window room,

fairly large dinette area, kitchen, and standard camper back door. Intended for small import trucks such as Datsun and Toyota, it can be adapted for several other short-bed pickups. Actually comes as plans with kits for the separate parts. A breakdown of costs:

Plans and patterns package	$ 10.00
Trailer fastening kit (includes nails, screws, bolts, corner beading)	17.50
Aluminum skin kit	196.00
Window kit	108.00
Entrance door kit with screen	95.00
Roof vent/baggage door kit	10.95
Sink/plumbing kit	59.00
Lavatory kit	23.00

Complete catalog ($1.) of many kits and plans for recreational vehicles and accessories. Many of their plans (typical price, $10.) can be used with their kits for parts of the camper as described above.

DELTA PRODUCTS, INC.

P.O. Box 1147
Grand Junction, Colo. 81501

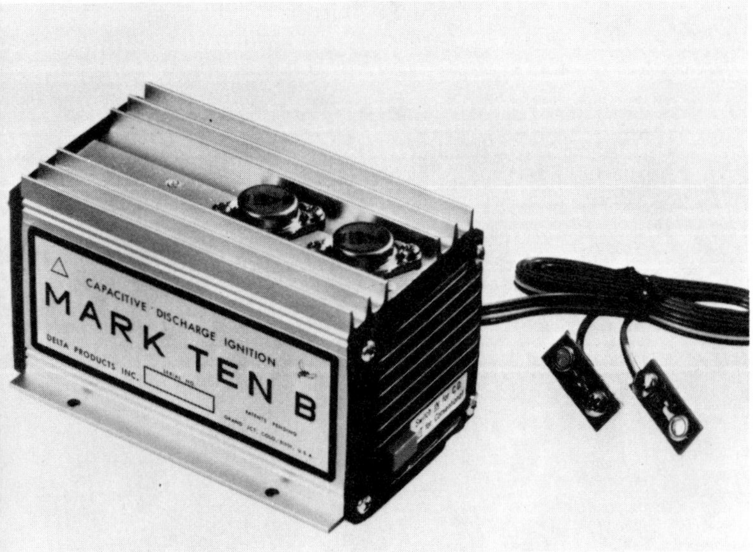

MARK TEN-B CAPACITIVE DISCHARGE IGNITION KIT

The CD ignition increases the power delivered to spark plugs and gives better firing characteristics with variation in engine speed. Also, since the points don't carry large current, you need fewer tune-ups. One of our staff built the Delta and was extremely pleased with the performance. On the other hand, other people claim that you should not change any characteristics of your engine; that is, your car was designed to run with a particular energy from the spark plug and you will get in trouble by messing around. We are not ready to enter into this controversy, but the kits offered below seem to be good, if you think you want CD ignition.

The Mark Ten-B CD Ignition kit involves straightforward circuit-board assembly. Easily installed, this has been one of the standard CD kits for years. Excellent, easy-to-follow instructions. $64.95 postpaid.

Company also offers a simpler version—the Mark Ten ($34.95)—but we recommend the Mark Ten-B because it includes switch for instant return to conventional ignition (for tune-ups, etc.).

OTHER SOURCES

American Motorsport Mfg.
P.O. Box 268
Costa Mesa, Calif. 92627
Motorcycle kits. Catalog ($1.).

Anderson Engineering
Epsom, N.H. 03239
Kits, parts, and components for electronic ignition systems. Catalog (10¢).

Beco, Inc.
P.O. Box 686
Salem, Va. 24153
You can save 50% by assembling Beco's ignition capacitive discharge and voltage regulator kits. Information (free).

Bird Automotive
P.O. Box 793
Fremont, Neb. 68025
Standard and deluxe roadster kits for Ford and Chevrolet V-8 engines. Brochure ($1.).

Braco Mfg. Co.
P.O. Box 26186
Denver, Colo. 80226
Kits for tractors, tow trailers, karts, and 1- and 2-passenger cars. Catalog (free).

Brown's Motorsports
19 Central St.
Worcester, Mass. 01608
Kits for mini bikes, motorized, midget cars, karts, and all terrain vehicles.

Byco Distributing Co.
P.O. Box 6241
Omaha, Neb. 68106
Mini-bike kits with 3½ h.p. engine. Catalog (50¢).

Cal Automotive, Inc.
8044 Lankershim Blvd.
North Hollywood, Calif. 91605
Features fiberglass autobodies for roadsters of the twenties. Catalog ($1.).

California Choppers
730 N. Anaheim Blvd.
Anaheim, Calif. 92805
A unique kit to convert your own motorcycle into a chopper. Catalog (free).

California Speed and Sport Shop
298 Jersey Ave.
New Brunswick, N.J. 08901

One of the largest suppliers in the East for kart, motorcycle, and mini-bike kits. Catalog ($1.).

C-D Systems
P.O. Box 484
Berkeley, Calif. 94701

Capacitive discharge ignition kit for cars and trucks. Brochure (free).

Comstock Camper and Trailer Supply
Box 646
Parsons, Kans. 67357

Three pickup, cover kits for easy assembling. Information (25¢).

Crower Cams & Equipment Co.
333 Main St.
Chula Vista, Calif. 92011

Quality cam kits and an engine stand kit with a universal adapter. Catalog ($1.).

Curtis Dyna-Products Corp.
Box 297
Westfield, Ind. 46074

Kits for making an air-cushion vehicle for traveling over land and water. Photos and prices ($1.).

Custom Cycle Delight, Inc.
8846 Alondra Blvd.
Bellflower, Calif. 90706

Kit to make your own chopper. Catalog ($2.).

Eastern Enterprises, Inc.
509 West Washington Blvd.
Los Angeles, Calif. 90015

Select from three models of mini-bikes and mini-cycles with or without engines. Catalog (25¢).

Don Garlit's Hi-Performance World, Inc.
3420 West Main St.
Tampa, Fla. 33607

Carries a large selection of hot rod hardware kits including cams, headers, and manifolds. Catalog ($1.).

Hank the Crank
7253 Lankershim Blvd.
North Hollywood, Calif. 91605

Kits for hot rod hardware. Catalog ($2.).

Hoosier Machine Products Co.
314 S.E. 6 St.
Pendleton, Ore. 97801

If heavy driving is slowing your Jeep engine down, why not repower it? Hoosier offers kits for power and transmission conversions. Rear axle conversion kits also available. Catalog (free).

Kel Manufacturing
2131 South Dupont Dr.
Anaheim, Calif. 92806

Trike kit with fiberglass body and upholstered seat. Just bolt on to your VW or Porsche engine and transaxle. Catalog (free).

K & P Mfg.
330 South Irwindale Ave.
Azusa, Calif. 91702

Kits for dune buggies, karts (they're the oldest and largest manufacturer of karts) and mini-bike kits. Information literature ($1.).

Motesa Motors, Inc.
3657 Beverly Blvd.
Los Angeles, Calif. 90004

Easy-to-assemble motorcycle engine kit from Spain. Brochure (free).

North American Imports
2325 Cerro Gordo P.O. Box N
Mojave, Calif. 93501

Motorcycle kits.

Rayjay Industries, Inc.
2602 East Wardlow Rd.
P.O. Box 207
Long Beach, Calif. 90801

A turbocharger kit for your VW that will double its horsepower. Information (free).

Scat Enterprises
P.O. Box 4096
121 West Hazel St.
Inglewood, Calif. 90302

High-performance kits for small cars. Catalog ($2.).

Schmieder Motors
RD # 1
Doylestown, Pa. 18901

Go-kart kit without engine. Information (25¢).

Side Strider, Inc.
1588 Arminta Unit 25
Van Nuys, Calif. 91406

You can finally take that third person along on your motorcycle trip. Side Strider offers a sidecar kit for your motorcycle. Takes an hour to assemble and attach the first time. After that only a few minutes to detach. Brochure (free).

Stanley W. Tull Co., Inc.
Sport Div.
1620 Harmon Place
Minneapolis, Minn. 55403

Offers one go-kart kit. Catalog ($1.50).

Wheel Specialties
2130 E. Orangewood Ave.
Anaheim, Calif. 92806

Variety of chopper kits. Information (free).

As soon as the Volkswagen Bug arrived on our shores, Americans took it to their hearts. And as soon as we received the economical little Bug into our hearts, we started trying to change it. Some of us have gone so far as to put high powered engines under those beetle-shaped hoods and turn the Bugs into racing cars.

Now comes the opposite kind of alteration. Convert the exterior of your gas-saving popular vehicle and dress it up to look like an upper-class auto. Conversion kits are available to let you do everything from adding a Rolls-Royce grille to removing the entire body and putting on one that looks like a playboy prince's daydream.

Chances are, if you're anything of a VW nut, you probably love to tinker with the car. You've always known you'd get around to taking apart that self-consciously ugly little exterior, anyway. Would you like, do you dare, to replace it with a purple swoop-fendered Grand Prix Special? Take a look at some of the kits offered in this section, and see if they can tempt you to get into the body-building business. Remember to do a little practice tinkering first, before you sell the old Beetle shell to the junk man. It hasn't yet become fashionable to drive the people's car with no body at all.

FRIZZELL'S ELECTRIC TRANSPORTATION

Old Claremont Rd. RFD - Box 245
Charlestown, N.H. 03603

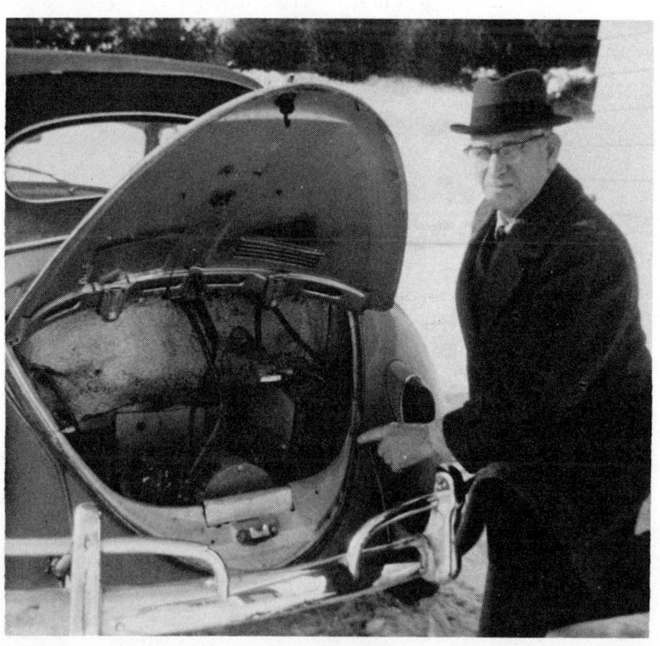

ELECTRICAL CONVERSION FOR VOLKSWAGEN

Everyone talks about pollution, but who does anything about it? Some people merely think about whether a car can run electrically. Mr. Theodore J. Frizzell thought about electric transportation and, fortunately for you, he developed an answer. An ingenious method whereby you can electrify a small car. Mr. Frizzell can supply you with the GE 36 v. direct current motor, the 36 v. battery charger, and a kit of patented control components, including motor bracket, speed control panel with micro-switches, solenoid panel with six solenoids, resistance coils, protective fuse, wiring, and detailed instructions.

There are many important reasons for wanting to electrify your small car, reasons that we read about in our daily newspapers, reasons like pollution-free driving, economy, and smooth action.

Mr. Frizzell is quick to caution that you never get far from home due to the need to recharge the batteries. So, if electrifying your small car is something you've been wondering about and wanting to do, send for Mr. Frizzell's kit. Kit of patented control components: $300.

BAY PRODUCTS CORP.
14211 North East 18 Ave.
North Miami, Fla. 33161

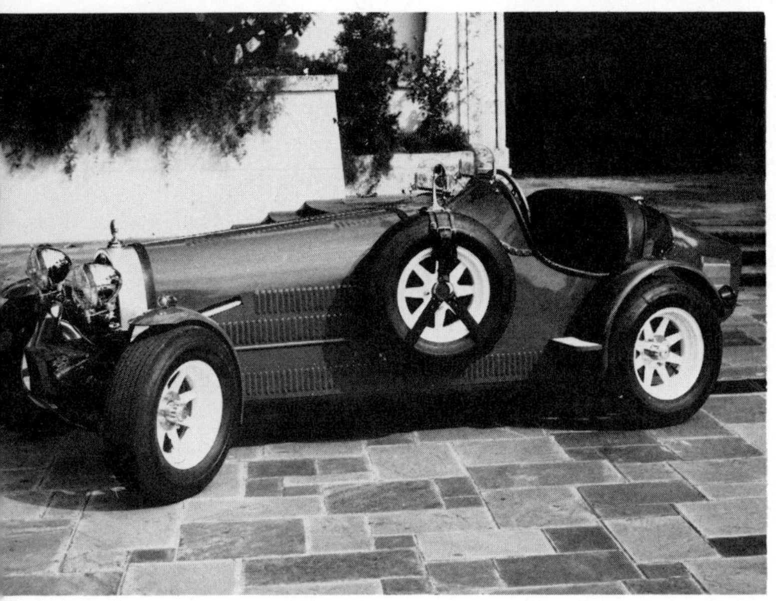

REPLICA 1927 BUGATTI 35B-VW CONVERSION KIT

This beautiful replica is made from a 2-piece fiberglass body with the louvers and rivets molded in, fiberglass side and body panels, and fenders as well as many accessories (radiator assembly, dash overlay, windscreen, headlights, all supports required for frame, body, and gas tank, etc.). Many accessories (Bugatti-type wheels, taillights, seat covers, etc.) are extra. All together you should figure on $1,000. to $1,250. for a complete job, especially if you want the convertible top kit. (You probably need a garage anyway—a 1927-type convertible top can't possibly work well.) If you want this classy item, you must invest substantial work as you really have to take a VW pretty much apart. The whole conversion will probably take several months and the car will be inoperable after the first ten minutes. If you've never messed with cars, this is not for you. There's a certain amount of heavy work, metal cutting, and welding certain parts may be advisable. Molded in colors available: Racy Red, Bright Golden Yellow, Bugatti Blue, Racing Green, Jet Black, or Snow White. Fits any year VW Beetle (not Super Beetle) or Karmann Ghia chassis. Bugatti kit: $750. Convertible top kit: $125. 8-spoke Bugatti-type wheels: $55. Shipping-$45. (Georgia) $100. (Arizona)

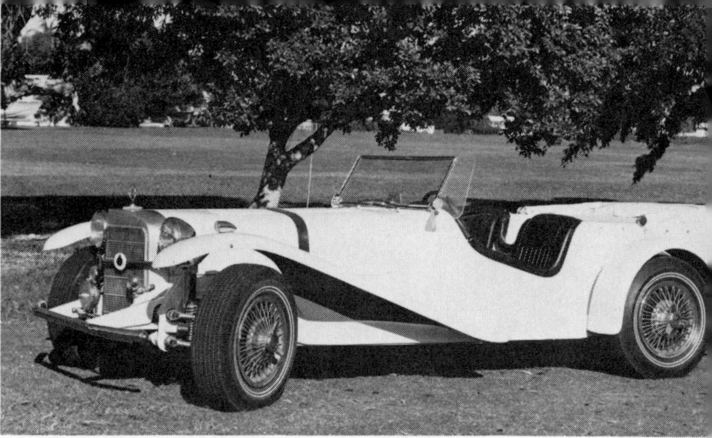

GAZELLE REPLICA-VOLKSWAGEN CONVERSION KIT

In production at the time of writing. Intended as complete kit to include as standard: a convertible top, side curtains, chromed folding windshield, chromed radiator, headlight, taillights, side running lights, and full upholstery. It is a copy of the 1929 Mercedes Benz SS and is made to fit right onto a Volkswagen chassis, without cutting the frame. Anticipated price: $1,700.

ELITE ENTERPRISES
210 East Third St.
Cokato, Minn. 55321

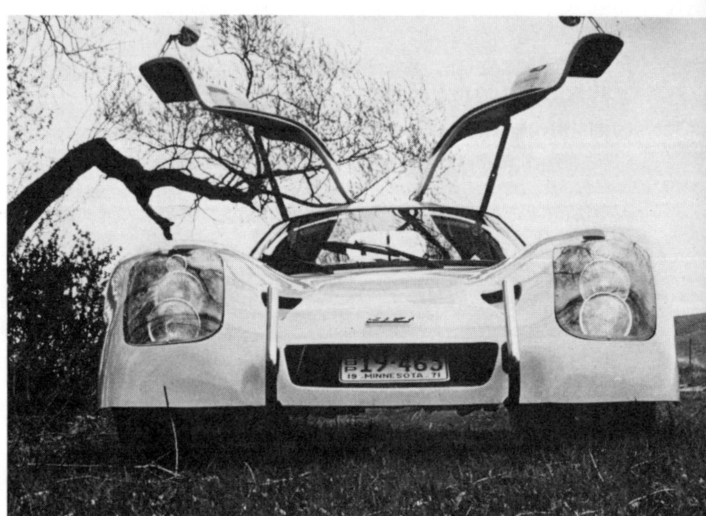

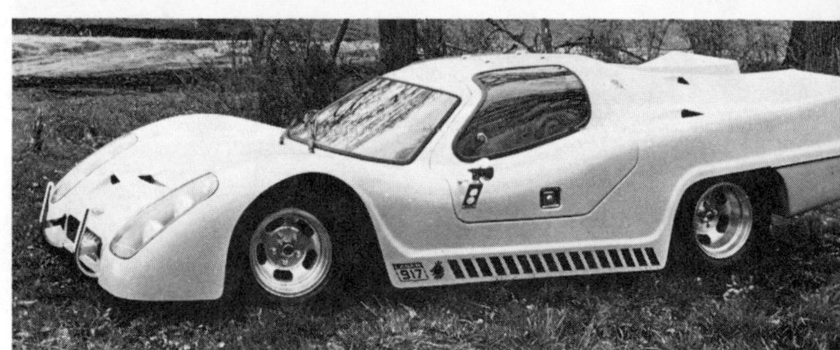

LASER 917

The car of tomorrow with the motor of today. The wildest of the VW kits. Complete down to Lemans-type seats. $1,895.

BRADLEY AUTOMOTIVE

7669 Washington Ave. South
Edina, Minn. 55435

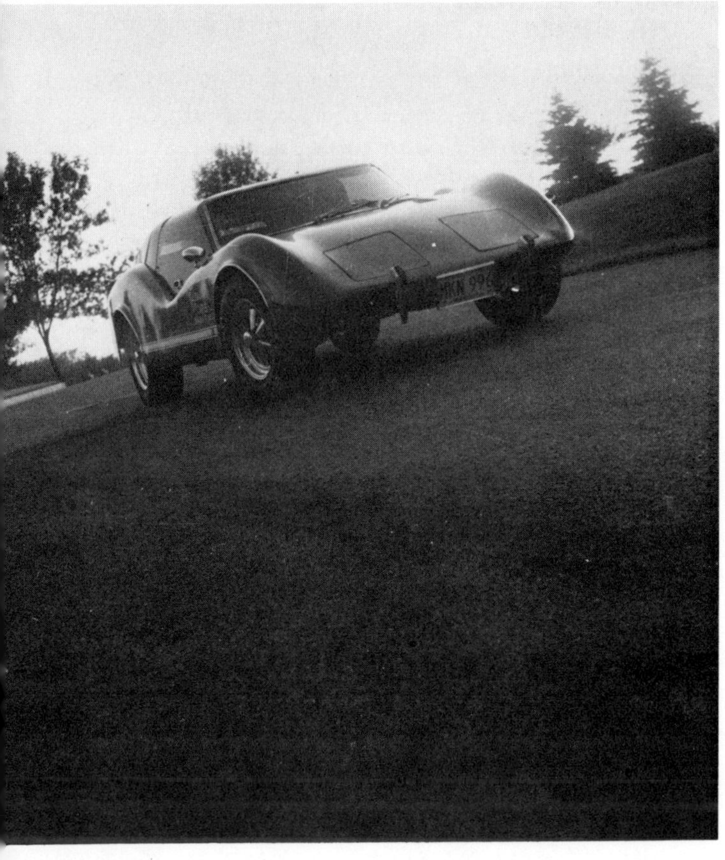

BRADLEY GT-VW CONVERSION KIT

Much less work is involved in putting this sports car body on your VW than, say, making it into the Bugatti replica—the price tag is also higher. The kit as sold contains everything that you need (except the Volkswagen). The only accessories are air conditioning, padded roll bar, and mag wheels. Offered as a basic kit and the same kit in preassembled form. "Everything in the kit is here, but it's assembled for you by factory-trained personnel. The same care that you would give the assembly is provided by Bradley. All that is left for you to do is to bolt it down, hook up the engine wires, install the steering, seats, and upholstery and drive it away." You can get an instruction manual with 150 detailed photos and diagrams for $10. (deductible from kit price). Prefinished body is available in General Metal Flake or solid colors. Bradley claims they sell more of these than all other conversion kit companies combined. GT kit: $2995. Air conditioning kit: $595. Roll bar: $150. Mag wheels: (set of four) $200.

P.V.T. PLASTICS CORP.

300 Richardson St.
Brooklyn, N.Y. 11222

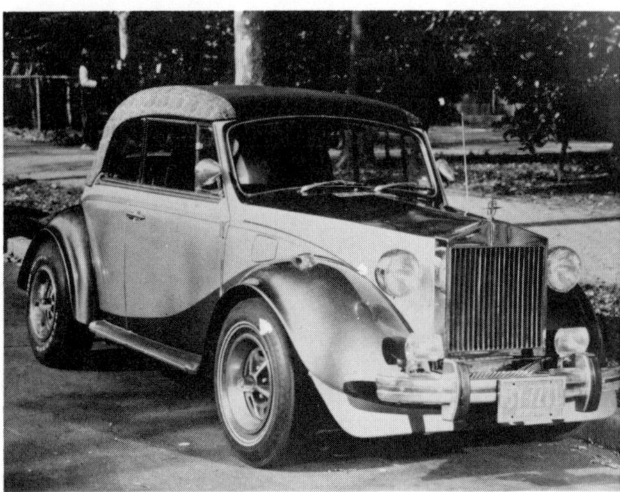

MINI-ROYALE VOLKSWAGEN CONVERSION KIT

Now you know who makes those Rolls grilles you see on Volkswagens? Did we really have to tell you that this company is located in Brooklyn? If this is your taste (sense of humor?) in cars, here it is: Complete kit includes hood grille, rear lid, four fenders, headlights, signal lights, bumper extension, and hardware. Fits any year Super or Standard Beetle. Kit: $568.

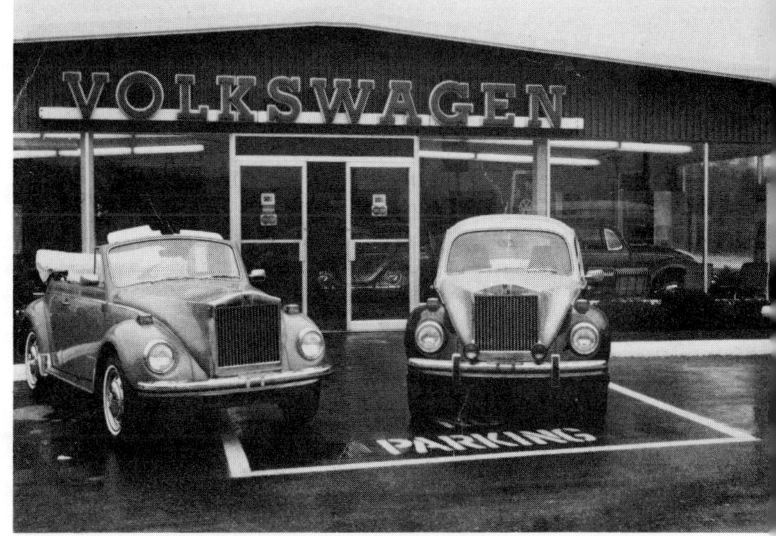

MINI-ROLLS/VW CONVERSION KIT

Fiberglass hood and grille only. Kit: $195.

Several other kits along this line. No information on how easy this conversion is but you do see a lot of them around. All orders are FOB factory, but probably if you want one of these items, you already live in Brooklyn.

VOKARO
VOPARD ENTERPRISES
Box M
Suisun City, Calif. 94585

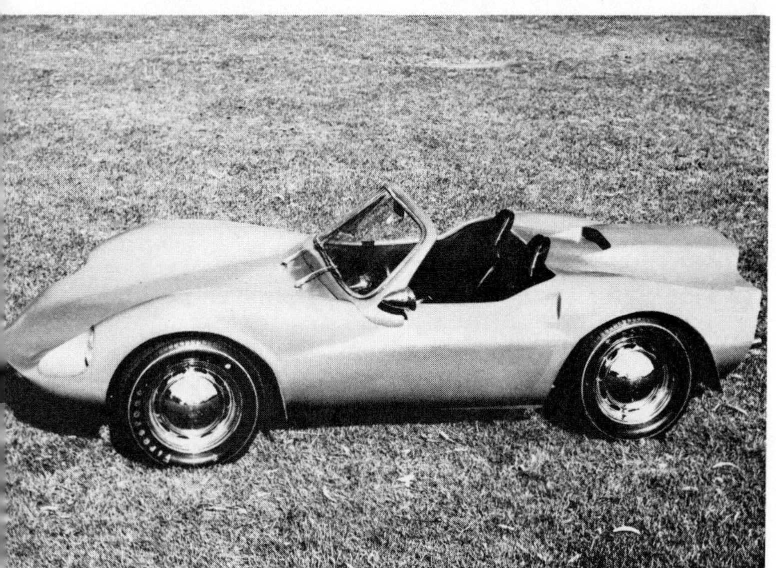

VOKARO SPORTS CAR-VW CONVERSION KIT

Fiberglass sports car kit contains inner shell that bolts on VW chassis, outer sports car body, windshield frame (for Karmann Ghia), bucket seats, and manual. We don't have enough information on difficulty of construction, but you must shorten the chassis. 5-piece fiberglass kit: $895. Seat upholstery (per pair): $84.90 Convertible top kit: $295. Dual quiet power exhaust: $79.95.

AUTOKIT INDUSTRIES
2725 Magnolia St.
Oakland, Calif. 94607

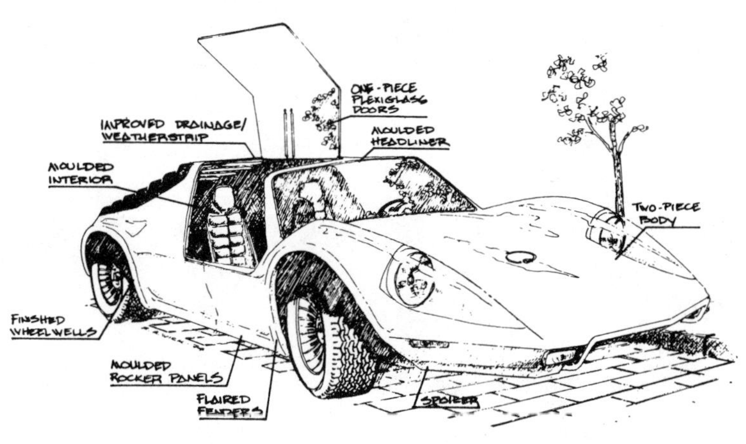

INVADER GT5/GT7 VOLKSWAGEN CONVERSION KIT

This is one of the simpler of the GT/sports car conversion kits—at least as described by the manufacturer, according to whom you: (1) remove 38 bolts from the VW bug; (2) clean and paint the chassis; (3) add hardware to unshortened chassis; (4) bond inner panel to outer shell; and (5) attach body to chassis with the 38 bolts. Completed car features gull-wing doors which can be removed to make a convertible, orthopedic bucket seats, and options like tilt-away steering wheel. Three kits are offered: Standard, Deluxe, and Super kit. The Deluxe kit actually contains things like the mounting kit and the hardware as well as the door and door assembly. Standard kit: $995. Deluxe: $1,595. Super kit (spare tire carrier kit, locking door handles, carpeting, dash kit, etc.): $1,995.

No doubt some of our readers were disappointed to find only domestic sources for kits. This chapter will serve as an explanation as well as a mini-directory to overseas sources. First for the explanation. We *don't* believe that everything good is domestic. However, in the case of kits, everything interesting we saw from overseas suppliers was also available here. It was available domestically either because a local manufacturer was making a comparable version or because an importer was selling it through a local company. Specifically, we see little use in going through the import hassle unless it's something exceptionally worthwhile. In all of our searching we found few kits overseas that were either a fantastic bargain or impressively unusual.

For those hardy souls who like the import game, we do offer a few recommendations. These are the firms, culled out of hundreds, that offer kits of some special merit. The same ground rules exist when ordering from abroad with the following few extras:

1. Prices change faster overseas. More specifically, they reprint catalogs less frequently, so inquire before ordering. The value of the dollar fluctuates, so include a few extra cents to account for that.

2. Don't forget customs costs if you are figuring on a saving. Add the duty, which you can find out by writing or calling your local customs office.

3. Watch out for language difficulties. As here, kit makers in Europe tend to be small companies. Try to avoid lengthy letters in English.

4. Allow plenty of time for delivery. Airmail on packages is usually prohibitively expensive. Sea mail can take a long time. Patience, please.

If the preceding has not totally discouraged you, we list a few sources below that you may find interesting. They are not presented in any particular order, but all are noteworthy for one reason or another.

CAMBRIDGE WOOLS

16-22 Anzac Ave.
Auckland, New Zealand

Even on the coldest of winter nights your feet will stay warm and dry in *sheepskin mocassins.* Cambridge offers them in kit form. They are exceptionally well made, the project is fun, and the end product will be worthwhile if your feet touch the floor in a cold climate.

PRISCILLA LOBLEY FLOWER KITS

Thorpe Lodge, Ealing Green
London, England W5

First-quality kits to make giant paper sunflowers, roses, and many other flowers. Tastefully produced and prompt attention to mail orders.

KLOCKARGARDENS HEMSLOJDAB

Olsbacka, 795 00
Rättvik, Sweden

It seems hard to imagine anyone would run out of needlepoint sources in the United States. However, this firm offers interesting abstract needlepoint kits. If you're past Bucilla, you may want to try your hand. Catalog is $1.

ART NEEDLEWORK INDUSTRIES

7 St. Michael's Mansions
Ship St.
Oxford, England

Heinz Kiewe, the company's owner, is sort of the Erica Wilson of Europe. He is the author of numerous needlepoint books. The kits are mostly of a historical nature, including designs by Mary, Queen of Scots. The prices are rather expensive but worth looking into for the serious needlepoint student. The catalog is $2.40.

H. A. C. SHORT-WAVE PRODUCTS
29 Old Bond St.
London, England

H. A. C. stands for Hear-All Continents. This is the goal of H. A. C. *shortwave kits.* They use miniature components and require some electronic experience. The quality is superior and prices better than many domestic kits. Catalog free.

OBLETTER SPIELWAREN
Karlsplatz 11-12
Munich, 2 Germany

First-quality precision German *model ships*, also a variety of *hobby kits* made in Munich and not exported. Expect to pay top dollar for these products. Stunning catalog is free.

PHILLIPS & PAGE
50 Kensington Church St.
London, England

If the "gravestone rubbing" kit in the Crafts section interested you, then read on. Phillips & Page makes more sophisticated kits than those available from the Boston source listed. "Rubbings" is quite a popular pastime in England. This firm has a whole store devoted to the activity. They offer a catalog of their kits for an international reply coupon (buy at the post office).

SELDON TAPESTRIES
10 Kings Mansions
Lawrence St.
London, England

If you'd like to needlepoint a picture of Aunt Jenny cooking turkey, try Seldon. They will custom-make a kit for you. Just give them an idea of the topic. It may take a little correspondence, but they do fine work.

HABITAT TORONTO
277 Victoria St.
Toronto, Ontario, Canada

The firm specializes in modern, low-priced home furnishings. Most everything is in finished form, but they do have some interesting *furniture* kits.

HAMLEY'S
200 Regent St.
London, England

Hamley's is Europe's largest *toy* store. Look for any number of new interesting kits for children in their free Christmas catalog.

WOOLCRAFT
4 Trading Building
Regina, Saskatchewan, Canada

A variety of craft items is offered. Many are different from domestic products. We especially suggest the *jewelry kits.* Catalog $1.

PAPERCHASE
216 Tottenham Court Road
London, England

Simple-to-construct *doll houses* and mobiles. Traditional British designs. Quite interesting.

ASHFORD HANDICRAFTS
P.O. Box 12
Rakaia
Canterbury, New Zealand

A *spinning wheel kit* at a reasonable $35. Comparable to wheels selling at over $150. Stateside. Relatively simple to assemble for even a Sunday carpenter.

The growth of the do-it-yourself and home hobby-craft industry has brought about a number of marketing changes. One is that kits are no longer the province of just the small specialty mail-order house. The large firms are starting to include items of this nature. Last year's Christmas catalogs from general mail-order houses included many kits. These firms change items more rapidly (some every month). Therefore, rather than show specific items, we supply the name and address of the company. They are listed this way because kit makers should know them, but it would be impossible to compile by item.

Catalogs you should get . . .

SUNSET HOUSE
Beverly Hills, Calif. 94713

WALTER DRAKE
Colorado Springs, Colo. 80901

MILES KIMBALL
Oshkosh, Wis. 54901

SPENCER GIFTS
Atlantic City, N.J. 08411

UNITED STATES PURCHASING EXCHANGE
5260 Vineland Ave.
North Hollywood, Calif. 91601

LILLIAN VERNON
510 South Fulton Ave.
Mt. Vernon, N.Y. 10552

STARCREST OF CALIFORNIA
3159 Redhill Ave.
Costa Mesa, Calif. 92626

IMPORTANT GENERAL SOURCES

SEARS, ROEBUCK AND CO.
303 East Ohio St.
Chicago, Ill. 60611

It's only natural that the world's largest mail-order company should feature numerous kits. Any serious kit builder should pore over the Sears catalog, for it features kits in every category. Their furniture and hobby kits are among the best. It sometimes takes a little persistence to obtain their catalog, but it's well worth the effort.

J. C. PENNY
P.O. Box 2056
Milwaukee, Wis. 53201

The great Penny chain has a wide variety of kits. Recently released is a catalog called "Creative Crafts Catalog." It's free and worth writing for.

F. A. O. SCHWARZ
Fifth Ave. at 58 St.
New York, N.Y. 10022

The world's largest toy store. Hundreds of craft and hobby kits. Also electronic kits for children. Anyone with kit builders under twelve in their family must write for a catalog.

HORCHOW COLLECTION
Box 34257
Dallas, Tex. 75234

The ultimate in mail-order catalogs. Includes items selected from such famed retailers as Cartier, Mark Cross, and Georg Jensen. Catalog ($1.) is four-color and tastefully prepared. Although mostly upscale gifts (e.g., Gazelle Horns in lucite base, $135.), there are a number of unusual kits. Recent catalogs feature Make-Your-Own-Christmas-Card kit, Needlepoint Dog Collar, and Junior Loom for Young Weavers.

Although it's fairly easy to buy kits through the mail, the most convenient way of all to shop is to join a club that sends you a catalog. In most cases, you pay a small membership fee and receive a regular magazine telling you about kits, books, and accessories you can buy. Needlework clubs have boomed in the last two or three years, but other kinds are starting to pop up, too.

Some clubs require you to buy a certain minimum number of items after you join. Others only charge for the catalog subscription, so that whether you buy everything or nothing is up to you. As the continued popularity of book clubs has shown, this is a good way to get to know what's available without fighting the crowds. If you're disappointed with what you get from these clubs, *mail it right back*. Almost all of them allow you ten or fifteen days' free trial.

BETTER HOMES AND GARDENS CRAFTS CLUB

P.O. Box 4724
Des Moines, Iowa 50336

CRAFT CLUB

When it comes to home projects, *Better Homes and Gardens* does it just about as well as it can be done. Their designs are almost always imaginative, and their plans are famous for being understandable and workable. Now, *BH&G* has a crafts club with a home bulletin every two months or so telling you what crafts kits are available. It works just like a book club. If you want the selection offered, do nothing, they send it. If not, check an alternate (or no kit) and send back the card. How-to books are also included as alternate selections. You can cancel after you buy two.

When you join the *BH&G* Crafts Club, they'll send you a bonus catalog for a dollar. This has the instructions for over 400 gifts like macrame belts, stuffed toys, purses, crochet goods, etc. Kits offered will be along the same line, but you'll have a large selection each month. The enrollment price is $1. Prices of individual kits will vary.

PACK-O-FUN

Park Ridge, Ill. 60068

PACK-O-FUN

Pack-O-Fun isn't a regular kit subscription service, but a monthly magazine about what might be called make-your-own kits. They call it scrapcraft, and it's the art of making something out of nothing, or nearly nothing.

To introduce you to their magazine and other kits that may be available, Pack-O-Fun offers a soap-decorating kit, can you imagine? They send you the sequins, beads, nylon net, everything you need to make novelty toys out of bars of soap. The kit is free with a subscription to the magazine. A one-year subscription costs $3.95.

ZYMEX'S CRAFT OF THE MONTH CLUB

900 West Vallecitos Blvd.
San Marcos, Calif. 92069

Here is a club for the craft enthusiast whose interest goes beyond needlework. You receive a craft kit every month (no choice—unfortunately, you have to take what they send). The kit you get may be for candlemaking, bead work, egg decorating, feathers, jewelry, ornaments, decoupage, corn husk dolls, and other crafts you haven't dreamed of yet. The advantage of this kind of club is the great variety of kits you'll get. Disadvantages are the lack of choice and the necessity to pay for each monthly kit before it arrives. If your payment doesn't reach the club in time, they'll send your next kit C.O.D. *Monthly* kit fee: $1.75.

ERICA WILSON
717 Madison Ave.
New York, N.Y. 10031

ERICA WILSON'S CREATIVE NEEDLEWORK SOCIETY

The most famous name in needlepoint has the largest needlepoint club; membership has just topped the 70,000 mark. Membership includes the quarterly newsletter, *The Creative Needle.* Members also receive a regular catalog from which they can order, but it takes a $10.-purchase per year to be a member.

GENERAL FOODS' CREATIVE VILLAGE STITCHERY
1112 Seventh Ave.
Monroe, Wis. 53566

CREATIVE VILLAGE STITCHERY

Ten different kinds of needlecraft kits brought to you by the makers of Log Cabin syrup. How did the food people get into the crafts kit business? It's hard to say, but the quality of their materials and plans ranks with the best. Every quarter (three months) you get a catalog plus a miniature sample kit. Order any or none of the kits pictured, whatever you like. You pay to subscribe to the catalog. If you want any of the kits offered, you are billed after you place your order.

Kits are available on needlepoint, crewel, embroidery, tapestry, toys, afghans, quilting, appliqué, macrame, and string art. The catalog also offers a selection of tools, supplies, and accessories. Color photographs help you choose among hundreds of kits each quarter. If you want to, you can send back the first book and sample kit and there's no charge. Or keep the kit and catalog. You'll receive three more during the rest of the year. Subscription price: $5.

NEEDLE ARTS SOCIETY
P.O. Box 23
Terre Haute, Ind. 47808

NEEDLE ARTS SOCIETY

An interesting idea for needlework kit fanciers. Each month you receive an offer of a sewing kit. They vary from stitchery to needlepoint to appliqué to macrame to quilting, to what have you. Like the Book-of-the-Month Club, if you don't respond, along comes your kit with a bill.

The idea follows the book clubs in every respect. They offer a free membership and then a regular service. The quality of the kits seems above average and the prices quite reasonable. The project is coordinated by Nan Comstock, editor of *McCall's Needlework and Crafts.* She seems to do an excellent job of selecting interesting and varied projects. A few typical selections are illustrated.

PRESCOTT LETTER
40 East 49 St.
New York, N.Y. 10017

An excellent kit newsletter positioned as a club. Members receive a six-time-a-year newsletter with information on new kits, reviews, do-it-yourself tips, and a well-written question and answer section. Membership is $5. a year. Send a self-addressed, stamped envelope for complete details.

Parents' Magazine's YOUNG MODEL BUILDERS' CLUB
P.O. Box 161
Bergenfield, N.J. 07621

YOUNG MODEL BUILDERS

Model building is one of the most instructive hobbies a child can have. It teaches patience, craftsmanship, and pride of achievement in a way no ready-made toy can do. Luckily, technology allows manufacturers to make better models all the time. Because of developments in plastic and molding, some of today's models have better detail at low prices than ever before.

If your child likes to build models or even if she thinks she might like it, here's a good idea. Enroll the child in the *Parents' Magazine* Young Model Builders' Club. When she enrolls, the young builder will receive a free tool kit containing scissors, file, cement, paint brush, thinner, and paints. She'll also get the first model kit. If you or the child are dissatisfied with the quality of the model, send it back. Otherwise, pay and receive a similar model kit each month at the same price. You are obliged to buy four kits when you join. After that you can quit any time. Price per model, $1.98 (plus postage and handling). Total obligation if you join: approximately $8. depending on postage charges.

IABBS

3183 Merrill
Royal Oak, Mich. 48072

INTERNATIONAL AMATEUR BOAT BUILDING SOCIETY (IABBS)

This group is the mail-order meeting ground for those wanting to build their own boats. Membership includes an informative magazine with full reports of boat-building news, designs, and facts of interest to hobbyists. Dues are $6. per year.

EAA

11311 West Forest Home Ave.
Hales Corner, Wis. 53130

EXPERIMENTAL AIRCRAFT ASSOCIATION

If your plane building is serious, check out EAA. With members around the world, you'll find worthwhile information. Annual meeting in Wisconsin and carefully researched monthly magazine. Dues are $15. per year.

USHGA, INC.

Box 66306
Los Angeles, Calif. 90066

GROUND SKIMMER CLUB

If you've made a glider from a kit, or even if you think you might want to, you'll probably want to join the United States Hang Glider Association (USHGA). For your membership dues, you get *Ground Skimmer* magazine plus voting privileges in the association. *Ground Skimmer* contains all the latest information on the sport of hang gliding, plus news of kits and new gliders you can build. Membership is $6. per year.

AUTO WORLD MODELERS

Box 961
Scranton, Pa. 18508

AUTO WORLD MODELERS CLUB

If auto building is your kit fascination, this is the last buck you need spend. Members receive news bulletins that have "how to" stories, photos of members' models, and tips and hints. Also included is a membership card and decals to use on your models. Membership is $1. per year, with no obligation to buy anything.

NATIONAL HANDCRAFT SOCIETY

1425 Grand Avenue
Des Moines, Iowa 50337

The best $1.25 you've ever spent. Each month you receive a handicraft kit. One month it may be the makings of an apron, the next month, the pieces to put together a jewelry box. Sometimes, when you open your kit, you'll find rich fabrics. Or pieces of sweet-smelling redwood, already cut to size. Sometimes there will be glowing mosaic tiles, and sometimes fine-grained leather. There will always be *everything* you need to make a charming and valuable keepsake.

$1.25 per month is all you pay. You get materials, instructions, even the glue if you need it. The secret to the low price is mass buying. If you're into handicrafts, don't miss this club. Write for further details.

HINTS ON BUYING AND BUILDING

HINTS ON BUYING AND BUILDING

<u>hints on buying kits</u>

In choosing a kit from the standpoint of saving money, you should bear in mind that while a manufacturer has reduced cost by selling you an unassembled kit rather than a finished product, there is a real expense in drawing up instructions, packaging the kit, etc. Therefore, do not assume that because an item is offered in kit form that it's a bargain. In most cases, you *will* save money on kits, but you should always comparison shop. Check the manufacturers' specifications, not only against other kits, but also against the assembled retail item. You should also calculate into the price of the kit the expense of tools you might need, although frequently these can be used again.

On the other hand, price is not the only reason for building a kit. In many cases, the manufacturer gives great thought to providing a pleasurable experience in the construction of the kit. We know an electronics expert in the army who has a multimillion dollar radar installation to play with, but last time we saw him on leave he was building a Heathkit amplifier and he thought it was the greatest thing he ever saw. You should investigate this aspect of kit building—many kits are of the bare-bones type and here price is an important consideration. Others are aimed at the pleasure of craftsmanship. Many manufacturers will sell you plans to their kits which are inexpensive and sometimes the price can be applied to the cost of the kit. In short, you should get as much information as possible before buying the kit. On large kits such as houses or expensive musical instruments, the manufacturer may have the names of people who have built the kit and you should take the trouble to contact them before investing a lot of money. Also, don't be afraid to pump the manufacturer for information, especially on large items. Most companies don't really want to sell you something that will make you unhappy.

One final consideration: know your supplier. Two kits may look identical yet one is twice the price. Consider if the materials and the manufacturer's reputation are the same. In researching this book we've ordered hundreds of kits. Some were of such inferior quality we had to delete them from the book. For example, we received needlepoint kits with too little yarn to complete the project. Most manufacturers are more than fair, but know your supplier, especially with expensively priced items.

<u>hints on putting kits together</u>

There are many reasons why people put kits together: they hope to save money over the store-bought item; they want to learn about a technique; or the kit offers some feature not available elsewhere; or, finally, because they enjoy putting it together. This last reason should really apply in any case. It is questionable how much you really save, or how much you learn if the construction of the kit is painful, and, even more important: you're not likely to do a good job if you're not enjoying it. Actually, it's surprising how many people who enjoy manual work set themselves up for *not* enjoying kit building and consequently ruin a kit or have a miserable time with it. There is really only *one* hint for building kits, and that is don't do it, unless you believe you will enjoy kit construction. This is not a trivial piece of advice: you must plan ahead for constructing any kit—the simplest kits—and avoid the two major reasons for kits failing. These are: (1) Lack of patience, and (2) Lack of proper tools and working conditions. With regard to the first, it is almost an absolute rule that if you need something immediately, don't try to build it (from a kit *or* from scratch). Of course, if it's a pot holder or something equally simple this doesn't apply, but then you don't need hints on how to knit a pot holder. However, if you're having a party in three days, and you need that coffee table, and you break out that kit that just arrived in the mail, you're not likely to get the most out of the kit, or have a very nice table. Much better to borrow a table and save the kit for a rainy month. The second major fault is actually related to the first: make sure you have the proper tools or materials before starting your kit, and make sure you have sufficient space to build it in. This even applies if you discover an unanticipated need halfway through a kit. Don't use the wrong yarn, don't use inferior solder, don't use pliers if you need a wrench, etc. It's amazing how many experienced kit makers can violate this rule in the enthusiasm to finish a kit. Have the self-control to stop and wait until you have the proper tool to finish the job, and you will be rewarded by the quality of the product. Several specific hints to help you enjoy the kit:

1. Always read the plans through carefully before beginning. Don't start until you have a good mental picture of exactly what you will have to do.

2. If a technique you are not familiar with is called for, practice on scrap material before doing it on the kit.

3. Organize the parts of the kit before you start. In a typical furniture kit, you might get 100 nails. If you're holding two pieces together with glue on them, you don't want to have to look for a 1¼″ nail. Egg cartons or plastic ice cube trays are good for separating and organizing small parts.

4. Don't ignore the possibility of getting help from the manufacturer. Despite trends in the opposite direction, American companies feel substantial accountability to their customers. This is especially true for kit manufacturers, many of whom were originally enthusiasts themselves. Therefore, if you have a complaint, contact the company. Moreover, companies are usually eager to help you in construction if you need assistance. A three-dollar long-distance call can save a fifty-dollar kit from ruin if it yields technical advice. Don't be embarrassed about contacting them either—most sell themselves, at least partly, as providing educational service. Conversely, you should try to avoid extreme demands on kit manufacturers, some of whom have very small outfits with relatively low profit margins. The basic idea is that most people involved in producing, selling, and buying kits are usually involved, to a greater or lesser extent, in labors of love and you should act accordingly.

INDEX